# Music

## FOR OUR TIME

Robert Winter
*University of California,
Los Angeles*

Wadsworth Publishing Company
Belmont, California
A Division of Wadsworth, Inc.

Music Editor: Suzanna Brabant
Assistant Editor: Julie Johnson
Editorial Assistant: Dana Lipsky
Production Editor: Sandra Craig
Managing Designer: Andrew Ogus
Print Buyer: Karen Hunt
Permissions Editor: Peggy Meehan
Development Editor: Everett Sims
Designer: Donna Davis
Copy Editor: Judy Johnstone
Photo Researcher: Stephen Forsling
Photo Captions: Pat Tompkins
Technical Illustrations: Susan Breitbard
Autography: Ernie Mansfield
Calligraphy: Georgia Deaver
Cover Painting: *At the Opera,* 1880, Mary Stevenson Cassatt. Oil on canvas, 31½ × 25½ in. Charles Henry Hayden Fund. Courtesy, Museum of Fine Arts, Boston.
Signing Representative: Diana Rothberg
Compositor: Graphic Typesetting Service
Printer: Vail-Ballou Press

Illustration credits are on page 722.

Printed in the United States of America
10  9  8  7  6  5  4  3  2  1
96  95  94  93  92

Library of Congress Cataloging-in-Publication Data

Winter, Robert, 1945–
    Music for our time / Robert Winter.
        p.    cm.
    Includes index.
    ISBN 0–534–13104–2
    1. Music appreciation    I. Title.
MT6.W636M9 1992
780—dc20                        91–27766
                                         CIP
                                         MN

*To Lois, Robert, and Julia*

# ABOUT THE AUTHOR

Raised in Florida and educated at Brown University (B.A.), the State University of New York at Buffalo (M.F.A. in piano), and the University of Chicago (Ph.D. in the history and theory of music), scholar/pianist Robert Winter has been a member of the music faculty at the University of California, Los Angeles, since 1974. He is the author, coauthor, or editor of four major books on Beethoven and many articles on compositional process and performance practice. He has been the recipient of several awards, including a Guggenheim Fellowship in 1983 and the 1985 Otto Kinkeldey Prize of the American Musicological Society for the best scholarly book in music (*The Beethoven Sketchbooks,* with Douglas Johnson and Alan Tyson).

Professor Winter is nationally known for his translation of state-of-the-art scholarship into accessible, entertaining public presentations. He has lectured and performed throughout the United States and Canada, including at the Smithsonian Institution in Washington, D.C., the Metropolitan Museum of Art and the 92nd Street Y in New York City, the annual Digital World Conferences, and five summer concert series at the J. Paul Getty Museum in Malibu, California, of which he is the music director. Professor Winter has also presented numerous live series (on Mozart and Beethoven, among others) on American Public Radio.

For the last three years he has worked with the Voyager Company on their CD Companion Series, which uses the new interactive media to explore music. His first project, Ludwig van Beethoven's Symphony No. 9, is considered a milestone in multimedia publishing. Igor Stravinsky's *The Rite of Spring* was released in January 1991, and a third program, on Mozart's String Quartet in C Major, K. 465, with the Angeles Quartet, was published as an interactive videodisc in August 1991.

# BRIEF CONTENTS

## Part One
### THE LANGUAGE OF MUSIC 1

Chapter 1 / Prelude 3
Chapter 2 / The Primacy of Rhythm 16
Chapter 3 / Melody and Harmony 26
Chapter 4 / Texture, Color, and Shape 38

## Part Two
### EARLY MUSIC (TO 1690) 61

*The Middle Ages (500–1430)—A Medieval World View: Historical and Cultural Background* 63
Chapter 5 / Medieval Monophony 69
Chapter 6 / Medieval Polyphony 95

*The Renaissance (1430–1600)—The Age of Humanism: Historical and Cultural Background* 119
Chapter 7 / Secular Music in the Renaissance 125
Chapter 8 / Motet and Mass 143

*The Early Baroque (1600–1690)—The Age of Absolutism: Historical and Cultural Background* 159
Chapter 9 / The Early Baroque in Italy and Germany 163
Chapter 10 / Early Opera 183

*Part Three*

## THE AGE OF TONALITY (1690–1910)  199

*The Late Baroque (1690–1750)—The Age of Enlightenment: Historical and Cultural Background  201*

Chapter 11 / Instrumental Music  203

Chapter 12 / Vocal Music  231

*The Viennese Classical Style (1750–1828)—The Age of Revolution: Historical and Cultural Background  261*

Chapter 13 / The Rise of the Symphony  266

Chapter 14 / Concerto and Quartet  286

Chapter 15 / Mozart's Operas  304

Chapter 16 / Beethoven's Heroic Decade  333

Chapter 17 / Beethoven's Late Style (1813–1827)  346

Chapter 18 / Toward Romanticism  357

*Romanticism (1829–1910)—The Cult of the Individual: Historical and Cultural Background  371*

Chapter 19 / Romanticism in Paris  377

Chapter 20 / Virtuosos and Pianists  393

Chapter 21 / Absolute Music and Popular Music  414

Chapter 22 / Romantic Opera in Italy  431

Chapter 23 / Romantic Opera in Germany  458

Chapter 24 / Nationalism; The Twilight of Romanticism  480

## *Part Four*
## THE TWENTIETH CENTURY 499

*The Age of Technology: Historical and Cultural Background 501*
Chapter 25 / Debussy and Stravinsky in Paris 507
Chapter 26 / Expressionism and Serialism in Vienna 534
Chapter 27 / American Music Comes of Age 570
Chapter 28 / Responses to Jazz; Neoclassicism 606
Chapter 29 / Émigres and Traditionalists 642
Chapter 30 / Where Do We Go from Here? 675

Glossary 711
Acknowledgments 722
Index 723

# CONTENTS

## *Part One*
## THE LANGUAGE OF MUSIC 1

Chapter 1 / Prelude 3

Living with Music 3

Universality and Diversity 7
How We Got Here 7

Thinking About Music 8

A Working Definition 9
Western Music and International Musics 9
Classical and Popular 9
The Fine Arts 11

Listening to Music 12

Four Key Components 12

Some Procedural Matters 15

Chapter 2 / The Primacy of Rhythm 16

Incidence and Duration 16

Regular Rhythm and Irregular Rhythm 17

Organized Rhythm 17

Beat 18
Meter 18

Simple Meters 18

Duple Meter 19
Triple Meter 19

Subdividing Beats 20

Duple Subdivision of Beats 20
Compound Meter 21
Irregular Meter 22

Tempo 23

Accent and Syncopation 24

Chapter 3 / Melody and Harmony 26

Four Essential Ingredients 27

Pitch 27
Interval 27
Octave 27
Scale 28

Vocal Melody 29

Instrumental Melody 30

Phrase, Period, and Cadence 30

Regular and Irregular Melody 31

Tune 32

Theme 32

Motive 32

Harmony 33

The Triad 33

Tonality 34

Diatonic Harmonies and
Chromatic Harmonies 35

Consonance and Dissonance 35

Harmonic Rhythm 36

Modulation 36

Chapter 4 / Texture, Color, and Shape 38

Texture 38

Color (Timbre) 39

  Strings 40

  Woodwinds 44

  Brass 46

Percussion 46

Keyboard Instruments 47

Period Instruments 48

Non-Western Instruments 49

Orchestration 51

Performance Directions 51

Interpretation 52

Shape 53

  Repetition, Contrast, and Variation 53

Musical Notation 54

Musical Style 59

## Part Two

# EARLY MUSIC (TO 1690) 61

*The Middle Ages (500–1430)—A Medieval
World View: Historical and Cultural
Background 63*

Chapter 5 / Medieval Monophony 69

The Greek Heritage 69

Music in the Church 72

Plainchant 73

  Marian Antiphon: *"Alma redemptoris mater"*
  ("Loving Mother of the Redeemer")
  (11th century?) 75

  Listening Guide 1: *"Alma redemptoris
  mater"* 76

Medieval Drama 78

  Hildegard of Bingen (1098–1179): From
  Scene 4 of *Ordo virtutum* (Play of the Virtues)
  (ca. 1152?) 79

  Listening Guide 2: *Ordo virtutum* 80

Secular Song 82

  Troubador Song: Countess of Dia, *"A una
  amante infidele"* ("To an Unfaithful Lover")
  (ca. 1160) 83

  Listening Guide 3: *"A una amante
  infidele"* 84

*Historical Window: A Medieval Monastery 86*

  Minnesänger Song: Walther von der Vogelweide (ca. 1170–1230): *"Unter der linden an
  der heide"* ("Under the Linden Tree on the
  Heath") (ca. 1200) 89

  Listening Guide 4: *"Unter der linden an
  der heide"* 90

Instrumental Music: Estampie (ca. 1300)  92

    Listening Guide 5: Estampie  93


## Chapter 6 / Medieval Polyphony  95

Organum  95

    Pérotin (fl. ca. 1200): Four-voiced organum, *Viderunt omnes* (All shall see) (ca. 1198)  96

    Listening Guide 6: *Viderunt omnes*  98

The Motet  99

    Anonymous Motet: *"O mitissima / Quant voi—Virgo virginum—Haec dies"* ("O most gentle / When I notice—Virgin of virgins—This is the day") (ca. 1275)  100

    Listening Guide 7: *"O mitissima / Quant voi—Virgo virginum—Haec dies"*  101

The *Ars Nova* in France  100

    Guillaume de Machaut (ca. 1300–1377): Gloria to the *Mass of Notre Dame* (1364?)  102

    Listening Guide 8: Gloria to the *Mass of Notre Dame*  103

*Historical Window: A Choirboy's Life at Notre Dame  106*

*Formes fixes* ("Fixed forms")  105

    Machaut: Ballade, *"Dame, comment qu'amez"* ("My lady, however little I may be loved") (ca. 1350)  109

    Listening Guide 9: *"Dame, comment qu'amez"*  110

The *Trecento* in Italy  109

    Giovanni da Firenze (fl.1340–1350): Caccia, *"Con bracchi assai"* ("With many dogs") (ca. 1345)  111

    Listening Guide 10: *"Con bracchi assai"*  112

    Francesco Landini (ca. 1325–1397): Ballata, *"Cara mie donna"* ("My dear lady") (1360?)  111

    Listening Guide 11: *"Cara mie donna"*  114

The Waning of the Middle Ages  116

    John Dunstable? (ca. 1390–1453): Ballata, *"O rosa bella"* ("Oh lovely rose") (ca. 1425?)  116

    Listening Guide 12: *"O rosa bella"*  117


## *The Renaissance (1430–1600)—The Age of Humanism: Historical and Cultural Background  119*


### Chapter 7 / Secular Music in the Renaissance  125

The Renaissance Style  125

Secular Song  127

    Gilles Binchois (ca. 1400–1460) or Guillaume Dufay (ca. 1400–1474): Rondeau, *"Je ne vis onques le pareille"* ("I have never seen the equal") (ca. 1454)  127

    Listening Guide 13: *"Je ne vis onques le pareille"*  128

    Heinrich Isaac (ca. 1450–1517): Lied, *"Isbruck, ich muss dich lassen"* ("Innsbruck, I must leave you") (ca. 1500?)  127

    Listening Guide 14: *"Isbruck, ich muss dich lassen"*  130

*Historical Window: An Unforgettable Feast at the Court of Philip the Good  132*

Josquin Desprez (ca. 1440–1521)  131

    Josquin: Frottola, *"El grillo"* ("The cricket") (ca. 1474)  134

    Listening Guide 15: *"El grillo"*  135

    Josquin: Canonic chanson, *"Baisez moy"* ("Kiss me") (ca. 1500)  136

    Listening Guide 16: *"Baisez moy"*  137

The English Madrigal  138

    Thomas Weelkes (ca. 1575–1623): Madrigal, "Those sweet delightful Lilies" (pub. 1597)  138

Listening Guide 17: "Those sweet delightful Lilies"  139

Instrumental Dance Music  139

Listening Guide 18: Dance Medley  141

Chapter 8 / Motet and Mass  143

The Motet  143

Guillaume Dufay: Motet, *"Supremum est mortalibus bonum"* ("The greatest good of mortals") (1433)  143

Listening Guide 19: *"Supremum est mortalibus bonum"*  144

The Mass  146

Josquin Desprez: Credo from the *Missa L'homme armé super voces musicales* (Mass on "The Man at Arms" at all the different pitches of the hexachord; ca. 1500)  146

Listening Guide 20: Credo from the *Missa L'homme armé super voces musicales*  148

Giovanni Pierluigi da Palestrina (ca. 1525–1594)  150

Palestrina: Credo from the *Pope Marcellus Mass* (pub. 1567)  151

Listening Guide 21: Credo from the *Pope Marcellus Mass*  155

*Historical Window: The Printing Revolution*  152

*The Early Baroque (1600–1690)—The Age of Absolutism: Historical and Cultural Background*  159

Chapter 9 / The Early Baroque in Italy and Germany  163

The Early Baroque Style  163

The Rise of Instrumental Music  166

Giovanni Gabrieli (1557–1612)  166

Gabrieli: Sonata XIX, from *Canzoni e Sonate* (pub. 1615)  167

Listening Guide 22: Sonata XIX, from *Canzoni e Sonate*  168

Girolamo Frescobaldi (1583–1643)  171

Frescobaldi: *Capriccio del Soggetto scritto sopra l'Aria di Ruggiero*, from Book I of Toccatas and Partitas (1614–1616, pub. 1637)  171

Listening Guide 23: *Capriccio del Soggetto scritto sopra l'Aria di Ruggiero*  170

*Historical Window: The "Early Music" Movement*  172

The Italian Continuo Madrigal  176

Claudio Monteverdi (1567–1643)  176

Monteverdi: *"Zefiro torna"* ("Zephyr returns") (Petrarch) from Madrigals, Book VI (1614)  177

Listening Guide 24: *"Zefiro torna"*  178

The First Great German Composer: Heinrich Schütz (1585–1672)  178

Schütz: *"Freue dich"* ("Rejoice") (ca. 1626)  180

Listening Guide 25: *"Freue dich"*  181

Chapter 10 / Early Opera  183

Monteverdi: Orfeo's Ascent from Act IV of *Orfeo* (1607)  184

Listening Guide 26: Orfeo's Ascent from Act IV of *Orfeo*  186

Henry Purcell (1659–1695)  191

Purcell: Conclusion of *Dido and Aeneas* (1689)  192

*Historical Window: The First Public Musical Entertainments*  194

*Part Three*
# THE AGE OF TONALITY (1690–1910) 199

*The Late Baroque (1690–1750)—The Age of Enlightenment: Historical and Cultural Background 201*

Chapter 11 / Instrumental Music 203

The Late Baroque Style 203

The Concerto Grosso 206

Johann Sebastian Bach (1685–1750) 207

> Bach : Brandenburg Concerto No. 2 in F Major (ca. 1718) 208
>
> Listening Guide 27: Brandenburg Concerto No. 2 in F Major 210

The Solo Concerto 213

Antonio Vivaldi (1678–1741) 213

> Vivaldi: "Autumn" from *The Four Seasons*, Op. 8 (ca. 1725) 214
>
> Listening Guide 28: "Autumn" 215

*Historical Window: The Genius of Stradivari 218*

The Suite 217

> Handel: Suite in D Major from the *Water Music* (ca. 1715) 218
>
> Listening Guide 29: Suite in D Major from the *Water Music* 220

The Trio Sonata 223

Georg Philipp Telemann (1681–1767) 223

> Telemann: Trio Sonata in A Minor from *Essercizii musici* (1740) 224
>
> Listening Guide 30: Trio Sonata in A Minor from *Essercizii musici* 225

Improvisation 225

Fugue 226

> J. S. Bach: Toccata and Fugue in D Minor for Organ, BWV 565 (ca. 1708) 227
>
> Listening Guide 31: Toccata and Fugue in D Minor for Organ 229

Chapter 12 / Vocal Music 231

Words and Music in the Late Baroque 231

Late Baroque Opera 232

George Frideric Handel (1685–1759) 233

> Handel: Recitative and Aria, *"Fammi combattere"* ("Go bid me combat") from *Orlando* (1733) 234
>
> Listening Guide 32: *"Fammi combattere"* 236

Jean-Philippe Rameau (1683–1764) 236

> Rameau: Jupiter's Descent from Act V of the opera *Castor et Pollux* (1737) 238
>
> Listening Guide 33: Jupiter's Descent from Act V of the opera *Castor et Pollux* 240

The English Oratorio 245

> Handel: From Part II of *Messiah* (1742) 246
>
> Listening Guide 34: From Part II of *Messiah* 247

*Historical Window: The Composer as Businessman 252*

The Cantata 250

> J. S. Bach: Cantata No. 78, *Jesu der du meine Seele* (Jesus, who hath my soul) (1724) 251
>
> Listening Guide 35: Cantata No. 78, *Jesu der du meine Seele* 256

*Contents*

*The Viennese Classical Style (1750–1828)—
The Age of Revolution: Historical and
Cultural Background 261*

Chapter 13 / The Rise of the Symphony 266

The Viennese Classical Style 266

Sonata Form 267

Anatomy of the Symphony 269

Franz Joseph Haydn (1732–1809) 270

   Haydn: Symphony No. 100 in G Major,
   "Military" (1794) 273

   Listening Guide 36: "Military" 274

*Historical Window: Haydn in London 280*

   Mozart: Symphony No. 41 in C Major, K. 551
   (1788) 283

Chapter 14 / Concerto and Quartet 286

Public Music and Private Music 286

The Piano Concerto 287

Wolfgang Amadeus Mozart (1756–1791) 289

   Mozart: Piano Concerto in C Major, K. 467
   (1785) 291

   Listening Guide 37: Piano Concerto in C
   Major, K. 467, First and Third
   Movements, 292

*Historical Window: Mozart in Letters 296*

The String Quartet 299

   Haydn: String Quartet in D Major, Op. 76,
   No. 5 (1797) 300

   Listening Guide 38: String Quartet in D
   Major, Op. 76, No. 5, Second Movement 301

Chapter 15 / Mozart's Operas 304

Classical Opera 304

Mozart's Viennese Operas 305

   Mozart: Three Excerpts from *The Marriage
   of Figaro* (1786) 306

   Listening Guide 39: *The Marriage
   of Figaro* 311

*Historical Window: Mozart's Librettist 308*

Chapter 16 / Beethoven's
Heroic Decade 333

Beethoven to 1812 334

*Historical Window: A Beethoven Academy 336*

   Beethoven: Symphony No. 5 in C Minor,
   Op. 67 (1804–1808) 338

   Listening Guide 40: Symphony No. 5 in C
   Minor, Op. 67, First Movement 340

   Beethoven: Piano Concerto No. 4 in G Major,
   Op. 58 (1805–1806) 343

Chapter 17 / Beethoven's Late Style
(1813–1827) 346

Beethoven After the Heroic Decade 346

   Beethoven: Piano Sonata in C Minor,
   Op. 111 (1822) 348

*Historical Window: Beethoven's Pianos 350*

   Beethoven: String Quartet in C-sharp Minor,
   Op. 131 (1826) 355

Chapter 18 / Toward Romanticism 357

The "Classicizing" Style 357

Franz Schubert (1797–1828) 358

The German *Lied* 360

   Schubert: *"An Silvia"* ("To Silvia"),
D. 891 (1826) 361

   Schubert: *"Gretchen am Spinnrade"*
("Gretchen at the Spinning Wheel"),
D. 118 (1814) 368

   Schubert: *"Rastlose Liebe"* ("Restless Love"),
D. 138 (1815) 370

   Listening Guide 41: Three Songs 362

*Historical Window: A Schubertiad 366*

***Romanticism (1829–1910)—The Cult of
the Individual: Historical and Cultural
Background 371***

**Chapter 19 / Romanticism in Paris 377**

Romantic Style Traits 377

Paris in the Nineteenth Century 380

Hector Berlioz (1803–1869) 382

Berlioz's Style 384

   Berlioz: *Symphonie fantastique* (1830) 385

*Historical Window: Moods and Music 388*

**Chapter 20 / Virtuosos and Pianists 393**

The Rise of Virtuosity 393

Nicolò Paganini (1782–1840) 394

   Paganini: Solo Violin Caprice,
Op. 1, No. 9 (ca. 1805) 396

   Listening Guide 42: Solo Violin Caprice,
Op. 1, No. 9 397

The Romantic Piano 397

*Historical Window: A Pianistic Duel 400*

Franz Liszt (1811–1886) 398

   Liszt: Concert Étude after Paganini, *La Campanella* ("The Little Bells") (1838) 404

   Listening Guide 43: *La Campanella* 405

Frédéric Chopin (1810–1849) 406

Chopin's Style 407

   Chopin: Étude in G-sharp Minor, Op. 25,
No. 6 (1832–1834) 408

   Chopin: Mazurka in D Major, Op. 33, No. 2
(1837) 409

   Chopin: Nocturne in E Major, Op. 62, No. 2
(1846) 410

   Listening Guide 44: Nocturne in E Major,
Op. 62, No. 2 411

Clara Wieck (1819–1896): Romance in
G Minor, Op. 11, No. 2 (1839) 411

   Listening Guide 45: Romance in G Minor,
Op. 11, No. 2 412

**Chapter 21 / Absolute Music and
Popular Music 414**

Absolute Music in the Romantic Era 414

Robert Schumann (1810–1856) 415

   Schumann: Piano Concerto in A Minor,
Op. 54 (1841, 1845) 416

Felix Mendelssohn (1809–1847) 418

   Mendelssohn: Piano Trio in D Minor, Op. 49
(1839) 419

*Historical Window: Where Were the Women? 420*

Johannes Brahms (1833–1897) 424

   Brahms: Variations on a Theme by Haydn,
Op. 56a (1873) 425

The Rise of Popular Music 426

Johann Strauss, Jr. (1825–1899)  427

  Strauss: Waltz, *Voices of Spring,*
Op. 410 (1883)  428

  Listening Guide 46: *Voices of Spring,*
Op. 410  430


Chapter 22 / Romantic Opera in Italy  431

Italian Opera Before Mid-Century  431

Giuseppi Verdi (1813–1901)  434

  Verdi: Act III from *Rigoletto* (1851)  436

  Listening Guide 47: *Rigoletto*  438

  Franz Liszt: Piano Transcription of the Act III
Quartet from *Rigoletto* (1859)  446

*Historical Window: "Viva Verdi!"  450*

Giacomo Puccini (1858–1924)
and Late Romantic Opera  449

  Puccini: Love Duet from Act I of *La bohème*
(1896)  453

  Listening Guide 48: *La bohème*  455


Chapter 23 / Romantic Opera
in Germany  458

Richard Wagner (1813–1883)  460

  Wagner: Love Duet from Act II of *Tristan und
Isolde* (1856–1859)  463

Listening Guide 49: *Tristan und Isolde*  469

*Historical Window: The Music Critic  477*


Chapter 24 / Nationalism; The Twilight
of Romanticism  480

Nationalism Outside the European
Mainstream  480

Bedřich Smetana (1824–1884)  481

  Smetana: *The Moldau* from *Má Vlast (My
Fatherland)* (1874)  482

  Listening Guide 50: *The Moldau*  484

Russian Nationalism  485

Modest Musorgsky (1839–1881)  485

  Musorgsky: *Pictures at an Exhibition*
(1874)  486

*Historical Window: Composers in the Movies  490*

Peter Tchaikovsky (1840–1893)  488

  Tchaikovsky: Fantasy Overture, *Romeo
and Juliet* (1881)  492

The Twilight of Romanticism  493

Gustav Mahler (1860–1911)  494

  Mahler: First Movement from the Symphony
No. 6 in A Minor (1903–1904)  496

## Part Four

# THE TWENTIETH CENTURY  499

*The Age of Technology: Historical and Cultural Background*  501

Chapter 25 / Debussy and Stravinsky in Paris  507

Avant-Garde Paris  507

Wagnerism  509

Claude Debussy (1862–1918) 509

Debussy: *Prelude to "The Afternoon of a Faun"* (1892–1894)  511
Listening Guide 51: *Prelude to "The Afternoon of a Faun"*  512

*Historical Window: The Exposition Universelle of 1889*  516

Les Ballet Russes  519

Igor Stravinsky (1882–1971)  522

Stravinsky: Part I from *The Rite of Spring* (1913)  524
Listening Guide 52: *The Rite of Spring*  526

Chapter 26 / Expressionism and Serialism in Vienna  534

Secessionism, Freud, and Expressionism  535

Arnold Schoenberg (1874–1951) and Atonality  537

Schoenberg: *Vergangenes (The Past)* from *Five Pieces for Orchestra*, Op. 16 (1909)  539
Listening Guide 53: *Vergangenes*  540

Schoenberg: *"Nacht"* ("Night"), from *Pierrot lunaire (Pierrot of the moon)*, Op. 21 (1912)  542

Listening Guide 54: *"Nacht"*  544

Anton Webern (1883–1945)  546

Webern: Nos. 3 and 4 from *Five Pieces for Orchestra*, Op. 10 (1911–1913)  547
Listening Guide 55: Nos. 3 and 4 from *Five Pieces for Orchestra*, Op. 10  548

Alban Berg (1885–1935)  549

Berg: Act III from *Wozzeck* (1917–1922)  550
Listening Guide 56: *Wozzeck*  554

*Historical Window: The Society for Private Musical Performances*  562

The Development of Serialism  564

Webern: Symphony, Op. 21 (1928)  566
Listening Guide 57: Symphony, Op. 21 (1928)  568

Chapter 27 / American Music Comes of Age  570

Early American Music  570

John Philip Sousa (1854–1932)  573

Sousa: March, "The Stars and Stripes Forever" (1897)  573
Listening Guide 58: "The Stars and Stripes Forever"  575

Charles Ives (1874–1954)  576

Ives: "Putnam's Camp, Redding, Connecticut" and "The Housatonic at Stockbridge" from *Three Places in New England* (1912?–1930?)  579
Listening Guide 59: "Putnam's Camp, Redding, Connecticut"  580

Aaron Copland (1900–1990)  582

Copland: Suite from *Appalachian Spring* (1944)  584

Jazz: A Uniquely American Music  587

Ragtime  588

Scott Joplin (1868–1917): "Gladiolus Rag" (1907)  589

Listening Guide 60: "Gladiolus Rag"  591

The Blues  592

Ferdinand "Jelly Roll" Morton (1885–1941): "Dead Man Blues" (recorded 1926–1927)  593

Listening Guide 61: "Dead Man Blues"  595

*Historical Window: The New Orleans Brass Band*  596

Louis "Satchmo" Armstrong (ca. 1898–1971): "West End Blues" (1928)  594

Listening Guide 62: "West End Blues"  599

Swing Bands  598

Duke Ellington (1899–1974): "Harlem Air Shaft" (1940)  599

Listening Guide 63: "Harlem Air Shaft"  601

Bebop  602

Charlie "Bird" Parker (1920–1955): "Bloomdido" (1950)  602

Listening Guide 64: "Bloomdido"  603

Modern Jazz  604

Chapter 28 / Responses to Jazz; Neoclassicism  606

Jazz and Art Music  606

Stravinsky: "Three Dances" from *A Soldier's Tale* (1918)  607

Listening Guide 65: "Three Dances"  608

George Gershwin (1898–1937)  611

Gershwin: From Act I, Scene 1 of *Porgy and Bess* (1935)  613

Listening Guide 66: *Porgy and Bess*  614

Musical Theater in America  619

Leonard Bernstein (1918–1990)  621

Bernstein: Two Excerpts from *West Side Story* (1957)  622

Listening Guide 67: *West Side Story*  624

Neoclassicism  630

*Historical Window: The Boston Symphony*  634

Stravinsky: Third Movement from the *Symphony of Psalms* (1930)  636

Listening Guide 68: *Symphony of Psalms*  639

Chapter 29 / Émigrés and Traditionalists  642

The Émigrés  643

Edgard Varèse (1883–1965)  643

Varèse: *Ionisation* (1929–1931)  644

Listening Guide 69: *Ionisation*  645

Béla Bartók (1881–1945)  647

Bartók: Concerto for Orchestra, First and Fourth Movements (1944)  650

Listening Guide 70: Concerto for Orchestra  653

*Historical Window: Musicians and War*  656

Traditionalists  659

Sergei Rachmaninoff (1873–1943): *Rhapsody on a Theme of Paganini* (1934)  659

Benjamin Britten (1913–1976): *Peter Grimes* (1945), Act III, End of Scene 1 through Scene 2  661

Listening Guide 71: *Peter Grimes*  663

Music for Films  670

Bernard Herrmann (1911–1975): Music from the Film *Journey to the Centre of the Earth* (1959)  672
Listening Guide 72: Music from the Film *Journey to the Centre of the Earth*  673

Chapter 30 / Where Do We Go from Here?  675

A Permanent Avant Garde?  675

Pierre Boulez (b. 1925): *Le marteau sans maître* (The hammer without a master) (1954)  676
Listening Guide 73: *Le marteau sans maître*  677

The Electronic Age  679

Karlheinz Stockhausen (b. 1928): *Song of the Youths* (1954–1956)  680
Listening Guide 74: *Song of the Youths*  682

The Birth of Rock 'n' Roll  685

*Historical Window: The Home Electronic Music Studio*  686

Rock in the 1960s: The Age of the Beatles  689

The Beatles: *Sgt. Pepper's Lonely Hearts Club Band* (1967)  692

Rock in the 1970s and 1980s  693

The Pioneer Spirit  694

John Cage (b. 1912): *Aria with Fontana Mix* (1958)  695

The Postmodernist Age  697

György Ligeti (b. 1923): *Lux aeterna* for 16-Voice A Capella Mixed Chorus (1966)  697
Listening Guide 75: *Lux aeterna*  698

Ellen Taaffe Zwilich (b. 1939): "Eyesight" from *Passages* for Soprano and Instrumental Ensemble (1981)  699
Listening Guide 76: "Eyesight"  700

Minimalism  701

John Adams (b. 1947): "News Has a Kind of Mystery" from *Nixon in China* (1987)  703
Listening Guide 77: "News Has a Kind of Mystery"  704

Other Contemporary Styles and Trends  706

Where Are We Headed?  708

Segmented Audiences  708
Centrifugal Styles  709
Vanishing Boundaries  709
More Technology  709
Dynamic Stasis  709

Glossary  711

Acknowledgments  722

Index  723

# PREFACE

A good textbook serves as an "amplifier" for a good teacher. *Music for Our Time* strives to be just that: an up-to-date and easy-to-use amplifier that enhances instructors' effectiveness and students' understanding.

I wish to emphasize *understanding*. As someone who, at the university level, came to the field of music from physics, I was puzzled from the beginning by the notion of "music appreciation." I had never encountered a course in "physics appreciation" or, for that matter, any course that ended in "appreciation." It was only when I started teaching that I began to understand the forces in our cultural life that lead to the appreciation of music and art being viewed as a self-sufficient goal. It struck me then and it strikes me now that "appreciation" is a desirable by-product of study in any field—but that the primary goal must always be understanding. Understanding leads to skillful and attentive listening—our ultimate goal. To this end, *Music for Our Time* is dedicated.

I understand music as an art with roots deep in the cultural soil that nourishes it. Accordingly, I do not believe that we must choose between understanding music in purely aesthetic terms and approaching it in terms of its social, political, and economic contexts. The more we know about the one, the more we can learn about the other. We study the historical context of a musical work to gain insight into the way its environment shaped it; we study a work's aesthetic content to understand how a composer shaped—and sometimes transcended—that environment. *Music for Our Time* is organized to serve these twin goals.

## Historical Context

Introductory essays to each main section describe in real-life terms the age about to be covered. Along with crisp, relevant portraits of individual composers, each stylistic epoch and musical genre is presented in terms of its social background and function. Newcomers to music understand plainchant better when they learn that the church fathers believed it would foster a proper devotional attitude, that its resonant acoustics simulated heavenly voices, and that it helped worshipers to memorize the liturgy. They find it easier to deal with the conventions of eighteenth-century opera when they understand that these works were designed to glorify the nobility who financed them. They benefit from knowing that the demise of tonality in the early twentieth century coincided with the demise of centuries of monarchical rule.

To create a sense of historical immediacy, 26 Historical Windows offer vivid closeups of pivotal historical moments or developments in music. Examples include "The Life of a Choirboy at Notre Dame," "An Unforgettable Feast at the Court of Philip the Good," "A Schubertiad," "Where Were the Women?" and "The Home Electronic Music Studio." Ten easy-to-read maps (including maps of the United States and of the world) refer to the persons who are discussed in each section and show *where* they were active. The nearly 175 illustrations are keyed to specific points in the text and carry captions that invite browsing.

## Listening Skills

Throughout *Music for Our Time,* students are encouraged to strengthen their listening skills. Starting from the assumption that students have little or no background in music, Chapters 2 (on rhythm), 3 (on melody and harmony), and 4 (on texture, color, and shape, with tips on following notation) introduce the language of music in a logical, graded fashion. To illustrate this language, an 85-minute elements audiotape cassette that accompanies each copy of the book presents almost 90 customized examples, including "signatures" of 36 Western and non-Western instruments. For instructors who choose not to use precious class time teaching fundamentals, these early chapters and the tape can be self-teaching. Chapters 2–4 can also be assigned by section. The working vocabulary established in these early chapters is used consistently throughout the book. Technical terms are defined and indexed at their first appearance and are brought together in a comprehensive glossary at the end of the book. Each instance of musical notation makes a point that benefits directly from visual representation, with arrows, explanatory text, and other symbols used liberally to elucidate ideas in a way that does not require a detailed reading knowledge of music.

Although listening guides are more common today than they were a decade ago, they are still often treated as "supplements" rather than as a central tool. Some instructors fear that students will become overreliant on listening guides. But how many of us learned to ride a bicycle without first using training wheels? True, the goal is to dispense with such aids as soon as possible, but at the outset they help beginners to move ahead confidently on a steady course. Hence, I have provided Listening Guides for virtually all of the 95 works discussed—77 in the main text (which accounts for the slightly greater length of *Music for Our Time* over other texts), 16 in the Study Guide and Instructor's Manual. They work in real time, linked via to-the-second elapsed times to significant events (15–25 seconds apart on average) within the complete work. Boldfacing of structural pillars prevents students from being inundated by detail and enables instructors, depending on their aims, to assign an appropriate depth. For vocal compositions, English translations appear directly under the original texts rather than in the facing columns that even trained musicians have difficulty following.

## Recordings

Of the 95 works covered, 81 are contained in the eight-CD or cassette set, in performances carefully chosen for their effectiveness in the classroom. Some 400 "index" marks encoded on the record set and noted down the left side of each Listening Guide enable instructors with index-capable CD players (a feature found on most mid-price machines manufactured today) to go directly to a structural juncture without affecting the elapsed-time readout for the whole excerpt.

The 14 works discussed in the text but not included in the recording set are all standard works that belong—in their entirety rather than excerpted—in even modest record libraries. As an aid to instructors, Wadsworth Publishing Company will provide supplemental recordings of these works (such as Mozart's *Jupiter* Symphony, Berlioz's *Symphonie fantastique,* and Musorgsky's *Pictures at an Exhibition)* at discount prices through the PolyGram music library. These performances are keyed to the Listening Guide timings in the Study Guide and Instructor's Manual.

## Repertoire

Although the choice of repertoire is a highly personal one, I have been guided by several principles. First, I have favored composers and works on the cutting edge of major style changes. Second, I have not hesitated to include music by composers omitted from most texts whose contributions seem, in my view, important. You will find, for example, works by Frescobaldi, Schütz, Rameau, and Paganini in works guaranteed to fuel students' interest. Third, instead of relegating popular music (including jazz and rock 'n' roll) to a tacked-on section, it is integrated into the main text. (Students do not "appreciate" the message that popular music is somehow inferior to Western art music.)

Fourth, I have treated the contributions of women to Western music—both as composers and performers—as equally integral to the text. Over the last two decades a host of scholars have heightened our awareness both of the contributions made by women and of the obstacles to their participation. The recording set includes works by Hildegard of Bingen, the Countess of Dia, Clara Wieck, and Ellen Taaffe Zwilich. The Historical Window in Chapter 21 considers in detail the dilemma faced by women musicians, focusing on the careers of Fanny Mendelssohn and Clara Wieck.

Finally, this is not a book on Western music parading as a book on world music. Having taught for eighteen years at an institution with one of the oldest and most distinguished ethnomusicology programs in the world, I have benefited greatly from interaction with my world-music colleagues (two of whom perform superbly on the elements cassette). But I believe it is patronizing to tack on a chapter purporting to cover world music and pretend that one has done justice to vast repertoires and cultures covering millenia. Yet *Music for Our Time* incorporates some of the broader methodologies of world-music scholars and remains mindful of the enormous debt of Western music to outside influences. In Chapter 1, I draw a careful distinction between world musics and Western music, and in Chapters 3 and 4 I use non-Western musics to illustrate key points about musical language. From Chapter 25 on (Debussy and Stravinsky), the text displays an increasingly global frame of reference to reflect the increasingly global nature of Western music.

## Organization

Although the organization of *Music for Our Time* is linear and chronological, the book lends itself readily to use in a nonlinear fashion. Instructors may begin, for example, with The Age of Tonality without any loss in coherence or clarity. The Instructor's Manual includes suggestions for differing timetables (one quarter, one semester, two quarters) and sequences, both chronological and nonchronological.

## Supplementary Aids

Unlike many such supplements, the student Study Guide for *Music for Our Time* has been carefully developed to work in concert with the text itself. The Study Guide is the work of Katherine Rohrer, a scholar and highly successful teacher of the introductory courses at Columbia and Princeton who became intimately familiar with *Music for Our Time* as a valued reviewer during the development of the book. Combining a remarkable grasp of the material with an equally remarkable feel for communicating about music to students of all backgrounds, Dr. Rohrer has created an engaging, often humorous Study Guide that is sure to spark and maintain student interest outside of class.

The instructor's manual is often treated as an afterthought in the publication process, in part because the person most qualified to write it—the author of the main text—is frequently the least willing. Inspired by Dr. Rohrer's example, I have undertaken the Instructor's Manual myself. It includes general suggestions for the successful teaching of introductory music courses, specific chapter-by-chapter teaching tips, supplementary Listening Guides for all the pieces not covered by Listening Guides in the main text, and a test-item file of some 1,200 handily referenced questions created by the author. The test items are also available in computerized form from Wadsworth.

It is a commonplace that we live in the midst of an information-processing revolution. The revolution is now coming to music education, with benefits unimaginable just a short time ago. For the last three years I have helped launch the Voyager Company's pioneering CD Companion Series, which uses the new consumer CD-ROM and laserdisc technologies. In the course of creating interactive learning programs on Beethoven's Ninth Symphony, Stravinsky's *The Rite of Spring*, and Mozart's "Dissonant" Quartet, I have come to appreciate the potential of this technology for empowering both instructors and students.

The Voyager Company is publishing Macintosh software that I have prepared containing interactive versions of all 95 Listening Guides. This software can be used in conjunction with the eight-CD set and the supplementary CDs offered by PolyGram through Wadsworth. An instructor with a Macintosh computer and a Macintosh-compatible CD-ROM drive can, for example, bring up a Listening Guide on the screen, click on any portion, and hear it instantly. Classroom use can be enhanced by projecting the Macintosh screen onto an electronic blackboard, or individual students can prepare and review assignments in a multimedia lab. Details about the necessary hardware, tips for implementation, and information about ordering the software are included in the Instructor's Manual. This new technology is optional and is in no way a prerequisite for using *Music for Our Time*.

## Acknowledgments

Development editors are now standard fare in the textbook business, but few have played a more pioneering or distinguished role over the last decades than Everett Sims. Throughout the long process of writing this book, his unfailing support and good humor consoled me in many a dark hour. His unyielding credo of "immediate comprehensibility" gives this first edition whatever directness and clarity it may possess.

In return for a hearty handshake and a sandwich, my students and colleagues (most of them at UCLA) cheerfully contributed their performing talents to the preparation of the elements audiotape cassette that accompanies this book. To Kelly Parkinson (violin), Andrew Picken (viola), Adrienne Grossman (cello), Eric Werner (double bass), Marcelo Millan (lute), Lawrence Schwedler (classical guitar), Kathleen Moon (pedal harp), Iris Gross (flute and piccolo), Jessica Hoffman (oboe), Margaret Gilinsky (English horn), Laurence Lew (clarinet), Amanda Walker (bass clarinet), Peggy Smith (bassoon), Rand Clark (contrabassoon), Kathleen Maxwell (alto saxophone), Carolyn O'Keefe (trumpet), Ruth de Sarno (French horn, and my capable assistant), James King (trombone), Chris Anderson (tuba), Aaron Smith (a percussion decathlon: timpani, bass drum, snare drum, cymbals, triangle, gong, tubular bells, tambourine, castanets, xylophone, marimba, and vibraphone), Scott Schlesinger (chamber organ), Diana

Vassall (concert organ), Tsun-Yuen Lui *(qin)*, and Ali Jihad Racy *(mijwiz)*, a collective but heartfelt thanks. Special thanks go to my colleague, Professor Thomas Lee, Director of the UCLA Wind Ensemble, for his generous support, and to Michael Schwartz of the Voyager Company for postproduction assistance.

Sheryl Fullerton at Wadsworth has known me longer than either of us cares to acknowledge. What I can happily acknowledge is her unstinting support, alternately warm or tough as circumstances required. Suzanna Brabant took over as editor along the way and proved equally ingenious in keeping the project (and the author) moving ahead. Both have my deep admiration, affection, and appreciation. Sandra Craig in editorial production and Andrew Ogus in art and design performed their never-ending tasks with special aplomb. The entire production staff exemplifies the professionalism that I have come to associate with Wadsworth. At PolyGram Records, Tom Laskey and crack engineer Andrew Nicholas displayed the determination of salmon swimming upstream, resulting in a recording set of which we can all be proud.

To the reviewers of the manuscript in its various incarnations, I owe an unredeemable debt of gratitude: Ann Anderson, University of Minnesota, Duluth; Jack Ashworth, University of Louisville; Jeanne Belfy, Boise State University; Howard Brahmstedt, Tennessee Tech University; Martha Braswell, University of Georgia; Lester Brothers, University of North Texas; Lance Brunner, University of Kentucky; Gregory Carroll, University of North Carolina, Greensboro; Peter Gano, Ohio State University; Aubrey Garlington, University of North Carolina, Greensboro; William B. George, San Jose State University; Donna Dee Hardy, Shippensburg University; David Josephson, Brown University; Mark L. Lusk, Pennsylvania State University; Margaret McArthur, Texas A&M University; James McCray, Colorado State University; Jann Pasler, University of California, San Diego; William A. Payn, Bucknell University; Phil Perrin, Gardner-Webb College; Katherine Powers, University of California, Santa Barbara; Martha Rearick, University of South Florida; Christopher Reynolds, University of California, Davis; Katherine Rohrer, Princeton University; Homer Rudolf, University of Richmond; John Schwartz, Lock Haven University; Ronald Steele, University of Massachusetts at Amherst; K Marie Stolba, Indiana University–Purdue University at Fort Wayne; Anne Swartz, Baruch College, City University of New York; and Stephen Willier, Temple University. These colleagues will note their positive influence on many a page throughout the book. My failure to satisfy their laudable standards reflects in no way on them.

Only my wife, Julia, and my children, Darin and Kelly, know what sacrifices were occasioned by the writing of this book, because the greatest sacrifices were theirs. I plan to spend the nineties making it up to them.

Robert Winter

# Chapter 1

## PRELUDE

*A*lmost everyone likes music of one kind or another; where they differ is in what they like best. Some prefer the latest hits on the Top 40 charts; others prefer the favorites of twenty years ago. Some prefer a particular kind of music, such as jazz or opera. Some are deeply moved by the music they hear in a church or a synagogue, others by the blare of a rock 'n' roll band. Some prefer the lush strains of a 150-piece orchestra; others prefer the private strumming of a guitar (or perhaps singing in the shower). (See Figure 1.1.)

## LIVING WITH MUSIC

There are almost as many kinds of music as there are people to enjoy it. You have only to turn the dial of your radio across the AM and FM bands to experience the remarkable variety of contemporary musical fare. In large cities like New York or Chicago or Los Angeles you will find stations that cater to many different tastes:

- Top 40s pop-rock (also called CHR [contemporary hit rock]: Paula Abdul, Madonna, George Michael).
- Mainstream rock 'n' roll (called corporate rock by critics: Bon Jovi, the Rolling Stones, Fleetwood Mac, Bruce Springsteen).
- Hard rock and heavy metal bands (Aerosmith, Metallica, Anthrax).
- Alternative rock (where styles such as rap [M. C. Hammer, Public Enemy] got their start).
- Soul music (best known through the recordings on the Motown label, including the Supremes, Stevie Wonder, the Commodores, and Michael Jackson).
- Soft rock (ranging from Neil Diamond and Carly Simon to classic rock like the Beatles and Bob Dylan).
- Reggae (Bob Marley and the Wailers, Black Uhuru, heavy influence in Police).

*Part One   The Language of Music*

FIGURE 1.1 "Music is in the air—you simply take as much of it as you want," observed Sir Edward Elgar, the composer of the Pomp and Circumstance March that figures in countless graduation ceremonies. Indeed, music surrounds you, from the radio jingles that stick in your head to the massed sonorities of a symphony orchestra. Whether as a listener or a performer, you participate in a mode of communication that takes many forms. Opposite page: Gunther Herbig leads the Detroit Symphony Orchestra in Carnegie Hall; a teenager creates a tune on her guitar; the rock band U2 appears on the British TV show "The Tube." This page: A high school chorus in Ulster County, New York, rehearses for a performance with the Hudson Valley Philharmonic.

- Jazz (from rhythm & blues to New Orleans/Dixieland, mainstream, and contemporary styles).
- Country (sometimes called country-western, though the two are largely unrelated: Patsy Cline, Hank Williams, Jr., Emmylou Harris, Dwight Yoakam).
- Classical (such composers as Mozart, Beethoven, and Tchaikovsky).
- New Age (a recent entry; artists on the Windham Hill and Private Music labels).
- Ethnic music (such as *mariachi* among Latinos and *zydeco* among Cajuns).

This enormous range of styles—and our list is by no means complete—reflects the cultural and ethnic diversity that is so much a part of being American. (See Figure 1.2.)

You are probably familiar with at least one of these categories. If you live in an area where one type predominates (for example, country music around Nashville, Tennessee), you may be familiar with only that one type. If your exposure has been greater (whether by choice or by accident), you may have heard several or even most of these varieties. But it is unlikely that anyone—even a professional musician—could claim to have an intimate knowledge of all the varieties of music being performed and enjoyed in America today. Moreover, the combinations are endless. The singer Aretha Franklin, for example, combines elements of gospel, jazz, and soul.

*Part One   The Language of Music*

FIGURE 1.2 "Jazz is a language. It is people living in sound. Jazz is people talking, laughing, crying, building. . . . In other words, living." Substitute "American music" for "jazz" in Willis Conover's remarks, and it's obvious how jazz reflects central elements of American music—people from different cultures expressing themselves in different ways. Opposite page: A jazz ensemble conveys the joy of making music; country singer Dwight Yoakum; *mariachi* musicians serenade a family. This page: A New Orleans gospel choir.

## Universality and Diversity

We can take in this rainbow of musical colors by simply spinning a radio dial or visiting a record store, and with only a little more effort we can find specialty recordings (and, on many college campuses, live performances) of "international musics" from India and Japan, Africa and Indonesia.

So we find ourselves faced with a paradox: Music is indeed a universal language, but a language that is expressed in countless regional dialects. As with spoken dialects, none of us is likely to become fluent in more than a few. Yet all musical dialects share an essential feature: They all consist of sounds organized to express the range of human feelings, from sheer pleasure to religious devotion, from ecstatic love to blind rage. Hence music is a language of both universality *and* diversity.

## How We Got Here

Today we take the diversity of our music for granted. But things have not always been this way. If, for example, you had been a contemporary of the Austrian composer Wolfgang Amadeus Mozart living in Vienna during the last quarter of the eighteenth century, you would have heard symphonies, concertos, chamber music, dance music, sacred music, and operas. But this seeming diversity of styles is far less than the rich diversity of twentieth-century styles. Moreover, most of

the styles in Mozart's time shared common features. By modern standards, Mozart's own music was performed in public infrequently.

You probably would not have heard any of the music of Johann Sebastian Bach, who had died a half century earlier. Mozart and a few of his contemporaries knew some of Bach's music, but most Viennese had little interest in listening to the music of a dead composer. Indeed, after a few performances during Bach's lifetime his *St. Matthew Passion* went unperformed for almost 75 years because no one thought that any work, however splendid, deserved a permanent place in the repertory. Until about 1800, both listeners and patrons demanded a steady stream of new compositions; after a work had enjoyed a brief vogue, it generally passed into oblivion.

What happened to bring us the enormous diversity we enjoy today? First, over the last century and a half, Western audiences have come to prefer music from the past over newly composed music. In our list of musical styles, more than half are from the past. People have become more curious about their cultural heritage, and many listeners find in the musical styles of the past a kind of refuge from contemporary music. They charge, for example, that many of today's composers of classical music have "forgotten" their audiences.

Second, before about 1800 the enjoyment of music was more readily available to some people than to others, with access tied closely to wealth or social status. The emergence of a prosperous middle class during the nineteenth century opened music to the public at large. Today, the enormous array of regular concert series (unheard of in Mozart's time) in even small communities gives music lovers a chance to hear the music of Mozart and Bach performed many times every year. Indeed, it is likely that a public performance of some Mozart work is taking place somewhere in the world every minute of the day—a phenomenon that would doubtless astonish Mozart himself.

Third, the rapid technological advances of the twentieth century have opened up to us an extraordinary range of cultural experiences. Compact discs, cassette tapes, videodiscs, and interactive computer programs have put the music of the centuries at our fingertips. Imagine Mozart's amazement if he could witness someone jogging along to a disco version of his G-Minor Symphony on a Sony Walkman! Radio and television, live concerts, and recording have brought music into the life of anyone who cares to listen. Compared to our ancestors, we live in a musical paradise.

## THINKING ABOUT MUSIC

Not everyone agrees about what music really is. Many listeners, when they hear a new work for the first time, remark "Why, that's not even music!" But what they generally mean is "I'm not familiar with that music." Most people immediately associate a violin with music, but not a siren. Actually, some twentieth-century composers have used sirens in their compositions. (We shall study one such work, *Ionisation*, by Edgard Varèse.) Only cultural prejudice excludes the siren while admitting the violin. Granted, a siren intended to warn people of imminent danger cannot be regarded as music. Music is quite different from the mere use of sounds to transmit information (Morse code, for example).

## A Working Definition

If we are to take into account the entire sweep of Western music, from the Middle Ages to our own century, we will need a sufficiently broad definition: Music is sound (including silences!) organized to express a wide variety of human emotions. At its most basic level, music is designed to move us.

## Western Music and International Musics

The *Western tradition* has nothing to do with country-western, which is based on regional American boundaries. Rather, it refers to a centuries-old worldview. The ancient Greeks, who modestly put themselves at the center of the world, described everything to their west (most of Europe) as "Western" and everything to their east (the Middle East and Asia) as "Eastern." And it was the Greeks who provided the philosophical basis for much of European civilization. The colonists from Europe who settled North America in the seventeenth and eighteenth centuries continued to regard themselves as Western. To be sure, it is stretching things a bit to say that the United States is part of the West when, for example, San Francisco is closer to Tokyo than it is to London or Paris. Still, Americans continue to think of their culture as Western.

Over the centuries, Western music has responded repeatedly to the influence of non-Western cultures. Instead of adhering to traditional forms over long periods of time, as have most non-Western cultures, Western composers have chosen to experiment, modifying familiar styles and developing new ones. Beginning around A.D. 1000 they broke radically with non-Western cultures by introducing music in more than a single voice as a regular feature in their compositions, and ever since then they have moved restlessly and inventively in new directions.

In the chapters ahead, we shall refer frequently to non-Western influences on Western music: Near Eastern, Asian, African, and Latin American. But we shall limit ourselves to their impact on the Western tradition rather than trying to describe them in detail. Familiarity with one tradition fosters interest in others.

## Classical and Popular

Most people think of classical music as music performed in a concert hall before an audience that sits attentively for a couple of hours while a group of soberly dressed men and women sit on the stage playing old-fashioned instruments like violins, oboes, and timpani. They think of popular music, on the other hand, as music that invites movement (in dance and aerobics classes), that serves as a pleasant background for conversation, and that exploits modern technology (electric guitars, microphones, 24-track studios). Classical music suggests fine wine in crystal glasses; popular music suggests foaming beer in heavy mugs. Like all stereotypes, this one contains a grain of truth, while at the same time it distorts reality.

To begin with, the expression *classical music* is really a misnomer. After the Second World War, music commentators began to use the phrase to refer to a group of frequently played works by eighteenth- and nineteenth-century composers from Bach to Tchaikovsky, but there was never any consensus on which works were "classics" and which were not. That narrow definition excluded a great deal of fine music composed before Bach and after Tchaikovsky. More recently, the phrase *art music* has come into use to describe music whose primary intent is personal expression rather than mass appeal.

Even so, it is not always easy to distinguish art music from popular music. Historically, that distinction is very recent. Much of the music we now regard as art music was immensely popular in its own day. At least until the time of Beethoven (who composed his major works after 1800), the composer's primary aim was to please the patron or the group for whom a work was composed. If they were not pleased, the work was judged a failure.

The gulf between art music and popular music first set in with the rise of the middle class in the nineteenth century. The Industrial Revolution, which had begun in England a century before, eventually brought a dramatic increase in leisure time and, with it, an almost insatiable demand for pleasant, enjoyable music. Among the first composers to respond to that demand were members of the Strauss family, to whose waltzes, polkas, and galops Vienna danced away the second half of the nineteenth century. The orchestra that played that music was identical to the orchestra that played the symphonies of Anton Bruckner and Gustav Mahler—composers of art music. Moreover, Johannes Brahms, a most visible composer of art music, could write popular waltzes without compromising his reputation.

Only in our own century has the distinction between "art" and "pop" hardened. Modern composers are trained to specialize and are expected to pledge their allegiance to either serious or pop music. Only a few intrepid souls, like Leonard Bernstein, have dared to challenge this insistence on either/or, at the constant risk of ridicule from both camps. The 1980s brought a few signs of a thaw in this cold war, but a great many of our cultural and economic institutions seem to have a vested interest in its continuation.

True, some music has an immediate appeal for listeners—dance music, for example, which dates back at least a thousand years. Other music must be heard over and over again before it can be fully appreciated. But who can say which of the enormously varied works of jazz are art music and which are popular music? If Mozart were living in the United States today, he might very well be composing jazz or movie music rather than operas or string quartets or piano concertos.

Although most of the music we will be talking about in this book is traditionally classified as art music, what we are really interested in is music that has stood the test of time—popular as well as art.

## The Fine Arts

Ever since the Renaissance, music has been regarded as one of the fine arts. This broad term embraces human endeavors that have as their goals such intangibles as enjoyment, satisfaction, the capturing of beauty or mystery, the expression of feeling, and self-revelation. Taken together, the fine arts make up the realm of experience that we characterize as *aesthetic* rather than practical.

It is very difficult to measure aesthetic values or to demonstrate the impact of aesthetic considerations on, say, the gross national product. When budgets are drawn up and priorities established, these intangibles tend to be overshadowed by more pressing needs, such as agricultural price supports, oil depletion allowances, or armaments. Yet if we take the long view of history, civilizations are remembered more for their achievements in the arts than for their practical accomplishments. Tourists in Paris may pay a visit to Napoleon's tomb, but they are likely to be more interested in the art treasures of the Louvre or the impressionist paintings in the Musée d'Orsay. Great art endures after politicians and industrialists have been forgotten. Agriculture and industry make it possible for us to live; art helps us to understand *why* we live.

Generally it is easy to distinguish between the fine arts and more practical human activities. A road crew repaving a highway is hardly engaged in a fine art, nor is a stockbroker purchasing 1,000 shares of General Motors. The composer of a symphony, however, is unquestionably engaged in a fine art. Sometimes the distinction is harder to draw. We might argue that watching Stefi Graf make a perfect passing shot on the tennis court, or Michael Jordan complete a reverse slam dunk on the basketball court, is aesthetically as pleasing as watching a ballet dancer execute a jeté (a dance step) in Tchaikovsky's ballet *Swan Lake*.

FIGURE 1.3   An *aulos* player decorates this ancient Greek amphora. A reed pipe, the *aulos* was associated with the cult of Dionysus, the god of wine. To the Greeks, from whom we get the term *music, mousike* meant any art inspired by one of the nine muses; Euterpe was the muse of music.

In fact, the ancient Greeks regularly accompanied their athletic contests (the forerunners of our Olympic Games) with music played on a reed instrument called the *aulos* (Figure 1.3.) The principal difference between classical ballet and basketball is that basketball, like most sports, is played with the object of winning, whereas ballet exists solely for the visual and aural pleasure it affords. But a clever sports fan might argue that an exhibition by the Harlem Globetrotters, where winning plays no part, qualifies as a fine art. Almost every area of human endeavor includes some dimensions that are not strictly functional. From automobiles to overcoats, from lampposts to bathtubs, it is the aesthetic appeal of an object that matters as well as what the object does. Indeed, for many people the capacity for aesthetic enjoyment is what separates us from the rest of the animal kingdom. The fine arts are at the center of being human.

The fine arts include dance, theater, and the visual arts as well as music, and each art encompasses many modes of expression. Dance is not only ballet but also tap dancing, ethnic dance, and modern dance. Theater includes formal tragedies and comedies, street theater, improvisation, and mime. The visual arts encompass photography as well as painting and sculpture. Music includes the varieties we have mentioned in this chapter and many we have not mentioned. The motion picture has incorporated several of these elements into a composite art form, much as Romantic opera did in the nineteenth century.

Within each of the fine arts, we can further distinguish between *creators* and *performers*. A playwright is a creative artist, while an actor is a performing artist. A composer is a creator, while a singer or a violinist or a conductor is a performer who translates the composer's written notations into sound. In a sense, a skillful performer is a creator as well. Ideally there is a close collaboration between the two. Sometimes one person is both creator and performer, as were Mozart and Franz Liszt in earlier times and Bruce Springsteen in our own.

Ultimately, the role of both composer and performer is to serve the *listener*. Listeners play an active part in the fine art of music when they choose what radio stations to support, what concerts to attend, and what recordings to buy. And listening, too, is an art—an art that engages both heart and mind.

## LISTENING TO MUSIC

We listen to music for many reasons: for relaxation, for stimulation, for re-creation of past experience. Sometimes music elicits feelings of joy or sorrow or awe. And sometimes we listen to music for the music itself—the power of a *rhythm* by Bach, the development of a *theme* by Beethoven, or the unfolding of a *melody* by Tchaikovsky (concepts we shall discuss in Chapters 2 and 3). But how can the formal study of music enrich these varied experiences? We can best answer this question by examining four components that are essential to musical understanding. Without the elements of concentration, feelings and intellect, words, and historical context, you can have occasional flings with music but no long-term relationship.

### Four Key Components

**Concentration.** Under what circumstances do you ordinarily listen to music? Are you in a situation where you feel comfortable? Can you give the music your undivided attention? Are you well rested and relaxed? If you are a typical listener, your answer to most of these questions is no. Contemporary lifestyles do not encourage the kind of concentration that leads to a deeply satisfying musical experience. Music serves as a pleasant background in supermarkets, restaurants, elevators, and movies. We hear "canned" music on every side, but rarely do we listen to live music. We accept as a matter of course lip-synched performances by pop singers on MTV. Music has become a packaged commodity dispensed by loudspeakers.

Listening to music is quite different from simply hearing it. Have you ever met people who nod their heads at whatever you say but who are not really there? They hear you, but they are not listening. Nothing much happens between you and such people. The same is true of music. It shares its secrets with us only if we are prepared to listen to what it has to say.

**Feelings and Intellect.** Many people are apprehensive about studying music in a serious way: "I enjoy music so much that I'm afraid I'll spoil my pleasure if I start to analyze and dissect it." But most people who hold this position overlook a fundamental condition of human existence. You may be deeply moved when you hear a work for the first time, but then you gradually discover that you cannot recreate that first experience upon each rehearing. You can choose either to move on to another work and hope for a similar experience, or you can delve more deeply into the work that moved you in the first place, searching for whatever made it so arresting. The analogy to human relationships is again instructive. We may be drawn initially to a person by physical attraction or by surface charm, but unless we build on these initial responses the relationship is doomed to either stagnation or termination.

Feelings and intellect, as it turns out, are not natural enemies but inseparable allies. Although an emotional reaction may spark our interest for a moment, without the exercise of intellect our feelings soon fade. Far from hindering feelings, the intellect is necessary to their very survival and growth. Suppose a particular passage in a piece gives you goose bumps the first few times you hear it. Learning about the musical devices that give that passage its effect will probably increase your admiration for both the work and its composer. More important, it will broaden your range of responses.

**Words.** Many people resist translating an emotional experience into words. And yet the only way we have of communicating about music is through words, however inadequate they may seem. Although the music must ultimately speak for itself, words can spark our curiosity and help us understand an experience.

Many of the words people use to talk about music are jargon, designed to impress rather than to convey anything of substance. Other words, however, provide us with conceptual handles. They are technical only in the sense that they specify a particular musical phenomenon. The term *triad*, for example, refers to a particular relationship among three notes; no other term does the job as accurately or as economically. Without such terms, we would have to resort to endless strings of nontechnical words, and even then we would never be sure we had conveyed precisely what we had in mind.

**Historical Context.** Because we live in a time of ceaseless change, even the recent past sometimes seems remote. It is hard for some of us to be enthusiastic about music composed by someone who lived a couple of centuries ago in a remote part of the world and who bore a strange name. The same is true of the

FIGURE 1.4 Portrait of
Johann Sebastian Bach
by Elias Gottlob Hauss-
man. Bach was 61 at the
time of this painting; he
died, completely blind,
four years later.

visual arts. Take, for example, the portrait of Johann Sebastian Bach made in 1746 (Figure 1.4). What kind of strange hairdo is that? Why does Bach look so stuffy? Why is he wearing a collarless coat with brass buttons and puffed sleeves? Why is he holding that piece of music so stiffly? Why is the whole portrait so somber?

Knowing something about the historical context helps us answer those questions. Bach, like most of his contemporaries, is wearing a powdered wig because it was customary to wash one's hair only every few weeks. The clothing he is wearing was the uniform of the skilled servant, the class to which Bach belonged. The piece of music he is holding was written to celebrate his admission to a prestigious honorary society, and a stiff, formal pose was customary for portraits on such occasions.

Historical context helps us to understand Bach's music, just as it helps us to understand Bach as a person. The first time we hear a Bach cantata we may be put off by the unfamiliar language, the strange symbolism of the text (even in translation), the alternation between two singing styles, and by other unfamiliar conventions. Once we understand those conventions, however, we can enter into the work and derive pleasure from listening to it. A sense of history enriches our musical understanding.

## SOME PROCEDURAL MATTERS

The next three chapters introduce the concepts that will enable you, with the help of your instructor and the accompanying cassette, to communicate verbally about the basic elements of musical style. You have been experiencing the elements of style—*rhythm* and *beat* and *meter*, for example—all your life. But now our goal is to translate those intuitive experiences into conscious ones. At first the listening exercises may seem like mere mental calisthenics, but as time passes you will notice that they are adding constantly to your listening pleasure.

For the time being, do not worry about the terms used to identify musical works. You do not need to know the difference between a "prelude," a "gigue," and a "sonata" in order to start sharpening your listening skills. You do not need to know whether Beethoven lived before or after Debussy. All you need to do is *listen*.

# *Chapter 2*

## THE PRIMACY OF RHYTHM

TAPE EXAMPLE 1a
Gershwin, "I Got Rhythm"

W hen we listen to a piece of music, whether for the first time or for the hundredth, we are listening at many different levels. Although each listener is more naturally attuned to some dimensions of music than to others, humans seem to respond most readily to rhythm. Why, for example, do we find George Gershwin's famous song "I Got Rhythm" (Tape Example 1a) so enjoyable? Most people would describe Gershwin's tune as "catchy" or "bouncy."

### INCIDENCE AND DURATION

The appeal of Gershwin's tune lies not in the individual sounds but in the *patterns* of sound he creates by manipulating two time-related dimensions: first, *when* each individual sound begins, known as its moment of *incidence*; and second, *how long* each sound lasts, known as its *duration*. **Rhythm** is the pattern in time created by the incidence and duration of individual sounds.

If you have ever watched a tugboat pulling a passenger liner out of a harbor (perhaps on television or in the movies), you heard a series of sharp, well-separated blasts sounded by the tug. The moment of incidence is the precise moment at which each blast begins; the duration is the length of time the blast lasts. If you were to time the blasts with a wristwatch, you might find that the first blast began 10 seconds after the minute (its moment of incidence) and lasted for 10 seconds (its duration). The second blast might begin 5 seconds later, at 25 seconds after the minute (its moment of incidence), and might last only 5 seconds (its duration)—and so on, with successive blasts. By the time the tugboat released the liner and sent it on its way, you would have charted the *rhythm* of the tugboat blasts.

Notice the difference when an audience applauds a performance in a concert hall. Each member of the audience produces a series of brief claps; the moments of incidence are close together, and the duration of each clap is only a fraction of a second. When everyone claps at once, we hear a continuous wash of sound in which it is impossible to detect any pattern of incidence and duration.

The rhythm of most music falls between the blasts of a tugboat whistle and the applause of an audience. Not even highly trained musicians can identify the incidence and duration of every sound in a piece of music; instead, they single out the rhythmic patterns that emerge from the sounds. If they alter those patterns, they alter the music itself. Notice what happens when we alter the rhythm of the opening of Gershwin's "I Got Rhythm" (Tape Example 1b) while keeping the music identical in all other respects.

In this version the music sounds square and predictable rather than catchy and bouncy. Both versions have rhythm of a sort, just like any other succession of sounds—whether a symphony by Beethoven or a rush-hour traffic jam. What Gershwin meant by his title was "I Got *Catchy* Rhythm." Later on we will see what rhythmic feature makes Gershwin's song so catchy. But first we must examine two extreme types of musical rhythm.

## REGULAR RHYTHM AND IRREGULAR RHYTHM

You are driving down a highway and spot a blinking light at an intersection. Its predictable pattern of incidence and duration warns you to slow down. Its rhythm is regular. You pass safely through the intersection and drive on until you approach a great city sparkling against the night sky. The lights along the skyline seem to blink on and off at random. Their rhythm is irregular, suggesting the activity and excitement of the city.

We perceive musical rhythms *aurally* in much the same way as we perceive the rhythms of blinking lights *visually*. Listen first to a prelude by J. S. Bach (Tape Example 2). In most of this piece the incidence and duration of individual sounds are utterly regular and predictable. Toward the end we hear a faster passage, then a slower one, and finally a return to the opening speed. Now listen to the opening of Debussy's *Voiles* ("Sails") (Tape Example 3). Here the rhythmic pattern seems irregular, almost random. There is a leisurely unpredictability to the wind in these sails that keeps us off balance. (Actually, this seeming irregularity is highly organized; the irregular bits are repeated in a very regular pattern, although you may need several hearings to grasp it.)

Bach's Prelude and Debussy's *Voiles* are extreme examples of rhythmic regularity and irregularity. Most pieces exhibit a more limited mix of rhythms.

## ORGANIZED RHYTHM

Regardless of the mix between regular and irregular rhythms in a piece, not all the sounds that make up a rhythmic pattern are of equal importance. Rather, the rhythms of Western music tend to be *organized* and *hierarchical*—that is, they are arranged into specific groupings, and these groupings are arranged according to greater or lesser importance. To support that structure, composers use beat and meter.

## Beat

A **beat** is the basic unit of musical time. A beat in music is analogous to a human heartbeat and is therefore sometimes referred to as a *pulse*. Listen to the theme from the Andante of Beethoven's Piano Sonata in G Major, Op. 14 No. 2, in which the regular beat is clearly apparent (Tape Example 4). Listen to this excerpt several times until you can mark the beat by tapping with a pencil or with your finger. Make each tap coincide with the beginning of each new beat. Occasionally the beat seems to stop, and you may think you have lost it. But all this means is that more than one beat has taken place. If you continue to tap regularly, the music always "catches up." The beat continues whether or not it is marked by the incidence of a new sound.

Several non-Western musics consist of a succession of rhythmically undifferentiated sounds, with the beats strung together in an additive (though often highly complex) fashion. Much of the early sacred music known in the West as *plainchant* also lacks any pronounced rhythmic differentiation. Beginning around A.D. 1000, however, Western composers began to group beats together into larger, hierarchical units.

TAPE EXAMPLE 4
Beethoven, theme from the Andante of the Piano Sonata in G Major, Op. 14 No. 2

## Meter

**Meter** is the organization of beats into a regular, recurring pattern. In musical notation (the visual shorthand used to represent music), each recurrence of the pattern occupies a *measure*.* The first beat of each measure is the most highly stressed, and hence rhythmically the most important. Stressed beats provide the framework around which the measures and, consequently, the whole piece are organized. The regular use of metric patterns emerged around the twelfth century and lasted well into the twentieth century in art music. It is still a central feature of most popular music.

# SIMPLE METERS

Most music composed between A.D. 1200 and 1910 employs one of two simple meters: duple meter and triple meter.

*The British prefer the term *bar*; the terms are used interchangeably throughout this book.

FIGURE 2.1 "Left, right, left, right, left": A military band in march formation follows a clear two-step pattern.

## Duple Meter

**Duple meter** is the regular grouping of beats into twos. Pieces with two, four, or even eight beats per measure are in duple meter. In a sense, duple meter is an extension of the binary symmetry of the human body (two legs, two arms, two eyes, two ears). The boldest music based on this binary symmetry is the march (see Figure 2.1), as in "The Rifle-Regiment March" by John Philip Sousa (Tape Example 5). Familiar examples of duple meter are "Yankee Doodle" and "America the Beautiful." Duple meter occurs so frequently in Western music that it is sometimes referred to as "common time." From its beginnings as dance music in the 1950s, rock music also has been almost exclusively binary.

TAPE EXAMPLE 5
Sousa, opening of "The Rifle-Regiment March"

## Triple Meter

**Triple meter** is the regular grouping of beats into threes. Composers in the Middle Ages favored triple meter because it symbolized the Christian Trinity (Father, Son, and Holy Ghost). In fact, triple meter was regarded as the "perfect" meter, whereas duple meter was regarded as "imperfect."

Listen to a brief waltz by the nineteenth-century composer Franz Schubert (Tape Example 6). Notice how easily this music falls into triple meter. If you try to impose any kind of duple meter on this waltz, you will find that there is just no way of making it fit. A surprising number of well-known tunes are in triple

TAPE EXAMPLE 6
Schubert, Waltz in A Major

meter, including "The Star-Spangled Banner," "Happy Birthday," and "Take Me Out to the Ball Game."

Not all of these tunes begin on the first beat of each measure, which is known as the *downbeat*. We sing: "Oh— / SAY can you / SEE." The music of "Oh" anticipates the downbeat and is called an *upbeat*. Similarly, the first two syllables of "Hap-py / BIRTH-day to / YOU" are an upbeat, while "TAKE Me Out to the Ball Game" begins on a downbeat. (The terms *downbeat* and *upbeat* derive from the motions made by conductors, who indicate a downbeat by a downward motion and an upbeat by an upward motion.)

In each of these examples, the meter is quite easy to recognize. Although the meter of much of the music we will be listening to is equally clear, some composers favor music in which the meter is elusive or downright ambiguous.

TAPE EXAMPLE 7a
Beethoven, Andante, theme opening

Listen again to the beginning of Beethoven's Andante (repeated in Tape Example 7a) and see if you can determine whether it is in duple or triple meter. Count out loud:

2-beat measures: ONE-two/ONE-two/ONE-two/ONE-two
*or*
3-beat measures: ONE-two-three/ONE-two-three/ONE-two-three

TAPE EXAMPLE 7b
Beethoven theme in 2-beat units

TAPE EXAMPLE 7c
Beethoven theme in 3-beat units

If you have trouble organizing these beats, move ahead to Tape Examples 7b and 7c. Here each pattern is imposed on the same theme. As you count along, reinforce what you are hearing by moving your head or your hand to match the beat. You probably discovered that the triple meter does not fit at all. The stresses called for by the music turn up in all the "wrong" places, whereas the 2-beat pattern reinforces the natural stresses. (Beethoven actually specified 4-beat units to make the theme less choppy.)

## SUBDIVIDING BEATS

In addition to simple meter, there are two more complex varieties of meter, called *compound* meter and *irregular* meter. Compound meter is defined not only by the meters we have been discussing but also by the manner in which individual beats are subdivided. So before we address compound meter we must see how beats are subdivided.

### Duple Subdivision of Beats

Beats may be grouped together, but a single beat may also be divided into smaller units. We can think of these subdivisions as the rhythmic background, as opposed to the rhythmic foreground provided by meter. In Western music, subdivided beats evolved primarily in units divisible by two. A good way to demonstrate this to yourself is to take a pencil in each hand. (If you don't trust your ability to coordinate two rhythmic events, persuade a friend to wield one of the pencils.) With one hand, set up a slow, steady beat no faster than 60 per minute (one per second). Now tap along with the other hand. At first, keep both hands tapping together. Then double the number of taps by the second hand to two per beat while maintaining the original beat by the first hand. After you feel secure doing this, double the tapping rate of the faster hand once again to four taps per beat. (These are, by the way, the basic exercises that any rock drummer—or would-be conductor—must master.) Practice switching back and forth—for example, go directly from one to four taps and back again. If you have trouble doing this, listen to the demonstration in Tape Example 8.

Now listen to the continuation of the Beethoven Andante (Tape Example 9a), whose opening you heard in Tape Examples 4 and 7a–c. The basic beat is still the same. Now, however, instead of only one sound per pulse, each beat is subdivided into two evenly spaced sounds (the second of which receives slightly less emphasis than the first). Listen several times until you can identify these duple subdivisions of the beat.

Now move on to Tape Example 9b, in which Beethoven gives each beat four evenly spaced sounds. You will need a nimble tongue in order to count ONE-two-three-four aloud for each beat, but even if you cannot, you will be able to mark the four sounds mentally. An interesting thing happens at the very end of this example. Beethoven, having moved from one to two to four sounds per beat, suddenly reverts to the one sound per beat of the opening. He uses this device to remind us of where we started and also to play a little joke with the last sound (perhaps to wake up any listeners who might have dozed off).

Having mastered the moderate pulse of the Beethoven Andante, you might wish to tackle the opening of Beethoven's *Waldstein* Sonata (Tape Example 10). Here the basic pulse is considerably faster. At first, each rapid beat is subdivided into two parts. Then, about 20 seconds into the excerpt, the music makes a sudden, dramatic pause. When the music resumes, each beat is further subdivided into four parts. Even if you have worked as an auctioneer, you will probably not be able to count these subdivisions as fast as they occur. That their speed cannot be articulated verbally, but only felt by the body, gives this opening its tremendous drive.

Finally, at the end of the excerpt, the rhythmic process reverses itself: The four subdivisions per beat return abruptly to two per beat and then to one per beat (or even one per two beats), half that of the opening. So long as beats are subdivided according to the standard duple patterns illustrated by these Beethoven examples, Western ears have subsumed them within a duple- or triple-meter framework. But when the metric background is triple, both composers and performers have acknowledged a new category of meter.

## Compound Meter

**Compound meter** is the mixture of a triple metric background with either a duple or triple metric foreground. Listen to the opening section of the first

TAPE EXAMPLE 8
Subdivision of beats in duple patterns

TAPE EXAMPLE 9a
Beethoven, Variation 1 from the Andante of the Piano Sonata in G Major, Op. 14 No. 2

TAPE EXAMPLE 9b
Beethoven, Variation 3 from the Andante of the Piano Sonata in G Major, Op. 14 No. 2

TAPE EXAMPLE 10
Beethoven, opening of the Piano Sonata in C Major, Op. 53, *Waldstein*

TAPE EXAMPLE 11a
Haydn, exposition of the
opening movement of the
Piano Sonata in E Minor,
H. XVI/34

movement of Joseph Haydn's Piano Sonata in E Minor (Tape Example 11a). (In this example you will encounter three sudden silences, each signaled by a *fermata*\*—a favorite trick of this composer; each time the music resumes, it begins on the downbeat of a measure.) The immediate sense of meter comes from the rapid 3-note units, so it might at first seem that the Sonata is in simple triple meter. But if you listen carefully, you will discover that, on top of this pattern, moving only one-third as fast, is a slower duple grouping of two beats per bar. The 3-note groupings provide a triple background to the slower duple foreground:

TRIPLE BACKGROUND:

ONE-two-three-FOUR-five-six/ ONE-two-three-FOUR-five-six/

DUPLE FOREGROUND:

ONE————————TWO————————/ONE————————TWO————————/

In some music this relationship is reversed—that is, the meter has a duple background and a triple foreground. Listen to Tape Example 11a until you can hear both metric levels working separately and together. In Tape Example 11b, each level is counted with the music, first the triple background and then the duple foreground.

TAPE EXAMPLE 11b
Haydn, opening of the
Piano Sonata in E Minor
with background and fore-
ground levels of the com-
pound meter

## Irregular Meter

**Irregular meter** is the mixture at a single rhythmic level of more than one kind of metric grouping. For well over 700 years, Western composers worked with the possibilities (and within the limitations) of duple, triple, and compound meters. In our own century, composers have extended metric complexity even further. As we mentioned earlier, some contemporary composers of art music have dispensed with meter altogether. Others have combined traditional meter with new elements, producing novel, irregular meters. A delightful example is the fourth in a series of six *Dances in Bulgarian Rhythm* by the Hungarian composer Béla Bartók (Tape Example 12a). Notice that this piece is organized quite differently from our earlier examples. First, the metric background is irregular and "off balance"; there is no easily audible pulse. Yet the metric foreground is highly regular, with a slow pulse repeated more than 60 times in the course of the piece. *Irregular* groupings recur in a highly *regular* fashion, with each irregular group constituting a measure. Although it is relatively easy to detect the slower pulse, it is more difficult to determine just how the individual bars are organized. In Tape Example 12b the opening is played more slowly. At this slower speed you can hear that each bar is made up of eight beats. This might

TAPE EXAMPLE 12a
Bartók, Dance No. 4 in
Bulgarian Rhythm

TAPE EXAMPLE 12b
Bartók, opening of Dance
No. 4 played slowly

\*A *fermata* (notated as ⌢) can be applied to either a sound (which it extends beyond its written value by about half) or, as in this example, to a rest (which it extends by the same amount).

suggest a traditional background division of 2 + 2 + 2 + 2. Bartók's organization, however, is quite different. Instead of duple groupings, each measure is arranged 3 + 2 + 3. Here the irregularity occurs at the background level. But it may also operate at the foreground level or even simultaneously at both the background and foreground levels. An infinite variety of irregular meters is possible, limited only by the ingenuity of the composer and the skill of the performer.

Throughout most of Bartók's dance, the rhythmic arrangement has a perfect mirror symmetry:

STRESS:

ONE-two-three-FOUR-five-SIX-seven-eight

DURATION:

one     two          two          two          one

On each side of the two beats in the middle of each bar there is a 3-note group, one the inverse of the other. The first beats are organized *short-long* (a *short* receives one beat, a *long* receives two), while the last three beats are *long-short*; hence the mirror symmetry. Now listen again to Tape Example 12a and see if you can follow Bartók's unique arrangement.

## TEMPO

FIGURE 2.2  A traditional mechanical metronome. This device for indicating the exact tempo of a piece was popularized by Johann Maelzel, a German contemporary of Beethoven's.

**Tempo** (Italian for "time") is the speed of a piece of music. When we speak of the speed of an automobile or a train, the concept seems simple enough. But our perception of musical tempo is more complex, because it depends on the interrelationships among all three of the rhythmic characteristics we have described: *beat, meter*, and the *subdivision* of beats.

Beat has the greatest influence on our perception of tempo. We have already noted that the beat in music corresponds closely to the heartbeat of our body. When we check our pulse, we determine how many times per minute the heart is pumping blood into the circulatory system. At rest, healthy people have a pulse rate of between 60 and 80 per minute. (Some marathon runners have rates as low as 40.) In the Renaissance, when the notion of a regular beat was introduced, theorists recommended a *tactus* (Latin for "beat") of about 80 beats per minute to mirror the human body at rest. Under stress or physical exertion, the pulse rate may climb to 160 or higher. A musical beat is any pulse that falls between the extremes of roughly 40 to 180. The *metronome*, a mechanical device popularized around 1815, ticks off tempo in *beats per minute* (Figure 2.2). Many composers include numerical *metronome markings* along with their tempo markings. Because tempo markings were first used in Italy in the seventeenth century, in art music they are usually given in Italian. Most commonly, tempos fall within the bodily extremes:

| ITALIAN TEMPO MARKING | ENGLISH TRANSLATION | METRONOME MARKING IN BEATS PER MINUTE |
|---|---|---|
| Largo | Very slow | 40–50 |
| Adagio | Slow | 50–70 |
| Andante | Walking | 70–100 |
| Allegretto | Slightly fast | 100–120 |
| Allegro | Fast | 120–140 |
| Molto allegro | Very fast | 140–160 |
| Presto | Extremely fast | 160–180 |

Meter also affects our perception of tempo. Imagine, for example, two pieces with an identical tempo. One of them has four beats per measure, however, while the other has two. Even though the rate of individual beats is the same, the piece with two beats per measure will *seem* faster, because it has twice as many strong first beats as the 4-beat pattern.

Finally, the degree to which the beats are *subdivided* also influences our perception of tempo. Imagine the same two pieces with an identical tempo. The beats in one of them are subdivided into no more than two parts, while the beats in the other are subdivided into four parts. Again, the second piece will seem faster.

It is largely because of these subtle interrelationships among beat, meter, and subdivision that performers may interpret the tempo of the same piece in widely different ways.

## ACCENT AND SYNCOPATION

Beat and meter are the staples of rhythm. The two principal means of enlivening them are *accent* and *syncopation*. Both depend on regular meter for their effect; yet both serve to relieve the monotony that relentless metric regularity might produce.

An **accent** is a conspicuous and sudden emphasis given to a particular sound. The most common means of creating a musical accent is through a sudden increase in *volume*. Other means of creating an accent are *holding* the sound for slightly longer than notated, and *delaying* its attack slightly. These three devices are sometimes used in combination.

We use accents in our everyday speech. For example, rather than saying "The remake of the movie *Tarzan the Ape Man* was horrendous," we might say "The remake of the movie *Tarzan the Ape Man* was horRENdous." Although this verbal accent is not necessary to understanding, it adds to the impact of the comment.

The skillful use of accents in music has sometimes transformed mediocre ideas into memorable ones. A good example is the Scherzo from the Piano Sonata in

TAPE EXAMPLE 13a
Beethoven, opening of the
Scherzo from the Piano
Sonata in E-flat Major, Op.
31 No. 3, without accents

TAPE EXAMPLE 13b
Beethoven, opening of the
Scherzo with accents

E-flat Major, Op. 31 No. 3 by Beethoven, a clever manipulator of accent. This appealing piece can be counted most easily in two briskly subdivided beats per bar (ONE-and-two-and/ONE-and-two-and). First, listen to the opening without the accents (Tape Example 13a). Now, listen to the same excerpt with the accents called for by the composer (Tape Example 13b). In this example the first four accents all appear at the same place in the first and second, and in the fifth and sixth, bars: on the last *and*. They propel the music forward in a delightfully off-balance way. Their impact is greater because they occur *off* rather than *on* a main beat (these are actually examples of *syncopation*, discussed below). The two strong-beat accents that occur in the middle of the excerpt (during a kind of "waiting" passage) prepare for the return of the original idea, which then repeats the original pattern of off-beat accents. Although the passage is interesting even without the accents, Beethoven's version is more engaging.

**Syncopation** is the shift of an accent, within a well-defined meter, from strong beats to weaker beats or portions of beats (as in the first four accents in the Beethoven example). Syncopation is often linked with the origins of jazz, although it had been around for many centuries before. A catchy example is the ragtime "Euphonic Sounds" by Scott Joplin, which the composer subtitled "A Syncopated Two Step" (Tape Example 14a).

TAPE EXAMPLE 14a
Joplin, opening of
"Euphonic Sounds"

TAPE EXAMPLE 14b
Joplin, "Euphonic
Sounds" stripped of
syncopation

If you had difficulty identifying exactly where the syncopation occurs in "Euphonic Sounds," listen to a version stripped of syncopation (Tape Example 14b). (Nothing is altered except the rhythm!) In a way this is a more "correct" version—though far less interesting. Beats one and two are both marked by notes in the melody (the part you would hum or whistle). Joplin, however, placed the melody *off* the beat, with the left hand marking the meter on the strong beats. This opposition between clearly discernible meter and rhythmic displacement is what gives syncopation its effect.

If in reading this chapter you have developed a genuine feel for the various aspects of rhythm, you are now ready to move on to the two other principal elements of music, melody and harmony. (And you will know which aspect of rhythm makes Gershwin's "I Got Rhythm" so catchy.)

# Chapter 3

## MELODY AND HARMONY

We have defined rhythm as the pattern of sounds in time. But time also provides the framework for the two other building blocks of music: melody and harmony.

We learn early on that time flows in one direction. Although we sometimes speak of turning back the clock, the truth is, "time marches on" (if not necessarily in duple meter). Hence it is natural to think of time as one-directional. In our own lives, we are mostly aware of the passage of seconds, minutes, hours, days, years, and decades—what we call *successive time*.

But successive time is only one dimension of time. What we perceive as a succession of moments in our own lives are simultaneous moments in the lives of other people. When New Yorkers are going to bed, people in California are sitting down to dinner, and Hawaiians are just finishing lunch. When someone is laughing in one place, someone is crying somewhere else. Although we generally pay less attention to *simultaneous time* than to successive time, simultaneous time is no less real.

Music, too, is governed by these time-related dimensions. Sometimes music proceeds by a succession of single sounds. We call that dimension *melody*. **Melody** is the succession of single sounds in a coherent arrangement. We also refer to melody as *tune, theme,* or *voice*. Just what a "coherent arrangement" is depends on the cultural context and the taste of listeners. You might disagree with someone who calls the sounds produced by imitating a barking dog a "melody," but your disagreement would have more to do with taste than with definition.

If all music consisted of nothing more than single sounds in succession, then melody would be the only term we would need to describe it. But since about A.D. 1000, Western composers have been keenly interested in the simultaneous dimension of time in music, known as *harmony*. **Harmony** is the simultaneous playing of two or more different sounds.

Harmony is far more characteristic of Western music than it is of other international musics. Again, to deny that the simultaneous sounds arising from a traffic jam constitute harmony would be a matter of taste rather than a matter of definition. In this chapter we shall focus on the directions in which Western melody and harmony have developed.

# FOUR ESSENTIAL INGREDIENTS

To understand melody and harmony we must consider four concepts that are common to all musical systems: pitch, interval, octave, and scale.

## Pitch

**Pitch** is the high and low of sounds, measured in acoustical frequencies. If you are a woman, your natural speaking voice is probably higher than that of most men; if you are a man, your voice is probably lower than that of most women. Listen now to a succession of pitches on the piano that move from low to high and back to low again (Tape Example 15).

TAPE EXAMPLE 15
Pitch from low to high and back to low again

Frequency determines the pitch of a sound. The **frequency** of a sound is the number of times per second that the air carrying the sound vibrates as a wave. The higher the frequency, the higher the pitch. Unlike the random, continuous frequencies of sound we hear around us, most Western music consists of a predetermined set of *fixed pitches*.

Each of the 88 keys on the modern piano sounds a single pitch. Out of the infinite number of pitches* available, the piano can produce only those 88. Up to recent times the number of pitches available for music has been very limited. A fixed-pitch instrument such as the piano could never match the continuous range of pitches we hear in the songs of birds, for example. Electronic instruments (discussed in Chapter 30) introduced since the Second World War have greatly expanded the available range of pitches.

## Interval

An **interval** is the distance between two pitches. The interval is the same whether the pitches are played simultaneously or successively. With a finite number of fixed pitches, the number of available intervals is also finite.

## Octave

The universal interval found in virtually all musical systems is the octave. An **octave** is the interval in which one pitch is doubled (or halved) in frequency by another pitch. The ancient Greeks discovered that when they played a note whose frequency was exactly twice (or half) that of another note, the two notes appeared to duplicate each other. When the letter notation that we use today was developed in the Middle Ages, theorists assigned the same letter to notes an octave apart. Hence "middle C" refers to a specific note; if we say simply "C," no one can tell which of the seven different C's on the piano we mean. Listen to a succession of C's first played from low to high and then played simultaneously

*Pitches are also called *notes*, although that term may carry other meanings.

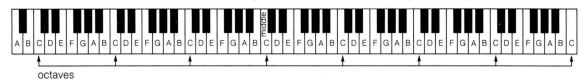

octaves

FIGURE 3.1 A full, modern keyboard includes more than seven octaves. Notice that all black notes have two designations; for example C-sharp and D-flat refer to the same note.

TAPE EXAMPLE 16
C's played successively from bottom to top of the keyboard, and then four played simultaneously

(Tape Example 16). Notice that regardless of whether they are played successively or simultaneously, each C duplicates the others at a higher or lower octave.

## Scale

While the octave is nearly universal, musical systems employ different *scales*. A **scale** is an array of fixed pitches between two notes an octave apart. The word *scale* derives from the Latin word for ladder, and each fixed note is analogous to a rung. A scale represents the actual pitches that might be chosen from among the many available for use in a particular composition. For the last five centuries or so, the octave in Western music has been divided into 12 equal *half steps* (also called *semitones*). The most frequently used scales consist largely of notes separated by two half steps, which have therefore been designated as *whole steps*.

When all 12 semitones are played successively, the resulting scale is called the *chromatic scale* (meaning "fully colored," that is, using all the available pitches). If you have access to a piano, you can hear what a chromatic scale sounds like by playing in succession all the pitches between any two notes an octave apart. Tape Example 17 demonstrates the sounds of the chromatic scale from middle C to the C above. The chromatic scale is so regular that it sounds just about the same no matter what note you begin on, so it has not been the most favored scale among Western composers. In fact, the development of Western scales began from the seven notes that, on a modern keyboard, are colored white. (Figure 3.1 shows the layout of the modern keyboard.) Regardless of where you begin, each scale built on the white notes contains five whole steps and two half steps (between B and C, and between E and F). Such seven-note scales were called *diatonic* scales, from the Greek for "proceeding (mostly!) by whole steps."

The ancient Greeks referred to different arrays of these diatonic scales as *modes,* and medieval theorists took up this terminology. Medieval and Renaissance melodies are assigned to one of several modes depending on a range of factors, including where they begin and—especially—where they end.

Around 1690 (and until about 1910 in art music), Western music settled on two diatonic patterns, known today as the *major* scale and the *minor* scale. The **major scale** consists of five whole steps plus half steps between the third and fourth, and the seventh and eighth, degrees.* If you begin with any C on the piano, the major scale consists of all the white notes (Tape Example 18). Each of these seven notes is assigned a letter of the alphabet, in this case C-D-E-F-G-A-B[-C]; the same letters are used for corresponding notes in higher and lower

TAPE EXAMPLE 17
Chromatic scale from middle C to the C above

TAPE EXAMPLE 18
Major scale starting on middle C

---

* *Degree* is a more precise term for *note* when we are referring to the steps of a scale; the eighth degree of a diatonic scale is an octave duplication of the first degree.

*Part One   The Language of Music*

octaves. The five black notes that fill out the octave are called *accidentals* (though they have nothing to do with chance or mishap); each black note can be either a *sharp* (a half step above the nearest white note; abbreviated ♯) or a *flat* (a half step below the nearest white note; abbreviated ♭). Hence C♯ is the black note one half step above C, and B♭ is the black note one half step below B. A major scale that starts on a note other than C uses anywhere from one to all five of these accidentals. Although most sharps and flats are black notes, the irregular physical layout of the Western keyboard allows for the possibility of a white sharp or flat—for example, E♯. (The note a half step above E is also a white note.)

The **minor scale** results from flatting (lowering by a half step) the third and sixth degrees of the major scale. Hence the C-minor scale consists of the notes C-D-E♭-F-G-A♭-B[-C]. (Listen to Tape Example 19a.) This form is referred to more specifically as the *harmonic minor scale.* Because the interval between the sixth and seventh degrees in the harmonic minor scale is an awkward-sounding step and a half, it is frequently smoothed out by raising the sixth degree in an ascending scalar passage (A♭ to A in C Minor) and lowering the seventh degree in a descending one (B to B♭ in C Minor). Because of its emphasis on smooth adjacent intervals, this form of the minor scale is called the *melodic minor scale* (Tape Example 19b).

Scales, as we have seen, consist of half steps and whole steps; movement by either of these steps is called *conjunct* or *stepwise motion.* Most melodies also employ intervals larger than a whole step; this kind of motion is called *disjunct* or, more simply, *motion by a leap.*

Although there is some scientific basis for our system, it is only one of many possible systems; Japanese music, for example, is built on a 5-note scale, and some scales in Arabian music use as many as 17 notes. Tape Example 20 presents one of the numerous 7-note scales (called *maqām*) used in Middle Eastern music. To Western ears, some of these pitches sound "out of tune." But again, this is a matter of taste, not tuning. To Middle Eastern ears, our two scales seem bland and limited.

Armed with the concepts of pitch, interval, octave, and scale, we can now turn to an exploration of melody and harmony.

TAPE EXAMPLE 19a
Minor scale starting on middle C

TAPE EXAMPLE 19b
Melodic minor scale starting on middle C

TAPE EXAMPLE 20
Middle Eastern scale

## VOCAL MELODY

Melody, especially sung melody, is the most expressive element of music. No instrument—not even the violin—can match the expressiveness of the human voice. Although we do not know what sort of music human beings first made, it was probably singing. Almost everyone is born with the instrument of voice, and that instrument is the most personal expression of ourselves.

What is a good melody? People's tastes in melody have differed from age to age, and from group to group. An operatic tenor sings melodies very different from those sung by a lead singer in a heavy metal band. Yet to their audiences both are pleasing.

## INSTRUMENTAL MELODY

There is no ironclad distinction between vocal and instrumental melody, nor is it always possible to determine whether a particular melody was vocally or instrumentally conceived. Nevertheless, instrumental melody—especially melody for keyboards and strings—is generally less bound to the rhythm of human breathing than vocal melody. Listen to the first half of the slow movement of the *Concerto in the Italian Style* for harpsichord by Johann Sebastian Bach (Tape Example 21). Throughout the more than two minutes this excerpt lasts, the melody presents only two breathing points. Not even the most deep-chested singer could manage that. Since a harpsichord—an instrument whose tone is produced by plucking strings rather than through air pressure—does not need to breathe as a singer does, the phrases can be considerably longer. Another characteristic of the harpsichord is that its sound begins to die away (known acoustically as *decay*) almost immediately after a note is struck. Hence the composer must keep "renewing" the melody in order to keep the music moving. Finally, the melody's *range* from low to high exceeds that of most human voices.

TAPE EXAMPLE 21
J. S. Bach, slow movement of the *Concerto in the Italian Style*, BWV 971

This excerpt also provides a good example of the complementary relationship between melody and accompaniment. **Accompaniment is the subordinate material that supports the melody.** This first portion of Bach's slow movement prepares the way for the melody that follows. Once the melody has been established, the introductory material functions as the accompaniment.

The melody is generally in the top voice, with the accompaniment supplying a harmonic foundation. But sometimes the composer places the accompaniment above the melody, as in this *Romance* by Clara Wieck (Tape Example 22). Whatever the arrangement, melody and accompaniment make for a mutually satisfying combination.

TAPE EXAMPLE 22
Clara Wieck, *Romance* in G Minor, Op. 11 No. 2

## PHRASE, PERIOD, AND CADENCE

In prose, the basic elements are the *sentence*, the *paragraph*, and the *punctuation* that marks the boundaries between sentences and paragraphs. In music the analogous units are the *phrase*, the *period*, and the *cadence*. A **phrase** is the musical equivalent of a sentence. A **period** is the musical equivalent of a paragraph.* The great majority of compositions written between 1200 and 1940 consist of a series of phrases organized into periods.

A **cadence** is the musical punctuation that separates phrases and periods from

---

*Strictly speaking, a phrase is more analogous to a clause, and a period is more analogous to a sentence, but it is easier to think in terms of the larger units of sentence and paragraph.

each other. Cadences within pieces are frequently followed by a brief silence, known in music as a *rest*. But melodic shape, harmony, and rhythm all work together to create a cadence, as in Tape Example 23. Many different passages could precede this idea but, regardless of their shape, the passage in our example is heard as an emphatic cadence.

TAPE EXAMPLE 23
Familiar cadence pattern

Depending on how emphatic it is, a cadence may function as a comma, a semicolon, or a period. The opening phrase of *Carnaval*, by Robert Schumann (Tape Example 24), repeats twice. Each time, the phrase ends with a slight pause called a *half cadence*. The end of the full period, however, concludes with a resounding *full cadence*.

TAPE EXAMPLE 24
Robert Schumann, opening of *Carnaval*, Op. 9

## REGULAR AND IRREGULAR MELODY

The easiest melodies to grasp are those with a regular structure. Listen to the first section of the *Impromptu* in G-flat Major by Franz Schubert, one of the nineteenth century's great melodists (Tape Example 25a). As with the duple meter and the duple subdivisions of beats described in Chapter 2, the basis of phrase structure in Western music is also duple. The first 8-bar phrase (which we will call *A*) consists of two 4-bar subphrases that begin alike; the subphrases, in turn, consist of smaller 2-bar units. The second phrase (which we will call *B*), also eight bars in length, is built from sections of 2 + 2 + 4 bars. It then repeats to round out an opening period 24 bars in length, with the shape *A* (4 + 4) — *B* (2 + 2 + 4) — *B* (2 + 2 + 4). (We will have more to say about *shape* in Chapter 4.) It is easy to keep track of phrase structure by counting the bars as in Tape Example 25b. Schubert has blurred the outlines of his melody by using only gentle cadences and by making the accompaniment continuous. The melody actually consists entirely of small, even-numbered units.

TAPE EXAMPLE 25a
Schubert, opening section of the *Impromptu* in G-flat Major, Op. 90 No. 3

In the opening 12 measures of Maurice Ravel's *Pavane for a Dead Princess*, we find a different approach to building a melody. As you listen to Tape Example 26a, notice how the smaller units work together to create a long, arched phrase. The duple regularity that marks the Schubert melody is absent here. Although the first two bars form a unit, the remainder of the first subphrase divides into 3½ + 1½ measures. Moreover, bar 5 "copies" bar 4 a step lower, in what is known as a *sequence* (Tape Example 26b). A **sequence**, which is the repetition of a musical idea at progressively higher or lower pitches,* adds to the irregularity of the melody. The second subphrase is another irregular 5-bar unit, which divides into two equal (but irregular) 2½-bar sections. Twice the melody "slows down" (in what is called a *ritard*), further contributing to the overall irregularity

TAPE EXAMPLE 25b
Schubert, opening of *Impromptu* with three 8-bar phrases counted out loud

TAPE EXAMPLE 26a
Ravel, opening of *Pavane for a Dead Princess*

TAPE EXAMPLE 26b
Ravel, measures 4 and 5 of the *Pavane*, showing a sequence

*A sequence may repeat more than once, although in most Western music three repetitions is the limit.

of 7(2 + 5 [3½ + 1½]) + 5 (2½ + 2½) measures. Although you probably cannot "feel" these divisions, Ravel makes this highly complex phrase structure seem natural, almost inevitable.

## TUNE

TAPE EXAMPLE 27
Gershwin, refrain of
"Someone To Watch over
Me"

A less formal way of referring to a catchy melody is to call it a *tune*. A good example is the refrain of George Gershwin's song "Someone To Watch over Me" (Tape Example 27). Although some people insist on distinguishing between a classical melody and a popular tune, art music is full of tunes—for example, those of Joseph Haydn in the Classical period. Gershwin's appealing tune is a beautiful melody as well.

## THEME

TAPE EXAMPLE 28
Haydn, opening of the
finale to the Piano Sonata
in E-flat Major, H. XVI/52

A **theme** is a self-contained melodic unit on which a composition is based. The main musical material of a piece generally consists of themes. Listen, for example, to the opening theme from the finale of Haydn's Piano Sonata in E-flat Major (Tape Example 28). This theme is made up of three closely related phrases separated by a cadence and a fermata. The second phrase repeats the first one a step higher (another example of sequence). The third phrase begins with the rhythm of the first two phrases and then concludes the theme with a series of rapid notes. Almost all of the material in the rest of the movement is derived from this initial idea.

## MOTIVE

TAPE EXAMPLE 29
Stravinsky, opening of the
*Serenade in A*

A **motive** is the smallest coherent unit of a musical idea. A theme, for example, may consist of one or more motives. Perhaps the most famous motive in all Western music is the ta-ta-ta-TUM that opens Beethoven's Fifth Symphony and that sounds again and again throughout the symphony. (We shall be studying this work in Chapter 16.) Igor Stravinsky's *Serenade in A* for piano also opens with a motive (Tape Example 29). Most of the material in this passage is derived from the 5-note motive that begins the theme: LONG-short-LONG-short-SHORT. The motive spins round and round like a cat chasing its tail and provides the basis for an entire theme.

Theme, motive, and melody (or tune) are points on a continuum rather than discrete entities. Together they suggest the enormous range of successive sounds.

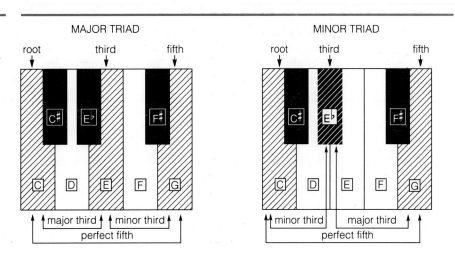

## HARMONY

Harmony, as we have seen, is the simultaneous occurrence of two or more different sounds (which we can now describe more precisely as *pitches*). While two such pitches create an interval, a **chord** is the simultaneous sounding of three or more pitches. (Some groupings of three or more sounds—for example, three adjacent semitones—might be called a "cluster" rather than a chord. But for the most part we shall be dealing with chords.) The earliest harmonies in Western music consisted of intervals but, as we shall see in Chapters 4 through 9, those intervals developed over the centuries into a family of chords known as *triads*.

### The Triad

From about A.D. 1500 on, Western harmony has been based on the triad. A **triad** is a chord consisting of three pitches constructed around intervals of interlocking thirds (on the white notes this amounts to choosing every other note; see Figure 3.2). These thirds may be either major thirds, consisting of four half steps, or minor thirds, consisting of three half steps. The two most common forms of triads are the *major triad* and the *minor triad*. If we reckon from the bottom note up, a **major triad** consists of a major third plus a minor third; a **minor triad** consists of a minor third plus a major third. When a triad (or, more frequently, a series of triads) is played successively rather than simultaneously, it is called an *arpeggio* (meaning "broken" chord). A **major chord** or **minor chord** refers more generally to a triad in which some or all notes have been duplicated at the octave (called *doubling*). Tape Example 30 gives a major chord and then an arpeggio based on that chord, followed by a minor chord and an arpeggio based on that chord.

TAPE EXAMPLE 30
Major and minor chords and arpeggios

# TONALITY

For about two centuries after triads emerged as the basis of Western harmony, major and minor harmonies were arranged in a coherent but open-ended fashion. Around 1690 a system coalesced that organized triads in a closed but no less flexible system. This system of *tonality* profoundly shaped musical developments for the next two centuries. Although tonality developed gradually and declined significantly in art music after about 1910, it is still the harmonic basis of popular music (and some recent art music as well). The very flexibility of tonality has been responsible for its widespread use.

**Tonality** is a harmonic system in which triads are arranged hierarchically around a central triad called the *tonic*.\* After the tonic triad, the most important triad in the hierarchy is the triad built on the fifth degree, called the *dominant* (V). A counterbalancing triad, built on the scale note a fifth below the tonic, is called the *subdominant* (that is, "under-dominant," but abbreviated as IV, since the note five degrees below the tonic is the octave to the one four degrees above; see also Figure 3.3).

Collectively these triads establish the *key*. For example, a piece in the "key of C" is built around a tonic triad on C, a dominant triad on G, and a subdominant triad on F. In addition to naming the key of a composition, we also specify its *mode*,[†] either major or minor, depending on which diatonic scale is used. To describe a tonal work fully, we give both its key and its mode—for example, "Symphony in C Major." As a simple means of reference, however, "key" generally indicates both the key and the mode.

Frédéric Chopin's brief Prelude in A Major (Tape Example 31a) provides an example of tonality at work. Most of the piece consists of a simple alternation between the dominant and tonic triads. This simplicity gives the "color chord" (a more complex chord outside the seven diatonic chords) in bar 12 its impact. The harmonies are distributed as follows (measure numbers are in parentheses):

V(1–2) — I(3–4) — V(5–6) — I(7–8) — V(9–10) — I(11) — COLOR CHORD (12) — ii(13) — V(14) — I(15–16)

Some listeners contend that they cannot distinguish between the major and minor modes. But notice the difference when the Chopin prelude is played in A Minor rather than A Major (Tape Example 31b). An even more dramatic difference can be heard in the popular seventh-inning-stretch song "Take Me Out to the Ball Game" (Tape Example 32). Although we may not always be able to identify an isolated tonal passage as being in major or minor, we can generally distinguish between them when they are played side by side. The frequent characterization of the major mode as "happy" and the minor mode as "sad" is

---

\*Abbreviated as "I." The triads built upon each degree of the scale are numbered accordingly, with I, II, and so on denoting a major triad, and i, ii, and so on denoting a minor triad.

[†]This use of "mode" is related to, but different from, its use by medieval musicians. See page 74.

FIGURE 3.3 Tonic, domi-
nant, and subdominant
triads, the most common
triads. You'll notice that
each of these triads
shares at least one note
with an adjacent triad.

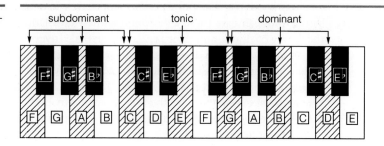

simplistic. It seems more useful to think of the major mode as bright and stable, and the minor mode as dark and unstable. These are generalizations, of course, but they have an acoustical basis.

## DIATONIC HARMONIES AND CHROMATIC HARMONIES

We have already introduced the terms *diatonic* and *chromatic* in our discussion of scales, but each term carries a harmonic connotation as well. **Diatonic harmonies** are those built on the seven degrees of whatever major or minor diatonic scale is being used. **Chromatic harmonies** are those built on, or using, the five nondiatonic degrees of the scale.

The minor mode is more unstable than the major mode, for two reasons. First, the minor third on which the minor triad is built is acoustically less pure than the major third on which the major triad is built. Second, the minor scale uses both the raised and lowered forms of the sixth and seventh degrees, and therefore employs 10 rather than 8 of the 12 chromatic notes. The first four bars of Chopin's C-Minor Prelude introduce all 12 notes of the chromatic scale (Tape Example 33). Even if you cannot identify each note, you can hear that Chopin's C-Minor Prelude is more chromatic than his A-Major Prelude.

TAPE EXAMPLE 33
Chopin, Prelude in C
Minor

## CONSONANCE AND DISSONANCE

Just as our eyes sort colors into relative shades of light and dark, so our ears sort harmonies into relative degrees of consonance and dissonance. **Consonant harmonies** sound pure, sweet, and stable. **Dissonant harmonies** sound impure,

**harsh, or unstable.** The purest consonances are the octave and the perfect fifth*; to our modern ears these also sound somewhat bland. Sweet consonances are the family of thirds, and their *inversions*, sixths. (Inversions are the result of turning an interval upside down.) A familiar example that uses almost entirely pure or sweet consonances is the theme of Mozart's Variations on *Ah, vous dirai-je, Maman,* which we know as "Twinkle, Twinkle Little Star" (Tape Example 34). The harshest dissonances are those constructed from the intervals of seconds and their inversions, sevenths. An example is the opening of Bartók's "Minor Seconds, Major Sevenths" (Tape Example 35).

Our full assessment of the dissonance level in a passage depends on factors beyond the raw intervals, such as what instrument plays what notes how loudly. Although these two examples present the extremes, they demonstrate the fundamental importance of both consonance and dissonance to musical expression. Until the early years of the twentieth century, it was expected that most dissonances would resolve to a consonance no more than a whole step away—for example, a minor seventh to a major sixth. Such a resolution is perceived as going from motion to rest or from instability to stability. Much of the energy of music derives from the tension and resolution inherent in dissonance and consonance.

TAPE EXAMPLE 34
Mozart, theme from the Variations on *Ah, vous dirai-je, Maman,* K. 265

TAPE EXAMPLE 35
Bartók, opening of "Minor Seconds, Major Sevenths" from *Mikrokosmos,* Vol. VII

## HARMONIC RHYTHM

Harmony is closely associated with rhythm. We can learn a great deal about the inner workings of a composition by tracking the rate at which the harmony changes and the degree of regularity with which it changes. The combined effect of these two factors is called **harmonic rhythm.** Two dissimilar examples will show the interaction between rate and regularity. In Tape Example 36, the Prelude in C-sharp Major by J. S. Bach, the harmony changes both frequently (about 90 times per minute) and regularly. Tape Example 37, the opening of Mozart's Sonata in C Major, reverses both trends. The rate of harmonic change is both considerably slower than in the Bach example and less regular. The example on the tape counts out these "changes" for the first few measures; see if you can keep track of them for the remainder of the excerpt.

TAPE EXAMPLE 36
J. S. Bach, Prelude in C-sharp Major from *The Well-Tempered Clavier,* Book I

TAPE EXAMPLE 37
Mozart, opening of the Piano Sonata in C Major, K. 330

## MODULATION

The flexibility of the tonal system derives from its ability to move readily from one key to another. In a tonal piece the more common procedure is to move away from the home key (also called the "tonic" key) to temporary "foreign"

*The perfect fourth, though technically a consonance, is often treated as a dissonance.

keys that ultimately resolve back to the home key. **Modulation** is the process of changing keys. A modulation is also said to have occurred when the key changes. Many listeners have trouble at first trying to detect such changes, because they are looking for a dramatic shift at a specific instant. Actually, most modulations take place smoothly (often imperceptibly) over several, or even many, seconds. They are more analogous to a sunrise than to a bolt of lightning. A tonal piece that lasts only a few minutes will accommodate fewer modulations than will a piece that lasts 20 minutes. As composers explored tonality, they discovered that they could write increasingly elaborate and lengthy pieces.

The opening of the Haydn E-Minor Sonata contains a clearly articulated (and uncharacteristically swift) modulation. The first phrase, through the first fermata, establishes E Minor as the home key. The second phrase, in the space of a few quick measures, modulates from E Minor to G Major. Haydn announces the arrival of the new key with a sudden loud outburst (Tape Example 38). Most modulations are neither as sudden nor as dramatic, but the importance of modulation in tonal music can scarcely be exaggerated.

TAPE EXAMPLE 38
Haydn, Sonata in E Minor, opening modulation

Although we have introduced melody and harmony separately, they are in fact interdependent. By "harmonizing" a melody in different ways, we can give it an entirely different cast, and we can build a wide range of melodies on identical harmonies. Rhythm, melody, and harmony are the building blocks of music. In the next chapter, our last on musical language, we examine ways in which composers give music its texture, color, and shape.

# Chapter 4

## TEXTURE, COLOR, AND SHAPE

Rhythm, melody, and harmony supply the raw materials of music. They are like the lumber and nails, the bricks and mortar, that go into a house. But a house must be finished inside and out before it is livable. Few people would choose to live for long in unpainted quarters, or in a house with the plumbing and wiring exposed. The texture of the materials and the colors inside and outside influence the aesthetic appeal of a house, and a unified plan—a shape—ensures that the house fulfills all the functions its inhabitants expect.

Similarly, without texture, color, and shape, even the most original music will sound lackluster and diffuse. Though texture, color, and shape complement one another, they operate at different levels of the listening experience. Texture and color lie on the surface of music; they may change from moment to moment. Shape, on the other hand, is something we comprehend only as we listen to an entire composition; shape is the underlying structure of music. We first consider the components of texture and color, and then of shape.

## TEXTURE

A piece of coarsely woven burlap feels rough, while a tightly woven rug made of the same threads feels smooth. In music, **texture** is the musical weave of a composition. In a work with only a single voice—that is, a single musical line, whether sung or played by instruments—the texture is simple. Such music is called *monophony* (pronounced "mo-*nof*-ony"), from the Greek for "single voice" (adjective: *monophonic*, pronounced "mo-no-*fon*-ik"). Monophony dominated Western music until about A.D. 1000.

In works with several voices—the kind of music that has dominated Western music since about A.D. 1000—the textures may vary from simple to highly complex. A texture in which all the voices move more or less together is called *homophony* (pronounced "ho-*mof*-ony"), from the Greek for "sounding alike" (adjective: *homophonic*, pronounced "ho-mo-*fon*-ik"). A good example is the final chorale from Johann Sebastian Bach's Cantata No. 78 (which we will return

TAPE EXAMPLE 39
J. S. Bach, chorale setting
of *Jesu der du meine
Seele*

to in Chapter 12), played on the harpsichord in Tape Example 39. Because the music moves smoothly from chord to chord, homophony is often referred to as the *chordal style*. The term *homophony* is also used to describe a melody with accompaniment, especially if the accompaniment is unobtrusive. (Recall the slow movement from Bach's Italian Concerto [page 30] or the opening of Schubert's *Impromptu* in G-flat Major [page 31].)

Textures in which the individual voices move independently of one another are called polyphonic or, more often, contrapuntal, meaning "point against point" (note against note). In *equal voiced counterpoint*, each voice employs similar material but at different times. The best-known variety of equal-voiced counterpoint is *imitative counterpoint* (often referred to simply as imitation). **Imitation** is the successive repetition in different voices of a prominent motive. The repetitions mimic the original motive. Each successive entry of the theme dominates for a time, but no single voice dominates for long. Overall, each of the voices can lay claim to equal importance. Listen to the equal-voiced Sinfonia in E Minor, also by J. S. Bach (Tape Example 40), and note the homogeneous blend of the three independent voices. At the very beginning, the upper voice dominates; at other times, the middle or lower voice comes to the fore. The overall impression is of three balanced voices, each contributing its share in a true musical partnership. We can admire the skill with which Bach creates such rich counterpoint using only minimal thematic materials.

TAPE EXAMPLE 40
J. S. Bach, Sinfonia in E
Minor

In *unequal-voiced counterpoint* (also called *non-imitative counterpoint*), independent voices of differing character compete for our attention. In a jazz ensemble, for example, the trumpet, clarinet, and trombone each play material suited to themselves. The resulting texture is a heterogeneous mix rather than a homogeneous blend, as in the chorus from Jelly Roll Morton's "Dead Man Blues" in Tape Example 41.

It is sometimes difficult to determine whether the texture of a particular passage is homophonic or contrapuntal. If we are struck more by the successive qualities of individual voices, we are hearing counterpoint; if we are drawn to the simultaneous harmonies, we are listening to homophony. What really matters, however, is recognizing how composers manage to develop a series of textural gradations. Just as we would not make a sack for a three-legged race out of satin or wear a formal shirt made of burlap, the skillful composer chooses an appropriate texture for each passage.

TAPE EXAMPLE 41
Chorus from "Dead Man
Blues"

## COLOR (TIMBRE)

Most of our examples so far have been performed on keyboard instruments. That has enabled us to focus on matters of rhythm, melody, and harmony that might otherwise be overshadowed by the most seductive dimension of musical color: *timbre* (pronounced *tam*-ber). **Timbre** consists of the acoustical properties of a sound and results from a phenomenon known as the *overtone series*. The airwaves that carry sound vibrate most strongly at the frequency known as the *fundamental;* this is the pitch the listener perceives. The fundamental, however, is accompanied by a spectrum of higher-pitched frequencies known as *overtones* (acousticians call them *partials*). It is the relative strength and distribution of these overtones that determine the timbre of a given sound. That is why two pitches with the same fundamental can sound very different.

In technical terms, timbre refers to the acoustical properties of a fixed, steady pitch. In general usage, however, the phrase *tone color* is often substituted, and that is the term we will use here. But remember that tone color refers to the acoustical properties of sound.

Nowhere is tone color more evident than in the sounds produced by different instruments, either alone or in combination. For many centuries Western music employed five instrumental families, each based on a different principle of sound production and each producing different tone colors. Those five families are strings, woodwinds, brass, percussion, and keyboards. In the following chapters we shall discuss the manner in which specific instruments function in actual compositions. Here we give a general introduction to the families of instruments.

## Strings

Bowed string instruments come closest to reproducing the expressiveness and subtle inflections of the most expressive of all instruments, the human voice. The tone color of string instruments is pure, yet warm and rich. Modern bowed string instruments consist of a wooden frame with four strings stretched between the end of the *fingerboard* (where they are attached by tuning pins) and the *tailpiece.* Just before the tailpiece the strings pass over a wooden *bridge* (see Figure 4.1). A bundle of bleached horsehairs stretched tautly between the ends of a wooden stick called the *bow* are drawn over one or more of the strings. The vibrations of the strings are transmitted though the bridge to the body of the instrument, which serves as a *soundboard.* The movement of the soundboard activates the airwaves, producing the tone we hear.

Originally the strings were made of sheep gut. On modern instruments strings are made of gut, metal, or synthetic material and are usually wrapped in metal (Figure 4.2). There are four progressively larger sizes of bowed string instruments: violin, viola, cello, and double bass (Figure 4.3). All of them have four strings tuned a fifth apart or, in the case of the double bass, a fourth apart.

TAPE EXAMPLE 42a–42d
Violin, viola, cello, and double bass

Tape Example 42 introduces, in succession, violin, viola, cello, and double bass.

String instruments can be plucked as well as bowed. On string instruments like the violin, plucking produces a special effect known as *pizzicato.* On string instruments like the Renaissance lute (distinguished by its rounded belly), guitar (a flat-backed member of the lute family), and harp (whose antecedents date back to the ancient Greeks), plucking is the only means of tone production. The lute and guitar have *frets*—raised strips of ivory, wood, or metal at right angles to the string (Figure 4.4)—along their necks to fix specific pitches. Their strings are generally made of nylon. Tape Example 43 presents the Renaissance lute (Figure 4.5), the classical guitar, and the modern pedal harp.

TAPE EXAMPLE 43a–43c
Renaissance lute, classical guitar, and modern pedal harp

FIGURE 4.1 A violin is created from some 70 parts, primarily in different types of wood: maple, sycamore, pine, ebony, and pearwood.

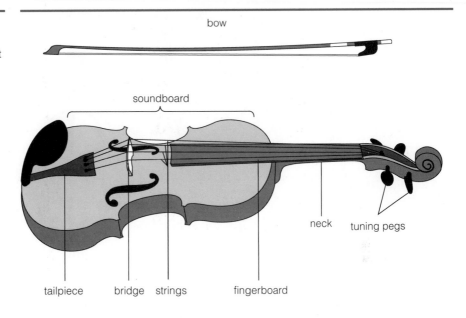

bow

soundboard

neck    tuning pegs

tailpiece    bridge    strings    fingerboard

FIGURE 4.2 "Holding a violin is like holding a young bird," said the violinist Yehudi Menuhim. "It is vibrating under your touch and you must hold it without squeezing it." The performer is also frequently the repair person—the cellist here is replacing a broken string.

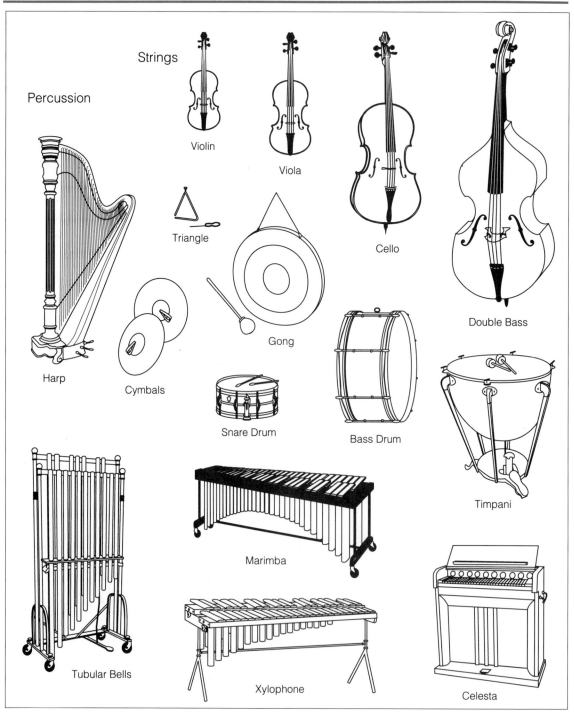

FIGURE 4.3 The modern orchestra contains more than two dozen different kinds of instruments from four principal families. Until the late eighteenth century, musicians in many orchestras played

*Part One The Language of Music*

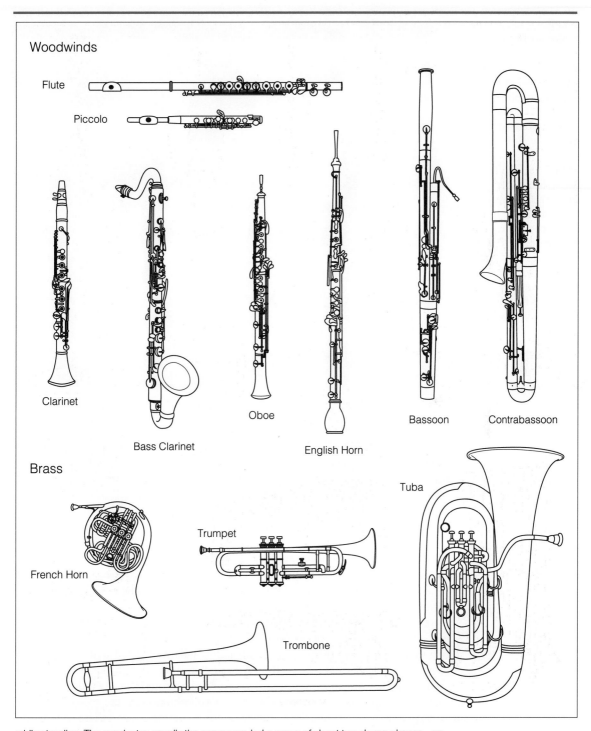

Woodwinds

Flute

Piccolo

Clarinet

Bass Clarinet

Oboe

English Horn

Bassoon

Contrabassoon

Brass

Tuba

French Horn

Trumpet

Trombone

while standing. The conductor, usually the composer, led a group of about two dozen players—as in the case of Franz Joseph Haydn.

FIGURE 4.4 (left) A heavily decorated Italian guitar, with ten well-marked frets, made in Venice in the early seventeenth century. The large amount of ivory suggests that elephants were not yet a protected species.

FIGURE 4.5 (right) This Renaissance lute is another ancestor of today's six-string guitar, whose roots stretch back to ancient Egypt. The Romans brought the instrument to Spain, where it flourished. The lute gets its name from the Arabic *al-'ud*, meaning "the wood."

## Woodwinds

Originally, all woodwinds were made of wood. Woodwinds produce their sounds by means of vibrating air columns in conical tubes. There are various ways of setting the air in motion. With the flute (made today of metal), the player blows across a hole near the end of a closed tube. With *single-reed instruments* like the clarinet, the player blows through a mouthpiece, one side of which consists of a thin, vibrating cane reed. The oboe and bassoon, which use a single reed folded into two opposing sections, are known as *double-reed instruments* (Figure 4.6). Many oboe and bassoon players make their own reeds.

The flute, oboe, and bassoon play "at pitch"—that is, the pitch they produce is the same as the pitch notated on the score. The clarinet, however, is one of several "transposing instruments." In the two common sizes of the modern clarinet (B$^\flat$ and A), the pitch produced is either a whole step (in the B$^\flat$ instrument) or a minor third* (in the A instrument) below what is notated on the score. The two varieties of clarinet (the mellow A clarinet and the more brilliant B$^\flat$ clarinet) are holdovers from an earlier period in which numerous sizes existed.

Each of the four main woodwinds (flute, oboe, clarinet, bassoon) has a

*Three half steps.

FIGURE 4.6 The names of the oboe and bassoon suggest their sounds. *Oboe* is from the French *hautbois*, meaning "high wood." *Bassoon* derives from the Italian *basso,* or "low."

smaller or a larger relative. The diminutive piccolo is pitched an octave higher than the standard flute and produces a brilliant, sometimes shrill, tone. It is a descendant of the wooden fife used in seventeenth-century military ensembles. The bass clarinet is pitched an octave lower than the standard B♭ clarinet. The English horn and contrabassoon are deeper versions of the oboe and bassoon.

Saxophones, invented by the Belgian instrument maker Adolphe Sax in the 1840s, combine the single reed of the clarinet with the metal body of brass instruments. Although they have never caught on in symphony orchestras as Sax had hoped, saxophones are an integral part of modern wind, military, and jazz ensembles. Some of the greatest jazz performers, such as Charlie Parker, have been saxophonists.

TAPE EXAMPLE 44a–44e Piccolo and flute, oboe and English horn, clarinet and bass clarinet, bassoon and contrabassoon, and alto saxophone

Because of their varied materials and means of sound production, the wood-winds offer a great variety of tone colors, from the silvery flute to the mellow clarinet, from the piercing oboe to the good-humored bassoon to the reedy but metallic saxophone. Tape Example 44 introduces, in order, piccolo and flute, oboe and English horn, clarinet and bass clarinet, bassoon and contrabassoon, and alto saxophone.

FIGURE 4.7 Germany, not France, was the site of the early musical development of the French horn. Here the principal French horn player of the Los Angeles Philharmonic plays a solo line while the remainder of his section anticipates their next entry. Playing the French horn without cracking requires iron lips and steel nerves.

## Brass

The instruments of the brass family were first used in hunting and warfare. The player blows through a cup-shaped mouthpiece into a series of metal tubes. Since brass instruments have no reeds, players must use their lips to create the vibrations. It takes years of practice to develop a reliable lip technique. Brass instruments come in many shapes and sizes (Figure 4.3). The trumpets are the most brilliant and varied. The larger, widely flared French horn produces a mellow, rich tone (Figure 4.7). The slide trombone is unique among instruments in its ability to produce a continuous spectrum of pitches (a feature that has endeared it to jazz musicians). The tuba, introduced in the mid-nineteenth century, quickly established itself as a mainstay of the brass family. Tape Example 45 presents the trumpet, French horn, trombone, and tuba.

TAPE EXAMPLE 45a–45d
Trumpet, French horn, trombone, and tuba

## Percussion

The percussion family is the most varied of all. Percussion instruments produce sounds by being either struck, rattled, or scraped. In addition to a large array of drums, they include cymbals, triangle, gong, tubular bells, tambourine, castanets, xylophone, marimba, vibraphone, and celesta (most shown in Figure 4.3).

Like the members of the brass family, many percussion instruments were first used in military ensembles, where they reinforced the strong duple meter to which soldiers marched. Percussion instruments emphasize rhythm and tone color rather than pitch. Tape Example 46 presents a wide array of modern percussion instruments.

TAPE EXAMPLE 46a–46m
Timpani, bass drum, snare drum, cymbals, triangle, gong, tubular bells, tambourine, castanets, xylophone, marimba, vibraphone, and celesta

FIGURE 4.8  A few modern performers have played the interior of the piano, directly plucking or striking the strings with their fingers or with mallets to produce new sounds.

## Keyboard Instruments

Keyboard instruments include the piano (and the *fortepiano*, its eighteenth-century predecessor), the clavichord, the harpsichord, the organ, the accordion, and electronic keyboards. (You have heard the piano, fortepiano, and harpsichord in some of the tape examples.) Strictly speaking, the piano is a percussion instrument, because its tone is produced by hammers striking string stretched over a soundboard. (We included the celesta, a keyboard instrument, in the percussion family.) Moreover, the harpsichord is a plucked string instrument, and the organ is a wind instrument. But all keyboard instruments share the ability to play polyphonic music. Ten fingers can play up to 10 notes—and sometimes more—simultaneously. Consequently, keyboard instruments are commonly viewed as a separate family.

In design the piano and harpsichord are related to the harp. When a harp is placed on its side, its profile is identical to that of the inside of a harpsichord or piano (Figure 4.8). Unlike a harp, however, those instruments have a large wooden soundboard that amplifies the sound.

TAPE EXAMPLE 47a–47b
Seventeenth-century
chamber organ, modern
concert organ

FIGURE 4.9 The Fisk
organ at the House of
Hope Presbyterian
Church, St. Paul, Minne-
sota, includes 70 separate
hand stops.

The organ is the oldest keyboard instrument. Hydraulic organs were built by the ancient Greeks, and portable organs have been used since the Middle Ages. Since the seventeenth century, organs have been equipped with a series of hand *stops* (Figure 4.9), each of which activates a different tone color. The reed stops on an organ produce tones in much the same way as a woodwind instrument. When the organist depresses a key, a small opening permits air under pressure to pass through an open pipe to which a reed is attached, and the vibrating reed sets the air column in motion. Other stops emulate brass instruments, the flute, and even the human voice. Until the Industrial Revolution the organ was (along with ornate clocks) one of the most complex machines produced by western Europeans. In a sense, the organ was the first musical synthesizer, although electric organs and synthesizer keyboards produce their tones by electronic means.

Organs are built in many sizes and produce many different sounds. Tape Example 47 contrasts two very different organs: a chamber organ built to seventeenth-century specifications, and a large contemporary concert organ.

## Period Instruments

One of the most interesting developments in recent years has been a resurgence of interest in *period instruments*. A **period instrument** is an instrument of a type that was in use at the time a work was originally performed.* (Such instruments

*Some writers refer to these as "original" or "authentic" instruments, but both of these terms have inappropriate connotations.

may be from the period itself, or they may be replicas constructed according to period practices.) This distinction has come about because almost all of the instruments in use today have developed from earlier versions. Continual modification and development have been characteristic of Western instruments since the earliest times. For example, eighteenth-century trumpets and French horns were valveless, all the woodwinds had many fewer keys than they do today, and string instruments and bows were constructed and used differently. The modern piano is very different from both the harpsichord and the early piano. (In Chapter 17 we trace the development of the piano during Beethoven's lifetime.) Even singing styles were different in earlier centuries, with less emphasis, for example, on *vibrato* (small but rapid fluctuations in pitch used to intensify a sound).

Period-instrument enthusiasts argue that the works of Bach, Mozart, Beethoven, and Berlioz cannot be fully appreciated unless we hear them on the instruments for which their composers wrote. But there is no way to guarantee that works performed today on period instruments will sound exactly as their composers intended. To some extent the choice of instrument(s) is a personal one that involves trade-offs. The valveless eighteenth-century French horn, for example, produces a purer sound on many tones than its modern counterpart, but it cannot play an even chromatic scale. The classical violin produces a more transparent tone than the modern one but is hard to hear in a large concert hall.

In choosing the recordings for this book, we have taken no stand one way or the other. Rather, we have chosen what we regarded as the most effective performances, whether on modern or period instruments.

## Non-Western Instruments

Western music has come full circle. With its roots deep in Middle Eastern and Byzantine cultures, Western music developed along a largely independent path for more than a thousand years. But the interest in folklore and anthropology that arose at the end of the nineteenth century has triggered a renewed interest in the music and instruments of eastern Europe, Asia, the Middle East, and Africa. Composers today borrow freely from the music of other cultures, and Western listeners enjoy this music for its own sake.

Unlike Western instruments, many non-Western instruments have remained remarkably stable over long periods. The Chinese *qin* (or *ch'in*, pronounced "chin"; Figure 4.10) is a member of the zither family that dates back to at least the eighteenth century B.C. Today's instrument differs little from that of nearly four thousand years ago. The qin consists of a shallow wooden box with seven silk strings tuned to degrees of the pentatonic (five-note) scale (on our modern piano, about G-A-C-D-E-G-A). Its dimensions (3.65 Chinese inches, for the number of days of the year) and shape (a convex soundboard to symbolize heaven; a flat bottom board to symbolize earth) are part of an elaborate symbolism. The qin's delicate plucked sound (including "sliding" tones that are possible on fretless instruments like this) is well suited to the expression of subtle moods.

FIGURE 4.10 Wearing traditional garb, Tsun-Yuen Lui performs on the Chinese *qin*, a long zither associated with culture and intellectuals.

FIGURE 4.11 Ali Jihad Racy, a virtuoso on more than a dozen Middle Eastern instruments, plays the *mijwiz*. Performing on this folk instrument requires an almost superhuman degree of breath control.

The Middle Eastern *mijwiz* (Figure 4.11), also known as the double clarinet, is a folk instrument whose antecedents date back to ancient times, when it may have been used in funeral processions. It consists of two separate pipes joined together, one providing a *drone* (a sustained tone, or tones, below the melody and common to much folk music) and the other providing the melody. The performer keeps both instruments going by a remarkable process known as "circular breathing," in which no breath appears to be taken.

TAPE EXAMPLE 48a–48b Qin (China), mijwiz (Middle East)

Tape Example 48 presents in succession the sounds of both the qin and the mijwiz.

## Orchestration

When composers complete a piece of music, they usually write it down in a **score**, a permanent visual record that serves as a guide for performers (see Musical Notation later in this chapter for more details). Composers set down not only which notes to play but also what instruments are to play them. This process is called **orchestration** (or **scoring**). For some composers the act of orchestration is inseparable from the act of composition; for others it is a separate process.[*] Recordings of rock music may consist of up to a hundred tracks of music, each recorded (or, as the arrangers say, "laid down") one at a time over a simple skeletal version.

During the Middle Ages and Renaissance, it would not have occurred to a composer to specify the instruments that were to be used in the performance of a piece. Composers left that to the performer, who drew on conventional practice and on the instruments or voices available at the time. In the seventeenth century composers began to specify the particular instruments that were to perform in a work. And in the Romantic era (from about 1830 on) composers grew almost obsessed with orchestration. Some twentieth-century composers favor instrumentation that is uniquely their own.

## Performance Directions

Performers need to know more, however, than *what* notes are to be played *when* and by *which* instruments. They also need to know *how* these notes are to be played. Composers provide performance directions covering the "how" of music by specifying articulation, dynamics, expression, and phrasing.

**Articulation.** **Articulation**[†] is the manner in which adjacent notes are connected or separated. Three types of articulation became standardized early in the eighteenth century: (1) *legato*, the seamless connection of adjacent notes, also referred to as a slur; (2) *non-legato*, the slight separation of adjacent notes; and (3) *staccato*, the marked separation of adjacent notes.

Why do we use Italian words for concepts that could be expressed perfectly well in English? Performance directions were first introduced into musical scores

---

[*]In the movie industry, for example, some people earn top salaries as *arrangers* of other people's music. They take the skeletal score supplied by the composer and render it as a lavish *arrangement*.

[†]Musicians sometimes call this "touch," referring to the manner in which they handle their instruments.

during the seventeenth century by Italian musicians (recall our discussion of tempo, page 23), and by the mid-eighteenth century the Italian expressions had become standardized throughout Europe. (Only France, which has always resisted cultural domination, held out.) After the final defeat of Napoleon Bonaparte in 1815, Beethoven—in a burst of chauvinism—began to use German for his performance directions. But succeeding generations usually returned to Italian. Although many English-speaking composers today write performance directions in their native language, Italian is still commonly used by composers of art music.

**Dynamics.** **Dynamics** refers to the relative softness or loudness of a note or passage. Although dynamics range from the barely audible to the deafening, all are gradations of *piano* (abbreviated *p*; Italian for "soft") and *forte* (abbreviated *f*; Italian for "loud"). The abbreviation *pp* means "very soft"; *ppp* means "very, very soft"; *mf* (from *mezzo forte*) means "medium loud"; *ff* means "very loud"; and so forth. Beginning in the eighteenth century, composers called for gradual shifts from one dynamic level to another in either a *crescendo* ("growing louder") or a *decrescendo* ("growing softer"). All dynamics must be played in a manner appropriate to the composition; a *forte* in a seventeenth-century work, for example, means something very different from a *forte* in a nineteenth-century work.

**Expression.** **Expression** is the general character of a passage or work, ranging from *cantabile* ("singing"), to *marcato* ("marked"), to *dolce* ("sweetly"), to *con brio* ("with fire"). Performers must translate these rather general directions into actual performance.

Tempo, which we discussed in Chapter 2, is yet another aspect of musical expression. Composers have gone to great lengths to specify exactly what tempos they want. Perhaps the most extreme example is Beethoven's marking for the Kyrie of his Mass in C: *Andante con moto assai vivace quasi Allegretto ma non troppo*, roughly, "fairly slow with motion but very lively and a little fast but not too much."

**Phrasing.** **Phrasing** is the manner in which a performer organizes and presents the parts of a composition. Two persons relating the same story, for example, might choose to emphasize certain aspects and de-emphasize others. In the same way, two performers may phrase the same piece of music quite differently. We admire musical phrasing that is clear and compelling, the same qualities we admire in a storyteller.

## Interpretation

Regardless of how meticulous a composer is in specifying performance directions, the performer must have some freedom in interpreting them. **Interpretation** is the manner in which the performer executes the composer's performance directions. No two performances of the same work sound exactly alike, although we may prefer one performance to another. In the twentieth century some composers, viewing performers as unnecessary "middlemen," have composed directly onto audiotape with electronic instruments whose sounds vary only according to the acoustical environment in which the tape is played. In spite of an inevitable degree of conflict between composers and performers, however, most composers still prefer to entrust the interpretation of their creations to live performers.

Listen now to the opening of Beethoven's celebrated *Appassionata* Sonata for Piano (Tape Example 49) and notice how articulation, dynamics, and expression markings (noted in the performance) come into play.

TAPE EXAMPLE 49
Beethoven, opening of the Sonata in F Minor, Op. 57, *Appassionata*

## SHAPE

Ordinarily we think of shape as the appearance of a figure in space—a human figure or a mountain range. If something has a shape, we assume that we ought to be able to see it. But shape has to do with time as well as with space. The shape of our lives, for example, is outlined by infancy, childhood, adolescence, adulthood, and old age. Similarly, the shape of a piece of music is outlined by the stages through which it passes, from beginning to end. **Musical shape** is the interrelationship through time of the sections of a piece.

Composers have used many standardized shapes, or **forms**, over the centuries. Sonata, rondo, theme and variation, binary, ternary, *da càpo*, strophic—these are only some of the forms we shall encounter. Musical forms, unlike cookie-cutters, do not produce exactly the same shape every time. Two pieces with the same form might nevertheless differ in many details. The supreme test of a composer's skill is the manner in which he or she shapes music over time. Composers like Mozart and Beethoven have maintained their popularity in part because of their unparalleled mastery of shape.

Throughout this book, we use Listening Guides to outline the shapes of the works we are discussing. These guides will help you follow a work on first or second hearing, but remember that they are intended only as aids. The ultimate goal is for you to comprehend the music on your own.

### Repetition, Contrast, and Variation

Shape in Western music is based on three techniques. The first two are opposites and the third is a synthesis. The first is *repetition*, in which a brief idea, an entire theme, or even a complete section is repeated. The second is *contrast*, in which one idea is followed by a different idea—for example, homophonic by contrapuntal, major mode by minor mode, loud by soft, fast by slow, serious by comic. *Variation* is the *repetition* of an idea but with some degree of *contrast*. Over the years, each new means of creating musical shape has simply applied repetition, contrast, and variation in new ways.

TAPE EXAMPLE 50a
Chopin, Nocturne in F
Major, Op. 15, No. 1

Listen to the Nocturne in F Major by Chopin (Tape Example 50a) and note how repetition, contrast, and variation determine its shape. At first you may find it difficult to concentrate on the musical shape of an entire composition. With a little persistence, however, you will find that it is one of the most intriguing dimensions of the listening experience. Notice that this work consists of three distinct sections. The first and the third are nearly identical; this is an example of repetition. The middle section contrasts dramatically with the other two. If we use letters to represent the sections (a conventional practice), we can describe the shape of this piece as *A-B-A*. (This 3-section arrangement is called *ternary form*.) We use capital letters to refer to sections: *A*-Section, *B*-Section, etc.

To represent phrases within major sections, we use lower-case letters. For example, we can indicate the phrases within Chopin's *A*-Sections like this: *a-b-a-c-c-a*. Repetition and contrast come into play within each *A*-Section just as they do in the whole piece. The opening *a*-phrase occurs three times, interspersed by two contrasting phrases (*b* and *c*), the second of which (*c*) repeats.

TAPE EXAMPLE 50b
Chopin, Nocturne in F
Major, opening of the *a*-
phrases of the *A*-Section
at their first and second
appearances

Chopin uses variation as well as repetition and contrast. For example, when he repeats the opening *a*-phrase (Tape Example 50b), he embellishes the melody by adding some new tones. We represent the varied repetition of the *a*-phrase as *a'*. In fact, Chopin subjects several phrases of his Nocturne to variation. We can represent the overall shape of the piece as follows:

$$A(a\text{-}b\text{-}a'\text{-}c\text{-}c'\text{-}a') \longrightarrow B(d\text{-}e\text{-}d\text{-}e') \longrightarrow A'(a\text{-}b\text{-}a'\text{-}c\text{-}c'\text{-}a')$$

This may seem like a complicated way of viewing a relatively short piece, but repetition, contrast, and variation dictate the shape of even a simple composition like this one.

## MUSICAL NOTATION

For almost a thousand years, Western music was transmitted orally, without benefit of written notation. Many non-Western musics still rely largely on oral tradition. The worlds of jazz and popular music abound with stories of outstanding performers who did not, or do not, read music. But beginning in the ninth century, Western composers began to record their music in handwritten manuscripts. The earliest notated music offered only rudimentary guidance on the pitches that were to be sung (Figure 4.12). During the late Middle Ages and the Renaissance, composers devised ways of indicating both rhythm and pitch in their scores (Figure 4.13). Around the mid-seventeenth century, composers began to specify instrumentation, though they rarely provided performance directions (Figure 4.14). During the nineteenth century the density of performance directions in musical scores increased dramatically until, in the works of

*Part One   The Language of Music*

FIGURE 4.12 Musical notation with neumes from a tenth-century manuscript compiled in the monastery at St. Gall, Switzerland. It is believed that these cryptic signs provided no information about the rhythm.

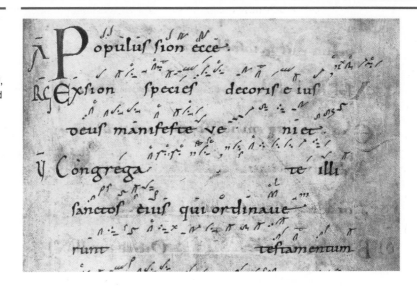

FIGURE 4.13 In his 1531 book of *19 Musical Songs* for keyboard, the French publisher Pierre Attaignant indicated the rhythms with great precision.

Gustav Mahler, almost every group of notes seems to be accompanied by a performance direction of some kind (Figure 4.15).

The musical examples in this book are not full scores with detailed notation. You would need such scores only if you were planning to become a conductor or an arranger. Instead, the examples are *reductions* that present the crucial pitches in condensed form. Details are omitted so as not to detract from the main points. You do not need to be able to read music in order to follow the discussions, but the musical examples will help you to identify important points. After a little practice, you will know what to watch and listen for.

FIGURE 4.14 "Concerto Entitled 'The Night,' " handwritten about 1730 by Antonio Vivaldi, shows instrumentation: flute or violin (stave 1), violin I (stave 2), violin II (stave 3), bassoon (stave 4), and bass (stave 5).

The accompanying score of Chopin's Nocturne is a piano score rather than an orchestral reduction, but the notational conventions are the same. Here we show the first nine measures of the piece. The brackets at the left enclose two sets of horizontal lines called *staves* (singular *staff*). Each bracket groups the two staves together into a *system*. In a piano score like this, the upper staff is usually played by the right hand, and the lower staff by the left hand. The *treble clef* (𝄞) in the upper staff shows pitches that are mostly *above* middle C. The *bass clef* (𝄢) in the lower staff shows pitches that are mostly *below* middle C. The relative pitches of individual notes are indicated by how high or low the round *noteheads* appear on the staff—or above or below the staff. The vertical *bar lines* divide the music into even measures. The symbol to the right of the clefs tells the musician what key the piece is in (see page 34). The two numbers that appear after the clefs are called the *time signature*. The upper number tells us how many beats each measure is to receive. Here each measure receives three beats. The lower number tells us the value of the note that receives each beat. Here the notes are quarter notes. The metronome marking at the head of the piece tells us that there should be about 69 quarter notes per minute (top of page 58):

*Part One   The Language of Music*

FIGURE 4.15  Closing page of the score of the first movement of Gustav Mahler's Symphony No. 8. This symphony requires a mammoth orchestra (including a large pipe organ), three vocal choirs (one a children's choir), and seven vocal soloists. In the space of a few seconds, the dynamics change from loud *(f)* to very soft *(pp)* to extremely loud *(ff)*.

With some sense of meter and tempo, you will find that you can follow this score even though you cannot "read" every detail. The open noteheads represent the notes that are of longest duration. The filled-in noteheads with one or more horizontal *beams* across the top or bottom of the note's *stem* represent notes of shorter duration. The tiny note at the beginning of the last measure, called a *grace note*, borrows its short duration from either the preceding note or the following note. Chopin (who was a fine pianist) gives a wealth of performance directions and phrase markings to indicate dynamics and expression, including pedal indications. The 𝄻𝄞𝄡. in the example above indicates that the damper pedal is to be depressed. The ❋ indicates that the pedal is to be released.

# MUSICAL STYLE

**Musical style** is the result of the interaction among rhythm, melody, harmony, texture, color, and shape. Every piece of music has a style of its own, though the individual elements of style vary considerably from one piece to another. As your awareness of these elements increases, you will find yourself relating to music at deeper and deeper levels, beyond what may at first have been a purely visceral response. After a time you may come to enjoy a work that you found uninteresting at first. Or you may discover a work that moved you on first hearing has lost some of its appeal. Or you may find that your deeper awareness of the musical style of a work has confirmed your initial response. In any case, the experience of listening to music will grow more rewarding as time passes and will help you appreciate why, over the centuries, men and women have found in music an endless source of pleasure and fulfillment.

# Part Two

## EARLY MUSIC
## (TO 1690)

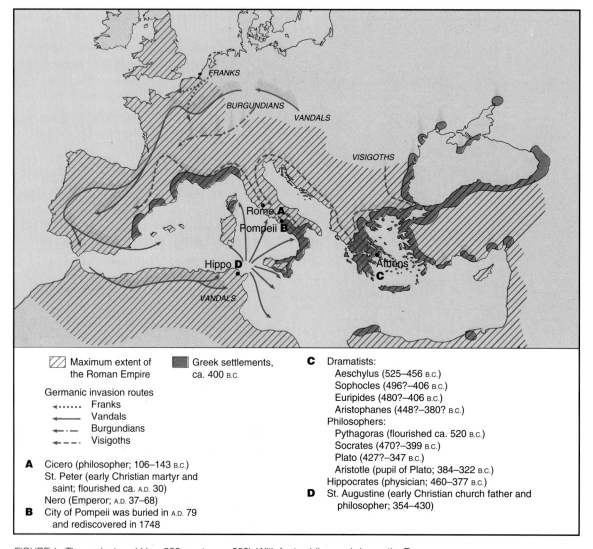

Maximum extent of the Roman Empire

Germanic invasion routes
◄······ Franks
◄—— Vandals
◄—·— Burgundians
◄——·—·. Visigoths

Greek settlements, ca. 400 B.C.

**A** Cicero (philosopher; 106–143 B.C.)
St. Peter (early Christian martyr and saint; flourished ca. A.D. 30)
Nero (Emperor; A.D. 37–68)
**B** City of Pompeii was buried in A.D. 79 and rediscovered in 1748

**C** Dramatists:
Aeschylus (525–456 B.C.)
Sophocles (496?–406 B.C.)
Euripides (480?–406 B.C.)
Aristophanes (448?–380? B.C.)
Philosophers:
Pythagoras (flourished ca. 520 B.C.)
Socrates (470?–399 B.C.)
Plato (427?–347 B.C.)
Aristotle (pupil of Plato; 384–322 B.C.)
Hippocrates (physician; 460–377 B.C.)
**D** St. Augustine (early Christian church father and philosopher; 354–430)

FIGURE 1   The ancient world (ca. 500 B.C. to A.D. 500): With foot soldiers and slaves, the Roman army so expanded the empire's boundaries that it was vulnerable to attacks on dozens of remote outposts.

# THE MIDDLE AGES (500–1430)

## *A Medieval World View*

*T*he foundations of Western culture lie in the Greek and Roman civilizations that flourished between the fifth century B.C. and the fifth century A.D. (map, Figure 1). Around 500 B.C. the Greek city state of Athens instituted a limited democracy, the first in the West and the model for virtually all later experiments. In a remarkable flowering during the fifth and fourth centuries B.C., Athens produced the dramatists Aeschylus, Sophocles, Euripides, and Aristophanes; the philosopher/teachers Socrates, Plato, and Aristotle; and the physician Hippocrates. Probably no other city—with the exception of Renaissance Florence—can claim to have been home to such talent over so brief a period. The Greeks also excelled in the visual and plastic arts. The Parthenon, a temple to the goddess Athena, epitomized the classic Greek ideals of balance and symmetry (Figure 2).

By the middle of the third century B.C. the Romans had brought the Italian peninsula under their control, and over the next century they expanded their empire to include Macedonia (northern Greece), northern Africa, Asia Minor, and Gaul (corresponding roughly to present-day France and Germany). Driven by conquest, the Romans slowly but inexorably overextended their reach. In the middle of the third century A.D., the first "barbarians" (as the Romans called them because of their strange language and uncouth manners and dress) invaded western Europe. In the fourth century, hordes of nomadic barbarians called Huns swept out of their Asian homelands and terrorized western Europe. Under their chief, Attila, they raided Gaul and Italy in search of plunder and tribute (A.D. 433?–453). In the path of the invading Huns were several Germanic tribes, notably the Franks, Visigoths, Vandals, and Burgundians. The Visigoths themselves sacked Rome in 410, and a Burgundian, Odoacer, deposed the last Roman emperor in 476.

The fall of Rome marked the beginning of the Middle Ages—an expression introduced by Renaissance humanists who regarded the centuries between the

FIGURE 2 This famous image of the Parthenon (ca. 447–438 B.C.) is incomplete. Sections of the temple originally were painted red and blue; sculpted figures had colored hair and eyes. A model of harmony and order, the temple was built with sophisticated refinements of proportion that may be invisible to the casual observer. In architecture, as in music, we see or hear more when we understand the structure in context.

fall of Rome and the revival of interest in literature and art in the fifteenth century as the Dark Ages. Actually, many significant cultural advances took place during that period.

The various Germanic tribes who found their way into Gaul during the fifth century assimilated the tribes already established there. The society that emerged relied on large councils or assemblies to record important contracts and decisions, a practice that led to our jury system. Each tribal chief was served by a *comitatus* ("following") made up of young warriors who fought for him in return for his protection. The Germanic tribes established "guilds" that at first served only social functions but eventually developed into the medieval craft guilds.

Earlier invaders had remained in an area only until they exhausted its natural resources and then moved on. The Germanic tribes, however, devised new techniques for farming the hard topsoils of northern Europe. They introduced a heavier plow and designed a harness that did not—as earlier ones had—strangle the horses as they pulled. They introduced the single-family farm and the feudal manor, two institutions that provided the basis of Europe's agricultural economy for the next thousand years. Under the "three-field" system, they let one-third of their farmland lie fallow at any one time, making it possible for them to cultivate the same land year after year.

In the wake of the barbarian invasions, three major religions emerged: Roman (Catholic) Christianity in western Europe, Orthodox Christianity in Asia Minor, and Islam in the Middle East and North Africa. The spread of Christianity served to stabilize the society of western Europe. And, though the head of the Roman Church, the Pope, lived in Rome, thousands of missionaries carried the faith across Europe. (See the map of the medieval world, Figure 3.)

FIGURE 3 Some bright spots in the Dark Ages: Although Paris, Florence, and Rome had already emerged as major centers of learning and education, small communities such as Bingen and St. Gall were also important centers of learning.

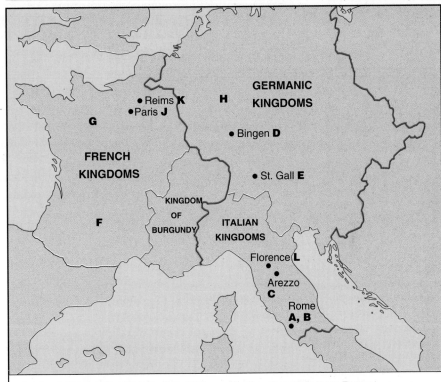

| | | | |
|---|---|---|---|
| **A** | Pope Gregory the Great (ca. 540–604) | **G** | Trouvères in northern France (twelfth and thirteenth centuries) |
| **B** | Charlemagne (742?–814); crowned Holy Roman Emperor in 800 | **H** | Minnesänger in Germany (twelfth through fourteenth centuries) |
| **C** | Guido of Arezzo (music theorist; born ca. 991, died after 1033) | **J** | Cathedral of Notre Dame, center of early polyphony Pérotin (composer; flourished ca.1200) |
| **D** | Hildegard of Bingen (abbess, mystic, writer; 1098–1179) | **K** | Guillaume de Machaut (composer; ca. 1300–1377?) |
| **E** | Monastery of St. Gall (peak in tenth century) | **L** | Francesco Landini (composer; ca.1325–1397) Giotto (painter; ca. 1266–ca. 1337) |
| **F** | Troubadors in southern France (eleventh through thirteenth centuries) | | |

FIGURE 4 Charlemagne was the first emperor of the Holy Roman Empire, which exercised power in Europe to varying degrees until Napoleon dissolved it a thousand years after Charlemagne. A collector of Greek and Latin manuscripts, Charlemagne supported schools where manuscripts were copied and lavishly illuminated. Manuscripts for the emperor, who did not know how to write, frequently featured gold letters on purple parchment.

Christianity spread through both conversion and force. Both were at work in the career of Charlemagne, "Charles the Great" (742?–814; Figure 4), the Christian king of the Franks. When his brother died, Charles first annexed his lands (disinheriting the brother's two sons) and then invaded northern Italy and Spain. For 30 years he waged war against the tribe of pagan Saxons, employing forced conversions, wholesale massacres, and mass relocation. In 800 Charles rushed to defend the Pope against threats of deposition by the Romans, and on Christmas Day the Pope crowned Charles the first emperor of the Holy Roman Empire. Charlemagne administered his vast empire wisely. He permitted conquered peoples to retain their own laws. He made thousands of former slaves "freemen"—a revolutionary concept—and reduced their military obligations. He strove to educate the clergy and to preserve classical literature while struggling to perfect his own command of Latin. His posthumous fame (probably exaggerated) provided the model for Napoleon in the nineteenth century.

The most active arm of the Roman Church was the monastery. Monasticism (the ascetic ideal of withdrawing from the world to devote oneself to worship) is common to many religions. Among early Christians, the Irish embraced the monastic ideal most fervently, though by the fifth century there was a bewildering variety of monastic orders throughout Europe.

An Italian monk named Benedict (480?–543?) brought uniformity to the movement. As a student in Rome, he was appalled by the vice he witnessed and fled to the wilderness. In 529 he founded a community at Monte Cassino, where late in life he drew up a set of guidelines for monastic life. According to those guidelines the leader of a monastery, called the *abbot,* was to be appointed for life and could not be replaced. Though he was obliged to consult with all the members of his monastery, he had full authority over them. Benedict set up eight regular times for daily worship: about 3:00 A.M., daybreak, 6:00 A.M., 9:00 A.M., 12 noon, 3:00 P.M., twilight, and just before retiring. These services were known collectively as the *Divine Office.* Each member took lifetime vows of poverty, chastity, and obedience, and no member could leave one monastery and move to another.

Many monasteries fortified themselves against the threat of plunder, and the security they afforded doubtless helped them to recruit new members. Monasteries were self-supporting communities, with their own fields, vineyards, stables, and livestock (see the Historical Window in Chapter 5).

Gradually, Christianity imbued society with a sense of the value of human life. Although life for most people was still brief and harsh, even the humblest peasants could now believe that they would be rewarded in an afterlife for their suffering on earth.

One of the most significant contributions of the monasteries was the preservation and cultivation of writing, an inheritance from the Greeks and Romans.

FIGURE 5 As medieval cities grew, urban cathedrals needed to be fire resistant; brick or stone replaced wooden roofs. The heavy masonry of the Romanesque Notre Dame la Grande in Poitiers, France, required great support, but medieval engineers had not yet worked out what art historian Frederick Hartt describes as "a three-way balance among great church size, stable vaulting, and adequate illumination."

The monks took advantage of the recently developed *codex* (a group of loose leaves bound together into a single volume) to organize and preserve the fruits of their studies. Many of their manuscripts are adorned with elaborate and painstaking *illuminations* (Color Plate 1). Building on the writings of Aristotle, Plato, and the mystical *Confessions* of the early Christian theologian St. Augustine (354–430), the monks cultivated the philosophy of *scholasticism,* whose chief goal was the reconciliation of faith and reason.

Beginning in the eleventh century, great cathedrals began to rise throughout Europe, most of them built under the direction of monastic orders. From about 1050 to 1150, the Romanesque style of architecture prevailed, a blend of classical Roman forms, Byzantine architecture, and bold innovations. Romanesque cathedrals have huge facades with towers, massive barrel vaults (arched structures forming a ceiling), and tall, narrow windows (Figure 5). Toward the

*The Middle Ages*

FIGURE 6 A pinnacle of Gothic style: the Cathedral of Reims in northern France. Its construction spanned most of the thirteenth century. Nearly every surface of the facade is peopled with sculpture. As art historian H. W. Janson described it, "The exterior of the cathedral begins to look like a dovecote [a pigeon roost] for statues."

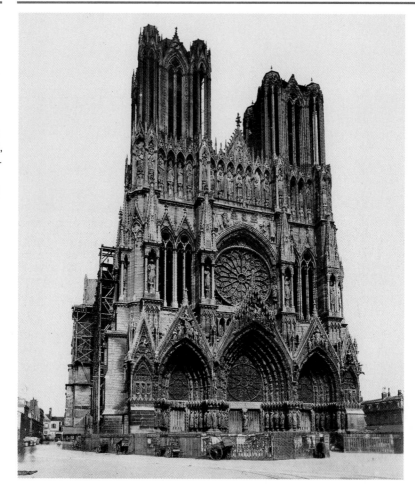

middle of the twelfth century, the Romanesque style gave way to the Gothic style (another label applied by Renaissance humanists, in reference to the Gothic barbarians), marked by lightness and soaring spaces. Supporting buttresses relieved the walls of their load and made possible wide expanses of stained glass (Figure 6). It was within such structures that Western music enjoyed its first great flowering.

# Chapter 5

## MEDIEVAL MONOPHONY

*I*magine for a moment that two thousand years from now an archaeologist is trying to decipher references to an ancient game she has stumbled across that had apparently been called "baseball." She has managed to piece together 14 box scores (though none is complete) from between 1850 and 2415 (when the game died out), several statistical yearbooks, several bats (all with parts of their handles missing), a few dozen photographs of players, discussions of the game in two philosophical books from the period, and a French translation from about 2500 of the first four chapters of an early rule book (the table of contents indicates that there were originally seven). This is the situation we find ourselves in today as we try to understand ancient Greek music.

## THE GREEK HERITAGE

What survives are about 14 incomplete melodies; several theoretical treatises; several *auloi* (early wind instruments) lacking mouthpieces; a few dozen vases with pictures of instrumentalists; discussions in philosophical treatises by Plato and Aristotle; and four of seven parts of two Greek treatises in a translation by the Roman Boethius from around A.D. 520. Still, despite this scanty evidence, scholars have not been reluctant to speculate about Greek music.

We know that music played an important role in classical Greece. Musician/poets competed in contests of skill, and music was sung in the tragedies of Euripides and to accompany processions of atonement or supplication. Music seems to have been cultivated by amateurs as well. In mythology, Orpheus could soften even the stoniest heart by singing to the accompaniment of his lyre (Figure 5.1). Greek music was predominantly monophonic, though singing at the octave (that is, singing the same melody an octave apart) may have occurred, and there may have been some use of drones (a long-held note beneath the melody). A group of vocalists or instrumentalists may have performed varying versions of the same melody simultaneously, in what was known as *heterophony* (from the Greek for

FIGURE 5.1 Orpheus, the famed musician and poet of Greek mythology, charmed listeners with his playing. Such was his skill with the lyre that Orpheus used it to try to persuade the gods to release his bride, Eurydice, from Hades—and he nearly succeeded.

"different voices"). For the Greeks, music was a science that, along with arithmetic, geometry, and astronomy, formed what the Middle Ages called the *quadrivium,* the fourfold path to the knowledge of "essences" (entities unaffected by material substances).

Three Greek scales, though based on the octave, perfect fifth, and perfect fourth, contain intervals both narrower than our half step and wider than our whole step. The scales were organized into modes such as Dorian, Phrygian, and Lydian, terms that suggest regional origins. The Greek philosopher and teacher Pythagoras (fl. ca. 520 B.C.) made elaborate measurements of the sounding lengths of strings and discovered that the primary intervals of the octave, fifth, and fourth use ratios of 1:2, 2:3, and 3:4 (Figure 5.2). These discoveries, reported in the writings of Boethius, probably had little influence on Greek music, but they had considerable influence in later centuries on the development of Western music.

Plato spoke of music's *ethos,* its power to arouse emotions or incite behavior. In *The Republic,* his dramatic dialogue on the character of the ideal state, he has this exchange take place:

"What then, are the dirge-like scales? Tell me, for you are a musician." "The Mixolydian," he said, "and the intense Lydian, and others similar to them."

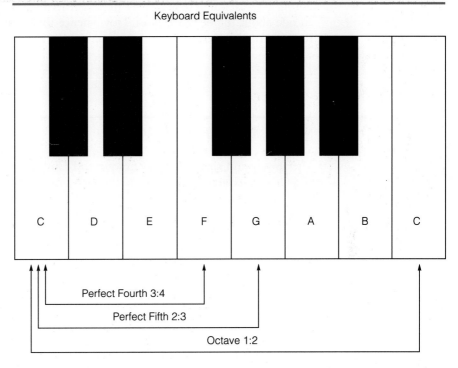

FIGURE 5.2 Pythagorean string ratios and their modern keyboard equivalents: *Superparticular ratios* refer to ratios of adjacent intervals (1:2 or 2:3, for example). Except for the octave, the ratios on modern keyboards vary slightly from the pure proportions of Pythagoras.

"These, then," said I, "we must do away with. For they are useless even to women who are to make the best of themselves, let alone to men."

Elsewhere in this dialogue, the speaker says that "the devotees of unmitigated gymnastics turn out more brutal than they should be, and those of music softer than is good for them." The best musician "blends gymnastics with music." We cannot be sure how widely Plato's rather conservative views were shared.

We know that the Romans, who subjugated the Greeks in the second century B.C., cultivated music enthusiastically, under strong Greek influence. Musicians playing brass instruments accompanied military legions in battle, but Roman philosophers complained about the corrupting influence of music played in theaters and for entertainment. Much of that music was performed by immigrant Greeks, and the wandering musicians of the Middle Ages carried on the musical tradition of those early performers.

Roman historians tell us that the emperor Nero (A.D. 37–68) had a passionate interest in music. He made an intensive study of music and took part in competitions in which the contestants sang to the accompaniment of the *kithara* (a plucked-string instrument in the shape of a lyre). Since the competitions were public and the winners were decided by the level of applause, we can imagine that Nero fared well. The biographer Suetonius (A.D. 69–ca. 140) reports that, during a devastating fire in A.D. 64 that destroyed half of Rome, Nero had sung an ode about the destruction of Troy—hence the phrase "Nero fiddled while Rome burned." Nero blamed the fire on the Christians.

## MUSIC IN THE CHURCH

The towers and spires of Romanesque and Gothic cathedrals reached toward heaven and declared to everyone in the surrounding countryside that here was a place where order and stability reigned. The Church exercised earthly authority in the name of a higher authority and did much to bring order to society after centuries of chaos.

One evidence of that order was the standardization of the liturgy, which comprises all the texts and rituals used in worship services. Gradually the clergy built an entire church year around a calendar that celebrated such major events as the Annunciation (Mary's visitation by the angel Gabriel informing her that she is to be the mother of Christ), Nativity (Christ's birth), Resurrection (Easter), Ascension (Christ's ascent into heaven), Pentecost (the visitation of the Holy Spirit seven weeks after the Resurrection), and Trinity (the formation of the holy trinity—God the Father, God the Son, God the Holy Spirit). These milestones gave Christians a way of marking their progress through life.

From the time of St. Peter in Rome (ca. A.D. 30), the central ritual in the Christian faith was the celebration of the Mass, during which the bread and the wine are consecrated as symbols of the body and blood of Christ. The liturgy of the Mass consists of two categories. First, the *Ordinary* contains the five items that are part of every celebration of the Mass:*

- *Kyrie:* a threefold repetition, derived from the Byzantine Church, of "Lord have mercy," "Christ have mercy," "Lord have mercy."
- *Gloria:* an extended hymn of praise.
- *Credo:* the recitation of doctrinal beliefs.
- *Sanctus:* an acclamation offered during the blessing of sacramental bread and wine.
- *Agnus Dei:* a concluding prayer for peace.

The second, much larger category is the *Proper,* which contains the items in the Mass that vary according to the time in the liturgical year. The parts of the Proper associated with major feast days were often extremely ornate.

In addition to the Ordinary and the Proper, the Roman liturgy contains the Divine Office celebrated by members of monastic orders.

*An exception is the Requiem Mass, or Mass for the Dead, which has its own structure.

# PLAINCHANT

These liturgical categories had one thing in common: They were all sung.* The practice of singing during religious services dates back at least to the ancient Jewish temples. The Book of Psalms is attributed largely to King David (fl. ca. 980 B.C.), who was celebrated for his musical prowess. Several of the Psalms refer specifically to singing:

> Praise the Lord! For it is good to sing praises to our God; for he is gracious, and a song of praise is seemly. (Psalm 147)

> Praise the Lord! Sing unto the Lord a new song. . . . (Psalm 149)

Other references in the Book of Psalms are to an even earlier practice of instrumental accompaniment:

> Praise him with the sound of the trumpet; praise him with lute and harp!
> Praise him with timbrel and dance; praise him with strings and pipe!
> Praise him with sounding cymbals; praise him with loud clashing cymbals!
> (Psalm 150)

From the time of its founding in the early fourth century, the Byzantine Church also called for much of its liturgy to be sung. The Roman Church assimilated both Byzantine and Jewish influences.

In the West, the music sung during services became known in Latin (which remained the official church language for centuries) as *cantus planus,* or "plainchant." All plainchant was monophonic unison singing, either by solo voice or choir.

The early church fathers encouraged the use of plainchant because they believed that it fostered a proper devotional attitude among worshipers. In the vast interiors of the cathedrals, the music rebounded from the stones of the arches and vaultings and rose in what seemed a chorus of heavenly voices. Moreover, plainchant made it easier to memorize the liturgy.

Around the eighth century, in an effort to establish authority for the Roman plainchant, writers began to credit Pope Gregory the Great (ca. 540–604; Figure 5.3) with having composed much of it himself. Though Gregory helped consolidate the Roman practice, he was probably not a composer. Even so, the music came to be called "Gregorian chant," and for centuries it was an essential part of Catholic worship. It was altered substantially during the seventeenth and eighteenth centuries but was restored toward the end of the nineteenth century. The Second Vatican Council (1963) reduced the role of Gregorian chant in favor of more active participation by the congregation, though plainchant is still sung in the more traditional Catholic churches.

Since plainchant was transmitted orally from generation to generation, we

---

*This does not mean that the entire service was sung. Readings from the Scripture and other spoken portions were also an integral part of the service.

FIGURE 5.3 Although Pope Gregory the Great was probably too busy with his other duties to write down "Gregorian chant," as portrayed here, he did encourage others to copy and disseminate the chant.

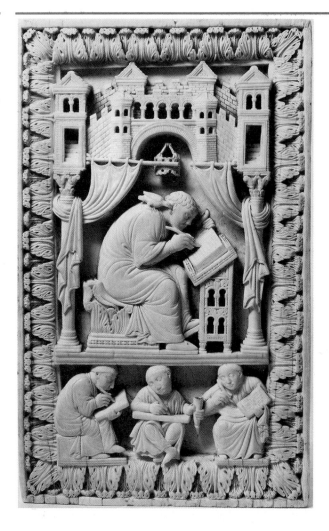

know little about the details of its performance. The earliest precise system of plainchant notation dates from the tenth century, when an Italian monk and theorist, Guido of Arezzo (born ca. 991; died after 1033), assigned red and yellow lines to specific pitches. The notation in all the early sources offers few indications about rhythm, and serious debates (never fully resolved) have arisen between advocates of a *mensural* ("measured") system, in which some notes are sung twice as fast as others, and advocates of freer and more declamatory rhythms, such as the monks at Solesmes in France.

Plainchant was organized around a series of "modes" whose subtleties were earnestly debated by medieval theorists. They derived the general concept from the Greeks and assigned Greek names to the modes—Dorian, Phrygian, Lydian, and Mixolydian (Figure 5.4)—in the mistaken belief that they corresponded to actual Greek scales. Like a scale in the modern tonal system, a mode was classified

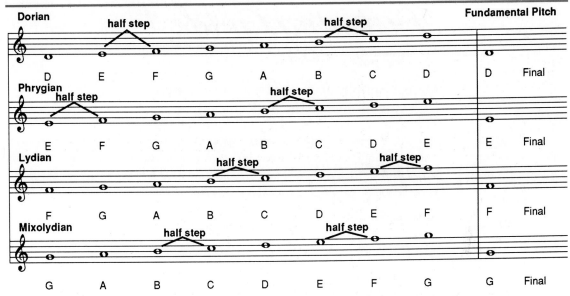

**FIGURE 5.4** The four principal medieval modes use the same seven notes corresponding to the white notes on the modern keyboard. They differ in their finals, ranges, and relative location of half steps.

according to its *final*, or concluding note (corresponding roughly to the tonic note in a tonal scale). Unlike a scale, the same final could belong to two modes depending on the *range* of the mode. This variety permitted melodies of surprising subtlety and complexity.

The modes arose during the ninth century as part of an effort to codify the vast body of plainchant melodies that already existed. With its passion for organization, the Church strove to impose a systematic order on an unwieldy and varied repertoire. The miracle is that so many of the melodies could be made to fit this modal system.

## Marian Antiphon: *"Alma redemptoris mater"* ("Loving mother of the Redeemer") (11th century?)

Mary, the mother of Jesus, has occupied a special place in Christian worship from the earliest days of the Church (Color Plate 2). The Gospel of Luke (written ca. A.D. 70–90) speaks of her importance, and around A.D. 100 Bishop Ignatius of Antioch wrote of her "mysteries to be loudly proclaimed." In both the Byzantine Church and the Roman Church, various feast days came to be associated with Mary, and by the sixth century more than a thousand such feasts were being celebrated.

A special group of plainchants associated with Mary grew up as part of the Divine Office. These are the four Marian antiphons, each of which is assigned to a season of the year. Antiphons were originally plainchants that framed the singing of a psalm. The term derives from the earlier practice of singing psalms "antiphonally"—that is, with two alternating choirs. In the Marian antiphons, however, neither of these practices survives.

## Marian Antiphon: *"Alma redemptoris mater"* ("Loving mother of the Redeemer")

CD 1, TRACK [1]
TAPE 1A, TRACK 1
DURATION: 1:38

*Although it flows smoothly from beginning to end in a predominantly neumatic style, "Alma redemptoris mater" divides into four sections, the last three of which contain varied descents from the highest note. The most extended melisma occurs on "Al-[ma]" at the very opening, underscoring Mary's "loving" nature.*

*Form: Sectional*

| LOCATION / TEXT | TIME | COMMENTS |
| --- | --- | --- |
| **SECTION 1** | | |
| **1** *Alma redemptoris mater,* <br> Loving mother of the Redeemer, | **0:00** | Long melisma on first syllable. Climbs from final to highest note, and back. |
| *quae pervia caeli porta manes,* <br> who art the open door into heaven, | 0:14 | Melisma on *"porta manes."* |
| **SECTION 2** | | |
| *et stella maris, succurre cadenti,* <br> and star of the sea, aid thy people, | **0:28** | Descends from the highest note down to *a.* |
| *surgere qui curat populo;* <br> who fall but strive to stand again; | 0:39 | |
| **SECTION 3** | | |
| **2** *Tu quae genuisti,* <br> Thou who gave birth, | **0:46** | Descends from the highest note to the final. |
| *natura mirante,* <br> to nature's amazement, | 0:52 | Neumatic setting. |
| *tuum sanctorium genitorem;* <br> to the holy Creator; | 0:59 | |
| **SECTION 4** | | |
| *Virgo prius ac posterius,* <br> yet ceased not to be a virgin, | **1:07** | Descends, largely in a neumatic setting, from the highest note to the final. |
| *Gabrielis ab ore* <br> receiving from Gabriel's lips | 1:19 | |
| *sumens illud "AVE," peccatorum miserere.* <br> that greeting ["Ave"], have mercy on us sinners. | 1:25 | *"Miserere"* is set syllabically. |

Perhaps the most beautiful of the Marian antiphons is *"Alma redemptoris mater"* ("Loving mother of the Redeemer"; Listening Guide 1), one of the few early plainchants to be ascribed to a particular author. It is thought to have been written by Hermann of Reichenau (1013?–1054), better known as Hermannus Contractus (Herman the Cripple), though certain stylistic features suggest a date about a century later.

*"Alma redemptoris mater"* is an example of the Lydian mode, which spans the octave from f to f$^1$.* The manuscript sources for this plainchant, however, specify that the b's are to be sung as b$^\flat$'s, a practice that became common during the eleventh century. The Lydian mode with b$^\flat$ corresponds exactly to the pitches of our major scale. The melody of *"Alma redemptoris mater,"* however, is treated very differently from what we would expect in a traditional tonal melody. Except for one brief rise outside the mode, the melody remains within the octave above the final. This plainchant consists of four sections. The first section rises from the final to f$^1$ an octave above and then descends again. The other three sections consist of highly embellished descents from f$^1$. Section 2 descends only to a, but Sections 3 and 4 descend to the final.

We find in this music examples of the three types of text setting that were common in early plainchant. The first section opens with an elaborate **melisma, in which a single syllable** (here *"Al-[ma],"* a reference to Mary's loving nature) **is sung to more than five or six notes** (our melisma contains 14 notes). At the other end of the spectrum we find *syllabic* writing, in which each syllable receives only a single note (see the following example). Between these two extremes is *neumatic* writing, in which a syllable receives several notes. These categories represent points on a continuum, and the music moves freely from one style to the other.

A practice common to many plainchants was the use of melodic patterns, or formulas, that are repeated in the course of the melody. An example is the third phrase of Section 1 *(quae pervia caeli)*, whose nine notes differ only slightly from the eight notes of the second phrase in Section 4 *(ac posterius)*:

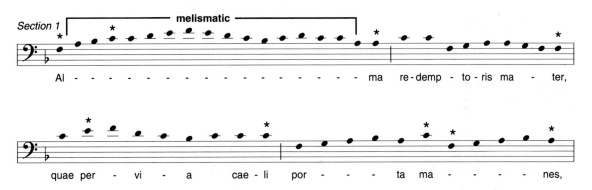

*To indicate pitches precisely, musicians assign them letters and numbers within each octave. Beginning with the lowest c on the piano, the octaves are CC, C, c, c$^1$, c$^2$, c$^3$, c$^4$, and c$^5$. Our plainchant spans the range from a fifth below c$^1$ (called "middle c") to a fourth (fifth) above.

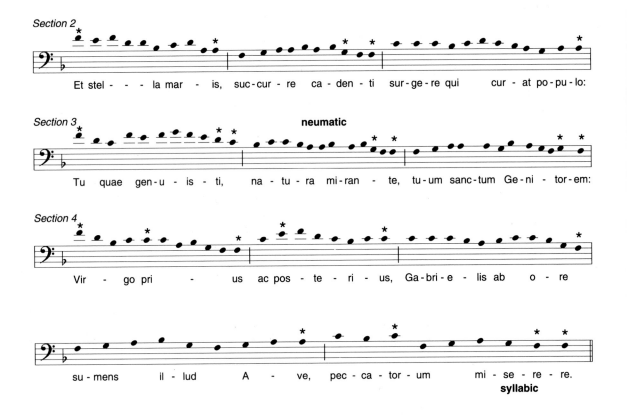

*Section 2*

Et stel - - - la mar - is, suc-cur - re ca - den - ti sur-ge-re qui cur - at po-pu - lo:

*Section 3*                                          **neumatic**

Tu quae gen-u - is - ti, na-tu-ra mi-ran - te, tu-um sanc-tum Ge-ni - tor-em:

*Section 4*

Vir - go pri - us ac pos - te - ri - us, Ga-bri-e - lis ab o - re

su - mens il - lud A - ve, pec - ca - tor - um mi - se - re - re.

**syllabic**

Such repetitions lend the plainchant a sense of serenity and balance.

Plainchant was notated with *neumes* (see Figure 4.12) rather than with note values and barlines. Consequently most modern transcriptions use noteheads with neither stems nor barlines, making it easier to follow the gentle rise and fall of the lines. In our performance some of the notes (marked here with an asterisk) are held longer than others, either for emphasis or because they come at the end of a phrase.

## MEDIEVAL DRAMA

In addition to the liturgical plainchant, poet/composers from the tenth century on created imaginary dialogues that told a story in more vivid terms. Most of these dialogues had to do with Christmas or Easter and grew out of melodies called *tropes*. A **trope** was an addition to the plainchant, either a new text to fit an existing melisma, a textless melody to enrich an established plainchant, or a new text and melody that prefaced an established plainchant or were inserted between lines as a kind of gloss. Troping reflected the desire of composers to venture beyond the constraints of established texts and plainchants.

One such trope associated with the Easter Mass begins with the line spoken to the three Marys by one of the angels at the tomb of Jesus: *"Quem queritis?"* ("Whom do you seek?"). This dialogue was gradually expanded into a self-sufficient *liturgical drama* between these characters, complete with its own text and monophonic melodies.

Liturgical dramas were influenced by the *vernacular dramas* presented by roving minstrels who freely mixed secular texts, instrumental music, and plainchant. A popular example is *Robin and Marion* by the thirteenth-century composer Adam de la Halle, written around 1283 to entertain French soldiers during Christmas festivities. In songs and dances, *Robin and Marion* tells the story of an amorous encounter between a shepherdess and a roving knight. Although its dramatic organization is rather loose and informal, *Robin and Marion* marks the start of a development that led around 1600 to the emergence of opera.

Liturgical dramas proved extremely popular, so much so that in the sixteenth century they were banned by the Vatican as corruptions of plainchant. Some of them had become so elaborate that they were staged outside of liturgical services. One of the most popular types was the *morality play*—a drama set to music to illustrate a moral point, such as the struggle between good and evil. The first composer of a morality play was Hildegard of Bingen (1098–1179), an abbess in southern Germany.

## Hildegard of Bingen (1098–1179): From Scene 4 of *Ordo virtutum* (Play of the Virtues) (ca. 1152?)

Because the chief officials of the Church were males, plainchant was usually associated with male voices and was written by male composers. Nevertheless, we know of several women who sang and composed plainchant. Hildegard's aristocratic parents offered their tenth child, as was the custom, to the Church, whose service she entered at age eight. She and a small group of followers lived with her teacher, the abbess Jutta, in a Benedictine monastery. After Jutta's death in 1136, Hildegard was elected abbess and around 1150 she succeeded—against the wishes of the local abbot—in founding an independent convent at Rupertsberg, in southwestern Germany (see the map on page 65).

Hildegard regarded herself as an instrument through which God spoke in mystical visions. With the help of two colleagues she recorded these visions in illuminated manuscripts, one of which was titled *Scivias* ("Know the Ways"). Hildegard also wrote books on theology, medicine, and the physical sciences and carried on a voluminous correspondence with many political and religious leaders, who eagerly sought her advice.

Hildegard was active as a poet and composer as well and wrote more than 150 monophonic melodies. In her 90-minute morality play, *Ordo virtutum* (Play of the Virtues; Listening Guide 2), perhaps written for the dedication of the convent church in 1152, a Soul *(Anima)* succumbs to the temptations of the Devil

# *Listening Guide 2*

## HILDEGARD OF BINGEN (1098–1179):
## From Scene 4 of *Ordo virtutum* (Play of the Virtues)

CD 1, TRACK 2
TAPE 1A, TRACK 2
DURATION: 4:31

*The characters sing in a variety of styles suited to their roles, accompanied by instruments that represent the dramatic action. The reverberation of sound in the recording is characteristic of a large cathedral.*

*Form: Dialogue*

| TEXT | TIME | COMMENTS |
|------|------|----------|
| **DEVIL:** | | |
| 1 *Que es, aut unde venis?* <br> Who are you, where do you come from? | **0:00** | Spoken. Denied the gift of song, the devil has only a spoken part in the play. |
| *Tu amplexata es me, et ego foras eduxi te.* <br> You were in my embrace, I led you out. | | |
| *Sed nunc in reversione tua confundis me—* <br> Yet now you are going back, defying me— | | |
| *ego autem pugna mea deiciam te!* <br> but I shall fight you and bring you down! | | |
| **PENITENT SOUL:** | | |
| *Ego omnes vias meas malas esse cognovi, et ideo fugi a te.* <br> I recognized that all my ways were wicked, so I fled you. | 0:22 | The weakened but penitent spirit sings in a syllabic/neumatic style that repeats melodic formulas. She is accompanied by a drone in the fiddle and heterophonic counterpoint in the flute. |
| *Modo autem, o illusor, pugno contra te.* <br> But now, you trickster, I'll fight you face to face. | | |
| *Inde tu, o regina Humilitas, tuo medicamine adiuva me!* <br> Come, Queen Humility, with your medicine give me aid! | | |
| **HUMILITY (TO VICTORY):** | | |
| *O Victoria, que istum in celo superasti,* <br> O Victory, you who once conquered this creature in the heavens, | 1:31 | Dramatic ascent to *"Victoria."* |
| *curre cum militibus tuis et omnes ligate Diabolum hunc!* | | |

| TEXT | TIME | COMMENTS |
|------|------|----------|
| run now, with all your soldiery, and all of you, blind this fiend! | | |
| VICTORY (TO THE VIRTUES): | | |
| *O fortissimi et gloriosissimi milites,*<br>Bravest and most glorious warriors, | 2:01 | Accompanied by a drone on the organ. |
| *venite, et adiuvate me istum fallacem vincere.*<br>come, and help me to vanquish this deceitful one. | | |
| THE VIRTUES: | | |
| **2** *O dulcissima bellatrix, in torrente fonte*<br>O sweetest warrior, in the scorching fountain | 2:32 | Sung by the chorus of 16 virtues. More stepwise than the preceding solo melodies. Accompanied by a drone on the fiddle. |
| *qui absorbuit lupum rapacem—*<br>that swallowed up the rapacious wolf— | | |
| *o gloriosa coronata, nos libenter*<br>o glorious crowned one, how gladly | | |
| *militamus tecum contra illusorem hunc.*<br>we will fight at your side against that trickster. | | |
| HUMILITY (TO THE VIRTUES): | | |
| *Ligate ergo istum, o Virtutes preclare!*<br>Bind him then, you shining Virtues! | 3:12 | Neumatic style. Second half of phrase repeats the first half. Accompanied by flute. |
| THE VIRTUES: | | |
| *O regina nostra, tibi parebimus,*<br>O our queen, we obey you, | 3:28 | Sung by the chorus in a more syllabic style. |
| *et precepta tua in omnibus adimplebimus.*<br>and we will carry out your orders completely. | | |
| VICTORY: | | |
| **3** *Gaudete, o socii quia antiquus serpens ligatus est!*<br>Comrades, rejoice, the age-old snake is bound! | 3:49 | Sung in the highest register in neumatic/melismatic style. Accompanied by bells. |
| THE VIRTUES: | | |
| *Laus tibi, Christe, rex angelorum.*<br>Praise be to you, Christ, king of the angels. | 4:18 | Chorus. Upward leap on *"rex"* (king) and melisma on *"angelorum"* (angels). |

but is rescued through the intervention of the sixteen virtues (Knowledge-of-God, Humility, Discipline, Compassion, Mercy, Victory, Discretion, Patience, Charity, Obedience, Faith, Hope, Chastity, Innocence, World-Rejection, and Heavenly Love).

For her play Hildegard wrote 82 chantlike melodies that rely more heavily than *"Alma redemptoris mater"* on a group of melodic formulas, which she combined in a variety of ways. All the parts were sung by the nuns, except that of the Devil, who was presumably played by the monastic priest Volmar (who administered the sacraments to the nuns and served as Hildegard's secretary). The Devil, who is denied the gift of song, can speak only in a rasping voice. Hildegard assigned the simplest, most syllabic passages to the chorus of Virtues and the most elaborate and melismatic to Victory and other important protagonists.

Because all that survives of medieval dramas is a set of notations that specify little more than pitch, their performance requires considerable historical imagination. In our excerpt (in which the penitent Soul breaks with the Devil and returns to God), such instruments as the medieval fiddle (a fretted violin), flute, organ, and bells have been added to enrich the symbolism. For example, Hildegard associated the sound of stringed instruments with the Soul's struggle back to light. For medieval musicians the flute symbolized the presence of God. Bells were a symbol of rejoicing. These instruments provide either a drone (page 69) or heterophonic accompaniments to the vocal line. Both in extent and texture, medieval drama represents the richest and most elaborate form of medieval music.

## SECULAR SONGS

We know that men and women in medieval days were fond of songs based on secular texts, but we know little about what those songs were and how they were performed. The reason is that most of them were created spontaneously, performed as the occasion arose, and only rarely written down. Many of them were written by poets who knew nothing about musical notation but who knew how to catch the attention of listeners by singing their own poems. The few songs that have survived were written down only a century or more after they were composed.

From the twelfth through the fourteenth centuries courtly and lyric poetry flourished in many parts of Europe. In the north of France were the *troubadours,* who recited or sang their poetry in Provençal, a French dialect. In the south were the *trouvères,* who recited or sang in French. And in Germany were the *Minnesänger,* successors of the troubadours. Much of the music that accompanied their singing has been lost, and only about one-tenth of the roughly 2,500 troubadour poems that have come down to us have musical settings.

All these poets sang of "courtly love," usually the love of a man for an unobtainable woman of impeccable virtue. This convention arose from the tradition of Marian worship in the Church, and many of the Church's teachings about love—selflessness, devotion, a willingness to sacrifice—found expression in the poetry of courtly love.

These poets have often been pictured as carefree minstrels wandering from castle to castle singing for their supper, and they often presented themselves that way in their poems. It now appears that most of them were aristocrats, though others, including some of the most famous, were gifted commoners.

## Troubadour Song: Countess of Dia, *"A una amante infidele"* ("To an Unfaithful Lover") (ca. 1160)

During the Middle Ages aristocratic women enjoyed considerable freedom and power. For example, in 1132 Eleanor of Aquitaine (ca. 1122–1204) inherited a duchy larger than the kingdom of France, and she held it together until her death at the age of 82. In the thirteenth century French barons, in a desperate attempt to keep the French throne from passing to an English claimant, declared that inheritances could no longer pass through the female line, a prohibition that quickly caught on.

Aristocratic women in medieval France received about the same musical education as men. Some of them, known as *trobairitz,* traveled about singing and accompanying themselves on harps, fiddles, and guitars. The *jongleresses* of southern France seem to have been especially free to travel. Women continued to compose music until the introduction of polyphony around 1000. For the next three centuries, since the theoretical training required for polyphony was available almost exclusively in monasteries, few women composed music.

Little is known about the countess who composed "To an Unfaithful Lover" (Listening Guide 3), though a contemporary poem suggests that she may have been Beatrice (Beatriz de Dia), the wife of William I of Poitiers and the lover of Raimbaut d'Orange. Only five of the poems attributed to her have survived, but we know that "To an Unfaithful Lover" (perhaps Raimbaut) was popular in the Middle Ages. The subject of the poem is variously described as "arrogant," "malevolent," "unsociable," and "hard," but also, as the author ruefully confesses, a man of considerable appeal and charm.

As is true of many troubadour songs, the pitches of the melody of "To an Unfaithful Lover" are specified but the rhythms are not. With so little to go on, anyone who performs the song today must improvise both the delivery and the accompaniment.

The song consists of several poetic *stanzas* (the units of verse into which a poem is divided), each set to the same music. Such a song is said to be in *strophic form* (a "strophe" is synonymous with a "stanza"). In each performance the singer would present as few or as many stanzas as she wished. (Our example, which follows, includes the first and the last of five stanzas.)

Further, each stanza within the song is organized musically as a *bar form,* which consists of two identical units *(A-A)* that conclude with a refrain *(B)*— hence *A-A-B.* The refrain was frequently the longest section of such songs and

*(Text continues on page 89.)*

# Listening Guide 3

## COUNTESS OF DIA: Troubadour Song, *"A una amante infidele"* ("To an Unfaithful Lover")

CD 1, TRACK 3
TAPE 1A, TRACK 3
DURATION: 5:08

*The performers have made several choices not specified in the manuscript sources. The song opens with a lengthy solo on the lute, a fretted, plucked-string instrument with a long neck and rounded back. The vocalist sings each line of text as a solo, followed by an improvised echo in the lute. The shawm (an early double-reed wind instrument with a powerful, shrill sound) and tambourine provide instrumental interludes between the stanzas. Finally, the vocalist speaks the tornada over an improvised accompaniment.*

*Form: Strophic, with bar-form stanzas*

| | TEXT | TIME | LOCATION / COMMENTS |
|---|---|---|---|
| **1** | [Improvised introduction] | **0:00** | Played on the lute. |
| **2** | STANZA 1 | | |
| | *A chantar m'er de so qu'eu no volria:*<br>I must sing of something about which I would rather not: | **0:55** | **A-Section.** Improvised break at the end of each half-phrase. |
| | *Tant me rancur de lui cui sui amia;*<br>But I have much to complain of concerning him whose lover I am; | 1:05 | |
| | *Car eu l'am mais que nulha ren que sia:*<br>Because I love him yet I have not found favor with him: | 1:16 | **A-Section.** |
| | *Vas lui no·m val Merces ni Cortezia,*<br>Neither by my Gratitude nor my Good Manners, | 1:24 | |
| **3** | *Ni ma beltatz ni mos pretz ni mos sens:*<br>nor my beauty, nor my worth, nor my wit: | 1:36 | **B-Section.** A few strummed chords inserted during the vocal line. |
| | *Qu'atressi·m sui enganad' e trahia*<br>I have been deceived and betrayed | | |
| | *Com degr'esser, s'eu fos desavinens.*<br>as I would have been were I devoid of charm. | 1:52 | Repeats the music of the last line of the *A*-Section. |

| TEXT | TIME | LOCATION / COMMENTS |
|------|------|---------------------|
| [Instrumental interlude] | **2:06** | Improvised from a related but independent melody. Lute joined by shawm and tambourine. |

**4**   STANZA 5

| | | |
|------|------|---------------------|
| *Valer mi deu mos pretz e mos paratges,*<br>I must be able to depend on my worth and my noble birth, | **3:46** | *A-Section.* |
| *E ma beutatz e plus mos fins coratges:*<br>And my beauty, and even more on my sincere heart: | 3:55 | |
| *Per qu'eu vos mand, lai on es vostr' estatges,*<br>This is why I send over to you in your lodgings, | 4:04 | *A-Section.* |
| *Esta chanson, que me sia messatges!*<br>This song, that serves as my messenger! | 4:12 | |
| *E volh saber lo meus bels amics gens,*<br>I would like to know, my beautiful and sweet friend, | 4:24 | *B-Section.* |
| *Per que vos m'etz tant fers ni tant salvatges;*<br>Why regarding me you have been so unsociable and so harsh; | | |
| *No sai si s'es orgolhs o mals talens?*<br>Is it pride or ill will? | 4:42 | Repeats the music of the last line of the *A-Section.* |

**5**   TORNADA

| | | |
|------|------|---------------------|
| *Mas aitan plus volh li digas, messatges,*<br>But what I would most like you to tell him, messenger, | **4:53** | Spoken over the improvised accompaniment. |
| *Qu'en trop d'orgolh an gran dan maintas gens!*<br>Is that too much pride can hurt many people! | | |

## A MEDIEVAL MONASTERY

The monastery built during the ninth century in the tiny village of St. Gall in Switzerland was one of the most famous in western Europe. St. Gall himself was thought to have been one of several Irish monks who visited the area in the early seventh century. The local duke, after tolerating three years of vigorous proselytizing by the monks, at last ordered them to leave. Illness prevented St. Gall from leaving with his companions, however, and he retired to a steep cliff overlooking a river. There he resolved to spend his last days in fasting and prayer. He lived long enough to win fame as a preacher and managed to convert many of the local residents to Christianity. When he died, he was buried with some of his relics in a tiny hermitage he had built for himself.

After his death, St. Gall's reputation spread far and wide and pilgrims came to visit the hermitage. By the middle of the eighth century, two priests, a deacon, and 47 monks had taken up residence at the hermitage, now vastly expanded, and in time a Benedictine abbey was erected near the original site. Under Abbot Gozbert (d. 836), St. Gall was transformed into one of the most impressive monasteries in Europe. Although little of the structure survives, the original plans have been preserved. They reveal a design that was typical of large, prosperous abbeys at the time (Figure 5.5). The sanctuary had stained-glass windows and chandeliers, and the altars were decorated with gold and silver and covered with expensive cloth. Frescoes (plaster painted while fresh, creating deep, rich images) adorned the walls. St. Gall lay only a few miles from the intersection of two major trade routes, and visitors filled the sanctuary to attend the two Masses celebrated each day.

Nearby were a well-stocked library, several large kitchens (for guests of varying social status), an inn for pilgrims and one for noble guests (another arrangement hard to reconcile with Christian beliefs), a bakery and brewery, artisan workshops, a flour mill, a woodturning shop, a wheelwright's shop, a barn (with room for sheep, goats, cows, horses, and pigs), a school, a hospital, and numerous outbuildings.

During its prime in the tenth century, the abbey received countless bequests of land and even whole monasteries. Some of these bequests were no doubt made by pious Christians, though others were probably made in the hope of selling supplies to the hundreds of people who now lived at the abbey. (Some donors specified that their bequests were to go into effect only after their deaths.) It is difficult to reconcile all this with the Benedictine vow of poverty, but the abbots doubtless felt that the abbey's wealth testified to the glory of God.

*continued*

FIGURE 5.5 Plans for the monastery of St. Gall (ca. 820)—a design for a self-sufficient community, complete with a cemetery that doubled as an orchard. The calefactory was a heated sitting room; in the almonry, alms were distributed to the poor.

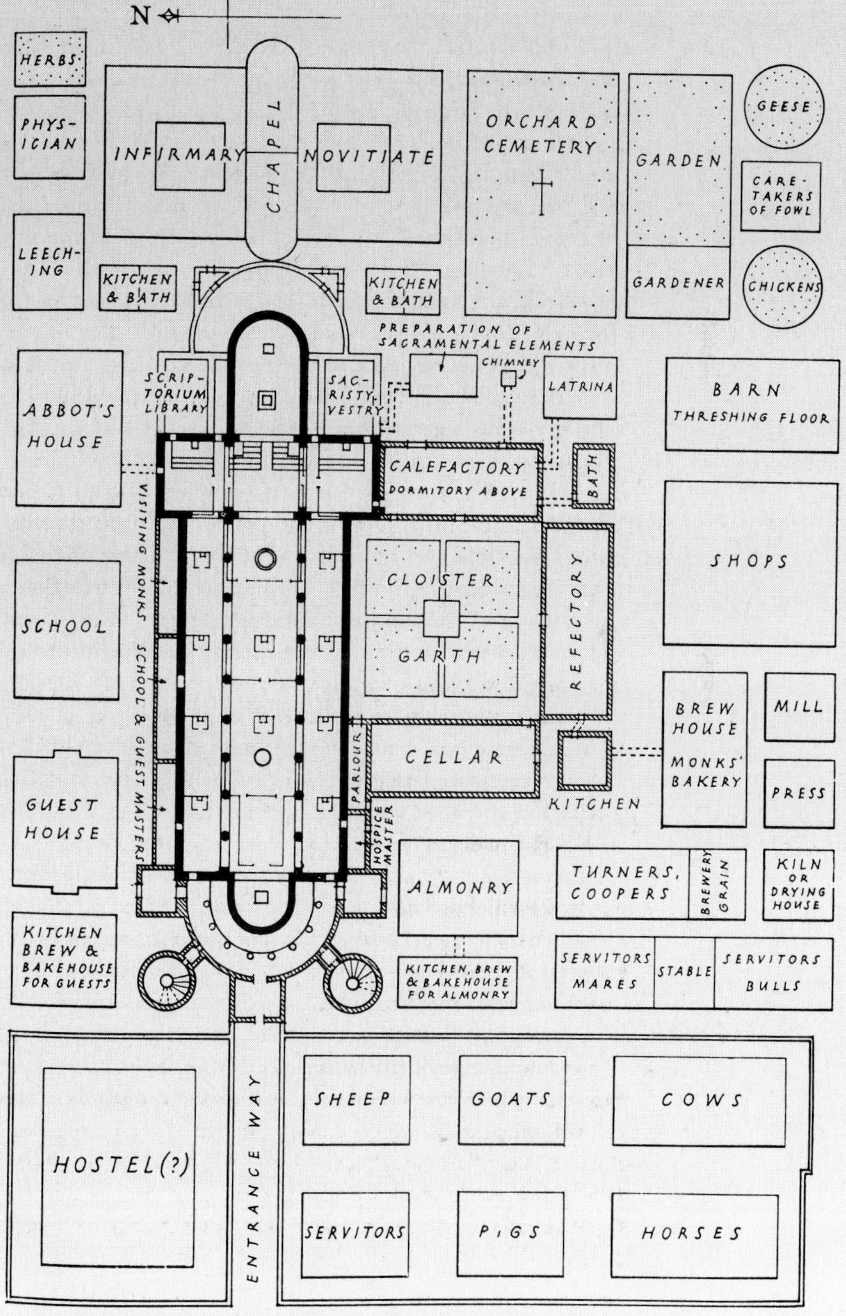

In the famous school at St. Gall, founded in the eighth century, apprentices learned to read and write and to copy and illuminate manuscripts in the "scriptorium" (the writing room). The monks studied the movement of the sun and stars and kept abreast of the most recent developments in science. They could study painting, architecture, sculpture, weaving, and spinning as well.

The curriculum also included instruction in the theory and composition of music, as evidenced by the rich collection of music manuscripts that has survived. One monk, Notker Balbulus (Notker the Stammerer; ca. 840–912), was a well-known musician at St. Gall who, according to one account, introduced a form of chant known as *sequence,* long syllabic settings of unrhymed verses based on lengthy melismas from the chant. Notker's aim, according to the account, was to help the monks memorize long musical passages.

Over time, the abbots turned over much of the farming to apprentices or neighboring peasants in order to free time for scholarly pursuits. They stocked their library with books in Latin and Greek and collected German literature. (Most of the abbots were members of the German nobility.)

St. Gall was not immune from the violence of the outside world, however. One ninth-century abbot, who kept a chronicle that has come down to us, reminds us of the fragility of medieval life—and also reminds us that the Christian dictum to "turn the other cheek" had its limits:

The Saracens, whose nature it is to be strong in the mountains, molested us and our dependents from the south to such an extent that, having gained possession of our grazing lands and mountains, they even hurled javelins at the monks following the cross [i.e., in a procession] around the town. The Abbot's troops could not discover where they were hiding. One night he himself, accompanied by the boldest men from among the attendants, found where their hiding place was, and attacked them in their sleep with spears, sickles, and axes. Some were killed, others taken prisoner, and the rest escaped by flight; [the abbot] considered it useless to pursue them, since they ran over the mountains more swiftly than goats. But he drove the captives before him to the monastery. Since, however, they refused to eat or drink, they all perished. It will suffice to mention this as an example of the sufferings of that time . . . for if I were to list all the hardships which our community suffered at the hands of the Saracens, I should fill a volume.

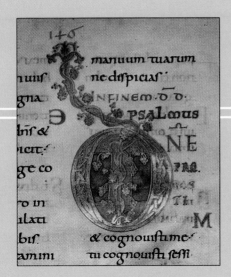

**COLOR PLATE 1**
*Two illuminations from the Golden Psalter (so-called because of its extraordinary decorations):* Domine *(left) and* Beatus vir *(right). The manuscript was created at the monas-* *tery of St. Gall in the ninth century. In such laboriously crafted medieval manuscripts, the richness of the decoration signifies the importance of the contents.*

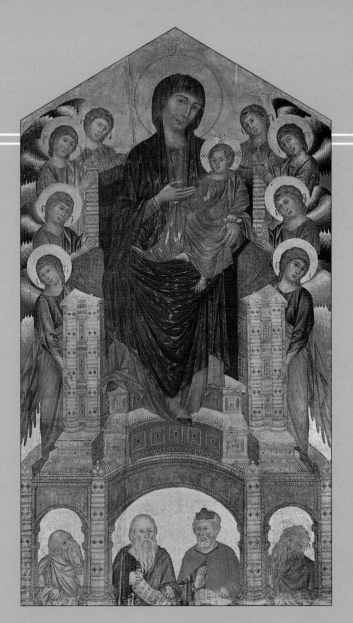

**COLOR PLATE 2**
*This imposing wood altarpiece*—Madonna Enthroned—*by the Florentine painter Giovanni Cimabue (ca. 1251–1302) stands nearly thirteen feet tall; it testifies to the central place of the Virgin Mary in medieval Christian worship. The altar panel is housed today in the Uffizi Gallery, commissioned during the Renaissance by Cosimo I.*

**COLOR PLATE 3**

The Raising of Lazarus, a fresco in Padua by Giotto (ca. 1266–1337), evinces a new feeling for human forms and dramatic shape. We feel that we could walk right into the scene; there is a clear distinction between the background and the foreground. Unlike earlier Byzantine-influenced artists, such as Cimabue, Giotto painted rounded figures in less rigid drapery. Adding to the realism of the scene is the woman covering her nose against the stench. During this same period, the stylistic leaps in Western music were as bold as those in painting.

**COLOR PLATE 4**
*A member of a distinguished family of painters, Gentile Bellini (1429–1507) excelled at depicting ceremonial processions* *such as this annual founder's day parade through the Piazza San Marco in Venice. The Venetian love of pomp and circumstance invariably impressed* *visitors. The festive spirit carried over to the music sung in the church in the picture's background.*

was often related musically to the *A*-Section. In "To an Unfaithful Lover," for example, the last line of the *A*-Section is identical to the last line of the *B*-Section.

The text of this song is in the style of a *canso*, the most prestigious type of courtly love poetry. The structure and rhyme scheme in a canso were improvised. Here the rhyme scheme (the rhyme patterns of the final syllables) of the 7-line stanzas is *a-a-a-a-b-a-b* and is coordinated with the music as follows:

| MUSIC | TEXT | STANZA 1 END RHYMES |
|---|---|---|
| *A*-Section | *a* | "volria" |
| | *a* | "amia" |
| *A*-Section | *a* | "sia" |
| | *a* | "Cortezia" |
| *B*-Section | *b* | "sens" |
| | *a* | "trahia" |
| | *b* | "desavinens" |
| | | (to music of the last line of the *A*-Section) |

The poem ends with a brief *tornada,* or half-stanza, to the music of the *A*-Section. Our poem presents a moral aphorism typical of a tornada: "But what I would most like you to tell him, messenger, is that too much pride can hurt many people!"


## Minnesänger Song: Walther von der Vogelweide (ca. 1170–1230): *"Unter der linden an der heide"* ("Under the linden tree on the heath") (ca. 1200)

Legend has it that when Frederick Barbarossa, the Holy Roman Emperor, married Beatrix of Burgundy in 1156, her retinue included a minstrel, Guiot of Provence, who introduced the troubadour art into Germany. Whether true or not, the *Minnesänger,* as the German troubadours came to be called, made significant contributions of their own. For example, the bar form in the song by the Countess of Dia was more common in earlier Minnesang than in troubadour song and may well have originated there.

Walther von der Vogelweide (literally, "Walter of the bird meadow") was one of the greatest singers and poets of his day. He was also a knight, though that rank carried little prestige in medieval Germany. He probably spent most of his time wandering from court to court, relying more on his talents than on his social station. Vogelweide is one of the models for the romanticized picture of the wandering minstrel.

Vogelweide probably composed the song in Listening Guide 4 around 1200, and it was already famous during his lifetime. Its stepwise, repetitive melody moves within a narrow range that suggests the influence of plainchant. The

# *Listening Guide 4*

CD 1, TRACK 4
TAPE 1A, TRACK 4
DURATION: 3:20

## WALTHER VON DER VOGELWEIDE: Minnesänger Song, *"Unter der linden an der heide"* ("Under the linden tree on the heath")

*In this performance, the singer has chosen to use a hushed, intimate tone. One could as easily imagine a bright upbeat performance to the same melody.*

*Form: Strophic, with bar-form stanzas*

| TEXT | TIME | LOCATION/COMMENTS |
|---|---|---|
| **1** [Instrumental introduction] | **0:00** | Opening flourish on the psalterium, a fretless plucked string instrument consisting of a shallow wooden box with about a dozen strings. |
| STANZA 1 | | |
| *Unter der linden an der heide,*<br>Under the linden tree on the heath, | **0:06** | **A-Section.** Strummed accompaniment. |
| *da unser zweier bette was,*<br>there was our bed for two, | 0:14 | **A-Section.** |
| *Da mugt ir vinden schone beide*<br>*gebrochen bluomen under gras.*<br>There you can see where the pretty flowers lie broken on the grass. | 0:21 | **B-Section.** Arpeggiated accompaniment. |
| *Vor dem walde in einem tal, tandaradei,*<br>Before the forest in the valley, tandaradei, | 0:35 | Return of strummed accompaniment. |
| *schone sanc diu nahtegal.*<br>sang beautifully the nightingale. · | 0:47 | Leads smoothly into the second stanza. |
| STANZA 2 | | |
| *Ich kam gegangen zuo der ouwe,*<br>I came through the green meadow, | **0:55** | **A-Section.** |
| *do was min friedel komen e.*<br>there where my lover awaited me. | 1:01 | **A-Section.** |
| *Da wart ich empfangen, here frouwe,*<br>*daz ich bin saelic iemer me.*<br>There I was received, blissful lady, as if I were eternally blessed. | 1:08 | **B-Section.** |

| TEXT | TIME | LOCATION/COMMENTS |
|---|---|---|
| *Kust er mich? wol tausentstunt, tandaradei,* <br> Did he kiss me? Just a thousand times, tandaradei, | 1:22 | |
| *seht wie roht mir ist der munt!* <br> see how red my mouth is! | 1:33 | Leads smoothly into the third stanza. |

**2**  STANZA 3

| TEXT | TIME | LOCATION/COMMENTS |
|---|---|---|
| *Do het er gemachet also riche* <br> There he made therefore | **1:40** | *A*-Section. |
| *von bluomen eine bettestat.* <br> from flowers a lovely bed. | 1:47 | *A*-Section. |
| *Des wirt gelachet innecliche,* <br> He will have a good laugh, | 1:54 | *B*-Section. |
| *kumt iemen an das selbe pfat.* <br> should someone chance along this path today. | 2:01 | |
| *Bi den rosen er wol mac, tandaradei,* <br> From the roses he probably can, tandaradei, | 2:08 | |
| *merken wa mirz houbet lac.* <br> tell just where my head lay. | 2:20 | Leads smoothly into the fourth stanza. |

STANZA 4

| TEXT | TIME | LOCATION/COMMENTS |
|---|---|---|
| *Daz er bi mit laege, wessez iemen,* <br> That he lay with me, anybody would know, | **2:28** | *A*-Section. |
| *(nu enwelle got!), so schamt ich mich.* <br> (God forbid!), I would be so ashamed. | 2:34 | *A*-Section. |
| *Wes er mit mir pflaege, niemer niemen* <br> *bevinde daz wan er unde ich,* <br> What he did with me, may no one ever know except for him and me, | 2:41 | *B*-Section. |
| *Und ein kleinez vogellin, tandaradei,* <br> and the little bird, tandaradei, | 2:54 | |
| *daz mac wol getriuwe sin.* <br> it will never say a word. | 3:07 | |

form, strophic with stanzas in bar form, is identical to that of "To an Unfaithful Lover." The narrator is a woman who describes an amorous encounter with her lover in the forest. The text reflects a prevailing medieval view of forbidden sex: It is all right to engage in such activities so long as you do not get caught!

## INSTRUMENTAL MUSIC: ESTAMPIE (ca. 1300)

Many early instruments seem to have been used primarily to accompany a singer. The estampie, however, which first appears in French manuscripts from the early years of the thirteenth century, is one of the earliest examples of purely instrumental music. The notation indicates that the melodies were not meant to be sung, and no text is given. The spirited tunes suggest that they were to be played on an agile instrument like the lute or the fiddle.

Almost all estampies are organized as a succession of independent sections, each containing a theme that is usually repeated only once but sometimes as many as five times. (In our performance the last section mixes three of the themes [see Listening Guide 5].) Each theme divides into two halves that are identical except for slightly different closes. The repetitions of the individual themes were probably played by different groups of instruments, as they are in our recording. The frequent doubling of the instrumental lines offers ample opportunities for heterophony. The *A*-Theme presents a refreshing asymmetry: Its first part has eight beats, while the second part has nine.

About one aspect of the estampie scholars disagree: Was it dance music? The fact that in some sources estampies were grouped with other dance pieces suggests that it was, and yet the term *estampie* (whose origins are obscure) does not itself suggest dancing. Our example, from a northern French manuscript from around 1300, certainly seems to invite dancing.

# Listening Guide 5

## Estampie

CD 1, TRACK 5
TAPE 1A, TRACK 5
DURATION: 4:47

*Since this musical form is inherently repetitive, the performers are called upon to crea. variety by orchestrating the simple monophonic lines. The melody instruments in th recording include the lute, guitar, fiddle, and lyra (a bowed string instrument hel vertically and usually played with a drone). Generally each theme is stated simply an then further instruments are added. The regular rhythmic accompaniment provided l the tambourine (from the fifth repetition of the A-Theme on) suggests music for dancin*

*Form: Sectional (Section 1, 2, 3, etc.)*

| | LOCATION | TIME | COMMENTS |
|---|---|---|---|
| 1 | Introduction | **0:00** | The mouth harp sets up the basic pulse of the piece. |
| | SECTION 1 | | |
| | A-Theme* | **0:04** | On the lute, 8-beat phrase plus 9-beat phrase. |
| | A | 0:14 | The same melody repeats in embellished form. |
| | A | 0:23 | Heterophonic melody now added on the guitar. |
| | A | 0:33 | Lute and guitar repeat the melody in embellished form. |
| | A | 0:42 | More instruments enter, including the fiddle and tambourine. |
| | A | 0:51 | The melody repeats with the same instruments. |
| | SECTION 2 | | |
| | B | **1:01** | Melody played by the lyra in sustained notes. |
| | B | 1:10 | Fiddle added above the lyra. |
| | B | 1:19 | The lute joins the lyra and fiddle. |
| | B | 1:27 | The guitar joins in as well. |
| 2 | SECTION 3 | | |
| | C | **1:36** | Sprightly tune played first by the lute. |
| | C | 1:45 | Played in parallel thirds between lute and guitar (an addition by the per- |
| | C | 1:53 | formers). Fiddle enters. |
| | C | 2:02 | Lyra enters with drone-like tones. |

*Because the themes repeat so frequently, we have omitted the term *theme* throughout this Listening Guide.

*continued*

# *Listening Guide 5 (Continued)*

| LOCATION | TIME | COMMENTS |
|----------|------|----------|
| D | **2:11** | Simple scalar descent in the bells. |
| D | 2:19 | Lute enters with an animated embellishment of the descent. |
| D | 2:28 | Fiddle and lyra enter. |
| D | 2:36 | The lyra plays the scalar descent in parallel fifths. |
| | | |
| **SECTION 5** | | |
| E | **2:45** | Tune in fiddle and lyra. Phrase contains an interruption. |
| E | 2:56 | The bells accent the interruption. |
| | | |
| **SECTION 6** | | |
| F | **3:05** | An 8-beat phrase plus a 10-beat phrase. Begins with the scalar descent, but |
| F | 3:14 | then introduces yet another interruption. |
| | | |
| **SECTION 7** | | |
| G | **3:24** | Animated theme in the lute. |
| D | 3:33 | Strong parallel fifths in the lyra. |
| G | 3:42 | Lute accompanied by slower tones in the lyra. |
| D | 3:51 | Strong parallel fifths in the lyra. |
| F' | 4:00 | A variant of the earlier theme. |
| G | 4:16 | The instruments fade into the distance. |

3

# Chapter 6

## MEDIEVAL POLYPHONY

Western music differs from the musics of other cultures in many ways, including its instruments, musical forms, and social functions. Yet only one difference is fundamental: the Western predilection for polyphony—that is, music for two or more independent voices. No one has yet offered a satisfactory explanation as to why composers in the West shared this predilection, which departed sharply from the paths followed by virtually all other musics.

## ORGANUM

At first, polyphony was used to provide simple embellishments to monophonic plainchant. Because of the special nature of polyphony, it was reserved for the most important feast days of the church year. In the earliest type of polyphony, singers accompanied plainchant at intervals of either the perfect fifth or the perfect fourth (page 70) above. After the 1:2 ratio of the octave, these two intervals have the lowest ratios of adjacent integers (2:3, 3:4, 4:5, and so on). The perfect fifth (for example, C-G) has a ratio of 2:3, and the perfect fourth (for example, C-F) has a ratio of 3:4. The fifth above any pitch represents its first and strongest overtone, and the fourth above *that* represents its next most powerful overtone.* Indeed, some scholars have suggested that the earliest polyphony resulted accidentally when singers confused two notes a fifth apart for the same note.

A plainchant embellished in this manner was known as an *organum* (pl. *organa*). The Greek word *organon* meant an instrument or an implement, and the Latin term *organum* may have referred to the medieval organ, an instrument

---

*You can verify the presence of these overtones with a simple experiment. Go to a piano and silently depress the G above middle C (a perfect fifth). This will raise the damper and allow the string to vibrate freely. Now strike the middle C forcefully and then release it while still keeping the G depressed. You will now hear the G even though it has not been struck. Its strings have been activated by sympathetic vibration, in which the overtone a fifth above C (G) sets the G-strings into motion. (The piano must be in good tune for this experiment to work.)

with limited range and a reedy sound. Gradually, however, "organum" came to refer to the vocal practice. Organum can refer either to a piece characterized by organum or, in the more limited sense, to the style of organum. Organum in which the voices move together both rhythmically and melodically is known as *parallel organum*. The first written evidence of this practice occurs in theoretical sources from the second half of the ninth century.

As organum developed, the upper voice (called the *vox principalis*) gained independence by singing melismas over the slower-moving lower voice (called the *vox organalis,* or "organ voice"). Eventually, three independent voices emerged—the slower-moving organ voice and two faster-moving voices above (called the *duplum* and *triplum*).

During the twelfth century the practice of *melismatic organum* flourished, especially at the most important church in France, the cathedral of Notre Dame of Paris. Here organa were written by two of the first composers to whom specific works can be ascribed. Those composers were Master Léonin and Master Pérotin.

## Pérotin (fl. ca. 1200): Four-voiced organum, *Viderunt omnes* (All shall see) (ca. 1198)

Originally a small Celtic village along the Seine River, Paris began to emerge as an important community around the fifth century as Christianity spread. In the sixth century, when the Merovingian King Clovis (a convert to Christianity) selected Paris as his residence, churches began to appear along the banks of the river (still referred to as Right Bank and Left Bank) and in the surrounding countryside. With the accession of Charlemagne as Holy Roman Emperor in 800, Paris began its long rise to eminence.

The foundations of the massive Gothic cathedral of Notre Dame date to the middle of the twelfth century (Figure 6.1). The cathedral stood next to a walled city on the right bank of the Seine and faced a university (chartered in 1200) on the left bank. Members of the university and the church cooperated to produce beautifully illuminated manuscripts and theoretical treatises on music. The university also fostered interest in Greek and Roman culture and in learning in general. A historian described Paris around 1210:

> Never before in any time or in any part of the world, whether in Athens or in Egypt, had there been such a multitude of students. The reasons for this lie not only in the admirable beauty of Paris, but also in the special privileges . . . conferred on the scholars. In that great city the study of the *trivium* and *quadrivium* was held in high esteem. But the throng pressed with special enthusiasm around the chairs where the Holy Scripture was taught, or where problems of theology were solved.

The most famous manuscript collection of music associated with Paris in the eleventh and twelfth centuries was the *Magnus Liber,* or "Great Book," which included the most elaborate examples of polyphony used at Notre Dame. According to contemporary accounts, this music was the work of Master Léonin,

FIGURE 6.1 *Harmony* and *proportion*, terms associated with music and architecture, often occur in descriptions of the Gothic Cathedral of Notre Dame ("Our Lady"). Kenneth Clark linked the two arts in his observation, "Opera, next to Gothic architecture, is one of the strangest inventions of Western man. It could not have been foreseen by any logical process."

who was active in Paris between 1163 and 1190. Most of the organa in the *Magnus Liber* are in two voices, though Léonin probably composed a well-known organum in three voices as well.

Léonin and his successor, Master Pérotin, are among the first composers we can identify by name. Master Pérotin revised Léonin's work to reflect new, more liberal rules governing harmony and dissonance. Indeed, the history of polyphony is a record of the gradual acceptance of new intervals, and consequently of new dissonances. Whereas in the earliest organa no intervals other than perfect fifths and fourths were permitted, Pérotin used a much broader range. With this greater freedom, he created pungent, spiky dissonances with the tenor (as the lowest voice had come to be called) and, in music for three and four voices, with each other—much like the vigorous, sharp lines of the Gothic cathedral itself.

Pérotin's most remarkable composition is an *organum quadruplum* (a four-voiced organum) that he probably wrote for the Christmas season in 1198. This is the first documented example of a work in four voices. In its length and complexity it far surpasses anything that had been created up to this time. Pérotin has the tenor hold the individual notes and syllables of the original plainchant for extended periods. (The term *tenor* comes from the Latin for "to hold.") He then assigns elaborate melismas on the same syllables to the three newly composed upper voices. The first syllable in the tenor lasts 46 seconds in our performance, and the first word *(Vi-de-runt)* lasts over two minutes. The individual upper lines repeat small melodic formulas over and over, which Pérotin groups in novel ways. The individual voices, which are quite independent, seem to have been added in separate layers rather than conceived of simultaneously, which helps to account for the surprisingly high level of dissonance. (See Listening Guide 6.)

# *Listening Guide* 6

**PÉROTIN:** Excerpt from the Four-Voiced Organum
*Viderunt omnes* (All shall see)

CD 1, TRACK 6
TAPE 1A, TRACK 6
DURATION: 4:32

*The first strong cadence appears on "-runt," though the tenor holds his note right through to the beginning of the next phrase. The only breaks in the texture occur at the junctures between organum and clausula and between organum and plainchant. The text of the organum portion is "Viderunt omnes" ("All shall see").*

*Form: Sectional (organum / clausula / organum / plainchant)*

| | STYLE / TEXT | TIME | COMMENTS |
|---|---|---|---|
| | ORGANUM | | |
| 1 | *Vl -* | **0:00** | Long-held chord of perfect fifths and fourths. |
| | | 0:09 | The three upper voices move together in sharply defined modal rhythms, creating sharp dissonances with the tenor and with one another. |
| | *DE -* | 0:48 | The upper voices grow more independent of one another. |
| | *RUNT -* | 1:13 | The rhythms in the upper voices grow increasingly complex. |
| | | 2:09 | Strong cadence followed by a pause. |
| | CLAUSULA | | |
| 2 | *OM -* | **2:15** | The tenor now moves for eight notes in faster modal rhythms with the upper voices. |
| | ORGANUM | **2:25** | The tenor returns to a long-held note in organum style. |
| | *NES* | 3:19 | Strong cadence, followed by a pause. |
| | PLAINCHANT | | |
| 3 | *fines terrae salutare* <br> salvation to the end of the earth | **3:25** | Long melismas on end syllables of *"terrae, salutare."* |
| | *Dei nostri:* <br> of our God: | 3:45 | Long melisma on *"Dei."* |
| | *jubilate Deo* <br> rejoice in God | 3:57 | Long melisma on *"Deo."* |
| | *omnis terra.* <br> all the earth. | 4:08 | Long concluding melisma on *"[ter-]ra,"* outlining two successive major triads. |

Pérotin's rhythms are as bold as his harmonies. Polyphony requires the careful coordination of individual voices, and rhythms are needed to ensure their vertical alignment. Like the varieties of melody (page 74), the varieties of rhythm were called *modes*. During the medieval period, six rhythmic modes were used that consisted of various combinations of longs and shorts. (The shorts are half the length of the longs.) A long and a short together created three beats, reflecting the "perfection" of the Holy Trinity. In *Viderunt omnes*, Pérotin favors the first rhythmic mode (LONG-short, for a total of three beats) and the fifth mode (LONG-LONG, with each long consisting of three beats).

For the first few minutes of this work, the rhythmic modes govern only the three upper voices. But when Pérotin reaches the part where the original plain-chant is melismatic (at *om-[nes]*), he speeds up the next eight notes in the tenor so that they move in closer coordination with the upper voices. For this brief span the tenor, like the other voices, is governed by the rhythmic modes. Such a section was known as a *clausula* (from the Latin for "close" or "conclusion"). The music, however, soon returns to the style of organum. Finally, at the end of our excerpt, the monophonic plainchant returns to finish off the section. (No liturgical composition at this time was entirely polyphonic.) A performance of the entire work lasts almost 12 minutes, far longer than any single plainchant.

The Bishop of Paris described Pérotin's four-part organum as being sung by "four men walking in procession." In the vast cathedral of Notre Dame the effect must have been powerful indeed.

## THE MOTET

Pérotin's striking four-voiced organum suffered from one limitation: Its text was enunciated so slowly that it could scarcely be understood, and even a relatively short stretch of text went on for a considerable time. Soon medieval musicians began, in the process of troping (page 78), to add words to fit the music of the melismatic upper voices. The section of polyphonic pieces where they most often chose to do this was in the clausula, where all the voices were governed by modal rhythms. They then began to extract these newly texted clausulas from their set-ting within an entire piece and to designate them as independent pieces. Com-posers called such pieces *motets*, from the French *mot*, meaning "word"—a ref-erence to the added text.

Before long, composers began to extract only the tenor from a clausula, over which they provided new music *and* text. Sometimes they related the new text to the liturgical function of the tenor plainchant, but just as often they did not. To create a piece of even modest proportions, they found it necessary to repeat the brief tenor pattern, a practice that gave the piece some measure of coherence. In three-voiced motets composers often gave the duplum and triplum different texts (though usually on the same subject) that were sung simultaneously.

Even with repetitions of the tenor, early motets were considerably more mod-est in scale than Pérotin's monumental organa. Over the next three centuries, however, the motet was to grow into one of the most important types of vocal music.

Although the origins of the motet were in sacred music, composers soon supplied the upper voices with secular texts as well. Indeed, the distinction we make today between sacred and secular music was much less rigid in medieval times, as our next example shows in a dramatic way.

### Anonymous Motet: *"O mitissima / Quant voi—Virgo virginum—Haec dies"* ("O most gentle / When I notice—Virgin of virgins—This is the day") (ca. 1275)

Unlike the organum by Pérotin, much of the medieval music that has survived was written by composers whom we cannot identify. Such is the case with the motet *"O mitissima / Quant voi—Virgo virginum—Haec dies,"* whose cumbersome title results from the necessity of identifying it by all four of its texts. The tenor, *Haec dies,* is drawn from the melismatic portion (originally set as a clausula) of a popular Easter plainchant: "This is the day [which the Lord hath made; we will rejoice and be glad in it]" (Psalm 118:24). The duplum and the first triplum are set to newly composed quasi-liturgical texts addressed to the Virgin Mary. A variant manuscript source includes a secular triplum, in vernacular French, on the sadness felt by a heartsick lover toward a woman named Marion. The mixing of Mary and Marion would have seemed quite ordinary in medieval times. (See Listening Guide 7.)

## THE *ARS NOVA* IN FRANCE

The readiness of Western composers to experiment with current styles has often led them into conflict with defenders of the establishment. One of the earliest documented conflicts arose over the *ars nova,* or "new art," in fourteenth-century France. *Ars Nova* was the title of a treatise written by the composer Philippe de Vitry (1291–1361) around 1322. Actually, de Vitry was referring not to a new musical style but to new methods of notation that would free composers to draw on rhythms of greater complexity and flexibility than those of the *ars antiqua* ("old art"). Along with other innovations, de Vitry proposed the use of the *minim,* a note value only half that of the smallest currently acceptable value.

The first work that gives full play to de Vitry's reforms is the setting for part of a long poem that satirizes church corruption. *Roman de Fauvel* ("The Story of Fauvel") is an allegory about a deceitful character who is flattered by clerics and nobles, including even the Pope and the French king. The poem was probably written between 1310 and 1314 by Gervais de Bus, a member of the French court. One copy contains an elaborate musical setting that makes generous use of de Vitry's new notation.

# *Listening Guide 7*

## Anonymous Motet: *"O mitissima / Quant voi—Virgo virginum—Haec dies"* ("O most gentle / When I notice—Virgin of virgins—This is the day")

CD 1, TRACK 7
TAPE 1A, TRACK 7
DURATION: 1:24

*In our performance, this brief motet is heard twice, first with the sacred text found in the triplum of one source, and then with the secular text found in the triplum of another source. Typically, the tenor voice is doubled by an instrument, in this case a shawm. The rhythmic accompaniment on the* tabor *(a medieval drum) has been added in this performance.*

*Form: Repeating tenor*

| TEXT | TIME | COMMENTS |
|---|---|---|
| SACRED TRIPLUM (FIRST HEARING) | | |
| 1   *O mitissima Virgo Maria,* <br> O most gentle Virgin Mary, | **0:00** | The duplum and triplum share the same range. |
| *Posce tuum filium, ut nobis auxilium* <br> Ask thy son to give us aid | 0:09 | Triple meter, expressing the perfection of the Trinity. |
| *Det et remedium contra demonum,* <br> And a remedy against demons, | 0:21 | The tenor repeats exactly, to new music in the upper voices. |
| *Fallibiles astucias et horum nequicias.* <br> Their deceitful wiles and their iniquities. | 0:29 | |
| SECULAR TRIPLUM (SECOND HEARING) | | |
| 2   *Quant voi revinir d'esté la saison,* <br> When I notice the summer returning, | **0:41** | Secular text in vernacular French. |
| *Que le bois font retenir tuit cil oisillon,* <br> How the woods resound with merry bird-song, | 0:50 | |
| *Adonc pleur et soupir pour le grant desir* <br> Then I weep and sigh with a deep yearning | 1:01 | |
| *Qu'ai de la belle Marion qui mon cuer a en prison.* <br> For lovely Marion, who has my heart imprisoned. | 1:10 | |
| DUPLUM | | |
| *Virgo virginum, lumen luminum,* <br> Virgin of virgins, light of lights, | **0:00** | Sung simultaneously with the triplum. |

*continued*

| TEXT | TIME | COMMENTS |
|------|------|----------|
| *Reformatrix hominum, que portasti Dominum,*<br>Remaker of men, who hast borne the Lord, | 0:09 | The same text is sung both times. |
| *Per te, Maria, detur venia,*<br>Through thee, Mary, grant forgiveness, | 0:21 | |
| *Angelo nunciante, virgo es post et ante!*<br>As the angel announced, virgin before and after! | 0:29 | |
| TENOR | | |
| *Haec dies*<br>This is the day [which the Lord hath made] | **0:00**<br>0:21 | Voice doubled by the shawm.<br>Tenor pattern repeats. |

About this same time, Pope John XXII issued a papal bull (an official pronouncement) decrying the "disciples of the new school" of music. Despite the Pope's protests, composers all over Europe adopted de Vitry's innovations during the following decades.

### Guillaume de Machaut (ca. 1300–1377?): Gloria to the *Mass of Notre Dame* (1364?)

Machaut ranks as the greatest French poet/composer of the fourteenth century. When he was about 23, he became secretary to John of Luxembourg, King of Bohemia, and probably accompanied him on military expeditions between 1327 and 1330. By that time Machaut had written his first compositions. In 1346 John was killed in battle, and Machaut spent the next 30 years in the service of the highest members of the nobility. In 1361 even Emperor Charles V paid him a visit at his home.

Machaut is the first Western composer to ensure that his music would be preserved for posterity. He collected his complete works in a set of lavish manuscript volumes that were clearly meant to enshrine his artistic legacy. Because Machaut excelled in virtually every form of fourteenth-century music, his works fully warranted these unusual measures.

Machaut's *Mass of Notre Dame* (Listening Guide 8) is the first complete polyphonic setting of the entire Mass Ordinary. A mature and accomplished work, it

# *Listening Guide 8*

## MACHAUT: Gloria to the *Mass of Notre Dame*

CD 1, TRACK ⬚8⬚
TAPE 1A, TRACK 8
DURATION: 4:46

*Although Machaut relies mainly on a uniform chordal style, he introduces considerable harmonic and rhythmic variety. The unifying descending scalar pattern is shown by <u>underlinings</u> in the Text column. The movement divides into four sections (indicated by rules) separated by three clear cadences.*

*Form: Sectional, with unifying themes*

| | TEXT | TIME | COMMENTS |
|---|---|---|---|
| **1** | *Gloria in excelsis Deo,*<br>Glory to God in the highest, | **0:00** | Sung as plainchant. |
| | *Et in terra pax hominibus bonae <u>voluntatis</u>.*<br>And on earth peace to men of good will. | 0:08 | Mixed duple and triple meters.<br>Homophonic texture. |
| | *Laudamus te, Benedicimus te,*<br>We praise Thee, We bless Thee, | 0:27 | Intermediate cadence after first *"te."* |
| | *Adoramus te, <u>Glorificamus</u> te.*<br>We adore Thee, We glorify Thee. | 0:37 | |
| | | 0:46 | Instrumental bridge #1. |
| | *Gratias agimus tibi*<br>*propter magnam <u>gloriam tuam</u>,*<br>We give thanks to Thee for Thy great glory. | 0:48 | Duple meter. Full major triads on *"gratias"* and *"propter."* Section ends with a strong cadence. |
| **2** | *Domine Deus, rex <u>caelestis</u>,*<br>O Lord God, king of heaven, | **1:08** | New section. |
| | *Deus pater omnipotens.*<br>God the Father Almighty. | 1:17 | |
| | *Domine <u>fili</u> unigenite,*<br>The only begotten son, | 1:25<br>1:31 | Descending scale in the fiddle. |
| | *Jesu Christe.*<br>Jesus Christ. | 1:33<br>1:46 | Slow, long-held chords.<br>Instrumental bridge #2. |
| | *Domine Deus, Agnus Dei, <u>Filius</u> Patris.*<br>O Lord God, Lamb of God, Son of the Father. | 1:48 | Still in duple meter. Ends in a clear cadence. |

*continued*

| TEXT | TIME | COMMENTS |
|------|------|----------|

**3** *Qui tollis peccata mundi,*  
Who takes away the sins of the world, | **2:06** | New section.

*miserere nobis.*  
have mercy upon us. | 2:15  
2:20 | Instrumental bridge #3.

*Qui tollis peccata mundi,*  
Who takes away the sins of the world, | 2:22 |

*suscipe deprecationem nostram*  
receive our prayer. | 2:29 |

*Qui sedet ad dexteram Patris,*  
Who sits at the right hand of the Father, | 2:41 |

*miserere nobis.*  
have mercy upon us. | 2:50 | Ends in a clear cadence.

**4** *Quoniam tu solus Sanctus.*  
For Thou only art holy. | **2:57** | New section. Opens with full major triad.

*Tu solus Dominus.*  
Thou only art Lord. | 3:04 |

*Tu solus Altissimus, Jesu Christe.*  
Thou only art most high, Jesus Christ. | 3:09  
3:31 | *"Jesu Christe"* in soft, long chords.  
Instrumental bridge #4.

*Cum Sancto Spiritu,*  
Together with the Holy Ghost, | 3:33 | Changes to triple meter at *"Spiritu."*

*in gloria Dei Patris.*  
in the glory of God the Father, | 3:38 |

*Amen.*  
Amen. | 3:49 | Highly melismatic with liberal use of hocket.

includes other innovations as well. Machaut uses four voices throughout (from the bottom): tenor, *contratenor* ("against the tenor"), motetus (a holdover from the motet), and triplum. In the Kyrie, Sanctus, and Agnus Dei, he uses a technique now called *isorhythm*, in which a rhythmic pattern repeats independently of its pitches. In Machaut's day, such a rhythmic sequence was known as a *talea*.

It was imposed on the tenor voice (similar to the repetitions in a motet), often over an entire section or even over an entire composition. Machaut also uses a sequence of pitches that repeats independently of the rhythm, in what was called a *color* (kuh-*lor*). By overlapping talea and color, he achieves music of considerable intricacy.

In the Gloria, Machaut resorts to a *chordal style* (homophonic texture with harmonies consisting of chords) with bold chromatic harmonies that sound modern even to twentieth-century ears. He includes several major triads, though the triad (page 33) had not yet gained widespread acceptance. These harmonies are more the by-product of Machaut's independent *voice-leading* (the manner in which individual lines are shaped) than a desire to shock his listeners. Often, when a particular vocal line creates a harsh dissonance with another part, or when a vocal line contains an awkward melodic succession, the performer must decide whether to sing a given note as written or to raise or lower it to ease the dissonance or to smooth out the melody. Raising or lowering such notes was an application of *musica ficta* ("false" or "feigned" music), which was to play an important role in Western music till about 1600.

Machaut's rhythms in the Gloria also strike us as rather modern. He makes frequent use of minims and casts more than half the work in duple meter (what theorists still called "imperfect time"). Machaut organizes the final *Amen*, which contains one of the rare contrapuntal passages in the movement, as a *hocket*, in which two voices alternate in a series of short, hiccup-like entries punctuated by rests:

Machaut unifies the movement thematically by frequent repetitions of a descending scalar pattern and with a brief, recurring instrumental bridge that connects vocal sections. Certain harmonic progressions also recur. Such a level of organization was rare during the Middle Ages.

## *FORMES FIXES* ("FIXED FORMS")

During the fourteenth century composers of polyphonic secular music were every bit as innovative as composers of sacred music. Again the dominant figure was Machaut, rivaled only by the Italian Francesco Landini. Indeed, the great

# *Historical Window*

## A CHOIRBOY'S LIFE AT NOTRE DAME

Many of the plainchants and early polyphony we have been discussing were sung by neither men nor women but by young boys. The church fathers found scriptural justification for this practice in Psalm 8, which speaks of "Thou whose glory above the heavens is chanted by the mouth of babes and infants." The sweet, clear sounds of young voices added a tone of purity and innocence to the worship services. Moreover, the choirboys provided a pool from which future clerics could be drawn.

The cathedral of Notre Dame maintained about eight choirboys during the golden period of Notre Dame organum. A few of the boys were either poor orphans or sons of noblemen, though most of them came from artisan or merchant families in and around Paris. Boys were generally admitted at the age of eight, at which time they had to pass a musical audition and demonstrate evidence of a religious disposition. The parents were required to sign an irrevocable contract of six to ten years' duration, during which time the child could not be removed.

At the beginning of the fifteenth century, Jean Gerson, a theologian, published a *Doctrina*, or plan for the education and governance of the choirboys at the cathedral. Gerson's book, from which these excerpts are drawn, is presumed to describe practices from the twelfth and thirteenth centuries as well:

[1] Above all, the master should be the most upright person, because . . . the pupil will do nothing except that which he sees the master doing. . . .

[2] Moreover, let him frequently instill the word of exhortation of the love of God . . . because in and through the divine service they may ascend to Paradise and escape the cruel torments of Hell. . . .

[3] In addition, they are to be led to confession not just once each year, but four or six times. . . . And there should be an appropriate confessor instituted for them, because more prudence is often required in confessing well with them than with older people, so that they should not be examined too little or too much.

[5] Moreover, the master of music shall teach the boys at the statutory hours primarily plainchant and counterpoint . . . but no dissolute or ribald songs.

[6] Likewise we wish that one of the boys should always read during every meal from some useful book so that they might abstain from conversation and observe that admonition: "to speak few things during a meal."

[8] Likewise, each boy should inform on his comrade concerning the following things: if he has heard him speak French; if he has sworn; if he has uttered a lie or other falsehood; if he has said injurious things; if he has struck anyone; if he has risen too late; if he has babbled in church and done similar things. And if he has not accused the wrongdoer, he himself for him and with him is to be similarly punished.

[9] Moreover, all games are prohibited that lead to avarice, indecency or immodest noise, anger, or rancor, such as games of dice or chance. . . . Yet frequent and brief periods of recreation are to be given the boys, as for example shortly after the noon meal and after dinner, which times are of little use for other serious things.

[10] And let one master always be present.

[11] Moreover, we do not want the boys to go to any place or dwelling or church to sing unless by special license of the superiors. And then the master should be present to see that they do not indulge in too much food or otherwise behave themselves immodestly.

[15] They are to be prohibited from consuming too much food and drink in the morning and at other times through which the preservation of their voices may be hindered and the rule of sobriety infringed.

[16] In addition, in the choir they must sit apart from each other and not talk among themselves or with others. . . . And they should especially serve in silence and with appropriate decorum near the altar when the sacred mysteries of the Mass are celebrated without laughing, chattering, or making noises or indecent gestures among themselves or with others, but should serve just like angels of God so that all who see them might say: "these are truly angelic boys and such as the Immaculate Virgin ought to have in her church, the most renowned in all the world."

number of secular songs among the works of both composers marked the shift that helped lead to the Renaissance.

Poets and composers (often the same person, as in the case of Machaut) settled on three basic song patterns, known as *formes fixes* ("fixed forms"), which they had taken over from monophonic songs. At first, the patterns were poetic rather than musical. The three main forms were *ballade, virelai,* and *rondeau.* The 7-line ballade was the simplest, the 16-line virelai and rondeau the most complex. Over his career, Machaut composed 40 ballades, 32 virelais, and 20 rondeaux. The poets themselves developed other musical forms to fit their poems. Each form consisted of only two musical sections that were repeated in varying sequences.

The following diagram shows the relationship between text and music within a single strophe of each of the forms. A piece could have as many stanzas as the poet wished. The capital letters under RHYME SCHEME indicate refrain lines that are repeated in every strophe. The lower-case letters stand for the rhyme schemes themselves, and the letters to the right stand for the musical sections:

## MEDIEVAL SECULAR POLYPHONY

| Ballade | | Virelai | | Rondeau | |
|---|---|---|---|---|---|
| *Rhyme Scheme* | *Music* | *Rhyme Scheme* | *Music* | *Rhyme Scheme* | *Music* |
| a | A-Section | A | A-Section | A | A-Section |
| b | | B | | B | |
| a | A-Section | B | | B | B-Section |
| b | | A | | A | |
| b | B-Section | c | B-Section | a | A-Section |
| c | | d | | b | |
| C | | c | B-Section | A | A-Section |
| | | d | | B | |
| | | a | A-Section | a | A-Section |
| | | b | | b | |
| | | b | | b | B-Section |
| | | a | | a | |
| | | A | A-Section | A | A-Section |
| | | B | | B | |
| | | B | | B | B-Section |
| | | A | | A | |

✴ **Machaut: Ballade, *"Dame, comment qu'amez"***
**("My lady, however little I may be loved") (ca. 1350)**

This two-voiced ballade (Listening Guide 9) expresses a common theme of courtly love poetry and contains many of the features of the new style. These features are particularly evident in the vocal line, which includes two minims (shown here as eighth notes, with a single beam) and a long melisma interrupted by rests:

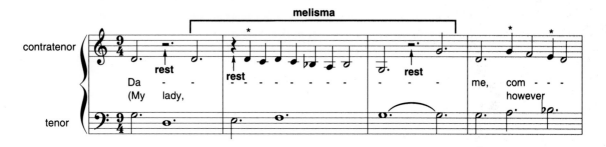

Moreover, Machaut takes a freer approach to dissonance than did composers of the *ars antiqua*. In this first phrase alone, four notes create unprepared dissonances (shown by * in the example), three of them on strong beats. The various rhythmic modes are mixed so freely that they are barely distinguishable. The result is a rich, expressive melodic line that takes many unexpected turns. (Our performance is accompanied by a medieval harp; in Machaut's time the singer and accompanist would probably have been the same person.)

## THE *TRECENTO* IN ITALY

Some historians refer to developments in fourteenth-century Italy as extensions of the French *ars nova*. Others prefer a label that applies specifically to Italy. The most widely used term is *trecento*, which means simply "the 1300s," even though the period referred to extended from 1325 to about 1425.

# Listening Guide 9

**MACHAUT:** Ballade, *"Dame, comment qu'amez"*
("My lady, however little I may be loved")

CD 1, TRACK 9
TAPE 1A, TRACK 9
DURATION: 1:51

*Although the rhythms feature both a triple foreground and background, the melody line contains so many syncopations and irregular groupings that little sense of meter comes through. Instead, the melody unfolds with a kind of intricate spontaneity that was the envy of Machaut's contemporaries.*

*Form: Ballade (A-A-B)*

| LOCATION / TEXT | TIME | COMMENTS |
|---|---|---|
| **A-SECTION** | | |
| 1 *Dame, comment qu'amez de vous ne soie,* My lady, however little I may be loved by you, | **0:00** | Long opening melisma; break at end of phrase. |
| *Si n'est il riens qui tant peust grever,* Yet there is nothing that could cause me so much pain, | 0:14 | Long closing melisma. Fuller close at end of phrase. |
| **A-SECTION** | | |
| 2 *Moy ne mon cuer, com ce que je savoie* Me and my heart, than seeing that you wished | **0:37** | Same music as the first section. |
| *Que voissiés autre que mi amer;* To love another more than myself; | 0:52 | Long melisma on *"amer."* |
| **B-SECTION** | | |
| 3 *Car riens conforter,* For nothing could ever comfort me, | **1:15** | The *B*-Section is about three-quarters the length of the *A*-Section. Its melody has smoother contours. |
| *Ne me porroit jamais ne rejoir;* Nor bring me joy; | 1:21 | |
| *S'il avenoit, fors seulement morir.* Were this to happen, only death. | 1:32 | |

During that time, Italian composers were following their own inclinations. Whereas the French style favored refined, subtle structures, the Italian style was warmer and more spontaneous. The Italian gift for melody is everywhere apparent, and composers incorporated the new rhythmic freedom of the French composers into a smoother texture.

### Giovanni da Firenze (fl. 1340–1350): Caccia, *"Con bracchi assai"* ("With many dogs") (ca. 1345)

The Italian *caccia* (pl. *caccie*) is a slightly bizarre form that attracts attention mainly because of its uniqueness. Only about 25 caccie survive, and only about a half dozen of them fit the pure form. A caccia is a work in three voices. The top two voices (both music and text) are in *canon* with each other—that is, one voice systematically follows the other at a specified time interval. The bottom voice (the tenor) is an independent line that provides a harmonic underpinning. The word *caccia* means "hunt" or "pursuit," and most caccie have to do with hunting.

We are familiar with such smooth canons as "Row, Row, Row Your Boat," but the canon in a caccia is anything but smooth. Each voice enters only after a considerable interval. And once it has entered it is interrupted by unexpected rests and by rhythmic bursts preceded or followed by longer note values, further punctuated by entries in the other voice. In Firenze's caccia (Listening Guide 10), the disjointed lines and the canonic answers reflect the excitement and hectic pace of the hunt.

Almost nothing is known about the life of Giovanni da Firenze (sometimes called Giovanni da Cascia), though he probably worked in northern Italy. The river "Adda" referred to in this caccia is near Milan. The caccia itself consists of two canonic strophes that end with a rhymed couplet called a *ritornello,* or "return," though the text occurs only once. The ritornello is also cast as a canon.

### Francesco Landini (ca. 1325–1397): Ballata, *"Cara mie donna"* ("My dear lady") (1360?)

Landini excelled as a poet, a composer, a singer, an organist, and an instrument maker. The son of a painter who belonged to the school of Giotto (Color Plate 3), Francesco lost his sight during childhood after an attack of smallpox. Despite his blindness, however, he built and tuned organs and became a celebrated organist and composer.

The *ballata* (pl. *ballate*) derived from the French virelai *(A-B-B-A-A),* one of the *formes fixes.* Like the virelai, it consists of only two musical sections. The second section, the *pieda,* is almost as long as the first but carries only half as

# Listening Guide 10

## GIOVANNI DA FIRENZE: Caccia, *"Con bracchi assai"* ("With many dogs")

CD 1, TRACK [10]
TAPE 1A, TRACK 10
DURATION: 3:20

*The timings in square brackets represent canonic entries following the first statement of the text line. The entries are elusive, just like the birds being hunted. The mention in the last line of Dido and Aeneas refers to a storm that broke while these lovers were hunting.*

*Form: Canonic*

| LOCATION / TEXT | TIME | COMMENTS |
|---|---|---|
| STANZA 1 | | |
| 1 *Con bracchi assai e con molti sparvieri* | **0:00** | Long-held first syllable. |
| With many dogs and with many falcons | [0:07] | Second voice enters in canon. |
| *Uccellavam su per la riva d'Adda,* | 0:20 | The lowest voice is played on the sackbut |
| We were hunting birds along the banks of | [0:28] | (a precursor of the trombone). |
| the Adda, | 0:27 | |
| *E qual diceva, "Da, da!"* | [0:34] | |
| And one shouted, "Come on!" | | |
| *E qual, "Vacia, Varin, Torna, Picciolo."* | 0:34 | |
| And one [called the dogs], "Vacia, Varin, | [0:42] | |
| Torna, Picciolo." | | |
| *E qual prendea le quaglie a volo, a volo,* | 0:45 | |
| And one was catching quails in flight, in | [0:52] | |
| flight, | | |
| *Quando con gran tempesta un'acqua venne.* | 1:01 | |
| when a great storm broke and the rain came. | [1:08] | At 1:11 the canon ends to prepare a |
| | | cadence. |

| LOCATION / TEXT | TIME | COMMENTS |
|---|---|---|
| STANZA 2 | | |
| 2   *Non corser mai per campagna levrieri,*<br>No greyhound ever ran through the fields, | **1:24**<br>[1:32] | Same music as Stanza 1. |
| *Come facea ciascun per fuggir l'acqua.*<br>As we did to escape the rain. | 1:44<br>[1:52] | |
| *E qual diceva, "Da' qua! Dammi 'l mantel!"*<br>One shouted, "Over there! Give me my<br>cloak!" | 1:50<br>[1:58] | |
| *E tal, "Dammi 'l cappello!"*<br>And another, "Give me my hat!" | 1:58<br>[2:06] | |
| *Quand'io ricoverai col mio uccello*<br>I found shelter with my falcon in a place | 2:08<br>[2:16] | |
| *Dove una pastorella il cor mi punse.*<br>Where a shepherdess pierced my heart. | 2:25<br>[2:32] | At 2:35 the canon ends. |
| RITORNELLO | | |
| 3   *Sola era li, onde fra me dicea,*<br>She was there alone, whereupon I said to<br>myself, | **2:48**<br>[2:50] | Begins another canon. |
| *"Ecco la pioggia, ecco Dido e Enea."*<br>"Here comes the rain, here are Dido and<br>Aeneas." | 2:59<br>[3:01] | At 3:10 the canon ends to prepare the<br>final cadence. |

# Listening Guide 11

## LANDINI: Ballata, *"Cara mie donna"* ("My dear lady")

CD 1, TRACK 11
TAPE 1B, TRACK 1
DURATION: 3:51

*Landini's ballata is in three voices. In our performance the two lower voices are played by a sackbutt and a shawm. The three stanzas of the poem are divided unequally. The A-Section (the* ripresa*) constitutes an entire stanza, while the B-Section (the* pieda*) sets only half a stanza. The* volta *supplies new text to the music of A.*

Form: Ballata *(A-B-B-A-A)*

| LOCATION / TEXT | TIME | COMMENTS |
|---|---|---|
| **STANZA 1 / A-SECTION [ *RIPRESA* ]** | | |
| 1   *Cara mie donna, i'vivo oma' contenta,* <br> My dear lady, I now live contented, | **0:00** <br> **[2:57]** | Melismas at beginning and end of phrase. |
| *Ch'anzi mi vo'sofrir la mie gran doglia* <br> for with your full approval I suffer great pain | 0:14 <br> [3:11] | Melisma at end of phrase; ends with an under-third cadence. |
| *Che con tuo piena voglia* <br> rather than attempt to find solace | 0:28 <br> [3:26] | Moves largely in a chordal style. |
| *Cercar grati' al disio che mi tormenta.* <br> for the desire which is tormenting me. | 0:36 <br> [3:34] | Ends with an under-third cadence. |
| **STANZA 2 / B-SECTION [ *PIEDA* ]** | | |
| 2   *Come degio da te gratia volere* <br> I must seek gratification from you | **0:51** | Melisma at end of phrase; ends with an under-third cadence. |

much text. Of Landini's 154 known works, 132 are ballate—the most progressive of all the trecento forms (Listening Guide 11).

Although the syncopations and complex rhythms of the French virelai are still apparent, Landini's vocal line and texture are smoother and the accompanying voices and the melody are more closely coordinated. His colorful cadences are marked by a characteristic melodic shape, in which the seventh degree of the modal scale proceeds down to the sixth degree before rising up a third to the tonic note, as in this ending of Landini's *A*-Section:

| LOCATION / TEXT | TIME | COMMENTS |
|---|---|---|
| *Di quel piacer che turba la tuo mente,* <br> through that pleasure which troubles your mind, | 1:07 | Melisma at end of phrase; ends with an under-third cadence. |
| *B-SECTION* | | |
| *Che pur che tu me 'l die nol posso avere,* <br> and unless you give it to me, I cannot have it, | **1:28** | Same music as above. |
| *Po'che con pena l'animo 'l consente.* <br> since I could not receive it otherwise. | 1:44 | |
| STANZA 3 / A-SECTION [*VOLTA*] | | |
| 3   *Però ch'i' t'amo si perfectamente* <br>    But I love you so perfectly | **2:07** | Same music as at the beginning. |
| *Che come che del donno i'mi sia vago,* <br> that though I am desirous of the gift of yourself, | 2:21 | |
| *Poco nel cor m'apaga,* <br> my heart has little pleasure, | 2:35 | |
| *Pensando ch'apagata te non senta.* <br> knowing that you do not feel happy about giving it. | 2:42 | |
| [Repeat of opening *A*-Section with Stanza 1] | | |

This cadence was so closely associated with Landini that it came to be known as the Landini cadence, or (because of its rise to the tonic from the interval a third below) as the "under-third" cadence.

## THE WANING OF THE MIDDLE AGES

The fourteenth century had produced music of great complexity and intellectual force. The use of new techniques like isorhythm, in conjunction with long, syncopated vocal lines, had carried music to new levels of sophistication. Then, toward the end of the century, a group of composers in southern France carried the new music to extremes. Though still working within Machaut's *formes fixes*, they developed a style of melodic and rhythmic extravagance that made Machaut's music seem tame by comparison. This complexity spread even to the accompanying voices. One of those composers was Jacob de Senleche, whose *La harpe de melodie* ("The Harp of Melody") is notated in the form of a harp and demands that the performer solve a difficult, irregular canon. A treatise at the end of the century referred to such music as *ars subtilior,* "refined art." Soon a reaction set in against what many regarded as excesses rather than refinements. The Middle Ages was drawing to a close, and the music of the next generation would reflect a new aesthetic.

### John Dunstable? (ca. 1390–1453): Ballata, *"O rosa bella"* ("O lovely rose") (ca. 1425?)

The music of the English composer John Dunstable carries hints of the new Renaissance style that was about to emerge. We know almost nothing about Dunstable's life, though he may have accompanied the Duke of Bedford to France between 1422 and 1435. We know his death date only from his tombstone (later destroyed by fire): "In the year 1453, on the day before Christ's birthday, the star passed over into the heavens." (Dunstable may have been active as an astronomer in his later years.)

Only about 50 pieces can be definitely ascribed to Dunstable. Many of the works ascribed to him are probably not his, and other works ascribed to "the Englishman" may very well be his. One of the most haunting love songs of the early fifteenth century, *"O rosa bella"* (Listening Guide 12), has been credited to Dunstable, though some scholars find it too progressive to be his. Dunstable's younger contemporary John Bedyngham has been suggested, but his authorship is no more certain.

*"O rosa bella"* is unmistakably English, however. The prominence in the harmonies of soft thirds and sixths reflects the longstanding preference of English

# *Listening Guide 12*

## DUNSTABLE: Ballata, *"O rosa bella"* ("O lovely rose")

CD 1, TRACK 12
TAPE 1B, TRACK 2
DURATION: 4:21

*The instrumental accompaniment on our recording is played by a "consort of viols," a family of fretted string instruments held vertically.*

*Form: Ballata, but performed as through-composed stanzas*

| | TEXT | TIME | COMMENTS |
|---|---|---|---|
| **1** | [Introduction] | **0:00** | Viol consort. Ends in an under-third cadence. |
| | STANZA 1 | | |
| | *O rosa bella, o dolce anima [amica] mia,*<br>O lovely rose, O my sweet soul [friend], | **0:18** | Lyrical, nonmelismatic line. |
| | *non mi lassar morire in cortesia.*<br>did not let me die in courtly love. | 0:30 | Under-third cadence at *"morire."* *"In cortesia"* treated elaborately and with repetition, ends with full "major" triad and dramatic pause. |
| | *Ay lasso mi dolente dezo finire*<br>Woe is me! Must I end hurt by you | 1:06 | Threefold repetition of *"Ay lasso."* Under-third cadence on *"dolente."* |
| | *per ben servire, e lialmente amare.*<br>for true service, and royal love? | 1:35 | Long melisma on *"amare,"* leading to an under-third cadence. |
| **2** | [Introduction] | **2:08** | Repeat of opening in viol consort. |
| | STANZA 2 | | |
| | *O dio d'amore che pena è questa amare,*<br>O god of love, how painful is this love, | **2:27** | The lowest voice is now sung as well as played on the viol. |
| | *vedi ch'io moro tutt' hora per sta giudea.*<br>you see that I am dying all the time because of this traitress. | 2:40 | Ends with same major triad and dramatic pause. |
| | *Soccoremi ormai del mio languire!*<br>Save me now from my suffering! | 3:17 | Threefold repetition of *"Soccoremi."* Under-third cadence on *"ormai."* |
| | *Core del corpo mio non mi lassar morire.*<br>Heart of my body, do not let me die. | 3:46 | Melisma on *"morire,"* leading to an under-third cadence. |

composers for these "impure" intervals. They produce a certain sweetness and give the work a modern sound. For example, the harmony that ends the first half of the first stanza is unmistakably major, while the harmony that begins the second half is unmistakably minor. We might even be tempted to regard stretches of this music as being "in the minor mode."

Though it was called a ballata, "O rosa bella" does not fit that poetic pattern. Some performers treat each stanza as if it were *through-composed*—that is, without internal repetitions. The very uniqueness of the work may explain why many fifteenth-century composers found it so fascinating.

In addition to the unusual form, all three lines share in the thematic material of the upper line, especially in the imitative opening:

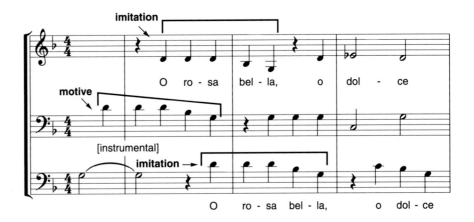

Not until the last quarter of the fifteenth century did this kind of imitation become common.

Most manuscript sources from this period provide only one of the musical voices with words. In the sources for "O rosa bella," however, both the highest and the lowest voices are provided with words throughout, and our performance exploits this feature in the second strophe by adding a singer.

And yet "O rosa bella" looks to the musical past as well as to the future. Each strophe contains four under-third cadences,* and the bottom two parts continue to cross each other frequently. "O rosa bella" is best regarded as an exquisite work that straddles the Middle Ages and the Renaissance.

---

*While the under-third cadence lasted into the sixteenth century, it was gradually supplanted by other types of cadences.

# THE RENAISSANCE (1430–1600)

## *The Age of Humanism*

HISTORICAL
AND CULTURAL
BACKGROUND

*T*he Renaissance marks the beginning of modern Western civilization. Many of the concepts on which our contemporary culture rests—the liberal arts, scientific method as a means of understanding the universe, political diplomacy, religious pluralism, national literatures, the masterpiece in art, genius—have their roots in the Renaissance.

Like many other historical labels, the term *Renaissance*—from the Latin (and old French) for "rebirth"—was applied after the fact by nineteenth-century historians, who used it to describe the flowering of cultural life that began in Italy at the end of the fourteenth century and spread throughout Europe in the fifteenth and sixteenth centuries. The Renaissance was more evolutionary than revolutionary. Medieval scholars had been interested in classical antiquity, but in the Renaissance that interest grew deeper and more sustained.

Nevertheless, Renaissance men and women saw themselves as having emerged from a dark, superstitious past. They felt a new urge to explore their world, an urge dramatized by the voyages of Christopher Columbus (1492–1502), Vasco da Gama (1497–1499), and Ferdinand Magellan (1519–1521). Rather than viewing life as a trial to be endured in hope of a blissful hereafter, they focused on the here and now.

The greatest achievement of Renaissance thought was the philosophy of *humanism*, in which the study of man and human capabilities is central. The term *humanities* comes from Cicero's assertion that the study of humanity *(humanitas)* is the proper goal of life. Throughout the Middle Ages, theologians and philosophers had wrestled with the reconciliation of human-centered Greek thought and God-centered Christian theology. Renaissance men and women, however, were less concerned with reconciling classical and Christian thought than with bringing theology into line with the new spirit of scientific inquiry. They were intensely curious about every aspect of human life.

FIGURE 1 (left)
In *The Prophet* (also known as *Zuccone*—"Baldy" or "Pumpkin Head"), completed in 1425, Donatello portrays an unidentified but distinctly human figure. The realistic detail and classical costume reflect Renaissance artists' interest in ancient Rome and Athens.

FIGURE 2 (right)
Despite its biblical source, which is hardly alluded to, Michelangelo's *David* pays homage to a heroic ideal of a modern man, not a saint or divinity.

The cultural center of the Italian Renaissance was Florence. Its prophet was the poet Francesco Petrarch (1304–1374), whose sonnets and canzones reflect a deep knowledge of Greek culture and laid the foundation for the modern Italian language. The first great Renaissance architect, Filippo Brunelleschi (1377?–1446), traveled to Rome to study the ruins of antiquity and then incorporated the lessons he learned into his designs. The sculptor Donatello (ca. 1386–1466), in works like *The Baldhead* (Figure 1), transformed Greek models into vivid, realistic figures. Both Brunelleschi and Donatello pioneered the novel technique of three-dimensional perspective. Donatello's student Michelangelo (1475–1564) celebrated the nude human body that the Middle Ages had sought to conceal (Figure 2).

The supreme Renaissance genius was the Florentine painter, sculptor, architect, musician, engineer, and scientist Leonardo da Vinci (1452–1519), the illegitimate son of an Italian notary and a peasant girl. Da Vinci excelled first as a painter before turning to architecture (as in the dome of the Milan Cathedral). He experimented with the ingredients of the plaster that make up a fresco, and his blend is partly responsible for the deterioration of one of his most sublime creations, *The Last Supper*. He studied the human body at the hospital of Santa Maria Nuove and produced a series of detailed anatomical drawings (Figure 3) that represent a brilliant blending of art and science. He designed flying machines and huge equestrian statues. For da Vinci, technology and art were indistinguishable. Driven by an insatiable curiosity, he embodied the ideals of an entire age.

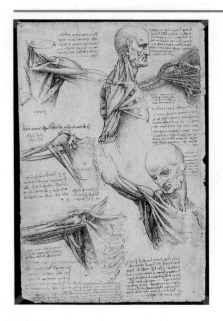

FIGURE 3 As his drawings illustrate, da Vinci thought an artist needed to understand the laws of nature, such as what governed the movement of muscles or water. For da Vinci, the chief aim of art was to show mankind's spiritual nature through physical depictions.

On a more mundane level, *The Courtier* (pub. 1528), a fascinating and widely read book by the Italian soldier and statesman Baldassare Castiglione (1478–1529), portrayed the ideal sixteenth-century gentleman as someone well educated in the humanities (including music as well as Greek and Latin), proficient in arms, chivalrous in love, and skilled in sports such as gymnastics. A gentleman sought individual expression, self-awareness, and worldly experience, and generations of Europeans aspired to be that "Renaissance man."

Castiglione's book was printed from movable type, a product of the revolutionary printing process that developed in Germany in the second half of the fifteenth century and spread quickly to Italy, France, and then England. Beginning with Petrarch in the fourteenth century and culminating with the plays of William Shakespeare (1564–1616) in the sixteenth century, the Renaissance was an age of great literature. Printing meant that people of modest means now had ready access to the works of these and other writers. By 1500 more than 15 million copies of books on a wide range of subjects had been printed in Europe.

Humanistic thought and the advent of printing encouraged Martin Luther (1483–1546; Figure 4) and other scholars to restudy the scriptures on their own. That study led to the Protestant Reformation, which began in 1517 with Luther's nailing of his Ninety-Five Theses to the door of the castle church in Wittenberg, Germany. After a year of intense negotiations, Luther refused to recant his criticisms, and the Roman Church underwent the first of a series of schisms that undermined its authority.

In Florence, the late Renaissance was presided over by a brilliant, ruthless

FIGURE 4 Martin Luther spearheaded the Protestant Reformation, a protest intended to reform the Roman Catholic Church. Part of what drove this devout German priest to criticize the church publicly was the corruption he observed on a visit to Rome in 1510.

politician and patron of the arts, Cosimo de' Medici (1519–1574; Figure 5). Of obscure origins, the Medici were a family of merchants and bankers who suppressed the guild merchants and artisans of Florence and seized power for themselves. Cosimo became heir to the ducal succession at age 19 when his predecessor was assassinated by a family member. He immediately assumed absolute authority and had his opponents either imprisoned or beheaded. One of those imprisoned was Niccolò Machiavelli (1469–1527), a Florentine writer and statesman whose *The Prince* (pub. posthumously in 1532) is seen by some scholars as an endorsement of the amoral, calculating tyrant.

And yet Cosimo was a generous and constant patron of painters, sculptors, poets, and musicians. He sponsored the creation of the Boboli Gardens, completed the Pitti Palace, and commissioned Giorgio Vasari's Uffizi Gallery (Figure 6), in which he housed many magnificent works of art. Cosimo epitomizes the powerful secular ruler and served as a model for generations to come.

The map in Figure 7 shows the geographical divisions and some of the important personages of western Europe in the Renaissance.

FIGURE 5 A dashing portrait of the young Cosimo I de'Medici by Jacopo da Pontormo. The swaggering pose was designed to counteract threats to the Medicis' hold on power.

FIGURE 6 Cosimo I commissioned Giorgio Vasari to design the Uffizi, offices for his government and the home of many of Cosimo's commissioned art works. Using an exaggerated U shape, Vasari created a dramatic tunnellike effect; one end of the building opens onto a large square; the other end faces the Arno River.

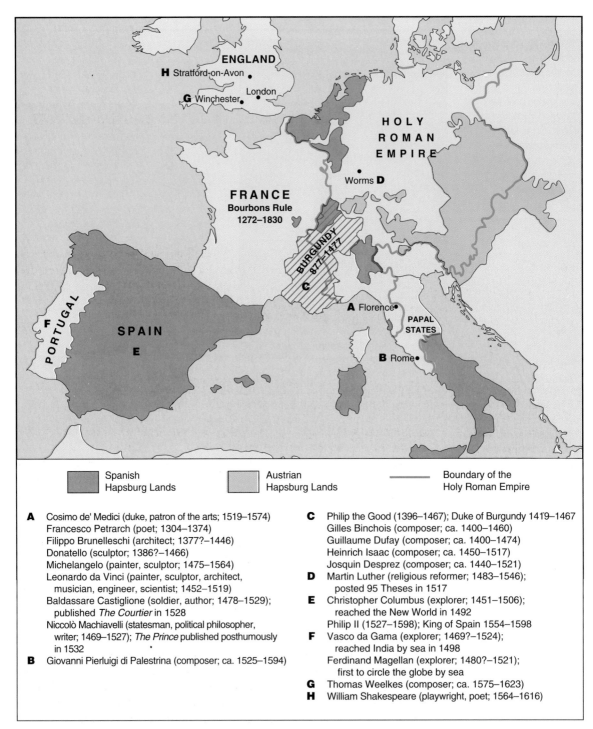

FIGURE 7  Discovering new worlds: The Renaissance was an era of exploration,
as these achievements indicate.

The map contains the following labels and text:

ENGLAND
**H** Stratford-on-Avon
**G** Winchester · London

HOLY ROMAN EMPIRE

Worms **D**

FRANCE
Bourbons Rule
1272–1830

BURGUNDY
877–1477
**C**

**A** Florence

PAPAL STATES

**B** Rome

F PORTUGAL

SPAIN
**E**

Legend:
- Spanish Hapsburg Lands
- Austrian Hapsburg Lands
- ——— Boundary of the Holy Roman Empire

**A**  Cosimo de' Medici (duke, patron of the arts; 1519–1574)
Francesco Petrarch (poet; 1304–1374)
Filippo Brunelleschi (architect; 1377?–1446)
Donatello (sculptor; 1386?–1466)
Michelangelo (painter, sculptor; 1475–1564)
Leonardo da Vinci (painter, sculptor, architect, musician, engineer, scientist; 1452–1519)
Baldassare Castiglione (soldier, author; 1478–1529); published *The Courtier* in 1528
Niccolò Machiavelli (statesman, political philosopher, writer; 1469–1527); *The Prince* published posthumously in 1532
**B**  Giovanni Pierluigi di Palestrina (composer; ca. 1525–1594)

**C**  Philip the Good (1396–1467); Duke of Burgundy 1419–1467
Gilles Binchois (composer; ca. 1400–1460)
Guillaume Dufay (composer; ca. 1400–1474)
Heinrich Isaac (composer; ca. 1450–1517)
Josquin Desprez (composer; ca. 1440–1521)
**D**  Martin Luther (religious reformer; 1483–1546); posted 95 Theses in 1517
**E**  Christopher Columbus (explorer; 1451–1506); reached the New World in 1492
Philip II (1527–1598); King of Spain 1554–1598
**F**  Vasco da Gama (explorer; 1469?–1524); reached India by sea in 1498
Ferdinand Magellan (explorer; 1480?–1521); first to circle the globe by sea
**G**  Thomas Weelkes (composer; ca. 1575–1623)
**H**  William Shakespeare (playwright, poet; 1564–1616)

# Chapter 7

## SECULAR MUSIC IN THE RENAISSANCE

round 1430 composers embarked on what was to emerge as a major shift in musical style. The fifteenth and sixteenth centuries, a time of innovation and revitalization, marked the beginning of modern Western music.

## THE RENAISSANCE STYLE

Renaissance composers did not suddenly abandon the styles of the past, however. They continued to use plainchant as the basis of sacred polyphony, in a relationship that grew even more rigorous and complex during the Renaissance. And they continued to draw on courtly love poetry as texts for their secular music.

Still, the Renaissance was a time of innovation. One of the most far-reaching departures from the past was the gradual adoption of the triad as the basic sonority. Triads extended the range of intervals that were regarded as consonant (page 97). Medieval theorists had accepted as consonant the intervals of the octave, perfect fifth, and perfect fourth and had consigned all other intervals to varying degrees of dissonance. While major and minor triads are bounded by a perfect fifth (Figure 7.1), a **triad** also includes two overlapping thirds—intervals formerly regarded as dissonant. In spite of their higher ratios of 4:5 and 5:6, these intervals, including the sixths that result when triads are inverted, were now gradually accepted as consonances.

Despite this apparent extension of former dissonances, to most modern listeners Renaissance harmonies seem milder than medieval harmonies. One reason is that we have been conditioned to hear triads, with their thirds and sixths, as sweet and full sounds and tend to hear fifths and fourths as empty and spare.

Another reason has to do with the manner in which medieval and Renaissance music was composed. In three-voiced medieval music, for example, the only relationships governed by strict rules regarding admissible intervals were those

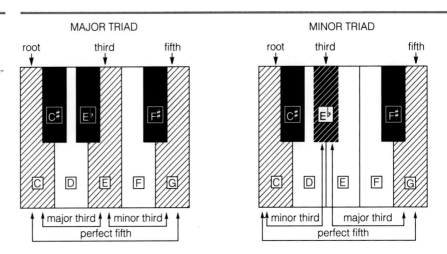

FIGURE 7.1 During the Renaissance, triads—especially major triads—gradually became the prevailing sonority. The interlocking thirds of a triad had been regarded by medieval theorists as dissonances.

between the tenor and the duplum, or the tenor and the triplum. The relationship between the duplum and triplum was relatively unregulated and accounts for many of the dissonant clashes that occur in medieval music.

Renaissance composers gradually replaced this successive method of composition with simultaneous composition, in which individual voices were subordinated to the need for triads or other consonant intervals on strong beats. Dissonance among all the voices was closely regulated. Renaissance music therefore sounds smoother, and hence less dissonant, than medieval music.

Moreover, in medieval music the individual voices are more or less independent of one another, whereas in Renaissance music they are closely coordinated. Composers began to experiment with assigning the same theme to different voices and discovered they could achieve a powerful effect by stating a theme in one voice and then restating it successively in the other voices. The result was imitative counterpoint (Chapter 4), which had become the predominant texture by about 1500.

In medieval polyphony, the voices often occupied the same range, which meant that they overlapped in performance and were difficult to distinguish. During the fifteenth century composers increasingly assigned each vocal part to its own range. They placed the contratenor below the tenor, where it developed into the bass line, a range that medieval composers had seldom explored.

In a literary age, composers paid close attention to the relationship between words and music. In a technique known as **word painting,** they used musical figures not only to express the general sense of a text but also to represent specific images—falling, sighing, weeping, rejoicing, and so forth.

The Renaissance in music began not in Italy but in the duchy of Burgundy, encompassing northeastern France, Belgium, and Holland (see map, page 124). Under the patronage of Philip the Good (reigned 1419–1467) and Charles the Bold (reigned 1467–1477), Burgundian musicians came to dominate the musical life of Europe.

# SECULAR SONG

The various *formes fixes* of the *ars nova* experienced different fates. The ballade and virelai disappeared rather quickly, while the rondeau remained in favor among Burgundian composers until about 1470. Gradually, composers turned to the newer, more freely structured French chanson and to the German *Lied* ("song," pronounced "leedt") and the Italian or English madrigal. We turn now to five representative works.

## ✳ Gilles Binchois (ca. 1400–1460) or Guillaume Dufay (ca. 1400–1474): Rondeau, *"Je ne vis onques le pareille"* ("I have never seen the equal") (ca. 1454)

The two most celebrated Burgundian composers of the first three-quarters of the fifteenth century were Gilles Binchois and Guillaume Dufay. Binchois, who is remembered mainly for his secular songs, seems to have been attached to the Burgundian court for most of his career. Dufay began his professional life at a Burgundian cathedral and then traveled widely, singing for five years in the papal chapel in Rome. By 1440 he had returned to Burgundy with a reputation as a gifted composer of both secular and sacred music. Because Binchois and Dufay are often mentioned together in the sources, we cannot be sure which of them was the composer of certain works. But both were central figures in the rise of a more direct and accessible style of popular song.

The rondeau *"Je ne vis onques le pareille"* (Listening Guide 13) is one of the few secular songs we know to have been sung on a specific occasion, in this instance the "Feast of the Pheasants" held by Philip the Good in 1454 (see Historical Window on page 132). For most of the song the upper voice carries the melody and remains consistently above the two lower voices. For a few bars at the beginning of the *B*-Section the two upper voices exchange ranges.

The *B*-Section ends with an under-third cadence, though near the end of the *A*-Section that same cadence is prolonged through an expressive melisma on *"da-[me]"* ("lady"). The song opens and closes on pure octaves, fifths, and fourths, but more than a third of the measures begin with full triads, and another third include intervals of a third or sixth. Although there is no imitation, the smoothly contoured lines seem to have been conceived simultaneously. Our purely vocal performance of the song reveals the new lyrical qualities of the Renaissance style.

## Heinrich Isaac (ca. 1450–1517): Lied, *"Isbruck, ich muss dich lassen"* ("Innsbruck, I must leave you") (ca. 1500?)

During the Middle Ages, musical activity in Germany had been less vigorous than in France or Italy, and German composers were slower to exploit the more sophisticated uses of polyphony. But an event that took place in 1477 was to

# *Listening Guide 14*

### ISAAC: Lied, *"Isbruck, ich muss dich lassen"*
### ("Innsbruck, I must leave you")

CD 1, TRACK 14
TAPE 1B, TRACK 4
DURATION: 3:12

*This song consists of short phrases separated by rests and sung in a homophonic, syllabic style. The sole melisma and the repetitions of text are reserved for the last line of each stanza.*

*Form: Strophic*

| TEXT | TIME | LOCATION / COMMENTS |
|---|---|---|
| **STANZA 1** | | |
| *Isbruck, ich muss dich lassen,* <br> Innsbruck, I must leave you, | **0:00** | **A-Section.** Syllabic text setting; full homophonic, triadic texture. |
| *ich fahr dahin mein Straßen* <br> I travel down my streets | 0:11 | |
| *in fremde Land dahin.* <br> to foreign lands. | 0:20 | |
| *Main Freud ist mir genommen,* <br> My joy is taken from me, | **0:25** | ***A'*-Section.** |
| *die ich nit weiß bekummen,* <br> and I know not where I shall find it | 0:34 | |
| *Wo ich im Elend bin.* <br> when I am in need. | 0:43 | Contains the only melisma, on *"E-[lend]."* <br> The line repeats as an echo at 0:54. |
| **STANZA 2** | | |
| *Groß Leid muß ich yetz tragen,* <br> Great suffering I must now bear, | **1:08** | **A-Section.** Two tenors in canon. The overlapping voices create a continuous texture. |

adic style was soon incorporated into the Protestant hymns of Martin Luther and his followers.

Our performance draws on two different versions of the song. The first and third stanzas are from the homophonic version, with accompaniment by two lutes and harp. The middle stanza is a canonic version between two voices that may or may not have been written by Isaac himself.

*Part Two   Early Music (To 1690)*

| TEXT | TIME | LOCATION / COMMENTS |
|------|------|---------------------|
| *das ich allein thu klagen*<br>and can only confide | 1:16 | The phrases are modified to keep the canon intact. |
| *dem liebsten Bulen mein.*<br>in my dearest love. | 1:24 | |
| *Ach Lieb, nun laß mich Armen*<br>My love, now on poor me | **1:32** | **A′-Section.** |
| *im Hertzen dein Erbarmen,*<br>in your heart have pity, | 1:38 | |
| *daß ich muß von dannen sein!*<br>because I must go away! | 1:47 | |

STANZA 3

| | | |
|------|------|---------------------|
| **3** *Mein Trost ob allen Weyben,*<br>My comfort over all other women, | **2:02** | **A-Section.** Return to the first version, but with a more ornamented instrumental accompaniment. |
| *dein thu ich ewig bleiben,*<br>I shall always be yours, | 2:13 | |
| *stet trew, der Ehren fromm.*<br>always faithful, and honoring you. | 2:22 | |
| *Nun muß dich Gott bewahren,*<br>Now may the Lord protect you, | **2:27** | **A′-Section.** |
| *in aller Tugendt sparen,*<br>and preserve your virtue, | 2:36 | |
| *bis daß ich wider komm!*<br>until I come again! | 2:44 | Contains the same melisma, now on *"wi-[der]."* Line repeated as an echo at 2:56. |

# JOSQUIN DESPREZ (ca. 1440–1521)

From time to time a composer so dominates an age that it comes to be identified with him. In the early nineteenth century, Beethoven is an example. In the fifteenth and sixteenth centuries such a composer was Josquin Desprez (Figure 7.2), who was born around 1440 in a small Burgundian town just across the

# *Historical Window*

## AN UNFORGETTABLE FEAST AT
## THE COURT OF PHILIP THE GOOD

**During the Middle Ages and early Renaissance, the royal courts of Europe moved almost constantly from place to place in response to the dictates of war and diplomacy. Though the dukes of Burgundy, for example, maintained palaces in Brussels, Bruge, and Arras, they spent much of their time in travel.**

**Along the way they entertained by staging lavish feasts. Almost any occasion would do—a visiting dignitary, a name day, a peace treaty. One of the most extravagant feasts was staged in Lille by Philip the Good on Sunday, February 17, 1454. Constantinople, the capital of the Byzantine Empire, had just fallen to the Turks and Philip had vowed to launch a crusade to repel the infidels. To muster support, he arranged what has become known as "The Feast of the Pheasants."**

**The festivities began with a grand procession of princes decked out in black velvet and diamonds and accompanied by musicians. On reaching the center of town they engaged in a joust, in which two knights were seriously injured. They then moved on to a banquet in the great hall of the Hôtel de la Salle. There, in a structure built to represent the interior of a church, four musicians sat playing an organ. Elsewhere, 28 musicians sat in a huge mock pastry playing popular songs. In an Indian jungle, animated animals stalked their prey.**

**When the banquet proper began, hundreds of onlookers in the galleries peered down at the guests below. Great platforms carrying food were lowered from the ceiling. For the meat course there were more than 40 different dishes; serving carriages moved about the hall offering a total of 82 dishes.**

**The entertainment consisted of a series of interludes with music, and each new event was announced by trumpeters. Choirboys sang a *Benedictus*, a shep-**

French border. We know almost nothing about his childhood or schooling, but we do know that by 1459 he was working for a low salary at the cathedral in Milan. Soon, however, under the patronage of a member of the ducal family, he became one of the best-paid musicians in Milan. When his patron was assassinated, he accepted the patronage of Cardinal Ascanio Sforza (1455–1505), the brother of his former patron.

Josquin lived for a time in France, and in 1503 he apparently moved to the court at Ferrara after being hunted down by a talent scout sent out by the duke. The scout assured the duke that Josquin's presence would "place a crown upon herd played a new tune on the bagpipes, and vocalists sang a selection of secular songs. A horse dressed in pink silk trotted backwards, and a juggler kept two daggers and a sword in the air while an acrobat balanced upside down on the juggler's shoulders.

A beautiful white stag with gilt antlers then appeared, accompanied by a boy dressed in a crimson velvet coat and a black hat. The boy sat on a silk rug and sang ("in pure voice") *"Je ne vis onques le pareille,"* accompanied by the stag! Along the way, a medieval morality play, *The Adventures of Jason*, was performed. The climax of the evening, announced by the musicians, was an elaborate spectacle in which a woman riding an elephant begged to be rescued from Saracens dressed as giants (a pointed reminder of the hated Turks).

At the conclusion of the spectacle, heralds brought in a live pheasant wearing a collar of gold embedded with precious stones and pearls. The pheasant was a symbol of oath-taking, and each nobleman swore an oath that he would march with Philip and follow his commands. Illness was the only route of escape.

At last, the great doors opened to admit a company of torchbearers accompanied by musicians playing tambourines, harps, and lutes. With them was a simply dressed woman bearing the legend "God's Grace." Accompanying her were 12 knights dressed in black tights, tunics, and hats, each escorting a woman in crimson petticoats edged in fur, and wearing a necklace of precious jewels. The women, who represented the Twelve Virtues of medieval theology (Faith, Hope, Love, Truth, Justice, Understanding, Prudence, Courage, Temperance, Strength, Ardor, and Generosity), committed themselves to Philip's undertaking.

Finally, wines and spices were passed around in great bowls. The winner of the joust was acclaimed, and another joust was announced for the following day.

this chapel of ours," although an earlier letter from another scout, in 1502, suggests that Heinrich Isaac had been the first choice:

> To me he [Isaac] seems very well suited to serve Your Lordship, much more so than Josquin, because he is of a better nature among his companions and will compose new works more often. It is true that Josquin composes better, but he composes when he wants to, and not when one wants him to, and he is asking 200 ducats in salary, while Isaac will come for 129—but Your Lordship will decide what should be done.

FIGURE 7.2 This woodcut of Josquin Desprez was made 90 years after his death. Although this portrait does not suggest it, Josquin and Leonardo da Vinci were contemporaries, and both, as leading artists in their fields, worked for the Sforza family, which ruled the Duchy of Milan.

Around 1504, Josquin returned to his birthplace, where he continued to compose almost to the end of his life.

Josquin excelled in every genre of the period, sacred or secular, retrospective or progressive, popular or learned. More than any other composer of the time, he developed the texture of imitative counterpoint that was to characterize the music of the sixteenth century. This technical mastery expressed a range of human feelings that was unknown in music before Josquin. He was admired by all as the greatest composer of his age. Our age views Josquin as perhaps the first modern musical genius. We turn now to two of his secular works.

### Josquin: Frottola, *"El grillo"* ("The cricket") (ca. 1474)

Josquin's *"El grillo"* (Listening Guide 15) is in a popular Italian style called the *frottola,* a precursor of the Italian madrigal. The texts and music of these songs were generally popular and light in tone. Some scholars have suggested that the text of *"El grillo"* alludes to a certain Carlo Grillo, a singer in Cardinal Sforza's chapel in the 1470s. Others suspect that it pokes fun at the Cardinal himself. The humorous text is in keeping with the spirit of many frottolas.

*"El grillo"* is in *A-B-A* form; at the end of the *B*-Section the singers are simply instructed to repeat the *A*-Section. The basically homophonic texture is highly rhythmic, alternating between slow, drawn-out notes and faster, almost patter, tones. Although the *A*-Section ends and the *B*-Section begins and ends on pure octaves and fifths, the song opens with a full triad, and most of the harmonies also are full triads. The distribution of the clearly defined voices is familiar to modern listeners (from the top down): soprano, alto, tenor, and bass.

To suggest the cricket's "long verses," Josquin draws out the word *verso.* And for "The cricket sings just for fun," he tosses the music back and forth between

# *Listening Guide 15*

## JOSQUIN: Frottola, "*El grillo*" ("The cricket")

CD 1, TRACK 15
TAPE 1B, TRACK 5
DURATION: 1:26

*Even in this short, unpretentious work Josquin manages to characterize the words with sharply drawn music.*

*Form: A-B-A*

| TEXT | TIME | LOCATION / COMMENTS |
|------|------|---------------------|
| **1** *El grillo e buon cantore*<br>The cricket is a good singer | **0:00** | **A-Section.** Four-part vocal homophony. |
| *che tiene longo verso.*<br>who sings long verses. | 0:05 | Drawn-out notes and melismas on *"verso."* |
| *Dale beve grillo canta,*<br>The cricket sings just for fun, | 0:12 | Text tossed back and forth between the upper and lower parts. |
| *El grillo e buon cantore.*<br>The cricket is a good singer. | 0:19 | Dramatic pause at the end of the phrase. |
| **2** *Ma non fa come gli altri uccelli,*<br>But unlike the other birds who, | **0:26** | **B-Section.** Homophonic, softer and slower. |
| *come li han cantato un poco,*<br>after they've sung a little, | 0:31 | |
| *Van' de fatto in altro loco,*<br>fly off to another place, | 0:36 | Repeats the music of the first two lines. |
| *sempre el grillo sta pur saldo.*<br>the cricket always stays where he is. | 0:40 | |
| *Quando la maggior el caldo*<br>When the weather is really hot | 0:45 | Louder and bolder. |
| *alhor canta sol per amore.*<br>he sings only for love. | 0:50 | |
| **3** *El grillo e buon cantore*<br>The cricket is a good singer | **0:59** | **A-Section.** Begins louder than first time. |
| *che tiene longo verso.*<br>who sings long verses. | 1:04 | Drawn-out notes and melismas on *"verso."* |
| *Dale beve grillo canta,*<br>The cricket sings just for fun, | 1:12 | Text tossed back and forth between the upper and lower parts. |
| *El grillo e buon cantore.*<br>The cricket is a good singer. | 1:18 | Dramatic pause at end of phrase. |

the upper and lower parts. This kind of word painting was a prominent feature of secular music in the Renaissance. Throughout, the song is marked by an appealing spontaneity.

## ✳ Josquin: Canonic chanson, *"Baisez moy"* ("Kiss me") (ca. 1500)

During the late fifteenth and early sixteenth centuries the French chanson became the most popular form of secular vocal music in northern Europe. The chanson assumed a tremendous variety of forms, and no single form dominated. One of the shortest but most ingenious French chansons is Josquin's *"Baisez moy"* ("Kiss me"; Listening Guide 16), a spirited dialogue between two young people. The four-voiced version takes the form of a double canon, in which the two lowest voices (tenor and bass) are in canon with each other, as are the two highest voices (soprano and alto):

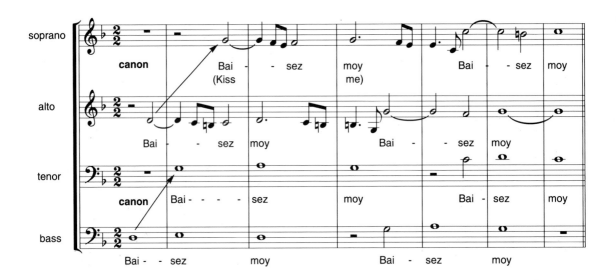

The *b*-phrase is even more unusual: All four voices share the same opening motive in what sounds like straightforward imitation, but they then continue with their individual canons.

The form is ingenious. There are five phrases altogether. Three times, the beginning of a phrase coincides with the beginning of the text line. Two times, it does not (shown by the letters that follow the arrows): $a—b \rightarrow a—b \rightarrow a'$. The final phrase cadences on a different harmony than the first. In an audacious display of harmonic freedom, Josquin ends the piece in a mode different from the beginning mode.

# *Listening Guide 16*

## J O S Q U I N :  Canonic chanson, *"Baisez moy"* ("Kiss me")

CD 1, TRACK ☐16
TAPE 1B, TRACK 6
DURATION: 1:34

*Aside from the opening, only the beginning of the b-phrases coincides with the beginning of the text lines.*

*Form(s): Double and triple canons: a-b-a-b-a' phrases*

| TEXT | TIME | LOCATION / COMMENTS |
|---|---|---|
| **1** *Baisez moy,*<br>Kiss me, | **0:00** | **a-phrase.** Double canon between tenor/ bass and soprano/alto, four voices. |
| *baisez moy, ma doulce amye,*<br>kiss me, my sweet friend, | 0:08 | **b-phrase.** Ascending imitation beginning with the bass. |
| *par amour je vous-en prie.*<br>for love, I beg you. | | At 0:17 the **a-phrase** begins to repeat in the middle of the text lines. |
| *Non feray.*<br>I will not. | | |
| *Et porquoy?*<br>And why not? | | |
| *Se je faisoie la follie*<br>If I indulged in this folly | 0:25 | **b-phrase.** Same ascending imitation as at 0:08. |
| *ma mère en seroit morrie.*<br>my mother would be shocked. | | At 0:36 the **a-phrase** begins again, only to cadence this time to a different harmony. |
| *Velà de quoy.*<br>That's why. | | |
| **2** *Baisez moy,*<br>Kiss me, | **0:46** | **a-phrase.** Triple canon, six voices. |
| *baisez moy, ma doulce amye,*<br>kiss me, my sweet friend, | 0:54 | **b-phrase.** Ascending imitation containing only two canons. |
| *par amour je vous-en prie.*<br>for love, I beg you. | | At 1:03 the **a-phrase** begins to repeat in the middle of the text lines. |
| *Non feray.*<br>I will not. | | |
| *Et porquoy?*<br>And why not? | | |
| *Se je faisoie la follie*<br>If I indulged in this folly | 1:12 | **b-phrase.** Same ascending imitation as at 0:54. |
| *ma mère en seroit morrie.*<br>my mother would be shocked. | 1:19 | |
| *Velà de quoy.*<br>That's why. | | At 1:28 the **a-phrase** begins again, only to cadence this time to a different harmony. |

Our performance includes a second performance of the chanson in a version for six voices. Because the canonic pairings are different in the two phrases and the *b*-phrase reduces to a double canon, some scholars have questioned whether it was written by Josquin. In any case, both settings cleverly conceal all the contrapuntal artifice.

## THE ENGLISH MADRIGAL

The madrigal arose in Italy during the sixteenth century (it had no connection to the Italian madrigal of the fourteenth century) and was in some respects the Italian counterpart of the French chanson. Its literary roots, however, were deeper and richer, drawing heavily on the poetic forms of Petrarch. Over time the madrigal developed into the most ambitious secular form of the Renaissance. Throughout the sixteenth century, *madrigal* was a generic term for the setting of many kinds of Italian verse. The Renaissance interest in text expression and word painting reached its highest level in the madrigal. In fact, word painting is so closely associated with the madrigal that it is sometimes referred to simply as a "madrigalism."

Whereas the French chanson was cultivated by composers all over Europe, the madrigal remained exclusively Italian until the last two decades of the sixteenth century, when a school of English composers adapted it to English verse forms. English madrigals were never as extensive or as complex as the late Italian madrigal (which we shall discuss in Chapter 9), but they are exquisite examples of pure vocal writing and of the close relationship between text and music.

### Thomas Weelkes (ca. 1575–1623): "Those sweet delightful Lilies" (pub. 1597)

Weelkes spent his life working at various courts and cathedrals outside London. His later life was marred by alcoholism, but while productive he was one of the most important English composers of both anthems (a favorite form of choral music in the English church) and madrigals. His first book of madrigals, from which our selection is drawn, was published in 1597 when Weelkes was still in his early twenties. Over the next decade he published three more collections containing more than a hundred works.

"Those sweet delightful Lilies" consists of two brief sections, each repeated once. The homophonic opening phrase of the *A*-Section is followed by the highly imitative setting of "Which nature gave my Phyllis." The *B*-Section moves to a darker mood in which a slow imitative motive culminates in a sharp dissonance on the word *anguish*. Throughout this work Weelkes displays the English predilection for sweet, full triads (Listening Guide 17).

# *Listening Guide 17*

**WEELKES:** English Madrigal, "Those sweet delightful Lilies"

CD 1, TRACK 17
TAPE 1B, TRACK 7
DURATION: 2:13

*Form: Two-part (A-B) with repeats*

| TEXT | TIME | LOCATION / COMMENTS |
|------|------|---------------------|
| **1** Those sweet delightful Lilies | **0:00** | *A*-**Section.** Frequent changes in meter. |
| Which nature gave my Phyllis. | 0:08 | Highly imitative texture. |
| | | |
| Those sweet delightful Lilies | **0:19** | *A*-**Section (repeat).** |
| Which nature gave my Phyllis. | 0:27 | |
| | | |
| **2** Ay me, | **0:40** | *B*-**Section.** Slow chords, sighing figures. |
| each hour makes me to languish. | 0:49 | |
| So grievous is my pain and anguish. | 0:55 | Imitative texture. Long-held notes on *"griev-[ous]."* Sharp dissonance on *"pain."* |
| | | |
| Ay me, | **1:23** | *B*-**Section (repeat).** |
| each hour makes me to languish. | 1:33 | |
| So grievous is my pain and anguish. | 1:38 | Long-held notes. Sharp dissonance on *"pain."* |

---

## ✳ INSTRUMENTAL DANCE MUSIC

Dance music was popular throughout the Renaissance, partly as a result of the wider distribution made possible by the printing of music (see the Historical Window in Chapter 8, page 152). Much of it still consisted of arrangements of popular vocal pieces, but there were also well-established instrumental forms based on courtly and popular dances. Here we look at five of the dozens of forms current at the time.

The *basse danse* was the most popular courtly dance during the Renaissance, especially at the Burgundian court. The dancers, in couples, moved in a dignified striding motion to a slow bass pattern that could support either duple or triple meter and that was unaffected by the speed of the upper parts. The *calata*, which

FIGURE 7.3 Peasants dance the branle to the accompaniment of a bagpipe in this late fifteenth-century illustration from a book of hours.

called for no particular steps, had a distinctive rhythm in the accompaniment (LONG/short-short-LONG / LONG-LONG-LONG) and a Spanish flavor in its harmonies. Dancers probably danced the calata as they were changing from one dance to another.

The *branle* was a group dance in which the dancers formed a line or a circle and often sang along with the music. Contemporary pictures suggest that high stepping was part of its vigorous movement (Figure 7.3). The *passamezzo* was a dignified dance in slow to moderate triple meter. The name of this dance may derive from the phrase *passo e mezzo*, which means "step and a half." Finally, the triple-meter *galliard*, which probably originated in northern Italy, was one of the fastest and sprightliest of the Renaissance dances.

The music for all these dances is simple and repetitive, consisting largely of repeating strains (*A-A-B-B*, etc.) that, on each repetition, the musicians were expected to vary (see Listening Guide 18).

Various instruments were used, including the viol and recorder (a flutelike wind instrument held vertically and producing a breathy but sweet sound) for intimate dances, and the piercing shawm for out-of-doors. Percussion instruments of some sort, though they are never specified, must have been used in many of these dances, especially the energetic branle and galliard. From the courtly basse danse to the rustic branle, dance music was a popular feature of social life in the Renaissance.

# *Listening Guide 18*

## Dance Medley

CD 1, TRACK 18
TAPE 1B, TRACK 8
DURATION: 7:51

*Although the first basse danse* (La Gatta) *seems faster than the second* (La Magdalena), *both use the same moderate beat. Just what the "Reprise" refers to is unclear.*

*Form: Repeating strains (varied)*

| LOCATION | TIME | COMMENTS |
|---|---|---|
| **1** BASSE DANSE: *LA GATTA* | | |
| *A*-Section* | **0:00** | Recorder and regal (small reed organ). |
| *A'* | 0:21 | Embellishment of preceding section. |
| | | |
| BASSE DANSE: *LA MAGDALENA* | | |
| *A* | **0:48** | Viol consort in dignified but ambiguous meter. |
| *A'* | 1:04 | Embellishment of preceding section. |
| *B* | 1:19 | Triple meter discernible. |
| *B'* | 1:33 | Embellishment of preceding section. |
| | | |
| *C* | 1:46 | Faster triple meter. |
| *C'* | 1:55 | Embellishment of preceding section. |
| *D* | 2:03 | |
| *D'* | 2:12 | Embellishment of preceding section. |
| | | |
| *C"* | 2:21 | Same tempo as preceding stanza, but more |
| *C"* | 2:30 | embellished. |
| *D'* | 2:38 | |
| *D'* | 2:47 | Embellishment of preceding section. |
| | | |
| **2** *CALATA ALA SPAGNOLA* | | |
| Short repeating phrases. | **2:59** | Lute in lively triple meter with tambourine accompaniment (called a "Basque drum"). |
| | | |
| **3** *BRANLE DE CHAMPAGNE* | | |
| *A* | **4:23** | Vigorous melody played on the shawm, |
| *A'* | 4:31 | accompanied by lutes, viols, and drums. |
| *B* | 4:39 | Contrasting section. |
| *B* | 4:48 | Repeat of contrasting section. |

*Since there are so many brief sections, we have omitted the term *section* from this Listening Guide.

*continued*

# Listening Guide 18 (Continued)

| LOCATION | TIME | COMMENTS |
|---|---|---|
| A | 4:56 | Embellishment of earlier section. |
| B | 5:04 | |
| **4** PASSAMEZZO D'ITALYE | | |
| A | **5:16** | Five viols play plaintive melody in slow duple meter. |
| | 5:36 | Embellished answer to preceding phrase. |
| A' | 5:56 | Embellishment of first statement. |
| | 6:16 | Embellished answer to preceding phrase. |
| REPRISE | | |
| A | **6:36** | Rapid duple meter. Recorder, viols, percussion. |
| A' | 6:58 | Highly embellished version of preceding section. |
| **5** GALLIARD | | |
| A | **7:20** | Same music as the Passamezzo but recast in lively triple meter. Tune in the recorder. |
| A' | 7:33 | Highly embellished, including a final flourish. |

# Chapter 8

## MOTET AND MASS

By the time of the Renaissance, composers had been writing polyphonic motets for centuries. The polyphonic Mass was a more recent form, but for composers of church music it quickly became a staple. These two forms were to dominate sacred polyphony for the next 150 years.

## THE MOTET

The medieval motet, though it was based on plainchant, employed vernacular texts as well as Latin texts. Composers of Renaissance motets, however, satisfied themselves with Latin. Although motets were not sung during the Mass, they could be used in any of the quasi-religious events that took place at a court or in a chapel. The motet demonstrates how thin—and often irrelevant—the line was between sacred and secular music. Although Renaissance motets used Latin texts and the techniques common to sacred music, they often dealt with secular themes.

During the fifteenth century motets were in either three or four voices, but by the middle of the sixteenth century five- and six-voiced motets had become common. All parts were intended to be sung, though instruments often doubled the vocal lines. Each voice usually moves within its own well-defined register, though voices may still cross occasionally.

### Guillaume Dufay: Motet, *"Supremum est mortalibus bonum"* ("The greatest good of mortals") (1433)

*"Supremum est mortalibus bonum"* (Listening Guide 19) is one of the few motets whose composition we can date precisely. In 1433, Pope Eugenius IV signed the Treaty of Viterbo with King Sigismund, who was crowned Holy Roman Emperor later that year. This motet was probably sung at an event marking the signing of the treaty.

DUFAY: Motet, *"Supremum est mortalibus bonum"*
("The greatest good of mortals")

CD 1, TRACK [19]
TAPE 1B, TRACK 9
DURATION: 8:01

*Although there is no imitation to speak of, the voices frequently begin their lines at different times, increasing the sense of independence. More than a half dozen under-third cadences serve to unify the piece. The sections are separated by ruled lines.*

*Form: Through-composed (5 sections)*

| | TEXT | TIME | COMMENTS |
|---|---|---|---|
| **1** | *Supremum est mortalibus bonum*<br>The greatest good of mortals is | **0:00** | Smooth 3-voiced texture, much parallel motion, under-third cadence. |
| | *Pax, optimum summi Dei donum.*<br>Peace, the best gift of God the Highest. | 0:17 | Long melisma on *"[do]-num,"* which ends with a full under-third cadence. |
| **2** | *Pace vere legem praestantia*<br>By true peace the rule of law | **0:37** | Ends with under-third cadence. |
| | *Viget atque recti constantia.*<br>And the constancy of right are strengthened. | 0:50 | Slower-moving tenor. |
| | *Pace die solutus et laetus*<br>In peace the day closes and joyous | 1:05 | Under-third cadence in mid-phrase. |
| | *Nocte somnus trahitur quietus.*<br>Deep sleep is brought by night. | 1:21 | Ends with full triad. |
| | *Pax docuit virginem ornare*<br>Peace taught the virgin to adorn | 1:34 | Sweet triads and thirds on *"virginem."* |
| | *Auro coman crinesque nodare.*<br>Her hair with gold and to bind her tresses. | 2:00 | Ends with full under-third cadence. |
| **3** | *Pace rivi psallentes et aves*<br>In peace the streams murmur psalms and the birds | **2:19** | Parallel motion, coordinated stop. |
| | *Patent laeti, collesque suaves.*<br>Are joyous, the hills are soft. | 2:31 | |

| *Pace dives pervadit viator* | 2:48 | Ends with under-third cadence. |
| In peace proceeds the rich traveller | | |
| *Tutus arva incolit arator.* | 3:02 | |
| And the ploughman tills his field in safety. | | |

---

**4** [Instrumental interlude]     **3:17**

| *O sancta pax, diu expecta,* | 3:32 | |
| O holy peace, day long awaited, | | |
| *Mortalibus tam dulcis, tam grata,* | 3:57 | Long closing melisma on *"[gra]-ta."* |
| So sweet to mortals, so welcome, | | |
| *Sis eterna, firma, sine fraude!* | 4:25 | Full triads. |
| Be eternal, certain, without deception! | | |
| *Fidem tecum semper esse gaude!* | 4:53 | Ends with under-third cadence. |
| May trust in thee always mean joy! | | |
| *Et qui nobis, o pax, te dedere* | 5:19 | Closing melisma on *"[de-de]-re."* Ends with under-third cadence. |
| And may they, o peace, that gave thee to us | | |
| *Possideant regnum sine fine:* | 5:46 | |
| Possess their power without end: | | |

---

**5** [Instrumental interlude]     **6:03**

| *Sit noster hic pontifex aeternus* | 6:13 | Contains two under-third cadences. |
| May our eternal pontiff be | | |
| *EUGENIUS ET REX SIGISMUNDIS.* | 6:38 | Smooth, homophonic thirds and triads. |
| EUGENIUS AND OUR KING SIGIS-MUND. | | |
| *Amen.* | 7:15 | Extended melisma in all voices. |
| Amen. | | |

The influence of Dunstable (page 116) and his English contemporaries is evident throughout this three-voiced work. It abounds in thirds and sixths, many of them moving in the parallel fashion the English favored. The most striking passage in the work is the line *"EUGENIUS ET REX SIGISMUNDIS"* ("EUGENIUS AND OUR KING SIGISMUND"). Of the ten chords used to set this line, five are full triads and only the first lacks a third.

Dufay divides this relatively lengthy, through-composed work into five sections separated by clear cadences. He still relies heavily on the under-third cadence that was abandoned by Josquin's generation. The final *Amen* receives an elaborate melisma in which some of the volatile rhythms of the Middle Ages persist. Although Dufay makes little use of imitation, the voices exhibit a smoothness and coordination characteristic of the new music of the Renaissance.

## THE MASS

The idea of polyphonic settings of the Mass Ordinary introduced by Machaut spread quickly throughout Europe. Because the Ordinary was part of virtually every celebration of the Mass, composers could count on frequent performances. In the fifteenth century Dufay wrote nine such Masses and by the end of the sixteenth century Giovanni Pierluigi da Palestrina had written more than a hundred.

To unify the disparate texts of the Ordinary, composers used a variety of musical techniques. Most commonly they built a Mass around a recurring melody known as a **cantus firmus** ("fixed melody"), usually placed in the tenor. As in the Middle Ages, the source for the cantus firmus was plainchant, though as early as the fifteenth century composers were using popular tunes as well. Some composers began with a cantus firmus which they then elaborated and embellished in a process known as *paraphrase*. The elaborate means of musical organization favored by Renaissance composers inevitably undermined the clarity and intelligibility of the Mass text. In longer texts such as the Credo, some composers even resorted to setting two lines simultaneously. Since the musical structure tended to overshadow the text, Renaissance settings of the Mass celebrate the creative powers of the composer as well as the glories of God.

We look now at two phases in the development of the Renaissance Mass.

### Josquin Desprez: Credo from the *Missa L'homme armé super voces musicales* (Mass on "The Man at Arms" at all the different pitches of the hexachord; ca. 1500)

Josquin composed Masses from his youthful days in Milan until his last years in semi-retirement. They were in such demand that Petrucci (see the Historical Window on page 152) devoted no fewer than three volumes to them. Josquin brought an astonishing range of techniques to these works. He wrote cantus firmus Masses and paraphrase Masses and canonic Masses. He borrowed melodies from plainchant, French chansons, popular songs, and *solmization* syllables ("La sol fa re mi," used to teach melodies).

The literal title of this work is "Mass on 'The Man at Arms' at all the different pitches of the hexachord." Let us take these two strange phrases one at a time. We do not know just when the song *"L'homme armé"* ("The Man at Arms") was written, or by whom, but by the middle of the fifteenth century it had become extremely popular. Composers had even begun to use it for the tenor voice in their settings of the Mass. By the end of the sixteenth century there were dozens of such settings. The very simplicity of the tune may have accounted for much of its appeal.

This tune appears and reappears in the tenor voice throughout Josquin's Mass. Instead of using it over and over on the same pitches, however, he subjects it to a systematic series of transpositions that cover all the usable degrees of the modal scale, known as the *hexachord* (6-note scale). Thus in the Kyrie the tune begins on C, in the Gloria on D, in the Credo on E, in the Sanctus and Osanna on F, in the first Agnus Dei on G, and in the third and final Agnus on A. Because the arrangement of the whole tones and semitones changes with each transposition, the character of the tune itself is transformed with each new movement. In the Kyrie and Benedictus, Josquin writes one of the voices in canon with the tenor.

## J O S Q U I N : Credo from the *Missa L'homme armé super voces musicales* (Mass on "The Man at Arms" at all the different pitches of the hexachord)

CD 2, TRACK [1]
TAPE 2A, TRACK 1
DURATION: 7:42

*The movements of this Mass are held together by Josquin's use of imitation. The listener is scarcely aware of the popular tune in the tenor, or of its being played backwards or in shorter note values. The three sections, separated by full cadences, are set off by ruled lines in the Listening Guide.*

*Form: Through-composed (3 sections)*

| | TEXT | TIME | COMMENTS |
|---|---|---|---|
| 1 | *(Credo in unum Deum,)* <br> (I believe in one God,) | **0:00** | Syllabic plainchant. (It was customary to open both Gloria and Credo this way.) |
| | *Patrem omnipotentem,* <br> The Father almighty, | **0:06** | Imitation in the two upper voices. |
| | *factorem caeli et terrae,* <br> maker of heaven and earth, | 0:15 | |
| | *visibilium omnium et invisibilium.* <br> and of all things visible and invisible. | 0:17 | Text begins in the bass voice. |
| | *Et in unum Dominum, Jesum Christum,* <br> And in one Lord Jesus Christ, | 0:36 | Imitation at 0:43. Melismas on *"Je-[sum]."* |
| | *Filium Dei unigenitum,* <br> the only begotten Son of God, | 1:01 | Two upper voices, extensive melismas. |
| | *et ex Patre natum ante omnia saecula;* <br> born of the Father before all ages; | 1:17 | Imitation in all but tenor voice. |
| | *Deum de Deo, lumen de lumine,* <br> God of God, light of light, | **1:46** | Imitation between short motives. |
| | *Deum verum de Deo vero;* <br> true God of true God; | | Bass holds a long note on *"vero."* |
| | *Genitum, non factum;* <br> begotten, not made; | 2:16 | Imitation in all but tenor. |
| | *consubstantialem Patri:* <br> consubstantial with the Father: | | Imitation in scalar ascent. |
| | *per quem omnia facta sunt.* <br> by whom all things were made. | | |
| | *Qui propter nos homines et propter nostram salutem,* <br> Who, for us men, and for our salvation, | 2:38 | Close imitation between soprano and bass. |

| TEXT | TIME | COMMENTS |
|------|------|----------|
| *descendit de caelis;*<br>came down from heaven; | | Extensive melismas leading to a full cadence. |
| **2** *Et incarnatus est de Spiritu Sancto ex Maria Virgine:*<br>and was incarnate by the Holy Ghost of the Virgin Mary: | **3:10** | Homophonic texture. Extensive imitation on *"ex Maria Virgine."* The cantus firmus is now sung backwards. |
| *Et homo factus est.*<br>and was made man. | 3:37 | In uppermost voice. |
| *Crucifixus etiam pro nobis,*<br>He was crucified also for us, | 3:57 | Motive in soprano repeated three times. |
| *sub Pontio Pilato,*<br>under Pontius Pilate, | 4:13 | Extensive imitation built on a scalar descent. |
| *passus et sepultus est.*<br>suffered and was buried. | 4:25 | Imitation in descending motive. |
| *Et resurrexit tertia die,*<br>And the third day he rose again, | **4:43** | Slow, chordal harmonies. |
| *secundum Scripturas.*<br>according to the Scriptures. | 5:05 | Soprano and tenor only. |
| *Et ascendit in caelum:*<br>And ascended into heaven: | 5:11 | Melody ascends to *"caelum"* ("heaven"). |
| *sedet ad dexteram Patris;*<br>He sits at the right hand of the Father; | 5:19 | Same music as preceding line, leading to a strong cadence on *"Patris."* |
| *Et iterum venturus est cum gloria,*<br>and he shall come again with glory, | 5:27 | Two- and three-voiced texture. |
| *judicare vivos et mortuos;*<br>to judge the living and the dead; | 5:36 | |
| *cuius regni non erit finis.*<br>and his Kingdom shall have no end. | 5:51 | Full cadence. |
| | | [Josquin omits part of the Credo text.] |
| **3** *Confiteor unum baptisma in remissionem pec-catorum.*<br>I confess one baptism for the remission of sins. | **6:08** | Imitation in two upper voices of lengthy, melismatic theme. The cantus firmus now appears in shortened note values. |
| *Et expecto resurrectionem mortuorum,*<br>And I await the resurrection of the dead, | 6:47 | Long-breathed, seamless texture to end. |
| *Et vitam venturi saeculi, Amen.*<br>and the life of the world to come, Amen. | 7:12 | Long melismas on *"Amen."* |

In the Credo (Listening Guide 20), Josquin begins by writing the cantus firmus in slower note values with long rests between phrases. In the second section (*"Et incarnatus"*) he extends the structure by writing the tune backwards, and in the third and final section (*"Confiteor"*) he presents the cantus firmus in note values one-third shorter. The density of the counterpoint means that the voices sing the same text together only occasionally, and then only for short periods. More often, two different lines of text are sung simultaneously. Josquin even omits the first 34 words of the third section. In short, he imposes the musical organization onto the text.

Despite all the contrapuntal devices, the movement flows smoothly from beginning to end. To introduce many of the text phrases, Josquin uses the new technique of imitation, which serves as a means of organization.

# GIOVANNI PIERLUIGI DA PALESTRINA (ca. 1525–1594)

In his own day and well into the nineteenth century, Palestrina's serene, contemplative music was regarded as the consummate example of late Renaissance polyphony. Later generations believed that it represented the ideal of *a cappella* singing (roughly, "as done in the chapel," signifying voices without instrumental accompaniment). Although this purely vocal sound was less valued during the Renaissance than later musicians thought, the ability to reproduce the Palestrina style was a prerequisite even for Romantic composers in the nineteenth century.

Palestrina is the name of a small town in the hills outside Rome, where the composer was probably born and where he received his early training. After serving until 1551 as organist in a local church, Palestrina accepted the first of several appointments in Rome's three major churches. While still in his mid-twenties he was appointed musical director of the Cappella Giulia (the chapel named after Pope Julius II, who had reorganized it as a place for training native musicians). Even though he was not a priest, Palestrina was dismissed from the papal choir because his marriage violated the rule of celibacy. After a time in the service of a wealthy cardinal, in 1571 he returned to St. Peter's in Rome (Figure 8.1), where he spent the last 23 years of his life. Between 1572 and 1581 he lost his brother, two sons, and wife to the Black Plague,* and for a time he considered entering the priesthood. But a new marriage to the well-to-do widow of a Roman merchant freed him from financial worries.

*A bacterial infection transmitted by fleas and infected rats, the Black Plague appeared as early as the fifth century B.C. in Athens. The most severe outbreak, however, began in Constantinople in 1334 and spread quickly throughout Europe, killing almost three-quarters of the population within 20 years. It continued to terrorize Europe until the late seventeenth century.

FIGURE 8.1 The building of St. Peter's stretched over 125 years, during which time the structure evolved from a Renaissance to a Baroque design and grew into the world's largest Christian church. Bramante, the first of four architects in charge of the cathedral, based his design completely on circles and squares. The architect Alberti maintained that these were the ideal shapes for sacred buildings, as the circle represented divine reason.

## Palestrina: Credo from the *Pope Marcellus Mass* (pub. 1567)

Palestrina's music was profoundly influenced by the Counter-Reformation, an effort by the Catholic Church to cleanse itself of corruption and to counter the successes of Lutheranism. The movement was centered in the Council of Trent, which began as an attempt to resolve differences between Protestants and Catholics. When the Council was formally convened in 1545, however, no Protestant delegates showed up. The Council continued to meet periodically over the next 18 years and spelled out in detail the doctrinal beliefs and practices of the Church.

In 1555 Pope Marcellus II (who reigned only three weeks) directed the members of the papal choir to sing in a dignified style that permitted the text to be clearly understood. One of his successors, Pius IV, even considered banning polyphony. In 1562 the Council laid down firm guidelines for the performance of music in the Mass:

> All things should be indeed so ordered that the Masses . . . may reach tranquilly into the ears and hearts of those who hear them, when everything is executed clearly and at the right speed. . . . The whole plan of singing in musical modes should be constituted

# THE PRINTING REVOLUTION

Today we are in the midst of a revolution in the way information is packaged, processed, and consumed. Some call it the "information revolution," others more prosaically the "computer revolution." In the fifteenth century, the introduction of printing with movable type had as profound an effect on life as the computer has had on life in the late twentieth century.

Before the end of the fifteenth century, books were written and bound by hand and the dissemination of music was limited, slow, and uncertain. Books were rarities to be preserved in the libraries of monasteries or wealthy aristocrats, and people traveled great distances to consult a particular book.

In the middle of the fifteenth century Johann Gutenberg (ca. 1397–1468) printed his famous Mazarin Bibles from hand-set type, spending several hours to set up a single page. The most widespread use of early printing was in making school primers, which by the end of the century were being turned out by the thousands.

Then, around the turn of the century, several innovative publishers began to produce books of printed music. Probably the earliest was the Italian Ottaviano Petrucci (1466–1539), who at 24 made his way to Venice, a center of the still primitive art of printing. Music symbols were hard to develop because, unlike block letters, they were of unusual design and often had to be tied together. In 1498 Petrucci petitioned the doge of Venice for an exclusive license to print *canto figurato* (measured music—that is, music with rhythm, as opposed to plainchant), claiming that he had succeeded where others had "long attempted in vain." It took him three years to get all the symbols together (notes, rests, clefs, accidentals, staves, texts). But in 1501 he published his "One Hundred Songs in Harmonic [i.e., polyphonic] Music," a collection of popular French chansons by contemporary composers. Over the next eight years he published editions of secular and sacred music at the astonishing rate of one every two or three months. Each page required three impressions: one for the staves, one for the notes and rests, and one for the text. And yet the alignment is precise in all his books (Figure 8.2).

During the Middle Ages and the Renaissance, most polyphonic music had been copied into part books, each containing the music of only a single part. No one performer had the score of an entire work. Petrucci published full scores as well as part books, a boon to students and performers alike. A war in which Venice took part seems to have forced him out of business in 1509.

Somewhat later, an enterprising bookseller, Pierre Attaignant (1494–1551

FIGURE 8.2 During the early sixteenth century, prosperous Venice was a center of printing as well as of musical composition.

or 1552), began experimenting with music printing in Paris. Unlike Petrucci, he focused at first on liturgical music and primers for schoolchildren. Then around 1527, he too began to publish secular music, for voices as well as in lute *intabulations* (numerically based notations of popular repertoire for lute).

In 1537 Attaignant succeeded in having himself appointed "Music Printer and Bookseller to the King." He later developed a method that made it possible to print notes and staff lines simultaneously, an advance that reduced printing costs sharply and widened the dissemination of printed music. Attaignant contributed to the popularity of the French chanson by publishing 36 volumes of chansons in runs of about a thousand each. When we compare this to the rate of copying by hand, it is clear that printing had begun to transform the musical life of Europe.

not to give empty pleasure to the ear, but in such a way that the words be clearly understood by all, and thus the hearts of the listeners be drawn to desire of heavenly harmonies, in the contemplation of the joys of the blessed. . . . They should also banish from church all music that contains, whether in the singing or in the organ playing, things that are lascivious or impure.

Palestrina responded to the Council's decree with his six-voiced (soprano, alto, two tenors, two basses) *Pope Marcellus Mass.* During the seventeenth century the story spread that this work had saved polyphonic music from being banished from Catholic services. There is no direct evidence to support the story, but Palestrina's setting satisfied the Vatican without sacrificing musical values.

Although it was customary to build a Mass based around borrowed melodies, Palestrina seems to have written the *Pope Marcellus Mass* without recourse to any pre-existing melodies. Instead, he focused on the clearest possible presentation of the text. To ensure clarity, he has all the participating voices start each line of text together, thereby curtailing the opportunities for imitation.

His use of other musical devices is limited as well. In the Credo (Listening Guide 21), for example, he limits melismas to an ascending or descending 5-note figure enunciated at the opening:

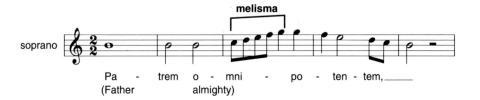

Palestrina unifies the movement by calling frequently on this simple figure (and its inversion). Indeed, the only extensive melisma in the Credo is the systematic, cascading imitation in six voices on *"Amen,"* based on a slower inversion of the melisma shown above.

To compensate for these self-imposed limitations, Palestrina richly "orchestrates" his six voices. He presents them in every conceivable combination, from duets in both adjacent and widely spaced voices to combinations of three and four voices. He reserves all six voices for the final cadences at the end of each of the four sections.

He uses full triadic harmonies throughout. In the Credo, the only section that does not begin or end on a major triad is the opening of the *"Crucifixus"* ("He was crucified"), which begins as a dark duet between tenor and bass. For Dufay the triad was an available sonority, for Josquin it was a central sonority, and for Palestrina it was almost the only sonority.

# *Listening Guide 21*

## PALESTRINA: Credo from the *Pope Marcellus Mass*

CD 2, TRACK 2
TAPE 2A, TRACK 2
DURATION: 8:45

*The four sections, separated by full cadences in the music, are set off by ruled lines in this Guide. Triadic harmonies predominate throughout. The Comments column merely hints at the rich variety of voice combinations. Note how much easier it is to follow this text than it is to follow the same text in Josquin's Mass (page 148). Even the staggered (successive) entries of the same text are easily understood.*

*Form: Through-composed (4 sections)*

| | TEXT | TIME | COMMENTS |
|---|---|---|---|
| **1** | *(Credo in unum Deum,)*<br>(I believe in one God,) | **0:00** | Syllabic plainchant. |
| | *Patrem omnipotentum,*<br>The Father almighty, | **0:07** | Full triadic harmonies, upper voices. Ascending melisma on *"-ni-[potentum]."* |
| | *factorem caeli et terrae,*<br>maker of heaven and earth, | 0:17 | Lower voices. Descends to *"terrae"* ("earth"). |
| | *visibilium omnium et invisibilium.*<br>and of all things visible and invisible. | 0:24 | Smooth chordal style. Listen for the ascending melisma in the bass. |
| | *Et in unum Dominum, Jesum Christum,*<br>And in one Lord, Jesus Christ, | 0:37 | First half of line repeated. |
| | *Filium Dei unigenitum,*<br>the only begotten Son of God, | 0:53 | Three middle voices. Moves in parallel descending harmonies. |
| | *Et ex Patre natum ante omnia saecula;*<br>born of the Father before all ages; | 0:59 | Five and four voices. Begins with a "minor" triad. Full cadence and brief stop. |
| | *Deum de Deo, lumen de lumine,*<br>God of God, light of light, | 1:12 | Staggered entry on *"De-[um]."* |
| | *Deum verum de Deo vero;*<br>true God of true God; | 1:20 | Staggered and overlapping voice entries. |
| | *Genitum, non factum;*<br>begotten, not made; | **1:37** | Chordal style. |
| | *consubstantialem Patri:*<br>consubstantial with the Father: | 1:42 | Ascending melisma. |
| | *per quem omnia facta sunt.*<br>by whom all things were made. | 1:51 | Full six-voiced texture, ascending melisma. |

*continued*

| TEXT | TIME | COMMENTS |
|------|------|----------|
| *Qui propter nos homines,*<br>Who, for us men, | 1:59 | Three middle voices. |
| *et propter nostram salutem,*<br>and for our salvation, | 2:05 | Three upper voices |
| *descendit de caelis;*<br>came down from heaven; | 2:11 | Extensive melismas on descending lines, leading to a full six-voiced triadic cadence and a pause. |
| **2** *Et incarnatus est de Spiritu Sancto*<br>and was incarnate by the Holy Ghost | **2:30** | Homophonic texture. Slow, full triads. |
| *ex Maria Virgine:*<br>of the Virgin Mary: | 2:54 | |
| *Et homo factus est.*<br>and was made man. | 3:07 | Six voices, leading to a full triadic cadence and a pause. |
| **3** *Crucifixus etiam pro nobis,*<br>He was crucified also for us, | **3:36** | This section is in four voices—soprano, alto, tenor, and bass. |
| *sub Pontio Pilato,*<br>under Pontius Pilate, | 3:48 | Loose imitation between soprano and tenor. |
| *passus et sepultus est.*<br>suffered and was buried. | 3:58 | Homophonic, ends in a rest to illustrate *"sepultus"* ("buried"). |
| *Et resurrexit tertia die,*<br>And he rose again on the third day, | 4:12 | Louder and higher. Staggered entry on *"tertia"* ("third") provides extra emphasis. |
| *secundum Scripturas.*<br>according to the Scriptures. | 4:21 | Tenor and bass only. |
| *Et ascendit in caelum:*<br>And ascended into heaven: | **4:29** | Four voices, ascending lines. |
| *sedet ad dexteram Patris;*<br>He sits at the right hand of the Father; | 4:36 | Three upper voices. |
| *Et iterum venturus est cum gloria,*<br>and he shall come again with glory, | 4:45 | Three lower voices. Following a pause after *"judicare"* ("to judge"), *"vivos et mortuos"* ("the living and the dead") is set in long-held chords. |
| *judicare vivos et mortuos;*<br>to judge the living and the dead; | | |

| TEXT | TIME | COMMENTS |
|---|---|---|
| *cuius regni non erit finis.*<br>and his Kingdom shall have no end. | 5:08 | Text repeated to illustrate "have no end," leading to a full triadic cadence and a pause. |

**4** *Et in Spiritum Sanctum, Dominum,*
And in the Holy Ghost, Lord,

| TEXT | TIME | COMMENTS |
|---|---|---|
| **5:36** | Returns to six voices, though only five used here. Upward melisma on *"Sanctum."* |
| *et vivificantem:*<br>and giver of life: | 5:45 | Text repeated for emphasis. Five upward and downward melismas to suggest "life." |
| *qui ex Patre Filioque procedit.*<br>Who proceedeth from the Father and the Son, | 5:58 | All six voices. More upward and downward melismas. |
| *Qui cum Patre et Filio simul adoratur*<br>Who together with the Father and the Son | 6:09 | Mostly the middle voices, staggered entries. |
| *et con glorificatur:*<br>is adored and glorified: | 6:22 | Outer voices, music parallels the end of the preceding line. |
| *qui locutus est per Prophetas.*<br>who spoke by the prophets. | **6:29** | Rich six-voiced texture. Long staggered melismas on *["Pro]-phe-[tas"]* ("prophets"). |
| *Et unum sanctam catholicam et apostolicam Ecclesiam.*<br>And one holy catholic and apostolic church. | 6:40 | Staggered voice entries. The music for the second line of text essentially repeats that for the first line. |
| *Confiteor unum baptisma in remissionem peccatorum.*<br>I confess one baptism for the remission of sins. | 6:55 | All six voices. Lengthy melismas on *["remissi]-o[nem"]* and *["pecca]-to[rum"]* ("remission of sins"). |
| *Et expecto resurrectionem mortuorum,*<br>And I await the resurrection of the dead, | 7:22 | Staggered entries. *"Resurrectionem"* repeated. Long melisma on *"mortuorum."* |
| *Et vitam venturi saeculi, Amen.*<br>And the life of the world to come, Amen. | 7:48 | Staggered entries. Text repeated for emphasis. Elaborate imitative melismas on *"Amen."* |

FIGURE 1 Europe in 1648. Although the Thirty Years' War was fought largely in Germany, it drew in Bohemia, France, Sweden, Denmark, and England against the power of the Hapsburgs.

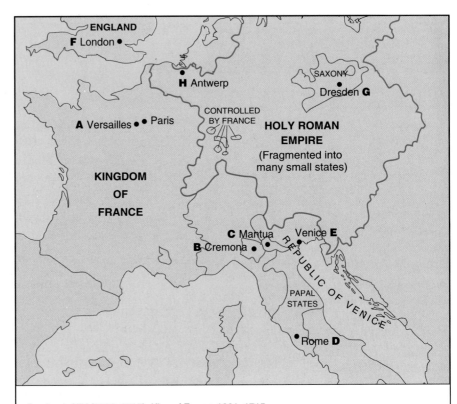

**A**     Louis XIV (1638–1715); King of France 1661–1715
**B**     Center of violin making
**C**     Claudio Monteverdi's opera *Orfeo* premiered in 1607
**D**     Galileo Galilei (astronomer, mathematician, physicist; 1564–1642)
        Girolamo Frescobaldi (composer; 1583–1643)
**E**     Center of early opera and music printing
        Giovanni Gabrieli (composer; 1557–1612)
        Monteverdi at St. Mark's, 1613–1643
**F**     Henry Purcell (composer; 1659–1695); *Dido and Aeneas* premiered in London in 1689
**G**    Heinrich Schütz (composer; 1585–1672)
**H**    Peter Paul Rubens (painter; 1577–1640)

# THE EARLY BAROQUE (1600–1690)

## The Age of Absolutism

HISTORICAL<br>AND CULTURAL<br>BACKGROUND

During the seventeenth century, known as the Age of Absolutism, families like the Hapsburgs in Austria, the Medicis in Italy, and the Bourbon family in France are commonly believed to have ruled Europe with unchallenged authority. That belief is based on an oversimplification, however.

The end of the sixteenth century and the first half of the seventeenth century were times of enormous upheaval in Europe (see map, Figure 1). Until the end of the sixteenth century, the organization of Europe had centered around the Hapsburg family, who ruled most of central and southern Europe. Their most powerful representative was Philip II (1527–1598), King of Spain from 1556 until his death.

After Philip's death, the Hapsburg grip loosened and war gradually spread throughout Europe. The most widespread and costly was the Thirty Years' War (1618–1648) that eventually dragged almost every European country and territory into its deadly grip. Nominally a religious war between Catholics and Protestants, virtually none of the aims held by any of the participants made any real sense, and the war ended only because the combatants had become exhausted.

It was a bloody war. Military strategist King Gustavus Adolphus of Sweden (1594–1632) introduced the *salvo,* in which attacking troops fired at the defenders all at once, causing them to break ranks. Adolphus also introduced a light cannon that could be moved swiftly into new battle positions. (A devout Christian, he forbade his troops to take part in the looting and raping that were common in seventeenth-century warfare; he himself died in battle at the age of 38.) Sieges of heavily fortified towns and cities often went on for months and sometimes years.

The Thirty Years' War disrupted the economies of most of Europe and crippled cultural and artistic growth. The country least affected was Italy, the scene of the most important advances in music during the seventeenth century.

FIGURE 2 A portrait of the king (at age 63) as absolute monarch. Louis XIV's palace at Versailles was oriented on the sun's east-west path. As Frederick Hartt explains, "It is no accident that the great event of each day at Versailles was the levée (rising), a term applied interchangeably to the appearance of the sun over the horizon and to the emergence of the Sun King from his bed."

After mid-century, order was once again restored in Europe and would last until the outbreak of the democratic revolutions in the last quarter of the eighteenth century. The French king, Louis XIV (1638–1715; de facto king from 1643, actual ruler from 1661), carried the concept of absolute rule to extraordinary lengths over the more than half a century of his reign (1661–1715). A skillful, scheming administrator, he exempted the nobility from taxes but made them financially dependent on him, thereby inviting court intrigue. He summed up his view of government in the famous phrase *L'état, c'est moi* ("I am the State"). Exhausted from years of war, Louis's subjects accepted his absolutist rule in lieu of further strife.

Under Louis, who was known as "The Sun King" (Figure 2), the French court became the model of sophistication, elegance, and etiquette to which all other courts in Europe aspired. In the 1660s Louis began the transformation of a sleepy village named Versailles into the setting for a magnificent palace sur-

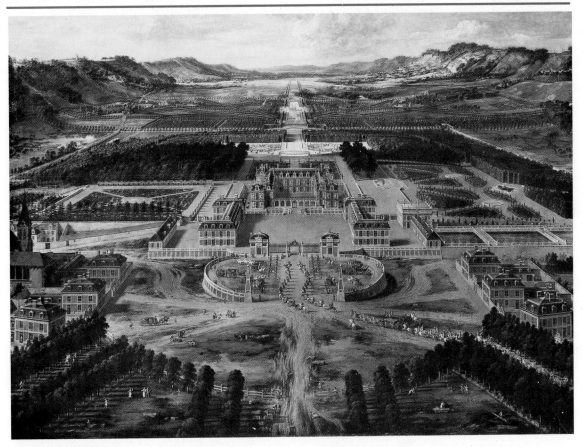

FIGURE 3 Miles of formal gardens, filled with fountains and statues, surrounded Versailles. They were essentially outdoor rooms, with nature under geometrical control.

rounded by fountains, reservoirs, and sculpture (Figure 3). In 1682 he moved his court to this splendid site. For the next century and a half, imitations of Versailles sprang up all over Europe, and French language and manners were cultivated at many foreign courts.

The seventeenth century quickened the pace of scientific inquiry. The Italian astronomer, mathematician, and physicist Galileo Galilei (1564–1642, the son of one of the founders of opera, Vincenzo Galileo) discovered natural laws of physics that laid the foundation for modern experimental science. Galileo built the first working telescope, with which he discovered that the moon had an uneven surface and that the Milky Way consisted of independent stars. In 1632 he published a book defending the Copernican solar system (in which planets revolve around the sun) as opposed to the Ptolemaic system (in which the sun and planets revolve around a stationary earth). Brought before a Papal Inquisition, he was forced to recant his unorthodox beliefs. Legend has it that as he arose from his knees at the end of the trial he muttered *"E pur si muove"* ("Nevertheless it [the earth] does move"). He was consigned to house arrest outside Florence for the rest of his life.

In view of the continuing advances in science, the use of the term *Baroque* in the arts seems ironic. The term derives from a word used in the sixteenth century by Portuguese jewelers for a "pearl of irregular shape." By the mid-eighteenth century, critics were using it to describe what they regarded as the extravagance and abandon of the architecture and music of the preceding years. The implication was that Baroque art was imperfect or eccentric, a negative connotation like that given to the earlier term *Gothic* in painting and architecture. Nevertheless, art historians adopted "Baroque" early in the twentieth century to characterize the entire period from about 1590 to 1750, and soon music historians adopted it as well. Over the years the term has become a standard historical label with no pejorative overtones, and today Baroque music is one of the most popular forms of art music.

The first Baroque music to be revived in the twentieth century was that of Arcangelo Corelli, Antonio Vivaldi, George Frideric Handel, and Johann Sebastian Bach. Since all of them were active during the last 60 years of this long era, their music came to be known, somewhat pretentiously, as "High Baroque," implying that it was somehow superior to the music of the seventeenth century.

Although there are important differences between the music composed before and after 1690, the terms *late* and *early* seem more useful. The early Baroque in music was marked by two influential developments: the advent of the *continuo* (coupled with a dramatic rise in instrumental music) and the birth of opera. In the next two chapters we consider these developments in turn.

# Chapter 9

## THE EARLY BAROQUE
## IN ITALY AND GERMANY

The seventeenth century witnessed dramatic changes in musical life throughout Europe, especially in Italy. Around 1600 musical style began to change more swiftly than the gradual change in style that had occurred between the end of the Middle Ages and the beginning of the Renaissance. Unlike the evolutionary Renaissance style, the Baroque style was the result of a genuine revolution.

## THE EARLY BAROQUE STYLE

The Renaissance had celebrated imitative vocal polyphony, as we have seen in the works of Josquin and, to a lesser extent, Palestrina. Musical textures of four, five, and even eight voices were the rule, and the text had been made subservient to the music. The decrees of the Council of Trent were a partial response to this domination of text by music.

In 1605 an Italian composer, Claudio Monteverdi, in the preface to his fifth book of madrigals, described a *seconda prattica* ("second practice"). Monteverdi's preface was a response to a sharp criticism made a few years earlier by a conservative theorist, Giovanni Maria Artusi. Firmly, Monteverdi pointed out that the *prima prattica* ("first practice") of imitative counterpoint sacrificed the meaning of the words to the music, and that the new techniques were intended to reverse that relationship—to make the music the servant of the text.

Monteverdi's new techniques included bold new harmonies and dissonances, but his main concern was to establish the ascendancy of text over music. One result of this new concern was a drastic simplification of vocal textures that music historians have dubbed *monody*. **Monody** (not to be confused with monophony) was a style of accompanied solo singing in which the meaning of the text was expressed in a flexible vocal line.

The development of monody was spurred by the humanist tradition in Florence, whose most distinguished representative was Count Giovanni de' Bardi

(1534–1612), a literary critic, poet, playwright, and composer. Bardi, who was passionately interested in the arts, hosted an informal club called a *camerata* made up of Florentine noblemen who came together from time to time to discuss poetry, astrology, music, and other "sciences." One of their favorite topics was the musical practices of the ancient Greeks. A member of the camerata, Vincenzo Galilei, carried on a lengthy correspondence at the time with Girolamo Mei, a Rome-based philologist whose music-loving patron had inspired him to study Greek texts in which music was discussed. Galilei became familiar with Mei's views on subjects ranging from abstract theories of tuning and scales to the implications of Greek music for "modern" music. Mei believed that the Greeks had favored a simple, expressive, declamatory style that was quite different from the polyphonic complexities of sixteenth-century music. Around 1578, Bardi mentioned the virtues of this simpler style of singing to Giulio Caccini, a Roman singer and composer living in Florence. In response, Caccini published in 1602 a collection of songs titled *Le nuove musiche* ("The New Music"). Some of the songs in this collection are *strophic variations,* in which a recurring harmonic pattern (a strophe, usually the same length as a stanza of text) supports a melody that is varied with each repetition. Other songs are in a style of free declamation over slow-moving harmonies, which Caccini called *musica recitativa* ("recited music," generally called "recitative"). These were the two most important forms of monody.

Mei was not a musician, a fact that doubtless contributed to his misreading of certain aspects of Greek practice. For example, there is no evidence that the Greeks gave harmonic support to their singing with an independent instrumental accompaniment or that they employed metrical schemes like those devised by Caccini. And there is certainly no evidence that the Greeks ever set a drama to music from beginning to end. Nevertheless, Mei and the members of Bardi's camerata, in their attempt to imitate the most attractive features of ancient practice, created an important new musical style.

One feature that developed around this time provided ready support for the new monodic style. This was the **continuo** ("continuous [sound]"), which furnished an unbroken musical scaffolding over which the vocal line unfolded. At the end of the sixteenth century, Baroque organists commonly played the bass line to sacred pieces and filled in the harmonies above. In the newer monodic style of secular singing, the harpsichord supplied an unbroken but often sparse accompaniment. Then, as vocal music grew more complex, the continuo came to be supplied not by just one instrument, but by a group of instruments that we call a "continuo group." In elaborate stage pieces this group might include more than a dozen plucked string or keyboard instruments.

The continuo was seldom written out in the score. Instead, it was merely suggested by a series of shorthand numbers below the bass line, called the **figured bass,** which the players then *realized* during performance (Figure 9.1). The degree of imagination and polish that players brought to this task provided a measure of their skill.

Just as the continuo supported the new forms of vocal music, so too it contributed to the rise of instrumental music.

## THE RISE OF INSTRUMENTAL MUSIC

FIGURE 9.2 A mid-seventeenth-century harpsichord by Girolamo Zenti. Today, the harpsichord is enjoying a revival of interest, although earlier ears would have agreed with the English conductor Sir Thomas Beecham (1879–1961), who said, "The sound of the harpsichord resembles that of a birdcage played with toasting forks."

During the seventeenth century instrumental music assumed for the first time a position of nearly equal importance with vocal music. The three most important instruments in that development were the organ, the harpsichord (Figure 9.2), and the violin. The organ and the harpsichord were ideally equipped to play the chords required by the continuo. The tone of the harpsichord is characterized by a sharp attack and a quick decay—well suited for emphasizing the regular rhythms that emerged in Baroque instrumental music. It gradually developed the capacity—especially in the hands of French composers—to function both as a solo instrument and an accompanying instrument.

The violin also achieved greater prominence during the early Baroque. The modern four-string version of this instrument had emerged early in the sixteenth century, an outgrowth of the medieval *rebec* and *fiddle*. The first great center of violin making was Cremona, a town in northern Italy (see map, page 158). Beginning with Andrea Amati (born ca. 1505), the artisans of Cremona turned out splendid instruments for two centuries (see the Historical Window in Chapter 11, page 218). The violin is an extraordinarily versatile instrument. In addition to emulating the expressiveness of the human voice, it can reproduce the *passage work* (passages consisting of rapid runs and scales) of a keyboard instrument. During the seventeenth century the violin, along with the viola and the cello (both of which emerged at about the same time as the violin), joined the organ and the harpsichord as the foundation instruments of the early Baroque.

Renaissance instruments had typically been grouped by homogeneous families of recorders, sackbutts, and so forth. In the Baroque, families of instruments gradually became more heterogeneous. For example, the modern woodwind family of flute, oboe, clarinet, and bassoon produces sounds in three different ways: by blowing across an opening, with a single reed, and with a double reed (Chapter 4). Although the modern wind family did not fully emerge until around 1750, the movement toward heterogeneous families was well under way by the end of the seventeenth century.

The orchestra as we know it, with its foundation of strings supplemented by various woodwinds and brass (frequently in pairs) and a pair of timpani, did not emerge until the eighteenth century. But the increased use of these instruments during the seventeenth century prepared the way. We now look at two examples of the emerging instrumental style.

## GIOVANNI GABRIELI (1557–1612)

Venice has long enjoyed a reputation as one of the most splendid cities of Europe. For centuries, Venetian life has centered around the magnificent church of St. Mark's (Color Plate 4). According to legend, the body of the Apostle St. Mark was brought to a small church on the site of St. Mark's in 827. Then, beginning in the eleventh century, a much grander structure, based on Byzantine models, was erected. This basilica, as it is called, was largely completed by the sixteenth century. St. Mark's looks out on a magnificent *piazza* (Italian for "square"), which Napoleon once called "the finest drawing room in Europe."

Starting in the 1560s, the doges of Venice maintained an instrumental ensemble to play during services in the Doge's Chapel. The ensemble consisted of three to six sackbutts and several wooden or ivory cornetts (precursors of the trumpet). There was also a male choir of about 25 voices, including 8 to 10 boy sopranos. Additional musicians were hired for special feasts and holidays, of which there were many. At a time when only small groups of instrumentalists and singers were being hired to perform in other cities, Venice attracted many fine musicians. One of the finest was Giovanni Gabrieli, who succeeded his uncle Andrea as organist at St. Mark's in 1585 after winning a competition for that post and who remained in Venice for the rest of his life.

Gabrieli is a transitional figure between the late Renaissance and the early Baroque, and elements of both styles are evident in his music. Before 1600 he wrote a large amount of music for voices and instruments intended for performance at St. Mark's, the best known of which is a collection of "sacred symphonies" published in 1597. This collection also includes 16 purely instrumental pieces. Indeed, Gabrieli wrote more instrumental music than his contemporaries and in 1615 published a monumental set of 20 "canzonas and sonatas." These works reveal the influence of the vocal style on instrumental music and at the same time point the way toward a distinctive instrumental idiom.

## Gabrieli: Sonata XIX, from *Canzoni e Sonate* (pub. 1615)

Gabrieli's most important instrumental works consist of canzonas and sonatas intended for performance during the Mass. At this time the term *sonata* (from the Italian *sonare*, "to sound") simply meant an instrumental piece as distinguished from a vocal piece. Gabrieli tailored these works, some of which call for 22 instruments (including brass, strings, and organ continuo), to the superb acoustics of St. Mark's vast interior.

Since the Renaissance it had been customary to divide the vocal choir into separate groups that sang from lofts along either side of the interior. The groups were almost 35 yards apart. Works for the largest *cori spezzati* ("divided choruses") were reserved for the most important feast days, such as the Mass celebrated on Founder's Day (preceded by a magnificent procession).

Apparently it was Gabrieli who hit upon the idea of applying the *cori spezzati* to instruments as well. His Sonata XIX (1615; Listening Guide 22), for example, calls for three choirs (as the instrumental groups also were called, in deference to their vocal origins), each anchored by three sackbutts and headed by a violin and viola (Choirs 1, 3) or a cornett and viola (Choir 2). Gabrieli exults in the varied contrasts that these choirs make possible. The virtuosic passages in the violins and cornetts contrast dramatically with the solemn choral style. Judging from the fast pace of the virtuoso passages, Gabrieli must have had great confidence in his instrumentalists.

# Listening Guide 22

## GABRIELI: Sonata XIX, from *Canzoni e Sonate*

CD 2, TRACK 3
TAPE 2A, TRACK 3
DURATION: 4:43

*The Sonata moves smoothly from section to section with scarcely a break, the first occurring well over halfway into the piece (breaks are shown by ruled lines in the Time column). From there to the end, the sections are shorter but fuller and increasingly embellished. The organization of the work is cumulative, moving from a single choir in a slow imitative texture to all three choirs with rapid embellishments.*

*Form: Cumulative*

| | LOCATION | CHOIR | TIME | COMMENTS |
|---|---|---|---|---|
| 1 | Theme head | 1 | **0:00** | In Trombone I, with Trombone III in close imitation. Characterized by even note values. |
| | | | 0:06 | Violin enters in imitation. |
| | | | 0:15 | Sackbut I enters in imitation. |
| | | 2 | 0:31 | The first dotted rhythms are introduced. |
| | | 3 | 0:59 | Leads to stronger dotted rhythms, here in a rising sequence. |
| | Theme head | 1, 2, 3 | **1:19** | Played in rhythmic diminution (twice as fast). |
| | | | 1:30 | Dotted rhythms trigger elaborately embellished lines in violin and cornett. |
| | | | 1:59 | Chain of slow dotted rhythms in a sequence. |
| 2 | Theme head | 3 | **2:16** | Strings. |
| | | 1–3 | 2:23 | Rapid figure played in imitation, leading to an elaborate, highly embellished cadence. |
| | | 1–3 | **2:39** | Follows the first sectional break in the piece. Motto rhythm in minor, with three massed choirs. |
| | | 1, 2, 3 | 2:45 | Dotted rhythms leading to highly embellished lines in violin and cornett. |
| 3 | Theme head | 1–3 | **3:23** | Motto rhythm beginning in the minor mode, full sonorities. |
| | Theme head | 3, 2 | **3:42** | Motto rhythm beginning in the major mode. |
| | | 1–3 | 3:51 | Sequences based on short dotted-rhythm pattern. |
| 4 | Closing Section | 1, 2, 3 | **4:12** | Cadential material repeated successively in each choir. |
| | | 1–3 | 4:21 | Elaborate, full cadence with massed choirs. |

An instrumental piece lasting almost five minutes was a rarity in the early Baroque. To support such dimensions, Gabrieli unifies the Sonata thematically with a single "theme head" that provides a rhythmic "motto": LONG-short-short-LONG (a formula common throughout the Renaissance). Like a motet, the piece begins in close imitation:

The Sonata moves smoothly from section to section with scarcely a break. The first break occurs over halfway into the piece. From then on, the articulations between sections occur more and more frequently, with each section richer and more embellished than the one before. Gabrieli indulges in the time-honored technique of *diminution,* in which a simple skeleton is embellished with smaller note values:

On its return, the theme head is played twice as fast as before. Gabrieli reserves the massed choir of instruments for two dramatic moments: following the first break in the texture (see the Listening Guide), and for the final cadence. The organization is cumulative: The work opens with a single choir in even rhythms, builds to dotted rhythms, moves to diminution of the head of the main theme, and concludes with rapid embellishments with all three choirs. The harmonies celebrate the sensuous fullness of richly scored triads. Dissonances occur only at cadences, and there only to intensify the fullness of the triads. The recording offers but a hint at how glorious this truly stereophonic work must have sounded within St. Mark's.

# Listening Guide 23

### FRESCOBALDI: *Capriccio del Soggetto scritto sopra l'Aria di Ruggiero* (pub. 1637)

CD 2, TRACK 4
TAPE 2A, TRACK 4
DURATION: 4:17

*The marked textural contrasts between the theme and each variation make this form rather easy to follow, even though you may not immediately grasp all the contrapuntal subtleties.*

*Form: Theme and variations*

| | LOCATION | TIME | COMMENTS |
|---|---|---|---|
| 1 | Introduction | **0:00** | 5-bar first phrase of *"Fra Iacopino"* played as melody only. |
| | | 0:10 | 5-bar first phrase repeated with simple ornamentation. |
| 2 | Theme | | |
| | *a* (4 bars) | **0:20** | *"Ruggiero"*-Theme begins. Straightforward, but with polyphonic accompaniment. |
| | *a'* (4 bars) | 0:28 | Differs from first phrase in its end cadence. |
| | *b* (8 bars) | 0:37 | Based on the *a*-phrase. |
| 3 | Variation 1 | **0:57** | In the major mode, but with frequent chromatic inflections to the minor. Melody of first phrase in the bass. Migrates to soprano for second phrase; appears in both bass and soprano in third phrase. |
| | Variation 2 | **1:35** | In triple meter. First part of each phrase accompanied by a written-out trill. Third phrase includes a jarring "passing note" in the melody. |
| 4 | Variation 3 | **2:24** | Fast, dancelike triple meter, suggesting a movement from a dance suite. Staccato touch. |
| | Variation 4 | **2:54** | Returns to duple meter. Rich, imitative texture in nearly continuous rhythms. |
| 5 | Variation 5 | **3:15** | Duple meter. Even fuller imitative texture in a higher register. |
| | [Reprise of theme] | **3:39** | Essentially a reprise of Variation 1. |

FIGURE 9.3 As organist at St. Peter's in Rome for 35 years, Frescobaldi was well known throughout Italy; his fame as a performer extended to Germany.

# GIROLAMO FRESCOBALDI (1583–1643)

The rise of instrumental music is documented most dramatically in the rise of keyboard music for organ, harpsichord, and (in England) virginal. One of the greatest keyboard composers and players of his day was the Italian Girolamo Frescobaldi (Figure 9.3), who until recently was an unjustly neglected composer. (His first full-length English biography appeared only in 1983.) Frescobaldi was born in the north Italian city of Ferrara, an active center of music in the Renaissance. Its reigning duke, Alfonso II d'Este, is said to have listened to music for two to four hours a day. Apparently a prodigy, Frescobaldi studied with the court organist Luzzasco Luzzaschi. When Frescobaldi was 14, Alfonso died and the court at Ferrara was disbanded.

Frescobaldi seems to have moved at about this time to Rome, where in 1607 he was appointed organist at an important church, Santa Maria in Trastevere. He traveled in the same year to Brussels, where he admired the beautiful harpsichords being made by the Ruckers family. In 1608 he became organist at Rome's largest and best-known church, St. Peter's, a position he held for the rest of his life. Except for a trip late in life to Florence, he seems to have spent most of his time in Rome with his wife Orsola and their four children. Nevertheless his fame as an improviser and composer, both during his lifetime and for a century afterward, was enormous. Stories, probably exaggerated, tell of thousands turning up to hear him play at St. Peter's.

## Frescobaldi: *Capriccio del Soggetto scritto sopra l'Aria di Ruggiero,* from Book I of Toccatas and Partitas (1614–1616, pub. 1637)

Frescobaldi wrote both sacred and secular works, many of which can be played on either the organ or the harpsichord. His *Capriccio del Soggetto scritto sopra l'Aria di Ruggiero* (literally, "Caprice written on the subject of Ruggiero's aria"; Listening Guide 23) is clearly intended for the harpsichord. Both the title and the structure of the piece require explanation. First of all, the *"Ruggiero"* is a bass pattern, with its implied harmonies, that was widely known to composer and listener alike. The pattern begins like this:

Frescobaldi based two keyboard compositions on the *"Ruggiero,"* and he was probably familiar with at least three sets of variations on the same pattern by earlier Italian composers.

*Capriccio,* meaning "whim" or "fancy," suggests a piece in which the imagination prevails over strict rules. And that is just what happens here. Before the piece proper begins, Frescobaldi offers up a few unaccompanied lines of a tune that any contemporary would have recognized as *"Fra Iacopino"* (the Italian

*(Text continues on page 176.)*

# *Historical Window*

## THE "EARLY MUSIC" MOVEMENT

Throughout most of Western history, composers wrote music either to satisfy a commission or to suit a specific event, such as a wedding. Neither composers nor their audiences expected a new work to be played very often, if ever, after its first performance. As a result, a great deal of music simply dropped out of sight. Then, in the 1860s in Germany, a new discipline arose known as *Musikwissenschaft*—literally, "science of music," but generally translated into English as "musicology." In the years since, musicologists have recovered much of the music of the past, and recently performers and scholars have launched what is known as the "early music" movement.

As musicologists searched out this long-forgotten music in libraries and archives, they found few clues to how it had originally been performed. Unlike paintings and statues, music takes place in time and must be brought to life each time it is performed. As we have seen, notation was very incomplete in early music, and the instruments to be used in performance were rarely specified. Even when the instruments were indicated (shawms or crumhorns, for example), often no specimens of them survived.

So musicologists (most of them German or French), instrument makers, and performers set about reinventing the styles of the past and instruments to match. They created a discipline called *Aufführungspraxis*, or "performance practice." In the English town of Haslemere, for example, Arnold Dolmetsch (1858–1940; Figure 9.4) set up a workshop to manufacture such "period instruments."* as the viola d'amore (a precursor of the viola), the lute, the clavichord, and the Baroque recorder.

Dolmetsch urged that period instruments be used for performances of early music even when modern instruments could be substituted. Today, students of early music disagree on whether such substitutions are desirable or even permissible. (Our recording of Gabrieli's Sonata XIX uses period sackbutts and cornetts, while our recording of Schütz's *Freue dich* uses modern trumpets and trombones.) Some argue that since we are more familiar with the sounds of modern instruments the use of period instruments makes the music sound "wrong" to our ears.

In fact, performers, audiences, and critics alike disagree on just how early music should be performed. If we have no reliable guides to tempos or dynam-

*Some writers use the terms *original* instrument or *authentic* instrument, but these can be misleading.

FIGURE 9.4 Arnold Dolmetsch in his Haslemere workshop, where instrumental types that had been as extinct as dinosaurs made music again.

ics, instruments, or, in some cases, even rhythms, then how can we be sure we are hearing what the composer intended, or anything even close to it? Clearly, taste must be the final arbiter.

In 1952 the American Noah Greenberg (1919–1966) founded a group called the New York Pro Musica that has done much to influence our taste in this matter. Instead of approaching early music in a tentative, almost apologetic fashion, Greenberg addressed it with enthusiasm and dramatic flair. His singers and instrumentalists (often the same persons, as in the Middle Ages and Renaissance) exhibited the same level of virtuosic skill as the best contemporary pianists or violinists. Greenberg even succeeded in producing brilliant performances of medieval liturgical dramas *(The Play of Daniel,* and later, *The Play of Herod).*

*continued*

FIGURE 9.5 Wanda Landowska, a flamboyant and charismatic performer, rekindled interest in the harpsichord. Confident of her ability to divine Bach's performance intentions, she once said to a colleague, "You go ahead and play Bach your way; I prefer to play him his way."

Another outstanding musician, the Polish Wanda Landowska (1879–1959; Figure 9.5), reintroduced the harpsichord at a time when virtually all early secular keyboard music was being performed on the piano. The instrument she used differed in many ways from period instruments, but her recordings of Bach's keyboard music (especially the *Goldberg Variations*) launched a harpsichord revival that continues to this day. In England, the harpsichordist Thurston Dart (1921–1971) did much to revive the keyboard music of the sixteenth through eighteenth centuries, including the repertoire of the French *clavecinistes* who flourished at the French court in the seventeenth and eighteenth centuries.

David Munrow (1942–1976) and Christopher Hogwood (b. 1941; Figure 9.6) also have been influential. Munrow's "Pied Piper" radio broadcasts over

FIGURE 9.6 In the late 1980s, keyboardist and conductor Christopher Hogwood became the most recorded classical artist in the world—all with period instruments.

the BBC and the concerts and recordings of his Early Music Consort of London in the 1970s brought early music to the attention of new audiences. (Munrow's group performed several of the works included in Chapter 6.) Hogwood, along with John Eliot Gardiner (b. 1943) and Roger Norrington (b. 1934), has carried the concept of early music well beyond the Baroque. Today we have recordings of Mozart's piano concertos on the *fortepiano*, and performances of Beethoven's symphonies, and even of Berlioz's *Symphonie fantastique*, on period instruments.

People who view the "early music" movement as a self-righteous return to an unattainable authenticity miss the point. At its best, the movement speaks to the way we re-invent and experience the past.

version of the well-known French folksong *"Frère Jacques"*). His piece consists of a remarkable combination of that tune with the bass pattern, the *"Ruggiero."* It would be as if a composer today were to write a piece combining "Take Me Out to the Ball Game" with "Chopsticks."

Frescobaldi does not present *"Fra Iacopino"* in its entirety but rather uses it as the basis of a free exploration. He treats the combination of the bass pattern and tune as a theme and variations. A **theme and variations** consists of the repetition of an independent harmonic pattern, whose first statement (the theme) presents an appealing tune with successive variations set off by rhythmic, melodic, and textural contrasts. Given the brevity of Frescobaldi's theme, the five distinctive variations (followed by a *reprise,* or "return," of the theme) encompass a remarkably broad range of expression. Following the straightforward theme, the first variation explores every chromatic nook and cranny of this overwise major-mode theme, with the melody of the first phrase in the bass. The second and third variations are in triple meter, with the latter in a dancelike style. The richly polyphonic fourth and fifth variations return to duple meter, followed by the simpler reprise. Subjecting a tune to variations in this manner became a common practice in keyboard music and was to remain so for the next 250 years.

## THE ITALIAN CONTINUO MADRIGAL

In the sixteenth century, as we have seen, the term *madrigal* meant almost any secular song set to an Italian text. Composers of madrigals abandoned the simple, formal schemes of earlier types, like the frottola (page 134), and usually chose for their settings a brief poem consisting of a single stanza or else a single stanza from a longer poem. Around 1530 the first printed collection of madrigals was published in Rome by Philippe Verdelot, soon followed by another collection published by Costanzo Festa. These were four-to-six-voice madrigals in which the more complex polyphony of the northern style (with Josquin as the model) alternated with a simpler chordal style.

As time passed, the polyphony grew richer and more complex, and composers grew fonder of word painting, or madrigalisms. The Italian madrigal achieved its final form around the turn of the seventeenth century with the addition of the continuo to its texture. Such a madrigal, called a *continuo madrigal,* found its most brilliant expression in the works of Claudio Monteverdi.

## CLAUDIO MONTEVERDI (1567–1643)

Throughout his long life, Monteverdi kept abreast of all the latest styles and incorporated them into his own compositions. He brought to music a new level of emotional intensity that both impressed and offended his contemporaries. Monteverdi was born in Cremona (of violin fame) to a family of modest means who nevertheless saw to it that he received a solid music education. He was only 15 when his first works were published by a prestigious printing house in Venice.

By 1590 Monteverdi had joined the court of Duke Vincenzo I in nearby Mantua and was serving as a string player in the court ensemble. His reputation as a composer spread swiftly, and in 1600 he was attacked by Artusi (page 163). Though more a reformer than a revolutionary, Monteverdi became the champion of the "second practice." In eight masterly books of madrigals he summarized the entire madrigal tradition of the sixteenth century. Beginning in his fifth book, published in Venice in 1605, Monteverdi introduced the continuo into his madrigals. And in the seventh and eighth books he introduced "concertato" instruments such as the violin. Meanwhile, he had composed the first great Italian operas (to be discussed in Chapter 10).

Following the death of his wife in 1607 and the death soon after of a singer who had been a close friend, Monteverdi fell into a deep depression and returned to Cremona. His father requested Duke Vincenzo to release him from the Mantuan court, but Vincenzo refused. When Vincenzo died in 1612, Monteverdi was dismissed without warning. A year later, when the *maestro di cappella* (the music director, the highest music official at a court or cathedral) at St. Mark's died, Monteverdi—now in his mid-forties—was invited to apply and won the position. During his 30 years at St. Mark's, Monteverdi raised the quality of music performed there to new heights, and in his seventies he was still composing operas for the new opera house in Venice (see the Historical Window in Chapter 10, page 194).

## Monteverdi: *"Zefiro torna"* ("Zephyr returns") (Petrarch) from Madrigals, Book VI (1614)

Monteverdi wrote madrigal settings for many of Petrarch's poems. In *"Zefiro torna"* ("Zephyr returns"), Petrarch expresses the familiar contrast between the coming of spring and the lover's despair. In the first two stanzas he describes the gentle western breeze (the zephyr) that brings fair weather and fills all living things with love. Up to this point in Monteverdi's 5-voiced setting, the music suggests a celebration of spring, but in the third stanza, where Petrarch recalls his own unhappy experience with love, the music suddenly turns dark. In the fourth and final stanza he confesses that all the signs of spring are but a "desert" to him, and complains that the acts of women are like those of "terrible and savage" beasts. Here Monteverdi introduces powerful, unexpected dissonances, based on the previously forbidden interval of the *tritone* (three whole steps, known in the Middle Ages as the *diabolus in musica*—that is, "devil in music"), that lead to a poignant climax. As Monteverdi would have been happy to explain to Artusi, the dissonance is all in the service of the text (see Listening Guide 24).

# Listening Guide 24

## MONTEVERDI: Madrigal, *"Zefiro torna"* ("Zephyr returns")

CD 2, TRACK 5
TAPE 2A, TRACK 5
DURATION: 4:15

*The music of the first two stanzas is either identical or parallel. The third stanza brings a sudden and dramatic contrast in tempo and mood, though the full dissonances are not released until the last line of Stanza 4.*

*Form: Sectional (A-A'-B-C)*

| TEXT | TIME | LOCATION/COMMENTS |
|---|---|---|
| STANZA 1 | | **A-Section.** |
| 1 *Zefiro torna, e'l bel tempo rimena,* Zephyr returns and ushers in fair weather, | **0:00** | Dotted rhythms in close imitation; rapid melisma on *"tempo"* ("weather"). |
| *e i fiori e l'erbe, sua dolce famiglia,* flowers and grass, his charming companions, | 0:17 | Smooth rhythms, imitation. |
| *e garrir Progne, e pianger Filomena,* and warbling Procne and weeping Philomel, | 0:22 | Short imitative phrases. |
| *e primavera candida e vermiglia.* and the fresh and ruddy Spring. | 0:38 | Faster rhythms, imitation. |
| STANZA 2 | | **A'-Section.** |
| 2 *Ridono i prati e'l ciel si rasserena;* The meadows smile and the sky grows calm; | **0:50** | Same music that opens Stanza 1. |
| *Giove s'allegra di mirar sua figlia;* Jove rejoices to see his daughter; | 1:09 | Parallel but different music. |
| *l'aria, e l'acqua, e la terra è d'amor piena;* air, water, and earth are full of love; | 1:13 | Short imitative phrases. |

## THE FIRST GREAT GERMAN COMPOSER: HEINRICH SCHÜTZ (1585–1672)

In the sixteenth century, northern Germany was still a collection of petty principalities with no important cultural centers to rival those of France and Italy. The Dark Ages had lasted longer here than elsewhere, and Germany was just

| TEXT | TIME | LOCATION / COMMENTS |
|---|---|---|
| *ogni animal d'amar si riconsiglia.*<br>every living thing falls in love again. | 1:26 | Faster rhythms, longer imitative phrases. |
| STANZA 3 | | **B-Section.** |
| **3**   *Ma per me, lasso, tornano i più gravi sospiri,*<br>     But for me, alas, return the heaviest sighs, | **1:40** | Sudden turn to low registers, long-held notes, especially on *"sospiri"* ("sighs"). |
| *che dal cor profondo tragge*<br>which she who took the keys of my heart | 2:07 | |
| *quella ch'al ciel se ne portò le chiavi;*<br>to heaven drew from its depths; | 2:22 | Full cadence leads seamlessly to the C-section. |
| STANZA 4 | | **C-Section.** |
| **4**   *e cantar augelletti, e fiorir piaggie,*<br>     the singing of the birds, the blooming of the hillsides, | **2:42** | Smooth rhythms in triple meter, upper registers. |
| *e'n belle donne honeste atti soavi*<br>and gracious acts of fair, noble ladies | 2:52 | |
| *sono un deserto,*<br>are to me a desert, | 3:02 | Slow, arpeggiated melody, still major mode. |
| *e fere aspre e selvaggie.*<br>and [acts] of harsh and savage beasts. | 3:18 | Five powerful, unexpected dissonances based on tritones. Dissolves to a final cadence on a full major triad. |

beginning to enter the mainstream of European life. Until the start of the seventeenth century, there were few German composers of any international renown. Heinrich Schütz (Figure 9.7), however, was a composer whose talents would not be equaled until the appearance of Johann Sebastian Bach a century later. Schütz brought to his style a rigorous structure and intellectual profundity that would mark German music well into the twentieth century.

Although his life was marked by hardship and tragedy, Schütz displayed cour-

FIGURE 9.7 Heinrich Schütz used German texts for the great majority of his sacred works, fulfilling Luther's desire to replace Latin with the vernacular. Although infant mortality was as high as 50 percent in seventeenth-century Europe, people who lived to Schütz's advanced age were common.

age and humor throughout his 87 years. As a child, he showed an early talent for music, especially for singing. When a visiting aristocrat heard the 13-year-old boy sing, he persuaded the parents to let him take the youth back with him to Kassel. There Schütz received a solid education that included instruction in French, Latin, and Greek, and he later enrolled in the University of Marburg. When another aristocrat offered to pay his expenses for a trip to Venice to study with Giovanni Gabrieli, Schütz happily accepted his offer. He stayed on in Venice and studied with Gabrieli for some two years until the latter's death. Many of his later compositions reflect his efforts to reconcile the sensuous Italian style with the rigorous, contrapuntal German style.

On his return to Germany, Schütz served as second organist in a ducal court until the Elector of Saxony, Johann Georg I, heard of his talents and spirited him off to Dresden. For a time, the Elector pretended that he was just "borrowing" Schütz but then insisted on keeping him on because he could not find anyone else "as good." Schütz stayed in Dresden for more than 40 years, although the Elector permitted him to accept invitations for short trips. With the Elector's death in 1757, Schütz, now 72, was given his freedom and spent the last 15 years of his life composing new works and revising earlier ones.

## Schütz: *"Freue dich"* ("Rejoice") (ca. 1626)

*Freue dich* (pronounced "*froi*-yuh deek," with a "soft" final *k*), which Schütz wrote for a wedding celebration in 1626, is an example of his synthesis of the Italian and German styles. The ensemble is typically Italian. It consists of a quintet of sackbutts and cornetts (played here by modern trombones and trumpets; see the Historical Window on page 172). The four-part mixed chorus is identical to one of the choral dispositions Gabrieli used in Venice. In the *cori spezzati* tradition (page 167), Schütz exploits the contrasts between chorus and soloists—as, for example, in the first line, which moves from solo voice to full chorus to antiphonal chorus, with alternating voices (see Listening Guide 25).

Schütz contrasts the diatonic harmonies of the phrase *"Freue dich"* with the rich chromaticism of *"Sie ist lieblich."* Into these four syllables Schütz packs an extended chromatic passage worthy of Monteverdi. He also contrasts the homophonic settings of *"Freue dich"* with the imitative settings of "and blessedly sweet like a deer" and "Let her love satisfy thee at all times," distinguishing between the free imitation of those passages and the rigorous imitation of "and delight yourself in every way with her love":

# Listening Guide 25

## SCHÜTZ: *"Freue dich"* ("Rejoice")

CD 2, TRACK 6
TAPE 2A, TRACK 6
DURATION: 4:44

*Schütz organizes the piece by using the A-Section as a frame and by partially repeating it in the middle. The music alternates between homophonic and contrapuntal textures, and between vocal and instrumental forces. The Italian influence is apparent in the chromatic word painting of "lieblich" ("lovely").*

*Form: Sectional (A-B-A-C-A)*

| TEXT | TIME | LOCATION / COMMENTS |
|---|---|---|
| **1** *Freue dich des Weibes deiner Jugend.* Rejoice with the wife of thy youth. | **0:00** | **A-Section.** Countertenor* solo. Sets up pattern of minor to major triads. |
| *Freue dich des Weibes deiner Jugend.* | 0:10 | Full chorus, trumpet ornamentation. |
| *Freue dich des Weibes deiner Jugend.* | 0:20 | Antiphonal chorus, text repeats, leads to pungent brass cadence. |
| **2** *Sie ist lieblich,* She is lovely, | **0:45** | **B-Section.** Rich chromatic progressions in successively descending voices. |
| *wie eine Hinde,* like a roe, | 1:08 | Cadence pattern. |
| *Sie ist lieblich,* | 1:17 | Chorus, led by the soprano. |
| *wie eine Hinde,* | 1:25 | Cadence pattern. |
| [Sinfonia] | 1:31 | Same chromatic harmonies and cadence. |
| *und hold selig, wie ein Rehe.* and blessedly sweet, like a deer. | 2:00 | Imitative scalar patterns in voices and brass. Cadences on full major triad. |
| **3** *Freue dich des Weibes deiner Jugend.* Rejoice with the wife of thy youth. | **2:17** | **A-Section.** Like the second statement of the first section. |
| **4** *Lass dich ihre Liebe allezeit sättigen;* Let her love satisfy thee at all times; | **2:28** | **C-Section.** Freely imitative at close time intervals. |
| *und ergetze dich allewege in ihrer Liebe.* | 2:52 | New, highly rhythmic figure in the trumpets. |
| and delight yourself in every way with her love. | 2:56 | Chorus in systematic imitation of trumpet theme. |

*A naturally high male tenor whose range is roughly the same as that of an alto.

*continued*

| TEXT | TIME | LOCATION / COMMENTS |
|---|---|---|
| | 3:10 | Trumpets enter before choral passage has ended. |
| *und ergetze dich allewege in ihrer Liebe.* and delight yourself in every way with her love. | 3:27 | Chorus in systematic imitation of trumpet theme. Cadences softly on a major triad. |
| **5** *Freue dich des Weibes deiner Jugend.* Rejoice with the wife of thy youth. | **3:56** | ***A*-Section.** Restatement, countertenor solo. |
| *Freue dich des Weibes deiner Jugend.* | 4:07 | Full chorus, brass ornamentation. |
| *Freue dich des Weibes deiner Jugend.* | 4:17 | Antiphonal chorus, same pungent cadence, concluding on a full major triad. |

Schütz manages to make this "learned" style sound effortless and spontaneous. Systematic counterpoint of this sort would be typical of German music for the next two centuries.

# Chapter 10

## EARLY OPERA

From the fifteenth century on, the ducal courts of Italy had been celebrating weddings, births, and the visits of dignitaries with elaborate spectacles that combined pageant and music. The most resplendent of those courts was at Florence. There, in 1600, the festivities celebrating the marriage of Maria de' Medici (the duke's daughter) and King Henry IV of France lasted for almost two weeks (Figure 10.1). Every day, the guests were regaled with a succession of musical entertainments.

Beginning in 1518, it became customary in Florence to insert four brief musical entertainments between the five acts of a spoken play (usually a comic play). Such an entertainment was called an *intermedio* ("intermission"; pl., *intermedii*). While this practice may seem bizarre to us, it made sense in Renaissance terms. The play preserved the "unities of time," while the musical entertainments had no sense of time or place and functioned simply as breaks during the drama. The earliest intermedii required no stage characters at all and probably lasted only a few minutes. Gradually stage characters became common, and musical scenes were added to the beginning and end of the drama as well, creating six separate entertainments. The intermedio continued this gradual evolution until what had once been a series of unconnected scenes was brought together into a coherent narrative with music throughout.

A parallel development occurred in the *pastoral play,* a type of escapist drama peopled by shepherds and mythological figures and designed to amuse the aristocracy. Such plays were regularly accompanied by songs and choruses that gradually became more and more elaborate.

Underlying both of these developments was the mistaken belief of the members of Bardi's camerata (page 163) that ancient Greek drama had been set to continuous music, a practice they wished to emulate. The intermedio and the pastoral play, along with such musical forms as monody and the concerted madrigal, all led to a hybrid dramatic form set to music throughout and accompanied by scenery, dramatic staging, and dancing. By 1600, this form had become known as *opera* (plural of the Latin *opus,* a "work"). An **opera,** then, is a drama set to music. The characters perform on a stage, much as actors do in a play, but they sing their lines instead of simply speaking them. The text, known as the *libretto* (Italian for "little book"), is written to accommodate the requirements of a musical setting. Costumes and stage sets suggest the time and place of the action. We turn now to two early masterpieces of opera.

FIGURE 10.1 Peter Paul Rubens painted 21 allegorical scenes of Maria de Medici's life, including her marriage by proxy to Henry IV. Rubens abandoned work on a series about the king when the queen failed to pay for the works celebrating herself that she had commissioned.

## Monteverdi: Orfeo's Ascent from Act IV of *Orfeo* (1607)

The first truly great opera is *Orfeo,* which Claudio Monteverdi composed in 1607 for the court at Mantua. Although the new genre had only recently been "invented," in this work Monteverdi achieved an astonishingly high level of dramatic and musical integration. While relying heavily on the freely declaimed style of recitative, he also made extensive use of the chorus and of strophic variation.

Monteverdi and his *librettist* (the author of the libretto), Alessandro Striggio, adapted the story of Orfeo (in English, "Orpheus") and Euridice from Greek mythology as preserved in Renaissance plays. Indeed, Orfeo was the subject of the first two preserved operas, composed by Jacopo Peri and Guilio Caccini (the composer of *Le nuove musiche;* page 164). In Striggio's adaptation (which draws on the librettos of the earlier works), Orfeo, a poet and musician, is about to be married to his beloved Euridice when a messenger arrives with the news that she has been bitten by a snake and has died. Grief stricken, Orfeo resolves to descend to the underworld to demand that Pluto, god of the underworld, return Euridice to him. With his lyre, he charms the Furies who guard the entrance into letting him pass. Proserpina, Pluto's wife, urges Pluto to release Euridice. Pluto agrees, but only on condition that Orfeo not look back at her until they have reached the land of the living. Fearing that he has been tricked, Orfeo decides that "what Pluto forbids, Love commands" and turns to look at Euridice. As he does so, she vanishes. In the last of five acts, the god Apollo persuades Orfeo to join him in the heavens, where he can gaze forever "upon her beautiful likenesses in the sun and the stars."

It is tempting to view this myth as a lesson in how the absence of self-discipline leads to ruin. But we get a sense that Orfeo is *supposed* to look at Euridice, that only by losing her in this way can he come to terms with the eternal human ambivalence about death and separation. His demand for Euridice's return is not a literal one; rather, it is a symbol of the struggle that all humans must go through when the death of a loved one intrudes upon life.

Monteverdi's orchestra calls for an unusually large continuo group consisting of two harpsichords, two double basses, a double harp, two archlutes (large lutes), two chamber organs, two bass viols, and a regal (a reed organ with a snarling tone). For the melody instruments, he calls for ten violins, two soprano violins, two cornetts, a clarino (a long trumpet with a high range), a soprano recorder, and three muted trumpets. Monteverdi provides only scant notation and few dynamics or phrase markings, leaving the orchestration largely to the performers.

The Prologue is sung by the "Spirit of Music," who, "in sweet accents, knows how to calm every troubled soul." For this music Monteverdi uses strophic variation. Each of the five stanzas is set to music in which the harmonies and phrase structure remain the same but in which the recitative-like melodic lines are varied with each musical strophe—not unlike theme and variations. The melodies are expressive and free. Monteverdi engages in word painting in his treatment of the words "sweet," "troubled," "anger," and "frozen." The strophes are separated by *ritornelli* (repeating instrumental refrains; singular, *ritornello*) played first by the strings and then by other instruments.

The most moving scene in the opera occurs in Act IV, when Pluto tells Orfeo that he can take Euridice with him on condition that he not look back at her. In the first part of the scene, Proserpina, Pluto's wife, prevails upon her husband to release Euridice. (Pluto is accompanied by the pungent reed organ.) When Pluto agrees, four Spirits join in a rich chorus (where Listening Guide 26 begins): "Today, pity and love triumph in Hell." The First Spirit announces the arrival of Orfeo, whose entrance is accompanied by an animated string ritornello. In three varied strophes, Orfeo declares that his lyre has the power to change "every heartless mind in the infernal regions." Then, as he and Euridice begin their

*(Text continues on page 190.)*

# *Listening Guide 26*

## MONTEVERDI: Orfeo's Ascent from Act IV of *Orfeo*

CD 2, TRACK 7
TAPE 2B, TRACK 1
DURATION: 8:55

*This dramatic scene illustrates the power of monody (used by the Spirits, the suspicious Orfeo, and Euridice) to express feelings. Orfeo's initial joy takes the form of three strophic variations which are abruptly cut short by his mistrust—expressed in recitative—of the infernal spirits. The chorus that opens and closes this excerpt functions as a moral voice, commenting on the action from the vantage point of an outside observer.*

*Forms / Techniques: Chorus, strophic variation, recitative*

| | STYLE / TEXT | TIME | COMMENTS |
|---|---|---|---|
| **1** | CHORUS: | | |
| | *Pietade, oggi, e Amore* <br> Pity, today, and love | **0:00** | Deep rich voices, homophonic texture. |
| | *Trionfan nel'Inferno.* <br> triumph in Hell. | | Tempo increases, brass added. |
| | FIRST SPIRIT: | | |
| | *Ecco il gentil cantore,* <br> Behold the noble singer, | **0:26** | Simple recitative, accompanied by archlute. |
| | *Che sua sposa conduce al ciel superno.* <br> who leads his wife to the skies above. | | Inflection to minor on *"superno"* ("above"). |
| **2** | [RITORNELLO] <br> [STROPHE 1] | **0:40** | Strings, sprightly dotted rhythms, major harmonies. |
| | ORFEO: | | |
| | *Qual onor di te sia degno,* <br> What honor is worthy of you, | 0:49 | Steady harmonies in a walking tempo. |
| | *Mia cetra onnipotente,* <br> my omnipotent lyre, | | |
| | *S'hai nel tartareo regno* <br> that you have succeeded in changing | | |
| | *Piegar potuto ogni indurata mente?* <br> every heartless mind in the infernal regions? | | |
| | [RITORNELLO] <br> [STROPHE 2] | **1:04** | Strings. |
| | *Luogo avrai fra le più belle* <br> You shall have a place among the most | 1:13 | |

| STYLE / TEXT | TIME | COMMENTS |
|---|---|---|
| *Imagini celesti,*<br>beautiful images of the heavens, | | |
| *Ond'al tuo suon le stelle,*<br>where, to your tones, | | |
| *Danzeranno in giri or tardi or presti.*<br>the stars will dance in circles, slowly or quickly. | | Word painting on *"giri"* ("circles") and *"presti"* ("quickly"). |
| [RITORNELLO]<br>[STROPHE 3] | **1:28** | Strings. |
| *Io per te felice a pieno,*<br>Made completely happy by you, | 1:36 | Continuo supplied by archlutes. |
| *Vedrò l'amato volto,*<br>I shall see the beloved face, | | |
| *E nel candido seno de la mia donna oggi sarò raccolto.*<br>and on her snow-white bosom today I shall rest. | | |
| [Interrupted!!] | | |
| *Ma mentre io canto, oimè!*<br>But even while I sing, ah me! | 1:53 | Muted singing returns to recitative. Chamber-organ continuo, colored by minor triads. Singing muted. |
| *chi m'assicura, ch'ella mi segua?*<br>who can assure me that she is following? | | |
| *Oimè, chi mi nasconde*<br>Ah, who may be hiding from me | 2:04 | Emotional outburst. |
| *De l'amate pupille il dolce lume?*<br>the sweet light of those beloved eyes? | | |

3    *Forse d'invidia punte, le deità d'Averno,*
     Perhaps, pricked by envy, the gods of Hades,

                                                                         2:13        Sudden passionate outburst.

| | TIME | COMMENTS |
|---|---|---|
| *Forse d'invidia punte, le deità d'Averno,*<br>Perhaps, pricked by envy, the gods of Hades, | **2:13** | Sudden passionate outburst. |
| *Perch'io non sia qua giù felice appieno,*<br>in order to deny me happiness here below, | | |
| *Mi tolgono il mirarvi,*<br>prevent me from gazing on you, | | |
| *Luci beate e liete,*<br>beauteous and radiant eyes, | | The emotion subsides briefly as Orfeo thinks of his beloved. |

*continued*

| STYLE / TEXT | TIME | COMMENTS |
| --- | --- | --- |
| *Che sol col sguardo altrui bear potete?* <br> one glance from which renders another happy? | | |
| *Ma che temi, mio core?* <br> But what do you fear, oh my heart? | **2:40** | Another passionate outburst. |
| *Ciò che vieta Pluton, comanda Amore.* <br> What Pluto forbids, Love commands. | | |
| *A nume più possente,* <br> A more powerful divinity, | 2:52 | Ends in an embellished cadence. |
| *Che vinci uomini e dei,* <br> who conquers both men and gods, | | |
| *Ben ubbidir dovrei.* <br> I must obey. | | |
| *[There is a noise behind the screen.]* | | |
| *Ma che odo? Oimè lasso!* <br> But what do I hear? Ah me! | 3:05 | In an increasingly agitated style, with the vocal line climbing steadily. |
| *S'armann forse a miei danni* <br> Perhaps the love-crazed furies | | |
| *Con tal furor le Furie innamorate* <br> are preparing to harm me by | | |
| *Per rapirmi il mio ben? Ed io 'l consento?* <br> snatching my treasure from me? Can I allow it? | | |
| *[Orpheus turns and looks back.]* | | |
| *O dolcissimi lumi, io pur vi veggio, io pur . . .* <br> O sweetest light, finally I behold you. I do . . . | 3:23 | Halting, vocal line over long chords in chamber organ. |
| *ma qua eclissi, oimè, v'oscura?* <br> but what eclipse, ah me, obscures you? | 3:40 | Outburst on *"ma qua."* |
| THIRD SPIRIT: <br> 4 *Rott'hai la legge, e se' di grazia indegno.* <br> You have broken the law and are unworthy of mercy. | **3:46** | Bass, delivered in stern tones over the reed organ. |

| STYLE / TEXT | TIME | COMMENTS |
|---|---|---|
| EURIDICE: | | |
| *Ahi, vista troppo dolce e troppo amara,* <br> Ah, vision too sweet and too bitter, | **3:54** | Anguished, chromatic dissonances. Sung to strummed chords in a slow, static style. |
| *Così per troppo amor dunque mi perdi?* <br> Thus through too much love do you lose me? | | |
| *Ed io, misera, perdo il poter più godere,* <br> And I, poor wretch, lose all hope of enjoying | | Sharp dissonance on *"misera."* |
| *E di luce e di vita, e perdo insieme,* <br> Light and life, and lose, at the same time, | | |
| *Te, d'ogni ben più caro, o mio consorte.* <br> You, more precious than all that is good, oh my consort. | | Ends with an embellished cadence. |
| FIRST SPIRIT: | | |
| *Torn'a l'ombre di morte, infelice Euridice,* <br> Return to the shadows of death, miserable Euridice, | **4:53** | Tenor, accompanied again by the reed organ. |
| *Né più sperar di riveder le stelle,* <br> never hope again to see the stars, | | |
| *Ch'omai sia sordo a prieghi tuoi l'Inferno.* <br> From here on Hell turns a deaf ear to your prayers. | | |
| ORFEO: | | |
| 5   *Dove te'n vai, mia vita? Ecco, io ti seguo.* <br> Where are you going, my life? I shall follow you. | **5:13** | Momentarily bright and intense. Accompanied by the harpsichord. Becomes increasingly chromatic, with more minor harmonies. |
| *Ma chi me 'l niega, oimè? Sogno o vaneggio?* <br> But what prevents me, ah me? Dreams or ravings? | | |
| *Qual occulto poter di questi orrori,* <br> What occult power among these horrors, | | |
| *Da questi amati orrori,* <br> These beloved horrors, | | |
| *Mal mio grado mi tragge e mi conduce* <br> Drags me against my will and leads me | | |

*continued*

| STYLE / TEXT | TIME | COMMENTS |
|---|---|---|
| *A l'odiosa luce?*<br>to the loathsome light of day? | | |
| *(Sinfonia à 7)* | **5:46** | Brass instruments in imitation and sequence. |
| CHORUS:<br>*È la virtute un raggio di celeste bellezza,*<br>Virtue is a ray of celestial beauty, | **6:28** | Heavily imitative. Minor chords. |
| *Pregio dell'alma ond'ella sol s'apprezza.*<br>Prize of the soul, through which alone it can<br>be appreciated. | | More animated, major chords. |
| *Questa di temp' oltraggio,*<br>It does not fear the ravages of time, | | Energetic syncopations. |
| *Nom tem', anzi maggiore*<br>On the contrary, with more | | Extensive melisma on *"maggiore."* |
| *Nell'uom rendono gl'anni il suo splendore.*<br>but rather with time its splendor increases. | | |
| *Orfeo vinse l'Inferno e vinto poi*<br>Orpheus conquered Hell, but was conquered | 7:18 | Broad harmonies in lower voices. |
| *Fu dagl'affetti suoi.*<br>By his own passions. | | Homophonic texture, even rhythms. |
| *Degno d'eterna gloria*<br>Worthy of eternal glory shall be | 7:44 | Rich, rising harmonies and lines to portray<br>"eternal glory." |
| *Fia sol colui ch'avrà di sé vittoria.*<br>only he who is victorious over himself. | | |
| *(Sinfonia à 7)* | **8:10** | Same as the first *Sinfonia.* |

ascent, he is overcome with doubt and in free recitative wonders whether Euridice is following him. In a passionate outpouring he exclaims "What Pluto forbids, Love commands" and imagines that the "love-crazed Furies" are about to steal his bride.

As Orfeo turns back and Euridice vanishes, he sings in halting recitative with chromatic intervals and poignant pauses. When he is unable to continue, the Third Spirit (a bass) announces in gruff tones accompanied by the reed organ that Orfeo is "unworthy of mercy." Euridice, in her second speech of the opera (she appears only briefly in Act I), expresses her grief at losing her chance for "light and life" and at losing Orfeo as well. She sings in anguished chromatic lines over static harmonies in the chamber organ.

The Fourth Spirit (a tenor), over the reed organ, consigns Euridice forever to "the shadows of death." In tortured, chromatic lines of his own, Orfeo pledges to follow her back to the underworld but is dragged into "the loathsome light of day." Immediately, the brass play an extended seven-voice sinfonia and the full chorus declares the moral of the story: "Orfeo conquered Hell, but was conquered by his own passions." The act ends with a repeat of the sinfonia.

Throughout *Orfeo,* the emotional pace is swifter than the dramatic action itself. Monteverdi evokes the rapidly shifting emotions by moving deftly among chorus, strophic variation, simple and embellished recitative, and instrumental ritornello and sinfonia. The simplicity of the story masks a profound expression of human feelings.

## HENRY PURCELL (1659–1695)

FIGURE 10.2  Henry Purcell's interest in dramatic music is evident in his remark: "Musick is the exaltation of poetry. Both of them may excell apart, but surely they are most excellent when they are joyn'd, because nothing is then wanting to either of their proportions; for thus they appear like wit and beauty in the same person."

The English composer Henry Purcell (pronounced *pur*-sul; Figure 10.2) excelled in a variety of genres: dramatic music, sacred and secular vocal music, and instrumental music. Though his life was short, he created an impressive number of memorable works. Many believe that he was the greatest English composer of all time. At the very least, he was the culmination of a long line of development in English music.

Purcell's father was a "Gentleman of the Chapel Royal" who sang at the coronation of King Charles II in 1661. His uncle sang in the choir at Westminster Abbey, and one of his brothers also was a musician. For much of his life, Purcell worked as "organ maker and keeper of the king's instruments."

Most of our scant knowledge of Purcell's life comes from notices on his published works. We do know, however, that he was esteemed by his contemporaries. The full choirs of Westminster Abbey and the Royal Chapel performed at his funeral, and he was buried in a place of honor near the Abbey organ.

Outside London, most musical life was limited to the parish church, where congregations were content with simple hymns and congregational singing. Wealthier parishes might commission sacred anthems that called for both choirs and instruments, and wealthy aristocrats maintained ensembles that played the latest instrumental music imported from Italy.

But the most splendid music was to be heard at the royal court in London, with its choirs and its ensembles of strings, brass, winds, and percussion. For special occasions, such as coronation days and St. Cecilia's Day, Purcell was commissioned to write elaborate anthems to be sung before the royal court. Purcell's works span the entire range of music then in vogue, from elaborate choral and orchestral music to simple works for amateurs to play at home. He wrote over 60 anthems and more than 150 independent songs.

Purcell was drawn to vocal music, especially to dramatic music. He wrote incidental music and songs, infused with both lyricism and power, for more than 40 plays. He seems to have been familiar with both early French and Italian opera During his lifetime there were even plans to bring Italian opera to London. Had Purcell lived even into his mid-fifties, he probably would have taken part in the great wave of Italian opera presided over by Handel starting in 1711. Instead, he had to content himself with writing music for plays or what were called "semi-" or "dramatic" operas. These Restoration dramas featured spectacular staging with elaborate musical scenes. Some, called "masques," were "plays within a play." Others advanced the main action but had spoken dialogue rather than recitative. Purcell wrote or adapted five of these (the most popular were *King Arthur* and *The Fairy Queen*), which contain some of his most elaborate and effective music.

## Purcell: Conclusion of *Dido and Aeneas* (1689)

*Dido and Aeneas* is Purcell's only opera that is sung throughout. It was commissioned by Josias Priest, who ran a boarding school for indigent young women in Chelsea (a borough of London) for performance by student singers and instrumentalists. Though at least a few male singers must have been brought in, Purcell seems to have been inspired by writing for the modest abilities of the female students.

This three-act opera lasts just over an hour, and the orchestra consists only of strings and harpsichord. Although *Dido and Aeneas* is not the first completely sung English opera (John Blow's *Venus and Adonis* was staged a few years earlier), it is certainly the first great English opera.

Dido, the Queen of Carthage (on the northern coast of Africa), and the Trojan prince Aeneas (whose Greek city has been sacked and burned) have fallen in love after his rescue from a shipwreck. As the opera opens, Dido confesses to her handmaiden Belinda that "peace and I are strangers grown." She fears a calamity but "would not have it guess'd." In the second scene, a group of witches who hate Dido, "as we do all in prosp'rous state," plot her ruin. They send an elf disguised as Mercury (the messenger of the gods), who orders Aeneas to sail with his fleet that night.

In Act II the happy couple are out on a hunt when a ferocious storm, staged by the witches, forces them to return home. Finding Aeneas alone, the elf orders him to set sail and Aeneas reluctantly agrees. At the thought of leaving Dido, Aeneas confesses that he "with more ease could die." At the opening of Act III the sailors are making ready to depart and the witches are rejoicing in their success. Aeneas tries to console Dido, but she orders him to leave. When he persists and offers to defy the gods in order to remain with her, she replies that "'tis enough, whate'er you now decree, That you once had thoughts of leaving me." Here Purcell suggests the rift by keeping the vocal lines distinct. The argument climaxes in a passage in which Aeneas inverts each of Dido's rejections:

Rejected, Aeneas finally leaves. Dido now expresses her grief in a form much favored by English composers—the ground bass, which consists of a repeating bass pattern over which a melody unfolds. Here it consists of a 5-bar, chromatic descent that leads to a cadence:

Dido then sings a long, plaintive melody, also chromatic. She sings each of two sections twice. The second section—"Remember me, but ah! forget my fate"—consists of brief, sobbing outbursts that rise to a climax and then sink gently. (Whether she dies of heartbreak or by her own hand is left unclear.)

Like Corelli in Italy, Purcell weaves together various strands of seventeenth-century harmony into triadic tonality (which we take up in the next chapter). He uses the major and minor modes to suggest stability and instability, light and darkness. For example, in the chorus "Destruction's our delight," he exploits the major mode to suggest the witches' glee and sets Dido's farewell in the dark minor mode.

Throughout the opera the chorus plays a prominent role, serving as members of Dido's court, as witches, as sailors, and as Cupids. (Since there were only eight female roles, most of the girls in the school would have sung in the chorus.) Most of the choral passages are homophonic (as is "Destruction's our delight"), but a few are highly imitative, including the drawn-out final chorus of Cupids. To accommodate the amateur singers, Purcell made the rhythms easy to remember:

# Historical Window

## THE FIRST PUBLIC MUSICAL ENTERTAINMENTS

For hundreds of years secular music was rarely heard outside the noble courts of Europe. (Today, with our ready access to music, it is hard to imagine such a time.) Then, in 1637, the first opera house, the Teatro San Cassiano, opened in Venice. This was probably the first time that anyone with the price of admission had the opportunity to listen to secular music in a public place. Over the next 30 years, seven more opera houses opened in Venice, and soon there were opera houses from Milan in the north to Naples in the south.

It was appropriate that Venice took the lead. The city had long been a center of innovation in music and other arts, and the Venetians were (and still are) shrewd entrepreneurs. One visitor remarked that operas "are the industry of the people, the wealth of the country itself, from whence it seems that they have had their origins and where equally it will suffice to say that they perform them more as business than pleasure."

Opera was less than four decades old when the Teatro San Cassiano opened its doors. Even in that brief period, however, the staging of operas had become extraordinarily elaborate. Here is a contemporary description of a 1637 production of the opera *Andromeda* (Andromeda is the wife of Perseus, who in the opera rescues her from a sea monster):

> The curtain disappears. The scene was entirely at sea. In the distance was a view of water and rocks so calculated that its naturalness (although feigned) moved the spectators to question whether they were in a theater or at a real seashore. The scene was quite dark except for the light given by a few stars which disappeared one after another, giving way to Aurora [the goddess of the dawn], who came to make the prologue. She was dressed entirely in silver cloth with a shining star on her brow, and appeared inside a very beautiful cloud which sometimes grew large and sometimes small, and oh, lovely surprise! circled across the sky on the stage. . . .
>
> Then Juno [the goddess of marriage] came out on a golden car drawn by her peacocks, blazing in a coat of gold cloth with a superb variety of jewels on her head or in her crown. To the amazed delight of the spectators the car turned from right to left as it pleased. This character was, and was not, in a machine. He *was*, we must admit, since he was flying; he was *not*, since one saw no other machine but that of a flying body. . . .

FIGURE 10.3 The elaborate backstage machinery (left) required for the staging Giovanni Leqrenzi's *Germanico su Reno*, produced in Venice in 1675. When the dazzling set (right) was in place, the audience could surrender to the special effects just as we do in a modern cinema.

The scene turned in a moment from the wood to the seascape. Neptune [the god of the sea] appeared and Mercury [the messenger god] came out to meet him in a wonderful machine. Neptune was on a great silver shell drawn by four sea horses and a sky blue mantle covered him. [Later in the opera] the sea monster came out. This animal was made with such beautiful cunning that, although not real, he put people in terror. Except for the act of tearing to pieces and devouring, he did everything as if alive and breathing. Perseus [the son of Zeus] arrived on Pegasus [a winged horse] and, with three blows of a lance and five with a rapier, he overthrew the monster and killed it. . . .

The sky opened and one saw Jove [Juno's husband, the supreme god of the Greek pantheon; also known as Jupiter] and Juno in glory with other divinities. This great machine descended to the ground to the accompaniment of a concerto of voices and instruments truly from heaven. The two heroes, joined to each other, were conducted to the sky. Here the royal and ever worthy occasion had an end.

*continued*

Such descriptions convey the same fascination with special effects that exists in motion pictures today. As with early horror films like *King Kong*, the technicians apparently had trouble making certain effects (the monster's "tearing to pieces and devouring") look entirely realistic. What is remarkable about these seventeenth-century effects, of course, is that they were achieved entirely with human-powered cable-and-pulley systems (see Figure 10.3). Audiences came expecting to be thrilled, and they were seldom disappointed.

Such spectacular productions drew visitors to Italy from all over Europe. The English traveler John Evelyn (1620–1706) wrote this account of an evening at the opera in Venice in 1646:

This night, having with my Lord Bruce taken our places before, we went to the Opera where comedies and other plays are represented in recitative music by the most excellent musicians vocal and instrumental, with a variety of scenes painted and contrived with no less art of perspective, and machines for flying in the aire and other wonderful motions; taken together it is one of the most magnificent and expensive diversions the wit of man can invent. . . . This held us by the eyes and ears till two in the morning.

Although most of the solo writing is in recitative, it varies from simple declamation over slow-moving harmonies to embellished passages with elaborate accompaniments. Much of the harpsichord continuo must be improvised, as Purcell himself probably did at the first performance. Throughout our excerpt, the vocal lines and the instrumental accompaniment are punctuated by dotted rhythms that suggest the conflict between Dido and Aeneas and the command supposedly issued by Jove. (By mid-century the French had created an instrumental overture associated with royalty, whose slow introduction featured dotted rhythms.)

Purcell's music is far better than either the prosaic libretto or the modest circumstances of *Dido*'s composition warranted. Despite the sketchy characterizations (Aeneas, for example, is scarcely established), his music conveys intense emotions with a convincing directness.

After its initial performance, two centuries were to pass before *Dido and Aeneas* was performed again. Today it is a staple of professional and amateur companies the world over.

# *Part Three*

## THE AGE OF
## TONALITY
## (1690–1910)

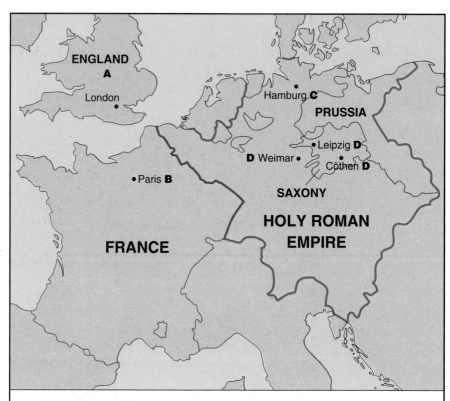

FIGURE 1 Western Europe during the Age of Enlightenment.

———— Boundary of the
Holy Roman Empire

**A** Sir Isaac Newton (mathematician, physicist; 1642–1727); published *Principia* in 1687
John Locke (philosopher; 1632–1704); published *Essay Concerning Human Understanding* in 1690
George Frideric Handel (composer; 1685–1759)
Samuel Johnson (writer; 1709–1784); published *Dictionary of the English Language* in 1775
**B** Denis Diderot (1713–1784); editor of *Encyclopédie* from 1745–1772
François Voltaire (philosopher, writer; 1694–1778)
Jean-Philippe Rameau (composer; 1683–1764)
**C** Georg Philipp Telemann (composer; 1681–1767); in Hamburg from 1721
**D** Johann Sebastian Bach (composer; 1685–1750); in Weimar 1708–1717; in Cöthen 1718–1722; in Leipzig 1723–1750

# THE LATE BAROQUE (1690–1750)

## The Age of Enlightenment

*I*n the waning years of the seventeenth century, the Hapsburg family in Austria and the Bourbon family in France ruled much of Europe with a firm hand. The rest of Europe was divided into hundreds of petty principalities locked in constant squabbles.

About 90 percent of the European population lived harsh, short lives as peasants or urban laborers. Beset by war, famine, and plague (the last outbreaks of the Black Death occurred in the 1720s), they had little time or opportunity for cultivating music seriously. (Moreover, what music they knew was passed on orally and is lost to us.)

But for more fortunate Europeans, the first half of the eighteenth century was a time of extraordinary philosophical, political, and cultural ferment. These were years in which the foundations of our modern democratic institutions were being laid. Indeed, the American Revolution of 1776 had its roots in the work of a small group of intrepid intellectuals and scientists who presided over what historians call the *Age of Enlightenment* (see map, Figure 1).

The Enlightenment rested on an optimistic belief in the ability of men and women to solve the perennial problems of humanity through rational discourse and on the conviction that disciplined minds could unlock nature's secrets through scientific inquiry. Sir Isaac Newton, for example, based his celebrated *Principia* (1687) on mathematics and experiment rather than on what he referred to contemptuously as "speculation."

In his *Essay Concerning Human Understanding* (1690), the English philosopher John Locke proposed that the newborn infant was a *tabula rasa*, or "empty slate," who, with the aid of reason and experience, could discover the underlying pattern and order of the universe. On the heels of a century marked by witchcraft and black magic, Locke's thesis had strong appeal for advocates of the Enlightenment. The French scholar Denis Diderot (1713–1784), who assumed the editorship of the *Encyclopédie* in 1745, symbolized the desire of scientists and thinkers to define and expand the base of knowledge. The

201

FIGURE 2  Instead of citing divine intervention to explain historical events, in his social histories Voltaire wrote of natural causes in the development of science, the arts, and philosophy. Ever the skeptic, he observed, "History is nothing more than a tableau of crimes and misfortunes."

English writer Samuel Johnson's (1709–1784) massive *Dictionary of the English Language* (1755) reflected a desire to codify and organize a rich and complex language.

The most passionate advocate of the Enlightenment, however, was François Voltaire (1694–1778; Figure 2). The son of a notary, Voltaire studied law at the University of Paris. Twice during his early years he was thrown into the Bastille by powerful aristocrats whose anger he had incurred. Devoted to the principles of fairness and justice, Voltaire spent the rest of his life writing satirical attacks on the abuses of power. He rejected the formal God of the Church and professed belief in a deity based on reason rather than on faith. His most celebrated work, the drama *Candide* (1759), pokes fun at philosophers who ponder unanswerable questions rather than attending to life's pressing problems. When Voltaire died at the age of 84, he was refused a church burial until a sympathetic abbot intervened.

And yet the Enlightenment was not a democratic movement. Louis XIV, as we have seen, governed as an absolute ruler. Absolutism continued under Louis XV and ended only with the execution of Louis XVI in 1793. Over these years, European dukes and princes did their best to imitate the lavish scale and style of the French regime. But in laboratories and studies all over Europe, scientists and philosophers continued to reflect and to write, whether supported, opposed, or ignored by their governments.

# Chapter 11

## INSTRUMENTAL MUSIC

The stylistic roots of Baroque music, as we have seen, were primarily vocal. Late Baroque music, by contrast, was significantly influenced by the new instrumental styles. This may seem an odd way to characterize a period that produced an enormous amount of music meant to be sung, but even that music bears the strong stamp of the instrumental style.

## THE LATE BAROQUE STYLE

Take, for example, the most obvious characteristic of late Baroque music, its *regularity*. Both the meter and the rhythm of this music are constant and well marked. Late Baroque melodies begin and remain at a steady, often high level of energy, rarely rising to a pronounced peak. Such melodies are well suited to music played by ten fingers on a keyboard instrument. A singing voice, on the other hand, moves more naturally in a succession of phrases toward a climax.

Or take *continuity*. A violinist can prolong a musical line indefinitely, as often happens in late Baroque music, but a singer is obliged to take a breath every so often. Or, finally, take the so-called motion by leaps that is also characteristic of many late Baroque melodies. A keyboard player can execute bold leaps, especially in rapid passages, with far greater ease than a singer can. In fact, eighteenth-century singers were expected to negotiate instrumentally conceived lines of such length and complexity that they had to stay in constant training; the best performers were genuine superstars who were accorded the acclaim reserved today for sports heroes.

Regular meter, continuous lines, and motion by leaps make for music that is highly charged. We often tap our feet when we listen to late Baroque music in response to its exuberance. It is not surprising that fans of rock 'n' roll, in which strong, regular meter prevails, also enjoy music by Bach, Handel, and other late Baroque composers.

The themes of late Baroque music are clear-cut and compact, sometimes little more than a motive. As we listen to a typical movement, we feel that we have heard all the principal thematic material within the first 5 or 10 seconds. In the passages that follow, the themes and motives are prolonged by a single-minded process known as **spinning-out** (a clumsy translation of the German *Fortspinnung* used by most English-language writers), in which an idea, or fragments of it, is extended through *repetition* and *variation*. Late Baroque composers tend to exhaust the possibilities of a single musical idea in one movement and then turn to a completely different idea in the next. To compensate for the lack of thematic variety within a movement, they often introduce a profusion of closely related voices in counterpoint. Not until the last half of the eighteenth century did composers regularly resolve the demands of two or more contrasting themes *within* a single movement.

As in the early Baroque, the keyboard player (a harpsichordist or an organist) provided the foundation of the continuo group. As harmony became increasingly triadic and as the range of dissonance widened, the continuo group assumed greater responsibility for supplying these elements. The continuo reflects the passion of late Baroque composers for filling in every nook and cranny of musical space. The regular, rapid harmonic rhythm of late Baroque music helps to create and sustain its high energy and compelling momentum.

The late Baroque consolidated the system of tonality, which had evolved gradually throughout the seventeenth century. Tonality exhibited a logic and a scientific rigor (especially evident in the writings of composer/theorists like Jean-Philippe Rameau, whom we shall meet in Chapter 12) that reflected the spirit of the Enlightenment. Before tonality, only a limited range of triads sounded "in tune." The reason is that in the Western scale a small discrepancy in the overtone series prevents all the fifths from being pure. The emergence of tonality coincided with dozens of proposals by music theorists for a more precise tuning of scales that would enable composers to write in a wide range of keys. Between 1722 and 1742 Johann Sebastian Bach wrote two "well-tempered" sets of preludes and fugues that traversed all 24 keys.

Most important, tonality gave composers a way of fashioning more ambitious structures for instrumental compositions. Before the late Baroque, most instrumental pieces had been short, like popular music today. Some vocal pieces were a good bit longer, but there the words supplied the scaffolding. With the advent of tonality, composers could devise more sustained, standardized forms. In their externals these forms were simple and flexible, challenging composers to fill them out in an imaginative way.

Regularity, the single-minded development of one idea at a time, tonality, and standardized forms were all manifestations of the late Baroque passion for *order*, a passion shared by the philosophers and scientists of the time. Even the formal gardens of the eighteenth century reflect this desire to impose order on everything in the environment (Figure 11.1).

Late Baroque composers wrote their instrumental music for small groups of performers. The largest **ensemble** (a group of musicians performing together) seldom numbered more than 15 or 20 players rather than the 60 to 90 common in modern symphony orchestras. The string family, which had developed rapidly

FIGURE 11.1 Around 1700, the formal gardens of Chatsworth in Derbyshire, England, featured parterres, statues, and fountains inspired by those at Versailles. At one point, Chatsworth employed a battalion of 80 gardeners to keep nature manicured.

during the seventeenth century, formed the core of Baroque ensembles, although such instruments as the high trumpet, the oboe, the recorder, and the pipe organ were prominently featured. Baroque instrumental music is very colorful, and yet the success of individual musical ideas does not usually depend on a specific tone color. Composers freely arranged their works and those of others for different instrumental combinations. Moreover, the continuo supplies a continuous wash of sound in Baroque music that tempers the prominence of individual tone colors.

In socially progressive England there was an upsurge of amateur orchestras during the late Baroque. There instrumentalists performed for their own pleasure the new music from Italy, Germany, and France. On the Continent, however, most musicians were employed by the church, by towns and cities, or by wealthy patrons. Those who could afford to maintained bands of horn and trumpet players to accompany them on the hunt (Color Plate 5) or in battle. Rulers who were especially fond of music maintained a staff of household musicians to play at banquets and receptions. Because this music was performed indoors, often in intimate surroundings, it became known as **chamber music.** The term comes from the German *Kammer,* a small room well suited to performances by a handful of musicians.

Whether ensemble music or chamber music, there were three principal varieties of late Baroque instrumental music:

- The **concerto** (from the Italian *concertare,* "to agree, to get together"). The major form of ensemble music, calling for one or more soloists.
- The **suite.** A loosely organized series of stylized dances or dance-related movements, suitable either for chamber or ensemble performance.
- The **sonata.** A chamber work for one or more soloists; the most common type was the trio sonata.

In addition to these formal types, two important compositional techniques characterize much of the music written during this period: *improvisation* and *fugue.* We shall examine all these types and techniques through the music of four of the most celebrated composers of the late Baroque.

## THE CONCERTO GROSSO

Originally the term *concerto* had been applied to both vocal and instrumental music. By the late seventeenth century, however, it had come to mean a purely instrumental work. The concerto evolved in three different directions: the *concerto grosso,* the *concerto ripieno,* and the *solo concerto.* The earliest was the concerto grosso, which emerged in the last years of the seventeenth century as the most important form of ensemble music. It grew out of smaller chamber works, and the term **concerto grosso** referred to a "large consort [group]" of performers, as distinguished from the **concertino,** or "little consort" of solo instruments. By the time Arcangelo Corelli's 12 Concerti Grossi, Op. 6,* were published in 1714, the phrase had come to signify a composition in several movements built on the interplay between the concerto grosso and the concertino. Corelli's concerti grossi exploited the rich sonorities of the strings as well as the new system of tonality. Although Corelli's work was probably composed for use in the most festive services of the church year, the music was quickly assimilated, especially in England, into the expanding repertoire of private and amateur orchestras. Gradually, the large group came to be known as the *tutti* ("all") or, more frequently, as the *ripieno* ("full"). By the early eighteenth century, the concerto grosso had become standardized into a three-movement form in a fast-slow-fast arrangement.

The other two varieties of concerto explored the extremes of the concerto-grosso texture. The **concerto ripieno** was a work written for the full ensemble; it specified no concertino and included few passages for a reduced ensemble. The

*Op. stands for *opus,* Latin for "work." During the seventeenth century, music publishers adopted the practice of assigning an opus number to each of a composer's successive works.

**solo concerto,** on the other hand, reduced the concertino to a single instrument and played the soloist off against the ripieno. Until about 1720 the concerto grosso was the dominant form.

## JOHANN SEBASTIAN BACH (1685–1750)

Bach (see Figure 1.4, page 14) is considered by many to have been the greatest composer of the Baroque era, and by almost all to have been the most powerful musical intellect in the Western tradition. He dominated every form of late Baroque music except opera (Chapter 12). Born in the Lutheran region of north-central Germany, Bach belonged to a family that included generations of musicians. In his immediate family he was the last of eight children, only four of whom survived infancy—a typical mortality rate in the eighteenth century. Bach had the encouragement of his family; given the number of his musical relatives, it would be surprising if young Sebastian had chosen to become anything *other* than a musician.

Bach had a difficult childhood. By the time he was 10, both his parents had died and he went to live in a nearby town with an older brother, Johann Cristoph, an organist. Here Bach received his first, and perhaps his only, keyboard lessons. When he reached 15, his brother's growing family found itself cramped for space and he was sent to a church school in the northern German town of Lüneburg. There he earned his keep by singing (as a soprano, until his voice changed) and by providing instrumental accompaniments on the harpsichord and violin. Despite the uncertainties of these early years, Bach received a broad liberal education, including instruction in Greek and Latin.

Shortly after his eighteenth birthday, Bach was offered his first position, as organist at a church in the town of Arnstadt. Evidently he had already become a skilled performer, because most of his musical duties in Arnstadt were as a performer rather than a composer. During his four years there he married his second cousin, Maria Barbara Bach.

After another brief stint as a church organist, Bach spent the next 14 years (1708–1722) in the employ of two wealthy aristocrats. He served first with Duke Wilhelm Ernst in the nearby town of Weimar, where he acted as organist and, eventually, as concertmaster (leader of the Duke's instrumentalists). The Duke greatly admired Bach's playing, and Bach is believed to have composed much of his organ music, as well as a considerable amount of sacred vocal music, while in Weimar. After eight years at Weimar, he learned of a more challenging position as *Kapellmeister* (leader of both instrumentalists and singers) at the court of Prince Leopold of Cöthen. Determined to move on, he demanded his release in such bold terms that he enraged his employer. It may be hard for us to understand today, in a time when many musicians are superstars, but in Bach's day a court musician—even a *Kapellmeister*—enjoyed a status little different from that of a cook or other high-level servant. So angered was the Duke at his organist's presumption of independence that he had Bach clapped into jail for almost four weeks and then dismissed him in disgrace. Prince Leopold was nevertheless delighted to receive Bach in Cöthen, where he was to remain for six years. Stimulated by the active and varied musical life at Cöthen, Bach turned more earnestly to composition. He completed his famous set of six Brandenburg Concertos during this period.

Prince Leopold, an enthusiastic lover of music, frequently took his *Kapellmeister* and a small group of musicians along with him on trips. On returning from one of those trips, Bach learned that his wife, who had borne seven children, had died suddenly and was already buried. Now in his mid-thirties, Bach next year married a young singer, Anna Magdalena Wilken, with whom he found great happiness and who bore 13 more children. Several of Bach's offspring became composers and musicians of distinction, among them Carl Philipp Emanuel Bach and Johann Christian Bach.

At this same time Prince Leopold married a woman who had little interest in music, and shortly his own interest began to wane. Bach, with his role at the court diminished, decided it was time to move on once again. In 1722 he applied for the recently vacated position of *Kantor* (choirmaster) at St. Thomas's Church in Leipzig, a post similar to that held in Hamburg by the better-known Georg Philipp Telemann (see page 223), whom Bach had met and admired. In fact, the Leipzig town council first offered the post to Telemann and another musician, and Bach was accepted only after both had withdrawn.

As *Kantor,* Bach was expected to produce original compositions for both the church and the town. His duties also included instructing the students of the Thomas School, a chore he disliked. He refused to teach Latin and was obliged to pay a substitute. Moreover, he was dissatisfied with the musicians who were available to play his music—students and townfolk, for the most part. For much of the 25 years he spent in Leipzig, Bach remained at best on civil terms with the members of the town council, and frequently he quarreled openly with them. Even so, he managed to produce a series of masterpieces that would have been extraordinary under the best of conditions.

### Bach: Brandenburg Concerto No. 2 in F Major (ca. 1718)

Bach's most famous set of instrumental works consists of six concertos known as the Brandenburg Concertos, which Bach called *Concerts avec plusieurs instruments* ("Concertos with various instruments"). Although Bach presented these concertos to the Margrave of Brandenburg in 1721, he had written them some years before (Figure 11.2). They were never performed by the Margrave's musicians, and the manuscript languished in the Margrave's library until his death. (Bach had doubtless performed the concertos in Cöthen and perhaps in Weimar as well.)

These six concertos encompass every dimension of the contemporary Italian concerto. Numbers 1, 3, and 6 are ripieno concertos. No. 2 is a concerto grosso. Numbers 4 and 5, though nominally concerti grossi, contain elements of the solo concerto as well (solo violin in No. 4 and solo harpsichord in No. 5). Even

FIGURE 11.2  A page
from the first movement
autograph of Bach's Bran-
denburg Concerto No. 2.
In the style of the day,
Bach dedicated his six
new concertos to "His
Princely Highness the
Margrave of Brandenburg,
from his very humble and
faithful servant Johann
Sebastian Bach." He
asked the Margrave not to
despise the "small talent
God has given me."

where they fit traditional forms, Bach's instrumental combinations are unusual. No. 6 includes the lower strings but no violins. In No. 5 the concertino includes a harpsichord, previously restricted to the continuo group. At a time when the typical concertino included a few strings and perhaps a recorder or an oboe, Bach's rich concertino in No. 2 includes trumpet, recorder,* oboe, and violin.

Bach's treatment of the concerto forms themselves was equally innovative. The first movement of Concerto No. 2 is cast in **ritornello form.** The ritornello ("recurring theme") is a theme played by the entire ensemble (ripieno) at intervals throughout the movement. By convention, a movement in ritornello form must open and close with a statement of the ritornello in the tonic key. It also returns in shortened form at intervals throughout the movement. Although the ritornelli are not note-for-note repeats, they provide a sturdy framework for the movement as a whole.

The sections between the occurrences of the ritornello are known as *episodes* and are played by the concertino. An episode may utilize entirely new material or may draw on material from the ritornello. Within the movement, there can be as many statements of the ritornello, and as many episodes, in as many keys as the composer wishes. Ritornello form was one of the most common organizational schemes in late Baroque instrumental music. Indeed, Bach transferred the ritornello concept to other genres such as choral music (as we shall see in the next chapter).

In the first movement of the Concerto No. 2 (Listening Guide 27), Bach makes a careful distinction between the material assigned to the ripieno and that assigned to the concertino. The ritornello (always assigned to the ripieno) consists of four short phrases of two measures each. In the first three phrases the

---

*A predecessor of the flute, the recorder was held vertically and the player blew through a mouthpiece.

# Listening Guide 27

## J. S. BACH: Brandenburg Concerto No. 2 in F Major, first movement

CD 2, TRACKS 8–10
TAPE 2B, TRACKS 2–4
DURATION: 5:04

*For ease of reference we have numbered the appearances of the ritornello (always played by the ripieno) and the concertino, as well as the seven parallel cadences (shown in bold-face in the Time column) that occur on six of the seven degrees of the F-Major scale. Bach's rapid alternations between ritornello and concertino are supplanted as the movement progresses by lengthier statements of both. Except for a rest after Cadence No. 6, the movement is rhythmically continuous throughout. The arrows (→) in the Location column show where two successive events are texturally continuous.*

*Form: Ritornello*

| | LOCATION | TIME | COMMENTS |
|---|---|---|---|
| 1 | Ritornello No. 1 → | **0:00** | Full statement of the ritornello in the tonic key. |
| | Cadence No. 1 | **0:15** | First statement of the unifying cadence. |
| | Concertino No. 1a (Violin) | 0:20 | First statement of the concertino theme. |
| | Ritornello No. 2a | 0:26 | Fragmentary statement of the ritornello opening. |
| | Concertino No. 1b (Oboe) | 0:31 | Second statement of the concertino theme. |
| | Ritornello No. 2b | 0:36 | Fragmentary statement of the ritornello. |
| | Concertino No. 1c (Recorder) | 0:41 | Third statement of the concertino theme. |
| | Ritornello No. 2c | 0:46 | Fragmentary statement of the ritornello. |
| | Concertino No. 1d (Trumpet) | 0:51 | Fourth statement of the concertino theme. |
| | Ritornello No. 2d → | 0:56 | Third and fourth bars of the ritornello. |

second measure repeats the first measure, either exactly (first phrase) or nearly exactly (second and third phrases). The fourth phrase provides a strong cadence. The first and third phrases share similar rhythms, as do the second and fourth. The theme begins and ends on the same note. Together, these correspondences create a symmetrical and sturdy theme:

Ripieno violin, concertino recorder, oboe, and violin

**first phrase**

| LOCATION | | TIME | COMMENTS |
|---|---|---|---|
| **2** | Cadence No. 2 | **1:06** | In C Major, the fifth degree (dominant) of F Major. |
| | Concertino No. 2 (Trumpet) | 1:11 | Even higher than the first statement. |
| | Ritornello No. 3 → | 1:17 | First two bars of ritornello, minor mode, trumpet trill. |
| | Sequence → | 1:21 | A threefold descending sequence. |
| | Cadence No. 3 | **1:34** | In D Minor, the sixth degree of F Major. |
| | Ritornello No. 4 → | 1:39 | An elaborate development. |
| **3** | Cadence No. 4 | **2:26** | In B-flat Major, the fourth degree (subdominant) of F Major. |
| | Concertino No. 3 (Recorder, Violin, Oboe, Trumpet) | 2:30 | The most elaborate episode of the concertino, including all four solo instruments. |
| | Ritornello No. 5 → | 2:51 | Another elaborate development. |
| | Sequence → | 3:14 | A slightly different version of the same descending sequence. |
| | Cadence No. 5 | **3:27** | In G Minor, the second degree of F Major. |
| | Ritornello No. 6 → | 3:32 | Another extensive development, in which the concertino instruments play a prominent role. |
| **4** | Cadence No. 6 | **4:15** | In A Minor, the third degree of F Major. Followed by the first full rest in the movement. |
| | Ritornello No. 7 → | 4:20 | Begins with a unison statement of the beginning of the ritornello theme before adding a final developmental episode featuring the concertino. |
| | Cadence No. 7 | **4:55** | In the tonic key. |

second phrase

third phrase

fourth phrase = cadence

With its ornamental trill and nearly continuous rhythms, the theme assigned exclusively to the concertino is well suited to solo performance:

The organization of the movement is more systematic than just an alternation between ripieno and concertino. Each degree of the F-Major scale except the seventh receives one of the ritornello cadences. At the beginning of the movement the alternations between ritornello and concertino are rapid, serving to introduce each of the four solo instruments (violin, oboe, recorder, and trumpet, in that order). As the movement progresses, the statements of the ritornello and the concertino become lengthier and more complex. For example, the central episode of the concertino presents all four instruments in successive imitation. The sixth statement of the ritornello (dominated by the instruments of the concertino) elaborates on all four phrases of the ritornello. Twice in the course of the movement Bach presents a threefold descending sequence of the kind that tonality had made possible.

The two remaining movements exhibit equally original structures within the conventional framework. The slow movement uses only three instruments from the concertino (recorder, oboe, and violin; the trumpet would have been too loud) and continuo. The movement is based almost entirely on a brief but expressive "sighing" theme:

This theme is treated in a series of continuous imitations between the three treble instruments—more than two dozen in less than three and a half minutes. Most composers would have settled for two instruments, but Bach preferred the richest possible counterpoint.

The unusual finale is dominated almost entirely by the concertino. It opens with a brilliant trumpet theme in the highest register (the trumpet has been silent during the slow movement):

Bach then brings in the theme imitatively in all the solo instruments, building from a single voice to four voices. He fragments the theme (as in measure 3—though without the trills) and elaborates on the fragments by introducing further imitation. Four sequential passages maintain the dancelike energy.

Each of the three movements makes use of such late Baroque features as regular harmonic rhythm and thematic spinning out, but each exhibits individual qualities that demonstrate Bach's extraordinary imagination. In spite of the richness and complexity of Bach's textures, there is a sense of balance and order. Moreover, players feel as if Bach wrote each part just for them; the Brandenburg Concertos are as much fun to play as they are to hear.

## THE SOLO CONCERTO

The solo concerto is a work in several movements in which a single soloist plays against the ripieno on a regular, contrasting basis. While still joining in the tuttis, the soloist replaces the concertino of the concerto grosso and functions even more prominently throughout. By the second decade of the eighteenth century, a three-movement, Fast-Slow-Fast plan had become standard. The solo concerto offered Baroque composers the maximum opportunity for virtuoso display in an instrumental work.

## ANTONIO VIVALDI (1678–1741)

While Bach's Brandenburg Concerto No. 2 represents the ordered, balanced phase of late Baroque music, the music of Antonio Vivaldi preserves some of its seventeenth-century extravagance. Vivaldi was born and raised in Venice. The "red priest" (as he was dubbed because of his red hair) was ordained in 1703. Poor health obliged him to give up active duties only a year later, and from that time on he devoted himself exclusively to music.

For 36 years (1704–1740), interrupted only by periodic journeys to promote his music, Vivaldi served as the resident composer, conductor, teacher, and head administrator of the Conservatory of the Pietà ("compassion") in Venice. This music school, like many others throughout Italy, was founded to shelter orphans and illegitimate children, of whom—if we are to believe the accounts of contemporary visitors—there were a great many. In 1730 one traveler reported that the Pietà sometimes housed as many as six thousand girls. Apparently the city fathers spared no expense in making the best musical training available to the residents of the Pietà, thereby contributing to the rich musical life of this festival-oriented city.

## Vivaldi: "Autumn" from *The Four Seasons*, Op. 8 (ca. 1725)

*The Four Seasons,* Vivaldi's most popular work, consists of the first 4 (all solo violin concertos) in a series of 12 concertos that make up his Op. 8. Vivaldi dedicated this work to Count Venceslao Marzin, who doubtless paid an honorarium for the privilege of having this charming music performed for his own pleasure by his private orchestra. The members of such ensembles were usually domestic male servants (coachmen, liverymen, cooks) who, in return for a small supplement to their salary, doubled as musicians. Wealthier nobles might support a small ensemble of full-time musicians who nevertheless were treated as servants. It is unlikely that these Vivaldi concertos were intended for church use.

The concertos in *The Four Seasons* are unusual in that each is accompanied by a poem characterizing the season portrayed in the music. Vivaldi keys each line of the poems to its exact location within the score. Music accompanied by a descriptive text in this manner is called **program music.**

In "Autumn," the third concerto of the group (Listening Guide 28), Vivaldi views the season as a time of celebration. The first movement, in ritornello form, is titled "Dances and Songs of the Countryside." It opens with a cheerful theme in the ripieno that is heard five times during the movement, either in the tonic or another key:

In the first movement of "Autumn," the solo violin episodes are accompanied only by a bass line. In the second episode, keyed to the line "and the liquor of Bacchus [the Greek god of wine] flows more and more freely," the soloist embarks on a spirited series of rapid arpeggios and scales that suggest the effects of the wine on the happy peasants:

# Listening Guide 28

## VIVALDI: "Autumn" from *The Four Seasons*

CD 2, TRACKS [11]–[13]
TAPE 2B, TRACKS 5–7
DURATION: I, 4:48;
II, 2:28; III, 2:57

*Vivaldi's ritornello form is considerably simpler in structure than Bach's. The focus is less on formal organization than on virtuoso display. The through-composed slow movement serves as an interlude between the fast-paced outer movements. The italic text in the Comments column is a translation of the programmatic commentary in the score.*

*Form: Ritornello (I, III); through-composed (II)*

| LOCATION | TIME | COMMENTS |
|---|---|---|
| **1** I. ALLEGRO (Fast) | | |
| Ritornello 1 (opening) | **0:00** | *The peasants celebrate with song and dance the joy of the rich harvest.* Full statement of the ritornello in the tonic key of F Major. Bright chords in square rhythms, homophonic texture. Frequent contrasts between loud and soft passages, as well as between ripieno and concertino. |
| Episode 1 (solo violin) | 1:00 | *And full of the liquor of Bacchus . . .* Spirited series of arpeggios and scales. Fragments of the ritornello at 1:13 and 1:16. Tempo then alternates between fast and slow. |
| **2** Ritornello 2 | **1:56** | In G Minor, the second degree of F Major. |
| Episode 2 (solo violin) | 2:17 | Extravagant figuration that moves in stops and starts. |
| Ritornello 3 | **2:41** | Free paraphrase in C Major, the fifth degree (dominant) of F Major. |
| Episode 3 (solo violin) | 3:01 | Rapid arpeggios. |
| **3** "Larghetto" (Rather slow) | 3:08 | *they conclude their merrymaking with a nap.* Slow, dreamy passage. |
| | 3:42 | The ripieno introduces a hypnotic, short-short-LONG-LONG rhythm. |
| **4** Ritornello 4 (closing) "Allegro molto" (Very fast) | **4:28** | In the tonic key and identical to the first part of the opening ritornello. |

*continued*

| LOCATION | TIME | COMMENTS |
|---|---|---|
| **1** II. ADAGIO MOLTO (Very slow) | **0:00** | *All are made to leave off singing and dancing by the season, which invites many to enjoy a sweet sleep.* Slow-moving chords in the muted strings. The harpsichordist improvises an arpeggiated continuo accompaniment. |
| | 1:33 | More slow-moving chords over a lengthy dominant pedal point; prepares for the next movement. |
| **1** III. ALLEGRO (The Hunt) Ritornello 1 (opening) | **0:00** | *At dawn the hunters leave their homes with horns and guns and dogs.* The fullest statement, in *a-b-a* form. Features sharply dotted rhythms and homophonic textures. |
| Episode 1 (solo violin) | 0:32 | Double stops in the violin. |
| Ritornello 2 | **0:45** | In the tonic key. |
| Episode 2 (solo violin) | 0:53 | Double stops moving, after a sequence, to rapid arpeggios. |
| **2** Ritornello 3 | **1:14** | In the dominant key. |
| Episode 3 (solo violin) | 1:22 | *The animal flees; they follow its tracks.* Rapid, ascending arpeggios. |
| | 1:29 | *Already terrified and tired by the great tumult of the guns and dogs, wounded it tries . . .* Ripieno *tremolos* (the rapid change of bow directions on the same pitch), ascending sequence in the soloist playing rapid scales and arpeggios. |
| Ritornello 4 | **1:44** | Brief statement in the dominant key. |
| Episode 4 | 1:52 | Rapid arpeggios by the soloist with simple accompaniment by the ripieno. |
| **3** Ritornello 5 | **2:04** | In the tonic key. |
| Episode 5 (solo violin) | 2:12 | Rapid scales by the soloist answered by tremolos in the strings. |
| | 2:19 | *feebly to escape, but exhausted, it dies.* |
| Ritornello 6 (closing) | **2:36** | Full ensemble. Last phrase played softly. |

**COLOR PLATE 5**

*As director of the
Beauvais and Gobelins
tapestry factories, Jean-
Baptiste Oudry (1686–
1755) created spec-* *tacular scenes glorify-
ing life at the royal
court. In this portion of
the series* Hunts of
Louis XV, *three riders
carry hunting horns.* *What kind of music do
you suppose they played?
Which of these hunters
do you think is the
king?*

**COLOR PLATE 6**

*A Stradivarius violin, created in 1691 from pine, curly maple, ebony, and pearwood. The proportions and contoured outlines of violins are among the most pleasing shapes that humans have devised.*

**COLOR PLATE 7**
Francesco Solimena's
Elidoro Expelled by
Time *contains the dra-*
*matic exaggerations*
*typical of Baroque style.*
*Solimena (1657–1717)*
*was a popular and*
*influential artist in*
*Naples. As with com-*
*posers, painters fall in*
*and out of fashion, and*
*Solimena is largely for-*
*gotten today.*

**COLOR PLATE 8**
In The Orgy *(ca. 1734),*
*a painting from the se-*
*ries called* The Rake's
Progress, *William*
*Hogarth satirized the*
*English upper class in a*
*way that would have*
*been unthinkable a*
*century earlier. (A* rake
*was the contemporary*
*term for a fashionable*
*ladies' man.) Note how*
*two of the women are*
*conspiring to take ad-*
*vantage of the rake.*

In the final episode they have drunk themselves into a stupor, and the music slows almost to a halt—only to be jolted awake by a final statement of the extroverted ritornello.

The slow second movement is a dreamlike interlude in rich, slow-moving harmonies that are abruptly terminated by the lively "hunt" of the finale, a favorite theme of Baroque composers and painters (see Color Plate 5). The form, as in the opening movement, is ritornello, which here takes a partly comic, partly gruesome turn. Beginning with the rapid triplets of the third solo episode, Vivaldi portrays the dogs chasing down the hapless fox, which, in the final episode, is heard to expire. None of this tragedy, however, inhibits the final boisterous return of the ritornello.

While Vivaldi's themes and larger structures are simpler than those of Bach, Vivaldi's music shows more theatricality and flair. Bach packs his concerto with counterpoint, a feature absent from Vivaldi's concerto. The contrasts between these two composers reflect the variety and range of the late Baroque style.

## THE SUITE

The **suite** consists of a loosely organized series of dances or dance-related movements. Although the number of movements varies, they are generally unified by key, and sometimes by common thematic material. Most of the dances were drawn from Renaissance models, but as time passed they became *stylized* and enriched and were clearly intended for listening rather than for dancing. Because the suite is made up of numerous shorter pieces, it is less weighty than either the concerto grosso or the solo concerto.

Most of the movements in a suite are organized in **binary form,** in which the first half of the movement ends in a half cadence (usually on the dominant) and then repeats before the second half is played. The second half ends with a cadence back in the tonic key and then repeats as well. Because the cadences that mark the end of each half are sometimes no more emphatic than the internal cadences, the repeats in binary form may be hard to detect. The balanced halves and their repetitions do, however, impart stability and symmetry to binary form.

The origins of the suite lie especially in music for solo guitar and keyboard. During the first half of the eighteenth century the keyboard suite was customarily built around four dance types: the *allemande* (from Germany), the *courante* (of French and Italian origin), the *sarabande* (of Latin American and Spanish origin), and the *gigue* (from England). But there were no hard-and-fast rules about what a suite should contain. This was especially true of the ensemble suite, whose orchestration was considerably richer and more varied than that of most concertos.

# *Historical Window*

## THE GENIUS OF STRADIVARI

Antonio Stradivari (1644?–1737) has long been regarded as the greatest violin maker ever to have practiced that craft. Along with other famous violin makers, Nicolò Amati (his teacher) and Giuseppi Guarneri ("del Gesù"), Stradivari was born and trained in the small northern Italian town of Cremona (see the map on page 158), which had specialized in the manufacture of violins since the sixteenth century. In a career that spanned almost seven decades, Stradivari built an extraordinary number of instruments, about 650 of which survive today. Though most of them are violins, they include some three dozen cellos and a dozen violas. Many of his instruments have surely been lost over the years. If we count only those that have survived, however, we find that he must have turned out almost one instrument a month. That would be a phenomenal output for a craftsman of average ability. For a craftsman of Stradivari's genius, it is astonishing.

We know very little about Stradivari's life; no authentic portrait survives. His parents bore an old Cremonese name, although they may have fled Cremona temporarily during an outbreak of famine and plague from 1628 to 1630. We can only infer the year of his birth from the labels on his instruments, many of which give both the year of manufacture and Stradivari's age. Before he was 20 years old Stradivari must have been apprenticed to Amati, for the label of his first surviving instrument (1666) declares that he was Amati's pupil. As an apprentice, he also made harps, lutes, mandolins, and guitars. In July

## Handel: Suite in D Major from the *Water Music* (ca. 1715)

George Frideric Handel, whose biography we shall consider in Chapter 12, wrote most of his music for the theater. Among his instrumental works, however, are two celebrated suites—the *Water Music* and *Music for the Royal Fireworks*—that are as popular today as they were in Handel's own day. Both were written for performance out-of-doors. One of Handel's contemporaries recorded his impressions of the first performance of the *Water Music*, presented before King George I of England around 1715:

> About eight in the evening the King repaired to his barge. . . . Next to the King's barge was that of the musicians, about 50 in number, who played on all kinds of instruments, to wit trumpets, horns, oboes, bassoons, flutes, violins and basses. . . . The music had been composed specially by the famous Handel . . . His Majesty's principal Court

1667 he married a young widow, Francesca Feraboschi, who bore six children, including two sons who both became violin makers, though they barely outlived their father.

In 1680 Stradivari moved into a modest workshop on the Piazza San Domenico, where he remained for the rest of his life. By the time Amati died in 1684, Stradivari was recognized as the foremost instrument maker of his generation, and from this time on he seems to have concentrated almost exclusively on violin making. In 1698 his first wife died, and the following year (at 54) he married Antonia Maria Zambelli, with whom he had five more children.

Stradivari constantly refined the design of his violins. Those from the 1690s, known as the "Long Strads," differed significantly from the smaller, less robust instruments produced by Amati. Most experts regard the first two decades of the eighteenth century as Stradivari's golden age. During these years he developed the characteristic orange-brown varnish that seems crucial to the look and sound of his instruments (Color Plate 6). That varnish has never been duplicated. After 1720 it seems that he could no longer procure the best-quality maple that went into the backs of his violins. Yet he was still producing exquisite instruments when he died at the age of 92.

Over the centuries Stradivari's instruments have been scrutinized and analyzed in the minutest detail, and yet no one has ever succeeded in matching their richness, responsiveness, and power. In our age of mass production, it is comforting to know that not every achievement of our ancestors can be improved upon or even duplicated. Today, one of Stradivari's instruments in good condition fetches more than $500,000 at auction.

---

Composer. His Majesty approved of it so greatly that he caused it to be repeated three times in all, although each performance lasted an hour. . . . The evening was all that could be desired for the festivity, the number of barges and above all of boats filled with people desirous of hearing was beyond counting.

In 1733 Handel assembled for publication the three separate suites that make up the *Water Music,* though apparently he had composed them earlier. The most lavish is the Suite in D Major (Listening Guide 29), which calls for (in addition to the usual complement of strings) two trumpets and two horns (both prominently featured), two oboes, bassoon, and timpani. It consists of five movements:

I. [Fast]. Though Handel gave it no heading, the first movement is a typical Allegro in duple meter that serves as an overture (a musical introduction).

# *Listening Guide 29*

## HANDEL: Suite in D Major from the *Water Music*, movements II, IV, and V

CD 2, TRACKS 14 – 16
TAPE 2B, TRACKS 8–10
DURATION: II, 4:12;
IV, 1:18; V, 3:25

*The da capo form of the second movement is one of the most easily heard forms. The third and fifth movements are in compact binary forms that repeat in their entirety three times, with the middle repetition restricted to winds and brass. Note the brevity of the individual sections in both of these movements!*

*Forms: II: Da capo; IV and V: Binary*

| | LOCATION | TIME | COMMENTS |
|---|---|---|---|
| **1** | II. [Allegro] | | Called the "Alla Hornpipe" in Handel's day. |
| | *A*-Section | **0:00** | Syncopated melody in the strings and woodwinds. |
| | | 0:17 | Theme opening repeated in the trumpets and horns. |
| | | 0:29 | Alternation between strings/winds and brass. |
| | | 0:50 | Theme rounded out in the entire orchestra. |
| | *A*-Section repeated | **1:04** | Try hearing the formal subdivisions on your own. |
| **2** | *B*-Section | **2:07** | Middle section; strings and winds only. Largely in the minor mode and characterized by fast, steady rhythms in the strings. |
| **3** | Da capo of *A*-Section | **3:05** | Returns to the major mode. Repeats the opening *A*-Section verbatim. |
| **1** | IV. [Bourrée] | | Labeled an "Air" by Handel. |
| | 1. First half | **0:00** | Full orchestra in a rapid duple meter, homophonic texture. |
| | First half repeated | 0:04 | |
| | Second half | 0:08 | |
| | Second half repeated | 0:17 | |

The pattern consists of a theme played by the trumpets and echoed by the horns. The movement ends with a slow *bridge* (a connective passage) that leads directly to the second movement.

II. Known in Handel's time as the "Alla Hornpipe," the second movement is a rapid dancelike movement in triple meter. The form is repetitive: a lengthy

| LOCATION | | TIME | COMMENTS |
|---|---|---|---|
| **2** | 2. First half | **0:25** | Winds and brass only. |
| | First half repeated | 0:29 | |
| | Second half | 0:33 | |
| | Second half repeated | 0:41 | |
| | | | |
| | 3. First half | **0:50** | Exact repetition of the first statement. |
| | First half repeated | 0:54 | |
| | Second half | 0:58 | |
| | Second half repeated | 1:07 | |
| | | | |
| **1** | V. [Minuet] | | Labeled a "Chorus" by Handel. |
| | 1. First half | **0:00** | Full orchestra in a moderate, dignified triple meter. |
| | First half repeated | 0:11 | |
| | Second half | 0:22 | Reduced forces, then the full orchestra. |
| | Second half repeated | 0:45 | |
| | | | |
| **2** | 2. First half | **1:07** | Winds and brass only. |
| | First half repeated | 1:18 | |
| | Second half | 1:29 | Alternation between winds and brass. |
| | Second half repeated | 1:51 | |
| | | | |
| | 3. First half | **2:14** | Exact repetition of the first statement. |
| | First half repeated | 2:25 | |
| | Second half | 2:36 | As before, reduced forces, then the full orchestra. |
| | Second half repeated | 2:58 | |

opening section that repeats, a contrasting section, and then a *da capo* (meaning "from the head [beginning]") of the opening section, hence *A-A-B-A*. Da capo form was a popular way for late Baroque composers to emphasize the regularity and symmetry of their music. Because Handel's syncopated main tune is so appealing, we welcome its frequent recurrences:

III. *Lentement* (Slowly). The third movement is an ingratiating movement in triple meter that features a persistent *dotted rhythm* (long notes followed by short notes, so called because in the score the longer notes are followed by dots):

The form of this movement is identical to that of the second movement: a first section that repeats, a contrasting section, and a da capo of the opening section.

IV. [Fast]. Labeled an "Air," the fourth movement is a *bourrée,* a rapid dance in duple meter probably derived from French folk dance. Handel specifies three orchestrations, each of which receives a complete statement:

1. Trumpets and violins.
2. Horns and oboes.
3. All together.

Hence the scheme of the entire environment looks like this: *A-A-B-B / A-A-B-B / A-A-B-B.* The phrases in this movement are extremely short. Each *A*-Section consists of four symmetrical bars (2 + 2), and each *B*-Section consists of eight. (You can count these bars at the rate of about one bar per second.) The regularity of this movement reminds us of its dance origins.

V. *Coro* (Chorus). Though again without a heading, this movement in dignified triple meter is a *minuet,* a French dance that was the most popular social dance in aristocratic society during the Baroque. Its phrase structure and form are identical to those of the fourth movement, with the same sequence of instrumental combinations.

Despite the rigid structure, the repetitiveness, and the simple harmonic language of these movements, Handel's melodic inspiration never flags. There is a spontaneity about the music that amazed and delighted his contemporaries no less than it does us.

## THE TRIO SONATA

The sonata was the only form of late Baroque chamber music that did not derive from the dance. Earlier, sonata had meant simply some form of instrumental music, but by the eighteenth century the term generally referred to a composition in several movements for one to four soloists. The most common variety was the **trio sonata,** which employs two upper voices of nearly equal range supported by a well-defined bass line. It is called a trio sonata because it has three musical lines. In performance, however, a trio sonata requires four musicians: two treble soloists, a cellist playing the bass line, and a harpsichordist filling out the continuo line. (In earlier times, the cellist was actually a gambist—a performer on the viola da gamba, a precursor of the cello.) One of the most prolific composers of trio sonatas was Bach's contemporary Georg Philipp Telemann.

## GEORG PHILIPP TELEMANN (1681–1767)

Today we think of Johann Sebastian Bach as the dominant figure of the late Baroque, but in Bach's own time the most celebrated German composer living in Germany was Georg Philipp Telemann. In the major biographical dictionary of the day, Telemann received four times as much space as Bach.

Born to an upper-middle-class north German family of teachers and clerics, Telemann followed his parents' wishes by enrolling as a law student in Leipzig. His classmates recognized his musical talents, however, and soon he had organized a *collegium musicum* (Latin for "music society"). With students and professional musicians serving as voluntary members and with Telemann leading, the society staged several public concerts in Leipzig, at a time when such concerts were still extremely rare.

For almost a half century, from 1721 to his death in 1767, Telemann served as the *Kantor* (choirmaster) of the *Johanneum* (a Protestant boys' school) and as musical director of the five main churches in Hamburg. As choirmaster, Telemann instructed the pupils (in Latin), supervised their behavior, and trained them to read and perform music. He was also expected to compose two new cantatas (a genre to which we shall turn in the next chapter) a week and to compose special music for induction ceremonies, church consecrations, civic celebrations (of which there were many), and visits by official guests. Yet he still found time to write operas (Hamburg boasted the only public opera house in Germany) and to run a second collegium musicum.

### Telemann: Trio Sonata in A Minor from *Essercizii musici* (1740)

Telemann's *Essercizii musici* ("musical exercises") consists of 12 trio sonatas that he wrote to satisfy the growing demand of amateur musicians for interesting works of moderate difficulty. In the A-Minor Sonata (Listening Guide 30), the two treble parts are played by a soprano recorder and a violin. The differences in tone color between the two instruments make it easy to follow the voices as they intertwine. Frequently, as at the beginning of the final Allegro, they relate through imitation:

At other times they play together in parallel thirds; at still other times they present contrasting counterpoint. Telemann maintains forward momentum by frequent use of sequences.

The four brief movements of the A-Minor Sonata follow the standard organization of the trio sonata: Slow-Fast-Slow-Fast. Telemann builds each movement around a single theme. None of the first three movements contains any internal repeats, but toward the end of each the opening material returns in the tonic key to provide a kind of frame. The final Allegro, the most ambitious of the four movements, is in a clear-cut binary form on a considerably larger scale than in Handel's suite. In the first half the recorder leads the violin in closely spaced imitation. In the second half, which starts from the dominant cadence of the first half, the roles are reversed, with the violin leading the recorder back to the tonic key.

Although this is not music for beginners, such works encouraged the interest of the amateur performers on whom future composers would depend more and more for their livelihood. Telemann's contemporaries admired his music for its naturalness, its lack of pretension and artifice.

# Listening Guide 30

**TELEMANN:** Trio Sonata in A Minor
from *Essercizii musici,* fourth movement

CD 3, TRACK 1
TAPE 3A, TRACK 1
DURATION: 3:07

*Focus first on the manner in which the two treble instruments interact. Then focus on the symmetrical manner in which the form unfolds. Note that the scale of this binary form is considerably larger than that of the minuet and bourrée in the Handel suite.*

*Form: Binary*

| | LOCATION | TIME | COMMENTS |
|---|---|---|---|
| 1 | IV. [Allegro] First half | 0:00 | Recorder followed in close imitation by violin. Cadences in the dominant key. |
| | First half repeated | 0:37 | |
| 2 | Second half | 1:15 | Roles reversed: violin takes the lead. Moves from the dominant key back to the tonic key. |
| | Second half repeated | 2:10 | |

## IMPROVISATION

**Improvisation** is a style of playing in which the performer presents and develops musical ideas on the spot, without a written score. Today this style is kept alive by such jazz performers as Oscar Peterson and Keith Jarrett. As we have seen, when Baroque performers played the continuo, they improvised from a kind of musical shorthand. Every keyboard player was expected to be proficient in this skill. Baroque singers and other instrumentalists also were expected to embellish or ornament their notated parts when appropriate. Freely structured types of keyboard compositions like the *fantasia* ("fantasy") and the *toccata* (from the Italian *toccare,* "to touch" a keyboard) preserved improvisations that a performer/composer did not wish to lose. Unlike today's performers of art music, who carefully prepare their performances beforehand, musicians in the late Baroque viewed improvisation as a cornerstone of their art.

Toccata and Fugue in D Minor, probably composed between 1708 and 1717 while he was employed as court organist to Duke Wilhelm Ernst of Weimar.

Bach's reputation during his lifetime rested not only on the phenomenal finger and foot technique of his organ playing but also on his remarkable powers of improvisation—the spontaneous, on-the-spot creation of music. The *toccata* was a time-honored style of keyboard playing based on improvisation. Although Bach ultimately wrote out the Toccata and Fugue in D Minor (Listening Guide 31), it almost certainly preserves the essence of such an improvisation.* The toccata is through-composed, which meant that Bach could pursue his ideas without restraint. In this opening section Bach alternates deftly between different keyboard figurations (scales, arpeggios, and thick chords), exploits range, and makes dramatic use of pauses. For example, the very opening features a series of brief but arresting figures that descend precipitously. Bach's generous punctuation of rests with fermatas permitted the sound to reverberate throughout the sanctuary:

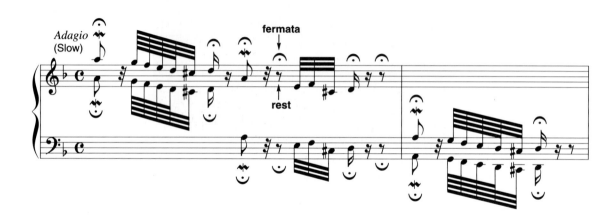

Bach's use of rests or long-held chords to link the sections, together with his frequent changes of tempo, reinforce the impression that this is an improvisation. He uses two *pedal points*—long-held tones played by the organist with the foot-operated pedal board—to build up richly dissonant harmonies that then resolve to major or minor triads.

In the four-voiced fugue that follows (whose subject is loosely related to material in the toccata), the first entry, though in the tonic key, begins on the dominant note (A) and is answered on the tonic note (D), then the dominant (A), and finally again on the tonic (D). This progression ensures that the harmonic momentum will be maintained. Bach builds his freewheeling subject on the rapid alternation between a stepwise pattern and a repeating pitch:

*Bach's "autograph"—that is, the version written in his own hand—does not survive, so we cannot be entirely sure that the eighteenth-century copies we have represent the original version.

# *Listening Guide 31*

## J. S. BACH: Toccata and Fugue in D Minor for Organ, BWV 565

CD 3, TRACK 2
TAPE 3A, TRACK 2
DURATION: 9:09

*The form of all three sections is dictated by Bach's love of surprise and spontaneous improvisation. Yet the overall work projects a feeling of unity and balance. The sections in the Toccata are all separated by dramatic rests whose function was at least partly to allow the rich sonorities to reverberate throughout the church. The seams between statements of the fugue subject and its episodes are much less clearly defined.*

*Form: Sectional (through-composed)*

| LOCATION | | TIME | COMMENTS |
|---|---|---|---|
| 1 | TOCCATA | **0:00** | Brief scale patterns descending dramatically, punctuated by rests and fermatas. |
| | | 0:19 | Over a pedal point, a richly dissonant chord builds upward, resolving to a major triad. |
| | | 0:34 | Rapidly ascending stepwise patterns, then treated in a descending sequence. |
| | | 0:56 | Another even more elaborate pedal point, resolving this time to a minor triad. |
| | | 1:16 | Brilliant passage work. |
| | | 1:31 | Cadence pattern alternating passage work with thick chords. |
| | | 2:06 | Brilliant passage work in rapid parallel sixths. |
| | | 2:22 | Final cadence in richly scored chords, resolving to a minor triad. |
| 2 | FUGUE | | |
| | Subject on dominant | **2:58** | Rapid alternation between a stepwise pattern and a repeating pitch. |
| | Answer on tonic | 3:04 | Higher than the first entry, and more extended. |
| | Answer on dominant | 3:22 | The highest entry, and the most extended. |
| | Answer on tonic | 3:56 | In the bass, played on the pedal board. |
| | Episode 1 | 4:11 | In the major, with thinner textures. Includes arpeggios that repeat in a question-answer pattern. |
| | Subject | 4:45 | In the treble, beginning on the dominant. |

*continued*

|   | LOCATION | TIME | COMMENTS |
|---|----------|------|----------|
| **3** | Episode 2 | **4:53** | Based on the arpeggios of Episode 1, now in minor. |
|   | Subject | 5:27 | In the bass pedals, accompanied by long trills. |
|   | Subject | 5:45 | In the middle voice, over a pedal point. |
|   | Episode 3 | 5:53 | Based loosely on fragments of the subject. |
|   | Subject | 6:20 | In the alto voice, over another pedal point. |
|   | Subject | 6:31 | In the bass pedals, played alone. |
| **4** | Episode 4 | **6:47** | Based on the arpeggios of Episode 1, now over a pedal point. |
|   |   | 7:27 | Unexpected, long-held chord. |
| **5** | TOCCATA FIGURATION RETURNS | **7:30** | Greatly extended series of cadences based on previous alternation between brilliant passage work and thick, heavy chords. |

The contrapuntal portions are broken up with toccata-like episodes that give extra force to the three returns of the fugal sections. Just when we expect the final cadence, Bach returns instead to the opening mood of the Toccata and ends in a blaze of fireworks. It must have been an electrifying experience to be present when Bach cut his imagination loose. Yet these very qualities of surprise and spontaneity which we so admire today were viewed by many of Bach's contemporaries, in an age of moderation and naturalness, as excessive.

# Chapter 12

## VOCAL MUSIC

The Enlightenment was an age of words, and the accomplishments of the great philosophers and scientists of the time depended in part on their command of the written language. It is no accident that the Enlightenment produced the first encyclopedia.

## WORDS AND MUSIC IN THE LATE BAROQUE

Although the idiomatic qualities of instruments played a major role in determining the shape and texture of late Baroque music, composers believed that the highest form of musical expression was achieved when music and words were brought together. At first glance, the uses to which words were put in the arts might appear to contradict the spirit of reason and scientific inquiry. Here is how the poet John Dryden, writing in 1687, describes the trumpet, flute, and violin in "A Song for St. Cecilia's Day":*

The trumpet's loud clangor
Excites us to arms,
With shrill notes of anger,
and mortal alarms.

The soft complaining flute
In dying notes discovers
The woes of hopeless lovers,
Whose dirge is whispered by the warbling lute.

Sharp violins proclaim
Their jealous pangs, and desperation,
Fury, frantic indignation,
Depth of pains, and height of passion,
For the fair disdainful dame.

---

*The English regarded St. Cecilia, an early Christian martyr and the supposed inventor of the organ, as the patron saint of music.

This is hardly an enlightened or reasoned view of either the instruments or of the emotions they are said to evoke. Dryden's images, which seem designed to stir the reader rather than to represent reality, are better suited to the theater than to the study. Baroque theater and painting were both built on emotions that are larger than life (Color Plate 7).

Yet it was precisely this extravagant tone that made a Baroque *text* (words set to music) so well suited to the musical style of the time. Late Baroque music, with its seamless textures, its dependence on harmonic sequences, and its insistence on treating one theme at a time, was an ideal vehicle for the representation of exaggerated emotions and moods. What we have is a paradox: A musical language based on tonality, a quasi-scientific system, was being used to represent very unscientific feelings. The paradox vanishes when we recognize that Dryden's emotional excesses are abstract representations rather than personal expressions of feelings.

During the early Middle Ages, most notated vocal music was written for performance in religious services. During the *ars nova* and Renaissance, however, a large number of secular vocal forms cultivated by the aristocracy came into prominence (discussed in Chapters 6 and 7), and this trend continued throughout the seventeenth century. Finally, in the late Baroque, vocal music written to be performed outside of religious services began to gain wide acceptance among the emerging merchant classes.

The three most popular types of vocal music in the late Baroque were the large-scale forms of opera, oratorio, and cantata, all of which shared certain patterns of organization. We look first at two very different manifestations of late Baroque opera, the Italian and the French.

## LATE BAROQUE OPERA

Late Baroque opera preserved some of the seventeenth-century fondness for extravagance and spectacle. The characters are larger than life, and the heroes are almost godlike in their heroism. Like Gary Cooper or John Wayne in a vintage western, they are models of virtue, without blemish or flaw. The nobility, who financed the operas, viewed these characters as extensions of themselves. The villains, without exception, are evil and treacherous. The plots serve to glorify aristocratic virtues, usually by means of a central character who is faced by a seemingly insurmountable problem but who overcomes it through courage, daring, and steadfastness.

Nevertheless, the librettos of late Baroque Italian opera differ in important respects from those of seventeenth-century opera. Under the leadership of two poets, Apostolo Zeno (1668–1750) and especially Pietro Metastasio (1698–1782), operas were purged of their overreliance on supernatural interventions, on machines, and on irrelevant (especially comic) episodes. Whereas the protagonists of seventeenth-century operas were often gods drawn from Greek or Roman mythology, the protagonists of Metastasio's dramas are generally historical figures with more complex personalities. Metastasio's reforms proved so popular that his 27 librettos were set almost a thousand times, and one of them was set 70 times. Most of them have a *lieto fine,* or "happy ending." This not only pleased audiences but also demonstrated that seemingly impossible situations could be resolved through the application of reason.

Metastasio introduced order and regularity into the libretto, which in turn affected the musical structure of Italian opera. Early Baroque opera was built on the new monodic style of recitative (page 164). Gradually composers began to emphasize certain portions of the drama by setting their texts as tuneful, stand-alone movements with independent musical structures. Composers called these new structures *arias* (from the Italian for "air," or "song"). The most common form was da capo, which we encountered in Handel's instrumental suite. Most Baroque arias are based on a single subject and, like late Baroque instrumental movements, express a single emotion. Although most arias were for a single voice, composers also wrote pieces for two or three soloists, in what were known as duets or trios. We can refer to all these stand-alone types as *set pieces.*

In the second half of the seventeenth century, composers had organized their operas freely, sometimes beginning and sometimes ending a *scene* (a dramatic unit) with recitative, and either including or not including a set piece in the course of a scene. Metastasio standardized this procedure. In so doing, he bore in mind that the hero and heroine in an opera were expected to have more arias than the subordinate characters, that the arias for each character were expected to be distributed more or less evenly over the drama, and that each character was expected to exit the stage after finishing his or her number. Within these constraints he organized his scenes around a succession of recitative-aria units, each sung by a single character. The characters appear one after the other, each furthering the action in a recitative and then, in an aria, making an emotional response to the action. Occasionally the singers come together in an ensemble. The scenes are usually grouped into three acts.

This form of Italian opera became the most popular form in Germany and England as well as in Italy. Composers generally referred to an opera on a libretto by Zeno, Metastasio, and others as a *dramma per musica* ("drama with music"). Occasionally they referred to such a work as an *opera seria* ("serious opera"), and this is the term that late-nineteenth-century historians adopted to characterize Italian opera of this period. Although the structure of an opera seria was more rigid and predictable than that of later forms of opera, the greatest composers of the period surmounted such limitations. No composer was more successful in doing so than George Frideric Handel.

## GEORGE FRIDERIC HANDEL (1685–1759)

Handel (Figure 12.1), who was born and raised in northern Germany, received his musical education in Italy, and spent most of his active career in England, exemplifies the cosmopolitan nature of late Baroque music. His father, a

FIGURE 12.1 George Frideric Handel was born in the same year and in the same province of Germany as J. S. Bach, but Handel wrote primarily for the concert hall, not the church. And he composed with a large audience in mind. For example, Handel scored his *Royal Fireworks Music* for a band accompanied by 101 cannons.

respected barber-surgeon (until the nineteenth century these two tasks were performed by the same person), was 63 when Handel was born. Determined that the boy study law, the father tried to block his access to music, despite his talent and inclination. In protest (or so the story goes), young Handel had a clavichord smuggled into the attic of their house.

His father died when Handel was 12. Though Handel was now free to do as he chose, he entered the University of Halle when he reached 18 and probably studied law for a year or two. After receiving a modicum of formal musical training in Halle, he went briefly to Hamburg, where he played in the opera orchestra and composed his earliest dramatic works. In 1706 he decided to follow the action and left for Italy. There he remained for almost five years, meeting Corelli in 1707 and building a reputation as a talented composer. While in Venice, he came to the attention of the north German House of Hanover, whose Elector was heir to the English throne and became King George I in 1714.* In 1710, Handel left Italy and signed on as *Kapellmeister* (musical director) to the Elector. He stipulated, however, that he be granted an immediate 12-month leave to visit England, where the entrepreneurial opportunities were said to be great. Returning to Germany in 1711, he persuaded the Elector to grant him yet another leave. From then on, except for infrequent journeys, he lived in England for the rest of his life. He was largely responsible for introducing Italian opera into England (see the Historical Window on page 252), and he invented the English oratorio almost singlehandedly.

A man of imposing presence and voracious appetites, Handel was sometimes the object of ridicule (as a foreigner, he probably never completely lost his Saxon accent). Yet his creative energy and persistence eventually brought him a degree of international fame experienced by few artists. Although it is hard to imagine, Handel seems not to have known Bach's music at all. Like Bach, he was a remarkable keyboard improviser; unlike Bach, he poured most of his creative energies into bringing human drama to life though music. He was first and foremost a man of the theater. Whereas Bach's music invites reflection, Handel's triggers an immediate response. Whereas Bach often appeals to the intellect, Handel appeals directly to the senses.

### Handel: Recitative and Aria, *"Fammi combattere"* ("Go bid me combat") from *Orlando* (1733)

Handel had written a few Italian operas before settling in England, and between 1711 and 1741 he wrote some three dozen more. That they are rarely performed today is a comment on the difficulties of performance and staging rather than on

*Eighteenth-century nobility did not use surnames as we do today. The House of Hanover was the extended family that ruled Hanover and its surroundings, and the "Elector" was the titular head of the House.

any deficiencies of the music. *Orlando* is generally agreed to be one of Handel's finest operas. The libretto is based on an epic poem by the Renaissance poet Ludovico Ariosto (1474–1533), a story "of dames, of knights, of arms, of love's delight, of courtesies, of high attempts" (not unlike a typical television mini-series). In the opera, Orlando, the nephew of Charlemagne, is deflected from war by his unrestrained passion for Angelica, the daughter of the Khan of Cathay. In the last of Orlando's third-act arias, *"Fammi combattere"* (Listening Guide 32), Angelica tries to dissuade Orlando from pursuing her by accusing him of loving a princess he has recently rescued. Orlando replies that he would sooner tear down walls, tame typhoons, or break magic spells than renounce Angelica.

Like most composers of this period, Handel wrote works with specific singers in mind. *Orlando* is the last opera in which Handel wrote the lead for the alto *castrato*\* Senesino (a nickname derived from his birthplace of Siena). A castrato combined the brilliance of the treble register with the power of the male voice. Although Senesino and Handel quarreled almost continuously (both were proud and stubborn) over a 13-year span, Handel nevertheless wrote many of his finest roles, including *Julius Caesar* (1724), for Senesino.

The brief recitative preceding the aria was known as *simple recitative,* because it calls only for the harpsichord to play occasional chords of short duration while the voice declaims the text freely. The recitative conveys the action of the scene: Orlando will obey the princess's command to leave, convinced that she will then know she has erred. In the aria he then gives expression to his feelings about leaving. Handel casts the aria in the most common variety of da capo form, in which the *A*-Section, entirely in the tonic key, is framed by an instrumental ritornello. Its text actually repeats three times, moving to the key of the dominant in the second repetition and back to the tonic in the third repetition. The *B*-Section jumps directly into a contrasting key (here in the minor mode), where it remains for two repetitions of the text. At the conclusion of the *B*-Section, the aria returns directly to the *A*-Section, which the vocal soloist then embellishes more elaborately than the first time.

In spite of its highly schematic form, Handel brings a wealth of melodic invention to the aria, accompanying it with the sprightly, regular rhythms of a *walking bass.* The soloist negotiates with seeming effortlessness a hazardous series of runs and trills that become more dense with each repetition of the text. The energy of these passages communicates the intensity of Orlando's feelings. Performances of such arias assured artists like Senesino financial rewards that often exceeded those of the composer.

---

\*The practice of castrating prepubescent boys to preserve their soprano register dates back to at least the mid-sixteenth century and persisted to the last years of the nineteenth century. Castratos played an important role in the first 150 years of operatic history and were not formally banned from the papal chapel until 1903. The performer on our recording, Drew Minter, is a natural male alto, called a countertenor in the Baroque.

# *Listening Guide 32*

**HANDEL:** Recitative and Aria, *"Fammi combattere"* ("Go bid me combat") from *Orlando*

CD 3, TRACK 3
TAPE 3A, TRACK 3
DURATION: 3:31

*This scene is divided clearly between the declamatory recitative and the melodic, closed aria. Note that, in the aria, each of the two parts of the A-Section (shown in the Comments column as the A1- and A2- Sections) states the text twice in its entirety. Similarly, the B-Section is divided into two parts, the second of which is vocally more elaborate. The vocalist was expected to provide the kind of elaborate embellishment that Drew Minter, our soloist, provides throughout.*

*Form: Da capo*

| LOCATION / TEXT | TIME | COMMENTS |
|---|---|---|
| RECITATIVE | | |
| 1 *T'ubbidirò, crudele;* <br> I'll obey thee, cruel one; <br><br> *E vedrai in questo Istante,* <br> And you shall know from this instant, <br><br> *Che della principesse* <br> That this princess <br><br> *Fui solo il defensor, ma non amante.* <br> I only defended, but never loved. | 0:00 | Declaimed over short, sporadic chords in the harpsichord. The goal of the entire recitative is the word *"non"* ("never") in the last line, where the soloist supplies a short but brilliant melisma. |
| ARIA | | |
| 2 *A*-Section | | |
| [Ritornello] | 0:19 | Brisk, appealing tune in the orchestra featuring a walking bass. |

## JEAN-PHILIPPE RAMEAU (1683-1764)

The French have always stood somewhat aloof from the mainstream of Western music. Whereas the Germans and the English embraced Italian opera, the French rejected it, complaining that it was too complex and shapeless. Ironically,

| LOCATION / TEXT | TIME | COMMENTS |
|---|---|---|
| *Fammi combattere* Go bid me to combat<br>*Mostri e Tifei,* Monsters and typhoons, | 0:34 | *A1*-Section. Straightforward setting based on the ritornello. Modulates to the dominant with an elaborate, brilliant melisma on *"combattere."* |
| *Novi Trofei*<br>New trophies | :04 | *A2*-Section. The elaborate melisma is now on *"valor."* Modulates back to the tonic. |
| *Se vuoi dal mio valor.*<br>That you wish of my valor. | | |
| [Ritornello] | 1:34 | In the tonic key. |

**3**   *B*-Section

| | | |
|---|---|---|
| *Muraglie abbattere,*<br>Walls I shall overturn, | **1:45** | In the minor mode (the key of the third degree). States the full text twice, with elaborate melismas in the second statement on *"incanti"* ("magic spells") and *"darti"* ("deeds"). |
| *Disfare incanti,*<br>I shall break spells, | | |
| *Se vuoi ch'io vanti*<br>If you wish that I | | |
| *Darti prove d'amor.*<br>By deeds prove my love. | | |

**4**   Da capo of the *A*-Section

| | | |
|---|---|---|
| [Ritornello] | **2:10** | Restated exactly as the first time. |
| *Fammi combattere*<br>*Mostri e Tifei,* | 2:18 | *A1*-Section. New embellishments. |
| *Novi Trofei*<br>*Se vuoi dal mio valor.* | 2:48 | *A2*-Section. New embellishments. |
| [Ritornello] | 3:18 | Rounds out the aria. |

it was an Italian by birth, Jean-Baptiste Lully (1632–1687), who created an indigenous French opera. Lully departed from Italian tradition by emphasizing dance and by relying less on set pieces. Jean-Philippe Rameau (Figure 12.2), Lully's successor, was even more innovative. No composer proved more successful in pleasing the growing public or creating a more dazzling synthesis of music, drama, and dance.

FIGURE 12.2 Rameau wrote theoretical essays expressing his view that music is based on universal principles of harmony derived from nature: "To enjoy the effects of music fully, we must completely lose ourselves in it; to judge it, we must relate it to the source through which we are affected by it. This source is nature."

In typical French fashion, Rameau defied convention throughout his career. He was the seventh of eleven children born to the town organist of Dijon (of mustard fame), a small village southeast of Paris. At first he acceded to his parents' wish that he study law. Then, when he reached 18, his parents relented—prompted perhaps by his dismissal from the Jesuit College where he was studying—and agreed to his becoming a musician.

Rameau drifted from place to place for several years, supporting himself as an organist. In 1715 he ended up at Clermont Cathedral in Clermont-Ferrand (a town in central France). After eight years there, he grew dissatisfied and decided to break his contract. First he refused to play the organ on a feast day, and then, when he was forced to perform, he flooded the cathedral with a torrent of harsh dissonances. Soon he was dismissed. During his years of wandering he had composed several sacred vocal works and had published a collection of harpsichord pieces and a book on theory. Now, almost 40, he faced an uncertain future.

Free of Clermont at last, Rameau made his way to Paris, where he stayed for the rest of his life. For the first few years he seems to have held no regular position, although he may have written some music for farces presented at town fairs. At age 43 he married a woman of 19. That same year he met a wealthy tax-farmer (someone who rented farmland and lived on the revenues) named Jean-Joseph Le Riche de la Pouplinière, a generous patron of the arts. Rameau now heard Lully's operas for the first time and became obsessed with the desire to compose operas himself.

Pouplinière kept a private orchestra, and his wife became a fervent admirer of Rameau's music. The couple eventually put their wealth and influence (including, from 1744 to 1753, an apartment on their estate) at the composer's disposal. For 22 years Rameau directed Pouplinière's orchestra and at the same time managed to turn out a major opera almost every year. He completed his first opera in 1733 at the age of 50; his librettist was 70. He also produced a series of treatises that furnished the theoretical framework for the new system of tonality.

Rameau remained an aloof, enigmatic figure to the end of his life. His wife once remarked that he never mentioned his first 40 years. A contemporary described his profile as "a sharp chin, no stomach, flutes for legs." In his old age Rameau spoke regretfully of the time he had devoted to composition, for he hoped to be remembered mainly as a theorist.

### Rameau: Jupiter's Descent from Act V of *Castor et Pollux* (1737)

Rameau took the story of Castor and Pollux from Greek and Roman mythology. Castor (a tenor) and Pollux (a baritone), twin brothers devoted to each other, are in love with the same woman, the fatally attractive Telaira. As the opera opens, Castor has just been murdered by the treacherous Linceus, whom Pollux has killed to avenge his brother's death. Pollux declares his love to Telaira, but she pleads with him to descend into the underworld to rescue Castor, whom she prefers. Torn between his love for Telaira and his love for his brother, Pollux agrees to risk the journey. At this point Jupiter declares that he will release Castor only if Pollux agrees to take his place.

When Pollux descends to the underworld, Castor is overjoyed to learn that he is to be released, but when he discovers that Pollux will have to remain behind he rejects the plan. At last he agrees to return to earth on condition that he will come back within 24 hours and change places with Pollux. Telaira's happiness at being reunited with Castor turns to despair when he tells her his plan, and she accuses him of not loving her.

Just when the situation seems hopeless, Jupiter—moved by the demonstrations of brotherly love—descends miraculously from Mount Olympus and announces that both Castor and Pollux can remain on earth. Moreover, he will make them both immortal by transforming them into stars in the heavens (along, incongruously, with the self-centered Telaira).

Today we would regard the sudden descent of a god to resolve a dramatic crisis as absurd. The French, however, continued to view as perfectly plausible the intervention of a *deus ex machina* (a "god from the machine," a reference to the stage machinery used to lower gods to the stage). For them it mirrored the wise intervention of a king, in this case Louis XV of France, and this sort of flattery doubtless helped composers win the king's favor. Despite the patently artificial plot and contrived staging, Rameau brought remarkable depth and humanity to the characters in this and other operas.

Although *Castor et Pollux* was only Rameau's second opera, it proved immensely successful. One contemporary raved: "This wonderful opera can be performed a hundred times without the slightest lessening in applause or enthusiasm of the public. At one and the same time it delights the soul, the heart, the intellect, the eyes, the ears and the imagination of the whole of Paris."

Our excerpt (Listening Guide 33), the dramatic high point of the work, includes the entrance of Jupiter, who descends quite literally on his eagle. Baroque operas are rarely staged today, and it is hard for us to imagine the excitement such an effect invariably aroused. Although the orchestra at Rameau's disposal numbered only about thirty musicians, he managed to provide a vivid musical accompaniment to the action on stage.

The scene begins after Castor's return from the underworld. An earthquake terrifies Telaira and Castor, who beg the "God of Vengeance" to put a stop to it. Telaira faints in Castor's arms, and he fears that she is dying. Rameau sets this passage in *accompanied recitative,* in which the characters declaim their lines while the full orchestra responds in brilliant fashion to the rapidly unfolding events.

This emotional passage gives way to a tender *symphony* (an instrumental interlude) that features two soothing flutes. In *arioso* style—a melodic style that retains the flexibility of recitative—Castor sings that "this harmonious music announces a more peaceable God." Sure enough, Jupiter (sung appropriately by a deep bass) touches down gently at the center of the stage. In simple recitative he announces his intention to grant both Pollux (who magically reappears) and Castor immortality. In the ensuing exchange, Pollux, touched by his brother's

*(Text continues on page 245.)*

# Listening Guide 33

## RAMEAU: Jupiter's Descent
## from Act V of *Castor et Pollux*

CD 3, TRACK 4

TAPE 3A, TRACK 4

DURATION: 10:54

*This excerpt contains all three vocal styles found in French late Baroque opera: simple recitative, accompanied recitative, and arioso. The arioso combines the melodiousness of the aria with the flexibility of recitative. The music is closely tailored to each dramatic situation: simple recitative for conversation (Jupiter, Castor, and Pollux at 3:19 ff.), accompanied recitative for dramatic situations (Telaira and Castor at the opening of the excerpt), and arioso for emphasis (Jupiter's final speech, 6:43 ff.).*

*Form: Through-composed*

| STYLE / TEXT | TIME | COMMENTS |
|---|---|---|
| ACCOMPANIED RECITATIVE | | |
| **1** *[Claps of thunder are heard.]* | **0:00** | Rapid scales and string tremolos. |
| TELAIRA: *Qu'ai-je entendu? Quel bruit! Quels éclat de tonnerre!* What do I hear? What noise! What thunder! | 0:08 | Agitated voice matched by frantic accompaniments. |
| *Hélas! c'est moi qui t'ai perdu!* Alas! I have lost you! | 0:19 | Tremolo accompaniments continue. |
| CASTOR: *J'entends frémir les airs,* I hear the airs trembling, | 0:26 | Accompaniment gradually subsides. |
| *je sens trembler la terre . . .* I feel the earth quaking . . . | 0:32 | Slow, steady chords in the orchestra. |
| *C'en est, j'ai trop attendu.* Enough, I have waited too long. | 0:42 | Reaches a cadence, followed by agitated string writing. |
| TELAIRA AND CASTOR: *Arrête, Dieu vengeur, arrête!* Stop, God of Vengeance, stop! | 0:52 | Sung together in sweet consonant harmonies. |
| CASTOR: *L'enfer est ouvert sous mes pas;* Hell is opening under my feet; | 0:59 | Orchestral accompaniment changes frequently to express the meaning of the text. |
| *la foudre gronde sur ma tête!* the lightning strikes down at my head! | 1:08 | |

| STYLE / TEXT | TIME | COMMENTS |
|---|---|---|
| *[Telaira faints in Castor's arms.]* | | Descending scale in violin. |
| *Ciel! O ciel! Télaïre expire dans mes bras!*<br>Heaven! Oh heaven! Telaira dies in my arms! | 1:14 | |
| *Arrête, Dieu vengeur, arrête!*<br>Stop, God of Vengeance, stop! | 1:23 | Powerful cry in the upper register. |
| ARIOSO | | |
| 2  *[A soft symphony is heard on the stage.]* | **1:32** | "Slow and gracious" music in the strings and flutes, resembling a slow minuet. |
| CASTOR:<br>*Mais, le bruit cesse . . . ouvrez les yeux!*<br>But the noise ceases . . . open your eyes! | 1:44 | The soft, tender music continues. |
| *A nos tourments la nature est sensible . . .*<br>On our torment nature has pity . . . | | |
| *Et ces concerts harmonieux*<br>And this harmonious music | 2:02 | |
| *Annoncent un Dieu plus paisible.*<br>Announces a more peaceable God. | 2:09 | |
| *[Jupiter descends to the stage on his eagle.]* | | The preceding music continues as the machines lower the god. |
| SIMPLE RECITATIVE | | |
| JUPITER:<br>3  *Les Destins sonts contents, ton sort est arrêté.*<br>The destiny is fulfilled, your fate has been decided. | **3:19** | Declamatory melody accompanied in simple recitative. |
| *Je te rends à jamais le serment qui t'engage,*<br>I rescind forever the oath that you took, | | |
| *Tu ne verras plus le rivage*<br>You shall not see the shore again | | |
| *Que ton frère a déjà quitté.*<br>Which your brother has already left. | | |
| *Il vit, et Jupiter vous permet*<br>He lives *[Pollux appears]*, and Jupiter grants you | 3:39 | |
| *le partage de l'immortalité.*  the mantle of immortality. | | Ends at 3:48 in a strong cadence. |
| CASTOR:<br>*Mon frère, ô ciel!*  My brother, oh heaven! | 3:51 | The simple recitative continues. |

*continued*

| STYLE / TEXT | TIME | COMMENTS |
|---|---|---|
| POLLUX: | | |
| *Dieux! je retrouve ensemble* | | |
| Gods, I find again | | |
| *tous les objets de mon amour!* | | |
| all the objects of my love! | | |
| CASTOR: | | |
| *J'allais te délivrer du ténébreux séjour;* | 4:02 | |
| I wished to free you from the dark dungeon; | | |
| *Mais le ciel enfin nous rassemble.* | | |
| But heaven at last unites us. | | |
| POLLUX: | | |
| *Quoi! malgré tout l'amour dont ton coeur est épris,* | 4:16 | The simple recitative continues. |
| What! Despite all the love within your heart, | | |
| *Tu me sacrifais la princesse qui t'aime?* | | |
| You sacrifice for me the princess who loves you? | | |
| *Quand j'ai volé vers toi, je fuyais ses mépris . . .* | 4:31 | The vocal line rises gradually in intensity. |
| When I came to you I fled from her contempt . . . | | |
| *Castor, tu m'as vaincu, je me vaincrai moi-même;* | | |
| Castor, you have defeated me, I shall defeat myself; | | |
| *Sois heureux! Je ne suis immortel qu'à ce prix.* | 4:51 | Peaks in intensity and descends to a cadence. |
| Be happy! I am only immortal at this price. | | |
| TELAIRA AND CASTOR: | | |
| *Quel généreux effort! quelle vertu suprême!* | 4:58 | Sung together in sweet consonant harmonies. |
| What a generous gesture! What supreme virtue! | | |
| POLLUX (TO CASTOR): | | |
| *Pour vaincre mon amour, il fallait à mon coeur,* | **5:07** | Simple recitative resumes. |
| To defeat my love, my heart needed | | |
| *Tes jours, ma gloire et son bonheur.* | | |
| Your life, my glory and her happiness. | | |
| *[points to Telaira]* | | Short descending scale in the cello. |
| *L'enfer n'aura qu'une victime:* | 5:19 | |
| Hell will have one victim only: | | |
| *J'ai vu Phébé descendre aux rives du trépas.* | | |
| I saw Phoebe descend to the shores of death. | | |

| STYLE / TEXT | TIME | COMMENTS |
|---|---|---|
| *Un malheureux amour l'entraînait sur mes pas,*<br>An unhappy love bade her follow my steps,<br><br>*Et l'amour a fait tout son crime.*<br>And her only crime was love. | 5:33 | |
| JUPITER:<br>*Palais de ma grandeur où je dicte mes lois,*<br>Palace of my grandeur where I dictate my laws,<br><br>*Vaste empire des Dieux, ouvrez-vous à ma voix!*<br>Vast empire of the Gods, oh hear my voice! | 5:47 | Elaborate figuration in the harpsichord. |
| [ *The heavens open and show forth the Zodiac. The sun begins to move. Clouds, with Mt. Olympus and the gods in the background.*] | 6:04 | Swirling passage in the strings. |
| *Tant de vertus doivent prétendre*<br>So much virtue shall claim<br><br>*Au partage de nos autels.*<br>A share of our altars. | 6:11 | Returns a last time to simple recitative. |
| *Offrons à l'univers des signes immortels*<br>Let us give an immortal sign to the universe<br><br>*D'une amitié si pure et d'un amour si tendre!*<br>Of friendship so pure and of love so tender! | 6:20 | |
| **5**   ARIOSO | **6:33** | Dotted passage in the full strings. |
| *Soleil sur le trône des cieux,*<br>Sun upon the throne of the skies, | 6:43 | Accompanied recitative returns. |
| *Arrête, suspends ta carrière*<br>Stop, interrupt your orbit | | Text repeated more passionately at 7:04. |
| *Et redouble encor la lumière*<br>And redouble again your splendor<br><br>*Pour éclairer de nouveaux Dieux!*<br>To glorify the new Gods! | | |
| | 7:24 | Another swirling passage in the strings. |
| *Descendez des sphères du monde,*<br>Descend from all spheres of the world, | 7:26 | The first of three parallel stanzas. Accompanied by the swirling figuration in the strings. |

*continued*

| STYLE / TEXT | TIME | COMMENTS |
|---|---|---|
| *Peuples répandus dans les airs!*<br>People floating in the air! | | |
| *C'est sur mon pouvoir que se fonde*<br>In my power is founded | 7:39 | |
| *L'ordre éternel de vos concerts.*<br>The eternal order of your harmony. | | |
| *Descendez des sphères du monde,*<br>Descend from all spheres of the world, | 7:53 | The second of three parallel stanzas. Largely in the minor mode. |
| *Peuples répandus dans les airs!*<br>People floating in the air! | | |
| *C'est du soleil la lumière féconde*<br>It is the fertile light of the sun | 8:05 | |
| *Qui forme tous vos feux divers.*<br>That lends you your fiery splendor. | | |
| *Descendez des sphères du monde,*<br>Descend from all spheres of the world, | 8:18 | The third of three parallel stanzas. *"Descendez"* repeated three times. Returns to the major mode. |
| *Peuples répandus dans les airs!*<br>People floating in the air! | | |
| *Que des astres unis tout l'éclat se confonde!*<br>All the splendor of the stars shall be united! | 8:36 | Opens with bold melodic sequence. |
| *C'est la fête de l'univers.*<br>It is the festival of the universe. | | Last line repeated for emphasis, concluding with a strong cadence. |
| [ *Balls of fire descend on clouds; spirits unite with the planets and the stars in an entertainment.*] | | Without a pause, the chorus enters. |
| **6** CHORUS OF THE STARS:<br>*Descendons des sphères du monde,*<br>Let us descend from the spheres, | 9:02 | Continues and elaborates on Jupiter's music in highly imitative textures. Chorus sings descending arpeggios on *"Descendons"* ("Let us descend"). Swirling string accompaniments on *"univers"* ("universe"). Slowing for emphatic final cadence. |
| *C'est la fête de l'univers.*<br>It is the festival of the universe. | | |
| *Qu'ici notre éclat se confonde!*<br>It is here that our splendor all unites! | | |
| *C'est la fête de l'univers.*<br>It is the festival of the universe. | | |

willingness to sacrifice his happiness, accepts the union between Castor and Telaira (even then, the tenor got the girl), who express their joy in a single line of sweetly consonant harmonies: "What a generous gesture! What supreme virtue!"

Pollux recounts the demise of Phoebe, his beloved, who was destroyed in her quest for him. Finally, Jupiter commands the heavens to open, which they obediently do to the accompaniment of a swirling passage in the strings. Finally, in an elaborate and richly orchestrated arioso passage, Jupiter celebrates the immortality of the three protagonists. We are left hanging as to whether they will live out their natural lives before taking their places in the firmament, but it is to their ultimate fate that Jupiter now speaks:

> Descend from all spheres of the world,
> People floating in the air!
> All the splendor of the stars shall be united!
> It is the festival of the universe.

On command, the stars—aided by more stage machinery—materialize and join in a final chorus of praise marked by considerable imitation. This concluding chorus, repeated from the Prologue, frames the action of the drama in much the same way that a ritornello frames an instrumental movement.

Throughout this extended scene, Rameau throws out tantalizing bits of melody without ever interrupting the drama for a set piece. Instead of stopping the action so that the characters can strike a static "aria pose," Rameau has them deliver their lines naturally. Without witnessing the elaborate scenery and staging Rameau brought to his operas, we may find it hard to appreciate their magnificence. Still, the music gives us a hint of what the audience must have experienced during these splendid productions.

## THE ENGLISH ORATORIO

The English oratorio is so closely associated with Handel that it might well be called Handelian oratorio. Its origins are operatic. As we have seen, Italian opera was one of England's major imports, and Handel introduced his first Italian opera to England in 1711. (The resourceful Handel released a flock of live sparrows during the performances!) During the 1730s two rival opera houses competed for London audiences until at last they put each other out of business. Adding to their difficulties was the success of English "ballad opera," in which popular tunes were worked into a story about common folk who poked fun at the pretensions of the upper classes. *The Beggar's Opera* of 1728, with text by John Gay and music arranged by John Christopher Pepusch, proved particularly popular. It was peopled by pickpockets, prostitutes, jailbirds, and other denizens of London's seamier quarters, all of whom ridiculed the pomposity of Italian opera as well as the political party in power.

Handel was a partner in one of the opera houses that failed. After that economic reversal, Handel—doubtless noting the success of ballad opera—concluded that London audiences might welcome dramatic presentations in English based on subjects with which they were more familiar. Acting on that belief, he created the **English oratorio,** a musical entertainment on a sacred subject (frequently drawn from the Bible) that blends the solo recitative and aria of Italian opera with rich passages for full chorus. Handel may have planned to stage his oratorios, but when the Bishop of London ruled that such performances would constitute a profanation of sacred subjects, Handel dropped the idea. Even so, the characters in Handel's oratorios relate vivid and dramatic stories. Most of the plots are based on familiar figures from the Old Testament, such as Esther, Saul, Samson, Joshua, and Solomon. Curiously, Handel's best-known oratorio, *Messiah,* is an exception to this rule.

## Handel: From Part II of *Messiah* (1742)

It is widely believed that Handel composed the oratorio *Messiah* for the Lord Lieutenant of Ireland as a benefit for Dublin charities. In any case, he wrote the entire work in London in the three weeks between August 22 and September 14, 1742, six weeks before he left for Dublin. Though *Messiah* was a great success there, its London premiere in 1743 was a failure. Finally, in 1750, when Handel offered *Messiah* at the first of a series of annual benefit performances for London's Foundling ("abandoned infant") Hospital, the work caught on, and soon it was being performed at every Advent season. Handel's librettist, Charles Jennens, who had assembled the text from passages in the Bible and the English Prayer Book, expressed disappointment with the music and grumbled that Handel should have taken a year to write it rather than three weeks.

Instead of telling a straightforward story, *Messiah* identifies Christ with the long-awaited Messiah. Still, the oratorio has a distinct dramatic flow. The Prologue, the first of its three parts, reviews the major Old Testament prophecies about the coming of the Messiah and concludes with the announcement of Christ's birth. The second part tells of Christ's suffering and rejection, his resurrection and ascent into heaven, and the ultimate triumph of Christianity on earth. The third part serves as an epilogue, expressing the promise of eternal life.

The musical forms Handel uses in *Messiah*—recitatives, arias (here called "songs"), and choruses—are the same sturdy forms he had used throughout his long career as a composer of operas. Here, however, he has the chorus serve a more dramatic purpose and reserves recitative for special situations. Throughout, he uses the forms with more flexibility than he did in his operas. With a few exceptions, most of the arias last only three or four minutes, with each line of text standing as an individual statement.

The final section of Part II (Listening Guide 34) culminates in the celebrated *Hallelujah Chorus,* and demonstrates the dynamic relationship between solo and chorus. The section opens with a vigorous song for the bass: "Why do the nations so furiously rage together, and why do the people imagine such a vain

# Listening Guide 34

## HANDEL: From Part II of *Messiah*

CD 3, TRACK 5
TAPE 3A, TRACK 5
DURATION: 9:14

*Handel displays great originality of form in* Messiah. *Neither of the two arias in this excerpt uses a da capo form, and the seven compact sections flow directly into one another. Numbers in brackets in the Time column signify repeats of blocks of text.*

*Form: Through-composed*

| TEXT | TIME | COMMENTS |
|---|---|---|
| **1**  AIR (BASS) | | |
| [Ritornello] | **0:00** | Strings play furious tremolo figures. |
| Why do the nations so furiously rage together, | 0:22 [0:34] | Elaborate melisma in second statement on "rage." |
| [and] why do the people imagine such a vain thing? | [0:47] | Elaborate melisma in second statement on "imagine." Leads directly to the following recitative. |
| SIMPLE RECITATIVE | | |
| The kings of the earth rise up, and the rulers take counsel together, against the Lord and his Anointed. | **1:03** | Accompaniment provided by short chords in the strings. |
| **2**  CHORUS | | |
| Let us break their bonds asunder, | **1:19** | Driving, detached theme treated in imitation. |
| and cast away their yokes from us. | 1:34 | Imitative texture, with elaborate melismas on "away." |
| Let us break their bonds asunder, | 1:56 | Driving, detached theme. |
| and cast away their yokes from us. | 2:16 | Imitative texture at close time intervals. |
| | 2:33 | Both lines simultaneously. |
| | 2:58 | Instrumental coda. Ends with a strong, clear cadence. |
| SIMPLE RECITATIVE | | |
| He that dwelleth in heaven shall laugh them to scorn: the Lord shall have them in derision. | **3:15** | Accompaniment by harpsichord and lower strings. |

*continued*

# Listening Guide 34 (Continued)

| TEXT | TIME | COMMENTS |
|---|---|---|
| **3**  SONG | | |
| [Ritornello] | **3:25** | Marked by a strong, insistent rhythm. |
| Thou shalt break them | 3:40 | |
| with a rod of iron, | | |
| thou shalt dash them in pieces | 3:51 [3:59] | Elaborate melisma on "potter's." |
| like a potter's vessel. | | |
| [Ritornello] | 4:11 | |
| Thou shalt break them | 4:20 | Similar to, but different from, the first section. |
| with a rod of iron, | | Elaborate melisma on "rod." |
| thou shalt dash them in pieces | 4:34 | Text repeated for emphasis. |
| like a potter's vessel. | | |
| [Ritornello] | 5:07 | Similar to the first ritornello; ends with a strong cadence. |
| **4**  CHORUS | | |
| [Instrumental introduction] | **5:26** | |
| Hallelujah, | 5:33 | Homophonic texture with characteristic rhythms on "Hallelujah." |
| for the Lord God | 5:52 | Repeated several times for emphasis. Trumpets and timpani enter. |
| omnipotent reigneth. Hallelujah. | | |
| The kingdom of this world is become | 6:42 | Homophonic texture, softer dynamic. |
| the kingdom of our Lord and of his | 6:52 | Sudden *forte*. |
| Christ; | | |
| and he shall reign for ever and ever. | 7:00 [8:06] | Imitative textures, proceeding from the bass up. |
| King of Kings and Lord of Lords. | 7:24 [8:18] | Trumpets and timpani; rising sequences. |
| Hallelujah. | | Dramatic pause before the final cadence. |

thing?" Originally, this aria was twice as long. To heighten its theatrical effect, however, Handel cut it in half (though most bass soloists prefer the full-length version!). Moreover, he reverses the conventional sequence of aria followed by recitative by having the solo end with a recitative, which is more appropriate to the text: "The kings of the earth rise up, and the rulers take counsel together, against the Lord and his Anointed."

The insistent chorus that follows carries on the sense of struggle: "Let us break their bonds asunder, and cast away their yokes from us." The third person plural of the text suggests choral treatment, and Handel masses the voices of the chorus around the hammering rhythm of the opening motive:

*Allegro e staccato* (Fast and detached)

Let us break their bonds a - sun - der, let us, let us break,

Two distinct musical ideas appear in alternation. The elaborate melisma on "away" in the second motive again suggests physical action. The simple recitative and aria for tenor that follow prepare the way for the rousing *Hallelujah Chorus* that concludes this part of *Messiah*. The tenor sings darkly of a Lord whose enemies shall be dashed "in pieces like a potter's vessel." Rather than a da capo aria, Handel provides a two-part form (*A-B*) with ritornelli at the beginning, middle, and end. Throughout the aria the accompaniment supplies a powerful rhythmic figure.

The chorus that breaks forth with a statement of faith in the eternal kingdom is dominated by jubilant repetitions of "Hallelujah." The straightforward diatonic harmonies and joyous tone of this thematically rich chorus contrast dramatically with the agitated orchestral ritornello and the jagged vocal line of the preceding aria. Jennens's framing of the text with the word "Hallelujah" may have suggested to Handel the famous rhythm that dominates the chorus.

Handel employs more subtle techniques as well. For example, he keeps the orchestral introduction light to heighten the impact of the trumpets, which have been silent up to this point. With "The kingdom of this world," he initiates a melodic descent that is answered by the stunning rising sequence on "King of Kings, and Lord of Lords":

*Allegro* (Fast)

chorus

The King - dom of this world

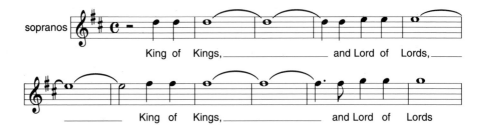

sopranos: King of Kings, _____ and Lord of Lords, _____

_____ King of Kings, _____ and Lord of Lords

He sets the line "And he shall reign for ever and ever" in the imitative style composers had used for centuries to suggest eternity. A lengthy trill on the second "EV[-er]" drives home the image of eternity. Indeed, Handel makes every line of this skillfully constructed verse memorable in its own right while at the same time making it appear part of a single strand of thought.

In 1743, King George II initiated the custom of rising during the performance of this magnificent chorus, an understandable response.

## THE CANTATA

Unlike most of the earlier composers, the greatest composer of Baroque church music, Johann Sebastian Bach, was a Protestant rather than a Catholic. The Protestant Reformation, launched by Martin Luther's Ninety-Five Theses in 1517, had divided Europe into two regions. Southern Europe, including Italy, Austria, and southern Germany, remained Catholic. In northern Europe, which included England, much of France, and northern Germany, the Protestants ("protestors") had broken away from the Catholic Church to embrace various forms of Protestantism, a more personalized faith. Before Luther's time, the Bible had been available only in Latin, a language that only the clergy commanded. To enable Christians to experience their faith more directly, Luther translated the Bible into vernacular German.

Try as they might, the leaders of the Lutheran church, as the Protestant church in northern Germany came to be known, could not—and probably did not wish to—abandon their Catholic legacy. The Lutheran service in the eighteenth century retained some of the ritual of the Catholic Mass and far exceeded it in length. Even some of the singing was still in Latin, the only language used in Catholic worship until the 1970s.

Bach and other Reformation composers introduced one genre that had no place in the Catholic service: the cantata. A **cantata** (from the Italian *cantare,* "to sing") is a poem set to music for voice(s) and instruments in several movements. The genre originated in seventeenth-century Italy, where it consisted of a series of modest, contrasting sections for solo voice and dealt mainly with secular subjects. Bach, along with Telemann and other Baroque composers, developed the cantata into a far more ambitious form. A typical Bach cantata, for example, contains up to seven movements expressing a unified religious theme and calls for several vocal soloists and a chorus. The cantata, like most vocal music of the late Baroque, was built around the two vocal styles inherited from Italian opera: aria and recitative. Within a cantata, as within an opera, these two styles generally alternate.

## J. S. Bach: Cantata No. 78, *Jesu der du meine Seele* (Jesus, who hath my soul) (1724)

One of Bach's duties in Leipzig was to produce a new cantata each week for St. Thomas's Church. This was a demanding chore: Of the more than 200 of his cantatas that survive, most call for both soloists and chorus (though he wrote several solo cantatas as well). For the first two years of his appointment Bach managed to keep up with this superhuman pace, though he sometimes borrowed from music he had written before. Not only did he have to write a new work each week; he also had to see that the parts were copied for the choir (12 to 16 singers) and the orchestra (12 to 18 strong) in time for the single rehearsal that preceded each Sunday performance.

The Lutheran service in Bach's day began at about 7 A.M. Sunday and generally ran for about three hours (or as long as five!). For the congregational singing and some of the choral singing, Bach could draw on standard music that was readily available. His own cantata usually came about a third of the way through this marathon service and lasted up to half an hour.

The text, and hence the tone, of each cantata was determined by where a particular Sunday fell in the church calendar, which was modeled on that of the Catholic Church (Chapter 5, page 72). The cantata we are about to discuss was composed for the "14th Sunday after Trinity," which usually falls in early September.

We would expect the music for, say, Christmas Sunday to be joyful. But what kind of music would be appropriate for the fourteenth Sunday after Trinity? The Lutheran church calendar specified a theme for each Sunday around which the whole service was to be organized, and for the fourteenth Sunday after Trinity the theme was the unworthiness of humankind and Christ's forgiveness. That was the theme Bach was responding to in Cantata No. 78.*

This cantata is of a type known as a *chorale cantata*. The chorale cantata begins and ends with a chorus based on a familiar melody and with a text in several stanzas, called a *chorale*. Many chorales, including Martin Luther's "A Mighty Fortress Is Our God," serve today as Protestant hymns. Cantata No. 78 takes its name from the chorale with which it begins and ends (see page 38). The inner sections are sung by soloists, who paraphrase the verses of the chorale while alternating between aria and recitative.

*Bach did not number his cantatas; the first editors of his complete works assigned the numbers more than a century after his death.

## THE COMPOSER AS BUSINESSMAN

Some people believe that all composers of art music have been poverty-stricken individuals, as if deprivation were a prerequisite to inspiration. Yet many great composers have been shrewd, successful businessmen. George Frideric Handel, though he suffered financial setbacks, was such a man.

Handel lived in a time of patronage, and while he was in Italy he had the support of Cardinal Ottoboni, Corelli's chief patron. Yet he chose to live in England, where entrepreneurs were encouraged. Even there, however, he continued to enjoy the security of patronage, accepting a regular pension from the King of £600 (about $10,000) per year in return for instructing the daughters of the royal family from time to time. While pocketing his pension, he launched a series of ambitious business ventures.

The first venture, supported in part by the King, was a bold scheme to establish a regular Italian opera company in London known as the Royal Academy of Music. Tickets were sold, on a lifetime subscription basis, for performances at the King's Theatre. One of Handel's tasks as music director was to recruit Italian singers to join the company. Among those most in demand were the *castrati* (page 235). Handel made regular trips to the Continent to attract singers to London, much as the management of a modern baseball team woos free agents.

For seven years Handel managed to hold together his fragile coalition of composers, singers, managers, librettists, stage designers, and machinists. His greatest problem was coping with the jealousies of the singers. One observer remarked drily, "It seems [as] impossible for two singers of equal merit to tread the same stage . . . as for two people to ride on the same horse, without the other being behind."

The so-called First Academy collapsed in 1728, but Handel was still determined to sell Italian opera to the London public. With a partner, he took over the King's Theatre and for eight more years struggled, in a Second Academy, to make it go. Then, in 1733 (the year in which Handel wrote *Orlando*), a rival opera company opened its doors. In a city that refused to support even one company, two were bound to fail, and they did. Yet somehow Handel managed to avoid bankruptcy and, perhaps thinking of his own future, became a charter subscriber to the Fund for the Support of Decayed Musicians, an early form (despite its grisly name) of a union pension fund.

With his operatic adventures at an end, Handel's tenacity and foresight impelled him to create the English oratorio, into which he incorporated many operatic elements. For one oratorio, *Saul*, Handel assembled a remarkable orchestra that included three trombones, a pair of double-bass kettledrums borrowed from the Tower of London, and a large, keyed glockenspiel (a keyboard instrument with tuned metal bars to produce the sounds). London audiences found such productions more thrilling than operas, with their tedious recitatives in a foreign language, and Handel resigned himself to satisfying the demands of public taste.

Soon he learned that he could make more money by having his oratorios performed only during the Lenten season (the six weeks before Easter) in a rented theater than he could by running a permanent theater for a full season. In fact, he could make as much as £700 from a single performance.

Handel derived additional income from the sale of his published works. Although English copyright laws at the time were far stronger than those of other European countries, he needed considerable skill to outwit unscrupulous publishers. As his finances improved, Handel contributed to the support of various charitable organizations. For example, as we have seen, he began to turn over the proceeds of his annual performances of *Messiah* to the Foundling Hospital.

Handel was admired and trusted by the people who worked for him. Singers were content to leave England after an engagement with nothing more than a promissory note, knowing that he would pay them promptly. When he died at the age of 74, he left more than £20,000, enough to take care of all his servants, surviving relatives (Handel never married), charities, and friends.

Throughout his long life, Handel kept his sense of humor. Once, when a friend complained about the wretched music being played at concerts in Vauxhall Gardens, Handel replied, "You are right, sir, it is very poor stuff; I thought so myself when I wrote it."

Like most of Bach's chorale cantatas, Cantata No. 78 consists of seven parts:

1. An extended opening chorus based on the chorale
2. An aria* (here a duet between soprano and alto, sung in Bach's day by boys)
3. A recitative and
4. An aria (for tenor)
5. A recitative and
6. An aria (for bass)
7. A concluding chorale (a straightforward harmonization of the melody, sung by the entire chorus)

These parts form a symmetrical structure:

<pre>
chorale [extended chorus]                          chorale [brief chorus]
     aria [duet]              aria                       aria
            recitative    recitative
</pre>

The first and last parts, sung by the full chorus, provide a sturdy framework for the entire composition.

Because the singers could not be expected to learn more than one new number each week, Bach assigned only one aria to each of the four soloists (soprano, alto, tenor, and bass). The arias proceed downward through the vocal range: soprano and alto (in the duet), then tenor, and finally bass. The tenor and the bass each sing both a recitative and an aria. Today we are so tune-oriented that we sometimes grow impatient during the recitatives as we wait for the melodic aria that follows. Yet some of Bach's most expressive vocal writing is to be found in his recitatives, particularly in the accompanied recitatives.

In keeping with the spirt of the time, the texts of Bach's cantatas are melodramatic and exaggerated. The members of the congregation were accustomed to powerful, sometimes gory images that would rouse them to religious fervor. Set in verse form with elaborate rhyme schemes, the texts provided a commentary on the scripture reading that regularly preceded the cantata. Bach managed to extract profound meaning from texts that themselves were highly stylized and formal.

In the magnificent opening chorus of Cantata No. 78, Bach combines elements of almost every style known to the late Baroque. The movement consists of almost 30 repetitions of a 4-bar, chromatically descending motive, introduced in the bass and then picked up by other voices:

*Bach referred to both solo arias and duets as arias.

Such a repetitive pattern is known as an **ostinato,** from the Italian word for "obstinate"; like the ground (the English term for ostinato) in Purcell's *Dido and Aeneas,* it repeats over and over. Bach varies the pattern with several *transpositions* (writing the same melody starting on another pitch) and with two *inversions* (writing a musical figure upside down; an extension of the interval inversion defined in Chapter 3). Over and around the ostinato, Bach imposes phrases of the chorale that will be heard in its entirety at the end of the cantata.

The movement also resembles ritornello form, with each of six sections (the beginnings of which are shown in the letters at the left below and reproduced in Listening Guide 35; identical letters signify identical music) headed by an orchestral ritornello. The slow, syncopated, dotted rhythm of the melody in the ritornello resembles that of a *sarabande,* as might be found in a French dance suite of the time.

At yet another level, Bach's chorus resembles bar form (*A-A-B* [through *E*]); the last section was frequently, as here, much longer than either *A*-Section that we noted in songs of the medieval troubadours and *Minnesänger* (Chapter 5). The musical setting of the first two lines of text (*A*-Section) is repeated for the second two lines (*A*-Section). Bach sets these four lines in an appropriately melancholy mood, with dark, minor-mode harmonies. The shift to the major mode in the next four lines brings the promise of salvation (the line-by-line translation produces a curious sentence structure):

| | | |
|---|---|---|
| *A*-Section | Jesus, who hath my soul through thy bitter death | Dark, minor harmonies. |
| *A*-Section | From the devil's dark hole and from spiritual distress | |
| *B*-Section | Dramatically rescued, | Includes bright major harmonies. |
| *C*-Section | And has reassured me | |
| *D*-Section | Through thy comforting word, | |
| *E*-Section | Be now, oh God, my guide! | |

The da capo duet for soprano and alto that follows contrasts strongly with the somber mood of the opening chorus. Here Bach uses a walking bass that is even more pictorial than the one in Handel's aria from *Orlando:*

Again, the music reflects the mood of the text:

We hasten with weak yet eager footsteps
Oh Jesus, oh Master for help unto you!
You seek patiently the sick and the misguided.
Ah! Hear how we
Lift our voices to ask for help!
Your blessed profile is to us a joy!

## J. S. BACH:  Cantata No. 78, first and second movements

### First Movement: Chorus

CD 3, TRACKS 6–7
TAPE 3B, TRACKS 1–2

DURATION: 5:31

*The* ostinato *repeats every 9–10 seconds (shown under Time). The larger sections (A–E) in ritornello form are shown under Location. Note that each section begins with an orchestral ritornello. The two A-Sections are musically identical, contributing to the bar form. First focus on hearing the four repetitions of the ostinato during the opening ritornello, and then shift your attention to the alternation between ritornello and chorus.*

*Form: Ritornello, organized around an ostinato*

| LOCATION / TEXT | | TIME | COMMENTS |
|---|---|---|---|
| 1 | A-SECTION: OPENING RITORNELLO | **0:00** | Orchestra only, *forte*. Ostinato in the bass. |
| | | 0:10 | *Piano.* |
| | | 0:19 | Ostinato in the oboes. |
| | | 0:28 | |
| 2 | CHORUS: | **0:38** | Imitative entries begin in the altos. |
| | *Jesu, der du meine Seele* | 0:47 | Full chorus. |
| | Jesus, who hath my soul | 0:56 | Ostinato inverted in chorus (ascending). |
| | *Hast durch deinen bittern Tod* | 1:05 | Return to original ostinato (descending). |
| | through thy bitter death | 1:14 | Full chorus. |
| 3 | A-SECTION: RITORNELLO | **1:23** | Orchestra only. |
| | | 1:33 | Ostinato in violins, countervoice in oboes. |
| 4 | CHORUS: | 1:42 | |
| | *Aus des Teufels finstrer Höhle* | **1:51** | Imitative entries begin in the altos. |
| | From the devil's dark hole | 2:00 | Full chorus. |
| | *Und der schweren Seelennot* | 2:09 | Ostinato inverted. |
| | and from spiritual distress | 2:19 | Return to original ostinato (descending). |
| | | 2:28 | Full chorus. |
| 5 | B-SECTION: RITORNELLO | **2:34** | Orchestra. Pedal point; ostinato in violins. |
| 6 | CHORUS: | **2:46** | Imitation in the chorus. |
| | *Kräftiglich herausgerissen,* | 2:55 | Ostinato in the basses. |
| | Dramatically rescued, | 3:04 | Full chorus; turn to the major mode. |
| 7 | C-SECTION: RITORNELLO | **3:12** | Orchestra. In the major mode. |

| LOCATION / TEXT | TIME | COMMENTS |
|---|---|---|
| CHORUS: | | |
| *Und mich solches lassen wissen* | 3:22 | Ostinato interrupted. |
| And has reassured me | 3:35 | Ostinato returns. Full chorus. |
| **8** *D*-SECTION: RITORNELLO | **3:44** | Orchestra. In the major mode. |
| | 3:53 | Ostinato interrupted. |
| **9** CHORUS: | | |
| *Durch dein angenehmes Wort,* | **4:02** | Ostinato returns in the voices, then is treated |
| Through thy comforting word, | | to elaborate imitation. |
| | 4:25 | Full chorus. |
| **10** *E*-SECTION: RITORNELLO | **4:32** | Orchestra. Ostinato interrupted, pedal point. |
| **11** CHORUS: | | |
| *Sei doch jetzt, o Gott, mein Hort!* | **4:50** | Imitation in the chorus. |
| Be now, oh God, my guide! | 5:05 | The ostinato returns in the full chorus. |
| **12** CLOSING [OPENING] RITORNELLO | **5:14** | Final statement, concluding in major. |

DURATION: 5:39

## Second Movement: Aria [Duet] (soprano and alto)

*The form of this duet is identical to that of the aria in Handel's* Orlando. *Note that the timings in the A- and B-sections refer to the beginning of each complete repetition of text. By contrast, the B-Section sets each line of text only once. The A-Section is framed by ritornellos, while the B-Section contains two internal ritornellos. Note that this duet calls for only a continuo accompaniment, which includes the organ and cello. The organist has only the walking bass and indications about the harmony, from which he fills out his own accompaniment.*

*Form: Da capo*

*A*-SECTION

| | | | |
|---|---|---|---|
| **1** | [Ritornello] | **0:00** | Establishes the walking bass. |
| | *Wir eilen mit schwachen,* | 0:17 | Overlapping imitation between soloists. |
| | *doch emsigen Schritten* | 0:39 | Second complete statement of the text. |
| | We hasten with weak yet eager footsteps | 1:06 | Third complete statement of the text. |
| | *O Jesu, O Meister, zu helfen, zu dir!* | 1:20 | Begins with *"zu dir,"* then fourth complete |
| | Oh Jesus, oh Master, for help unto you! | | statement of the text. |
| | [Ritornello] | 1:36 | Same as the first ritornello. |

*continued*

# Listening Guide 35 (Continued)

| LOCATION / TEXT | TIME | COMMENTS |
|---|---|---|
| **2**   B-SECTION | | |
| *Du suchest die Kranken und Irrenden treulich.* | **1:53** | Continues the imitative texture. |
| You seek patiently the sick and the misguided. | | |
| [Ritornello] | 2:16 | |
| *Ach! höre, wie wir* | 2:25 | Sung together in sweet minor harmonies. |
| Ah! Hear how we | | |
| *Die Stimme erheben, um Hilfe zu bitten!* | 2:36 | Imitation returns. |
| Lift our voices to ask for help! | | |
| [Ritornello] | [3:02] | |
| *Es sei uns dein gnädiges Anlitz erfreulich!* | 3:06 | With imitation. |
| Your blessed profile is to us a joy! | | |
| **3**   DA CAPO OF THE A-SECTION | | |
| [Ritornello] | **3:43** | Repeats the first A-Section exactly. |
| *Wir eilen mit schwachen,* | 4:00 | Overlapping imitation between the soloists. |
| *doch emsigen Schritten* | 4:22 | Walking bass in the organ. |
| We hasten with weak yet eager footsteps | 4:48 | Third statement of the text. |
| *O Jesu, O Meister, zu helfen, zu dir!* | 5:02 | Begins and ends with *"zu dir!"* |
| Oh Jesus, oh Master, for help unto you! | | |
| [Ritornello] | **5:17** | |

This **duet is in da capo form**, a form that Bach resorted to less often than most of his contemporaries.

The third section of the cantata, the tenor recitative, is a cry of self-condemnation saturated with correspondingly chromatic harmonies:

Ah! I am a child of sin,
Ah! I stray far and wide.
The curse of original sin
Will not leave me so long as I am human.
My impulses lead only to evil.
My soul asks: "Ah! Who will save me?" [etc.]

For the last lines, "Do not consider the sins which enrage thee," Bach moves from simple to accompanied recitative.

The tenor aria and the bass aria are both in ritornello form. The tenor aria is accompanied only by flute and *continuo*:

Your blood has cancelled my blame,
Has made my heart once again light
And set me free.
Should the devil now call me to battle,
Jesus will stand at my side,
So that I shall be heartened and victorious.

Reflecting the text, the bass recitative moves through four successive moods:

| | |
|---|---|
| *Somber* | "the wounds, nails, crown of thorns, and grave, the blows delivered to our Saviour"; |
| *Agitated* | "the horrifying judgment that condemns the damned"; |
| *Sustained and slower* | "you return to bless me, so that I know no pain"; |
| *Lyrical and slightly faster* | "My heart, consumed with grief yet freed by the blood you shed on the cross, give I now, Lord Jesus Christ, to you." |

For the second and fourth moods Bach again moves to accompanied recitative.

For the bass aria, Bach has the oboe join the solo singer in a virtuoso demonstration of breath control. Indeed, the spun-out vocal line suggests that Bach was writing more for the oboe than for the human voice (an oboist can get more mileage from each breath than can a singer). Twice in succession he has the bass sing 10 consecutive bars in moderate tempo without a single rest; this is something like swimming the length of a 40-meter pool underwater. Even if the singer sneaks a breath or two, he must maintain the illusion of continuity in order to make sense of the text: "When Christians believe in you, it will prove *eternally* impossible for any enemy to steal them out of your hands."

In the simple concluding chorale, Bach's skillful harmonization brings freshness to a tune that must have been familiar to every member of his congregation. Here all trace of gloom is dispelled:

Lord! I believe, help me in weakness,
Permit me not to fall into despair;
You, you can make me stronger,
When sin and death threaten.
I will trust thy goodness,
Until, after earthly struggle,
I come face to face with Thee,
In eternal bliss.

The extreme emotionalism with which these concepts are expressed in the text did not prevent Bach from imbuing them with depth and majesty.

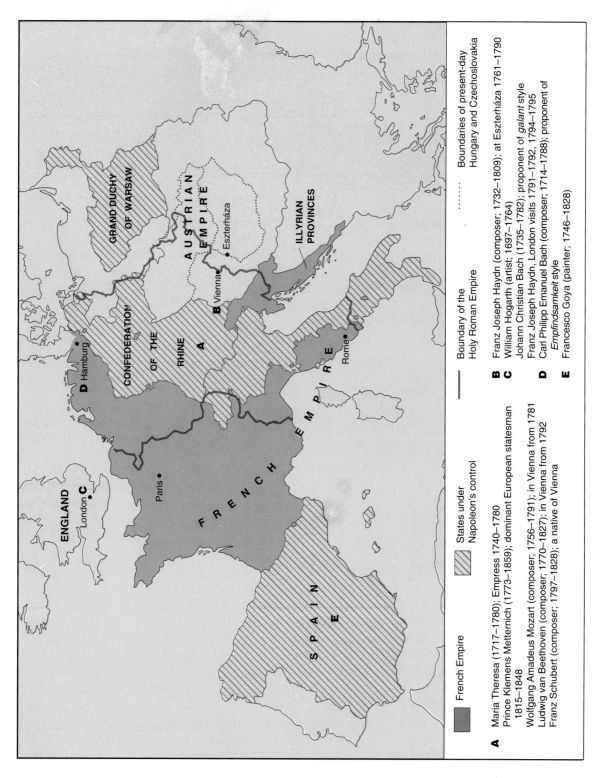

FIGURE 1 Western Europe in the Age of Revolution.

# THE VIENNESE CLASSICAL STYLE

## (1750–1828)

### *The Age of Revolution*

HISTORICAL
AND CULTURAL
BACKGROUND

*T*he history of Western music is a story of change and evolution, with the centers of musical activity shifting repeatedly from place to place. Paris in the twelfth century, Florence in the fourteenth, Venice in the seventeenth—for a time each was preeminent. Cities and courts vied openly for the services of the most renowned composers and performers of the day.

Yet no city dominated the musical scene as did Vienna for a brief but extraordinary period of about 50 years between 1780 and 1830. Vienna, the Hapsburg imperial capital and center of the Holy Roman Empire, first rose to prominence with the lavish celebrations of the Emperor Maximilian I in the early years of the sixteenth century. Austria stood at the crossroads of Germany, central Europe, and Italy, and its empire included large areas of what are now Hungary, Czechoslovakia, and Italy. Hapsburg power and influence culminated in the early eighteenth century during the reign of Charles VI. Attracted by the patronage of the royal family, the most gifted musicians of Europe made their way to Vienna (Figure 1).

Ironically, the political misfortunes of the Empress Maria Theresa early in her long reign (1740–1780) set the stage for the unprecedented flowering of musical life in Vienna. Embroiled in a series of costly wars, the Empress was unable to support the arts on the lavish scale of her predecessors. Around the middle of the century, a cultivated group of music lovers assumed the role of patrons. Most of these patrons (Prince Karl Lichnowsky, Prince Josef Lobkowitz, Prince Ferdinand Kinsky) were members of the aristocracy, and many were wealthy landowners. Some of them, however, belonged to the emerging class of merchants and businessmen who were to transform the social structure of Europe. Their appetite for music was insatiable, and many of them employed

261

FIGURE 2 Francisco Goya created a series of drawings inspired by the brutal behavior of Napoleon's army, which occupied Spain in 1808; the occupation generated a violent resistance movement. Goya's war scenes were revolutionary in depicting war as barbarous rather than glorious.

*Con razon ó sin ella*

domestic servants who could also double as musicians. (Austria still devotes close to 20 percent of its annual revenues to the arts.) Compared to the musical tastes of the Empress, the tastes of these new patrons were progressive, even revolutionary.

The intellectual achievements of the Enlightenment served further to undermine the long-standing authority of kings and queens, princes and princesses. People came to believe that reason was a surer guide than tradition. The English artist William Hogarth (1697–1764) criticized society in his satirical paintings of the English upper class (Color Plate 8; immortalized in Igor Stravinsky's 1951 opera, *The Rake's Progress*). The Spanish painter Francisco Goya (1746–1828) drew impassioned indictments of social injustice and man's inhumanity to man (Figure 2).

The political revolutions that marked the last years of the century were inevitable, with the American struggle for independence from the British (1775–1783) followed by the bloody French Revolution (1789–1799). The rise of Napoleon Bonaparte (1769–1821; Figure 3) in the aftermath of the French Revolution touched off a series of protracted wars (1803–1815) between France and its neighbors. A brilliant military and political strategist, Napoleon symbolized for Europeans both the ideals and the excesses of this age of revolution. Although the Austro-Hungarian empire was spared an internal revolution, all Europe became embroiled in the effort to curb Napoleon's expansionist

FIGURE 3 *Napoleon in His Study*, by the neoclassical artist Jacques-Louis David, was painted in 1812, when the emperor was at the height of his power. Years before, Napoleon had been so reluctant to pose for a portrait that his wife made him sit still by clasping him on her lap while the artist worked.

ambitions. After Napoleon's final defeat in 1815, Europe, under Austria's Prince Metternich, retreated into reactionary politics. But the issues of nobility and republicanism, of monarchy and democracy, of despots and liberators, continued to be debated throughout the first half of the nineteenth century.

Around 1730 the population of Europe began to expand at a rate unequaled before or since. The expansion was triggered in part by what has come to be known as the Industrial Revolution, though it was as much agricultural as industrial. In 1700, 80 percent of the English population lived on farms. By 1800, in part as a result of advances in farming techniques, only 40 percent were left in the countryside. Many of the displaced farmers and their families made their way to the cities and found work in busy factories that were themselves being mechanized. This social upheaval added to the political ferment of the period.

In 1800 Vienna boasted a population of about 250,000, tens of thousands of whom were employed by the monarchical government. After its founding as a Roman colony along the Danube, periodic flooding of the site had prompted the construction of a series of buffer canals. The modern city grew up along these canals. Outside the city stood a double set of semicircular fortifications. In 1809 Napoleon had most of them leveled when the Viennese refused to surrender. With its narrow streets radiating from public squares, the densely populated city took only about 20 minutes to cross by foot. A few miles outside the

FIGURE 4 An eruption of Mount Vesuvius in A.D. 79 buried the Roman towns of Pompeii and Herculaneum. The excavations of these sites in the mid-eighteenth century revived interest in the classical world. Almost all our surviving examples of Roman paintings are from these long-buried settlements.

walls was the famous *Wienerwald* ("Vienna forest"), where Beethoven often strolled. In and around the city flourished some 200 makers of musical instruments, including 130 piano makers. The equivalent would be for 6,000 instrument makers to be operating in New York City today!

More than a dozen important music publishers were active in Vienna at the turn of the century. Though they rarely published more than 300 copies of a work, the sales of hundreds of different items supported a robust market. During the summer, bands hired by the nobility roamed the streets playing light music. Dozens of composers supplied dance music for festive balls that celebrated everything from New Year's Eve to charities. Composers strove to supply works that would please, but the Viennese public displayed an independence (called "fickleness" by critics) that tried their patience.

Exactly when the Viennese Classical style arose and faded is hard to determine. The term *classical* was first used to describe the writings of two Germans, Johann Wolfgang von Goethe (1749–1832) and Friedrich von Schiller (1759–1805), who were active as poets, playwrights, and philosophers. During the late eighteenth century architects and painters frequently looked to the recently excavated Greek and Roman ruins of antiquity for inspiration. (Pompeii is perhaps the best-known example; see Figure 4.) For them these structures represented a balance and symmetry that later art historians referred to as *neoclassical*. The layout and architecture of Washington, D.C., was much influenced by this rekindled interest (Figure 5).

Hence the term *Classical*, like *Baroque*, came into use only after the period it describes had come to an end. Today the term *classical* is commonly used to

FIGURE 5 George Washington chose the location and the designer—French military engineer Pierre-Charles L'Enfant—for one of the world's few cities specifically planned as a national capital. In its early decades, the town in the wilderness on swampy land was short on neoclassical grandeur. Washington, D.C., was called "a mud-hole equal to the great Serbonian bog."

describe all art music, with the implication that "classical music" is somehow timeless. This is, of course, an absurd notion, just as absurd as the idea that all popular music is soon forgotten. Although some writers have advocated abolishing the term *Classical,* it is no more misleading than *Baroque.* And in the music of the four greatest proponents of Viennese Classicism—Joseph Haydn (1732–1809), Wolfgang Amadeus Mozart (1756–1791), Ludwig van Beethoven (1770–1827), and Franz Schubert (1797–1828)—we have some of the first music that has never gone out of fashion.

The Viennese Classical period generally refers to the entire span from about 1750 to 1828. Some writers identify a "high Classical" phase between about 1781 and 1815. Others describe the period after 1815 as "Romantic," although we will reserve that term for the more decisive style break that occurred around 1830. Modern-day audiences have become so familiar with the Viennese Classical repertory that it is hard for us to imagine the impact that music must have had on the audiences of the time. During the 30 years following the death of Bach in 1750, the musical language of Austria and Germany experienced a revolution no less profound than the social and political revolutions that were rocking Europe.

# Chapter 13

## THE RISE OF THE SYMPHONY

So strong and cohesive was the late Baroque style that, when it finally fell out of favor around 1750 (the process had been underway for at least 20 years), it took 30 years for a cohesive new style to replace it. During this lengthy *pre-Classical* phase, reactions against the earlier style took two forms.

The *galant* (French for "elegant, tasteful, correct, polite") style originated in France during the first half of the eighteenth century, but the term was soon applied to Italian and southern German music as well. *Galant* music is light, pleasant, and—at its best—charming. It favors tune-and-accompaniment textures rather than contrapuntal textures. Its phrases are more regular than spun out. Above all, *galant* music avoids strong displays of emotion.*

At the other extreme, the style of *Empfindsamkeit* (German for "sensitiveness") flourished in northern Germany around the middle of the eighteenth century. *Empfindsam* music is intense and brooding. It relies more on motives than tunes, favors textures that shift unpredictably, and indulges in emotional excess.

Two sons of Johann Sebastian Bach reflect the split personality of pre-Classical music. Bach's youngest son, Johann Christian (1735–1782), left Leipzig as a teenager to study in Milan, a center for Italian opera. He spent most of his career in London (he is sometimes called "the London Bach"), where he wrote works of a decidedly *galant* bent. Bach's eldest son, Carl Philipp Emanuel (1714–1788), remained in northern Germany and became the most important proponent of *Empfindsamkeit*.

## THE VIENNESE CLASSICAL STYLE

The Classical style that coalesced around 1780 incorporated features of both the *galant* and *empfindsam* styles and broke sharply with the late Baroque style. Late Baroque music was strongly influenced by keyboard and string techniques; Clas-

---

*Some writers have used the term *rococo* to describe this style. The roots of that term are in architecture, however; the term's only strong musical connection is with French ballet.

sical music depends more on a "singing" style. Late Baroque music employed complex themes; Classical music favors tunes of a popular character. Late Baroque music was based on continuity; Classical music is broken into clearly defined phrases, often divided into equal halves (2 + 2 or 4 + 4 bars, for example) arranged in question-and-answer patterns.

Late Baroque rhythms were square and maintained a uniform energy level; Classical rhythms are flexible and accumulate energy as the phrases unfold. The harmonic rhythm of late Baroque music was rapid and regular; the harmonic rhythm of Classical music is slower and irregular. (The breaking up of Baroque continuity and regularity gradually did away with the need for the continuo, though the practice persisted into the first years of the nineteenth century.)

Late Baroque textures were contrapuntal; Classical textures are variable and more homophonic. Late Baroque music used level dynamics with occasional bold contrasts; Classical composers introduced frequent, gradual changes in dynamics, which led to the replacement of the harpsichord by the piano. The instrumental colors of the late Baroque are uniform within a section or a movement; Viennese Classicism launched the modern orchestra, with its wide range of instrumental colors.

Some of the forms that became popular during the Classical period were already familiar in the Baroque. One such form was theme and variations (see Frescobaldi's *Capriccio* in Chapter 9, pages 170–171). The harmonic pattern of a Classical theme and variations usually outlines a simple form, such as binary form. Keyboard variations continued to enjoy special popularity.

A holdover from the Baroque dance suite was the *minuet,* generally in binary form, which found its way into almost every type of Classical music. The minuet was almost always followed by a trio, also in binary form, followed by a da capo (page 221) of the minuet. Out of the modest binary form we first encountered in Handel's suite evolved one of the most dynamic means of musical organization in the history of Western music.

## SONATA FORM

The hallmark of the Classical style was the sonata principle, commonly called *sonata form.* **Sonata form** is a style of composition based on successive stages of stability, tension, and resolution. An inherently dramatic style, it embodied the revolutionary spirit of the age. So pervasive was the influence of sonata form on virtually every category of music that Viennese Classicism is the only period in Western music ever spoken of as a single, uniform style.

Both words in the expression *sonata form* are somewhat misleading. Beginning in the late Renaissance, the generic term *sonata* was used for any instrumental music that had no program, or extramusical verbal description, associated with it—what we call today *absolute music.* Then in the late eighteenth century it came to mean an extended piece in several movements for solo keyboard, or a work for a soloist (such as a violinist) with keyboard accompaniment. Yet *sonata form* applies only to individual movements. Moreover, we find sonata form not only in sonatas but in trios, quartets, symphonies, concertos, and even operas. It occurs in fast movements and in slow movements, in opening movements and in concluding movements, in instrumental music and in vocal music.

The pairing of *sonata* with *form* occurred only in the mid-nineteenth century, well after the impulse behind its development had run its course. *Form* is misleading because it suggests that some sort of rigid, preconceived scheme was superimposed on the music. Actually, to the Viennese masters, sonata form was no more preconceived or schematic than the novel, whose development it paralleled.

Sonata form was a dynamic integration of harmonic, thematic, and rhythmic elements. Originating with the binary forms we examined in Chapter 11, it came to be used for compositions of much greater scale. Although we use the widely accepted term *form* in the following discussions, we must remember that to Haydn, Mozart, and Beethoven sonata form was a means to an end. Although they used broad formal divisions, the most important characteristic of sonata form was its flexibility. Having said that, we now outline those divisions.

**Exposition.** In sonata form the *exposition* corresponds to the first half of a binary form and usually repeats in the same manner (page 217). It introduces the principal thematic material of the movement and modulates away from the home key to provide dramatic conflict. The exposition usually consists of four phases, though they are more like points along a continuum than clearly separated units:

- *Primary area.* Presents one or more themes* that establish the tonic, or primary, key.
- *Transition.* An unstable section that modulates away from the tonic; transitions sound as if they are "in transit" or headed toward a new plateau.
- *Secondary area.* Presents one or more themes that temporarily establish the new, or secondary, key. In a movement in the major mode, this key is generally that of the dominant.
- *Closing area.* Confirms the new temporary key with a series of cadences.

**Development.** The development and the recapitulation correspond to the second half of a binary form. Composers often omitted the repeat of this second half, however, and performers often leave it out even when it is called for. The *development* is the most unstable section in a sonata-form movement and passes through the most remote tonalities. It develops or elaborates on material that was presented in the exposition, although it may include new material as well.

*A theme in a sonata-form movement is identified by its initial association with a key area. Thereafter it is referred to by means of that association. For example, a theme from the primary area that is then used in the development is identified as the "primary-area theme." This interrelationship between theme and key area is fundamental to sonata form.

The term *development* is both a label for a section and a technique. To Viennese composers, development as a technique meant subjecting the thematic material to fragmentation and harmonic sequencing. The development generally ends with a passage that prepares the return to the home key, called the *retransition*. The development is not obligatory; most frequently it is omitted in slow movements.

**Recapitulation.** The *recapitulation* affords a certain symmetry to the movement as a whole. It restates the material of the exposition, generally in the original order, but with a crucial difference: Thematic ideas that appeared in the exposition in a key other than the tonic now appear in the home key, resolving the harmonic conflict set up in the exposition.

An optional section, called the *coda* (from the Latin for "tail"), consists of a series of emphatic cadences designed to conclude the entire movement. Beethoven invested the coda with proportions that rivaled those of the three principal divisions of sonata form.

## ANATOMY OF THE SYMPHONY

Before 1750, secular instrumental music had usually been performed in informal or private settings before an invited audience. It was during the Classical period that the public concert, open to all who could pay for a ticket, first took hold. The most popular instrumental compositions in public concerts were the symphony and the piano concerto. For many people today, the symphony is so closely associated with public concerts that "going to the symphony" is almost synonymous with "going to a concert."

A **symphony** is an extended orchestral work in several movements. Its origins are in the early years of the eighteenth century, when several stylistic influences merged. The most important influence was the opera overture, a series of brief movements in a fast-slow-fast sequence. Composers experimented with this scheme throughout the 1760s and 1770s and at last settled on a four-movement plan:

I. An *Allegro*\*. This was generally the weightiest movement of the Classical symphony and was almost always in sonata form.

II. A *slow movement,* either in sonata form or in some simpler form such as ternary or theme and variations.

---

\*The clearest way to refer to a movement is by its position within the work: first, second, third, or fourth. But other terms are also common. The first movement may be referred to as the *opening Allegro;* the slow movement by its tempo marking (for example, *Andante*); the third movement as the *Minuet;* and the fourth movement as the *finale. Finale* (Italian for "end") was the generic term used throughout the eighteenth and nineteenth centuries for the last movement of any instrumental work.

# Listening Guide 36

## HAYDN:  Symphony No. 100 in G Major, "Military"

CD 3, TRACKS 8 – 11
TAPE 3B, TRACKS 3–6
DURATION: 24:00

*When you listen to these four movements, concentrate first on the* **boldface** *entries in the Time column that give each movement its shape; do not get sidetracked by the detailed comments. Once you have a feeling for the broad proportions, the details will fall into place. The start times for repeating sections are shown in brackets.*

DURATION: 7:30

### First Movement: Adagio/Allegro

*Form: Sonata*

| LOCATION | | TIME | COMMENTS |
|---|---|---|---|
| 1 | INTRODUCTION | | Adagio (Slow). |
| | | **0:00** | Soft strings with occasional winds. |
| | | 0:54 | Deflection to the minor mode, complete with trumpets and timpani. Resolution left hanging. |
| | | 1:06 | Returns abruptly to earlier mood, settling on a long pedal point that culminates in four loud chords with the full orchestra. |
| 2 | EXPOSITION | | Allegro (Fast). The entire section repeats. |
| | Primary area | **1:39 [3:15]** | Theme in the flute, accompanied by two oboes. The theme repeats in the strings. |
| | Transition | 1:53 [3:30] | Begins with a tutti explosion that leads to a modulating sequence. |
| | | 2:15 [3:51] | A long pedal point prepares the new key. |
| 3 | Secondary area | 2:27 [4:04] | Anticipated by long tones in flute and oboes, which then begin the theme of the primary area (monothematicism), but in the key of the dominant. |
| | | 2:39 [4:15] | A brief but powerful *forte* outburst. |
| | Closing area | 2:44 [4:21] | The theme (strings and then winds) is in the popular style. |
| | | 2:59 [4:35] | Loud, emphatic series of cadences in the new key, followed by a long rest. |
| 4 | DEVELOPMENT | | |
| | Closing-area theme | **4:53** | With rapid dynamic shifts, develops the head of the theme through a series of dramatic sequences and modulations. |
| | Primary-area theme and closing-area theme | 5:34 | First fragmented but then building to a dramatic *fortissimo*. |
| | Retransition | 5:58 | Suddenly soft, setting up the return to the opening material of the exposition. |

| LOCATION | TIME | COMMENTS |
|---|---|---|
| **5** RECAPITULATION | | |
| Primary area | **6:04** | Flute and oboes, as at opening of the exposition. |
| | 6:11 | Tutti outburst, replacing soft statement of primary-area theme and transition. |
| [Secondary area omitted] | | |
| Closing area | 6:27 | Theme in the popular style, now stated in the tonic key. |
| | 6:38 | Surprise chord, followed by emphatic cadences greatly expanded over the exposition (includes much of the transition, now redirected to the tonic). |

DURATION: 5:45

## Second Movement: Allegretto

*Form: Free variation of a theme*

*The two striking features of this movement are its alternation between (1) winds/strings and a full military ensemble and (2) the major mode and the minor mode.*

| | | | |
|---|---|---|---|
| **1** | *A*-SECTION | **0:00** | Theme in the major mode, *piano*. Alternates between two phrases (*a* and *b*), and between strings and winds. |
| **2** | *A'*-SECTION | **1:44** | Theme *forte* in the minor mode, with military instruments. Alternates with *piano* passages. |
| **3** | *A''*-SECTION | **2:48** | Theme back in the major mode, accompanied by pizzicato (in which the strings are plucked) strings. |
| **4** | | **3:26** | Theme, still played *forte*, aided by military instruments. |
| | | 3:38 | Winds, *piano*. |
| | | 4:06 | Theme, *forte* in the full orchestra. |
| **5** | CODA | **4:39** | Bold military call in the solo trumpet. |
| | | 4:51 | Furious timpani roll, final excursion to the minor mode. |
| | | 5:05 | Abrupt return to major mode. Sudden alternations between *piano* and *forte*, concluding triumphantly. |

DURATION: 5:42

## Third Movement: Menuetto. Moderato

*Movement form: Minuet/Trio with da capo of Minuet*
*Section (Minuet, Trio) form: binary*

*The minuet is in a moderate triple meter, with frequent contrasts between full, loud passages and softer passages. Typically for Haydn, the minuet is dominated by a single rhythmic figure (page 282).*

| | | | |
|---|---|---|---|
| **1** | MINUET | | |
| | *A* | **0:00** | The initial theme repeats in the full orchestra. |

*continued*

| LOCATION | TIME | COMMENTS |
|---|---|---|
| *B* | 0:23 [1:18] | |
| (*A* opening★) | 0:59 [1:55] | |

**2  TRIO**

| | | |
|---|---|---|
| *C* | **2:14** [2:26] | Sweet dotted-rhythm theme in winds and strings. |
| *D* | 2:38 [3:02] | Builds to a powerful *forte* chain of dotted rhythms. |
| (*C* opening) | 2:50 [3:14] | Played *piano*. |

**3  MINUET da capo** — Exactly the same as the first minuet.

| | | |
|---|---|---|
| *A* | **3:26** | |
| *B* | 3:48 [4:44] | |
| (*A* opening) | 4:24 [5:20] | |

★The return in the second half of a binary form to the opening theme of the first half (and always in the tonic key) produces *rounded binary form*. In practice these are miniature sonata forms.

DURATION: 5:00

*Fourth Movement: Finale. Presto*

*Form: Sonata*

**1  EXPOSITION**
Primary area

| | | |
|---|---|---|
| *a* | **0:00** [0:06] | Rollicking theme of popular character in rounded binary form. Strings only. |
| *b* | 0:12 [0:45] | Rapid alternations in the full orchestra between *forte* and *piano*. |
| *a* return | 0:39 [1:11] | Preceded by rests. Strings only. |
| Transition | 1:16 | *Forte*, based on primary-area theme. Closes out with a series of expectant rests. |

**2**  Secondary area — 1:42 — In the dominant. Over driving rhythms, snatches of tune tossed from register to register.

Closing area — 1:51 — Powerful *forte* cadences in the full orchestra.

---

**First Movement.**  The slow introduction (an option favored by Haydn) to the first movement prepares the listener for the drama to come. After the first several phrases, the music turns suddenly to the minor mode and heads toward a climax that is left hanging in midair. Just before the *Allegro*, a *fortissimo* abruptly follows a *pianissimo*. Unlike the contrasts in symphonies by *empfindsam* composers such as C. P. E. Bach, these opening contrasts are echoed at strategic structural junctures throughout the movement.

Following the *fortissimo* chord that concludes the introduction, the flute opens the exposition with an innocent tune (the prominence of the woodwinds is another indication of Haydn's "military" intent):

| LOCATION | TIME | COMMENTS |
|---|---|---|
| **3  DEVELOPMENT** | | |
| Bridge | **2:09** | Based on the rests that preceded the secondary area. Ends with rapid solo timpani strokes. |
| Primary-area theme | 2:15 | Begins *piano* in the minor mode. After a long rest, makes a dramatic crescendo. |
| Secondary-area theme | 2:34 | Alternates between *piano* and *forte*. Harmonically the farthest removed from the tonic key. |
| Bridge | | Includes smooth legato lines unlike anything else in the movement. |
| Primary-area theme | 3:01 | *Forte*, full orchestra in the minor mode. |
| Retransition | 3:17 | Based on the secondary-area theme, leading to a pedal point and another dramatic rest. |
| | | |
| **4  RECAPITULATION** | | |
| Primary area | **3:29** | Extensively rewritten from the exposition. |
| [Transition omitted] | | |
| **5**  Secondary area | 4:05 | In the tonic key. Snatches of the *forte* tune now accompanied by the military instruments. |
| Closing area | 4:11 | Rewritten from the exposition to incorporate the military instruments. |
| Bridge | 4:29 | Similar to the retransition. |
| | | |
| **6  CODA** | | |
| Primary-area theme | **4:34** | Much like the opening of the exposition. |
| Closing area | 4:45 | New closing themes based on the primary-area theme. Played *forte*, aided by the military instruments. |

Haydn was fond of these simple openings (though this one bears more than a passing resemblance to the tune that opens the slow introduction) and invariably transformed them into a boisterous transition. Here he introduces a kinetic passage in the transition to carry out the modulation from the primary key to the secondary key. The modulation extends over about 30 seconds, from the tutti explosion that launches the transition to the beginning of the secondary area. The music seems to be driving toward a particular goal.

Suddenly the kinetic motion ceases and gives way to the beginning of the secondary area. Instead of introducing a new idea, Haydn presents a variation on the tune from the primary area; he could get as much use out of a single thematic idea as other composers derived from several. This use of the same thematic material for both the primary and the secondary areas is called **monothematicism.** (Other themes can appear elsewhere in the movement.)

In Haydn's time, the gap between popular music and art music was still not pronounced. In any case, it is unlikely that Haydn had any firsthand knowledge of the popular music practiced by peasants. Rather, he crafted tunes whose four-square, repetitive phrase structure and diatonic—even static—harmonies conjured up rustic images for his urban audiences. There is probably a connection between this interest and the republican enthusiasms of the age. Typically, Haydn used such tunes to prepare for the close of the exposition, as in this symphony. Even here, however, he cannot leave the theme alone and has it jump up and down by octaves in successive phrases:

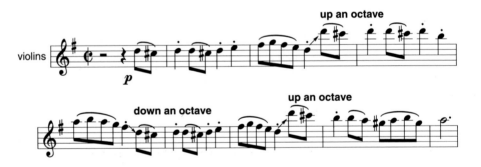

He then repeats the exposition without pause, affording listeners a second opportunity to familiarize themselves with the material.

After a dramatic 2-measure pause, Haydn begins his development in an entirely new key. He now subjects the jaunty little closing tune from the exposition to the most learned kinds of development. He starts as if he were going to run through it all over again. But then he settles on just its opening phrase, or head,* and develops it most elaborately. Another pause at mid-development

---

*Although there are several ways of referring to the parts of a theme or tune, throughout this book *head* will refer to the beginning of a theme, and *tail* to its end.

seems to signal the return of the primary-area theme, but Haydn now grafts its 3-note head onto the 5-note tail of the closing-area theme:

**primary-theme head** → **closing-theme tail**

Like the earlier sections of the development, it too builds to a resounding climax.

The instability of the development is followed by a return to the stability that opened the movement. This is the recapitulation, which Haydn prepares by bringing in the flute and oboes just before returning to the opening theme. Because this theme has already been heard twice in the exposition, Haydn now wisely abandons the monothematic principle and cuts straight to the closing tune, this time in the tonic key. Typically, he expands the rest of the closing material over what appeared in the exposition, though not enough to constitute a separate coda. Overall, the movement balances the serious and the jovial, the dramatic and the lyrical. The surprises are integrated into the whole.

**Second Movement.**   The movement that pleased Haydn's audience most at the premiere of Symphony No. 100, however, was the second-movement Allegretto, adapted, as we mentioned, from an earlier work. Here Haydn suddenly unleashes the trumpets, bass drum, triangle, and cymbals, none of which has been heard in the first movement. The effect is electrifying.

In form, this movement is as ingenious as it is simple. Haydn builds it around a single long-breathed theme (we show only the first 8 of 56 measures):

The theme is first heard *piano* in the major mode, then *forte* in the minor mode (with all the "military" instruments), and finally *piano* and *forte* in the major mode. (Haydn again gets a lot of mileage from a single theme.) Then an ominous trumpet call announces one final apocalyptic outburst in the minor, which is soon vanquished by the triumphant major. At the premiere, Haydn's London audience demanded and got an encore of this movement.

# *Historical Window*

## HAYDN IN LONDON

The Viennese saw Haydn as just another provincial *Kapellmeister*. Londoners hailed him as a hero. A week after his arrival in January 1791, he wrote—more in astonishment than as a boast—to Marianne von Genzinger: "My arrival caused a great sensation throughout the whole city, and I went the round of all the newspapers for 3 successive days. Everyone wants to know me. I have had to dine out six times up to now, and if I wanted, I could have an invitation every day. . . ."

To reach England, Haydn had to cross the English Channel, a harrowing experience, as he reported to Marianne von Genzinger:

On . . . New Year's Day, after attending early mass, I boarded the ship at 7:30 a.m. and at 5 in the afternoon I arrived, thank God! safe and sound in Dover. . . . For the first 4 whole hours, we had almost no wind, and the ship went so slowly that . . . we didn't go further than one single English mile, and there are 24 between Calais and Dover. Our ship's captain, in an evil temper, said that if the wind did not change, we should have to spend the whole night at sea. Fortunately, however, towards 11:30 o'clock a wind arose and blew so favourably that by 4 o'clock we covered 22 miles. Since the tide, which had just begun to ebb, prevented our large vessel from reaching the pier, 2 smaller ships came out to meet us as we were still fairly far out at sea, and into these we and our luggage were transferred, and thus at last, though exposed to a medium gale, we landed safely. . . . I remained on deck during the whole passage, so as to gaze my fill at that mighty monster, the ocean. So long as it was calm, I wasn't afraid at all, but towards the end, when the wind grew stronger and stronger, and I saw the monstrous high waves rushing at us, I became a little frightened, and a little nauseated, too. But I overcame it all and arrived safely on shore without (pardon me) vomiting.

Despite his enthusiastic reception, Haydn confided to Genzinger that he found English life somewhat disconcerting: "I wish that I could fly for a time to Vienna, to have more quiet in which to work, for the noise that the common people make as they sell their wares in the street is intolerable."

While he was in London, Haydn discovered that much of his early music was circulating in corrupt versions. On January 14 the *Morning Chronicle* noted:

Since Haydn's arrival in this country, he has discovered the REMAINS of several of his early Concertos [symphonies] that were first KIDNAPPED and afterwards most inhumanely ROBBED AND MANGLED by some of our ORIGINAL COMPOSERS. A Jury of AMATEURS has sat on the BODIES, and brought in a verdict—WILFUL MURDER BY PERSONS UNKNOWN.

Since there were as yet no copyright laws protecting music written outside England, these "murders" were perfectly legal.

Always eager to augment his income, Haydn offered keyboard lessons to members of the nobility at the rate of a guinea per lesson (about 50 dollars by today's standards). On hearing that he could demand such a fee, he remarked later to a biographer, "My eyes popped out of my head." But he found that teaching was not without its hazards: "If a singing-, pianoforte-, or dancing-master asks half a guinea per lesson, he demands that an entrance fee of six guineas be paid for the first lesson. This is done because during the winter many Scots and Irishmen take pride in having their children study with the best teachers, only to find that at the end they cannot pay the fee. The entrance fee is dispensed if the teacher charges a guinea, but the guinea must then be paid at every lesson."

During both of Haydn's London visits, Salomon staged a series of subscription concerts in the Hanover Square Rooms. This so-called Great Hall measured 79 × 32 feet and seated 800 persons. Some 1,500 people, including commoners as well as aristocrats, reportedly attended one of the concerts, with the overflow presumably standing. With its high-domed ceiling and resonant acoustics, the Great Hall was London's most popular concert hall. A contemporary reported that it "was the custom for the concert-giver to serve his audience refreshments gratis during the intermission between the first and second halves of the programme."

For each of his two visits (January 1791 to June 1792, and February 1794 to August 1795), Haydn composed six new symphonies, each of which received its premiere during the Salomon concerts. The sensation aroused by these performances was captured vividly by Charles Burney:

> Haydn himself presided at the piano-forte; and the sight of that renowned composer so electrified the audience, as to excite the attention and a pleasure superior to any that had ever, to my knowledge, been caused by instrumental music in England. All the slow middle movements were encored; which never before happened, I believe, in any country.

The greatest success of all was the premiere of the "Military" Symphony on March 31, 1794. By now it had become customary for Haydn's *New Grand*

*continued*

*Overture* (that is, his new symphony) to open the second half of a very long program that included almost two and a half hours of music. A review of a repeat performance a week later confirms the symphony's impact:

> Another new Symphony, by Haydn, was performed for the second time; and the middle movement was again received with absolute shouts of applause. Encore! encore! encore! resounded from every seat: the Ladies themselves could not forbear. It is the advancing to battle; and the march of men, the sounding of the charge, the thundering of the onset, the clash of arms, the groans of the wounded, and what may well be called the hellish roar of war increase to a climax of horrid sublimity! which, if others can conceive, he alone can execute; at least he alone hitherto has effected these wonders [*Morning Chronicle*, 9 April 1794].

Haydn returned to London for his second visit against the wishes of Prince Esterházy. The £1,200 he had earned from his first visit doubtless encouraged him, though he was by now quite wealthy. In England he found a combination of tradition and entrepreneurship that could not fail to fascinate this endlessly curious man.

---

**Third Movement.** As in Haydn's other London Symphonies, the minuet of this symphony is full of pomp and circumstance. The minuet proper is saturated with a characteristic motive of four fast notes followed by two slower but staccato notes:

*Moderato (Moderately)*

Although Haydn takes the thematic economy of the first two movements even further in the minuet, the ingenuity with which he extends and manipulates the motive prevents us from becoming bored. Haydn gives the aristocratic tune rich orchestration and maintains its momentum with an increasingly independent bass line, often in spirited counterpoint with the upper melody in the violins and winds. The jaunty dotted rhythms of the central trio and a brief outburst in the minor mode reminiscent of the first two movements interrupt the aristocratic pose briefly before the da capo of the minuet.

**Fourth Movement.** In the fourth movement, the Presto, Haydn returns to the sonata principle of the first movement but has it serve different musical ends. His emphasis is on good-humored play rather than on dramatic contrasts. He makes the rounded binary theme of the primary area considerably longer than in the opening Allegro and introduces an unexpected pause before the return of the primary-area theme:

The secondary area consists of thematic snatches tossed, like the proverbial hot potato, from instrument to instrument.

The development is shot through with slapstick surprises and sudden pauses (derived from the pause just shown; for Haydn, a rest was as thematic as a succession of pitches). This reeling imbalance is set right by the recapitulation, which triumphantly re-orchestrates the fragmentary theme of the secondary area. This is accomplished with the help of the military instruments that have been silent since the second movement. A coda closes the work in grand style.

Throughout this symphony Haydn shows his skill in manipulating his audience. He moves them to pathos one moment and to laughter the next. Though by this time he was 62 years old, his music has the exuberance of youth, and his powers of invention seem stronger than ever. Small wonder that he took London by storm.

## ✷Mozart: Symphony No. 41 in C Major, K. 551* (1788)

Wolfgang Amadeus Mozart (whose life and music we explore more fully in the next two chapters) wrote symphonies that differed sharply in style from Haydn's. While Haydn extracted the maximum use from each theme, Mozart favored movements with many themes. While Haydn's formal proportions are compact, Mozart's are expansive. While the surface of Haydn's music teems with surprises, Mozart's surfaces are smoothly contoured. Haydn favors bright, unusual combinations of instruments; Mozart favors smooth blends. While Haydn delighted in formal experimentation, Mozart preferred sonata form. Mozart was not above injecting humor, but for Haydn humor was a cornerstone of his art. They had at

*K. is an abbreviation for Ludwig Ritter von Köchel, whose catalogue, published in 1865 and revised several times since, sought to number Mozart's works in chronological order.

least one feature in common: From the 1780s on, both integrated music in a popular style into the sophisticated sonata form.

These qualities are all evident in Mozart's final symphony, No. 41 in C Major, the last of three composed in a remarkably short period during the summer of 1788. Though they rank among the finest symphonies of the period, Mozart—unlike Haydn—never heard any of these works performed. The *Jupiter* (as it was dubbed in the nineteenth century) Symphony lasts half again as long as Haydn's "Military" Symphony. Three of its four movements are in sonata form, and even the minuet could (like Haydn's) be construed as a miniature sonata form. The symphony's profusion of themes suggest a composer for whom melodic invention was as natural as breathing.

The opening phrase of Mozart's first movement takes the question-and-answer form that he favored:

He integrates large dynamic and textural contrasts such as this into symmetrical and balanced phrase structures. The music unfolds at a leisurely pace, with the primary and secondary areas set off by strongly articulated rests. Mozart rounds off the primary area, transition, and closing area with nearly identical material.

The theme of the secondary area unfolds in a pattern of increasing rhythmic activity:

This principle of "increasing animation" underlies many of Mozart's melodies and accounts in part for their irresistible flow. After the first bit of tune, the cellos and double basses, which provide part of the accompaniment, play the same figure a step higher. This interchangeability of theme and accompaniment is an important feature of the Classical style. An unexpected rest leads to a dramatic but brief deflection to the minor mode that makes the arrival at the closing area all the more satisfying.

Mozart, too, uses a popular tune as one of five (!) closing themes. Unlike the restless Haydn, however, he is content to present it in a straightforward manner:

Mozart opens the development with the same theme, though in a distant key. A small cadential theme that followed this tune in the exposition becomes the basis for an extended development. The density of imitation is almost fugal—an acknowledgment of Mozart's assimilation of Bach's music, which both he and Haydn had encountered at their friend Baron von Swieten's house in the early 1780s.

While Haydn's retransition leaves the listener guessing as to the exact moment of recapitulation, Mozart's retransition functions like a wave that crests at exactly the right moment. And unlike the considerable rewriting that takes place in Haydn's recapitulation (caused partly by its monothematicism), Mozart makes the minimal adjustments needed to create a large-scale symmetry between exposition and recapitulation.

Mozart's unusual slow movement calls for violins *con sordino* ("with mutes") and is shot through with offbeat accents, chromatic harmonies from the minor mode, rhythms that range from very slow to very fast, and syncopated melodies. Yet all these elements are integrated into a balanced, symmetrical form that flows exceptionally smoothly. Unlike many slow movements, Mozart's includes a full development section, one that exploits the minor-mode episodes from the exposition.

Smoothness also characterizes the lyrical minuet, whose trio makes ingenious use of a simple, 2-chord cadence pattern. Mozart's finale provides a fitting conclusion to his last symphony. Along with his customarily clear structures, it contains a brilliant synthesis of the symphonic style, the overture style of comic opera (which we shall discuss in Chapter 15), and Baroque counterpoint. Four highly contrasting themes are manipulated in a virtuoso fashion, culminating in the coda with the combining of all four in a texture that is simultaneously imitative and nonimitative. Only a Mozart seems to have been capable of juggling successfully so many elements at the same time.

The glory of the Classical style was that a single language could accommodate the expression of two such individual composers. In the next two chapters we explore further genres at which each composer excelled: string quartet for Haydn, piano concerto and opera for Mozart.

# Chapter 14

## CONCERTO AND QUARTET

During the 1830s and 1840s, concert series aimed at general audiences became increasingly popular, and success at public performances became a composer's principal means of recognition. Indeed, since the mid-nineteenth century, almost all art music has been composed for the concert hall or the opera house (Figure 14.1). So it may seem surprising that throughout the eighteenth and into the first decades of the nineteenth century composers consciously distinguished between music intended for the general public and music intended for private consumption.

## PUBLIC MUSIC AND PRIVATE MUSIC

For the general public, composers wrote operas (including concert arias derived from operatic models), symphonies, and solo concertos. The demand for music to satisfy this growing audience led to the rise of the Classical orchestra, which in the late eighteenth century generally consisted of pairs of oboes, bassoons, and horns (less frequently a flute or a pair of clarinets), first and second violins, violas, cellos, and double basses (the number of strings was generally fewer than employed today for the Classical repertoire). For more important occasions, trumpets and timpani might be added.

For private performances, composers wrote chamber music—solo keyboard sonatas and four-hand piano music (played by two performers at the same instrument), as well as duets, trios, quartets, and quintets—for voices with instrumental accompaniment or for instruments alone. It would never have occurred to Haydn or Mozart, for example, to perform a string quartet at a public concert. Although Salomon had Haydn's Op. 71 and Op. 73 string quartets performed at his London concerts in 1793, such performances were exceptional.

We can better understand a distinction that the Classical period took for granted by likening public music to a professional basketball game played in a large sports arena before a paying audience, and by likening private music to a pickup game played among friends. But whereas there might be a difference in the quality of play between the professional and the pickup game, Classical composers lavished equal care on both public and private music. If there are any

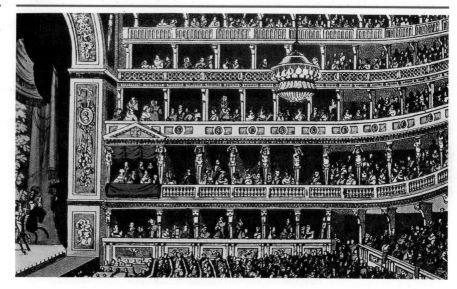

FIGURE 14.1 The Theater-an-der-Wien, a popular Viennese theater also used for music performance. In the twentieth century, designers have applied scientific understanding of acoustics to concert halls—with mixed results.

noteworthy differences, they lie, as we shall see in this chapter, in the experimental bent of private music and the greater attention paid to popular taste in public music. But exceptions to both generalizations are easy to find.

## THE PIANO CONCERTO

After the symphony, the best-known variety of public instrumental music in Vienna was the solo concerto. The mature form was fashioned almost single-handedly by Mozart (whose life we shall survey next). The solo concertos of Vivaldi and J. S. Bach (the two most gifted and prolific composers of concertos during the late Baroque) were cast predominantly in ritornello form (page 209). Mozart retained elements of this form, as well as the fast-slow-fast order of movements in the Baroque concerto, but he turned to the newly developed sonata form to invest all three movements with drama and complexity.

Mozart wrote concertos for violin, horn, and clarinet as well as for piano, but his more than two dozen keyboard concertos are his greatest achievement in the genre. The harpsichord concerto dates back to the beginning of the eighteenth century, about the same time the piano was invented in Italy. It was not until the late 1770s, however, that the piano's greater power and dynamic range enabled it gradually to supplant the harpsichord. The new instrument was able to render every shade of *forte* and *piano* (hence its early name, *fortepiano*), as well as various degrees of legato and non-legato. (In other respects the early piano was more closely related to the harpsichord than to our modern instrument; for an account of the piano's early development, see the Historical Window for Chapter 17 on page 350). Using scales and arpeggios, Mozart created marvelously varied figurations for the soloist. For him, the soloist was not an adversary but a scintillating partner in a fast-paced conversation.

The opening (and longest) movement of the concerto is generally in **sonata-concerto form,** which includes all the elements of a full sonata movement plus an orchestral ritornello that serves as introduction, as the bridge between exposition and development, and as the concluding frame of the movement. As in the concerto grosso (page 206), the opening ritornello rarely departs from the tonic key. However, it is greatly expanded, delaying the entrance of the soloist in order to introduce many of the important themes of the movement. The dramatic modulation in the exposition that follows is then dominated by the soloist. By expanding the proportions of sonata form into sonata-concerto form, Mozart achieved a wider range of interaction between orchestra and soloist.

Slow movements in the Classical concerto embraced a variety of forms, from ternary to sonata to sonata-concerto, and gave the piano a chance to display its new singing qualities. A popular choice for the finale was the *sonata-rondo,* a hybrid form that Mozart may have invented and was certainly among the first, along with Haydn, to perfect. Already in the seventeenth century the refrain form of the rondo *(A-B-A-C-A-D . . . A)* had become a popular means of organizing an operatic or instrumental number. With its recurring main theme, it is one of the easiest forms for listeners to follow. The typical rondo theme projected an appealing lightheartedness, like that in the finale of Haydn's Symphony No. 100 (which is nonetheless in sonata form). It is not hard to understand why Viennese composers were attracted to the idea of combining the popular flavor of the rondo with the drama of the sonata. In the chart that follows, keys are indicated by their scale degrees: the tonic key as "I" and the dominant key as "V."

| | *Section:* | *A* | *B* | | *A* | *C* | *A* | *D* | *A* |
|---|---|---|---|---|---|---|---|---|---|
| Rondo | *Key:* | I | other | | I | other | I | other | I |

| | *Section:* | Exposition | | | Development | Recapitulation | | Coda |
|---|---|---|---|---|---|---|---|---|
| Sonata | *Area:* | Primary—Secondary-Closing | | | | Primary—Secondary-Closing | | |
| | *Key:* | I | V | | other | I | I | I |

| | *Section:* | Exposition | | | Development | | Recapitulation | | Coda |
|---|---|---|---|---|---|---|---|---|---|
| Sonata-Rondo | *Section:** | *A* | *B* (Closing) | | *A* | *(C)* | *A* | *B* (Closing) | *A* |
| | *Key:* | I | V | | **I** | other | I | **I** | I |

The sonata-rondo differs in one major way from each of its prototypes. Borrowing from the rondo, the development in sonata form is now headed by a full statement of the *A*-Theme in the tonic. Borrowing from the sonata, the *B*-Theme of the rondo returns in the recapitulation in the tonic (as indicated by boldface letters).

*Part Three   The Age of Tonality (1690–1910)*

## WOLFGANG AMADEUS MOZART (1756–1791)

For many listeners, the concept of musical genius is synonymous with Mozart (Figure 14.2). Two centuries after his death the sheer beauty and perfection of his music continue to amaze and delight. By the time Mozart was six he could play the harpsichord and violin fluently, read difficult music at sight, and improvise to the amazement of family and friends. Beethoven was in his late twenties before he composed his first undisputed masterpieces; Bach and Handel were over 30, and Rameau and Haydn were near 50. Mozart was turning out masterpieces regularly by the time he was 21. He seems to have been incapable of writing a conventional phrase, and he excelled in every genre of his time. His accomplishments seem more miraculous in light of a personality that was in some respects contradictory and ineffectual.

The son of Leopold Mozart, a respected violinist and composer in the town of Salzburg, Wolfgang and his older sister Nannerl—the only two of seven children to survive infancy—came by their musical talents naturally. But even Leopold must have been startled when he came home and discovered his five-year-old son working away on a keyboard concerto! Prompted by his shrewd business sense and aware that Salzburg was too provincial to afford adequate rewards, Leopold decided to take his precocious children on the road. From 1762 to 1766 the Mozarts appeared at almost every major court of Europe, from Munich to Paris to London (where they stayed for 15 months). The two prodigies cheerfully performed solos and duets and improvised on the harpsichord or fortepiano for a fee, or at least in the hopes of one. (Leopold often wished their royal hosts would give them cash instead of gold watches, rings, and snuff boxes.)

When Nannerl reached puberty, the demand for her talents waned. In any case, Leopold probably never expected her to pursue a professional career. After they had been back in Salzburg for only nine months, father and son set out on a 15-month Italian journey that Leopold hoped would lead to profitable commissions. Wolfgang, in postscripts to his father's letters home, is already a discriminating observer of people but shows little interest in nature, ideas, or politics. His lack of political savvy was to cost him dearly in later years.

After less than five months at home, in October of 1771 the 16-year-old Mozart returned (as always, under the watchful eye of his father) to Italy to fulfill several commissions. His accomplishments, now those of a serious composer rather than a prodigy, continued to arouse wonder and amazement as well as envy and intrigue. Leopold, having provided for virtually all of his son's education, now set about finding him a position that would bring him some sort of steady income. They traveled to Vienna in 1773–1774, and Mozart began to write his first important symphonies and quartets. An audience was arranged with the Empress Maria Theresa, but it brought no offer of employment.

For the next three years Mozart lived in Salzburg, where he composed his first great piano concerto (in E-flat Major, K. 271). As an employee of the conservative Archbishop, he was expected to compose the kinds of music that he found least appealing. In August of 1777, finding the provincial atmosphere stifling, he asked rather insolently to be released. The Archbishop countered by releasing both Wolfgang and his father. But Leopold could not afford to leave, and so Mozart took off on another job-related journey, this time with his mother. In Munich, Mannheim, and Paris (where his mother died), Mozart's efforts to find a position worthy of his talents were met with polite but firm refusals. He returned empty-handed to Salzburg 16 months later, his heart broken by an unsuccessful love affair with a 16-year-old soprano.

Near the end of 1780, Mozart jumped at the opportunity to compose an opera, *Idomeneo*, for the court at Munich. The letters to his father during this period reveal Mozart's passion and affinity for the theater. The premiere of *Idomeneo* in January 1781 was a brilliant success, but once again no offers of a permanent post were forthcoming. Mozart must have rejoiced a few months later when the Archbishop of Salzburg summoned him to Vienna, the musical capital of Europe, to attend the celebrations surrounding the accession of Emperor Joseph II.

The thought of returning once again to Salzburg was too much for Mozart, and on June 9, after a month of acrimonious haggling, he was released from the Archbishop's service, "with a kick on my arse," as he wrote. His father was horrified by his son's behavior, but Mozart was confident he could make it on his own in Vienna. Moreover, he had fallen in love with Constanze Weber, the older sister of the soprano. They were married in August 1781 over Leopold's strong objections.

For his first several years in Vienna, Mozart's self-confidence seemed justified. His opera *The Abduction from the Seraglio,* which premiered in July 1782, was enthusiastically received. When the Emperor remarked that it had "very many notes," Mozart replied, "Exactly the necessary number, your majesty." Over the next six years Mozart produced a succession of masterpieces, including six piano concertos (among them the C-Major Concerto, K. 467), six string quartets dedicated to Haydn (who had become a close friend), and the irresistible opera buffa *The Marriage of Figaro* (Chapter 15). During a visit by Mozart's father early in 1785, Haydn declared, "I tell you before God and as an honest man that your son is the greatest composer known to me either personally or by name."

Mozart's successes in Vienna, however, were short-lived. In the spring of 1788 he was unable to sell a single set of parts for his masterful String Quintet in G Minor (K. 516). The tastes of the Viennese were capricious, but Mozart was also inept in promoting his own music. For a time he tried to support his family on a lavish scale that could not be sustained.* He and Constanze mismanaged his uncertain income, and they sank into debt. Mozart's last years were filled with pitiful entreaties for loans from a fellow freemason, Michael Puchberg (Mozart had joined a Masonic lodge in the early 1780s):

> In a week or two I shall be better off—for sure—but at present I am in need. Could you not assist me with a trifle? It would make all the difference at the moment. You would, at least for the moment, bring peace of mind to your true friend. . . .

Puchberg seems to have responded generously and tactfully to these persistent requests.

In December 1791, while at work on a *Requiem* (a Mass sung at a funeral service) commissioned by an anonymous caller dressed in gray, Mozart died, probably from complications of rheumatic fever. There is no evidence that he was poisoned by the Imperial Court Composer, Antonio Salieri, as was rumored at the time. Moreover, the myth that his funeral was the "poorest possible" and that he was dumped into a pauper's grave is untrue. Mozart received the kind of funeral accorded to all but the wealthiest citizens of Vienna, and burial in a common grave was customary at the time.

## ⭑ Mozart: Piano Concerto in C Major, K. 467 (1785)

The symphonies and piano concertos Mozart wrote during the 1780s were introduced at a series of subscription concerts known as "Academies" (see the Historical Window in Chapter 16, page 336). His C-Major Concerto (Listening Guide 37) was premiered on March 9, 1785, before an audience of some 200 subscribers, with the composer as soloist. Mozart's skill as a keyboard player, particularly in improvisation (similar to that practiced by jazz musicians), accounted for much of his initial success in Vienna.

The generous proportions of a sonata-concerto first movement could accommodate a profusion of themes (quite unlike Haydn's monothematicism!). Mozart's opening ritornello introduces several contrasting themes. The head of the first theme (*A*) is stated *piano* in simple arpeggiated triads at the outset:

*(Text continues on page 294.)*

---

*Constanze was pregnant much of their marriage, although only two children survived infancy.

# Listening Guide 37

## MOZART: Piano Concerto in C Major, K. 467, first and third movements

CD 4, TRACK 1
TAPE 4A, TRACK 1
DURATION: 14:04

### First Movement: Allegro

*Although the profusion of themes in this movement is somewhat intimidating, the logic with which Mozart uses them makes them easy to follow. He introduces four themes in the opening ritornello (the first of which recurs in several forms) and, in the exposition, two themes in the secondary area and three themes in the closing area. These themes meet varied fates. Some, like the first of the secondary-area themes, never recurs. Others, like Theme A of the opening ritornello, recur so frequently that they help support the entire structure.*

*Form: Sonata-concerto*

| | LOCATION | TIME | COMMENTS |
|---|---|---|---|
| **1** | OPENING RITORNELLO | | Orchestra only, entirely in the tonic key. |
| | Theme *A*  head | **0:00** | Soft, triadic figure in the strings. |
| | tail | 0:08 | More lyrical, with responses by winds and brass. |
| | head | 0:21 | Loud, tutti outburst. |
| | Theme *B* | 0:50 | Soft, marchlike theme featuring trumpets, flute, and oboe. |
| | Theme *A'* | 1:05 | A series of imitations based on the first bar of Theme *A*, building steadily in volume. |
| | Deflection | 1:19 | Tutti, unexpected deflection to the minor mode. |
| | Theme *C* | 1:34 | Soft rising chromatic scale heard especially in the flute. |
| | Theme *A''* | 1:55 | *Forte*, cadential. |
| | Theme *D* | 2:03 | A lyrical closing theme in oboe, bassoon, and flute. |
| | Lead-in | 2:15 | A short section introducing the piano soloist and smoothing the bridge from orchestral ritornello to solo exposition. |
| **2** | EXPOSITION | | |
| | Primary area    Theme *A* | **2:39** | Based on the opening soft statement of Theme *A*, with the orchestra playing the head, and the soloist the tail. |
| | Transition | 2:59 | New material featuring the soloist, moving mildly to the secondary key of the dominant. |

| LOCATION | TIME | COMMENTS |
|---|---|---|
| Secondary area | | |
|     Theme *E* | 3:29 | A sudden deflection by the soloist to the minor mode of the new key, concluding with a long run up the chromatic scale. |
| **3**      Theme *F* | **4:05** | The melodic payoff of the movement, introduced by the soloist. |
| Closing area | | |
|     Theme *G* | 4:32 | Based on Theme *A'*, but greatly expanded. |
|     Theme *H* | 4:52 | Rapid arpeggios in contrary motion in the soloist, reinforced by the orchestra. |
|     Theme *I* | 5:18 | A strong series of closely spaced cadences featuring the soloist, and culminating in a flurry of scales and arpeggios. |
| **4**   INTERMEDIATE RITORNELLO | | |
|     Theme *A'* | **6:02** | Tutti explosion. |
|     Theme *C* | 6:22 | Same rising chromatic scale. |
| **5**   DEVELOPMENT | | |
|     Bridge | **6:53** | Analogous to the original lead-in. |
|     Theme *B* head | 7:09 | Surrounded by figuration in the piano. |
|     Theme *I* head | 7:19 | The basis for most of the development, moving restlessly through a dramatic series of sequences. |
|     Retransition | 8:10 | Long pedal point on the dominant creates a strong feeling of expectancy. |
| **6**   RECAPITULATION | | |
|     Primary area | | |
|         Theme *A* | **8:25** | Identical up to the tutti outburst of the opening ritornello, which is then adjusted to remain in the tonic key. |
|         Theme *A'* | 8:44 | Now in the subdominant key. |
|     Secondary area | | |
| **7**     Theme *F* | **9:35** | Now in the tonic, but otherwise identical to the exposition. |
| Closing area | | |
|     Theme *G* | 10:02 | Based on Theme *A'*. |
|     Theme *B* | 10:41 | Heard for the first time since the opening ritornello. |
|     Theme *I* tail | 10:56 | We heard a great deal of the Theme-*I* head in the development, so Mozart omits it here. |

*continued*

| LOCATION | | TIME | COMMENTS |
|---|---|---|---|
| **8** | CLOSING RITORNELLO | | |
| | Theme *A* | **11:38** | Tutti culminates in a cadential chord that suspends motion temporarily, setting up the solo cadenza. |
| **9** | (Cadenza) | **12:02** | Provides the soloist with an opportunity to display skills at improvisation, taking themes from the movement as the starting point. |
| | Deflection | 13:26 | The tutti deflection to the minor mode, not heard since the opening ritornello. |
| | Theme *C* + Theme *A''* | 13:41 | The material that appeared near the end of the opening ritornello reappears to round out the movement. |

fast

### Third Movement: *Allegro vivace assai*

*The well-prepared recurrences of the cheerful rondo theme make the shape of this sonata-rondo easy to follow. Unlike the first movement, there are only three important themes.*

CD 4, TRACK 3
TAPE 4A, TRACK 3
DURATION: 7:20

*Form: Sonata-rondo*

| | LOCATION | TIME | COMMENTS |
|---|---|---|---|
| **1** | EXPOSITION | | |
| | Primary area - **A** | **0:00** | Rondo theme, in binary form, played by the orchestra. |
| | | 0:29 | Theme played briefly by the soloist. |
| | | 0:34 | Closing themes played by the full orchestra. |
| | Transition | 0:57 | Uses material from the rondo theme, with a gesture toward the minor mode at the close. |

This theme-head recurs almost like a refrain throughout the movement, serving as primary, closing, and even transitional material. Between its first and second occurrences is a marchlike theme ( *B* ) in the brass and winds:

| LOCATION | | TIME | COMMENTS |
|---|---|---|---|
| **2** | Secondary area - **B** | **1:37** | Another popular tune, played first by the orchestra and then by the soloist. |
| | Closing area | 2:11 | Slower theme marked by large intervals, played first by the soloist. |
| | Retransition | 2:24 | Prepares the return of the rondo theme. |
| **3** | DEVELOPMENT - **A** | | |
| | Rondo theme | **2:47** | In the tonic, alternating between soloist and orchestra. |
| | | 3:21 | Developments of the rondo theme, especially its head. |
| | | 3:56 | Brief deflection to the minor mode. |
| | Retransition | 4:24 | Also tinged with the minor mode. |
| **4** | RECAPITULATION - **A** | | |
| | Primary area | **4:34** | Rondo theme played first by the soloist. |
| | Transition | 4:48 | Rewritten to remain in the tonic. |
| **5** | Secondary area - **B** | **5:10** | As in the exposition, but in the tonic key. |
| | Closing area | 5:45 | As in the exposition. |
| **6** | (Cadenza) | **6:03** | Shorter than the cadenza in the first movement. |
| | Closing area **A** | 7:00 | Rondo theme converted into cadences by both soloist and orchestra. |

*C*

A chromatically ascending figure in the flute and oboe (*C*) provides the first of several closing themes:

# Historical Window

## MOZART IN LETTERS

With the invention of the telephone, and later the advent of computers, modems, and electronic mail, the art of personal correspondence—which extends back to the introduction of flax and hemp papers in thirteenth-century Europe—has been on the decline. Not all great men and women from the past have been great correspondents, and musicians are no exception. J. S. Bach, for example, wrote few letters, while Beethoven's letters deal mainly with business matters. But Mozart's are another matter; few composers have expressed themselves so vividly and frankly on so many aspects of life. Here are some samples of Mozart's epistolary art:

*To his sister, January 26, 1770:* I know nothing new except that Herr Gelehrt, the poet, has died in Leipzig and that since his death has written no more poetry.

*To his sister, August 24, 1771:* Above us is a violinist, under us also one, next to us a singing master who gives lessons, in the last room opposite ours is an oboist. That is good fun when you are composing! Gives one plenty of ideas.

*To his mother and sister from Milan, November 30, 1771:* So that you won't believe that I am sick I will write these two lines. Farewell. I kiss Mamma's hands. My greetings to all our good friends. I have seen four rascals hanged here in the cathedral square. They hang them just as in Lyon.

*To his sister, August 14, 1773:* I hope, my queen, that you are enjoying the highest degree of health and that now and then or, rather, sometimes or, better, occasionally or, better still, *qualche volta* ["sometimes"], as some say, of your important and urgent thoughts, which always issue from that most beautiful and trustworthy reasoning power, which you possess in addition to your beauty, although of such tender years and which of the above mentioned is almost never demanded from a women's gathering, you, O queen, possess in such a way as to put men and even oldsters to shame, a few will be sacrificed to me. Farewell. (P.S. Here you have something clever.)

*To his father upon the death of his mother, July 9, 1778:* Weep, weep and have a good cry, but finally take comfort. Remember that Almighty God has willed it thus—

and what can we undertake against Him? Let us rather pray to Him, and thank Him for seeing that it happened so well, for she died quite happily. In those distressing circumstances three things consoled me, namely my complete and trusting submission to the will of God—for through the experience of her very easy and beautiful death it seemed to me that in a moment she had become so happy (for how much happier she is now than we are) that at that moment I wished to travel with her. From this wish and from this longing developed finally my third consolation—the thought that she is not lost to us forever—that we shall see her again and live together far more pleasurably and happily than in this world. Only the time is not known to us, but that does not make me at all anxious. When God wills it, I am ready. Well, his heavenly and most holy will has been fulfilled. Let us say therefore a devout "Our Father" for her soul and proceed to other matters, for all things have their time.

*To his father, justifying his impending marriage to Constanze Weber, December 15, 1781:* You are horrified at the idea? But I entreat you, dearest, beloved father, to listen to me. . . . The voice of nature speaks as loudly in me as in others—louder, perhaps, than in many a big strong lout of a fellow. I simply cannot live as most young men do today. First of all I have too much religion; secondly, I have too great a love of neighbor and too many honorable feelings to seduce an innocent girl; and, thirdly, I have too much horror and disgust, too much dread and fear of diseases, and too much love for my health to fool around with whores. Therefore I can swear that I have never had anything to do with a woman of this type. . . . But my disposition, which is more inclined to a peaceful and domesticated life than to carousing—I, who from my youth have never been accustomed to looking after my own belongings, underwear, clothes, etc., cannot think of anything more essential to me than a wife.

*To his father, upon learning of his serious illness, April 4, 1787:* I certainly don't need to tell you how longingly I am hoping to receive some reassuring news from you. And I certainly hope for it, although I have made a habit of being prepared in all things for the worst. Since death, considered precisely, is the true goal of our existence, so I have become during the last few years so acquainted with this best and truest friend of mankind that his image is not only no longer terrifying to me, but is indeed very soothing and consoling.

This is followed by a cadential version of the Theme-*A* head (*A″*) and then a final closing theme (*D*), giving the ritornello an alternating pattern of *A-B-A′-C-A″-D*.

Mozart introduces two new themes (*E* and *F***) in the secondary area of the exposition. The first is a surprise move to the minor mode (already alluded to in a "deflection" in the opening ritornello), while the second is the most memorable tune of the movement:

Mozart reserves both of these new ideas for the soloist. The spacious closing area, which occupies more than 40 percent of the exposition, allows for an elaborate series of cadences (Themes *G*, *H*, and *I*) shared by soloist and orchestra.

After their initial appearance, some themes are strategically withheld to heighten the drama. For example, the marchlike theme (*B*) in the ritornello does not appear at all in the solo exposition, appears only as a brief fragment in the development, and is finally resolved with a full tonic statement in the recapitulation (the only time it is played by the soloist). The variation on the opening theme (*A″*) at the conclusion of the ritornello is withheld until the very close of the movement, providing a sturdy frame. Although the movement contains more than 30 musical events, Mozart manages to give the entire movement balance and symmetry. Neither the slow second movement nor the finale approaches the complexity of the opening Allegro.

In spite of the impression of seamless melody, the slow movement uses the same sonata-concerto form as the first movement. The sole anomaly demonstrates the composer's uncanny sensitivity to structure: The recapitulation omits the primary area. The theme of that area had dominated the opening ritornello, the primary area of the exposition, and the development section. Mozart decided that was enough and did not hesitate to ignore convention. (With the premiere of the Swedish film *Elvira Madigan* in 1969, this movement became, by art-music standards, a Top 40 hit.)

The finale is a sparkling example of the sonata-rondo. If this fusion of forms looks intellectual on paper, Mozart's handling of it is anything but—especially

---

*Although we generally associate themes with key areas in sonata form, the profusion of sections and themes in a Mozart concerto is most easily understood by labeling the themes consecutively (*A*, *B*, *C*, and so forth).

in the development, where he chooses to subject the opening theme to a witty fragmentation:

*Allegro vivace assai* (Fast and very lively)

No other composer in Mozart's time was capable of handling such large blocks of thematic material with such ease. This remarkable control served Mozart especially well in the grandest form of Viennese music, opera, the subject of our next chapter.

## THE STRING QUARTET

The most prestigious genre of private music in Viennese Classicism was the *string quartet*. A **string quartet** (Figure 14.3) is an ensemble of two violins, a viola, and a cello. The term *string quartet* is also used to describe a work written for such ensembles. Like the symphony, the string quartet emerged with the rise of the Classical style. The Baroque trio sonata (Chapter 11) foreshadowed the string quartet, especially in its use of two treble instruments of the same range (the violins). But the string quartet drew on other antecedents as well, including the *serenade* and the *divertimento,* lighter genres halfway between the Baroque suite and the four-movement Classical symphony.

Why four instruments rather than, for example, three or five? One reason may be that the most complex Classical harmonies, known as seventh chords, contain four pitches. Moreover, the combination of two violins, viola, and cello provides the full range of a Classical orchestra (except for the double basses, which generally reinforce the cellos an octave below).

And why strings rather than woodwinds or some other grouping? This is easier to answer. Strings are ideally suited to the expressive, intimate, balanced nature of chamber music. Although certain wind and brass instruments had recently migrated from the outdoors into the salon, it would be some time before they would approach the violin, viola, or cello in flexibility.

The Classical string quartet is generally built on the same four-movement plan as the symphony: a fast opening sonata-form movement, a slow movement, a minuet, and a quick finale.

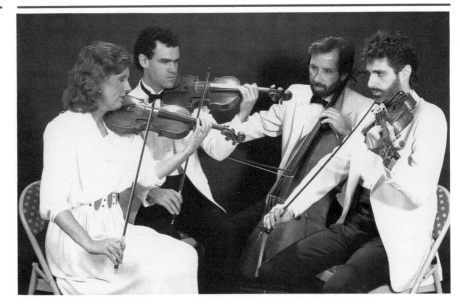

FIGURE 14.3 Haydn composed his first string quartets in the late 1750s. Within 25 years, this new format was very popular among composers and performers. Today string quartets (performed here by the Angeles Quartet) are a staple of the concert hall.

## ✴Haydn: String Quartet in D Major, Op. 76, No. 5 (1797)

Haydn made an even greater contribution to the development of the string quartet than he did to the development of the symphony. He was probably the first composer of genuine string quartets, and the more than 80 quartets that he wrote over almost four decades included many of the earliest masterpieces. With his love for experimentation and surprise, he found a superb medium in the grouping of four balanced solo instruments.

Haydn's experiments were truly radical. In the D-Major Quartet from Op. 76 (Listening Guide 38), Haydn—having now written more than 75 quartets—devised a novel succession of movements. Instead of opening with sonata form, he constructs the first-movement Allegretto as a ternary form built on a single ingratiating theme:

- *A-Section*. Presentation of the theme in moderate tempo.
- *B-Section*. Development of the theme in related keys (beginning with a readily audible shift to the tonic minor).
- *A'-Section*. Ornamented restatement of the theme in the tonic key.
- *Coda*. In a markedly faster tempo, using the head of the theme.

# *Listening Guide 38*

## HAYDN: String Quartet in D Major, Op. 76, No. 5, second movement

CD 4, TRACK 4
TAPE 4A, TRACK 4
DURATION: 8:42

*Aside from its unusual key, perhaps the most remarkable feature of this movement is its seamless flow from one section to the next, even between the exposition and the development. The monothematic structure of the entire movement contributes to this seamlessness.*

*Form: Sonata*

| LOCATION | TIME | COMMENTS |
|---|---|---|
| **1 EXPOSITION** | | |
| Primary area | **0:00** | Hymnlike theme in violin I. homophonic |
| Transition | 0:51 | Dotted rhythms over slow, steady chords. |
| Secondary area | 1:31 | Combines the head of the primary-area theme in the cello with the transition theme in Violin I. |
| Closing area | 2:07 | *Forte* outburst; based on the transition theme. |
| **2 DEVELOPMENT** | | |
| Theme from secondary area | **2:50** | Moves from major to minor; ends in a fermata. |
| Theme from primary area | 3:31 | False recapitulation; ends in the second fermata. |
| Retransition | 4:27 | Based on the transition theme; ends in the third fermata. |
| **3 RECAPITULATION** | | |
| Primary area | **5:31** | Exactly like the exposition. |
| Transition | 6:20 | Rewritten (and condensed) from the exposition so as to remain in the tonic key. |
| Secondary area | 6:37 | Now in the tonic key. |
| Closing area | 6:59 | Identical to the exposition, but in the tonic key. |
| **4 CODA** | **8:02** | Based on the transition theme. |

Although the coda is quite spirited, the movement lacks the tension-resolution characteristic of sonata form. The slow second movement explains why, for it is here that Haydn chooses to place the dramatic weight of the quartet. Not only is this Adagio half again as long as the opening Allegretto; it is a

# Historical Window

## MOZART'S LIBRETTIST

Few figures in music history have lived such eventful lives as Mozart's greatest librettist, Lorenzo da Ponte. Da Ponte's father was a Jewish leather dealer named Conegliano who, with his three small sons, converted to Christianity so that he could marry a Catholic. As was customary, the family took the name of the bishop in the town where they lived: da Ponte. The eldest son, Lorenzo, took the bishop's first name as well. Lorenzo received no formal education until he was 14 or 15, when he entered the local seminary. In 1768, at the age of 19, he took holy orders and became a professor of literature at a seminary in a small town near Venice. Four years later he moved to Venice, where he fell in love with a noblewoman. For a few years he was a professor of humanities at the seminary in nearby Treviso. In 1779 he was charged with adultery and was banned from the city for 15 years.

By 1781 da Ponte had visited Vienna for the first time. There he so impressed Joseph II that the Emperor appointed him as the librettist of a new royal opera company. Antonio Salieri, the most influential composer in Vienna, asked him to write a libretto for him, but the opera failed and Salieri withdrew his support. Just when da Ponte first met Mozart is unknown, but in 1786 da Ponte adapted the French comedy *Le Mariage de Figaro* and credited Mozart with suggesting it. In 1787 da Ponte regained Salieri's favor after providing him with another libretto. In that same year he also wrote the libretto for Mozart's *Don Giovanni*. Da Ponte probably drew on his own experience in creating the central character; for many years he had been a friend of Giacomo Casanova, the notorious eighteenth-century libertine (whose name is today synonymous with a personality complex). In 1788 da Ponte provided Mozart with a third and final libretto for *Così fan tutte*, a humorous account of fidelity and fickleness.

Mozart died in 1791, and Joseph II died a year later. Left without supporters, da Ponte was dismissed from the imperial service and moved to London, where in 1793 he was appointed librettist at the King's Theatre. In that post he traveled throughout Europe recruiting singers for the company, much as Handel had done 75 years before. He also launched several unsuccessful business ventures, including an Italian bookstore and a printing press. Partly to escape his creditors, he sailed to America in 1805 with Nancy Grahl, with whom he had several children.

Now in his mid-fifties, da Ponte proved once again that he could readily adapt to new circumstances. He first settled in New York City, where he opened a grocery store. Eventually he taught Italian in several mid-Atlantic states. In

1825 he began to teach at Columbia College (today Columbia University), thus becoming the first Professor of Romance Languages in the United States. That same year, he coached a New York production of *Don Giovanni*, doubtless a gratifying experience for the old poet. Although rumors of his unsavory past circulated from time to time, he was lionized by culture-hungry Americans eager to meet "the man who had known Mozart."

By today's standards da Ponte was well traveled; by the standards of his own day, his travels were phenomenal. In 1823 he began to set down a memoir of his eventful life and was working on a fifth volume at his death in 1838. Although the contents are both selective and subjective, they provide a vivid picture of nearly a century of European and American life. Here is an excerpt, somewhat condensed:

There was a certain Bussani, who was a jack-of-all-trades save that of an honest man. Having heard that I had woven a ballet into my *Figaro*, he ran straight to the Count and in a tone of righteous indignation cried: "Excellency, the poet has put a ballet into his opera!" The Count sent for me at once and, frowning darkly, launched into this dialogue:

"So, the *signor* poet has used a ballet in *Figaro*!"

"Yes, Excellency."

"The poet does not know that the Emperor has forbidden dancing in his theater?"

"No, Excellency."

"In that case, *signor* poet, I will tell you now."

"Yes, Excellency."

"And I will tell you further, *signor* poet, that you must take it out!"

"No, Excellency."

"Have you the libretto with you?"

"Yes, Excellency."

"Where is the scene with the dance?"

"Here it is, Excellency."

"This is what we do."

Having said that, he took the two sheets from my manuscript, laid them carefully on the fire, and returned the libretto to me. The dress rehearsal was to be held that day. I invited the Emperor personally, and he came—and with him half the aristocracy of Vienna. The first act was well received, but at the end of it there comes a pantomimed scene between the Count and Susanna, during which the orchestra plays and the dance takes place. But all one could see was the Count and Susanna gesticulating. Since there was no music, it looked like a puppet show.

*continued*

"What's all this?" exclaimed the Emperor. His Majesty sent for me, but instead of answering the question, I handed him my manuscript, in which the scene was restored. The Sovereign glanced through it and asked why the dancers had not appeared. My silence conveyed to him that there was some intrigue at work. He turned to the Count and asked him to explain. He, spluttering, said that the ballet had been left out because the opera had no dancers.

"Can't they be found at some other theater?" inquired His Majesty. The Count replied that they could. In less than half an hour 24 dancers had arrived. By the end of the second act the scene which had been suppressed was ready to be tried.

ousy in the fourth act. The Countess deplores the Count's behavior but takes heart when he repents. Mozart deftly matches his music to the development of each character.

Mozart relies heavily on ensembles throughout *Figaro,* from the opening duet to the seven-character finale of the second act. He steps up the tempo of the simple recitatives and makes swift transitions between the recitatives and the arias. In *Idomeneo,* Mozart had structured many of the arias and even ensembles in sonata form, and the recapitulations had often repeated large blocks of text, undermining the forward motion of the drama. In *Figaro,* Mozart replaced sonata-form arias with flexible, irregular arias that responded more readily to the dramatic action. When he repeats lines of text, it is for a dramatic purpose.

A good example of this innovative approach is our first excerpt, the aria of infatuation, *"Non so più cosa son"* ("I no longer know what I am"), which Cherubino sings to Susanna in Act I (Listening Guide 39). Having just reached the stage of adolescent awareness, Cherubino* is enamored of the Countess— indeed, as he admits, of "every woman in the castle." For this aria, da Ponte supplied Mozart with four irregular stanzas of 4, 4, 7, and 2 lines each.

In the first stanza (musically the *A*-Section) Cherubino expresses his agitation in a series of breathless exclamations ("First I'm feverish, then I'm freezing. Every woman makes me blush."). The melody reaches the tonic note only at the very end. The heightened intensity of the second stanza ("my heart pounds"; the *B*-Section) prompts a modulation to the dominant, reminiscent of the move to the secondary area in sonata form. Mozart highlights the word *"desio"* ("desire") with a chromatic appoggiatura that is soon repeated to different harmonies. *(Text continues on page 326.)*

*Like many such roles in Mozart's time, Cherubino is sung by a woman; hence the expression "trousers role." The *cherub* in Cherubino's name is a humorous reference to his youthfulness.

# *Listening Guide 39*

## MOZART: Three Excerpts from *The Marriage of Figaro*

### Excerpt 1: Act I, No. 6: *"Non so più cosa son"* ("I no longer know what I am")

CD 4, TRACK 5
TAPE 4B, TRACK 1
DURATION: 2:40

*Cherubino's aria illustrates Mozart's new flexibility in treating dramatic situations. Instead of adapting the text to a preconceived formal scheme, Mozart adapts the forms to the dramatic needs of the text. In this aria, he imbues each stanza with a different character to portray Cherubino's mercurial mood changes. (In the third stanza, separate lines have been placed on the same line to save space.)*

*Form: Sectional (A-B-A-C-C'-D)*

| [STANZA] / TEXT | TIME | LOCATION / COMMENTS |
|---|---|---|
| CHERUBINO: | | |
| **1** [1] *Non so più cosa son, cosa faccio,* <br> I no longer know what I am, or what I'm doing, <br><br> *Or di foco, ora sono di ghiaccio.* <br> First I'm feverish, then I'm freezing. <br><br> *Ogni donna cangiar di colore,* <br> Every woman makes me blush, | 0:00 | **A-Section.** Rapid, breathless singing. |
| *Ogni donna mi fa palpitar.* <br> Every woman makes my heart pound. | 0:10 | Repeated for emphasis, leading to a cadence, followed by a modulation to the dominant. |
| [2] *Solo ai nomi d'amore di diletto,* <br> At the very mention of love, <br><br> *Mi si turba, mi s'altera il petto,* <br> I am aroused, my heart pounds, <br><br> *E a parlare mi sforza d'amore,* <br> There speaks to me the power of love, | 0:19 | **B-Section.** In the key of the dominant. More sustained vocal line than the preceding section. |
| *Un desio ch'io non posso spiegar.* <br> A desire that I cannot explain. | 0:32 | Chromatic line repeated for emphasis, leading to a cadence. |
| [1] *Non so più cosa son, cosa faccio . . .* <br> I no longer know what I am, or what I'm doing . . . | 0:48 | **A-Section.** Repeated in its entirety. |
| **2** [3] *Parlo d'amor vegliando, parlo d'amor sognando,* <br> I speak of love when awake, I speak of love when asleep, | 1:06 | **C-Section.** Delivered as a reverie. |

*continued*

| [STANZA] / TEXT | TIME | LOCATION / COMMENTS |
|---|---|---|
| *All'acqua, all'ombra, ai monti,*<br>To the water, to the shadows, to the hills, | 1:17 | More agitated, with a repeated figure leading to a fermata. |
| *ai fiori, all'erbe, ai fonti, all'eco, all'aria, ai venti,*<br>to the flowers, to the grass, to the fountains,<br>to the echo, to the air, to the breezes, | | |
| *Che il suon de' vani accenti portano via con sè.*<br>So that my great longings may be carried with them. | 1:27 | Cadence with another fermata at the melodic peak. |
| [3] *Parlo d'amor vegliando, parlo d'amor sognando,*<br>I speak of love when awake, I speak of love when asleep, | **1:39** | **C'-Section.** Lyrical variation on the preceding C-Section. |
| *All'acqua, all'ombra, ai monti,*<br>To the water, to the shadows, to the hills, | 1:45 | Stronger sense of closure than first statement. Ends with another fermata. |
| *ai fiori, all'erbe, ai fonti, all'eco, all'aria, ai venti,*<br>to the flowers, to the grass, to the fountains,<br>to the echo, to the air, to the breezes, | | |
| *Che il suon de' vani accenti portano via con sè.*<br>So that my great longings may be carried with them. | 1:59 | Half cadence with another fermata at the melodic peak. |
| 3   [4] *E se non ho chi m'oda,*<br>And if no one will listen, | **2:14** | **D-Section.** Adagio. |
| *Parlo d'amor con me.*<br>I'll speak of love to myself. | 2:28 | Allegro vivace. |

## Excerpt 2: Act I: Recitative and Aria (No. 9), "Non più andrai, farfallone amoroso" ("No longer, amorous butterfly")

CD 4, TRACKS 6 – 7
TAPE 4B, TRACKS 2–3
DURATION: 1:16, 3:38

*This excerpt contrasts the rapid, real-life pace of recitative and the reflective character of the aria. In the recitative the drama is paramount; in the aria the music governs the pacing and structure. The A-Section of the aria functions like a refrain, while the continuity in the B-, C-, and D-Sections is provided largely by the orchestra.*

*Form: Recitative: Through-composed*
*Aria: Sectional (A-B-A-C-D-A-D)*

[RECITATIVE]

| | TIME | |
|---|---|---|
| FIGARO:<br>*Evviva!* Hurrah!<br>SUSANNA:<br>*Evviva!* Hurrah!<br>BASILIO:<br>*Evviva!* Hurrah! | **0:00** | Halfhearted cheers when the Count blesses the wedding but announces he must delay it briefly. The harpsichord accompaniment throughout is simple and unobtrusive. |

| [STANZA] / TEXT | TIME | LOCATION / COMMENTS |
|---|---|---|
| FIGARO:<br>*E voi non applaudite?* Why don't you cheer him? | | |
| SUSANNA:<br>*E afflitto poveretto, perche il padron lo scaccia dal castello.*<br>He's upset, poor little thing, because the count has banished him from the castle. | | |
| FIGARO:<br>*Ah, in un giorno sì bello!* Ah, on such a beautiful day! | | |
| SUSANNA:<br>*In un giorno di nozze!* On a wedding day! | | |
| FIGARO:<br>*Quando ognuno v'ammira!*<br>When everyone will admire you! | | |
| CHERUBINO:<br>*Perdono, mio signor!* Forgive me, my lord! | 0:16 | Lyrical request and brusque rejection. |
| COUNT:<br>*Nol meritate.* You don't deserve it. | | |
| SUSANNA:<br>*Egli è ancora fanciullo.* He's only a child. | | |
| COUNT:<br>*Men di quel che tu credi.* You'd be surprised. | | |
| CHERUBINO:<br>*E ver, mancai; ma dal mio labbro alfine—*<br>Truly, master; and even a child can repeat what he hears— | | |
| COUNT:<br>*Ben, ben, io vi perdono; anzi farò di più:*<br>Very well, I forgive you; I'll do even more: | | |
| *vaccante è un posto d'uffizial nel reggimento mio,*<br>there's an officer's post vacant in my regiment, | 0:32 | Abrupt delivery signals punishment rather than forgiveness. |
| *io scelgo voi, partite tosto, addio.*<br>I appoint you to it, go at once, good-by. | | |
| SUSANNA, FIGARO:<br>*Ah, fin domani sol!* Oh, let him remain today! | 0:39 | Sweet parallel singing. |
| COUNT:<br>*No, parta tosto.* No, he must go at once. | | |
| CHERUBINO:<br>*A ubbidirvi, signor, son già disposto.*<br>I am ready, signor, to carry out your wishes. | | Sung with resignation. |
| COUNT:<br>*Via per l'ultima volta la Susanna abbracciate.*<br>Come, for the last time embrace Susanna. | | |

*continued*

| [STANZA] / TEXT | TIME | LOCATION / COMMENTS |
|---|---|---|
| *[Cherubino embraces Susanna.]*<br>COUNT *[aside]*:<br>*Inaspettato è il colpo.* This blow is unexpected.<br>FIGARO:<br>*Ehi, capitano, a me pure la mano.*<br>Well, captain, shake my hand. | | |
| *[softly to Cherubino]* | | |
| *Io vo' parlarti pria che tu parta.*<br>I want to speak to you before you go. | 0:59 | Whispered privately, then sung publicly. |
| *[with feigned joy]* | | |
| *Addio, picciolo Cherubino!* Farewell, little Cherubino! | | |
| *Come cangia in un punto il tuo destino!*<br>How changed in a moment is your destiny! | | Sets up the aria that follows immediately. |
| [ARIA] | | |
| FIGARO: | | |
| **1**   [1] *Non più andrai, farfallone amoroso,*<br>No longer, amorous butterfly, will you go<br>*Notte e giorno d'intorno girando;*<br>Flitting around night and day; | 0:00 | **A-Section.** Jaunty, marchlike theme. |
| *Delle belle turbando il riposo,*<br>Disturbing ladies' sleep,<br>*Narcisetto, Adoncino d'amor!*<br>You little Narcissus, Adonis of love! | 0:09 | Smoother ascending arpeggios, with text repeated for emphasis. |
| [2] *Non più avrai questi bei pennacchini,*<br>No longer will you have your plumes,<br>*Quel cappello leggero e galante,*<br>That smart and jaunty cap,<br>*Quella chioma, quell'aria brillante,*<br>Those curls, that brilliant air,<br>*Quel vermiglio donnesco color!*<br>That pink, feminine complexion! | 0:24 | **B-Section.** The orchestra assumes a leading role, with the voice as a commentator. At 0:47 the first three lines of text repeat. |
| **2**   [1] *Non più andrai, farfallone amoroso . . .*<br>No longer, you amorous butterfly . . . | 0:58 | **A-Section.** Repeated in its entirety. |

| [STANZA] / TEXT | TIME | LOCATION / COMMENTS |
|---|---|---|
| [3] *Fra guerrieri, poffar Bacco!*<br>Among soldiers, by Jove!<br><br>*Gran mustacchi, stretto sacco,*<br>Large mustaches, tight tunic,<br><br>*Schioppo in spalla, sciabola al fianco,*<br>Shoulder arms, sword at your side,<br><br>*Collo dritto, muso franco,*<br>Neck straight, expression serious,<br><br>*Un gran casco o un gran turbante,*<br>A big helmet or a big turban, | **1:20** | **C-Section.** Short, speechlike interjections, with the continuity supplied by the orchestra. |
| *Molto onor, poco contante!* Much honor, little pay! | 1:42 | *"Poco contante"* repeated for emphasis. |
| [4] *Ed in vece del fandango, una marcia per il fango,*<br>And in place of the fandango, a march through the mud, | 1:48 | Ascending line in a crescendo. |
| *per montagne, per valloni, colle nevi e i sollioni,*<br>Over mountains, through valleys, in snow and sun,<br><br>*Al concerto di tromboni, di bombarde, di cannoni,*<br>To the sound of trumpets, of bombardments, of cannons,<br><br>*Che le palle in tutti i tuoni, all'orecchio fan fischiar.*<br>And bullets always thundering, and whistling past your ears. | 1:54 | **D-Section.** Principal tune in the orchestra, with the voice providing commentary. |
| [2 rearranged]<br>*Non più avrai questi bei pennacchini,*<br>No longer will you have your plumes,<br><br>*Non più avrai quel cappello,*<br>No longer will you have that smart and jaunty cap,<br><br>*Non più avrai quella chioma,*<br>No longer will you have those curls,<br><br>*Non più avrai quell'aria brillante.*<br>No longer will you have that brilliant air. | 2:11 | Text of the *B*-Section sung over a repeating pattern that prepares the return of the *A*-Section. |
| [1] *Non più andrai, farfallone amoroso . . .*<br>No longer, you amorous butterfly . . . | 2:28 | **A-Section.** Repeated in its entirety. |
| [Tail] *Cherubino all vittoria, alla gloria militar!*<br>Cherubino, on to victory, on to military glory! | 2:49 | **D-Section.** Same music as before but with different text.<br>*continued* |

315

## Excerpt 3: Stages 3–7 from the Act II Finale

CD 4, TRACK 8

TAPE 4B, TRACK 4

DURATION: 13:07

*The Act II finale shows Mozart adapting the harmonic principles of sonata form to a lengthy dramatic passage. In the first two stages, the Count has accused his wife of infidelity, only to discover that Susanna, not Cherubino, is concealed in the closet. Embarrassed, he begs for forgiveness, setting the stage for Figaro's boisterous entrance (where our excerpt begins). Each new twist in the drama is incorporated into a carefully designed key scheme that ultimately returns to the temporary tonic of E-flat Major. The music consists of neither recitatives nor conventional set pieces but of a seamless flow of short, flexible sections.*

*Form: Sectional with strong harmonic organization*

| LOCATION / TEXT | TIME | TEMPO / COMMENTS |
|---|---|---|
| STAGE 3 | | |
| **1** [*Figaro enters.*] | **0:00** | ALLEGRO. In G Major, three sudden fifths higher than the previous stage. In a boisterous, down-to-earth style. |
| FIGARO: | | |
| *Signori, di fuori, son già i suonatori.* | | |
| My Lord, what excitement, the musicians are already here. | | |
| *Le trombe sentite, i pifferi udite;* | | |
| Hear the trumpets, listen to the flutes; | | |
| *Tra canti, tra balli de' vostri vassalli,* | | |
| All the singing, all the dancing of your servants, | | |
| *Corriamo, voliamo le nozze a compir.* | | |
| Let's hurry, we want to celebrate our wedding. | | Text repeated for emphasis. |
| COUNT: | | |
| *Pian, piano, men fretta,* Hush, hush, less fuss, | **0:18** | Strong contrast between the unenthusiastic Count and the ebullient Figaro. |
| FIGARO: *La turba m'aspetta!* The crowd is waiting for me! | | |
| COUNT: | | |
| *Pian, piano, men tretta,* Hush, hush, there's no hurry, | | |
| *Un dubbio toglietemi in pria di partir.* | | |
| Relieve me of one doubt before you go. | | |
| SUSANNA, COUNTESS, FIGARO: | | |
| *La cosa è scabrosa—com'ha da finir?* | **0:27** | Different feelings expressed simultaneously. Hints of the minor mode convey the ladies' anxiety. |
| This matter is delicate—how will it all end? | | |
| COUNT: | | |
| *Con arte le carte convien scopir.* | | |
| Now's the time to play my trump card. | | |

| LOCATION / TEXT | TIME | TEMPO / COMMENTS |
|---|---|---|
| **2** STAGE 4 | | |

COUNT:

*Conoscete, Signor Figaro, questo foglio chi vergò?*  
Do you know, Master Figaro, who wrote this letter? — **0:45** — ANDANTE. In C Major, now headed *back* toward the tonic key.

FIGARO:

*Nol conosco. Nol conosco.* I don't know. I don't know. — 0:58 — Fragmented phrases express his stupefaction.

SUSANNA:

*Nol conosci?* You don't know? — 1:05 — Insistent repetition of short phrases by all the characters.

FIGARO:

*No!* No!

COUNTESS:

*Nol conosci?* You don't know?

FIGARO:

*No!* No!

COUNT:

*Nol conosci?* You don't know?

SUSANNA, COUNTESS, COUNT:

*Nol conosci?* You don't know?

FIGARO:

*No! No! No!* No! No! No!

SUSANNA:

*E nol desti a Don Basilio?* Wasn't it for Don Basilio? — 1:16 — Parallel line to the Count's question, now in G Major.

COUNTESS:

*Per recarlo—* To give him—

COUNT:

*Tu c'intendi?* Now you understand?

FIGARO:

*Oibò, oibò!* Not at all, not at all!

SUSANNA:

*E non sai del damerino—*  
And you don't know about the young woman— — 1:24 — Same structure as the previous question.

COUNTESS:

*Che stasera nel giardino—* Who, this evening, in the garden—

COUNT:

*Già capisci?* Now you remember?

FIGARO:

*Io non lo so.* Not a word.

COUNT:

*Cherchi invan difesa e scusa,*  
You're searching in vain for a defense and an excuse, — 1:32 — Two identical lines of music followed by a strong cadence.

*continued*

| LOCATION / TEXT | TIME | TEMPO / COMMENTS |
|---|---|---|

*Il tuo ceffo già t'accusa,* but your face accuses you,

*Vedo ben che vuoi mentir.* I can see that you are lying.

**3**

FIGARO:

*Mente il ceffo, io già non mento.*

My face may lie, but I don't know.

SUSANNA, COUNTESS:

*Il talento aguzzi invano.*

You sharpen your wits in vain.

*Palesato abbiam l'arcano—non v'è nulla da ridir.*

We've told all the secrets—there's nothing left to joke about.

**1:45** — Intensely lyrical passage that builds to a climax and then a cadence.

COUNT:

*Che rispondi?* What is your answer?

**2:04** — Short, repetitive phrases.

FIGARO:

*Niente, niente!* Nothing, nothing!

COUNT:

*Dunque accordi?* Then you admit it?

FIGARO:

*Non accordo!* I don't admit it!

SUSANNA, COUNTESS:

*Eh, via, chetati, balordo—* Be quiet, you idiot—

*la burletta ha da finir.*

this joke must come to an end.

**2:12** — Sung in parallel thirds.

FIGARO:

*Per finirla lietamente e all'usanza teatrale,*

To end things happily, as is customary in the theater,

*Un'azion matrimoniale le faremo ora seguir.*

with a wedding we will now round it off.

**2:21** — The same music and key as the Count's opening question to this stage.

SUSANNA, COUNTESS, FIGARO:

*Deh signor,* Pray, my Lord,

*nol contrastate, consolate i miei (lor) desir*

don't resist us—grant us (them) our (their) wishes.

COUNT *[aside]:*

*Marcellina! Marcellina! Quanto tardi a comparir.*

Marcellina! Marrcellina! How late you are.

**2:39** — To fresh text in the tonic, repeats previous lyrical passage two times (text four times), building to the emotional climax of the finale to this point.

*[Antonio, rather drunk, enters with a flowerpot.]*

| LOCATION / TEXT | TIME | TEMPO / COMMENTS |
|---|---|---|

**4**    STAGE 5

ANTONIO:

*Ah, Signor! Signor!* Ah, my Lord! My Lord!

COUNT:

*Cosa è stato?* What has happened?

ANTONIO:

*Che insolenza! Ch'il fece? Chi fu?*
How outrageous! Who has done it? Who was it?

SUSANNA, COUNTESS, COUNT, FIGARO:

*Cosa dici? Cos'hai, cosa è nato?*
What did you say? What's wrong, what happened?

ANTONIO:

*Ascoltate!* Just listen!

SUSANNA, COUNTESS, COUNT, FIGARO:

*Via parla di sù!* So tell us!

ANTONIO:

*Dal balcone che guarda in giardino,*
From the balcony overlooking the garden,

*Mille cose ogni dì gittar veggio.*
A thousand things I see thrown every day.

*E poc'anzi può darsi di peggio,*
But today it was much worse,

*Vidi un uom, signor mio, gittar giù.*
I saw a man, my lord, thrown down.

COUNT:

*Dal balcone?* From the balcony?

ANTONIO:

*Vedeti i garofani!* Just look at my carnations!

COUNT:

*In giardino?* Into the garden?

ANTONIO:

*Si!* Yes!

SUSANNA, COUNTESS *[to Figaro]*:

*Figaro, all'erta!* Figaro, attention!

COUNT:

*Cosa sento?* What am I hearing?

SUSANNA, COUNTESS, FIGARO *[to each other]*:

*Costui ci sconcerta, quel briaco, che viene a far quì?*
He threatens us, this old drunkard, what's he doing here?

**3:20** — ALLEGRO MOLTO. In F Major, another fifth closer to the tonic key. The characters sing over rapid, swirling triplets in the orchestra—a texture that continues throughout this stage.

These two lines are repeated.

**3:37** — Delivered in a rapid-fire, patter delivery that rises to an appropriate level of indignation. The dullness of Antonio's vocal lines matches his general witlessness.

*continued*

| LOCATION / TEXT | TIME | TEMPO / COMMENTS |
|---|---|---|
| COUNT: | | |
| *Dunque un uom! Ma dov'è gito?* | 3:58 | Declaimed over the orchestral |
| You said a man! But where's he gone? | | triplets. |
| ANTONIO: | | |
| *Ratto, ratto il birbone è fuggito;* | | |
| Rats, rats, the rascal fled; | | |
| *ed ad un tratto di vista m'uscì.* | | |
| and in a flash was out of my sight. | | |
| SUSANNA *[to Figaro]:* | | |
| *Sai che il paggio!* It was the page! | 4:05 | |
| FIGARO *[to Susanna]:* | | |
| *So tutto lo vidi!* I know it, I saw him! | | |
| *[laughs loudly]* | | |
| *Ah ah ah ah!* Ha ha ha ha! | | |
| COUNT: | | |
| *Taci là!* Quiet there! | | |
| FIGARO: | | |
| *Ah ah ah ah!* Ha ha ha ha! | | |
| ANTONIO: | | |
| *Cosa ridi?* What are you laughing at? | | |
| FIGARO: | | |
| *Ah ah ah ah!* Ha ha ha ha! | | |
| COUNT/ANTONIO: | | |
| *Taci la! / Cosa ridi?* Quiet there! / Why are you laughing? | | |
| *Tu sei cotto dal sorger del dì!* | | |
| You're drunk from dawn to midnight! [repeated] | | |
| COUNT: | | |
| *Or ripetimi: un uom dal balcone?* | 4:22 | Antonio's answers are exact rep- |
| Now, repeat to me: a man from the balcony? | | etitions of the Count's ques- |
| ANTONIO: | | tions. |
| *Dal balcone*—From the balcony— | | |
| COUNT: | | |
| *In giardino?* Into the garden? | | |
| ANTONIO: | | |
| *In giardino.* Into the garden. | | |
| SUSANNA, COUNTESS, FIGARO: | | |
| *Ma signore, se in lui parla il vino!* | | |
| But My Lord, it's the wine in him that's talking! | | |

COUNT:
*Segui pure, nè in volto il vedesti?*
Go on, didn't you see his face?
ANTONIO:
*No nol vidi.* No, I didn't see it.
SUSANNA:
*Ola, Figaro, ascolta, Figaro, ascolta!*
Attention, Figaro, listen, Figaro, listen!
COUNT:
*No?* No?
ANTONIO:
*Nol vidi.* I didn't see it.
FIGARO *[to Antonio]:*

| | | |
|---|---|---|
| *Via piangione, sta zitto una volta!* | 4:44 | Rising sequence, as in Antonio's |
| Look you hick, shut up for a minute! | | first major speech. |

*Per tre soldi far tanto tumulto!*
For three cents this is much too much fuss!

*Giacche il fatto non può stare occulto,*
I can't conceal the secret any longer,

*Sono io stesso saltato di lì.*
It was I who jumped into the garden.

| | | |
|---|---|---|
| COUNT: | | |
| *Chi? Voi stesso?* Who? You yourself? | 4:56 | Rapid exchanges among charac- |
| SUSANNA, COUNTESS: | | ters. |

*Che testa, che ingengo!* What a mind, how ingenious!
FIGARO:
*Che stupor!* What a surprise!
ANTONIO:
*Chi? Voi stesso?* Who? You yourself?

> SUSANNA, COUNTESS:
> *Che testa, che ingengo!* What a mind, how ingenious!
> FIGARO:
> *Che stupor! Che stupor!*
> What a surprise! What a surprise!

COUNT:
*Già creder nol posso.* I still can't believe it.
ANTONIO:
*Come mai diventasti sì grosso?* How did you get so large?

*continued*

| LOCATION / TEXT | TIME | TEMPO / COMMENTS |
|---|---|---|
| COUNT:<br>*Già creder nol posso.* I still can't believe it. | | A half cadence. |
| ANTONIO:<br>*Dopo il salto non fosti così.*<br>After you jumped you weren't like that. | 5:08 | Vocal lines are descending scales. |
| FIGARO:<br>*A chi salta succede così.*<br>That always happens after someone jumps. | | |
| ANTONIO:<br>*Ch'l direbbe!* Who'd have thought it? | | |
| SUSANNA, COUNTESS:<br>*Ed insiste quel pazzo?* Why does that lunatic persist? | | |
| COUNT [to Antonio]:<br>*Tu che dici?* What do you say? | | |
| ANTONIO:<br>*A me parve il ragazzo.* To me it looked like that boy. | | |
| COUNT [violently]:<br>*Cherubin?* Cherubino? | | Sudden minor harmonies. |
| SUSANNA, COUNTESS:<br>*Maledetto, maledetto!* Damnation, damnation! | | |
| FIGARO:<br>*Esso appunto, da Siviglia a cavallo quì giunto, da Siviglia ov'ei forse sarà.*<br>Of course, he must have ridden here from Seville, perhaps he's come from Seville today. | | |
| ANTONIO:<br>*Questo no, questo no chè il cavallo io no vidi saltare di là.*<br>That no, that no, I didn't see a horse jump out the window. | 5:30 | Simple scalar descent. |
| ⎡ COUNT:<br>*Che pazienza, finiam questo ballo!*<br>Give me patience, let's finish this ballet!<br>SUSANNA, COUNTESS:<br>*Come mai! Giusto ciel, finirà!*<br>What's this? Good heavens, be done!<br>COUNT:<br>⎣ *Finiam questo ballo!* Let's finish this ballet!<br>[to Figaro] *Dunque tu?* Then it was you? | | |
| FIGARO:<br>*Saltai giù . . .* I jumped out . . . | | |

| LOCATION / TEXT | TIME | TEMPO / COMMENTS |
|---|---|---|
| COUNT: *Ma perchè?* But why? | | |
| FIGARO: *Il timor.* I was afraid. | | |
| COUNT: *Che timor?* Afraid of what? | | |
| FIGARO: *Là rinchiuso aspettando quel caro visetto,* I was locked in there, waiting to see my sweetheart, | 5:46 | Rising sequence. |
| *tippe, tappe un susurro furo d'uso, voi gridaste,* suddenly bang, bang, furious noises, you shouting, | | |
| *lo scritto biglietto, saltai giù dal terrore confuso,* the letter I'd written, I jumped down confused by fear, | | On *"saltai,"* the tempo slows suddenly and the orchestral triplets cease. |
| *e stravolto m'ho un nervo del piè.* and I strained a nerve in my foot. | | |

**5**  STAGE 6

| | TIME | TEMPO / COMMENTS |
|---|---|---|
| | **6:11** | ANDANTE. In B-flat Major, the key of the dominant. |
| ANTONIO: *Vostre dunque saran queste carte, che perdeste.* Then this paper that was lost will be yours. | 6:21 | The orchestra's regular rhythmic pattern creates the continuity. |
| COUNT: *Olà, porgile a me.* Hey, give it to me. | | |
| FIGARO: *Sono in trappola.* Now I'm trapped. | | |
| SUSANNA, COUNTESS: *Figaro, all'erta.* Figaro, listen. | | |
| COUNT: *Dite un po', questo foglio cos'è?* Tell me, what is this paper? | 6:39 | |
| FIGARO: *Tosto, tosto, n'ho tante, aspettate.* Right away, right away, I have so many, wait a second. | | |
| ANTONIO: *Sarà forse il sommario dei debiti?* Perhaps it's a list of your debts? | | Sung on the same pitch. |
| FIGARO: *No, la lista degli osti.* No, a list of the wedding guests. | | |
| COUNT: *Parlate! [to Antonio]* Speak up! *E tu lascialo.* And you leave him alone. | | |

*continued*

| LOCATION / TEXT | TIME | TEMPO / COMMENTS |
|---|---|---|
| SUSANNA, COUNTESS / FIGARO: | | |
| *Lascialo / Lasciami e parti.* | 7:06 | The separate sentiments are |
| Leave him / Leave me alone and get lost. | | expressed simultaneously. |
| ANTONIO: | | |
| *Parto sì, ma se torno a trovarti . . .* | | |
| OK, I'll go, but the next time I find you . . . | | |
| FIGARO: | | |
| *Vanne, vanne, non temo di te.* | | |
| Beat it, beat it, I'm not afraid of you. | | |
| | | |
| *[Antonio exits.]* | | |
| COUNT: | | |
| *Dunque?* Well, then? | 7:29 | The ladies' words are declaimed |
| COUNTESS *[aside to Susanna]*: | | staccato. |
| *Oh ciel, la patente del paggio!* | | |
| O heavens, the page's commission! | | |
| COUNT: | | |
| *Dunque?* Well, then? | | |
| SUSANNA *[aside to Figaro]*: | | |
| *Oh ciel, la patente!* O heavens, the commission! | | |
| COUNT *[sarcastically to Figaro]*: | | |
| *Coraggio!* Courage! | | |
| FIGARO: | | |
| *Uh, che testa, un che testa, questa è la patente,* | | Figaro's "recall" is symbolized |
| Oh, how silly. That's the commission | | by a modulation to the minor |
| | | mode. |
| *che poc'anzi il fanciullo mi diè.* | | |
| that the boy gave me a while ago. | | |
| COUNT: | | |
| *Per che fare?* For what purpose? | 7:56 | As Figaro invents his explana- |
| FIGARO: | | tion, the orchestra gradually |
| *Vi manca—* It lacked— | | works its way back toward the |
| COUNT: | | temporary tonic key. |
| *Vi manca?* It lacked? | | |
| COUNTESS *[aside to Susanna]*: | | |
| *Il suggello.* The seal. | | |
| SUSANNA *[aside to Figaro]*: | | |
| *Il suggello.* The seal. | | |
| COUNT: | | |
| *Rispondi!* Answer me! | | |
| FIGARO: | | |
| *E l'usanza—* It's customary— | | |

COUNT:

*Su via, ti confondi!* Go on, confound you!

FIGARO:

*E l'usanza di porvi il suggello.*
It's customary to seal a commission.

COUNT:

*Questo birbo mi toglie il cervello,*
This rascal will drive me crazy,

*tutto, tutto è un mistero per me.*
everything, everything is a mystery to me.

SUSANNA, COUNTESS:

*Se mi salvo da questa tempesta,*
If I survive this storm,

*più non havvi naufragio per me.*
there will be no more shipwreck for me.

FIGARO:

*Sbuffa invano e la terra calpesta!*
Let him rave in vain and stamp the ground!

*Poverino, ne sa, men di me.*
The poor guy knows less about this than I do.

            The orchestra and Figaro arrive triumphantly back in the tonic key.

8:28    In a closing section, the four characters express three sets of feelings simultaneously. The passage ends in a clear cadence.

**6**   STAGE 7

*[Marcellina, Don Basilio, and Bartolo enter.]*

MARCELLINA, DON BASILIO, AND BARTOLO:

*Voi signor, che giusto siete, ci dovete or ascoltar.*
My Lord, you who are just must listen to us now.

COUNTESS, SUSANNA, FIGARO:

*Son venuti a sconcertarmi, qual rimedio a ritrovar?*
They've come to make trouble, what remedy can be found?

COUNT:

*Son venuti a vendicarmi, ed io mi sento a consolar.*
They've come to avenge me, and how relieved I feel.

FIGARO:

*Son tre stolidi, tre pazzi, cosa mai vengono a far?*
They're three idiots, three fools, what are they doing here?

COUNT:

*Pian, pianin senza schiamazzi, dica ognun quel che gli par.*
Quiet, quiet! Without commotion, let each state his case.

9:18    ALLEGRO ASSAI. Back in the overall tonic key of E-flat Major. The three new characters sing together in order to present a united front.

*continued*

# *Listening Guide 39 (Continued)*

| LOCATION / TEXT | TIME | TEMPO / COMMENTS |
|---|---|---|
| MARCELLINA *[pointing to Figaro]*:<br>*Un impegno nuziale ha costui con me contratto,*<br>A marriage agreement this man contracted with me, | 9:50 | The words are sung in a rapid patter style. |
| *e pretendo che il contratto deva meco effettuar.*<br>and I claim that he must honor the contract.<br>SUSANNA, COUNTESS, FIGARO:<br>*Come? Come?* What? What?<br>COUNT:<br>*Olà, silenzio, silenzio, silenzio! Io son quì per giudicar.*<br>All right, quiet, quiet, quiet! I'm here to judge.<br>BARTOLO:<br>*Io da lei scelto avvocato, vengo a far le sue difese.*<br>I, this lady's chosen counsel, am here to protect her interests. | 10:07 | Follows the same form as Marcellina's segment. |
| *Le legittime pretese, io vi vengo a palesar.*<br>Her legitimate claims I've come to lay before you.<br>SUSANNA, COUNTESS, FIGARO:<br>*E un birbante!* He's a scoundrel!<br>COUNT:<br>*Olà, silenzio, silenzio, silenzio! Io son quì per giudicar.*<br>All right, quiet, quiet, quiet! I'm here to judge.<br>BASILIO:<br>*Io com' uom al mondo cognito,*<br>I, as a man well known to the world, | 10:24 | Follows the same form as the first two segments. |
| *vengo quì per testimonio del promesso matrimonio*<br>come here to testify to the promise of marriage | | |
| *con prestanza di danar.*<br>made against a loan of money. | | |

---

The first stanza then repeats to the original music, providing temporary closure. Mozart treats the opening of the third stanza (the *C*-Section) as a reverie, or afterthought. But as Cherubino enumerates all the items to which he speaks of love, he becomes agitated again, hammering each one home with a persistent figure:

*Allegro vivace*
(Fast and lively)

all'ac - qua, all' ombra, ai monti, ai fio - ri, all'erbe, ai fon - ti, all'e - co, all'aria, ai ven - ti,
(to the water, to the shadows, to the hills, to the flowers, to the grass, to the fountains, to the echo, to the air, to the breezes)

SUSANNA, COUNTESS, FIGARO:
*Son tre matti!* They're three idiots!
COUNT:
*Olà, silenzio! Lo vedremo, il contratto leggeremo.*
All right, quiet! We shall see, let's read the contract.

*Tutto in ordin deve andar.*
Everything must proceed in order.

| | | | |
|---|---|---|---|
| 7 | SUSANNA / COUNTESS / FIGARO:<br>*Son confusa/o, son stordita/o.*<br>I'm bewildered, I'm dazed.<br>MARCELLINA, DON BASILIO, COUNT, BARTOLO:<br>*Che bel colpo! Che bel caso!*<br>What a beautiful stroke! What a lovely case!<br>SUSANNA / COUNTESS / FIGARO:<br>*Disperata/o, sbalordita/o.*<br>We're miserable, we're dumbfounded.<br>MARCELLINA, DON BASILIO, COUNT, BARTOLO:<br>*È cresciuto a tutti il naso.*<br>We'll make them pay through the nose.<br>SUSANNA / COUNTESS / FIGARO:<br>*Certo un diavol dell'inferno qui li ha fatti capitar!*<br>Surely an infernal devil is plotting against us!<br>MARCELLINA, DON BASILIO, COUNT, BARTOLO:<br>*Qualche nume a noi propizio qui ci ha fatti capitar.*<br>A propitious god has brought us here. | 10:47 | PIÙ ALLEGRO. In an elaborate closing section, the characters alternate between singing their separate lines simultaneously and singing as a separate trio (Susanna, Countess, Figaro) or quartet (Marcellina, Basilio, Bartolo, the Count). There is much textual and musical repetition. At 12:40, the tempo becomes Prestissimo [As fast as possible]. | |

The fermata at the end of the fifth line of the stanza neatly divides Cherubino's moods. Mozart emphasizes Cherubino's instability by repeating this stanza to a more lyrical version of the earlier music, all the while strengthening the sense of cadence. With the first line of the fourth stanza (the *D*-Section), Cherubino drifts into a reverie again but snaps out of it with the last line. The aria gives full play to the unpredictable swing of Cherubino's emotions, but at the same time it is musically coherent. In a few brief minutes Mozart gives us a convincing impression of adolescent love.

Most of the arias and ensembles in the opera are preceded by recitative. Rather than involving only one or two characters, as was common in opera seria,

Mozart's simple recitatives are often little ensembles in themselves. Such is true of the recitative that begins our second excerpt. As it opens, the Count has agreed to the marriage of Figaro and Susanna but insists on a slight delay to prepare a proper celebration. They respond with halfhearted "hurrahs" (where our excerpt begins). Figaro then turns to the dejected Cherubino, who has been caught by the Count hiding in Susanna's room (where he overheard the Count making advances to Susanna). Cherubino begs the Count for forgiveness, which the Count grants after some hesitation. But the Count then presents Cherubino with a commission that requires him to join one of the Count's regiments near Seville. Susanna and Figaro plead that Cherubino be allowed to remain until the wedding, but the Count insists that he leave immediately. Resigned, Cherubino declares his readiness to leave and embraces Susanna one last time. Figaro whispers that he wants to see him before he goes and then comments loudly on the sudden change in Cherubino's circumstances.

All of this action takes place in less than 90 seconds, probably faster than it would in real life. The characters declaim their lines over occasional arpeggiated harmonies supplied by the harpsichord. Yet the vocal lines express the sentiments of the text, from Cherubino's plaintive request for forgiveness to the Count's abrupt responses.

The speed with which the action has unfolded in the recitative prepares the way for Figaro's expansive aria, *"Non più andrai"* ("No longer amorous butterfly"), that concludes Act I. To the rhythms of a military march, Figaro describes with good-humored relish the life Cherubino can now expect to lead ("Instead of [dancing] the fandango, a forced march through the mud . . ."). The aria contains four irregular stanzas of 4, 4, 6, and 8 lines, concluding with a 2-line tail that serves as a summary. Mozart treats the poetry with considerable freedom, repeating the second stanza in a paraphrase and beginning the *D*-Section in the middle of the fourth stanza. The *A*-Section in this *A-B-A-C-D-A-D* form functions like a refrain. In the *B*-, *C*-, and *D*-Sections much of the continuity is provided by the orchestra rather than by the singer. This is especially true of the *D*-Section, where Mozart reduces the voice to a singsong patter while introducing a new march theme in the orchestra:

He uses this jaunty theme once again for the last stanza and has it appear by itself as Figaro and Cherubino march offstage to conclude the act. The aria bristles with action; both the words and the music give Figaro an opportunity to reveal his character through gesture and movement. We can see him taunting Cherubino, who tries his best to ignore the jibes. This is a very different sort of aria from the arias of Baroque opera.

Mozart's use of recitative and aria in *Figaro* is highly innovative, yet the most remarkable section of the opera is the 22-minute Act II finale, which relies on neither recitative nor aria. Instead, Mozart provides a series of tiered ensembles that begins with two characters and concludes with seven. While teeming with melodies that could each support a conventional set piece, Mozart keeps them short and flexible in order to maintain the dramatic pace. He combines, in essence, the virtues of both recitative and set piece. The scene begins with the Count's demand that the Countess open a closet in her dressing room where he suspects Cherubino is hiding. The Countess refuses and the Count leaves to get a crowbar. Before going, he locks all the doors to the room and takes the Countess with him. Susanna, who has been hiding elsewhere in the room, jumps out and lets Cherubino escape through a window into the garden. Susanna then slips into the closet. The action now proceeds through seven stages.

- *Stage 1* [Allegro, E-flat Major]. In sputtering dotted rhythms, the angry Count berates his wife and accuses her of infidelity. She protests her innocence in smooth, lyrical phrases. Threatening to run Cherubino through with his sword, the Count opens the closet door, only to discover—Susanna!

- *Stage 2* [Molto andante, B-flat Major]. Susanna steps outs of the closet, to the amazement of both the Count and the Countess. The music reflects their reaction with a deliberate, repeated, almost hypnotic rhythm (LONG-short-short-short-short / LONG-LONG). The music modulates to the dominant as the Count apologizes to his wife. As the surprise wears off, the tempo switches to Allegro; emboldened, Susanna and the Countess sing together in parallel thirds:

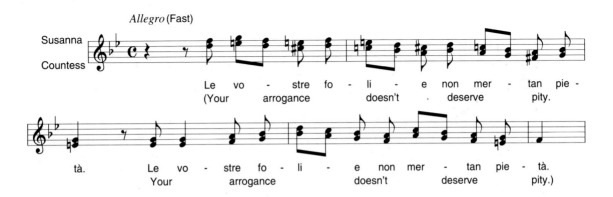

# Historical Window

## A BEETHOVEN ACADEMY

Today, a season of symphony or chamber music would be unthinkable without one or more works by Beethoven. In any major city there are dozens of live performances of Beethoven's music every season. Moreover, there are countless recordings of his works. The Fifth Symphony alone has been recorded more than a hundred times, and a well-stocked record store keeps at least a dozen versions on hand.

And yet, during Beethoven's 35 years in Vienna, the public had only about a dozen opportunities to hear concerts devoted largely or entirely to his music—an average of about once every three years. These infrequent events took the form of an *Akademie* ("academy"), a concert organized and presented by a composer or performer (often the same person) for his own benefit (Figure 16.3). While the profits accrued to the organizer, so did the risks and responsibilities.

First, the organizer of an academy would have to arrange for a place where the concert could be presented. Since there were no regular concert halls in Vienna until the 1870s, this was usually a theater. He then had to go through the bureaucratic ritual of obtaining a government permit before he could arrange to have posters and publicity notices printed up and distributed. He sold the tickets himself, usually from his own lodgings. Since there were no permanent concert orchestras in Vienna, he hired the players and arranged and paid for the copying of all the parts. Finally, he conducted the all-day rehearsal that generally preceded the performance. Somewhere along the way he had to find time to compose all the music that was to be played.

In December 1808, Beethoven presented an academy that ranks as one of the most remarkable concerts ever staged. On one program he offered premieres of his Fifth and Sixth Symphonies; his Fourth Piano Concerto;* two movements from his Mass in C; a solo piano improvisation; and the Choral Fantasy for Piano, Chorus, and Orchestra. The music alone required three hours to perform. We can get some idea of the event from this firsthand account by Johann Friedrich Reichardt:

> I accepted with heartfelt thanks the kind offer of Prince Lobkowitz to let me sit in his box. There we continued in the bitterest cold, from half past six to half past ten, and experienced the truth that one can easily have too much of a good thing—and still more of a loud thing. Nevertheless, I could no more leave the box before the end than could the exceedingly good-natured and delicate Prince, for the box was in the first balcony near the stage, so that the orchestra with

*This was probably the second performance of the work, since Beethoven may already have performed it at Prince Lobkowitz's in March 1807.

FIGURE 16.3 A playbill of a musical academy on December 23, 1806, in Vienna features works by Beethoven, Mozart, Handel, and Cherubini. Writing to his publisher, Beethoven defended his December 1808 academy: "What chiefly angered the musicians was that when they made careless mistakes in the simplest, most straightforward passages in the world, I suddenly stopped them and shouted *play that again*—which had never happened before; at which the audience showed its delight."

Beethoven in the middle conducting it was below us and close by; thus many a failure in the performance tried our patience greatly. Poor Beethoven, who from this, his own concert, was realizing the first and only scant profit that he could find in a whole year, had encountered much opposition and almost no support in the rehearsals and performance. Singers and orchestra were composed of mixed elements, and it had been impossible to arrange a single full rehearsal for all the pieces to be performed, all filled with the greatest difficulties.

Beethoven had written the Choral Fantasy at the last minute to provide a suitable close to the concert. There had been little time to rehearse it, however, and at the performance the winds went astray. Beethoven was obliged to stop the orchestra and start again, much to the consternation of the players. Although the orchestras of the time consisted of a mix of professionals and amateurs, there is no reason to assume that the performances lacked freshness or flair.

We do not know how much Beethoven earned from his 1808 concert, though earnings from an academy he presented in 1800 had been enough to support him comfortably for two years.

declared himself emperor of all the French, Beethoven tore up the dedication of his symphony and remarked, "So he, too, is like all the others." The *Eroica* lasts about 50 minutes in performance, more than half again as long as the symphonies Beethoven had been writing only a few years earlier.

Beethoven wrote many of the works that are most often performed today in the years from 1803 through 1812. They include the Third through the Eighth Symphonies, the Fourth and Fifth Piano Concertos, the Violin Concerto, five string quartets (including three dedicated to Prince Razumovsky, the Russian ambassador to Vienna), the opera *Fidelio,* seven piano sonatas (including the *Waldstein, Appassionata,* and *Les Adieux*), two piano trios, and the first great cello sonata (in A Major, Op. 69).

It was during these years, which the English writer Alan Tyson has dubbed "the heroic decade," that Beethoven tried to come to grips with his advancing deafness. In an informal will* addressed to his two brothers and set down during the summer of 1802, he had spoken of his infirmity:

> Though born with a fiery, active temperament . . . I was soon compelled to withdraw from society, to live life alone. If at times I tried to forget all this, oh how harshly was I flung back by the doubly sad experience of my bad hearing. Yet it wasn't possible for me to say to people, "Speak louder, shout, for I am deaf!" Ah, how could I possibly admit an infirmity in the *one sense* that ought to be more perfect in me than in others, a sense that I once possessed in the highest degree.

Throughout these years Beethoven seemed to be preoccupied with heroism. While still at work on the *Eroica* he began his only opera, *Fidelio,* which recounts the daring of Leonore (disguised as a man, Fidelio), who rescues her unjustly imprisoned husband, Florestan. In 1807 Beethoven wrote an overture to the tragedy *Coriolan,* the story of a hero who chooses death over a life in which he can no longer sustain his ideals. And in 1809 he wrote an overture and incidental pieces for the play *Egmont* by the German writer Johann Wolfgang von Goethe. *Egmont* is based on the life of a sixteenth-century Dutch statesman who was falsely arrested and beheaded for treason. Through these characters Beethoven may have found the courage to face his own misfortune.

We turn now to two works from Beethoven's heroic decade: a symphony and a piano concerto. Although Beethoven did not invent either of these types of music, he invested each of them with intensified content.

## ✸ Beethoven: Symphony No. 5 in C Minor, Op. 67 (1804–1808)

Beethoven was almost 30 before he completed his first symphony and his first string quartet, the two genres in which he was certain to be compared with Haydn and Mozart. No work is more closely identified with a composer than

---

*Known as the *Heiligenstadt Testament,* after the village near Vienna where Beethoven wrote it. He never sent it to his brothers.

Beethoven's Fifth Symphony (Listening Guide 40), which was first performed at a remarkable concert in 1808 (see the Historical Window on page 336). Its key of C Minor was a key that Beethoven favored to symbolize conflict, and he returned to it more than a dozen times over the next decade.

**First Movement.** The rhythm of the opening motive—three shorts and a long (ta-ta-ta-TUM)—suggests an explosive energy that leads after a fermata to another repetition:

Beethoven had learned from Haydn how to make the greatest use of a single theme, though not even Haydn had dared to base an entire movement on just one theme. Beethoven even derives the theme head of the secondary area from the opening motive, though here he balances the three shorts with three longs:

The opening rhythm dominates the accompaniment as well, as in this passage from the secondary area:

The theme head of the primary area contains four notes (and only two pitches), and the theme head of the secondary area contains only six notes (and four pitches). Such snatches of material would seem too tiny to be further fragmented. Yet, in the development, Beethoven reduces the 6-note head to five notes, then to two (the two long notes—4 and 5 in their order of appearance in the original theme), and finally to just one (the second of the long notes). He makes the fragmentation even more apparent by alternating the strings and the winds in different registers:

# *Listening Guide 40*

## BEETHOVEN: Symphony No. 5 in C Minor, Op. 67, first movement

CD 4, TRACK [9]
TAPE 4B, TRACK 5
DURATION: 7:13
[with repeated exposition]

*The headlong drive of this movement should not obscure Beethoven's careful attention to structure. The fermatas, for example, articulate the opening of the exposition, the recapitulation, the development, and the final cadence in the coda.*

*Form: Sonata*

| | LOCATION | TIME | COMMENTS |
|---|---|---|---|
| **1** | **EXPOSITION** | | |
| | Primary area | **0:00 [1:28]** | Opens with 4-note motive articulated by two fermatas. |
| | | 0:18 [1:46] | Third, and longer, fermata. |
| | [Transition] | 0:36 [2:04] | No break in texture. |
| **2** | Secondary area | **0:46 [2:14]** | Head of theme stated by the horns. |
| | Closing area | 1:19 [2:47] | Same rhythm as the opening. |
| **3** | **DEVELOPMENT** | | |
| | Primary-area theme | **2:56** | Opens, like the exposition, with a fermata. |
| | Secondary-area theme | 3:33 | Six notes. |
| | | 3:38 | Six notes. |
| | | 3:43 | Five notes. |
| | | 3:45 | Two notes. |

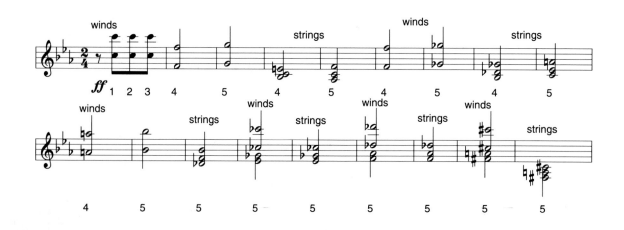

340     *Part Three   The Age of Tonality (1690–1910)*

| LOCATION | | TIME | COMMENTS |
|---|---|---|---|
| | | 3:54 | One note. |
| | | 4:05 | Six notes! |
| | | 4:08 | One note. |
| | Retransition | 4:12 | Fortissimo repetition of the opening rhythm creates a considerable sense of expectation. |
| **4** | **RECAPITULATION** | | |
| | Primary area | **4:18** | Played by the full orchestra. |
| | | 4:27 | Oboe countermelody leading to brief cadenza and third fermata. |
| | [Transition] | 5:02 | Same passage reinterpreted to remain in the tonic key. |
| **5** | Secondary area | **5:12** | Head of theme stated by the bassoons.* |
| | Closing area | 5:49 | Same rhythm as the opening. |
| **6** | CODA | **5:57** | Begins without a break. |
| | Themes from primary and secondary areas | 6:13 | Combines the *pitches* of the primary-area theme and the *rhythm* of the secondary-area theme. |
| | Opening of primary area | 7:05 | Sounds as if the movement were starting over again. |

*This may have been because valveless horns in Beethoven's day could not play in both E-flat (the key of the exposition) and C (the key of the recapitulation). Most modern orchestras substitute horns in the recapitulation, though this robs the movement of an important color contrast.

It is impossible to identify a theme on the basis of a single chord played in isolation. So to demonstrate that the chord has been extracted from the original 6-note theme, Beethoven repeats the original six notes in the middle of the 1-chord fragments. This time he alternates orchestration, registers, *and* dynamics to reinforce the point:

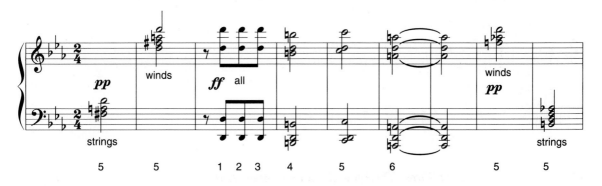

The recapitulation, which is embellished by a countermelody and a cadenza-like flourish in the oboe, leads without pause into the coda. In the development, Beethoven has, through fragmentation, reduced the secondary-area theme to a single note. In the coda, rather than fragmenting one idea, he combines elements of two ideas: the first four *pitches* of the primary-area theme with the *rhythm* of the secondary-area theme (three shorts and three longs):

He has the end of the coda repeat the opening of the movement. This time, however, the fermatas set up a final cadence. Beethoven manages, in just over seven minutes, to express a torrent of emotions with only a few terse motives.

**Second Movement.** Beethoven begins the second movement, the Andante, with a lyrical theme shared by the strings and the winds and then subjects it to five free variations. The movement opens innocently enough. However, just when a cadence seems imminent, the theme pauses for a moment and then breaks triumphantly into a new key with the full orchestra. The technique is simple but powerful. Beethoven groups the variations in a manner reminiscent of sonata form. He places the minor-mode variation in the middle, where it functions as a development. The theme then returns in its most elaborate variation, sounding like a recapitulation. The elaborate, lengthy coda finally tames the earlier outbursts.

**Third Movement.** By Beethoven's time the courtly minuet that accompanied the rise of the string quartet and the symphony had been gradually supplanted by the more dynamic *scherzo* (Italian for "joke"), a faster movement in triple meter. Haydn, in his string quartets from the 1780s, was one of the first composers to use the scherzo. Beethoven introduced scherzos into his Third, Fifth, Seventh, and Ninth Symphonies, combining the spirit and wit of Haydn's scherzos with his own symphonic style. In the Scherzo of his Fifth Symphony, he adds a new note of mystery. The opening in the cellos and basses is halting and tentative, pausing twice on fermatas that recall the opening of the first movement. This tentativeness gives way to a series of bold hammerlike tones in the horns:

Earlier composers had made little effort to link the successive movements of their symphonies. In this Scherzo, however, Beethoven repeats these "three-shorts-

and-a-long" from the first movement and uses them again just before the recapitulation in the finale. Clearly he wanted his listeners to experience the symphony as a unified work rather than as a succession of discrete movements.

A mock fugue in the Trio briefly relieves the somber mood. When the Scherzo returns, the theme is played pizzicato, adding to the sense of mystery. Instead of bringing the movement to a conclusion, Beethoven introduces a mysterious bridge that erupts into the finale—another way of unifying the symphony.

**Fourth Movement.** In straightforward sonata form, the major-mode finale dispels the turbulence of the first three movements. The theme of the primary area is simple and square, and the progressions from primary area to transition to secondary area to closing area are clearly delineated. Once again, Beethoven derives the theme of the secondary area from the opening of the first movement:

The tempo of the coda increases to Presto, and an elaborate series of cadences brings the symphony to a satisfying conclusion. While the Fifth Symphony is scarcely longer than one of Haydn's London Symphonies, Beethoven brings a new vigor and intensity to the symphonic form. The triumph of the major mode over the minor mode in the fourth movement completes a journey that began with the opening motto of the first movement. This sense of progression from movement to movement would have puzzled Haydn or Mozart. Though the symphony has no explicit program, its sustained statement about heroism helps explain its enduring popularity.

## Beethoven: Piano Concerto No. 4 in G Major, Op. 58 (1805–1806)

Beethoven's early reputation as a pianist gave way only gradually to his reputation as a composer. Between 1794 and 1809 he completed five piano concertos, ranging from the chamber music proportions of the B-flat Concerto, Op. 19, to the heaven-storming assaults of the *Emperor* Concerto, Op. 73. Like Mozart, he wrote these works to display his talents as a performer as well as a composer. Later, as his deafness grew more severe and he could no longer hear well enough to play with an orchestra, he lost interest in the concerto.*

**First Movement.** Instead of having the orchestra begin the ritornello, Beethoven opens the first movement with a simple question posed by the soloist and

---

*In fact, Beethoven never performed his last piano concerto, the Fifth. A sixth, begun in 1815, never progressed beyond sketches.

answered by the orchestra (Theme *A*). Hence the interaction between soloist and orchestra begins immediately. The 3-note upbeat to the second bar (identical to the rhythmic pattern that opens the Fifth Symphony) and the subsequent even, articulated eighth notes figure prominently throughout the movement. The orchestra brings the opening idea to a climax that spills over into a marchlike tune, modulating with each repetition (Theme *B*):

With this modulation in the opening ritornello, Beethoven was again departing from earlier practice.

Before the orchestra launches the exposition, the soloist plays an elaborate lead-in. Beethoven heightens the excitement of the transition by introducing rapid note values in the solo part:

A new theme in the strings, soon elaborated by the piano, marks the arrival of the secondary area (Theme *G**). Again, just when a cadence seems imminent, the reintroduction of the modulating theme from the opening ritornello delays it and sets up an elaborate closing area to the exposition. The writing for the soloist is spirited and wide-ranging.

The development is based largely on the rhythmic patterns of the two opening bars of the movement. This time they are played by the orchestra while the soloist weaves a series of improvisatory arpeggios around them. After a furious chromatic scale in the piano that cadences to near stillness in C-sharp Minor—the key most remote from the original tonic of G Major—Beethoven gradually works back to a retransition dominated by the fleet triplets of the transition. At the moment of recapitulation the soloist plays a *fortissimo* transformation of the opening.

Although Beethoven was a renowned improviser, he wrote out two different cadenzas for the first movement of this concerto. The one heard here surges in waves of sound that were certain to dazzle Beethoven's audience. Beginning from a point of repose at the end of the cadenza, the rhythm of the opening bars

*As in Mozart's piano concerto, we have labeled the themes consecutively in the Study Guide.

in the orchestra accompanies a cascade of scales and arpeggios by the soloist to close out the movement.

**Second Movement.** The second-movement Andante, one of Beethoven's most unusual slow movements, consists of a dialogue between strident, dotted-rhythm octaves in the orchestra and a serene chorale in the piano. He directs the pianist to play *una corda* ("one string"*), creating an ethereal, distant sound. One writer has speculated that Beethoven meant to portray Orpheus taming the furies on his trip to the underworld to reclaim Euridice. The gentle soloist does indeed tame the orchestra, which proceeds without pause into the sonata-rondo finale.

**Third Movement.** The bouncy rondo theme of the third-movement finale begins in the "wrong key"—the subdominant instead of the tonic—rather like someone who staggers and then regains balance. With its pedal-point bass, the theme of the secondary area provides a stabilizing counterbalance. Lasting for 12 measures, the pedal point imitates the drone of a hurdy-gurdy. The entire movement sparkles with lively conversation between piano and orchestra, as in this segment from the transition:

More than a decade after the apparent demise of the Viennese Classical style, Beethoven had carried it to new levels of complexity and power. By 1810 he was the most famous composer in Europe, even though public success eluded him in opera, the genre most associated with popular acclaim. From time to time he complained that the Viennese audiences were unappreciative and talked of moving to Paris, but a consortium of patrons guaranteed him a lifetime annuity if he would remain in Vienna. He accepted and never traveled more than a few miles from the city.

*This effect is not possible on the modern piano, whose shift mechanism moves at most to two strings. See the Historical Window in the next chapter.

# Chapter 17

## BEETHOVEN'S LATE STYLE

## (1813–1827)

fter the completion of the Eighth Symphony in the fall of 1812, Beethoven's phenomenal productivity fell off sharply. Before that time he had composed on average more than two and a half hours of music a year. From 1812 until his death in 1827, he composed only about 50 minutes a year.

---

## BEETHOVEN AFTER THE HEROIC DECADE

Even Beethoven had begun to exhaust the possibilities of the Viennese Classical style. Composers such as Carl Maria von Weber (1786–1826) and Franz Schubert (1797–1828) were starting to write in a freer, more chromatic style. The Italians, after being eclipsed in opera by Mozart, had begun a new phase of development whose leader was Gioacchino Rossini (1792–1868). Between about 1813 and 1817, Beethoven's own style became rather tentative and experimental. He wrote little original music and concentrated instead on arranging folk songs (in return for a handsome fee) for the Scottish collector and publisher George Thomson. Then, around 1818, Beethoven began to compose once again, writing music that was even more personal and expressive than his earlier works.

Beethoven's unsettled personal life must surely have contributed to his diminished productivity during these years. A deepening relationship between Beethoven and Antonie Brentano, a married woman he met in 1810, seems to have reached a turning point in the summer of 1812, when she apparently offered to leave her husband (and perhaps her two young daughters) in order to live with him. This was probably the occasion of a famous letter he wrote to *meine unsterbliche Geliebte* ("my immortal beloved"). In the letter, without explaining why, Beethoven states that he is unable to accept her offer. Either he was unwilling to break up her family or he was unable to deal with the intimacy implied by unconditional love. Four years later, he wrote: "Unfortunately I have no wife. I found only one, whom no doubt I shall never possess."

In 1815, Beethoven's brother Karl died of tuberculosis, leaving a nine-year-old son. Although there is no evidence that the child's mother, Johanna, was an unsuitable parent, Beethoven launched a series of protracted, costly legal battles to wrest the child from her. Because the Viennese mistakenly assumed that the Dutch "van" before his surname indicated nobility (as "von" did in Austria), he managed to avail himself of the court system reserved for the nobility. The child's mother, a commoner, had little chance of winning the suit.

In 1819, while he was offering testimony to the court, Beethoven inadvertently admitted that he was not of noble birth, and his case was immediately referred to the lower courts. Though enraged and humiliated, he nevertheless persisted until he received sole custody of the child in 1820. Beethoven proved to be a woefully inadequate parent, however, and the young man tried to commit suicide in the summer of 1826. At last Beethoven abandoned his attempt to create a family of his own.

During the latter stages of this struggle, Beethoven was at work on his *Missa solemnis*, Op. 123, a work he referred to as "my greatest." Although he composed this Mass for the impending coronation of his close friend and pupil, the Archduke Rudolf, as Bishop of Ölmutz, he seems to have regarded it in part as atonement for his harsh treatment of Johanna.

From 1818 on, Beethoven was clinically deaf. From that year until his death, more than 130 "conversation books" have survived.* These were small notebooks in which people wrote down what they wanted to say to him. (Reading these entries is rather like hearing one side—though perhaps the less important one—of a phone conversation.) Deafness intensified Beethoven's sense of isolation, though it did not diminish his creative powers.

About the time he was composing the *Missa solemnis*, Beethoven embarked on several other ambitious projects. Among them are the last 4 of his 30 (discounting 2 early works) piano sonatas; a masterful set of variations for piano, Op. 120, on a "flyspeck" of a theme by the Viennese publisher Antonio Diabelli; and the Ninth Symphony, which took him more than six years to write. In the last movement of the Ninth Symphony, Beethoven uses a choral setting of the revolutionary *Ode to Joy* by the German playwright and poet Friedrich von Schiller. Even more powerfully than the *Missa solemnis*, the Ninth Symphony expresses Beethoven's deep longing for universal brotherhood.

On May 7, 1824, Beethoven produced an academy in Vienna that featured the premieres of the Ninth Symphony and three movements of the *Missa solemnis*. It had been over 10 years since an audience had heard Beethoven's music in a public concert of his own, and the Viennese cheered loudly even though they were somewhat puzzled by the music. They also witnessed the poignant spectacle of the deaf composer trying to conduct his own music. It was Beethoven's last public appearance.

During the last three years of his life, Beethoven returned to the more intimate genre of the string quartet. He was an accomplished player of the violin

---

*There were originally almost 400, but Beethoven's friend Anton Schindler destroyed most of them, probably to protect his own image.

and the viola, as well as the piano, and even his earliest string trios, from the 1790s, reveal that he was thoroughly at home writing for strings. In 1800 he had published six string quartets (his Op. 18), which were compared favorably to the best quartets by Haydn and Mozart. And during his "heroic decade" he had written five more quartets, including the three "Razumofsky" Quartets. By 1825, however, Beethoven had written no quartets for 15 years. He wrote the first three of the "late quartets," Op. 127, Op. 132, and Op. 130 (in that order), to fulfill a commission from a Russian nobleman and amateur cellist, Prince Nicholas Galitzïn.* But the last two (Op. 131 and Op. 135) were written entirely at his own prompting. Toward the end of his life, Beethoven carried out some preliminary work on a tenth symphony.

For over a century the music of Beethoven's "late style" was believed to be beyond the reach of all but a few connoisseurs. Greater familiarity has won that music widespread popularity and genuine veneration.

## Beethoven: Piano Sonata in C Minor, Op. 111 (1822)

The piano figured prominently in Beethoven's music throughout his life (see the Historical Window on page 350). Although today his 30 piano sonatas are a staple of every concert pianist's repertoire, none of them is believed to have been performed in public during his lifetime. Beethoven transformed the solo sonata from a modest composition popular among amateurs into a genre of high artistic and technical demands. He wrote his first important keyboard sonatas during his early years in Vienna and completed his last sonata almost 30 years later.

Op. 111 marks the final phase of Beethoven's preoccupation with C Minor. In the Fifth Symphony, the major-mode finale seems to signal a hard-earned triumph. Like that symphony, this sonata begins in C Minor and ends in C Major, but it follows a different plan. Rather than a struggle, its two movements are studies in contrast. The sonata-form first movement is terse and harsh, and the second movement is a series of richly inventive variations on a songful theme (labeled *Arietta*). The second movement relies on persuasion rather than force.

**First Movement.** The movement opens with a slow introduction, more characteristic of a symphony than a sonata, whose dotted rhythms and jagged rhythms create an effect that is more disturbing than elegant. The harmonies shift abruptly from one diminished-seventh chord (among the most dissonant harmonies available to a Classical composer) to another, supported by large leaps and rapid arpeggios. The arrival of the dominant pedal point, which normally signals the end of the introduction, brings further harsh dissonances. A growling trill in the bass leads without the customary pause into the Allegro con brio, which constitutes the main portion of the movement.

Instead of beginning with a tune and accompaniment, the primary area begins with three powerful, disjunct octaves preceded by a rapid, 3-note upbeat:

*The Prince never paid Beethoven for these works.

*Allegro con brio ed appassionato* (Fast, with fire and passion)

Throughout the movement the three short-short-LONG octaves serve as a motto that inaugurates the transition and closing areas and saturates the development section. Beethoven repeats the motto in the primary area and then introduces rapid runs that span more than three octaves. The transition continues the two-voiced texture and halts suddenly on a bare octave in the bass that introduces the secondary area.

After a brief lyrical passage, a sudden downward rush on a diminished-seventh chord leads to an energetic closing theme in the bass, patterned once again on the motto. The exposition closes with a furious chromatic run in octaves that reinforces the aggressiveness of the entire movement:

During the last 12 years of his life, Beethoven made a close study of the music of Handel and J. S. Bach. He became intensely interested in fugue and integrated it into Classical forms in a highly original manner. In the first movement of this sonata, the development is a compact fugato in three voices, based again on the motto. The motto also dominates the retransition, which brings back the diminished-seventh chords from the introduction. The recapitulation arrives in thunderous doubled octaves, filling out the treble range that was largely absent from the exposition. Only in the brief coda, which slips quietly into the major

*(Text continues on page 354.)*

# *Historical Window*

## BEETHOVEN'S PIANOS

The modern piano (Figure 17.1b) is very different from the pianos Beethoven and his contemporaries used. A modern concert grand is about nine feet long and weighs more than 1,200 pounds. It is anchored by a cast-iron plate located inside the wooden frame, strong enough to withstand the force created by the strings (steel wire in the treble, steel wire wound with copper in the bass) under tension, which may exceed 12 tons. The instrument has a range of $7\frac{1}{3}$ octaves (88 notes), from AAA to $c^5$. The mechanism by which energy is transferred from the keys to the strings (called the "action") involves almost 20 moving parts per note (Figure 17.1a). The hammers are covered with thick, hard slabs of felt. The modern piano is designed to produce a tone that is full, long-lasting, and even throughout its range.

The *fortepiano** of Beethoven's youth (Figure 17.1d) was just over seven feet long and had a range of only five octaves, from FF to $f^3$ (61 notes). It was made entirely of wood and weighed only about 175 pounds. The tension on the frame was about two tons. The action—known as a Viennese action—was simple and direct, involving only three moving parts per note (Figure 17.1c). The tiny hammers consisted of wooden cores covered with thin layers of leather or buckskin. This instrument was ideally suited to the music of Mozart and his contemporaries. Its tone was light, clear, and crisp, with well-defined registers.

Even during Beethoven's lifetime the piano underwent rapid growth in response to the increasing size of orchestras and concert halls. From a small chamber ensemble around 1750, the orchestra had grown to as many as 80 players a century later. All the instruments of the orchestra increased in both range and size during this period.

Around 1800, the 5-octave Viennese fortepiano acquired another fifth (to $c^4$) in the treble and gained about 75 pounds in weight. A few years later it acquired another fourth (to $f^4$) and grew in weight to almost 300 pounds. Finally, around 1816, the range was extended down a fourth to CC, made possible by the introduction of wound strings. This newest version weighed more than 350 pounds and exerted as much as six tons of tension on the frame, which was still made of wood. In less than 20 years the fortepiano had doubled in size and weight.

The extension of the lower range reflects the intimate relationship between composers and technology during the early years of the nineteenth century. The

---

*The customary designation for the Viennese piano until about 1815, when Schubert and other composers began calling it (for reasons that are not clear) the *pianoforte*. The *forte* was dropped toward the end of the nineteenth century. Both terms refer to the piano's ability to play both loud (*forte*) and soft (*piano*), as opposed to the harpsichord, which can change its volume only by the coupling or de-coupling of sets of strings.

pitch of a string is determined by its material—iron (today steel) or brass—the sounding length and diameter, and the tension. Length, diameter, and tension are related exponentially: To calculate any of these variables, the others must be squared. A piano would sound most evenly throughout its entire range if all its strings were of the same diameter and tension. But to achieve that, the sounding length of the lowest string would have to equal the length of a football field!

**a**

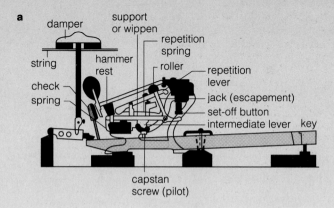

**b**

**c**

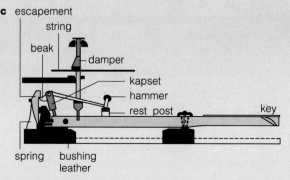

**d**

FIGURE 17.1 (a) This maze of interconnected levers gives a performer enough leverage to accelerate the hammer quickly, producing a large tone. (b) The design of the concert grand piano has changed little since this 1892 Steinway was built. (c) Before pianos had to fill large performing spaces, the simplicity and directness of the Viennese action provided an unsurpassed vehicle for intimate expression. (d) This 5-octave Viennese fortepiano from about 1800 by Ferdinand Hofmann raises the dampers (strips of felt that dampen the strings) with a knee lever. Pulling a small hand stop inserts a thin layer of cloth (called a moderator) between the hammer and the strings, producing a distant, veiled sound.

*continued*

The maximum length of the modern piano, 7½ to 9 feet, seems to have been imposed by the average size of rooms and by the need to move a piano in and out of buildings with ease. So builders compensated for the relative shortness of the lower strings by making them thicker. They discovered, however, that beyond a certain thickness a string becomes so stiff that it produces only a dull thud.

Viennese composers got along for many years with a lower limit of FF. But as Beethoven and others began to chafe under this restriction, the builders (who were also the designers) at last adopted the wound-wire technology that the English had been using on small pianos since the eighteenth century. The wound string consists of a core wire identical to the other strings and a clockwise copper wrapping at right angles to the core wire. The thin core preserves flexibility, while the wrapping adds the diameter needed to produce the five lower tones down to CC.

Beethoven's earliest use of a note below FF coincided with the appearance of the first pianos capable of producing that lower range (Figure 17.2). In his score for the A-Major Sonata, Op. 101, completed in November 1816, Beethoven calls attention to his use of a newly available note, as if to remind the player that it is not a misprint:

contra E

During this time Beethoven enjoyed a close relationship with a prominent Viennese piano maker, Johann Andreas Streicher, and his wife Nanette (Frau Streicher was herself the daughter of a piano maker highly praised by Mozart). In July 1817 Beethoven wrote to Nanette Streicher, "Although I have not always used one of your pianos, since 1809 I have always had a special preference for them—only Streicher would be able to send me the kind of piano that I require." Despite growing deafness, Beethoven probably talked regularly with piano makers about such matters as range, touch, and pedaling devices. Shortly after the publication of his "Moonlight" Sonata in 1802, he wrote to his friend Nicholas Zmeskall, "The whole flock of piano makers have been swarming around me in their eagerness to serve me. . . . Each of them wants to make me an instrument just as I would like it."

In Vienna, a city of 250,000, there were more than 200 piano makers, and it is likely that every family of ambition in Vienna aspired to the ownership of a fine piano, especially if there were daughters whose ability to play would make them better marriage candidates. There is no evidence that Beethoven ever purchased a piano himself. In 1803 a French builder presented him with an instrument, and in 1817 an English builder gave him another. He could probably borrow a Viennese instrument whenever he needed one. Toward the end of his life he is said to have remarked that the piano "is and remains an inadequate instrument." This does not mean that Beethoven would have preferred our modern instrument, any more than Rembrandt would have preferred to paint with acrylics or Michelangelo to work in plastic. Like all artists, Beethoven worked with what was available. Were he alive today, he would be composing for our modern instruments—and writing very different music.

FIGURE 17.2 This 6½-octave fortepiano by Conrad Graf, with range down to CC, features no fewer than five foot pedals: damper, moderator, shift (moves the keyboard over so that the hammers strike fewer strings), bassoon (lowers a parchment tube filled with buckshot onto the bass strings), and Janissary (strikes a padded mallet to the soundboard, a brass rod against the bass strings, and three brass bells—simultaneously!).

# *Historical Window*

FIGURE 18.3 Many of Schubert's songs were inspired by the most celebrated poet of his time, Johann Wolfgang von Goethe (1749–1832), who wrote, "In music the dignity of art seems to find supreme expression. There is no subject matter to be discounted. It is all form and significant content. It elevates and ennobles whatever it expresses."

## A SCHUBERTIAD

Rather than staging public concerts, as Mozart and Beethoven had before him, Schubert preferred to present his works in more intimate settings. Some of his pieces were introduced in semipublic *salons* in the homes of admirers, which he probably attended (see Figure 18.3). Others were introduced by singers or instrumentalists in their own public concerts, although few of Schubert's works were of the sort they preferred—concertos, for example. During the 1820s the most significant musical events for Schubert seem to have been spontaneous. In a letter of January 1821, written by Schubert's friend Josef Huber to his fiancée, Huber reports on an evening in St. Pölten, a suburb of Vienna:

> Last Friday I was wonderfully entertained. . . . Franz [Schober, a friend of Schubert's] invited Schubert and fourteen of his good friends for the evening. A bunch of Schubert's splendid songs were sung, which he accompanied, lasting until after 10 in the evening. Afterwards we drank punch supplied by one of the guests and, since there was a great deal, the already happily disposed guests became even merrier. It was 3 o'clock in the morning before we took leave of each other. . . . For this I would gladly forsake all that is called entertainment.

In October of the next year such an evening is referred to for the first time as a "Schubertiad," a coinage that appears repeatedly in the diaries and correspondence of Schubert's friends.

FIGURE 18.4 In 1825, Vogl and Schubert traveled to Salzburg, where they performed at small, private gatherings. Writing to his brother, Schubert observed, "The way Vogl sings and I accompany him . . . at such moments we seem to be at *one* with each other."

Early in 1817, Schubert met Johann Michael Vogl, a leading tenor/baritone in the Viennese opera. A man of wide interests and learning, Vogl became an ardent and influential champion of Schubert's songs. For a time in the early 1820s the towering Vogl and the diminutive Schubert (who was only about five feet tall) were seen together so frequently that they were caricatured by Schubert's friend Moritz von Schwind (Figure 18.4). The earliest mention of Vogl's participation in a Schubertiad appears in November of 1823. Over the next several years these events were held weekly (generally on Thursdays), numbering in the hundreds before Schubert's death. We should not conclude that they consisted only of a little singing followed by lots of drinking. Often a dinner was served, and there were readings of poetry and plays, with the guests playing various roles. Participants in the Schubertiads mention other activities as well:

- Performances of Schubert's four-hand piano music. Like the *Lied*, this was a genre that had occupied a minor place during the eighteenth century, but which Schubert raised to considerable importance. The pieces ranged from marches in a popular vein to large sonatas, fantasies, and sets of variations.
- Dancing, for which Schubert improvised waltzes and other popular types. More than 400 of these pieces survive, and many others were probably never written down.
- A party game known as *tableaux vivantes* ("living pictures"). This was a popular pastime that gave amateurs with aspirations to acting a chance to perform (the contemporary equivalent might be charades).

*continued*

- Another party game known as "tossing the blanket," in which one person was thrown into the air from a blanket, after which those holding it scurried to prearranged positions to create a pattern (such as a star) before catching the airborn subject on his or her return to earth.

The most distinguished host of the Schubertiads was Joseph von Spaun, an attorney who had once furnished the schoolboy Schubert with music paper. An entry from Franz von Hartmann's diary captures the spirit of a Schubertiad held at von Spaun's during the Christmas season of 1826:

I went to Spaun's, where there was a big, big Schubertiad. On entering I was received rudely by Fritz and very haughtily by Haas. There was a huge gathering. Gahy . . . played four hands gloriously with Schubert, and Vogl . . . sang almost 30 splendid songs. . . . As I was in a particularly excited state of mind today, I was moved almost to tears by the trio of the fifth march [for four-hand piano], which always reminds me of my dear, good mother. When the music was done, we ate with great relish and then danced. . . . I danced twice with Betty and once with each of the ladies Witteczek, Kurzrock, and Pompe. At 12:30, after a warm farewell with the Spauns . . . we saw Betty home and went to the "Anchor" [a tavern], where we still found Schober, Schubert, Schwind, Derffel, and Baurnfeld. Jolly. Then home. To bed at one o'clock.

melody makes it seem to float. He also frames the melody with an independent piano accompaniment whose left hand offers sharp counterpoint to the vocal line. All these elements contribute to the natural, effortless quality of the melody.

## Schubert: *"Gretchen am Spinnrade"*
## ("Gretchen at the Spinning Wheel"), D. 118 (1814)

When he was only 17, Schubert composed a setting for *"Gretchen am Spinnrade,"* D. 118 (Listening Guide 41), a poem from Goethe's *Faust,* in which he captures the mood of Faust's beloved as she longs for his return. It is Schubert's first undisputed masterpiece in the genre of *Lied.* The song is unified by a stream of sixteenth notes in the piano (marked *ligato,* or "connected") that represent the humming of Gretchen's spinning wheel (the voice sings the upper staff, and the pianist plays the two lower staves):

*Nicht zu geschwind* (Not too quickly)

sempre legato

pp

sempre staccato

Mei - ne Ruh_____ ist hin,
(My peace is gone,)

The upper note in the left hand (marked *sempre staccato*, or "always short") suggests the regular rhythm of Gretchen's treadle.

Schubert organizes the song around Goethe's threefold restatement of the first stanza. The vocal melody unfolds in three waves (Stanzas 1–3, 4–7, and 8–11), each of which begins identically but then develops in different directions, in what can be called *modified strophic form*. Throughout the first three stanzas Gretchen speaks of her heavy heart and distressed mind and likens the world to a grave. After repeating the first stanza (Stanza 4\*), she dwells in the fifth through seventh stanzas on Faust's lofty bearing, his smile, his powerful eyes, his magical voice, the pressure of his hands. As her excitement mounts, the vocal line climbs ever higher. Finally she imagines his kiss. At that moment the staccato left hand drops out, as if she has stopped her spinning, and the treadle comes to a halt:

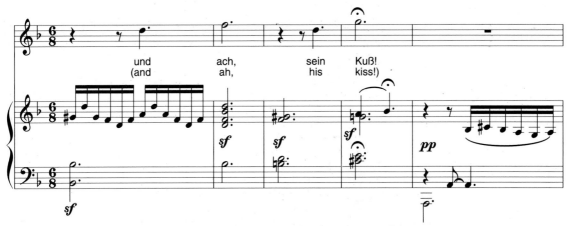

und ach, sein Kuß!
(and ah, his kiss!)

sf sf sf pp

sf

As the lingering kiss ends, the spinning resumes. In the third and final strophe, Gretchen lapses back into despair. Aided by chromatic harmonies, she becomes more and more agitated, longing to "kiss him as much as I wished." The music accelerates in tempo and rises to its highest pitch as Gretchen

\*Though they are identical poetically, we number them separately for easy reference.

"swoons under his kisses." Although Goethe's poem ends here, Schubert rounds out his setting with a laconic return of the first two lines ("My peace is gone, my heart is heavy") sung to the opening music; Gretchen's longing will continue.

### Schubert: *"Rastlose Liebe"* ("Restless Love"), D. 138 (1815)

A year later, Schubert composed a setting for another of Goethe's poems, *"Rastlose Liebe"* (Listening Guide 41). The breakneck tempo and chromatic harmonies of the setting capture the impetuosity of the poem. The poem's three agitated stanzas make Schubert's through-composed setting the logical choice. Schubert accompanies the first and third verses with a torrent of fast legato notes in the right hand and marked staccato notes in the left hand—as he had done in *"Gretchen am Spinnrade,"* though to very different effect. Even though the setting is through-composed, Schubert uses several subtle techniques to unify the song. For example, the tune for the lines *"Alle das Neigen von Herzen zu Herzen"* in the middle stanza is echoed in the lines *"Krone des Lebens, Glück ohne Ruh"* in the last stanza:

Moreover, the short-short-LONG rhythm in the left hand accompanies all three stanzas:

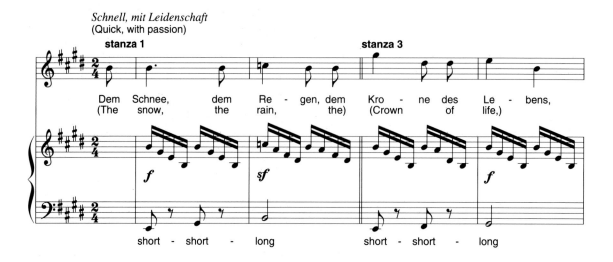

# ROMANTICISM (1829–1910)

## The Cult of the Individual

*M*ost of the terms used to label style periods in the arts came into use only after the periods themselves had run their course. By contrast, people were using the term *Romanticism* throughout the long period it describes. Poets spoke of romantic love, and we still refer to a movie or a novel—or someone we find attractive—as romantic. Many of the ideas and attitudes common to Romanticism survive to this very day.

Romanticism reflected the egalitarian ideals of the French Revolution and the reaction against the rationalism of the Enlightenment. Its roots reach much deeper, however. The word *romantic* derives from the medieval French for "romance," an imaginative tale written in a Romance language rather than in Latin (as in some early accounts of King Arthur). As a description of something wild or fanciful, the word *romantic* first appears in English literature during the seventeenth century.

In 1797 the German writer Friedrich von Schlegel (1772–1829) wrote: "That is romantic which depicts emotional matter in an imaginative form." In England, the Romantic movement achieved its fullest expression in the *Lyrical Ballads* of William Wordsworth (1770–1850) and Samuel Coleridge (1772–1834). Wordsworth wrote that poetry springs from "the spontaneous overflow of powerful feelings." The English poet and artist William Blake (1757–1827) wrote mystical poetry illustrated with fantastic images (Figure 1) that appealed to the imagination of later Romantics. In 1830 a young French novelist and playwright, Victor Hugo (1802–1885), wrote *Hernani,* a sprawling melodrama that centers around the efforts of three men to win the heart of one woman. With this play, Hugo broke with the rigid conventions of earlier French drama and set off an intemperate battle between the "classicists" and the "romantics."

Common to all these developments was an emphasis on the individual imagination. That emphasis, together with a defiance of authority, reached its peak

FIGURE 1 *The Ghost of Samuel Appearing to Saul* is one of Blake's illustrations of the Bible, which he considered the "great code of art." Blake based his long, prophetic poems of mythology on the idea of the "Universal Man."

FIGURE 2 (opposite) Europe in the Age of Romanticism. Even more so than in the Renaissance, musicians were on the move.

during the nineteenth century. Creative artists no longer strove to please aristocratic patrons and insisted instead on serving their own artistic vision. Even when artists did accept patronage—as when Richard Wagner accepted the support of King Ludwig II of Bavaria—they did so on their own terms. (See Figure 2 for a map of Europe in the Age of Romanticism.)

Romantic writers, painters, and composers shared a fascination, almost an obsession, with the past. In the 1820s the Scottish writer Sir Walter Scott (1771–1832) published almost a dozen popular novels set in medieval times, among them *Ivanhoe* (1820). In the Romantic view of the Middle Ages, gallant knights followed a chivalric code in the service of idealized women—a view evident in the canvases of the French painter Eugène Delacroix (1798–1863) (Color Plate 9). Later in the century the French composer Hector Berlioz drew on Greek and Roman mythology for his opera *The Trojans,* and the German composer Richard Wagner looked to Nordic mythology for his vast cycle of operas, *The Ring of the Nibelungen.*

*Part Three   The Age of Tonality (1690–1910)*

**A** Friedrich von Schlegel (writer; 1772–1829)
E. T. A. Hoffmann (composer, writer; 1776–1822)
**B** William Wordsworth (poet; 1770–1850)
Samuel Coleridge (poet; 1772–1834)
William Blake (poet, artist; 1757–1827)
William Turner (painter; 1775–1851)
Charles Darwin (naturalist; 1809–1882); published
  *On the Origin of Species* in 1859
**C** Sir Walter Scott (novelist; 1771–1832)
**D** Hector Berlioz (composer; 1803–1869)
Frédéric Chopin (composer; 1810–1849)
Victor Hugo (writer; 1802–1885)
Georges Bizet (composer; 1838–1875)
**E** Johannes Brahms (composer; 1833–1897);
  in Vienna from 1865
Johann Strauss, Jr. (composer; 1825–1899)
Gustav Mahler (composer; 1860–1911);
  in Vienna from 1899

**F** Felix Mendelssohn (composer; 1809–1847)
**G** Bedřich Smetana (composer; 1824–1884)
**H** Otto von Bismarck (politician; 1815–1898)
**J** Modest Musorgsky (composer; 1839–1881)
Peter Tchaikovsky (composer; 1840–1893)
Nikolai Rimsky-Korsakov (composer; 1844–1908)
**K** Edvard Grieg (composer; 1843–1907)

Musicians' travels:
- - - - - - -   Nicolò Paganini (1782–1840)
– – – – –   Franz Liszt (1811–1886)
―――   Robert Schumann (1810–1856) and
  Clara Wieck (Schumann) (1819–1896)
••••••••••   Giuseppe Verdi (1813–1901)
– – – – – –   Richard Wagner (1813–1883)

Romantics also shared a fondness for grotesque themes. Hugo's *The Hunchback of Notre Dame* (1831), which has been made into a movie four times, tells the story of a deformed bell ringer during the fourteenth century. The *Nibelungen* of Wagner's *Ring* are a race of ugly dwarfs who stand guard over a priceless treasure. Romantics were fascinated with the supernatural, especially its darker sides. Beginning with Carl Maria von Weber's opera *Der Freischütz* (1821), composers from Berlioz to Verdi to Wagner found a role for the devil in their works. And no Romantic career seemed complete without a setting of at least a portion of Goethe's *Faust*.

The Romantics' preoccupation with the past arose in part from nostalgia for what they viewed as a more peaceful, chivalric age. Only nostalgia could transform the turbulent Dark Ages into a time of peace and gallantry. At the same time, however, historians were turning to the scholarly study of political and cultural history, bringing the past into the present.

Another enthusiasm of the Romantics was the worship of nature. In the eighteenth century, Jean-Jacques Rousseau (1712–1778), the Enlightenment philosopher and composer who contributed entries on music to Diderot's *Encyclopedia,* had described an unspoiled state of nature in which man existed as a "noble savage." Eighteenth-century rationalists viewed nature as innocent and bucolic, often using a shepherd to typify natural man.

To nineteenth-century Romantics, however, nature was an awesome force to be feared as well as admired. A soft-spoken English naturalist, Charles Darwin (1809–1882), devised a theory of natural selection (published in 1859 as *On the Origin of Species*) that depicted nature as an arena of perpetual struggle for survival. The landscapes of Caspar David Friedrich (1774–1840) in Germany and the seascapes of William Turner (1775–1851) in England testify to the fascination exercised by the powerful forces of nature, such as violent storms at sea (see Color Plate 10).

These new directions in the arts were accompanied by profound social changes, in which new forms of freedom competed with new forms of oppression. The Industrial Revolution that had begun in England in the late eighteenth century now gave rise to smokestack industries that spewed their ashes over cities and countryside. More and more people abandoned their farms for the promise of greater security and comfort in the cities. Instead, they found congestion, poverty, and crime, and many factory owners took advantage of the seemingly limitless supply of cheap labor, including child labor (Figure 3).

The art of warfare made ominous advances as well. Earlier wars had been fought by armies of paid mercenaries who faced each other far from population centers. But Napoleon assembled hordes of soldiers motivated by patriotism rather than money. By mid-century soldiers carried arms capable of destroying targets that were barely visible. The Gatling gun, the predecessor of the modern machine gun, was tested during the American Civil War. When a series of

FIGURE 3 Child labor was widespread in the textile industries, where lace and intricate weaves required nimble little hands. For these poorly paid children, little more than slaves, a typical workday could last 18 hours. In 1850, a Factory Act in England limited children's workdays to 10½ hours.

revolutionary movements, born out of the failed promises of the French Revolution, swept across Europe in 1848, they were ruthlessly suppressed with little concern for civilian casualties.

The *colonialism* that had begun two centuries before now culminated in *imperialism*. The British, French, and Germans, convinced that Europeans had a mission to govern the "lesser" races of the world (many of whom had complex cultures at least as old as any European culture), brought most of Africa, India, and the Middle East under their rule. Institutionalized slavery, though by no means an American invention, almost destroyed the young republic.

In politics, nationalism was the predominant force. The unification of Italy (known as the *Risorgimento,* or "resurgence") in 1861 brought together dozens of small principalities that had long endured the yoke of the Austro-Hungarian Empire. A newly united Germany, under the iron-fisted leadership of Otto von Bismarck (1815–1898), defeated the French handily in 1871.

By the end of the century, the 70-hour work week common in factories at mid-century had been shortened to 60 or even 50 hours. For the first time in history workers could spend a few hours in pursuits other than the feeding and clothing of their families. Leisure time fueled the demand for music and led to the first permanent orchestras (in Leipzig, Vienna, Paris, Berlin, London, New York, and Boston) and the nine-month concert season.

The idea that education should not be limited to the upper classes also gained support during the Romantic era. England still favored the privileged classes, but even there schooling was more accessible than it had been in earlier centuries. Access to education encouraged the spread of egalitarianism. The American Civil War (1861–1865) was fought in part over the principle that, regardless of race, no person should be enslaved by another. Women, who for centuries had been confined to the home, won new though still limited opportunities to develop their creative talents, in music and in other arts as well (see the Historical Window for Chapter 21 on page 420).

These new freedoms transformed the relationship between artist and society. Richard Wagner took part in the revolutions of 1848. Franz Liszt played benefit concerts for flood victims. Giuseppe Verdi was elected to the first Italian senate. Having rejected the support of patrons, composers were obliged to devise new ways of earning a living. Robert Schumann founded and edited a leading music journal. Felix Mendelssohn conducted an orchestra and helped found a conservatory of music. Composers spoke to their audiences in words as well as in music. Hector Berlioz reviewed music regularly for several Parisian journals. Liszt published a biography of Chopin. Wagner wrote volumes of polemics setting forth his views on music.

The earliest references to Romanticism in music appear in the writings of E. T. A. Hoffmann (1776–1822), an accomplished composer as well as a writer. (Hoffmann added the initial "A" for "Amadeus," out of admiration for Mozart.) For Hoffmann, even Haydn, Mozart, and Beethoven were "romantics." In 1813 he wrote,

> Beethoven's music sets in motion the lever of fear, of awe, of horror, of suffering, and wakens just that infinite longing which is the essence of Romanticism. He is accordingly a completely Romantic composer. . . .

Hoffmann was not alone in his view of the "romantic" Beethoven, but most historians detect a more decisive break with the musical past around 1830, when the center of musical activity shifted from Vienna to Paris. Although Romanticism in the visual and dramatic arts had run its course by mid-century, it persisted in music for another half century, partly because it had emerged later and partly because Romanticism in music encompasses so many different styles.

**COLOR PLATE 9**
*Although the female representing "Liberty" in Eugene Delacroix's* Liberty Leading the People *may appear* *more sensuous than idealistic, these ragtag soldiers leading the July 1830 Paris uprising are the Romantic counterpart to medi-* *eval knights serving an idealized woman. Delacroix depicted himself as the rebel with the rifle.*

**COLOR PLATE 10**
*Romantics were fasci-
nated with the violent,
irrational side of na-
ture, as in J. M.W.
Turner's* Fishermen
upon a Lee Shore, in
Squally Weather
*(1802). Turner's work
displays the blurred
boundary in Romanti-
cism between a sketch
and a completed
composition. A con-*
*temporary critic found
the painting was an
"admirable sketch, but
we have doubt whether
Mr. Turner could make
it a good finished
picture."*

**COLOR PLATE 11**

*In the summer of 1978, the author ended a long search by stumbling into a small clearing containing the composing hut built by Gustav Mahler in 1899 at Maiernigg on the Wörthersee. Here he composed his Fourth through Eighth Symphonies and many orchestral songs. Mahler needed quiet: The hut has two-foot-thick walls and heavy insulation. At least twice a day he climbed the steep hill from his lakeside home to work here in splendid isolation. In the summer of 1907, the Mahlers abandoned Maiernigg abruptly after the death of their daughter Maria from scarlet fever and the discovery that Mahler had a serious heart condition.*

**COLOR PLATE 12**
*In 1874, a disgruntled critic attending a new group show in Paris coined the term* impressionism *from the title of Claude Monet's* Impression: Sunrise *(painted two years earlier). One critic wrote of this painting, "Wallpaper in its earliest stages is more finished." Monet actually carefully studied optics. His seascape seems vast, but it measures only 17 1/2" X 21".*

# Chapter 19

## ROMANTICISM IN PARIS

The musical style of the late Baroque had been very similar from one country to another. The musical language spoken by Vivaldi in Italy was readily understood by Bach in Germany and by Rameau in France. Composers sometimes alluded to foreign influences, as did Bach in his *Concerto in the Italian Style,* but those influences were less important than the shared elements. The Viennese Classical style was even more homogeneous. Haydn's French pupil Ignace Pleyel once published some of Haydn's works as his own, and years later Haydn himself believed that Pleyel had written them. The styles of both the late Baroque and Viennese Classicism were truly period styles.

## ROMANTIC STYLE TRAITS

By contrast, Romantic composers were determined to be original. They strove to create a musical language that was uniquely their own. It is far easier to distinguish between the styles of Berlioz and Brahms, for example, than it is to distinguish between the styles of Haydn and Mozart. Some Romantic composers devised styles that departed radically from the styles of the past, while others favored more conservative styles. Some wrote almost nothing but piano music (Chopin), operas (Verdi and Wagner), or symphonies (Mahler). Hence it is more useful to speak of "Romantic style traits" than of a single Romantic style.

Romantic music gravitated to the miniature and the monumental. Chopin wrote preludes that last less than a minute; Mahler wrote a symphony whose first movement lasts three-quarters of an hour. Some composers used dynamic extremes that range from the barely audible to the ear-splitting. And some began and ended their pieces "in the middle," suggesting that the music had been going on for some time before the listener stumbled in, and that it might continue indefinitely.

Although the Viennese Classicists had shown little interest in art forms other than music, Romantic composers enjoyed close associations with painters and

FIGURE 19.1 This parlor gathering to listen to Franz Liszt (whose gaze is fixed on a monstrous bust of Beethoven) includes the writers Alfred de Musset, Victor Hugo, George Sand, and Countess Marie D'Agoult, plus the composers Berlioz and Rossini. In his *Memoirs*, Berlioz expresses a Romantic notion of music: "Which of the two powers, love or music, is able to lift man to the sublimest heights? . . . Love cannot express the idea of music, while music may give an idea of love. Why separate the one from the other? They are the two wings of the soul."

writers (see Figure 19.1). They regarded music itself as an experience with extra-musical dimensions, and their concern for the intellectual and emotional content of music led them to compose a substantial amount of program music (page 214). They believed, in fact, that music was more capable of expressing human feelings than any other art form. Some program music tells a story—for example, Berlioz's *Symphonie fantastique* and Richard Strauss's *Don Quixote*. More often it expresses a mood. Sometimes it served merely as incidental music during the course of a stage drama. Although the practice of linking music and drama dates back to the Renaissance, it became common in the nineteenth century.

The Viennese Classicists had slowed the expansion of harmony and dissonance advanced by Baroque composers. Romantic composers took up that expansion enthusiastically. In some respects, the heir to the harmonic language of J. S. Bach was neither Mozart nor Beethoven but Wagner, whose first important works date from almost a century after Bach's death. Romantic composers favored complex, chromatic harmonies and a high level of dissonance. They valued chords not just for their function but for their "color" as well.

Some of them, including Johannes Brahms, abandoned the metric regularity of the preceding century and introduced original rhythms that subverted the prevailing meter. Others, like Felix Mendelssohn, favored regular meters and regular rhythms that were reminiscent of the late Baroque. To express the ebb and flow of human feelings, Romantic composers and performers treated tempo freely with techniques such as *rubato*.

Moreover, Romantic melodies and themes are longer and more open-ended than those of Viennese Classicism. Often they move forward in waves toward a single climax. Instead of following a symmetrical pattern, they unfold irregularly. Many Romantic themes, again like Baroque themes, grow out of the first few bars of a composition and are then developed. They are developed, however, not through fragmentation, as in Classical music, but through extension and elaboration in a technique known as *developing variation*.

Romantic composers also relied on the technique of *thematic transformation,* which preserves the essential pitch identity of a theme but alters its character. Although this technique resembles the theme and variations of Classical composers, it is structurally freer and serves as a unifying device.

With a technique known as *thematic anticipation,* Romantic composers introduce fragments of a theme before presenting it in its entirety—the reverse of Classical practice. By moving from the fragmentary to the fully expressed statement, Romantics invited the audience to share in the creative act.

Each of these techniques, though subtle, contributed to the sense of unity toward which the Romantics strove. Romantic composers did not insist that the unity of a composition be audible; there is ample evidence that they took special delight in hidden relationships.

Romantic melodies seem uniquely suited to the particular instrument for which they were written. Frédéric Chopin, for example, wrote piano melodies that sound as though they could be sung. But the moment you try to sing them, you realize that their vocal quality comes through only on the piano. Moreover, attempts to arrange Chopin's works for orchestra have been singularly unsuccessful.

Indeed, tone color is perhaps the most distinctive trait of Romantic music. This emphasis on color was supported by the emergence of the virtuoso orchestra during the nineteenth century. Several of the century's most brilliant orchestrators, including Berlioz and Wagner, played no solo instrument at a professional level. Their instrument was the orchestra itself. Almost every orchestral instrument underwent dramatic changes during the nineteenth century, and new instruments such as the saxophone were introduced.

Before the Romantic period, the leader of the violins and the keyboard continuo player provided whatever direction was needed during a performance. But the complex colors and shifting tempos of Romantic music demanded that someone take responsibility for balancing and coordinating the performance. That person was the *conductor.* By the end of the century the dominant role of the conductor in "interpreting" a piece of music was firmly established.

Usually, when a new musical style emerges, it is accompanied by a new form that eventually becomes dominant—for example, ritornello form in the Baroque and sonata form in the Classical period. Given their insistence on individuality and spontaneity, however, Romantic composers were reluctant to accept the restrictions inherent in any one form. True, under the influence of Beethoven's undiminished prestige, many of them continued to work in sonata form. Even then, however, they felt free to alter its proportions or to give it a thematic emphasis quite at odds with the balanced harmonic/thematic framework of the Viennese Classicists. The "inner form" of a work mattered more than its "external form."

By the end of the nineteenth century, every major European city (and several American ones) boasted a permanent orchestra. For at least nine months a year they offered regular subscription concerts designed to appeal to the middle classes. And they turned more and more to the music of the past. The music of J. S. Bach was restored to the repertory by a remarkable performance of his *St. Matthew Passion* organized in 1829 by the 20-year-old Felix Mendelssohn. The music of Mozart, Beethoven, and Schubert had never left the repertory. Even as they advocated the "music of the future," composers sensed that their music would henceforth be measured against great works of the past.

Perhaps the most popular musical form during the Romantic era was opera, which aroused much the same interest as movies do today. Many of the most famous opera houses of the world, some of them large enough to accommodate 3,000 people, were built during the nineteenth century.

Although Vienna retained its reputation as a major center of music after 1830, it was soon eclipsed by a city known for its sophistication and its remarkably varied cultural life. The center of musical Romanticism in the nineteenth century was Paris.

---

## PARIS IN THE NINETEENTH CENTURY

Paris, as we have seen, has had a long, distinguished musical tradition. When the French Revolution broke out in 1789, Paris was a thriving metropolis. In 1800 Paris had a half-million inhabitants (twice the size of Vienna); by mid-century its population had grown to a million, and a decade later to a million and a half.

During his years as emperor (1804–1815), Napoleon embarked on an ambitious construction program in Paris that included the Arch of Triumph (Figure 19.2) and the imposing obelisk in the Place Vendôme. Later in the century, Napoleon III (Bonaparte's nephew, emperor from 1852 to 1870) appointed Baron Georges Haussmann to plan the city's expansion in more orderly fashion (Figure 19.3). Haussmann created a plan of broad, tree-lined boulevards radiating from central squares, with open spaces that afforded striking views, and with great urban parks. He built four railway stations around the inner city, easing access and avoiding congestion, and preserved such historic structures as the cathedral of Notre Dame. The grand result was a city both visually pleasing and highly efficient.

Throughout the nineteenth century Paris attracted a brilliant array of talented artists. Among them were the French painters Jean Ingres, Théodore Géricault, Eugène Delacroix, Honoré Daumier, and Edouard Manet; the architects Charles Garnier and Henri Labrouste; and the writers Victor Hugo, Honoré de Balzac, and George Sand (pseudonym of Aurore Dudevant). Others came from all over Europe. Some of them, including the German writer Heinrich Heine, the Italian composer Gioacchino Rossini, and the Polish-French composer Frédéric Chopin, settled permanently in Paris. Others came in search of fame.

In opera, especially, Paris was dominant. It supported half a dozen opera

FIGURE 19.2 Built between 1806 and 1836, the Arc de Triomphe, Place de l'Etoile, marks the intersection of 12 radiating avenues and one end of the broad Champs Elysees. (The Louvre is at the other end.) The massive arch is 164 feet high and 148 feet wide.

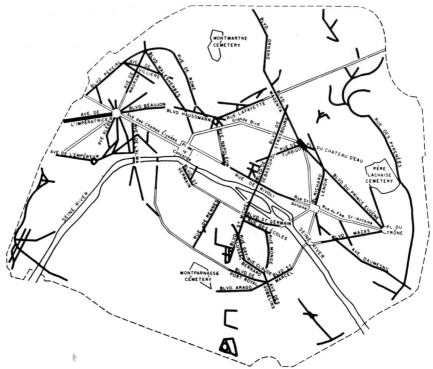

FIGURE 19.3 The streets marked in black on this map of central Paris were built during Haussman's years as city prefect and planner (1853–1870). His design focused the city on its main institutions, both visually and in terms of function. Haussman's achievements included improving the sewer system.

houses, including the Opéra Comique, the Théâtre Lyrique, and the Théâtre Italien. Two of the most important composers of Italian opera—Gaetano Donizetti (1797–1848) and Vincenzo Bellini (1801–1835)—came to Paris to promote their *bel canto* ("beautiful singing") operas, which displayed the expressive, sensuous qualities of the human voice. Success in Paris won singers international fame for their mastery of bel canto. Giacomo Meyerbeer (1791–1864), a German-born composer who spent much of his time in Paris, put together an amalgam of operatic styles known as *grand opera*. His subjects, both exotic *(Robert the Devil)* and historical *(The Huguenots)*, together with his gigantic casts and elaborate staging, were vastly popular with Parisian audiences. Meyerbeer's operas had a strong influence on the leading composer of late-nineteenth-century German opera, Richard Wagner, who himself journeyed to Paris in pursuit of success.

Despite the brilliance and sophistication of the artistic community, however, the Parisian public, like the Viennese public of an earlier time, often failed to support the newest trends in musical styles. Hector Berlioz, the only French composer among the major Romantic composers living in Paris, felt that rejection most keenly.

## HECTOR BERLIOZ (1803–1869)

Hector Berlioz

Hector Berlioz cut a flamboyant figure: He stood six feet tall (very tall for his time) and had wavy red hair, penetrating eyes, and unbounded energy. In his *Memoirs* he described his life as "arduous and turbulent." In many respects, Berlioz was the quintessential Romantic composer.

Berlioz was born in a small town near Grenoble in southeastern France, the oldest child of a respected physician. He attended a private school for a short time but received most of his education from his father, a man of wide interests and a lover of literature. In his *Memoirs* Berlioz recalls his reactions at the age of 10, while reading Virgil's *Aeneid* with his father:

One day I remember being deeply troubled by the line: "Now the Queen had for some time been troubled by the pangs of love." I struggled bravely on until we came to the great turning point of the drama. When I reached the scene in which Dido expires on the funeral pyre, surrounded by the gifts and weapons of the betrayer Aeneas, and pours forth on the bed . . . the bitter stream of her life blood, and I had to pronounce the despairing cries of the dying queen, "thrice raising herself upon her elbow, thrice falling back" . . . and I had to describe . . . the anguish of the disastrous love that convulsed her to the depth of her being, the cries of her sister, her nurse, . . . and that agony so terrible that even the gods are moved to pity—my lips quivered and I could scarcely stammer the words. Finally, at the line: as Dido "sought light from heaven and moaned as she found it," I was completely overcome and broke down. I could not read another word.

More than 40 years later he realized a lifelong ambition by turning parts of Virgil's epic into an opera, *The Trojans.*

Berlioz's father, despite his enlightened views, insisted that young Hector travel to Paris to study medicine. Berlioz studied valiantly for two years, but he could not suppress his passion for music. For the next five years, denied family support, he worked at odd musical jobs. At the age of 23 he entered the Paris Conservatory, where one of his teachers described him as a student who "betrayed dangerous tendencies." On his third attempt he won the prestigious Prix de Rome, a prize awarded annually by the Conservatory to subsidize two years of study in Rome.

In the fall of 1827, while watching a performance of Shakespeare's *Hamlet* by a visiting English troupe, Berlioz became infatuated with Harriet Smithson, an Irish actress who was playing Ophelia. Though he could scarcely understand a word she said, he wrote later that "the impression made on my heart and mind by her extraordinary talent, nay her dramatic genius, was equalled only by the havoc wrought in me by the poet she so nobly interpreted." In 1832, after rejecting Berlioz's approaches for years, Harriet Smithson consented to attend the premiere of his *Symphonie fantastique,* a work in which she recognized herself as the heroine. After a stormy courtship that lasted some 18 months, they were married.

In 1828 Berlioz attended performances of Beethoven's Third and Fifth Symphonies, which he described as "opening before me a new world of music, as Shakespeare had revealed a new universe of poetry." Between 1832 and 1842 he presented several concerts of his music every year, all at his own expense. The Parisian public found his music eccentric and even "incorrect," however, and the concerts were poorly attended. Earning almost nothing as a composer, he began to write music criticism to meet his expenses. Berlioz was a brilliant and often biting critic, and many of his writings, including *Evenings with the Orchestra* (anecdotes exchanged by pit musicians "during the performance of bad operas"), have been reprinted many times.

Berlioz's works were well received outside France, however, and in 1842 he made the first of many concert tours. To ensure performances of satisfactory quality, Berlioz himself became a skillful conductor. Over the next two decades he traveled to Belgium, Germany, Austria, Hungary, England, and Russia and everywhere was met by enthusiastic audiences. Remembering the indifference of the Paris audiences, he wrote: "In Paris music is a god—so long as only the puniest sacrifices are required to feed its altars." Still, in 1846 Berlioz, now a composer of international fame, chose Paris for the premiere of his monumental choral work, *The Damnation of Faust,* based on Goethe's drama:

> Faust was offered twice to a half empty hall. The cultured Parisian public, supposedly fond of music, stayed comfortably at home, evincing as little interest in my new work as if I had been the most obscure student at the Conservatory. For all the people that attended those two performances at the Opéra-Comique, it might as well have been the most wretched opera in the company's repertoire. . . . Nothing in my artistic career ever wounded me more deeply than this unexpected indifference.

Although Berlioz lived on for 20 more years, he presented only three further performances of his music in Paris.

Throughout his life Berlioz suffered from extreme mood swings that today would be diagnosed as manic-depressive illness (see the Historical Window on page 388). In 1848, exhausted by his struggle for acceptance but still wielding a feisty pen, he began to write his *Memoirs*. In 1865 he had 1,200 copies printed at his own expense and directed that they were to be distributed only after his death.

## BERLIOZ'S STYLE

Although Berlioz viewed himself as a disciple of Beethoven, he made a decisive break with the past. He wrote no chamber music. All his important works are either vocal or program music. Of the four works that Berlioz called symphonies, all are programmatic: the *Symphonie fantastique* (1830), *Harold in Italy* (1834, based on the epic poem *Childe Harold* by the English Romantic poet Lord Byron), *Romeo and Juliet* (1839, based on his beloved Shakespeare), and the *Grande symphonie funèbre et triomphale* (1840, *Grand Funereal and Triumphant Symphony,* written for a public ceremony).

The traditional categories of opera, symphony, concerto, and song meant little to Berlioz. *Harold in Italy,* with its important solo viola part, resembles a concerto, while *Romeo and Juliet,* called a "dramatic symphony," veers toward opera. Berlioz's imagination was fired by the great literature of all ages: Virgil, Shakespeare, Goethe, Hugo, and Byron.

In a sense, Berlioz invented the modern orchestra. Unlike almost every important composer since Bach, he was not a keyboard player (though he played the guitar passably). He conceived his ideas in orchestral terms and wrote an encyclopedic *Treatise on Instrumentation and Modern Orchestration* (1843) that is still consulted by composers and conductors.

Following a long French tradition, Berlioz built his compositions on a monumental scale. The *"Tuba mirum"* ("The trumpet shall sound") from his *Requiem* (1837) calls for four brass choirs, one in each corner of the hall, in addition to the main orchestra and chorus. His *Te Deum* (1849) requires an organ at one end of the church, an orchestra and two choirs at the other end, and a third choir in between. Berlioz once wrote:

> It is above all the scale of the movements, the breadth of style and the formidably slow and deliberate pace of certain progressions, whose goals cannot be surmised, that give these works their particularly "gigantic" character and "colossal" dimension. The consequence of such vastness of scale is that the listener either misses the point altogether or is overwhelmed by a powerful emotion.

When Berlioz's critics accused him of writing "without melody," he countered that his melodies were "unlike the desperately trivial little tunes which the riff-raff of the musical world understands by the term." His rhythms—especially in accompaniment figures—are sometimes so regular as to be hypnotic and at other times so unpredictable as to throw the listener off balance. Although his music is not particularly dissonant, he loved to juxtapose unrelated triads. His harmonies have less forward drive than those of his German contemporaries, but they are more colorful.

Berlioz described his style in this 1858 letter to a prospective biographer:

> The predominant features of my music are passionate expression, inner intensity, rhythmic animation, and a quality of unexpectedness. When I say passionate expression, I mean an expression bent on reproducing the inner meaning of its subject, even when that subject is the opposite of passion, and the feelings to be expressed are gentle and tender. . . . To perform [my works] well, everybody concerned, especially the conductor, must *feel* as I feel. This requires a combination of irresistible verve and extreme precision, a controlled vehemence, a dreamlike sensitivity, an almost morbid melancholy, without which the essential character of my phrases is falsified or even destroyed. For this reason I generally find it extremely painful to hear my works conducted by someone other than myself.

Despite this intensity, Berlioz managed to keep his sense of humor. In this same letter he tells of an encounter with a powerful prince:

> One day in Vienna Prince Metternich asked me whether it was I who "composed music for five hundred players?" To which I replied: "Not always, Your Excellency. Sometimes I use only four hundred and fifty."

## Berlioz: *Symphonie fantastique* (1830)

Berlioz's audience was hardly prepared for a symphony titled *fantastique* ("based on fantasy" or "fanciful"). They were even less prepared to have the composer distribute a printed program at the premiere that chronicled his well-known obsession with Harriet Smithson. (The numbers in brackets key events described in the program to the Listening Guide in the Study Guide.)

> *Program of the Symphony.* A young musician of morbidly sensitive temperament and fiery imagination poisons himself with opium in a fit of lovesick despair. The dose of the narcotic, too weak to bring about death, plunges him into a deep sleep accompanied by the strangest visions, during which his sensations, his feelings, his memories are translated into musical thoughts and images. The loved one herself has become a melody to him, like an *idée fixe* [obsession] that he encounters and hears everywhere.

> *Part I: Reveries, Passions.* [1] He recalls first that sickness of the soul, that *vague des passions* [wave of passion], those depressions, those groundless joys that he experienced before [2] he first gazed on his beloved; [3] then the volcanic love that she suddenly inspired in him, his delirious anguish, his frenzied suffering, [4] his jealous rages, [5] his reversion to tenderness, [6] his religious consolation.

## MOODS AND MUSIC

Creativity has been linked with madness since the beginnings of recorded history. The Greek philosopher Aristotle (384–322 B.C.) wrote:

> All who have been famous for their genius, whether in the study of philosophy, in affairs of state, in literary composition, or in the cultivation of the arts, have been inclined to insanity, as Hercules, Ajax, Bellerophon, Lysander, Empedocles, Socrates, and Plato.

The Renaissance composer Orlando de Lassus (1532–1594) suffered from what contemporaries described as a *melancholia hypochondriaca* ("melancholy hypochondria") that produced chronic anxiety and depression. The Italian madrigalist Carlo Gesualdo (1561–1613) endured bouts of mania and depression, referred to as the *affetto napoletanissimo* ("Neapolitan affliction"). The eighteenth-century poet Thomas Chatterton, who committed suicide at the age of 17, wrote:

> By our own spirits we are deified:
> We poets in our youth begin in gladness;
> But thereof comes in the end despondency and madness.

During the nineteenth century, with its emphasis on creativity, the incidence of mood disorders seems to have quickened. Among Romantic composers who suffered from mood disorders were Robert Schumann, Hector Berlioz, Gustav Mahler, Hugo Wolf, Anton Bruckner, Peter Tchaikovsky, Alexander Scriabin, Edward Elgar, and Sergei Rachmaninoff.

According to several recent studies, the incidence of mood disorders among artists (poets and painters have been studied most frequently) is almost seven times greater than it is in the general population. One explanation is that the manic phase of manic-depressive illness—especially the milder form known as hypomania—is accompanied by increased fluency and frequency of creative ideas, the ability to function well on a few hours of sleep, a high energy level, and a great depth and variety of emotions. The long spells of depression that inevitably follow are nevertheless a high price to pay for these creative spurts.

No Romantic composer described the trials of mood disorders more eloquently than Hector Berlioz, as in this 1832 letter to the composer Gasparo Spontini:

> The perpetual agitation in which I have been living, the heartbreak, the storms of every kind that have thundered over me for the past year, must serve as my

excuse. I have hardly ever been in Rome for two months at a time, constantly scurrying off to Florence, Genoa, Nice, or Naples, on foot across the mountains, with no other aim than to tire myself, distract my mind and more easily resist the "spleen" that was tormenting me. It would be tedious for you to learn the causes of the moral sickness from which I am no means cured as yet.

In his *Memoirs,* Berlioz gives this description of his affliction:

It was about this time in my academic career [1831–1832] that I again became vulnerable to that frightful affliction—psychological, nervous, imaginary, what you will—that I will call the plague of isolation. I experienced my first attack when I was sixteen. One fine May morning I was sitting in a field in the shade of a clump of large oaks, at La Côte Saint-André, reading Montjoie's novel *Manuscript found at Posilippo.* . . . The Rogation* procession was passing near by; the voices I heard were the peasants', chanting the prayer to the saints. . . . The procession halted at a wooden cross decorated with leaves; I watched the people kneel while the priest blessed the land. Then it moved slowly off and the melancholy intoning was resumed. . . .

Silence . . . the faint rustling of wheat in the soft morning breeze . . . the loving cry of quail calling to their mates . . . a bunting pouring forth its songs from the top of a poplar . . . profound peace . . . the dull beating of my own heart. . . . Life seemed so distant, a thing apart from me. . . .

And the fit fell upon me with appalling force. I suffered agonies and cast myself on the ground, groaning and clutching the earth wildly, convulsively tearing up handfuls of grass and wide-eyed innocent daisies, struggling against the crushing sense of absence, against a deathly isolation.

Yet such an attack does not compare with the tortures that I have known since then in ever-increasing measure.

What can I say that will give some idea of the action of this abominable disease? . . .

There are, moreover, two kinds of spleen;† one ironical, mocking, passionate, violent, and malignant; the other morose and wholly passive, when one's only wish is for silence and solitude and the oblivion of sleep. For anyone possessed by this latter kind, nothing has meaning, the destruction of the world would hardly move him. At such times I have wished that the earth were a shell filled with gunpowder, to which I would put a match for my entertainment.

*In the Catholic Church, the three days of prayer preceding Ascension Day (marking Christ's ascension into heaven).
†Until late in the nineteenth century, the spleen (a gland that filters blood) was thought to be the seat of negative emotions.

*continued*

# Historical Window (Continued)

Berlioz's impassioned account constitutes a textbook description of manic-depressive illness and its recurrent nature. Berlioz died embittered after a lifetime with only temporary periods of relief. Robert Schumann was committed to an asylum when he was 46, where he probably died of self-starvation. Hugo Wolf, the greatest songwriter of the late nineteenth century, was committed to an asylum at the age of 37, was released for two months, and was recommitted after attempting suicide. He died there at age 43.

Are we to assume that an artist's creativity depends on violent mood swings? Of course not. Many great artists have exhibited a stable temperament throughout their life—J. S. Bach, for example. And many people who suffer mood disorders display an utter lack of creativity. Modern researchers have learned that whole classes of mental disorders, including manic-depressive illness, are largely inherited and that many of them can be controlled with drugs that act as "enablers" rather than as sedatives. If Berlioz had been stabilized on lithium after his first adolescent attack, would he have composed his *Symphonie fantastique* or his *Requiem?* We cannot say. Preliminary research seems to suggest, however, that artists function more, rather than less, creatively when they are in a state of mental health than when they are in the grip of an unpredictable and terrifying disease.

Making only a gesture toward a transition, Berlioz combines the secondary and closing areas (based on the head of the *idée fixe*). Were it not for the repetition of this exposition, we would scarcely suspect that the movement is in sonata form. The development treats briefly the head of the *idée fixe* and the last bars of the secondary/closing area. Then Berlioz introduces a new, macabre idea consisting of ascending and descending chromatic scales. This unexpected digression reaches a brusque climax followed by three full bars of silence.

Without preparation, Berlioz ushers in a full statement of the *idée fixe,* which sounds for all the world like a recapitulation—except that it is not in the tonic. The eventful coda, which occupies almost two-fifths of the movement, presents the *idée fixe* in several guises, including a climactic full statement in the tonic (characterized by brilliant use of the cornet as a melody instrument) that erases the memory of the strange recapitulation. The movement closes with pensive restatements of the *idée fixe* and a final cadence marked *religiosamente* ("religiously"). Though it bears little resemblance to Classical sonata form, this movement makes for brilliant theater, with or without a program.

**Second Movement: A Ball.** The waltz, a dance of German origin, had become popular throughout Europe by the 1820s, but Berlioz is perhaps the only composer to incorporate a formal concert waltz into a symphony. Here its festive character could be easily adapted to his literary program. The ternary form is framed by an introduction and a coda. The introduction, which takes up where the first movement left off, allows time for choosing partners, as was the custom at balls. The fluid melody of the *A*-Section (which is varied and reorchestrated at the repeat of *A*) is followed in the *B*-Section by the encounter with the beloved and is echoed at the beginning of the coda. The striking orchestration of this movement calls for "at least" four harps; Berlioz preferred as many as could be fitted onto the stage.

**Third Movement: Scene in the Country.** In a departure from convention, Berlioz makes the middle movement of this symphony the longest. Again he makes use of ternary form with coda. Here, however, he provides an additional frame by introducing a dialogue between the English horn (presumably representing a male shepherd) and the oboe (presumably representing a female). The tender theme of the *A*-Section rises an octave and a half to its climax, and the recurrence of the *idée fixe* in the *B*-Section is punctuated by "painful premonitions" in the bassoons and lower strings. The repeat of the *A*-Section is considerably freer than it was in the second movement, in keeping with the Romantic preference for originality over straight repetition. Throughout, the movement unfolds at a pace suggestive of a lazy summer afternoon.

**Fourth Movement: March to the Scaffold.** The brilliantly orchestrated March, based on the alternation of two contrasting themes, created a sensation when the symphony was first performed. The introduction whispers a short-LONG-short rhythm that turns out to be the first bar of the "brilliant and solemn" *B*-Section. The orchestration features the full complement of brass, built on a foundation of blaring tones in the bass trombones. The minor-mode *A*-Section consists of "somber and fierce" scales in the cellos and basses that, at their final repeat, turn nimbly into upward scales to suggest the ascent of the condemned lover to the scaffold. His last glimpse of the *idée fixe* is interrupted by the swift fall of the guillotine, and we can almost hear the severed head rolling as three timpanists play furious rolls in the final bars.

**Fifth Movement: Dream of a Witches' Sabbath.** Berlioz's program spells out the course of the finale in some detail. Several examples of thematic anticipation contribute to its nightmarish quality. The "strange noises and groans" of the introduction are expressed in disembodied rhythms, rapid tremolo or detached figures in the muted strings, and muffled percussion rolls. The arrival of the beloved (on a broomstick?) is announced by the *idée fixe* transformed irreverently into an Irish jig (a reference to Harriet?) in the raucous E♭-clarinet, soon doubled by the shrill piccolo. After the "funeral knell," the first of two main sections intones the *Dies irae* that announces the day of judgment for the murderer ("Day of wrath, that dreadful day, when heaven and earth shall pass away"). Through a series of rhythmic diminutions, Berlioz transforms each of the three phrases of the sacred hymn into the jig rhythm—a connection that would not have been lost on Berlioz's largely Catholic audience:

**Dies irae in conventional notation**

**Dies irae as a jig**

As the witches celebrate the execution of the lover, the second main section introduces a spirited Sabbath Round in the form of a mock fugue. A lengthy build-up prepares for the final "combination" of the *Dies irae* and Sabbath Round promised in the program. Berlioz has the coda echo some of the eerie effects of the introduction by directing the violins and violas to play "with the wood of the bow," achieved by turning the bow over. With a series of surprisingly cheerful cadences, this burlesque comes to a riotous conclusion.

Berlioz described Harriet Smithson's reaction to the 1832 premiere of this symphony:

> The symphony began and produced a tremendous effect. The brilliant reception, the passionate character of the work, its ardent, exalted melodies, its protestations of love, its sudden outbursts of violence, and the sensation of hearing an orchestra of that size close to, could not fail to make an impression—an impression as profound as it was totally unexpected—on her nervous system and poetic imagination, and in her heart of hearts she thought, "Ah, if he still loved me!"

Their marriage was over within six years (he spoke little English and she less French), but in this symphony Berlioz had created a lasting work whose mix of striking originality and brilliant execution has never been surpassed.

# Chapter 20

## VIRTUOSOS AND PIANISTS

oday the term *virtuoso* is used very loosely to describe a skillful performer, especially one who can play difficult passages flawlessly. Biographical sketches in concert programs routinely describe performers as "brilliant virtuosos," and performers are admired as much for their "virtuosity" as for their ability to play expressively.

*Virtuoso* had quite a different meaning when the term first came into use in Italy during the sixteenth and seventeenth centuries. Then it meant a person of distinction in any of the arts, whether music, poetry, or architecture. Its Latin root, *virtu,* means "excellence" or "worth." A virtuoso in music was someone who was skilled not only as a performer but also as a composer and theorist (someone who wrote about the structure and language of music). During the late Baroque a distinction arose between the theoretical virtuoso, who explored the intellectual dimensions of an art, and the practical virtuoso, who was primarily a skillful performer. With the rise of the concerto and the aria-dominated opera, the term *virtuoso* came to mean a soloist with exceptional technical abilities.

## THE RISE OF VIRTUOSITY

During the nineteenth century the focus shifted from the virtuoso soloist to the concept of *virtuosity,* which referred to the complete mastery of one's instrument, especially the command of an extraordinary technique. Franz Liszt, one of the greatest performers of the Romantic era, maintained that "virtuosity is not a by-product, but an indispensable element of music."

Romantic composers demanded a higher level of instrumental mastery than had earlier composers. During the two centuries before Beethoven, keyboard composers had relied largely on scales and arpeggios. In passage work consisting of fast, even notes, the number of notes to be played per second rarely exceeded eight, and the performer played only one note at a time. Because most chords were within easy reach of the fingers, the music fell naturally under the hands.

Romantic composers of keyboard music continued to use scales and arpeggios, but they used them in more complex and chromatic patterns, often requiring that a black key be played with the thumb. Their passage work requires the performer to play up to twelve notes per second instead of eight, a dramatic increase. In rapid passages a single hand may have to play two simultaneous notes—thirds or sixths or octaves—in succession. Many chords consist of widely spaced notes that demand great stretches of the hand. Whereas earlier music favored the three middle fingers of each hand, Romantic music requires the equality and independence of all ten fingers. The performer needs strength and flexibility as well as dexterity and command of nuance.

Performers in earlier times acquired their techniques along the way, in the course of playing the standard repertoire. Then, around 1800, composer/performers began to publish *studies* (in French, *études*) designed to help amateurs develop particular performance skills. Forty years later, the étude had emerged as the vehicle of a "transcendental technique" attained only by the greatest virtuosos.

Virtuosity was not limited to solo performers. Challenged by the works of composers like Hector Berlioz, Richard Strauss, and Gustav Mahler, the orchestra became a virtuoso instrument in its own right. Members of the orchestra were expected to perform in perfect ensemble passages that soloists of the eighteenth century would have deemed almost unplayable. This preoccupation with virtuosity was part of a historical evolution that had been going on for two centuries. It received a dramatic boost during the Romantic era from Nicolò Paganini, a brilliant violinist whose influence extended over much of the century.

## NICOLÒ PAGANINI (1782–1840)

Born into a poor family in the fishing town of Genoa, Paganini began to study the violin at the age of 7. His father insisted that he practice from morning till night, denying him food if he faltered. By the time he was 13 he had become so proficient that one of Italy's leading violinists declined to take him as a pupil, saying, "My boy, I can teach you nothing."

From the age of 18, Paganini supported himself by giving concerts and playing in orchestras, but several years were to pass before his playing began to attract widespread attention. Finally, after a concert in Milan in 1813, one critic wrote, "He is undoubtedly the foremost and greatest violinist in the world. His playing is truly inconceivable. He performs certain passage work, leaps, and double stops that have never been heard from any violinist." Audiences were so astonished by the sounds that emanated from Paganini's instrument that it was rumored he was in league with the devil (Figure 20.1) or was the illegitimate son of noble parents. Paganini made no effort to quell the rumors.

In the spring of 1828 Paganini, now in his mid-forties, traveled to Vienna and gave his first concert there at the end of March. Although the concert was poorly attended, word of his astonishing feats spread swiftly among the Viennese, who

FIGURE 20.1 Notice the violin-playing devils in this engraving of *Paganini's Dream*. Paganini's Caprices inspired studies and variations for the piano by Liszt, Schumann, and Brahms, and Chopin described the virtuoso violinist as "absolute perfection."

demanded again and again that he postpone his scheduled departure. By the time Paganini left Vienna at the end of July, he had given 14 concerts. So great was the excitement created by his performances that Schubert's only public concert, on March 26, was not even mentioned in the local press.

Paganini visited Warsaw in 1829 and Paris in 1831. Among those who heard him were two teenagers, Frédéric Chopin and Franz Liszt. On a return visit to Paris in 1838 he met Hector Berlioz, whose music so impressed him that he gave the impoverished French composer the considerable sum of 20,000 francs.

In his early concerts Paganini generally favored the works of composers other than himself. As time passed, however, he played more and more of his own music, perhaps because it gave him better opportunities to display his extraordinary techniques. These techniques included ricochet bowings (in which several notes are "bounced" in the same bowstroke), rapid multiple stops, harmonics,* left-hand pizzicato, more use of the upper register than was customary, and rapid passage work. Among his compositions are works for solo violin and orchestra (which he withheld from publication so that no one else could perform them), chamber music for strings, and works for solo violin. Though Paganini contributed no innovations in harmony or form, he was an effective composer for his instrument. The pieces that invariably dazzled his audiences were a set of 24 Caprices, Op. 1, for solo violin.

*A tone produced by stopping a string lightly so that an overtone is produced rather than the customary fundamental.

### Paganini: Solo Violin Caprice, Op. 1, No. 9 (ca. 1805)

Paganini wrote these caprices* while he was still in his early twenties. When he published them in 1820, he dedicated them to "the artists," but the violinists of the time declared them to be too difficult to play. Paganini convinced audiences all over Europe that they *could* be played, and to this day these caprices are the yardstick by which virtuosity on the violin is measured.

Each caprice attacks a technical problem, often of Paganini's own devising: wide-ranging arpeggios in No. 1, parallel octaves in Nos. 3 and 7, large jumps in No. 11, rapid scales in No. 17, and fast staccato passages in No. 18. The last caprice is a brief theme and variations that was borrowed by several Romantic composers, including Johannes Brahms and Sergei Rachmaninoff (see Chapter 29).

The ninth caprice (Listening Guide 42) is in the form of a simple rondo *(A-B-A-C-A)*. Although it is only two and a half minutes long, its detached style of playing poses three separate challenges to violinists. The *A*-Sections consist of a sprightly tune in double stops in the upper register that Paganini first directs to be played like a flute and then—in the lower register—like a horn. Both registers require dexterity and a highly developed sense of *intonation* (the degree to which a performer plays pitches accurately, or "in tune"):

In the *B*-Section, widespread triple and quadruple stops alternate with staccato notes that call for constant, rapid shifts of the bow:

The *C*-Section calls for successive ricochet bowings in which five notes are "bounced" in each bow stroke:

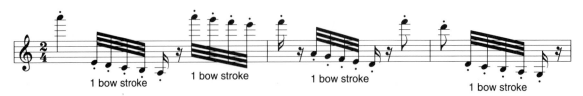

*A *caprice* is "an unmotivated whimsy," though Paganini's motivation in these pieces is quite apparent.

# Listening Guide 42

## PAGANINI: Caprice for Solo Violin, Op. 1, No. 9

CD 5, TRACK 1
TAPE 5A, TRACK 1
DURATION: 2:38

*The simple structure permits Paganini to focus on several technical challenges, including double stops, rapid scales, and ricochet bowing.*

*Form: Rondo (A-B-A-C-A)*

| | LOCATION | TIME | COMMENTS |
|---|---|---|---|
| 1 | *A*-Section | 0:00 | Rapid double stops, first in the upper register and then in the lower register. |
| | *B*-Section | 0:22 | Rapid alternation between triple/quadruple stops and single staccato notes. |
| 2 | *A*-Section | 0:49 | As at the opening. |
| | *C*-Section | 1:12 | Arpeggios in octave double stops alternate with rapid ascending scales. Followed by rapid ricochet bowing. |
| 3 | *A*-Section | 2:11 | As at the opening. |

Despite its fiendish difficulties, the directness of this music makes it highly appealing to audiences, especially if the violinist makes it all sound effortless.

## THE ROMANTIC PIANO

The instrument that brought opera and symphonic music into Romantic drawing rooms was the piano, whose popularity reached a peak around 1900. In 1830 fewer than 10,000 pianos were being produced annually; by the end of the century the number had risen to more than 500,000. Families that could not afford a grand piano bought at least a fashionable, heavily decorated square piano. The nineteenth century belonged to the piano, just as the 1960s belonged to the guitar and the 1980s and 1990s to the electronic keyboard.

The Romantic piano continued the development that had accelerated during Beethoven's lifetime. The Viennese pianos of Beethoven were challenged by the French pianos of Camille Pleyel and Sébastien Erard, who came to dominate the piano market by mid-century. With their stouter framing and "grand" or "double-escapement" actions (both of which permitted greater force to be applied to the hammer), these newer instruments were ideally suited to the public concerts that pianists began to offer. Even so, the Viennese and French (as well as English) instruments competed for the loyalty of pianists throughout the nineteenth century. Romantic composers and pianists demanded a variety of pianos by different makers to satisfy their desire for varied tone colors.

## FRANZ LISZT (1811–1886)

Liszt embodies many of the contradictions inherent in nineteenth-century Romanticism. A born showman and the forerunner of the twentieth-century rock star, he was also one of the most progressive composers of his time. While using his charisma and electrifying stage presence to further his own career, he also introduced audiences all over Europe to little-known music by other composers. As a Hungarian he championed the cause of an oppressed minority, but he was one of the most widely traveled and genuinely sophisticated musicians of the age. His personality combined deep spiritualism with unabashed hedonism.

Liszt was born into a Hungarian family that worked on the same Esterházy estate where Haydn had lived for 30 years. The Liszts believed they were descended from nobility, though there is no evidence to support that claim. Liszt began to show interest in music at the age of 6, and his father, a cellist in the court orchestra, began giving him lessons when he was 7. When he reached the age of 10, a group of Hungarian nobles provided funds for him to study in Vienna. There he studied piano for 3 years with Carl Czerny—who 20 years before had been a pupil of Beethoven. In 1823 Liszt's parents, hearing of the growing importance of Paris, moved there with their son. Over the next 5 years the teenaged Liszt traveled throughout France, England, and Switzerland, playing a grueling schedule of concerts. After the death of his father in a typhoid epidemic, he settled in Paris with his mother. There, while debating whether to enter the priesthood, he carried on love affairs with two countesses.

In 1830, the day before the premiere of the *Symphonie fantastique*, Liszt met Berlioz for the first time. The diabolical aspects of Berlioz's symphony influenced many of Liszt's own compositions (among them three *Mephisto* waltzes for piano; a *Totentanz*, or "Death-Dance," for piano and orchestra; a setting of the *Dies irae;* the *Faust* and *Dante* symphonies; and the *Dante* Fantasy). Three months later he heard Paganini for the first time and was electrified by the virtuoso's performance. Although Liszt had begun a set of concert études on his own when he was 16, his keyboard writing was transformed by his exposure to Paganini. For the next three years he practiced 10 to 12 hours a day, determined to perfect a "transcendental technique" of his own. He eventually arranged six of Paganini's best-known pieces for piano.

Liszt set an even more daunting task for himself: the transcription of Berlioz's *Symphonie fantastique* for solo piano (Figure 20.2). A *transcription* is an arrange-

FIGURE 20.2 As a pianist and composer, Liszt tackled such ambitious projects as a transcription for solo piano of Berlioz's *Symphonie fantastique.* (The introduction to the Waltz is shown here.) Some of Liszt's studies were so difficult that he later simplified them. His *Grandes Etudes* (published in 1839) was reissued in 1852 in a less demanding form as *Etudes d'execution transcendante.*

ment of a work in one medium (such as the orchestra) for another (such as the piano). Given the demands that Berlioz's work makes on a full orchestra, it was courageous of Liszt to think he could reduce it to a version performed by a single musician playing a single instrument. The account of a contemporary conductor, Sir Charles Hallé, suggests how brilliantly he succeeded:

At an orchestral concert given by [Liszt] and conducted by Berlioz, the "March to the Scaffold" from the latter's *Symphonie fantastique,* that most resplendent orchestral piece, was performed, after which Liszt sat down and played his own arrangement for solo piano of the same movement, with an effect that surpassed even that of the full orchestra and created an indescribable furor. The feat had been duly announced in the program beforehand, a proof of his indomitable courage.

*Chapter 20   Virtuosos and Pianists*                                                         399

# A PIANISTIC DUEL

Throughout the nineteenth century, showmanship was an integral part of every soloist's technique. In Paris during the 1830s, more than 250 pianists vied for the approval of eager audiences. The two leading French piano manufacturers, Pleyel and Erard, set up showrooms in their factories that doubled as concert halls, holding about 400 people (Figure 20.3). Up to four times a week pianists were invited to demonstrate their talents, and journalists debated their merits as intensely as sports writers review the performances of NFL quarterbacks today.

Liszt, who had been playing for Parisian audiences since the early 1820s, was widely acknowledged as the leader of the pack. During his absence in Switzerland for much of 1835/1836, a visiting German pianist, Sigismond Thalberg (1812–1871), posed the first threat to Liszt's commanding position. Critics described Thalberg's playing as "refined" and "poetic," his passage work like "strings of pearls." As torrents of notes flowed from the piano, Thalberg seemed to sit motionless before the keyboard. In what was known as his "three-handed" technique, he would play a slow-moving melody with his thumbs while embroidering it above and below with streams of arpeggios.

For critics, the aristocratic Thalberg was a perfect foil to the high-strung Liszt. In 1837 a prominent Parisian critic, François-Joseph Fétis, praised Thalberg in terms so extravagant that a heated debate erupted in the press over the relative virtues of the two performers. Berlioz, reviewing a Liszt recital, wrote that "Liszt has proved that he is the pianist of the future." Liszt himself, against his better judgment, permitted Marie d'Agoult to publish under his name a scathing critique that dismissed Thalberg's compositions as "worthless." Fétis shot back that Liszt was "the product of a school that had outlived itself." When someone suggested to Thalberg that he and Liszt give a joint recital, Thalberg is said to have replied, "I do not like to be accompanied." The stage was set for a confrontation.

On Sunday, March 12, 1837, Thalberg played a matinée at the Paris Conservatory, which seated about 300 people. The next Sunday, Liszt rented the Paris Opéra House, and 3,000 people squeezed in. This was probably the first time in history that a pianist had played for an audience of more than several hundred people. Wrote one reviewer:

When the curtain rose and this slender young man appeared, so pale and thin—paler and thinner through the distance and the lights—alone with his piano on this immense stage . . . a kind of fear came over us. Our entire sympathies were enlisted by this madness, for only madness can produce great things. The entire

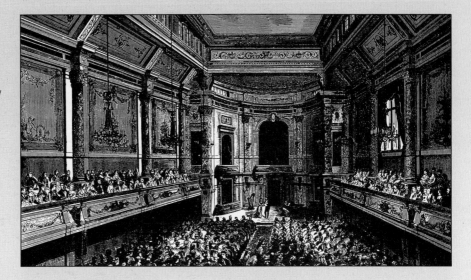

FIGURE 20.3 The nineteenth-century factory concert hall of Erard in Paris. The independent concert hall is a relatively new feature of cities. New York's Carnegie Hall, for example, just celebrated its centennial in 1991.

audience shared this anxiety, and each member listened to the first tones with a nervous ear. After the opening bar the victory was half won, for the piano sounded under Liszt's fingers like the voice of Lablache [the most famous bass of his generation].

Princess Cristina Belgiojoso, an Italian expatriate who had fled to Paris after being charged with treason in Italy, decided to capitalize on the controversy. She invited Liszt and Thalberg to play at a benefit on March 31 for a newly arrived group of Italian political refugees. It would have seemed uncharitable for either of them to refuse. So great was the public anticipation of this event that the Princess decided to charge 40 francs (the equivalent of more than a hundred dollars) per ticket. Several other pianists and singers appeared on the program, but they were scarcely noticed. Thalberg played a transcription he had made from Rossini's opera *Moses*, containing some of his most famous three-handed effects (Figure 20.4). Liszt countered with a dazzling transcription from the popular opera *Niobe* by the Italian Giovanni Pacini. Three days later, a review of the event appeared in the leading Parisian journal of the arts:

Never was Liszt's playing more controlled, more thoughtful, more energetic, or more passionate. Never has Thalberg played with greater verve and tenderness. Each of them prudently stayed within his musical domain, but each drew upon

*continued*

**FIGURE 20.4** Thalberg's "three-handed" compositions put the melody in the middle of the keyboard, switching from one hand to the other, with much use of thumbs, sustaining pedal, and embellished chords above and below. One cartoonist drew Thalberg as having ten hands.

every one of his resources. It was a worthy joust. The most profound silence fell over that noble arena. And in the end both Liszt and Thalberg were proclaimed victors by this glittering and sophisticated gathering.

Following their confrontation, Liszt and Thalberg became friends. Liszt played some of Thalberg's "worthless" works in his own concerts, and in a letter written many years after their duel, Liszt referred to Thalberg as "illustrious friend."

Princess Belgiojoso's own comment on the famous confrontation she had masterminded was a gem of tactfulness: "Thalberg is the finest pianist in the world; Liszt is the only one."

FIGURE 20.5 This caricature mocks audiences' reactions to Liszt's concerts. Liszt was unstinting in praising such contemporaries as Chopin, Schumann, Berlioz—and himself. In a letter to a friend in Vienna about his solo recital, Liszt noted, "Without vanity or self-deception, I think I may say that an effect so striking, so complete, so irresistible had never before been produced by an instrumentalist in Paris."

From 1838 to 1847 Liszt took to the road, appearing in hundreds of concerts in more than 170 cities throughout Europe and Asia Minor, from Naples in the south to Glasgow in the north, from Lisbon in the west to Constantinople and Moscow in the east. In 1840, he wrote to a friend, *"Le concert, c'est moi"* ("I am the concert"). He was referring to his innovation, the solo recital, in which a single musician performs the entire program. Previously, soloists had enlisted other performers to join them in their concerts, feeling that such collaboration was necessary to sustain the audience's interest. Women sometimes grew hysterical and even fainted at Liszt's concerts (Figure 20.5). According to some accounts, Liszt occasionally left his gloves behind when he walked off the stage, prompting his fans to fight over them.

In his concerts, Liszt played Beethoven's sonatas for audiences who had never heard them before. He also played many of his own works (most with programmatic titles), including elaborate transcriptions of operatic works by other composers. (We shall look at one of those transcriptions in Chapter 22.) His extended chromatic harmonies influenced composers from Chopin to Wagner.

In 1848 Liszt accepted a permanent appointment as conductor—still a novel position—of the Weimar court orchestra. There he championed the works of innovative composers like Berlioz and Wagner and found time to finish many of the piano works he had begun during his concert travels. He also composed several choral and orchestral works. His major innovation was the *symphonic poem,* a single-movement orchestral work with programmatic content. (A symphonic poem by Bedřich Smetana will be discussed in Chapter 24.)

In 1860, to escape the notoriety caused by a long-term liaison with a Catholic princess who could not obtain a divorce, Liszt moved from Weimar to Rome. From then until his death 25 years later, he spent his time conducting master classes in Rome, Weimar, and Budapest. The idea of inviting several pianists to play for a "master" who would then comment on each performance before the entire group was another of Liszt's innovations. In 1865 he took minor Catholic orders, though he never became a priest. He made his last public appearance as a pianist only a few weeks before his death.

## Liszt: Concert Étude after Paganini, *La Campanella* ("The Little Bells") (1838)

Unlike his transcription of Berlioz's *Symphonie fantastique,* in which Liszt had tried to be faithful to the original, his six Paganini études are free arrangements. He based five of them on Paganini's solo caprices, but for *La Campanella* (Listening Guide 43) he used the finale from Paganini's Second Violin Concerto (1826). This finale is an elaborate rondo with the shape *A-B-A-C-A-B-A-D-A.* Liszt confined himself to the first two of these sections, of which the *A*-Section (consisting of two repetitions of the same theme) is in the minor mode and the *B*-Section is in the major, and arranged them in a simple *A-B-A'-B'-A"-B'-A'''* pattern. The sections are varied with each repetition; even the repetitions of the theme *within* the *A*-Sections are varied.

In his violin concerto, Paganini suggests the sound of the *campanella* (a small church bell) by introducing the triangle* just before each repetition of his rondo theme (*A*), and by extending the range of the violin into its highest registers. Liszt's treatment is more daring: He represents the campanella throughout the *A*-Sections with a staccato pedal point in the uppermost voice, alternating between the pedal point and each melody note in the thumb:

The distances between the melody notes and the pedal point generally exceed the natural span of the hand, and in performance the right hand moves back and forth in a blur. (Liszt makes these passages slightly—but only slightly—easier to play by transposing Paganini's tune to a key with several black notes.) The *B*-Section maintains the detached leaps but with the color contrast of the major

---

*A small metal percussion instrument that makes a high-pitched ring when struck with a metal bar.

*Part Three  The Age of Tonality (1690–1910)*

# Listening Guide 43

## LISZT: *La Campanella* ("The Little Bells")

CD 5, TRACK 2
TAPE 5A, TRACK 2
DURATION: 5:04

*Note the ingenious manner in which Liszt varies and elaborates two simple themes, the first in the minor mode and the second in the major mode. All but one of the A-Sections consist of two statements of the same theme; each of the seven repetitions is progressively more elaborate and intense.*

*Form: Sectional (A-B-A'-B'-A''-B''-A'''-Coda)*

| | LOCATION | TIME | COMMENTS |
|---|---|---|---|
| 1 | Introduction | 0:00 | Tentative octaves create a sense of expectation. |
| | A-Section | 0:08 | First statement of the theme, in the minor mode. |
| | | 0:24 | Second statement of the theme, slightly embellished. |
| 2 | B-Section | 0:42 | Follows a brief rest, in the major mode. Concludes with an elaborate bridge back to the A'-Section. |
| | A'-Section | 1:24 | Third statement of the theme, now in the left hand. |
| | | 1:40 | Fourth statement of the theme, with three "bell" notes per melody note. |
| | B'-Section | 2:02 | Characterized by rapid repeated notes. |
| | | 2:32 | Chains of rapid chromatic scales. |
| 3 | A''-Section | 2:59 | Fifth statement of the theme with four notes per melody note. |
| | | 3:17 | Sixth statement of the theme (varied harmonically), with the first use of the low register in the left hand. |
| | B''-Section | 3:38 | Features brilliant repeated octaves, large leaps, and frequent changes of register. |
| 4 | A'''-Section | 4:24 | Seventh and final statement of the theme, played loudly in staccato octaves. |
| | Coda | 4:40 | Fiery octaves based on short-short-LONG rhythms. |

mode. Liszt's variations are elaborate. In the third occurrence of the A-Section, for example, the pedal point is extended to a 4-note trill for each note of the melody. The second occurrence of the B-Section features rapidly repeated notes and culminates in a shimmering cascade of chromatic scales.

In Paganini's concerto, the rondo ends as it began—with a straight restatement of the rondo theme. But Liszt's theatrical sense dictated otherwise. He plays the final statement of the rondo theme *forte* in thunderous octaves, appropriating the full bass register, which has been absent during most of the piece. A *con fuoco* ("with fire") coda ends the piece in a blaze of fireworks.

Instead of striving for complexity of structure, as had the Classicists before him, Liszt keeps the piece simple and popular in tone. He uses Paganini's rondo as a point of departure for his flights of fancy, focusing on brilliant effects rather than on structure. Even a full orchestra would have a hard time improving on Liszt's rainbow of colors.

## FRÉDÉRIC CHOPIN (1810–1849)

Liszt and Chopin, the two greatest pianists of the nineteenth century, were in many respects opposites. By temperament Chopin was reserved, even withdrawn. He showed little interest in concertizing or engaging in pianistic duels. Whereas Liszt eventually became a conductor, writer, and composer of orchestral and choral works, Chopin confined himself to the piano. Much of Liszt's music was programmatic, while Chopin let his music speak for itself. About all they shared was a fervor for the liberation of their oppressed homelands.

Chopin was born in Warsaw to a Polish mother and a French father, who taught French at the University of Warsaw. Nicolas Chopin had left France in 1787 at the age of 16 and never told his children that they had relatives in France. (Only after Frédéric had lived in Paris for several years did he discover them.) The young Chopin's talent was apparent from the time he was 6, but his family made sure that he received a solid education. Largely self-taught, he was naturally fluent at the keyboard. A masterful Piano Concerto in F Minor he wrote while still a teenager ranks as one of the most impressive accomplishments of any prodigy.

A visit by Paganini to Warsaw in 1829 had much the same effect on Chopin as Paganini's appearance in Paris was to have on Liszt. In the summer of that year, Chopin traveled to Vienna, where his performances were well received. A second journey the next year was a disappointment, however, and like so many other artists of his generation he made his way to Paris, where he lived for the rest of his short life.

Chopin supported himself in Paris by giving piano lessons to wealthy (mostly female) members of the aristocracy. He requested his students to leave their fees on the mantlepiece so as not to soil his hands. His phenomenal reputation as a pianist was based on less than three dozen public appearances over his lifetime, and he augmented his income by arranging for the simultaneous publication of his works in France, England, and Germany.

In 1836 Chopin met Aurore Dudevant, a novelist who wrote under the pen name of George Sand (Figure 20.6). An outspoken feminist with a lively intellect, Sand wore trousers on occasion, smoked cigars, and argued for personal freedom. Soon she and Chopin became lovers, and over the next nine years he

FIGURE 20.6 This drawing of Liszt and George Sand is by her son Maurice. In her memoirs, Sand described Chopin: "One would literally fight for his company. . . . His indifference to mercenary rewards, his pride and justifiable self-esteem as a sworn enemy of everything pertaining to vanity, bad taste, or insolent advertisement, the charm of his conversation . . . made him an interesting and delightful companion. . . . Back home at night, like a woman who takes off her makeup, he would put off all his animation and seductive power and submit to a night of fever and insomnia. . . . Chopin, this extreme type of artist, was not made for a long life in this world."

wrote some of his finest works. Their parting over a family dispute involving her children, followed by an ill-advised journey to England in 1848, may have hastened Chopin's death from tuberculosis at age 39.

## CHOPIN'S STYLE

Chopin never wrote a work that did not include the piano. Aside from 17 accompanied songs, a half-dozen pieces of chamber music, and another half-dozen for piano and orchestra, all of his almost 250 works are for solo piano. Only 7 contain more than a single movement, and most are short pieces that last only two to six minutes. This was the kind of music that found favor in the fashionable salons of Paris, where prosperous families invited composers and performers to play for small social gatherings. Chopin raised salon music far above its prevailing level of mediocrity.

Ever since childhood Chopin had been fond of the folk dances of his native Poland. Among them was the *mazurka*, a dance popular with a group outside Warsaw known as Mazurs (Figure 20.7). Its vigorous triple meter and strong offbeat accents inspired Chopin to write more than 50 mazurkas marked by great variety and refinement. Another Polish folk dance was the stately *polonaise*, which was danced and sung at weddings and other ceremonies. Chopin imbued it with a festive, often martial quality. Moreover, he raised both the waltz and the étude to new levels of importance. His 24 études of Op. 12 and Op. 25 are apt

FIGURE 20.7 Stamping feet, clicking heels, and spinning turns accented the mazurka, danced in a circle. Chopin's 58 mazurkas were directly inspired by this popular folk dance, but they were not written to accompany dancers.

piano counterparts to Paganini's 24 violin caprices. While he may have become familiar with the nocturne from the works of the Irish composer John Field, Chopin's nocturnes exhibit far greater depth and originality.

Like Mozart, whom he worshiped, Chopin placed great emphasis on melody, and his melodies are inseparable from his strong, colorful harmonies. Bar for bar, his music contains fewer pyrotechnics than Liszt's; still, many passages demand a virtuoso technique. Perhaps reflecting his veneration of J. S. Bach, many of his works incorporate a surprising degree of counterpoint. Rather than the equal-voiced counterpoint of Bach, however, Chopin chose to oppose two voices of different character in what might be called "Romantic counterpoint." He relied on simple forms (ternary, rondo), which he employed with great subtlety.

## Chopin: Étude in G-sharp Minor, Op. 25, No. 6 (1832–1834)

Chopin wrote his first étude soon after hearing Paganini's performances in Warsaw. Before he was 26 he had composed 24 études covering virtually every technical problem that confronted the Romantic pianist. In the Étude in G-sharp Minor, for example, he uses the popular Romantic device of playing melodies in parallel thirds, a practice derived from bel canto opera. The exotic key of G-sharp Minor, with its many black notes, makes it somewhat easier for the pianist to negotiate these twisting strands of chromaticism with the right hand, but it takes years of practice to manage them at Chopin's tempo:

Chopin introduces this same idea three times but each time has it lead in a different direction *(A-A'-A'')*. A coda takes the theme through a 4-octave chromatic descent, like a hot-air balloon being guided to a gentle landing. Apart from two brief *fortes,* the dynamic throughout is *sotto voce* ("in an undertone," another term derived from opera), and woe to the pianist who betrays the difficulties by pounding the keys.

## Chopin: Mazurka in D Major, Op. 33, No. 2 (1837)

Chopin's ebullient D-Major Mazurka is in a popular style known as the *kujawiak,* a ternary form characterized by strong accents on the third beat. The *A*-Section consists of six repetitions of a headlong, symmetrical 8-bar phrase, though Chopin avoids monotony by means of sharp dynamic contrasts and simple modulations. In the *B*-Section he shifts the rhythm to a LONG-short pattern on the first beat of each bar, enriching it with countervoices in the bass:

The exuberance of this work invites listeners to join in the dance. The coda begins with an *accelerando* ("acceleration") characteristic of the kujawiak, but then Chopin reverses field with a gentle *smorzando* ("dying away").

## Chopin: Nocturne in E Major, Op. 62, No. 2 (1846)

For Chopin the *nocturne* (French for "nocturnal") was a dreamy, meditative piece on which he lavished some of his most imaginative piano writing. In addition to the nocturnes of Field, Chopin may have been influenced by vocal duets of Rossini and Donizetti that were called nocturnes. The Nocturne in E Major (Listening Guide 44) is the last of 19 that Chopin wrote. Its external form is the same ternary form as that of the Mazurka in D Major, but here Chopin invests the form with greater contrast and variation. He builds the *A*-Section around a tender, lavishly embellished theme that gives way to a surprisingly intense, *agitato* ("agitated") *B*-Section. The theme of the *A*-Section consists of *a-a'-b-a''-c* phrases in which the two repetitions of *a* are elaborately varied. Chopin reharmonizes the *a*-phrase almost entirely in the final *A'*-Section. Indeed, the listener feels that Chopin might have engaged in dozens of further variations had he so chosen.

The *c*-phrase with which the *A*-Section ends masquerades as a closing theme before it blends seamlessly into the middle section. In the opening of this theme, the countervoice is as attractive as the main theme itself:

Chopin increases the intensity of the *B*-Section with a closely spaced imitation of the right-hand theme in the left hand—counterpoint that Bach would have admired. He abbreviates the final *A'*-Section to avoid tedium and to allow for the leisurely expansion of the *c*-phrase. Unlike almost all earlier ternary forms, not a single bar is repeated literally. Instead, Chopin alters each restatement and gives it its own colorful harmonies. The final cadence creates a sense of stillness and repose rather than a formal resolution.

Chopin is perhaps the only composer in the Western tradition whose self-imposed limitations do not disqualify him from being placed alongside first-rank composers like Bach and Mozart (whom he studied all his life). Having challenged generations of pianists, his works show no signs of losing their freshness and appeal.

# Listening Guide 44

## CHOPIN: Nocturne in E Major, Op. 62, No. 2

CD 5, TRACK 5
TAPE 5A, TRACK 5
DURATION: 5:05

*The ternary form of this work is identical to that of the D-Major Mazurka and many other pieces by Chopin, though here he handles the form with considerable freedom.*

*Form: Free ternary*

| | LOCATION | TIME | COMMENTS |
|---|---|---|---|
| **1** | *A*-Section | | |
| | *a*-phrase | **0:00** | Simple, tender theme. |
| | *a'*-phrase | 0:29 | Theme slightly embellished and reharmonized. |
| | *b*-phrase | 0:56 | Based on rhythm of the first bar of the *a*-phrase. |
| | *a"*-phrase | 1:23 | Elaborately embellished in two places. |
| | *c*-phrase | 1:52 | Sounds cadential but then dissolves into a bridge. |
| **2** | *B*-Section | | |
| | *d*-phrase | **2:26** | Agitated, *forte,* syncopated, imitative. |
| | *d'*-phrase | 3:01 | Similar agitated material transposed. |
| | Retransition | 3:32 | Melts away rather than creates anticipation. Slides back into the opening section. |
| **3** | *A'*-Section | | |
| | *a'''*-phrase | **3:44** | Altered and expanded. Soars to a *forte* climax. |
| | *c'*-phrase | 4:31 | Also altered and expanded but avoids a strong cadence. |
| | | 5:24 | Soft, understated cadence that dies away. |

## Clara Wieck (1819–1896): Romance in G Minor, Op. 11, No. 2 (1839)

Chopin and Liszt were not the only Romantic composers who wrote shorter pieces for piano. The form was especially popular in Germany, where its practitioners included Franz Schubert, Felix Mendelssohn, Fanny Mendelssohn, Robert Schumann, Johannes Brahms, and Clara Wieck. Clara Wieck (whose life as the wife of Robert Schumann we consider in the next chapter's Historical Window on page 420) was a gifted pianist and composer who wrote more than 15

# Listening Guide 45

## CLARA WIECK: Romance in G Minor, Op. 11, No. 2

CD 5, TRACK 6
TAPE 5A, TRACK 6
DURATION: 5:45

*Wieck uses the simplicity of ternary form as a framework for a free exploration of the possibilities of her themes.*

*Form: Free ternary*

| | TEXT | TIME | COMMENTS |
|---|---|---|---|
| **1** | *A*-Section | | Andante. |
| | *a*-phrase | **0:00** | Descending scalar melody placed in the left hand. |
| | *a'*-phrase | 0:14 | Melody moves into the right hand. |
| | *b*-phrase | 0:36 | Major mode, descends from the upper register. |
| | *a"*-phrase | 1:01 | Begins like the first phrase, then moves to a long pedal point that anticipates the *B*-Section. |
| | | | |
| **2** | *B*-Section | | Allegro passionato. |
| | *c*-phrase | **1:50** | Long, arching theme against a steady accompaniment. |
| | *c'*-phrase | 2:34 | Moves quickly to a climax, then pauses. |
| | Bridge | 2:49 | Begins tentatively, then expands into a rhapsodic melodic variant of the original *a*-phrase before wending its way back to the original theme. |
| | | | |
| **3** | *A'*-Section | | Returns to Andante. |
| | *a*-phrase | **3:35** | "Reorchestrated" by octave doublings. |
| | *a'*-phrase | 3:53 | Melody now in octaves. Moves in a new direction and then begins to dissolve. |
| | | | |
| **4** | Coda | **4:28** | Opens with a soft series of cadences using the *a*-phrase. |
| | | 4:48 | A last, passionate outburst using full chords and chromatic harmonies. |
| | | 5:09 | The *a*-phrase appears alone in the bass and leads to a gentle major-mode cadence. |

opuses of piano music. While some took the form of variations, a large number were *character pieces,* pieces on a modest scale that express a single overall mood. The term was sometimes used directly by Romantic composers, but it also applies to works with titles like *Romance, Caprice, Intermezzo,* and so forth.

The Romance in G Minor (Listening Guide 45) was one of three that Wieck published in 1839 as her Op. 11. No. 2 of the set displays the freedom that composers brought to this style. Its form—like many of Chopin's—is nominally ternary: an *A*-Section in the minor mode, a *B*-Section in the major mode of a related key, and a final return of the *A*-Section. Moreover, the phrases in the opening *A*-Section are arranged in an *a-a'-b-a"* pattern.

However, the piece sounds anything but schematic. After the opening 6-bar *a*-phrase (in which Wieck places the melody in the left hand), the *a'*-phrase expands through chromatic turns of the melody into 10 bars. The *b*-phrase, in the major mode, reshapes the downward scalar pattern of the *a*-phrase and expands further to 12 bars. The final *a"*-phrase expands to 22 bars that include a long pedal point on the dominant of the following *B*-Section.

Marked "Fast and passionate," the new *B*-Section unfolds as a long, arching melody whose next twist or turn cannot be anticipated. When it finally wends its way back to the *A*-Section, Wieck "reorchestrates" the entire theme on a grander scale. The coda makes one last chromatic outburst before the piece concludes in gentle major harmonies. This unpredictable work reflects the poetic imagination so prized by Romantic composers.

# Chapter 21

## ABSOLUTE MUSIC

## AND POPULAR MUSIC

Absolute music is instrumental music unaccompanied by any sort of program—the kind of music that dominated Viennese Classicism. Some historians make a sharp distinction between composers like Brahms, who wrote almost nothing but absolute music, and composers like Berlioz, who wrote almost nothing but program music. Actually, every Romantic composer wrote music with at least some hint of an accompanying program. Chopin, for example, though he never specified a program for any of his compositions, wrote pieces with evocative titles like *Nocturne* and *Ballade*. His four ballades were based loosely on epic poems by the Polish poet Adam Mickiewicz. Robert Schumann, in the early years of his career, wrote collections of short piano pieces bearing descriptive titles. And Felix Mendelssohn wrote incidental music to Shakespeare's comedy *A Midsummer Night's Dream* and orchestral overtures with such titles as *Fingal's Cave* and *The Hebrides*. Even Johannes Brahms wrote an *Academic Festival Overture* and a *Tragic Overture*.

## ABSOLUTE MUSIC IN THE ROMANTIC ERA

Romantic composers who favored program music are often considered more advanced than those who favored absolute music. And yet, though Brahms employed traditional forms, in his use of rhythms and in his treatment of themes, he anticipated twentieth-century practices. And Chopin's harmonies are more chromatic and evocative than those of the Viennese Classicists. Moreover, composers were no less audacious when they were writing absolute music than when they were writing program music.

Still, composers of absolute music seemed to favor such traditional forms as the symphony, piano concerto, string quartet, piano trio, and sonata. This is especially true of German composers, who saw themselves as heirs of Haydn, Mozart, Beethoven, and Schubert. In certain respects, that sense of obligation proved inhibiting. As we have mentioned, Brahms was so in awe of Beethoven that he was over 40 before he dared present his first symphony.

Though composers of absolute music remained faithful to traditional models throughout the century, they transformed both the characteristics and, in the case of chamber music, the social function of those models. We turn now to three eminent composers of absolute music.

## ROBERT SCHUMANN (1810–1856)

Robert Schumann was also one of the leading music critics of his day.

Robert Schumann, the son of a writer/publisher, displayed a keen interest in literature while still a child. He read widely in the books he found in his father's bookstore and experimented with writing poetry. After his father's death when Schumann was 16, he enrolled at his mother's urging in a liberal arts course of study at the University of Leipzig. He never attended a single lecture, however, and spent his time reading, sketching plans for novels, and improvising at the piano.

When he was 18, Schumann began to study with the celebrated piano teacher Friedrich Wieck. It was at this time that he met Wieck's nine-year-old daughter Clara (whose *Romance* we discussed in Chapter 20), whom he was to marry 12 years later. On Easter Sunday in 1830 Schumann heard Paganini play in Frankfurt and, like so many other young composers, fell under his spell. Like Liszt, he arranged several of Paganini's caprices for piano. While Schumann was still studying with Wieck, he persuaded his mother to allow him a six-month trial period as a performing pianist. Wieck had already become aware of Schumann's erratic behavior, and entries in Schumann's diaries suggest that he had begun to suffer the severe mood swings characteristic of manic-depressive illness.

After injuring two fingers on his right hand (perhaps as a consequence of using a mechanical device to strengthen his fingers), Schumann turned his full attention to composition and by 1839 had published 23 opuses of piano music. He had little formal training in composition, and his greatest successes in keyboard writing were collections of short pieces. The best-known is *Carnaval,* Op. 9, which Schumann subtitled "Little Scenes on Four Notes." He derived those notes from the name of the town of Asch, the home of Ernestine von Fricken, to whom he was briefly engaged. In German, *A* equals the note A; *s* is pronounced "es," the German for e♭; *C* equals the note C; and *h* in German equals b♮. *As* also means a♭ in German. Schumann uses combinations of these letters/notes—primarily *A-S* [e♭]-*C-H* [b♮], and *As* [a♭]—to open many pieces in the collection, indulging in the subtle unity that delighted the Romantics.

Schumann peopled his *Carnaval* with real and imaginary friends: Florestan and Eusebius (the extroverted and introverted sides of Schumann's personality), Pierrot and Arlequin (characters from the *commedia dell' arte,* a type of Italian street theater popular during the Renaissance), Chiarina (Clara Wieck), Estrella (Ernestine von Fricken), Chopin, and Paganini.

In 1834, Schumann and several of his friends founded a twice-weekly journal, the *Neue Zeitschrift für Musik* (*New Magazine for Music*), which he edited for 10 years. He was the first to praise Berlioz's *Symphonie fantastique* and the first to proclaim the genius of Chopin and Brahms. Though its circulation was only about 500 copies per issue, the magazine was considered highly successful.

In 1839, when Schumann and Clara Wieck announced their engagement, Clara's father took legal steps to block the union. After lengthy maneuverings on both sides, the court finally granted the couple permission to marry and they were united in September 1840. In a burst of creative energy that extended from the previous February to the end of the year, Schumann wrote almost 150 *Lieder*. The next 15 years were marked by similar periods of productivity, interrupted by long spells of depression and inactivity, accompanied by the ravages of syphilis.* Clara bore eight children during these years but still managed to carry on her career as a performing pianist (see the Historical Window on page 420).

Following his marriage, Schumann turned to more traditional instrumental genres, writing string quartets and a piano quintet. With Clara's encouragement he tackled orchestral music as well and composed four symphonies over the next decade. He also wrote music for chorus and orchestra to scenes from Goethe's *Faust* and sketched three movements that he brought together as his only piano concerto. In February 1854, after cycles of growing depression, Schumann threw himself into the Rhine River. He was rescued by fishermen and spent the last two years of his life in an asylum near Bonn, where he died. Though he was forbidden to see his wife, he was visited regularly by a devoted young composer, Johannes Brahms.

## Schumann: Piano Concerto in A Minor, Op. 54 (1841, 1845)

Like other of Schumann's Romantic works based on Classical models, his piano concerto took several years to complete. He wrote the first movement for Clara in 1840 as an independent "Fantasy" and added two more movements some five years later. Clara performed the concerto to acclaim throughout Europe both during his lifetime and after, and, as a work that explores poetic feelings rather than virtuosity, it remains one of the most popular works in the repertoire.

**First Movement.** Romantic though he was, Schumann organized the first movement around sonata form. Finding the opening ritornello of the Classical concerto too tedious, however, he opens with a bolt of lightning from the orchestra, followed by a series of dramatic dotted-rhythm chords by the soloist. From the very outset he sets up the conflict between orchestra and piano.

The lyrical themes of this movement are well suited to thematic transformation. For example, the brusque introduction gives way to a lyrical theme that rises to a double climax:

*Syphilis affected almost a quarter of the population in Schumann's time.

*Allegro affettuoso* (Fast and tenderly)

**1st climax**

**2nd climax**

*espressivo*
(expressively)

In the major mode, this theme serves as the principal idea of the secondary area. Schumann tightens the organization further by basing the closing theme on the first six notes of a theme from the transition:

transition

closing theme

*p*

*cresc.*

*f*

Ordinarily, a transition is inherently unstable, while a closing area is the most stable section of a movement. That would seem to call for a different theme in each section, but Schumann draws on the same thematic material for both.

Schumann also alters the proportions of the Classical sonata-concerto form. In place of the elaborate closing material common, for example, in the exposition of a Mozart concerto, he combines the brief closing material with the intermediate ritornello. Structural events succeed each other in a series of cinematic dissolves (like a camera shot that gradually becomes blurred): the intermediate ritornello dissolves into a nocturne-like transformation of the main theme to open the development. The nocturnal reverie in the development sets up a dissolve that Schumann interrupts with the dotted rhythms of the introduction— even more jarring the second time. Finally, a series of *Passionato* ("passionate") sequences dissolve into the recapitulation.

Instead of calling for an improvised cadenza in the Classical manner, Schumann provides an integrated, written-out cadenza that is an introspective exploration of the main theme rather than a virtuoso display. In the coda, the cadenza leads smoothly into a "quick-step" transformation of the same idea (rather like a march in a football halftime show). Whereas the first movement of a Mozart concerto uses many themes to create an operatic atmosphere, Schumann limits himself to three and focuses instead on thematic unity.

**Second and Third Movements.** The slow second movement, labeled an *Intermezzo* ("Interlude"), is in simple ternary form. The *A*-Section consists of a gracious dialogue between the soloist and orchestra. The *B*-Section introduces an expressive, singing theme in the cellos and violins, with comments by the soloist. The final *A*-Section recalls the head of the main theme from the first movement and leads without break into the sonata-form finale. The main themes of the first and last movements are subtly related:

**first movement**

**third movement**

Schumann was intrigued by the way in which triple meter could be broken into various duple subdivisions. In the remarkable orchestral theme of the secondary area, the basic triple meter is broken down into units of two beats each (the duple foreground shown below). Over this is a slower triple background; hence the first beat of the measure coincides with the normal "downbeat" only in every other bar:

| duple<br>foreground | 1 | 2 | 1 | | 2 | 1 | 2 | | 1 | 2 | 1 | | 2 | 1 | 2 | | 1 | 2 | 1 | | 2 | 1 | 2 | | 1 | 2 | 1 |
| triple<br>background | 1 | | 2 | | | 3 | | | 1 | | 2 | | | 3 | | | 1 | | 2 | | | 3 | | | 1 | | 2 |

Schumann carries this duple/triple ambiguity through the secondary and closing areas, with full, rich harmonies in the orchestra. In both the exposition and the recapitulation these areas encompass 75 bars of continuous arpeggios in the piano. The rhythmic complexities in the orchestra are very much in the Romantic manner, while the regular rhythms in the piano are reminiscent of the Baroque. The rhythmically graded phrases of Viennese Classicism are but a distant memory.

## FELIX MENDELSSOHN (1809–1847)

If prodigy were a measure of greatness, Mendelssohn would rank alongside Mozart. Mendelssohn was born in Hamburg (in the north of Germany) to a prosperous upper-class family of bankers. His paternal grandfather, Moses Mendelssohn, was one of the great Enlightenment philosophers who, in defiance of an edict forbidding Jews to learn German, was the first to translate substantial portions of the Old Testament from Hebrew into German. Mendelssohn's mother played the piano and sang, drew exquisitely, spoke four languages, and read Homer in the original Greek.

Felix Mendelssohn displayed a Mozartean prodigy as a child.

Mendelssohn's family encouraged his interest in music. Along with his older sister Fanny (see the Historical Window on page 420), Felix was tutored by some of the finest minds in Germany. He showed particular aptitude in music and painting and began composing at the age of 12. By the time he was 17 he had written two works that stand as monuments to youthful prodigy: a string octet (for double string quartet) and an overture to Shakespeare's *A Midsummer Night's Dream* that captures the elfin world of the play. Before he was 20 he led a performance of Bach's *St. Matthew Passion* in Berlin and launched a revival of interest in Bach's music.

In his early twenties Mendelssohn traveled to England, Scotland, and Italy (where he composed his popular "Italian" Symphony). At 26 he was appointed conductor of Leipzig's Gewandhaus Orchestra. During his six seasons in that post, he raised the number of annual subscription concerts and instituted the practice of inviting guest artists to perform with the orchestra. (Mendelssohn himself performed with the orchestra as pianist and organist.) During those years he composed several symphonies, the oratorio *Elijah,* several volumes of *Songs Without Words* (for solo piano), and some fine chamber music. He also founded the first conservatory of music and inaugurated evening concerts with student performers. The practices Mendelssohn introduced still form the core of professional training in music.

His death from a cerebral hemorrhage at the age of 39—mourned by music lovers throughout Europe and the United States—was hastened by the grueling rehearsal and performance schedule he had maintained throughout his adult life.

## Mendelssohn: Piano Trio in D Minor, Op. 49 (1839)

Like his idol Mozart, Mendelssohn wrote a great deal of chamber music, highlighted by six string quartets and two piano trios. The passionate lyricism of the Trio in D Minor for Violin, Cello, and Piano, Op. 49, has ensured its lasting popularity. It almost seems that he was writing for a concert hall rather than a drawing room. The music, especially the music for the piano, seems more suited to the public display of the concerto than to the intimacy of the sonata.

For this trio, Mendelssohn adopted a symphonic four-movement plan rather than the three-movement plan common to earlier piano trios. The first movement, in sonata form, overflows with melodies, even in the transition and development where Classical composers had favored nonthematic or fragmentary material. The lengthy melodies consist of a series of regular subphrases, and the rhythms suggest the regularity and continuity of the late Baroque rather than the carefully graded rhythms of Classical themes. The beautiful melody that introduces the secondary area, for example, consists of three repetitions (or near repetitions) of the same 4-bar phrase capped by a contrasting tail:

(*Text continues on page 423.*)

## WHERE WERE THE WOMEN?

As you may have noticed, Western music seems to have been dominated by males. For centuries the law courts treated women as if they were indeed the property of men. Bound to the home, they were expected to cater to their husbands and to produce and raise offspring (preferably males). On those rare occasions when they appeared in public, properly behaved women were accompanied by an escort.

Despite those severe restrictions, women have made significant contributions to the musical life of the West—although those contributions went largely unnoticed before the rise of women's studies in the 1960s. We have already mentioned the contributions of women to medieval music. Machaut (Chapter 6), for example, described a woman, Péronne d'Armentières, as "the best singer born in a hundred years."

During the Renaissance, despite its nurturing of humanistic attitudes, opportunities for women declined. Women were excluded from participation in church services and were denied access to music education, though a few were admitted to the new universities. Still, some women continued to perform secular music, many as skilled amateurs and a few as paid professionals. However, with the exception of composers like the seventeenth-century Venetian soprano, Barbara Strozzi (1619–ca. 1664), women confined their music-making to the home.

With the widespread political revolutions of the late eighteenth century, attitudes finally began to change, encouraged by the popularity of the piano in the home. By the middle of the nineteenth century several women had published *Lieder* and compositions for the piano. Two of the most talented were Fanny Mendelssohn Hensel (Figure 21.1), the older sister of Felix Mendelssohn, and Clara Wieck, the wife of Robert Schumann.

The Mendelssohn family acknowledged that Fanny was as gifted as her younger brother Felix. She is said to have performed Bach's *Well-Tempered Clavier* from memory by the time she was 13—a feat well beyond most musicians of the day. Her musical training was as good as that afforded to Felix. As she approached puberty, however, her father urged her to put her interest in music in its "proper" perspective. When she was 15, he sent her the following note:

FIGURE 21.1  Fanny Mendelssohn (1805–1847): A curtailed career in a short life. Fanny died a few months before Felix.

What you wrote to me about your musical occupations with reference to, and in comparison with, Felix was both rightly thought and expressed. Music will perhaps become his profession, while for you it can and must only be an ornament, never the basis of your existence. We may therefore pardon Felix some ambition and desire to be acknowledged in a pursuit which appears very important to him, because he feels a vocation for it, while it does you credit that you have always shown yourself good and sensible in these matters; and your very joy at the praise that he earns proves that you might, in his place, have merited equal approval. Remain true to these sentiments and to this line of conduct; they are feminine, and only what is feminine is an ornament to your sex.

Ironically, in most other respects Fanny's father was a socially progressive member of his generation.

Eventually Fanny married the painter Wilhelm Hensel. Although her family continued to discourage her from pursuing a career in music, she went on composing and appeared from time to time as a piano soloist. Only a few of her works were published under her name during her lifetime, though several of her songs appeared under Felix's name. She wrote more than 200 songs, piano pieces, and chamber works, most of them still unpublished. Those that have been published reveal a talented composer. Though she championed her brother Felix and served as his loyal confidante, she sometimes voiced her frustration. In 1836 she wrote: "If nobody ever offers an opinion, or takes the slightest interest in one's productions, one loses over time not only all pleasure in them but all ability to judge their value."

Clara Wieck's father Friedrich Wieck, a domineering, self-taught man, was an innovative and respected piano teacher. After his wife left him to return to her parents, he gained custody of their children.* Neglecting his sons, he directed his attentions to his eldest daughter, Clara. He even kept Clara's diary, either writing the entries himself or dictating them to her! Clara made her first public appearance as a pianist in Leipzig at the age of 9. In that same year she met Robert Schumann, who at 18 had come to Leipzig to consider whether or not to study with Wieck. After hearing Clara's brilliant playing, he decided to become Wieck's pupil. Clara made her first concert tour at 12 and published several compositions over the next few years. Robert used one of her themes as the basis for a set of impromptus. By the time she was 16, she was acclaimed as a virtuoso throughout Europe.

Their married life reflected the dilemmas faced by two-career couples today. Robert was more enlightened than most men of his generation, and when Clara went on tour in 1842 he stayed at home with their six-month-old daughter. "May this [separation] be worth the sacrifice and bring you joy as an artist," he

*In Saxony, the part of Germany where the Wiecks lived, children were considered the father's property.

*continued*

wrote. "You are still so young, and I cannot blame you if, as an artist, you do not want the hard work of your youth to be forgotten." Still, he was troubled: "Shall I neglect my own talent, in order to serve as a companion on your journeys? Should you allow your talent to lie fallow because I am chained to the paper and the piano?" Clara was pregnant every year between 1840 and 1854, and the responsibility of caring for seven children (one died in infancy and she suffered at least one miscarriage) cut deeply into her composing and concertizing.

Robert demanded absolute quiet when he was composing. Clara once complained, "My piano playing is falling behind again—this always happens when Robert is composing. Not even one little hour can be found in the day for me. If only I don't fall too far behind." And yet Clara made 139 formal appearances and many informal ones during her childbearing years. She missed her family while she was out on tour: "I long so dreadfully for you all that, if I could, I would turn around at once and joyfully run home."

Being married to a composer of genius seems to have made Clara doubt her own abilities: "I once believed that I possessed creative talent, but I have given up this idea. A woman must not desire to compose—there has never yet been one able to do it. Should I expect to be the one?" But on another occasion she wrote: "There is no greater joy than composing something oneself and then listening to it. . . . There is nothing which surpasses creative activity, even if one does it only for those hours of self-forgetfulness when one breathes totally in a world of sound."

Clara Wieck revolutionized the piano recital. After her husband's death, she went on tour again. But now, instead of playing the glittering works of salon composers, as was fashionable, she concentrated on the works of Mozart, Beethoven, Schubert, Schumann, and Brahms. There was no such thing as a concert manager at the time, so she had to make all the arrangements herself. She rented a piano and a hall, had tickets printed, arranged for publicity, and then appeared on stage as if playing were her only concern. She played the last of her more than 1,300 public concerts at the age of 72. Her performing career spanned six decades, longer than that of any other major nineteenth-century performer. In 1878 she accepted a teaching post at the Frankfurt Conservatory, and students flocked to her from all over the world. While shattering the gender stereotypes of her day, she maintained throughout her career the highest standards of excellence and integrity.

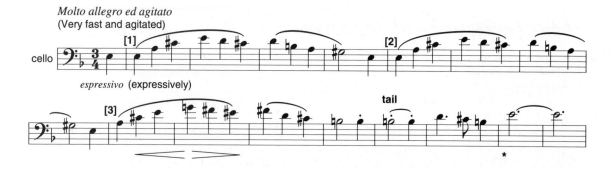

Mendelssohn conceals the symmetry of this 16-bar melody by having the piano begin its repetition two bars early, in the fifteenth bar (marked with an asterisk in the example). Mendelssohn seems so attached to these beautiful melodies that, in the development, he can only restate them rather than subject them to fragmentation.

The ternary-form second movement, marked *Andante con moto tranquillo* ("With moderate motion and calmly"), continues the lyricism of the first movement. The tender theme presented first in the piano begins with two parallel phrases with nearly identical rhythms:

When the theme recurs, Mendelssohn treats it as a soaring duet between violin and cello.

The third-movement Scherzo is light and fleet, a quality particularly favored by Mendelssohn. He casts it as a sonata-rondo, a form that earlier composers had reserved for finales.

In the sonata-form finale, all but one of the themes begin with the same LONG-short-short upbeat. The exception is a long, lyrical theme introduced in the development. Aside from a brief flurry of imitation in the development of the finale, this entire trio is built on a theme-and-accompaniment texture, with the themes shared equally by the three instruments.

Mendelssohn was more familiar with the musical past than were most of his contemporaries, and his forms and harmonies are more closely related to Classical models than are those, say, of Berlioz. But his reliance on lyricism rather than on motivic development places him squarely in the Romantic mainstream. Few composers have written with such apparent ease and naturalness.

# JOHANNES BRAHMS (1833–1897)

Johannes Brahms, a north German, became more Viennese than the Viennese.

Johannes Brahms, the second of three children, was born in the northern German industrial city of Hamburg to a woman of 43 and an army officer of 25. The father eventually became a double-bass player in the Hamburg city orchestra, the first of his family to become a musician. As a teenager, Brahms arranged music for a small dance orchestra in which his father played. He made his first appearance as a pianist at the age of 15. Already active as a composer, he sent some of his youthful works to Robert Schumann for comment, but the package was returned unopened.

At last, in the fall of 1853, he met Schumann, who, after hearing Brahms play several of his own works, wrote a famous article in the *Neue Zeitschrift für Musik* in which he proclaimed Brahms a "young eagle" pursuing "new paths" and prophesied greatness for him. After a brief stint as a choral conductor in Hamburg, Brahms moved to Vienna, where, except for occasional travels, he lived the rest of his life. He embraced the Viennese practices of taking long walks and spending leisurely hours in coffeehouses. Like many other Viennese composers, he spent his summers in picturesque western Austria. By his own admission, he felt the full weight of the Viennese musical tradition of Mozart, Beethoven, and Schubert.

Brahms was one of the few Romantic composers not attracted by either opera or program music. Most of his instrumental works fit the category of absolute music: four symphonies; four concertos; chamber music for two, three, four, five, and six players; and sonatas and character pieces for solo piano. He also wrote a large amount of accompanied and unaccompanied choral music; almost 200 *Lieder;* vocal duets; and vocal quartets with piano.

Because of his concentration on absolute music and his regular use of such traditional forms as sonata form and theme and variations, some view Brahms as a conservative (even a reactionary) composer in an age of innovators. Despite his seeming conservatism, however, he commanded a subtle, individual musical language. His use of rhythm is highly original. He was a master at shifting the major stress in a bar from the first beat to another beat and at overlaying conflicting rhythms. His harmonic language is richly ambiguous, and in harmonic invention he was equaled only by Wagner. Although he was born into the northern European instrumental tradition, Brahms became a great melodist in the Austrian tradition of Schubert. Some of his melodies, such as the *"Wiegenlied" ("Cradle Song"),* achieved the status of folk song during his lifetime, and his open-ended treatment of themes foreshadowed the practices of twentieth-century composers.

Much of Brahms's music is permeated by a sense of nostalgia, but he expresses that nostalgia in poignant resignation rather than in sentimentality. Brahms viewed himself—as did others—as the last steward of the great Viennese tradition. He drew a curtain over the past, but he did so with dignity and grace.

## Brahms: Variations on a Theme by Haydn, Op. 56a (1873)

In 1870, before Brahms had composed any of his symphonies or overtures, he was shown a collection of outdoor music for winds attributed to Haydn. The second movement was based on the so-called St. Anthony Chorale—a pilgrims' chant of anonymous origin. Brahms was so taken with the charming theme that he copied it into a notebook and three years later used it as the basis for a set of variations. Although it now appears that Haydn did not write the music from which Brahms took his theme, Brahms's work is still called *Variations on a Theme by Haydn.*

The theme is in rounded binary form with repeated halves (*a ://  b-a ://*). It displays the kind of asymmetry that delighted Brahms. Instead of a standard 8-bar phrase, the first half of the theme is 10 bars long, divided into two 5-bar halves:

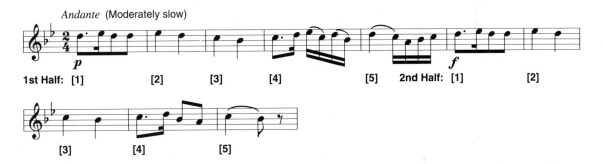

Theme and variations was a standard Classical form, though earlier composers had used it mainly for keyboard or chamber music. Brahms's straightforward structure consists of eight variations followed by a lengthy Finale. Rather than linking the variations, Brahms specifies a pause at the end of each to signal the start of a new variation. The Finale is a *passacaglia,* a Baroque technique in which a brief melodic idea repeats over and over while the other voices are varied freely. Paralleling the opening phrase of the theme, Brahms's passacaglia theme is also five bars long, and the pitches of the second and third bars (though two or three octaves lower) are identical to those of the original theme:

The first 13 repetitions are in the bass, the customary placement for a passacaglia theme. The theme then migrates in the minor mode to the treble instruments (oboes, horns, violins). After the seventeenth repetition, the theme returns in a spirited climax that concludes with a series of elaborate cadences.

Brahms explores a wider range of moods than did earlier composers of theme and variations. Instead of the traditional single variation in the minor mode, he supplies three (Nos. 2, 4, and 8). Only one of the variations, No. 1, is in the moderate tempo of the theme. Variations 3, 4, and 7 are slow, while Nos. 2, 5, 6, and 8 are fast. The fleet-footed Variation 5 is sparked by a kind of rhythmic displacement, or syncopation, for which Brahms is well known. Variations 3 and 7 introduce haunting new melodies that transcend the simplicity of the original theme. The final variation (No. 8), played with mutes,* never rises above a mysterious *pianissimo*.

Although Brahm's orchestration is not as flashy as that of Berlioz, it exhibits many warm, subtle touches. In Variations 2 and 4, and in portions of the Finale, Brahms makes skillful use of pizzicato effects in the cellos and basses. Perhaps the richest source of color in the work lies in his skillful enrichments of the original harmonies. Despite the frequent changes of mood and tempo, the variations move steadily toward the climax provided by the coda-like Finale. Although the variation technique itself is traditional, Brahms's sophisticated handling of it imbues the work with a thoroughly Romantic cast.

## THE RISE OF POPULAR MUSIC

Popular music is music that aims at immediate comprehension by listeners with no previous knowledge of musical theory or style. We must, however, add three caveats: (1) A great deal of art music also fits this definition. (2) Much popular music repays careful study. (3) Not all music written in a popular style is actually popular.

The term is most commonly applied today to American music starting from the time of Tin Pan Alley (around 1880) and extending to the present day. But, as we have seen, popular music has been performed since at least medieval times. Indeed, in earlier times most composers wrote *both* what we would describe as "art" and "popular" music. Josquin Desprez, for example, wrote popular chansons as well as Mass settings. In addition to symphonies and quartets, Haydn, Mozart, Beethoven, and Schubert wrote dance music for the elegant balls held in Vienna each year. Moreover, the people who attended the balls were pretty much the same people who listened to chamber music and attended symphony concerts.

Yet before the late nineteenth century a distinction between popular and art music was rarely made. (An exception were the tunes ground out on street corners by mechanical instruments like hurdy-gurdies and barrel organs, which

*A mute on a stringed instrument is generally a small three-pronged clamp made of wood (or, today, metal) that is attached to the bridge. By absorbing some of the tone, it creates a veiled, more remote sound.

were recognized as explicitly popular.) What has led to this distinction in our own time?

The answer is *specialization*. The first composers who specialized in writing popular music began to appear in the early years of the nineteenth century. In Vienna, in 1825, Johann Strauss, Sr. (1804–1849) put together an orchestra that played only at dances. The first in a line of distinguished composers of popular music, Strauss was the son of an innkeeper in one of the poorest sections of Vienna. Although he had studied with one of Beethoven's teachers, Strauss chose to write nothing but dance music. For a time he kept his band together by playing at the inns where the Viennese loved to congregate. Then, during an engagement at Zum Sperl (At the Sparrow's), a fashionable establishment in a Viennese suburb, Strauss's orchestra skyrocketed to prominence. Both Chopin and Wagner went to hear his music; Wagner called Strauss "the genius of Vienna's innate musical spirit." The Danish storyteller Hans Christian Andersen described a visit as follows: "He stood there in the middle of the orchestra, the heart of the entire waltz scene. The melodies seemed to be streaming out of him. His eyes were glistening. It was plain to see that he was both the life of this place and its leader."

In 1833 Strauss embarked on the first of many tours with his orchestra of 28 musicians. With their renditions of the latest dance crazes—waltzes, cotillions, galops, quadrilles—they created a sensation in France (where they aroused even Berlioz's admiration), Germany, and England. Audiences praised the precision and brilliance of the ensemble rather than the music itself. Almost all of Strauss's orchestral works were published in versions for piano solo and duet, with glittery title pages to catch the eye of the hordes of new piano owners.

## JOHANN STRAUSS, JR. (1825–1899)

Perhaps Strauss's greatest gift to the world was his eldest son. The elder Strauss tried to dissuade his son from taking up a musical career, but when the father ran off with a younger woman in 1842, Johann Jr. undertook his own musical education. Within a few years his orchestra of 24 musicians had emerged as his father's chief rival, and after his father's premature death Johann merged the two orchestras into one.

Strauss combined the rhythmic verve of his father's style with the lyrical tradition of Viennese music and replaced his father's short-breathed themes with long, arching melodies. By 1860, Strauss had become world-famous. In 1872 Patrick Gilmore, a Boston impressario, invited him to come to America for an "International Peace Jubilee" celebrating the end of the Franco-Prussian War. Strauss's music was performed by 10,000 instrumentalists, a chorus of 20,000, and 100 sub-conductors. This was true popularity.

Where did the enormous new audience for popular music come from? The Industrial Revolution had drawn masses of workers into the cities. Cooped up in factories all week long, they flooded into urban parks on weekends to be serenaded by outdoor bands in return for donations. Many factories formed brass bands of their own. Moreover, affluent city dwellers, aspiring to the cultural trappings of aristocracy, bought tickets to subscription concerts, joined the hundreds of amateur choruses that had sprung up all over Europe and the United States, or bought pianos along with sheet music and lessons to go with them. Technical improvements, together with higher sales, lowered the cost of printed music. Composers eagerly supplied pieces that resembled more serious genres but were easy to play and listen to.

The most popular form was the *operetta,* a light, entertaining version of Romantic opera. Among the most successful composers were Jacques Offenbach (1819–1880) in Paris and Johann Strauss, Jr., Franz von Suppé (1819–1895), and Franz Lehár (1870–1948) in Vienna. Works by Offenbach and Strauss still receive regular performances today. In Vienna, operettas commonly incorporated the dances so beloved by the Viennese. Mozart and Beethoven had written dance music to supplement their incomes, but for the composers in the Strauss family (of whom there were several), dance music brought both a handsome income and international fame. Strauss and Brahms were on cordial terms, though Strauss's fame far eclipsed that of Brahms. Popular music was here to stay.

## Johann Strauss, Jr.: Waltz, *Voices of Spring,* Op. 410 (1883)

Austria's major export during the nineteenth century was the waltz. The triple-meter waltz, which was introduced to Vienna in the early years of the nineteenth century, had developed out of the more robust, rustic *Ländler* (country dance). The waltz differed from group dances, however, in that waltzing couples danced face-to-face in close embrace (Figure 21.2). This shocking behavior was condemned in such pamphlets as *Proof That Waltzing Is a Primary Source of the Weakness of the Body and Mind of Our Generation* (1797).

Strauss composed hundreds of waltzes. Although they all followed the same general plan, he varied them in countless ways and invigorated them with a seemingly endless succession of ingratiating melodies. To catch the listener's attention, each waltz opens with a "curtain raiser"—a short, vigorous passage that sets up the OOM-pah-pah bass pattern common to all waltzes. (Viennese performances characteristically delay the second and third beats slightly.) In *Voices of Spring* (Listening Guide 46), Strauss then launches into a string of eight sections, most connected by a short bridge and each built on a single melody, arranged in chainlike fashion: *A-B-A-C-D-E-F-A*-Coda. Each section divides neatly into two halves. Sometimes the second half repeats the first half almost literally (Section *D*); at other times it expands considerably on the first half (Section *E*). Only the three *A*-Sections are in the tonic key.

The appeal of these melodies lies in their spontaneity and rhythmic surprise. The melody of the first section (*A*) unleashes 14 consecutive fast notes before pulling up short with a series of unexpected rests. The ascent from low to high heightens the impact of the rests:

FIGURE 21.2  The
waltzes of Strauss have
appealed to a wide audi-
ence. The composer
Maurice Ravel described
one of his own works as a
"kind of memorial to the
great Strauss, not
Richard, the other one,
Johann. . . . I delight in
those admirable rhythms."

Other melodies, such as that of the *C*-Section, combine sweetness (dolce) with syncopation, in which the first beats of bars 2, 4, and 6 are tied (that is, held over from the preceding beat rather than articulated again):

Strauss clothes the melodies in his favorite Viennese instrumental colors: strings, horns, and flutes. The "voices of spring" are the songs of birds, and the flutes supply appropriately chirping counterpoint in Sections *B, C, E,* and *F.* The horn, originally used to accompany the hunt, retained for the Viennese its sentimental association with the forest. The snare drum, used by Strauss to sharpen rhythms, was familiar from military bands.

Many of the techniques common to popular music appeared as well in the art music of the day. Brahms, for example, was fond of the same kind of syncopation that Strauss used in *Voices of Spring.* Moreover, the orchestras that performed both types of music were largely identical. But the composer of popular music was now an artistic and economic force whose influence would continue to grow.

# *Listening Guide 46*

## JOHANN STRAUSS, JR.:
### Waltz, *Voices of Spring*, Op. 410

CD 5, TRACK 7
TAPE 5A, TRACK 7
DURATION: 6:01

*The sections in this "waltz chain" are quite easy to follow. In spite of the additive, sectional form, Strauss manages to balance vigorous and lyrical sections and also to build a stirring climax.*

*Form:* Waltz chain *(A-B-A-C-D-E-F-A-Coda)*

| | LOCATION | TIME | COMMENTS |
|---|---|---|---|
| 1 | Curtain (short) | 0:00 | Vigorous rhythms that catch the listener's attention before settling into the OOM-pah-pah accompaniment. |
| | A-Section | 0:07 | Swirling, ascending melody in the strings that creates a slightly giddy feeling. |
| | B-Section | 0:35 | Slower but rhythmic theme marked by staccato notes on the downbeat. |
| | Bridge (short) | 1:10 | Leads back to the opening curtain. |
| 2 | A-Section | 1:19 | Identical to the opening A-Section. |
| | Bridge (short) | 1:47 | |
| | C-Section | 1:52 | Tender, lyrical theme in the strings, with commentary added by birdlike flutes. |
| 3 | D-Section | 2:33 | Strings and flute, characterized by a series of upward leaps. Theme repeats twice. |
| | Bridge (short) | 3:09 | Brief pedal point with snare-drum rhythms. |
| | E-Section | 3:12 | Begins with slow, tentative rhythms in horns and strings. Second half of phrase greatly expanded, then fades away. |
| 4 | F-Section | 3:58 | Buoyant theme accompanied by trills in the flute and a counter-voice in the horn. |
| | Bridge (short) | 4:32 | More elaborate than any of the previous bridges. Leads once again back to the opening curtain. |
| | A-Section | 4:41 | Identical to the opening A-Section. |
| | Coda | 5:11 | Accelerates, then pulls back. Features harp, flute, and snare drums. Ends with a cadence derived from the theme of the A-Section. |

# Chapter 22

## ROMANTIC OPERA

## IN ITALY

arly in the eighteenth century, opera began to move from the private theaters of the aristocracy to the public theaters of Europe's great cities. During the Viennese Classical period, splendid new opera houses opened their doors in Paris, London, Berlin, Vienna, and elsewhere, with the production costs borne by city governments, patrons, and entrepreneurs. By the end of the nineteenth century, opera had become the most popular form of entertainment in music history. Most cities with a population of 100,000 or more boasted their own opera houses and their own opera companies. Singers like Giuditta Pasta (1797–1865) and Pauline Viardot (1821–1910) enjoyed a celebrity accorded today only to sports heroes and movie stars (see Figure 22.1).

Unlike the sophisticated audiences of the eighteenth century, many of the people who flocked to the opera houses had no formal musical education. Before going to a new production they bought a libretto to familiarize themselves with the "story" (Figure 22.1). At its best, however, Romantic opera achieved intellectual prestige as well as popular appeal through its rich dramatic development. Both Mozart and Haydn had composed operas, but they spent much of their time writing instrumental music as well. Following the early lead of Rossini, however, many Romantic composers wrote almost nothing but operas. Writing operas had become the surest route to fame and fortune.

## ITALIAN OPERA BEFORE MID-CENTURY

We have seen that the Classical style in opera gave way to the Romantic style only gradually, with Classical forms and conventions surviving well into the nineteenth century. In Italian opera, Gioacchino Rossini (1792–1868) represents the first stage in this evolution. Rossini was born in 1792 in Pesaro, a village on the eastern coast of Italy. By the time he was 14 his family had moved to Bologna, where he was admitted to the prestigious *Accademia Filarmonica*, a society of

**RIGOLETTO**

MELODRAMMA IN TRE ATTI

DI

**F. M. Piave**

MUSICA DI

**GIUSEPPE VERDI**

DA RAPPRESENTARSI

**al Teatro Civico Carlo Felice in Genova**

**il Carnevale 1852-53**

**Milano**

DALL'I. R. STABILIMENTO NAZIONALE PRIVILEGIATO DI
**GIOVANNI RICORDI**
*Cont. degli Omenoni, N.1720*
e sotto il portico a fianco dell'I. R. Teatro alla Scala.
22752

FIGURE 22.1 Opera-goers routinely purchased librettos (right) beforehand to familiarize themselves with the plot. Leading opera singers, such as Giuditta Pasta (top) and Pauline Viardot (bottom), were celebrities, performing the "hit tunes" of their day. Today's best-known opera star, Luciano Pavarotti, once characterized his art: "Singing opera is controlled screaming."

accomplished professional musicians—a tribute to his musical precocity. He attended the Liceo Musicale, the local conservatory, for several years, where he received a solid musical background. It was here that he first encountered the music of Mozart, whom he later referred to as "the idol of my youth, the desperation of my middle years, the consolation of my old age."

Opera was now a thriving enterprise throughout Europe, especially in Italy. Theater directors frequently settled on the libretto and chose the cast for a new work only a few months before it was to be performed. Composers and singers rushed from theater to theater trying to keep pace with their demanding schedules. Rossini himself wrote his first opera at the age of 18, after another composer had failed to deliver a promised new work to a Venetian opera house. Between 1810 and 1829 Rossini turned out more than three dozen operas for 15 opera houses in Italy, Spain, and France, a remarkable pace that even he could not sustain indefinitely.

Between 1811 and 1819 Rossini wrote an average of three operas a year, often starting a new work less than a month before its premiere. He wrote his comic masterpiece, *The Barber of Seville*, for a theater in Rome in about three weeks. This pace took a toll on his health, and after the 1829 premiere in Paris of his most ambitious work, *William Tell*, he stopped composing operas altogether.

In 1816 several of Rossini's operas were performed in Vienna and took the city by storm, causing what became known as the *Rossini-Rummel* ("Rossini uproar"). For the next six years the popularity of Rossini's music dwarfed even that of Beethoven's. In March 1822, while on his wedding trip, Rossini visited Vienna for the first time and was hailed as a hero. Beethoven received him briefly and is said to have remarked, perhaps ruefully, that "he needs only as many weeks as the Germans need years to write an opera."

Rossini, though a reformer, retained much of Mozart's dramatic pacing and formal structure. The two most important Italian composers between Rossini and Verdi—Gaetano Donizetti (1797–1848) and Vincenzo Bellini (1801–1835)—broke sharply with tradition and transformed opera into a dazzling vehicle for vocal display. They favored the style of singing known as *bel canto* ("beautiful singing"): melodic, often florid, music sung by performers with naturally beautiful voices and flawless techniques. Like many other styles in music, bel canto was acknowledged only in its decline; in 1858, Rossini is said to have lamented, "Alas for us, we have lost our bel canto."

Mozart, of course, had written music that flattered the human voice. But Bellini and Donizetti went even further by emphasizing the melodic line, by simplifying the orchestral accompaniments, by limiting the harmonies, and by making the harmonic rhythm more predictable. The prolific Donizetti wrote 64 operas in less than 30 years. He favored historical subjects such as *Anna Bolena* (1830), about the ill-fated second wife of Henry VIII. Others drew on historical novels, such as *Lucia di Lammermoor* (1835?), based on Sir Walter Scott's *The Bride of Lammermoor*. Lucia's "mad scene"—in which she loses her mind when faced with the prospect of marrying a man she does not love—was the most famous Romantic example of this popular device. Bellini's career was considerably shorter than Donizetti's, and he completed fewer than a dozen operas. His long, arching melodies are more carefully crafted than Donizetti's and anticipate more closely the full-blooded Romantic opera that followed.

Composers of Baroque operas had unfailingly portrayed their protagonists as admirable, heroic figures. Their operas usually end with the happy resolution of a conflict arising from circumstances beyond the protagonists' control. Classical composers had introduced more complex, believable characters but, for the most part, retained the happy ending. Composers of Romantic operas, by contrast, favored complex characters who combine both desirable and undesirable traits and who often show some character flaw that leads to their downfall. The tragic endings of many Romantic operas arise from conflicts created by the characters themselves.

For example, in *Norma* (1831), Bellini's finest opera, the high priestess of the Druids,\* from whom the opera takes its name, is secretly married to Pollione, a Roman proconsul (a high-ranking military officer) with whom she has had two

---

\*The Druids were a religious cult that flourished in Gaul during Roman times.

sons. Pollione is passionately attracted to Adalgisa, a young virgin at the temple of Irminsul, and persuades her to flee with him to Rome. Overcome by guilt, Adalgisa confesses the plan to Norma, who confronts Pollione in a violent scene. Pollione, however, is unrepentant. Eventually, Norma and Pollione mount a funeral pyre in an act of atonement for their sins.

To achieve such complex characterizations, Romantic composers often set the struggles of their principal characters against a large backdrop of lesser characters. The quasi-historical operas of Giacomo Meyerbeer (1791–1864) were the most popular examples before Wagner of an epic genre the French called *grand opera. Les Huguenots* (*The Huguenots,* 1836), for example, recounts the massacre of a religious group on St. Bartholomew's Eve (a church celebration). Some of the battle scenes in this opera call for hundreds of participants. In Meyerbeer's last opera, *L'Africaine* (*The African Girl,* 1865, based on the life of the Portuguese explorer Vasco da Gama), Act III ends with a ship and its crew sinking on stage, a spectacle that created a sensation at the premiere (Figure 22.2).

The operas of Donizetti, Bellini, and Meyerbeer are performed less often today than they once were, but they were enormously popular during the first half of the nineteenth century. During the second half of the century, Italian opera was dominated by a composer whose reputation continues to grow: Giuseppe Verdi.

## GIUSEPPE VERDI (1813–1901)

Many operagoers regard the operas of Giuseppe Verdi as the perfect blend of musical and dramatic expression. The intensity of the characters and the urgency of the music create a powerful impact on audiences the world over.

Born in the northern Italian town of Roncole to a family of small landowners and tradespeople, Verdi took his first music lessons at the age of 3; by the time he was 9 he had taken over some of his teacher's duties. At 18 he tried to enter the Milan Conservatory but was turned down because he was four years over the age of admission.

After serving in several minor posts, Verdi turned to opera in his mid-twenties and had his first work produced at Milan's La Scala (Italy's premier opera house) in 1840. That first production was a failure. Within two months it was followed by the deaths of Verdi's first wife, son, and daughter. Despite these setbacks, Verdi made steady progress over the next decade. His first triumph came in 1842 with an elaborate grand opera, *Nabucco,* based on the life of the Babylonian king Nebuchadnezzar. Within eight years *Nabucco* had been produced in more than 15 countries. Over the next 15 years, Verdi composed 20 more operas, including three of his most popular: *Rigoletto* (1851), *Il Trovatore* (*The Troubadour,* 1853), and *La Traviata* (*The Fallen Woman,* 1853). In these operas and others, Verdi made several subtle references to the unification movement that was emerging in Italy, a movement in which he was to play an important role (see the Historical Window on page 450).

FIGURE 22.2 The Cecil B. deMille of the opera: The staging of Meyerbeer's operas were often more memorable than the music. Recounting one Meyerbeer opera, Chopin said it was magnificent—"Meyerbeer has won eternal fame"—and went on to describe in detail the sets rather than the music.

In 1847, while Verdi was in Paris, he renewed his acquaintance with the soprano Giuseppina Strepponi, whom he had met eight years before. After living with her for almost two years, he bought a large house in the small Italian town of Sant' Agata, where his ancestors had once lived. Giuseppina's arrival there set off gossip among the townspeople and prompted Verdi's former father-in-law to write him a reproachful letter. Verdi sent a terse reply: "It is my practice never to interfere, unless invited, in other people's business, and I expect others not to interfere in mine." In 1859 Giuseppe and Giuseppina were married in a private ceremony and remained nearly inseparable until her death some 40 years later.

After 1860 Verdi's production of operas declined sharply. Over the next 33 years he completed only five operas, though among them were three of his masterpieces: *Aïda* (composed for the opening of the Suez Canal in 1871), *Otello* (1887, based on the play by Shakespeare), and *Falstaff* (1893, based on Shakespeare's *The Merry Wives of Windsor* and *King Henry IV*). For many years Verdi felt that his works had not received the recognition they deserved. In 1863 the composer/librettist Arrigo Boito wrote: "Perhaps the man is already born who will elevate chaste, pure art on that altar now soiled like the wall of a brothel." An indignant Verdi believed that he had already proved himself to be that man. Apparently the rift was healed by time, for 24 years later Boito eagerly accepted an invitation to write the librettos for Verdi's last two operas, the dark tragedy *Otello* and the deeply human comedy *Falstaff*.

Verdi had an uncommon gift for melodies that are at once straightforward and subtle—melodies that beg to be whistled or hummed. He supported these melodies with bold harmonies and striking orchestrations. His concern with the staging of his operas also set him apart from his contemporaries. "Take great care over the staging," he wrote to the producers of his opera *Simon Boccanegra.* He went on to specify the precise location of a palace in the first scene and the exact sort of gauze that would suggest moonlight shimmering on water in the following scene.

A true Romantic, Verdi romanticized even his self-image, referring to himself as a simple peasant at heart. He remains one of the most appealing composers of the nineteenth century.

## Verdi: Act III from *Rigoletto* (1851)

A contemporary once noted Verdi's fondness for "ferocious and gloomy stories." That fondness is evident in *Rigoletto,* the first of three operas Verdi wrote in quick succession at mid-century. According to the practice of the day, the managers of an opera house would specify what libretto a composer was to use when they commissioned a new opera. But Verdi preferred to select his own subjects. In a letter to his librettist, he suggested that *Rigoletto* be based on the play *Le Roi s'amuse* (The King Amuses Himself) by the French playwright and novelist Victor Hugo:

> Oh, *Le Roi s'amuse* is the greatest subject and perhaps the greatest drama of modern times. Triboulet [the protagonist who becomes Rigoletto in Verdi's opera] is a creation worthy of Shakespeare!!! . . . Now going over the various subjects in my mind, *Le Roi* came on me like a flash of lightning, an inspiration, and I said to myself, . . . "Yes, by God, this one cannot go wrong."

Rigoletto is a taunting court jester embittered by having been born a hunchback. He lives at the court of a dissolute nobleman (the King of France in Hugo's play; the Duke of Mantua in Verdi's opera), who is in endless pursuit of his next female conquest. These two unsavory characters collide when the Duke sets his sights on a beautiful young woman he has seen in church. She turns out to be Rigoletto's only daughter, Gilda, whom Rigoletto has struggled to shield from the evil world. Rigoletto's love for Gilda is his only redeeming quality. When Rigoletto hires an assassin to kill the Duke, Gilda sacrifices herself in an effort to save the Duke's life.

The story unfolds swiftly and with a relentless inevitability. The opening scene of the opera reveals the extravagance of the Duke's court and hints at his corruption. (Like most male leads in Romantic opera, the Duke is a tenor.) While a dance band plays in the background, the Duke and his companions carry on in *parlante* ("speaking")—a rapid, uneven patter that suggests real conversation. Rigoletto taunts the courtiers whose spouses or daughters have been seduced by the Duke. One of them delivers a horrifying and prophetic curse.

In the next scene, Rigoletto encounters a professional assassin, Sparafucile, who offers his services should they ever be needed (for a fee, of course). Rigoletto orders his daughter to remain indoors except when she goes to church. The Duke, however, manages to enter their house and declares his love to the gullible young woman. Rigoletto, learning that the courtiers are about to abduct Ceprano's wife, is deceived into helping them abduct his own daughter, who is spirited away to the Duke's apartments. In the second act, Rigoletto learns that his worst fear has been realized: The Duke has seduced Gilda. In her infatuation, Gilda begs her father not to harm him.

Verdi knew that this opera would shock his audiences and make for great theater, but he knew too that the censors would object to his portraying a nobleman as dissolute. When Hugo's play opened in Paris in 1832, the French censors banned it almost immediately and it was not seen again for half a century.

At one point while Verdi was composing *Rigoletto,* the censors insisted that he make the Duke into a virtuous man. Verdi replied: "The courtiers' anger with Triboulet makes no sense. . . . The Duke is a zero. The Duke must be a complete playboy; otherwise there is no reason why Triboulet should be afraid to let his daughter out of concealment and therefore the drama is impossible." Eventually, Verdi's determination prevailed.

After its premiere, one critic complained that *Rigoletto* was "childish and ridiculous, full of vulgarity and eccentricity and without any ideas." The audience at the premiere hailed the opera, however, and *Rigoletto* has remained enormously popular ever since.

In the opening scene of Act III (where Listening Guide 47 begins), a desperate Rigoletto has taken Gilda to a spot overlooking a ramshackle inn on the outskirts of Mantua, where the Duke is meeting Maddalena, yet another potential conquest. Maddalena is the sister of the inn's owner, Sparafucile, whom Rigoletto—unbeknownst to Gilda—has hired to kill the Duke after he falls asleep. The scene opens quietly with a brief, minor-mode chorale-like passage in the strings. The dialogue that follows is delivered in simple recitative. Gilda admits to her father that she still loves the Duke. Her father leads her to an opening in a fence where, horrified, she watches the Duke, disguised as a cavalry officer, make advances to Maddalena.

The orchestra begins to play a striking theme and then stops abruptly. This is the cue for the Duke to sing a stirring aria, *"La donna è mobile"* ("Woman is fickle")—that recalls the sentiments he expressed earlier: a woman is "as fickle as a feather in the wind." If a man "confides in her, there goes his heart." The Duke's attitude toward women has shifted subtly. In the first act, women were playthings; now women are fickle and not to be trusted. Hence the man must desert the woman before she deserts him.

Like the Duke's first aria in the first act, *"La donna è mobile"* is divided into two equal stanzas of two phrases each. (Here, however, the *a*-phrase is not repeated at the end of each stanza, and the last four lines are the same as the first four lines.) The aria alternates between measures of notes of equal length (bars 1, 3, and so on) and measures with a sharp dotted rhythm on the first beat (2, 4, and so on):

# Listening Guide 47

## VERDI: Beginning of Act III from *Rigoletto*

CD 5, TRACK 8
TAPE 5A, TRACK 8
DURATION: 11:00

✛ *From the first lines of "La donna è mobile" ("Woman is fickle"), the structure of every aria or section in the quartet is a-a-b (or, in the Duke's second aria, a-a-b-c-b), giving it an unprecedented degree of unity and symmetry. The larger subdivisions (arias, sections) with A-A-B shapes are separated by ruled lines.*

*Form: Dramatic*

| | TEXT | TIME | LOCATION / COMMENTS |
|---|---|---|---|
| 1 | Instrumental Prelude | **0:00** | Low strings, chorale style, *pianissimo*, minor mode. |
| 2 | RIGOLETTO:<br>*E l'ami?* You love him?<br>GILDA:<br>*Sempre.* Always.<br>RIGOLETTO:<br>*Pure tempo a guarirne t'ho lasciato.*<br>But I've given you time to forget him.<br>GILDA:<br>*Io l'amo.* I love him.<br>RIGOLETTO:<br>*Povero cor di donna! Ah, il vile infame!*<br>Poor woman's heart! Ah, the scoundrel! | **0:53** | Simple recitative, with occasional chords from the orchestra. |
| | | 1:05 | Powerful orchestral chord on *"infame"* ("scoundrel"). |
| | *Ma ne avrai vendetta, O Gilda.*<br>You will be avenged, Gilda.<br>GILDA:<br>*Pietà, mio padre . . .* Have pity, my father . . .<br>RIGOLETTO:<br>*E se tu certa fossi ch'ei ti tradisse,*<br>And if you were sure that he was unfaithful, | 1:18 | More simple recitative. |
| | *l'ameresti ancora?* then would you still love him?<br>GILDA:<br>*Non so, ma pur m'adora.*<br>I don't know . . . but he adores me.<br>RIGOLETTO:<br>*Egli?* He does? | 1:29 | Soft orchestral chord on *"adora"* ("adores"). |

| TEXT | TIME | LOCATION / COMMENTS |
|------|------|---------------------|
| GILDA:<br>*Sì.* Yes.<br>RIGOLETTO:<br>*Ebben, osserva dunque.* Well, then watch carefully. | | |
| *[He leads her to an opening in the wall, and she looks in.]* | 1:45 | Recall of chorale music in strings. |
| GILDA:<br>*Un uomo vedo.* I see a man.<br>RIGOLETTO:<br>*Per poco attendi.* Wait a moment. | 1:56 | The pace picks up and the orchestra describes the Duke's entry. |
| *[The Duke enters, wearing the uniform of a cavalry officer.]* | | |
| GILDA *[with a start]*:<br>*Ah, padre mio!* Ah, father!<br>DUKE *[to Sparafucile]*:<br>*Due cose—e tosto.*<br>Two things—and make it snappy.<br>SPARAFUCILE:<br>*Quali?* What are they?<br>DUKE:<br>*Una stanza e del vino.* A room and some wine.<br>RIGOLETTO:<br>*(Son questi i suoi costumi!)* (Those are his habits!)<br>SPARAFUCILE:<br>*(Oh, il bel zerbino!)* (What a ladies' man!) | 2:07 | Return to simple recitative, but at a "snappier" pace. |
| | | Ends in a cadence. |

| | | |
|------|------|---------------------|
| 3 ✳ [Orchestral introduction] | 2:23 | Strings play a bright, popular tune in triple meter, breaking off on an expectant pause. |
| STANZA 1 | | |
| DUKE:<br>*La donna è mobile qual piuma al vento,*<br>A woman is as fickle as a feather in the wind, | 2:34 | **a-phrase.** Same melody as that just played in the orchestra. |
| *Muta d'accento e di pensier.*<br>Simple in speech and in mind. | | |
| *Sempre un amabile leggiadro viso,*<br>Always a lovable charming face, | 2:47 | **a-phrase.** Identical to the preceding phrase. |

*continued*

| TEXT | TIME | LOCATION / COMMENTS |
|---|---|---|
| *In pianto o in riso, è menzognero.*<br>In tears or in laughter, and a deceiving one. | | |
| *La donna è mobile qual piuma al vento,*<br>A woman is as fickle as a feather in the wind,<br><br>*Muta d'accento e di pensier.*<br>simple in speech and in mind. | 2:58 | **b-phrase.** Repeats the text of first *a*-phrase. Rises to a held climax on *accento* (''speech''), then descends to a cadence that repeats three times. |
| [Orchestral interlude, same as introduction] | | |
| STANZA 2<br>4 *È sempre misero chi a lei s'affida,*<br>Always miserable is he who gives himself up to her,<br><br>*Chi le confida mal caute il core!*<br>And if he confides in her, there goes his heart! | **3:28** | **a-phrase.** Same as in Stanza 1. |
| *Pur mai non sentesi felice appieno*<br>But no man ever feels really content<br><br>*Chi su quel seno, non liba amore!*<br>Who does not, in her arms, drink to love's health! | **3:39** | **a-phrase.** |
| *La donna è mobile qual piuma al vento,*<br>A woman is as fickle as a feather in the wind,<br><br>*Muta d'accento e di pensier.*<br>Simple in speech and in mind.<br><br>[Orchestral exit] | **3:52** | **b-phrase.** Identical to the first stanza (including text), except that the final cadence is embellished with a cadenza.<br>The orchestra begins by repeating the introduction, but then recedes with softer statements in oboe and bassoon. |
| SPARAFUCILE *[to Rigoletto]:*<br>5 *È là vostr'uomo . . . viver de' o morire?*<br>There's your man . . . shall he live or die?<br>RIGOLETTO:<br>*Più tardi tornerò l'opra a compire.*<br>I'll return later and settle the matter. | **5:04** | Delivered as *parlante.*<br><br>Orchestra comes to a soft, full cadence. |
| 6 DUKE:<br>*Un dì, se ben rammentomi,*<br>One day, if I recall correctly,<br><br>*O bella, t'incontrai.* I met you, pretty girl. | **5:22** | **A-Section.** Allegro tempo. *Parlante* style with brilliant melody in the strings, marked by trills and rapid repeated notes. |

| TEXT | TIME | LOCATION / COMMENTS |
|---|---|---|
| *Mi piacque di te chiedere e intesi che qui stai.*<br>I asked someone about you and was told you live here. | | |
| *Or sappi che d'allora sol te quest'alma adora.*<br>Let me say that ever since I have devoutly adored you. | | |
| GILDA:<br>*Iniquo!* The wretch! | 5:55 | An interjection.<br>*Parlante* style continues.<br>Both Maddalena and the Duke<br>sing in a patter style. |
| MADDALENA:<br>*Ah! Ah! . . . e vent'altre appresso*<br>Uh huh. And the twenty more since then | | |
| *Le scorda forse adesso?*<br>You have perhaps forgotten? | | |
| *Ha un'aria il signorino da vero libertino.*<br>I think my suave gentleman is something of a libertine. | | |
| DUKE *[trying to kiss her]:*<br>*Si—un mostro son—* Yes—I'm a monster— | | |
| GILDA:<br>*Oh padre mio!* Oh my father! | | |
| MADDALENA:<br>*Lasciatemi, stordito.* Leave me alone, you fool. | | |
| DUKE:<br>*Ih, che fracasso!* Hah, what a fracas! | | Builds to an agitated climax, at<br>which point the Duke holds out<br>the word *"chiasso."* |
| MADDALENA:<br>*Stia saggio!* Behave yourself! | | |
| DUKE:<br>*E tu sii docile, non farmi tanto chiasso.*<br>And you be docile, don't make such a fuss. | | |
| *Ogni saggezza chiudesi nel gaudio e nell'amore.*<br>The end of all wisdom lies in the joy of loving. | | Lyrical line sung in a considera-<br>bly slower tempo. |
| *[He takes her hand.]* | | |
| 7 *La bella mano candida!* Your pretty white hand! | 6:20 | *A-Section.* Grows directly out of<br>preceding line and resumes the<br>original tempo. |
| MADDALENA:<br>*Scherzate voi, signore.* You are joking, sir. | | |
| DUKE:<br>*No, no!* No, no! | | |
| MADDALENA:<br>*Son brutta.* But I am ugly. | | |
| DUKE:<br>*Abbracciami.* Embrace me. | | *continued* |

# *Listening Guide 47 (Continued)*

| TEXT | TIME | LOCATION / COMMENTS |
|------|------|---------------------|
| GILDA: | | |
| *Iniquo!* The wretch! | | |
| MADDALENA: | | |
| *Ebbro!* You're drunk! | | |
| DUKE: | | |
| *D'amore ardente!* With ardent love! | | |
| MADDALENA: | | |
| *Signor l'indifferente, vi piace canzonar?* | | |
| My cynical friend, you like to joke? | | |
| DUKE: | | |
| *No, no, ti vo' sposar.* No, no, I want to marry you. | | |
| MADDALENA: | | |
| *Ne voglio la parola.* I want your word of honor. | | Maddalena suddenly turns lyrical. |

| TEXT | TIME | LOCATION / COMMENTS |
|------|------|---------------------|
| DUKE *[ironically]*: | 6:40 | **(B-Section).** Over a long pedal |
| *Amabile figliuola!* Sweet child! | | point, the four characters sing |
| RIGOLETTO *[to Gilda, who has heard everything]*: | | together for the first time. They |
| *E non ti basta ancor?* Haven't you seen enough? | | set up the minor mode. |
| GILDA: | | |
| *Iniquo traditor!* Wretched traitor! | | |
| MADDALENA: | | |
| *Ne voglio la parola.* I want your word of honor. | | |
| DUKE: | | |
| *Amabile figliuola!* Sweet child! | | |

ARIA

| TEXT | TIME | LOCATION / COMMENTS |
|------|------|---------------------|
| DUKE: | | |
| **8** *Bella figlia dell'amore,* Beautiful daughter of love, | **6:56** | *A*-Section. *a*-phrase. Sweet, ardent melody in the major mode. |
| *schiavo son de' vezzi tuoi;* I am a slave to your charms; | 7:04 | *a'*-phrase. Simple accompaniment in strings and flute. |
| *con un detto sol tu puoi le mie pene consolar.* with a single word you have the power to console all my anguish. | | *b*-phrase. Climbs to a climax before descending. |
| *Vieni e senti del mio core il frequente palpitar;* Come, feel the wild beating of my lovesick heart; | | *c*-phrase. Moves to minor mode, climax on *"palpitar."* |
| *con un detto sol tu puoi le mie pene consolar.* with a single word you have the power to console all my anguish. | | *b*-phrase. Same text and music as preceding *b*-phrase. |

| TEXT | TIME | LOCATION / COMMENTS |
|------|------|---------------------|

**9**   MADDALENA:
*Ah! Ah! Rido ben di core;* Ah! That is laughable;

*chè tai baie costan poco.* such talk is cheap.

    **7:59**     **B-Section. a-phrase.** The Duke drops out as Maddalena sings a patter response.

GILDA:
*Ah, così parlar d'amore.*
Ah, to speak of love in such a way.

    Lyrical and anguished.

MADDALENA:
*Quanto valga il vostro gioco*
Just how much to value your flattery

    **8:06**     **a-phrase.** Identical to the preceding *a*-phrase.

*Mel credete, so apprezzar.* Believe me, I know how.

GILDA:
*A me pur l'infame ho udito!*
The wretch once spoke like that to me!

RIGOLETTO *[to Gilda]*:
*Taci, il pianger non vale;*
Hush, your tears are useless;

    **8:13**     **(b-phrase).** All four characters join in. At the end of the phrase, the Duke soars alone to the climax of his *c*-phrase.

GILDA:
*Infelice cor tradito, per angoscia non scoppiar.*
O wretched heart, betrayed, do not break from sorrow.

MADDALENA:
*Sono avvezza, bel signore, ad un simile scherzar.*
I'm familiar, handsome sir, with advances like these.

    From here to the end, the only new text lines are those added by Rigoletto.

**10**   DUKE:
*con un detto sol tu puoi le mie pene consolar.*
with a single word you have the power to console all my anguish.

    **8:42**     **A-Section.** The Duke's *"Bella figlia"* begins again, in four voices, with the voices from 7:59 as its counterpoint.

RIGOLETTO:
*Ch'ei mentiva or sei secura.*
Now you know he was lying.

    At **9:08** the first of two closing sections begins, also in *a-a-b* phrases. This theme repeats at 9:39.

*Taci, e mia sarà la cura la vendetta d'affretar.*
Be quiet and let me have the task of exacting vengeance.

    A final closing section begins at 10:08, also in *a-a-b* phrases.

*Pronta fia, sarà fatale; io saprollo fulminar.*
It shall be soon, and fatal; I shall strike him down.

    The quartet ends with Gilda singing a high D♭—not specified by Verdi!

*Allegretto* (Slightly fast)

La donna è mo-bi-le qual piuma al ven - to,
(A woman is fickle like a feather in the wind,)

In the *b*-phrase, Verdi reverses this relationship by placing the dotted rhythm on the odd-numbered measures:

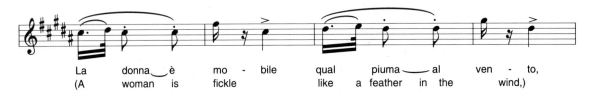

La donna è mo - bile qual piuma al ven - to,
(A woman is fickle like a feather in the wind,)

To create a sense of climax, Verdi replaces the downward direction of the *a*-phrases by the upward drive of the *b*-phrase. As the aria ends, the orchestra gradually recedes and Sparafucile re-enters the Duke's room with a bottle of wine and two glasses. He signals to Maddalena and then goes outside to talk to Rigoletto. Sure that his plan will work, Rigoletto rejects Sparafucile's offer to kill the Duke right away and tells him to wait until the Duke has fallen asleep.

The two couples on stage—the Duke and Maddalena, Rigoletto and Gilda—are now locked in cross-cutting conflict. The Duke wants to seduce Maddalena, but she resists. The Duke has deserted Gilda, who feels betrayed. Maddalena knows the Duke is not to be trusted but still finds him attractive. Gilda relinquishes her fantasies about the Duke but cannot repudiate the bond she feels to him. Rigoletto wants Gilda to acknowledge the Duke's disloyalty but is distressed by her pain.

To bring these conflicting passions together, Verdi hit upon a novel solution: a vocal quartet (Figure 22.3). Although we have to pretend that the characters cannot hear one another, the psychological truth is more compelling than the physical reality. As the quartet opens, the Duke is telling Maddalena a trumped-up story, Maddalena is putting him off, and Gilda is crying out in pain. (The style is somewhere between aria and *parlante*.) Although at first put off by the Duke's advances, Maddalena soon relents and requests the Duke's "word of honor" concerning his intentions. Finally Rigoletto joins in, and all four characters express their feelings simultaneously: Rigoletto his exasperation with his daughter, Gilda her rage with the Duke, Maddalena her pleas for fidelity—while the Duke calls her a "sweet child."

Verdi now gives the Duke yet a third aria. At first the Duke sings alone, forsaking the cynicism of *"La donna è mobile"* for more traditional entreaties, referring to Maddalena as a "beautiful daughter of love." The phrase structure is more complex than in the earlier arias *(a-a-b-c-b),* but again the melody rises to a climax near the end of the *c*-phrase. While the Duke drops out temporarily, the

FIGURE 22.3 Verdi's understanding of drama matched his musical talent. Complaining about a censored libretto of *Rigoletto,* he wrote, "I notice that Triboletto [later Rigoletto] is no longer to be ugly and hunchbacked!! A singing hunchback? Why not! . . . Will it make a good effect? I don't know; but . . . if I do not know, nobody knows, not even whoever has suggested this alteration. . . . The whole beauty lies in showing Triboletto as completely deformed . . . but inwardly passionate and full of love."

two women respond—Maddalena in a kind of patter more appropriate to opera buffa, and Gilda in sober, more lyrical anguish.

Before the women have finished, the Duke jumps back in and snatches the melody from them. As he repeats his stanza, all four characters sing together (the women with the melodies they have just sung):

*Duke:* Beautiful daughter of love, etc.

*Maddalena:* I'm familiar, handsome sir, with advances like these.

*Gilda:* O wretched heart, betrayed, do not break from sorrow.

*Rigoletto:* Be quiet and let me have the task of exacting vengeance.

Beginning with the Duke's *"La donna è mobile,"* Verdi unifies the action by organizing both set pieces and the phrases within them in *a-a-b* shapes. This extends to the two rich closing sections with which the quartet concludes.

The effect of four characters expressing such varied feelings at the same time electrified Verdi's audiences. After seeing a performance of the opera, Victor Hugo is said to have told Verdi that if he could achieve such an effect in a play he would be compared with Shakespeare. (In the ensuing action Gilda manages to substitute herself for the Duke. When Rigoletto opens the sack to dump the Duke's body into the river, he discovers his dying daughter. Monterone's curse has been fulfilled.)

FIGURE 22.4 Liszt praised his talented contemporaries, playing and promoting their work through his transcriptions. This transcription of Schumann's song *"Widmung"* ("Dedication") includes two parallel versions: Liszt's virtuoso transcription in large notes on the bottom and a more playable arrangement in small notes on the top.

## Franz Liszt: Piano Transcription of the Act III Quartet from *Rigoletto* (1859)

Despite the popularity of opera during the nineteenth century, relatively few people managed to attend live performances. Many who could not hear opera live were nevertheless eager to hear the "hit tunes" from the operas people were talking about. The nineteenth-century equivalent of the compact disc was the piano transcription—an arrangement for solo piano of an excerpt from an opera (or, less often, from a symphony or a song). Many transcriptions were written in a simplified version that amateur pianists could handle, though virtuosic passages were often provided as well (Figure 22.4).

The piano transcriptions made by such skillful musicians as Sigismond Thalberg and Franz Liszt are among their most brilliant compositions. Indeed, Liszt's transcriptions are as impressive and innovative as his original piano works. Liszt transcribed dozens of works by composers both living and dead, including many of Schubert's songs, all of Beethoven's symphonies, Berlioz's *Symphonie fantastique,* and operatic excerpts by Mozart, Bellini, Donizetti, Rossini, Meyerbeer, Verdi, and Wagner. When he played his transcriptions at recitals, his audiences could scarcely believe that what they heard was coming from a single instrument played by a single performer.

Aware of the popularity of *Rigoletto* during the 1850s, Liszt transcribed its most celebrated number, the Quartet from Act III. Although some of his transcriptions are faithful renditions of the original (like his transcription of Berlioz's *Symphonie fantastique*), his operatic transcriptions are "concert paraphrases" (as he called them). In these paraphrases he created his own structure and drew on material from various portions of the original work. He built his *Rigoletto* paraphrase around the second section of the Quartet (which begins with the Duke's aria, "Beautiful daughter of love"). In an elaborate introduction he quotes from passages sung by Maddalena and Gilda and then moves on to a harplike cascade of arpeggios that suggests the curtain rising before a performance:

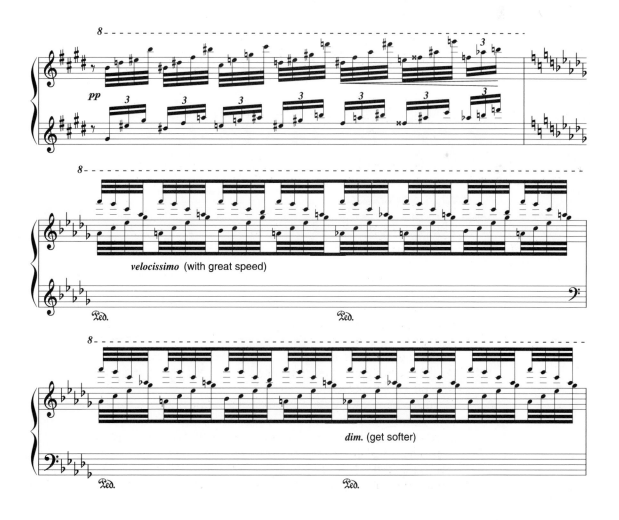

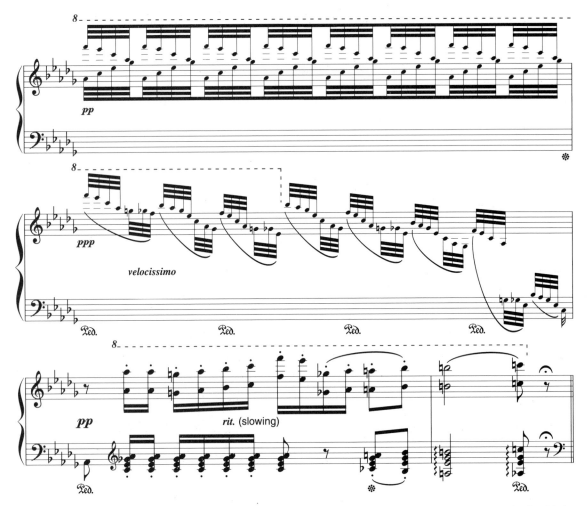

Liszt portrays each character with distinctive figuration. For example, he highlights the Duke's slow, languid melody with rapid-scale figures above (again in the small notes):

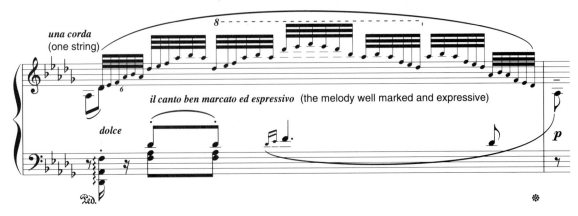

Later, he renders Gilda's "wretched heart, betrayed, do not break from sorrow" with rapid repeated octaves in place of the single tones of the vocal passage, as if to emphasize the "breaking":

Whereas Verdi prepares for the action to come by ending his quartet softly, Liszt closes out his paraphrase with a blaze of double-octave fireworks designed to dazzle his audience.

## GIACOMO PUCCINI (1858–1924) AND LATE ROMANTIC OPERA

As Romanticism waned, Verdi's shoes proved nearly impossible to fill. The composer who came closest was Giacomo Puccini, whose operas are as popular today as they were during his lifetime. More than any of his contemporaries, Puccini knew how to exploit the beauties of the human voice. His memorable, often

## "VIVA VERDI!"

The waves of nationalism that swept across Europe during the nineteenth century were powered by several forces. For many centuries the Austro-Hungarian empire had ruled over people who spoke different languages, including German, Hungarian, and Italian, and who had different cultural loyalties. Gradually, people who spoke a common language began to regain their sense of kinship. They took pride in their national costumes, their religious beliefs, and their modes of artistic expression. First here, then there, these regional populations resolved to overthrow their "foreign" rulers.

The quest for national identity was intensified by a widespread desire for political freedom. The motto of the French Revolution of 1789—Liberty, Equality, Fraternity—had not translated into democracies throughout Europe, and the political struggles in France had ended in 1830 (after a short-lived uprising) with the return, somewhat modified, of the monarchy against which the French had revolted. In 1848 uprisings broke out almost simultaneously from Copenhagen in the north to Palermo in the south; from Paris in the west to Budapest in the east (see map, page 373). Though these rebellions were soon put down, the longing for political freedom persisted.

In Verdi's Italy, a popular movement known as the *Risorgimento* ("resurgence") sought to recapture the grandeur and prestige of Renaissance Italy. At mid-century, however, two formidable obstacles stood in the way of Italian unification. First, the Austrians held the northern kingdoms of Lombardy (whose capital was Milan) and Venetia (whose capital was Venice). Second, the rest of Italy was fragmented into numerous independent states.

The island state of Sardinia took the lead in the struggle for unification. The king of Sardinia's constitutional monarchy was Victor Emmanuel, but its most influential and skillful politician was the prime minister, Camillo di Cavour. First, Cavour arranged an alliance with France and then, in 1859, tricked the French into joining in a war against the Austrians. The Austrians were defeated and had to give up both Lombardy and Venetia. Now Cavour turned to the recalcitrant southern kingdom of the "Two Sicilies" and in 1860 secretly connived with a band of Sardinian freedom fighters led by Giuseppe Garibaldi. At the head of a ragtag army of a thousand or so supporters known as "Red Shirts," Garibaldi marched on the Sicilian government. Cavour now led a more powerful army to Sicily and persuaded Garibaldi to throw his support behind the constitutional monarchy. In 1861, Cavour convened Italy's first parliament and, in another astute move, prevailed upon the immensely popular Giuseppe Verdi to serve as one of its members.

Verdi had already attracted the attention of Italy's politicians with references to the overthrow of tyranny in several of his early operas. In *Nabucco* (1842), for example, the Jews struggle against their captivity in Babylon. In *I Lombardi* (*The Lombards*, 1843), a renegade Italian passes strategic information to Christian crusaders who are trying to liberate eleventh-century Antioch from the Moslems. In *La Battaglia di Legnano (The Battle of Legnano)*, which Verdi wrote in the wake of the 1848 revolutions, the twelfth-century hero returns to Italy to join his countrymen around Milan in resisting the armies of the Holy Roman Empire.

When Verdi heard of the outbreak of revolution in Milan in 1848, he wrote from Paris to his librettist Francesco Maria Piave:

> Imagine whether I wanted to stay in Paris when I heard that there was a revolution in Milan! I left immediately when I heard the news, but I've been unable to see anything except those marvellous barricades. All honor to our great champions. Honor to all Italy, who at this moment shows true greatness.
>
> You can be sure that the hour of freedom has struck! The people insist on it . . . and there is no power on earth that can resist them.

Contrary to Verdi's prediction, however, the revolution fizzled out.

Verdi's music had the power to arouse patriotic fervor, as is shown by an event that took place at the premiere of *The Battle of Legnano*. Near the end of the third act, the hero, Arrigo, is locked in a tower to prevent him from joining his comrades in battle. Verdi suggests Arrigo's frustration with wildly displaced accents, as if someone were struggling to unlock a door. Trumpet calls sound from below, accompanied by cries of *"Viva l'Italia!"* ("Long live Italy!"). Over the confusion, Verdi introduces tremolo strings to suggest Arrigo's desperation. Finally, Arrigo leaps into a moat a hundred feet below and makes his escape. At this point an excited Italian sergeant in the audience is said to have jumped from the balcony into the orchestra pit below (no one was seriously hurt—or so the story goes).

Verdi's operas came to symbolize the struggle of the Italians against their oppressors. From Milan to Naples, an inscription was scribbled on the walls: "VIVA VERDI!" Those who scribbled the phrase used Verdi's name as an acronym for the Sardinian king who had launched the unification movement: *Victor Emmanuel Re di Italia* (Victor Emmanuel, King of Italy—Figure 22.5). Supporters of unification replaced the inscriptions as quickly as the authorities removed them.

*continued*

FIGURE 22.5  In the 1840s, Verdi responded to requests for operas with political themes with *Nabucco, I Lombardi, Attila,* and *La battaglia di Legnano.* These operas launched his great popularity in Italy.

**Despite his notoriety, however, Verdi disclaimed any political ambitions. He once wrote, "I know nothing of politics, and hope politics will leave me alone." When Cavour persuaded him to serve as a member of Italy's first parliament, Verdi remarked: "There are supposed to be 450 deputies in Italy. This is not true. There are only 449, for Verdi is no deputy."**

sentimental melodies and his colorful orchestrations frequently overshadow the narrow limits of the drama.

Puccini, who came from a family of church musicians, was trained as an organist. He sometimes surprised his congregations, however, by working Tuscan folk songs and snatches from Verdi operas into his playing. At the relatively late age of 22 he entered the Milan Conservatory, where his passion for opera became all-consuming. He once remarked, "The Almighty touched me with his little finger and said: 'Write for the theater, mind you, only for the theater!' And I have obeyed the supreme command."

His first success came in 1893 with *Manon Lescaut,* the story of a woman who leaves her older lover to elope with a younger man. Three of his 12 operas—*La bohème* (1896), *Tosca* (1900), and *Madama Butterfly* (1904)—are still in the standard repertory of major opera houses around the world. His last opera, *Turandot,* is based on an exotic Oriental legend. Left unfinished at his death, it contains some of his most beautiful music.

Like many composers of his generation, Puccini was profoundly influenced by a literary movement known as *verismo* (realism). Though rooted in nationalism, this movement favored lower-class characters caught up in lust, greed, hatred, betrayal, or revenge. The central character of *Manon Lescaut,* for example, is a woman of questionable reputation. Though Puccini's view of women was not a flattering one, more than half of his operas are named after their heroines. Almost without exception they are slaves to an erotic attraction that brings them to ruin and death. And yet within this narrow range, Puccini managed to create some of the most memorable characters in opera.

In *Tosca,* one of Puccini's four verismo operas, a singer, Floria Tosca, trying to save the life of her imprisoned patriot lover, finds herself blackmailed by Scarpia, the corrupt chief of the Roman police. She agrees to meet with him for a sexual encounter, but when he arrives she murders him. Earlier, Scarpia had arranged to have a firing squad use real bullets in what was to have been the mock execution of her lover. Learning that her lover has been killed, Tosca leaps off a parapet to her death. When Verdi closed *Rigoletto* with the discovery of Gilda's body in a sack, the scene stunned mid-nineteenth-century audiences. In verismo operas such as *Tosca,* however, grisly endings had become common.

Many other composers of the late Romantic operas show the influence of verismo. The most celebrated example is Ruggero Leoncavallo's *I Pagliacci* (*The Players,* 1892), in which Canio, the leader of a traveling circus, discovers that his wife is having an affair with another member of the troupe, whom Canio (playing the part of a clown) murders in the course of a live performance. In Georges Bizet's *Carmen* (1874), the heroine, who works in a cigarette factory, deserts her staid corporal, José, for a dashing bullfighter, Escamillo. In the last act, José, driven by jealousy, murders Carmen outside the amphitheater where Escamillo is about to perform.

Both Canio and Carmen shocked and titillated their audiences, though they are hardly sympathetic characters. Clearly verismo struck a responsive chord in the society of the time. It is not surprising that the first tabloid newspapers (the kind available today at supermarket checkout counters) appeared toward the end of the nineteenth century. At another level, by focusing on the underside of life, verismo drew attention to the social ills—poverty, crime, unemployment—that came in the wake of urbanization and industrialization.

## Puccini: Love Duet from Act I of *La bohème* (1896)

Puccini's sentimental melodrama, *La bohème (The Bohemian),* also reflects the influence of verismo. The characters of *La bohème* live in poverty in the heart of Paris. Mimi, the heroine, is a young woman suffering from consumption (tuberculosis) who ekes out a living by embroidering artificial flowers. The term *bohemian* was used to describe people, often artists, who had rejected bourgeois society and its materialistic goals. The cast includes a painter, a playwright, a musician, and a philosopher, all of them sympathetic characters who treat their poverty with lightness and humor.

Act I opens on Christmas Eve. The playwright Rodolfo cheerfully tosses his latest manuscript into the stove to warm their bitter-cold apartment. When the landlord Benoit marches in and demands his back rent, the artists goad him into admitting a harmless interest in other women and then throw him out in mock indignation. After Rodolfo's companions head downstairs, bound for Café Momus, Rodolfo hears a timid voice on the landing. Mimi enters, asking him to help her relight her candle. Rodolfo notices Mimi's fragile beauty. She leaves after a moment but returns almost immediately in search of her room key. Her candle blows out once again. Rodolfo slyly extinguishes his own candle and hides her key. He entreats her to tell him who she is, and she answers in a tender, melodious aria, *"Mi chiamano Mimi"* ("They call me Mimi").

By the time Mimi finishes, Rodolfo has decided that he is in love with her, though they have met only a few minutes before. When his friends, in a kind of ensemble recitative, shout from below, he urges them to go on ahead and save a place for two. Turning to Mimi, he declares his love. In the duet that follows (where Listening Guide 48 begins), Mimi professes her love for him. For the central action of the entire opera to spring from this casual encounter may stretch our credulity, but Puccini's music succeeds in making their love altogether believable.

Puccini uses recurrent motives to represent certain characters; for example, he uses the lively orchestral rhythm that accompanies the Bohemians' shouts from below to represent them throughout the opera:

But most of the time he proceeds with a succession of fluid melodies that build like a wave to a crest. The duet divides into three sections, the first and last melodic in character, the second declamatory. The first section ends in a clear cadence. In the second section, Rodolfo kisses Mimi, who protests halfheartedly. Their banter carries certain sexual undertones: Rodolfo suggests that it might be more pleasant if they stayed indoors and then asks what will happen when they return from the café. In the third section, which functions as a coda, Rodolfo holds out his arm to Mimi and, singing praises of love, they exit downstairs (and offstage) with Mimi holding a *pianissimo* high C (which many sopranos manage only at ear-splitting volume).

The melody of the first section moves in Puccini's typically broad, cumulative fashion. The orchestra introduces the melody, and then Rodolfo and Mimi take it up in the second phrase. The singers and the orchestra double (actually, quadruple) the melody, giving it an intense vibrancy known as "violinata":

# Listening Guide 48

## PUCCINI: Love duet from Act I
## of *La bohème (The Bohemian)*

CD 5, TRACK 10
TAPE 5B, TRACK 2
DURATION: 3:57

*Although the three sections differ in character, they blend smoothly together. Rather than placing the climax at the end, Puccini places it in the first section, with the second and third sections gently echoing the lovers' passion.*

*Form: Three sections*

| TEXT | TIME | LOCATION / MUSIC |
|---|---|---|
| **1** | **0:00** | **Section 1.** Melody in the orchestra, anticipating voices. |
| RODOLFO:<br>*O soave fanciulla . . .* O lovely girl . . . | 0:03 | Lyrical but flexible line. |
| MARCELLO *[from below]:*<br>*Trovò la poesia!*<br>He's found his poetry! | 0:05 | |
| RODOLFO:<br>*. . . o dolce viso di mite circonfuso alba lunar,*<br>. . . oh sweet face filled with the light of the rising moon, | | Swirling figures in the strings suggest the rising moon. |
| *in te ravviso il sogno ch'io vorrei sempre sognar!*<br>in you I see the dream that I would dream forever! | 0:20 | Builds steadily in volume and intensity. |
| **2** MIMI:<br>*Ah! tu sol comandi, amor!*<br>O, love alone shall command me! | 0:37 | Climax, both together, doubled by orchestra, *fortissimo*. |
| RODOLFO:<br>*Fremon già nell'anima le dolcezze estreme.*<br>Already passion sets my soul afire. | | |
| RODOLFO:<br>*Fremon già nell'anima le dolcezze estreme.*<br>Already passion sets my soul afire. | 1:01 | After Rodolfo's entrance, both sing together. The hot-blooded passion of the preceding phrase recedes. |
| *Nel bacio freme amor!*<br>Love quivers in a kiss! | | |
| *[Rodolfo tries to kiss Mimi.]* | | |
| MIMI:<br>*Oh! Come dolci scendono le sue lusinghe al core.*<br>O, how sweet his flattery sounds to my heart. | | |
| *Ah! tu sol commandi, amor!*<br>O, love alone shall command me! | | |

*continued*

| TEXT | TIME | LOCATION / MUSIC |
|------|------|------------------|
| **3** MIMI:<br>*No, per pietà!* No, please!<br>RODOLFO:<br>*Sei mia!* Be mine!<br>MIMI:<br>*V'aspettan gli amici.* Your friends are waiting for you.<br>RODOLFO:<br>*Già mi mandi via?* You send me away so soon? | **1:40** | **Section 2.** Declamatory lines sung over continuous, lush, widely spaced chords in the orchestra. |
| MIMI:<br>*Vorrei dir . . . ma non oso . . .*<br>I want to say . . . but I dare not . . .<br>RODOLFO:<br>*Di'.* Go on. | 1:55 | |
| MIMI:<br>*Se venissi con voi?* Might I come with you?<br>RODOLFO:<br>*Che? Mimi! Sarebbe così dolce restar qui.*<br>But? Mimi! It would be lovely to stay here.<br><br>*C'è freddo fuori.* It's cold outside. | 2:04 | Coquettishly. Orchestra halts momentarily. Melodic snatches in the clarinet and oboe. |
| MIMI:<br>*Vi starò vicina!* I shall be near you! | 2:29 | Tender and lyrical. |
| RODOLFO:<br>*E al ritorno?* And when we return? | 2:41 | Almost spoken. |
| MIMI:<br>*Curioso!* Wait and see! | | |
| **4** RODOLFO:<br>*Dammi il braccio, mia piccina.*<br>Give me your arm, my precious one.<br>MIMI:<br>*Obbedisco, signor!* I obey, sir! | **2:48** | **Section 3.** Lyrical passage in which a single melodic line is divided between the two characters. |
| RODOLFO:<br>*Che m'ami di'.* Say that you love me.<br>MIMI:<br>*Io t'amo!* I love you! | 3:00 | |
| [Orchestra] | 3:13 | Tender interlude in strings, flute, and harp. |
| BOTH:<br>*Amor! Amor! Amor!* Love! Love! Love! | 3:26 | The lovers sing a final soaring cadence while walking off-stage and the orchestra dies away. |

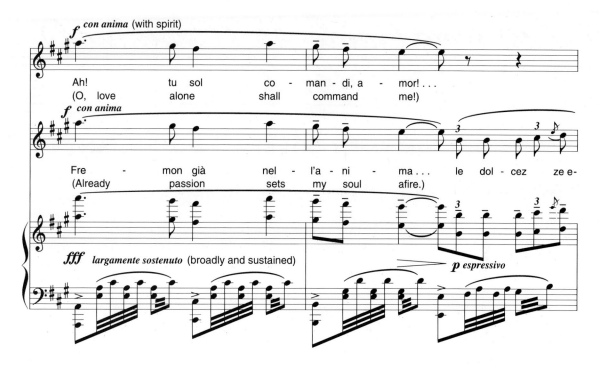

Later in the opera, Rodolfo decides that he cannot cope with Mimi's illness and he leaves her. He returns only as she lies dying. Mimi passively accepts Rodolfo's behavior and dies in his arms. There is an undeniable shallowness and sentimentality to the actions of the characters in *La bohème*, but the urgency and sincerity of Puccini's music compensate for the dramatic shortcomings.

# Chapter 23

## ROMANTIC OPERA IN GERMANY

After the death of Mozart in 1791, German opera languished for several years. Then the German composer Carl Maria von Weber (1786–1826) burst onto the scene with *Der Freischütz* (literally, "The Free Shot," of a magic bullet), whose Berlin premiere in 1821 created a sensation. Weber's father founded and operated a theater company that moved about like a traveling circus. Surrounded by the scenery and props, Weber developed a love of stage drama that was to persist throughout his life.

In his early twenties Weber had run across the story of Max, a young hunter who, fearful that he will fail a marksmanship test that will win him the hand of his fiancée, Agathe, sells his soul to the "black huntsman" (Samiel) in return for seven magic bullets. Max's scheme is discovered, and only through Agathe's selflessness and the intercession of a munificent prince is he redeemed. The supernatural elements in this story appealed strongly to Weber, though it was another 10 years before he transformed the story into an opera.

In its external form, *Der Freischütz* is a *Singspiel* in the Classical manner of Mozart's *The Abduction from the Seraglio* and *The Magic Flute*. But to that form Weber brought a blend of elements from Italian, French, and German operas. Although there are recitative/aria scenes similar in structure to those used by Mozart, Weber handles them with more flexibility. As Schubert had done in the *Lied*, Weber enriched the harmonic vocabulary of Viennese Classicism.

The most remarkable example of Weber's innovations is the scene that concludes the second act of *Der Freischütz*. The scene takes place in the wolf's glen, where the magic bullets are cast (Figure 23.1). Caspar, a comrade of Max's who is already in Samiel's power, has lured Max to the frightful glen in the hope of postponing his own demise, which is scheduled for the very next day. He calls anxiously for Samiel, who steps forth from the craggy cliffs and, rather than singing, sneers and shouts his way through his lines.

Throughout the scene a chorus of invisible spirits around the stage joins forces with strings playing tremolo figures to create an atmosphere of eeriness. From time to time the spirits, like Samiel, speak freely over the music, in a technique known as *melodrama*. (Beethoven had employed melodrama briefly in his opera *Fidelio*, but Weber's use is far more extensive.)

Each time a bullet is cast (marked by Samiel's chilling cry of each number, followed by an eerie echo), the orchestra introduces a striking new musical figure

FIGURE 23.1 Weber's *Der Freischütz* was enormously popular—even in Vienna, where censors eliminated Samiel, reset the story in the Middle Ages, and substituted crossbows for rifles. In a letter to his wife, Weber described a performance he attended: "There were not two passages played at the correct speed. . . . The choruses were excellent. The scenery very pretty, but most of it quite beside the point. The most elementary questions of stagecraft were ignored. . . . I don't understand how people can have liked the opera."

while wild beasts and birds rush about the stage. The sense of key is undermined by the almost constant presence of diminished-seventh harmonies that create an air of ambiguity. By the time we reach the seventh bullet, the terror felt by both Max and the audience is almost overwhelming. A torrential downpour, thunder and lightning, the shaking earth, an avalanche of rocks, trees being ripped from their roots—all remind us of the power of the evil to which Max has succumbed. The scene ends as abruptly as it began, leaving both the participants and the audience drained. Weber once commented, "Half the opera takes place in darkness. . . . These dark forms . . . are . . . reinforced by the musical forms."

When *Der Freischütz* was published, Weber called it a "Romantic opera." At the time of his death in London in 1826, no one seemed ready to carry his dramatic and stylistic innovations further. There was, however, a young musician growing up in Leipzig who would carry Weber's reforms to undreamed-of lengths. His name was Richard Wagner.

# RICHARD WAGNER (1813–1883)

Richard Wagner

For the generation of musicians who followed him, Richard Wagner represented the culmination of Romanticism. He carried to new levels the Romantic passion for bringing different art forms together, including music, drama, poetry, set design, staging, and architecture. This synthesis was enriched by Wagner's broad knowledge of literature and philosophy. Wagner's musical style, especially his treatment of themes and harmony, exerted a powerful influence on his contemporaries.

The youngest of nine children, Wagner was the son of a Leipzig police administrator whose family had included musicians since the seventeenth century. Wagner's father died when Wagner was six months old; less than a year later his mother married Ludwig Geyer, a portrait painter, actor, and poet, whose family also included musicians. Their marriage gave rise to a rumor that Geyer was Wagner's real father (a rumor Wagner denied).

Johanna Wagner and her new husband soon moved to Dresden, where from time to time the young Wagner visited the home of Carl Maria von Weber. In later years, Wagner was to credit Weber with "arousing a passion for music in me." At the age of 17, Wagner entered the *Gymnasium** in Leipzig, where he neglected his other studies to concentrate on the plays of Shakespeare, Goethe, and Schiller and the music of Mozart, Beethoven, and Weber. Before he was 20 Wagner had written both the libretto and the score of his first opera, *Die Hochzeit* (*The Wedding*), and he soon decided that he would always create his own librettos.

Like many other composers at the time, Wagner's driving ambition was to have an opera produced in Paris. He visited Meyerbeer in Boulogne, who promised to introduce him to the right people, but when Wagner arrived in Paris in 1839 he discovered that no introductions had been arranged. For a time he supported his family by making piano arrangements of operas and writing articles for popular journals. Despite his efforts, he spent a brief spell in debtor's prison. More determined than ever, in 1841 he completed *The Flying Dutchman,* based on the legend of a sea captain (Captain Vanderecken) who has been condemned to roam the seas until he finds a faithful woman. Happily for the struggling Wagner, the premiere of this opera in Dresden in 1842 was a great success.

Emboldened, Wagner embarked on two ambitious new projects tied even more closely to his interest in German/Norse legend and mythology. *Tannhäuser* (1842–1845) combines an ancient German legend about a Christian minstrel (Tannhäuser) who is seduced by the pagan goddess Venus, with a legendary account of a famous singing contest on the Wartburg (a German mountain). Its Dresden premiere in 1845 met with a mixed reception.

*Lohengrin* (1845–1848) is based on a medieval epic about a Knight of the

*In Germany and Austria the *Gymnasium* is roughly equivalent to the American high school, although a student who graduates from *Gymnasium* at age 18 has the equivalent of about two years of university study in the United States.

*Part Three   The Age of Tonality (1690–1910)*

Holy Grail* (Lohengrin) who intervenes in a royal feud in medieval Flanders. In the opera, Lohengrin's miraculous powers are symbolized by his entrance in a boat pulled by a magnificent white swan, a departure from reality that would have been unthinkable to Verdi. Lohengrin defends a woman who has been unjustly accused of murder and later marries her (in a ceremony that includes the familiar Wedding March). He makes it a condition that she never ask his real name. Unable to suppress her curiosity, she violates the condition, and Lohengrin leaves her. In Wagner's words:

> Lohengrin sought a woman who would believe in him, who would not ask who he was or from where he came, but would love him just as he was. . . . Doubt and jealousy prove to him that he is not understood but only adored, and tear from him the confession of his divinity, with which he returns, destroyed, into his isolation.

The theme of a faithful, utterly trusting woman, introduced in *The Flying Dutchman*, reappears in many of Wagner's later operas. Although Wagner was moving further and further from the kind of grand opera written by Meyerbeer, he still referred to these works as "Romantic operas."

In May 1849 a revolution broke out in Dresden. The authorities suspected that Wagner was one of its instigators, and he fled (with Liszt's help) to Switzerland to escape almost certain execution. While in exile he began to develop a mammoth project he had sketched out a few months before. What started as a single poem, *Siegfrieds Tod* (*Siegfried's Death*), was to culminate more than a quarter of a century later in the four-part *The Ring of the Nibelungen*. Wagner referred to the works that make up *The Ring* as "music dramas" to emphasize the equal importance of the dramatic and musical elements (but they are still called operas). *The Ring* is a vast, sprawling narrative based on a Norse myth in which the Rhinegold (a golden treasure in the Rhine River mined by dwarfs known as Nibelungen) brings misfortune to all who seek to possess it. According to some, *The Ring* is an indictment of industrialization and the corruption of modern civilization.

To help shape *The Ring's* 16 hours of music into a coherent whole, Wagner used a technique he had experimented with in *Lohengrin*. He associates a brief, open-ended motive in the orchestra with a particular character, object, event, or emotion in the drama. Wagner's disciples called such a motive a *Leitmotiv* ("leading motive," commonly rendered in English as *leitmotif*), a term that is still used. A given leitmotif may occur many times over the course of an opera, altered or transformed to suit the context. The names given to the leitmotifs (Magic Potion, Painful Longing, and so forth) by Wagner's disciples sound stilted today, but they serve as useful references.

Wagner builds these leitmotifs out of a rich array of chromatic harmonies that are more dissonant than those his contemporaries commonly used. Often he

---

*In medieval legends about King Arthur, Parsifal, and Galahad, the Holy Grail was the cup (or chalice) used by Jesus at the Last Supper. Its whereabouts would be revealed only to a pure knight free of all trace of sin or worldly ambition.

places a dissonance prominently on a strong beat and then resolves it to a consonance on a weak beat, in a pattern called an *appoggiatura*. Wagner's harmonic inventiveness exercised an almost mesmerizing (and sometimes suffocating) effect on composers later in the century.

Over this orchestral fabric of leitmotifs, Wagner provided the singers with a flexible, declamatory vocal line that he referred to (modestly) as *"unendliche Melodie"* ("unending melody"). Even more boldly than Verdi, he ignored the traditional distinction between recitative and aria. Unlike Verdi, however, he rarely gave his audiences a march, dance, or chorus to compensate for the absence of set pieces. Moreover, most of Wagner's operas are relentlessly serious in tone; he wrote only one mature comic work, *Die Meistersinger von Nürnberg* (*The Master Singers of Nuremberg;* 1868), in which he used an account of a singing competition as a thinly disguised attack on contemporary music criticism.

Not surprisingly, many listeners complained that Wagner's music was too radical. Wagner responded by publishing lengthy justifications of his efforts to create an authentically German music drama, referring to his music as *Zukunftsmusik* ("music of the future"). In a volume of essays titled *Opera as Drama* (1851), he outlined his vision of a *Gesamtkunstwerk* ("complete artwork"), in which the music, words, costumes, scenery, and staging all contribute to a single unified approach. He wrote: "Absolute music can express only enjoyment or endless yearning; it lacks action, the moral will. [Beethoven's] Ninth Symphony is the redemption of music into drama." Ignoring the fact that Beethoven's music was mostly absolute music, Wagner seized on the last movement of the Ninth Symphony as evidence that for Beethoven too the supreme form of expression was music combined with words.

In the early 1860s, a 17-year-old crown prince who was soon to ascend the Bavarian throne as King Ludwig II read Wagner's poem for *The Ring*. When Ludwig became king a few years later, he offered Wagner a sizable sum of money to complete the work. As time passed, Wagner decided that *The Ring* should be staged only in a theater designed to his own specifications. He had heard of a theater in the small central German town of Bayreuth that he felt might meet his needs, and he decided to buy it. After trying without success to raise the funds from his supporters, he undertook a series of grueling concert tours to raise the money himself. Despite his best efforts, he was still short of what was needed. Coming to the rescue once again, King Ludwig gave Wagner the equivalent of more than a million dollars to construct a new theater.

One of Wagner's last works, *Parsifal*, also based on the Holy Grail legend, was first performed at Bayreuth. By this time Wagner had equipped the theater with a special stage and orchestra pit that conformed to his ideas of the proper setting for his music dramas (Figure 23.2).

Wagner's successes were hard won. He pursued his vision with relentless (and sometimes ruthless) determination, and in personal matters he could display insensitivity and even callousness. He once had an affair with Mathilde von Wesendonk, the wife of a wealthy industrialist who had lent Wagner a substantial amount of money and who had put his summer house at Wagner's disposal. In the 1860s he entered into an affair with Cosima von Bülow, the daughter of

FIGURE 23.2 The orchestra pit at Bayreuth, set deep under the protruding stage. Wagner felt that, given its lofty subject, *Parsifal* needed "a stage to consecrate to it, and that can only be my remote Festival Theater at Bayreuth. *Parsifal* shall be given there and only there, to the end of time; it shall never be offered as an amusement to the audience of any other theater." Today *Parsifal* is staged around the world.

Franz Liszt and the wife of a leading conductor who had defended Wagner's cause. After bearing Wagner several children, Cosima finally divorced von Bülow and married Wagner.

Although Wagner's reputation as a composer has declined from the exalted level it had achieved by 1900, he is still regarded as one of the most original and influential composers of the nineteenth century.

### ✳Wagner: Love Duet from Act II of *Tristan und Isolde* (1856–1859)

With *Tristan und Isolde,* Wagner made a decisive break with the grand operas of Meyerbeer and the early operas of Verdi. For many listeners, this work is the most powerful and compelling of Wagner's music dramas. The story is based on a German adaptation of an Irish medieval legend. Sir Tristan, a young knight, is sent to Ireland to bring Isolde the Fair back to Cornwall as a bride for his uncle, King Mark. Earlier, Tristan had killed the Irish ruler, King Morold, to whom Isolde was betrothed; Tristan had been wounded in battle by Morold, and Isolde had nursed him back to health. When Tristan arrives to take her from her homeland, she recognizes him and resists his efforts to carry her off. On the boat returning to Cornwall, Isolde instructs Brangäne, her lady-in-waiting, to prepare a death potion for them both, which Isolde tells Tristan is a drink of atonement for the ill feelings between them. Instead, Brangäne serves them both a love potion that arouses an overwhelming passion between them. In Act II, after they have arrived in Cornwall, they meet at night outside King Mark's castle and sing rhapsodically of their love.

As dawn begins to break, King Mark and his hunting party arrive on the scene. Stunned by what he sees, Mark asks Tristan to explain his betrayal. Tristan's failure to answer enrages Melot, one of Mark's men, who wounds Tristan in a brief sword fight. Act III takes place at Tristan's castle on the island of Brittany, where his friend Kurnewal has taken the dying Tristan. Tristan hallucinates that Isolde has returned to him. Soon she arrives by ship and rushes to his side. Tristan dies and Isolde, grief-stricken, joins him in death.

Modern audiences may find it hard to accept the idea of love potions or to believe that a mortally wounded tenor can go on singing for almost an hour and that a lovesick woman can sing herself to death. But the drama of *Tristan und Isolde* operates at a level beyond the events it describes. It deals with the irrational forces of passion and yearning, symbolized by Brangäne's love potion. It is more than just a tragic love story. Almost from the beginning we sense that the intense passion of Tristan and Isolde will lead to self-annihilation. At the climax of their love duet in Act II (Figure 23.3), Tristan sings:

You Tristan, I Isolde, no more Tristan!

Isolde responds:

You Isolde, I Tristan, no more Isolde!

This surrender of self-identity is ultimately expressed in death. While the opera is not a love story per se, it is a powerful embodiment of romantic love.

The musical language Wagner chose for this drama is ideally suited to the theme. Endless longing is expressed in "endless melody." Before *Tristan und Isolde*, longer compositions (including operas) had been organized by phrases, with periodic cadences on the tonic chord of the home key (or the temporary home key). From Haydn to Schumann the musical distance between tonic cadences had grown steadily greater, but in *Tristan* Wagner extended it to unprecedented lengths. With the help of rich harmonies, he creates time after time the expectation of a cadence and then, at the last minute, turns it in a different direction, invariably intensifying it with an appoggiatura. Such a diverted cadence is called a *deceptive cadence.* Clearly, Wagner's goal was to overwhelm his audiences rather than just entertain them. Instead of proceeding in symmetrical blocks (like the banda music in *Rigoletto*), *Tristan* sweeps the listener along like a surfer riding the waves.

In the first scene of Act II, Brangäne, who gave the love potion to Tristan and Isolde in Act I, regrets her action and tries to temper Isolde's passion. But Isolde spurns Brangäne's efforts and orders her to extinguish the torch as a signal to Tristan. (Brangäne is too fearful and Isolde throws the torch to the ground herself.) When Tristan enters, they plunge headlong into a passionate dialogue:

TRISTAN: Isolde!

ISOLDE: Tristan! Beloved! Are you mine?

TRISTAN: Am I really holding you again?

ISOLDE: Can I embrace you?

TRISTAN: Can I believe it?

ISOLDE: At last! At last!

For the next 36 minutes the two dominate the stage while Brangäne watches nervously from a tower. In two nearly identical passages she warns that the protective night will soon pass—a poetic theme that dates back to medieval times.

Wagner divides their duet into three sections. The first section (of about 15 minutes) consists largely of impassioned exchanges, with the words tumbling out. In the transition from the first to the second section, Tristan sings of the night (a symbol of death as well as protection), gradually lowering the emotional level. An orchestral interlude (where Listening Guide 49 begins) separates the first and second sections. Tristan (following Wagner's detailed directions) "leads Isolde to a flowery bank, sinks before her on his knees, and rests his head on her arm." Later they both lie down, in which position they are expected to sing demanding music for 20 minutes.

The second section is built around a tender Love Duet leitmotif that Wagner had composed in 1857/1858 for a song titled "*Träume*" ("Dreams"—subtitled "Study for *Tristan and Isolde*"). The slow, irregular beat of the orchestral accompaniment gives the duet its dreamy quality:

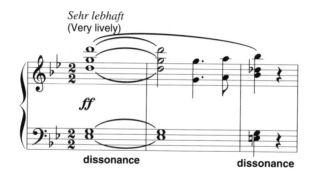

The love duet reaches a shattering climax with a powerful appoggiatura in the orchestra that repeats three times in rapid succession. As the lovers' passion mounts to near-frenzy, Brangäne's scream announces the approach of King Mark and his hunting party.

The love duet reveals Wagner's extraordinary emotional range and sense of dramatic pacing. There is almost no action. And yet Wagner manages to lift the lovers, and the audience, to higher and higher levels of emotional intensity. When King Mark and his hunting party burst on the scene, we are almost as emotionally wrung out as Tristan and Isolde.

# *Listening Guide 49*

## WAGNER: Love Duet from Act II of *Tristan und Isolde*

CD 5, TRACK 11
TAPE 5B, TRACK 3
DURATION: 21:20

*The two major sections (II and III) are shown in boldface type, the subsidiary leitmotifs in ordinary type. Wagner uses leitmotifs as flexible musical units to express a vast range of emotional shadings, expressed in waves of sound.*

*Form: Sectional, based on leitmotifs*

| TEXT | TIME | LEITMOTIF / COMMENTS |
|---|---|---|
| **1** [Orchestra] | **0:00** | Soft chords serve as an introduction. |
| **2** BOTH: | | |
| *O sink hernieder, Nacht der Liebe,*<br>O sink down upon us, night of love, | **0:15** | **II. Love duet.** Sighing melody built around a series of expressive appoggiaturas. |
| *gib Vergessen, dass ich lebe;*<br>make me forget that I live; | | |
| *nimm mich auf in deinen Schoss,*<br>hold me to your bosom, | | |
| *löse von der Welt mich los!*<br>free me from the world! | | |
| TRISTAN:<br>*Verloschen nun die letzte Leuchte . . .*<br>Extinguished now is the last glimmer . . . | 1:12 | The line builds slowly but steadily, rising to a climactic appoggiatura on *"welt-[erlösend]."* |
| ISOLDE:<br>*was wir dachten, was uns deuchte . . .*<br>of what we thought, of what we dreamed . . . | 1:23 | |
| TRISTAN:<br>*all Gedenken . . . all memories . . .* | 1:34 | |
| ISOLDE:<br>*all Gemahnen . . . all recollection . . .* | 1:40 | |
| BOTH:<br>*heil'ger Dämm'rung hehres Ahnen*<br>The glorious foretaste of holy twilight | 1:46 | |
| *löscht des Wähnens Graus welterlösend aus.*<br>extinguishes needless fears, as the world fades away. | | |

*continued*

| TEXT | TIME | LEITMOTIF / COMMENTS |
|------|------|----------------------|
| **3** ISOLDE:<br>*Barg im Busen uns sich die Sonne,*<br>The sun lies hidden in our breasts,<br><br>*leuchten lachend Sterne der Wonne.*<br>stars of bliss shine smiling. | **2:23** | Begins softly and rises again to an appoggiatura on *"Wonne"* ("bliss"). |
| TRISTAN:<br>*Von deinem Zauber sanft umsponnen,*<br>Gently enfolded in your spell,<br><br>*vor deinen Augen süß zerronnen . . .*<br>sweetly melting before your eyes . . . | **2:41** | Mirrors Isolde's preceding line, rising to an appoggiatura on *"zerronnen"* ("melting"). |
| **4** ISOLDE:<br>*Herz an Herz dir, Mund an Mund . . .*<br>heart to heart, lip to lip . . .<br><br>TRISTAN:<br>*eines Atems ein'ger Bund . . .*<br>bound together in one breath . . .<br><br>BOTH:<br>*Bricht mein Blick sich wonn'erblindet,*<br>my eyes grow dim, blinded with ecstasy,<br><br>*erbleichet die Welt mit ihrem Blenden . . .*<br>the world and its vanities fade away . . . | **3:01** | Peaceful Love leitmotif foreshadowed in a series of alternating phrases between the two lovers. |
| **5** ISOLDE:<br>*die uns der Tag trügend erhellt . . .*<br>the world which deceitful day illuminates for us . . .<br><br>TRISTAN:<br>*zu täuschendem Wahn entgegengestellt . . .*<br>to confront cheating illusion . . .<br><br>BOTH:<br>*selbst dann bin ich die Welt:*<br>I myself am therefore the world: | **3:31** | Painful Longing leitmotif in the oboe (opens Act II and used prominently throughout).<br><br>The phrase reaches its climax on *"Welt"* ("world"). |
| **6** *Wonne-hehrstes Weben, Liebe-heiligstes Leben.*<br>supremely blissful being, love-sanctified life, | **3:52** | Love Potion leitmotif (ascending chromatic scale from the Prelude to Act I) in the orchestra and Isolde. |
| **7** *Nie-wieder-Erwachens*<br>Never more awakening to<br><br>*wahnlos hold bewusster Wunsch.*<br>delusionless desire. | **4:23** | Love Duet theme recast as a coda. The lovers' union represented by their singing together. |

| TEXT | TIME | LEITMOTIF / COMMENTS |
|---|---|---|

**8** BRANGÄNE:
*Einsam wachend in der Nacht,*  
Watching alone in the night,  
**4:47**  Long, slow melodic line spun out over the sighing appoggiaturas in the clarinet.

*wem der Traum der Liebe lacht,*  
you to whom love's dream laughs,

*hab' der Einen Ruf in acht,*  
heed the cry of one  
5:39  Shifts to the minor mode. Countervoices in the violin.

*die den Schläfern Schlimmes ahnt*  
who foresees ill for the sleepers

*bange zum Erwachen mahnt.*  
and anxiously bids them awake.

*Habet acht! Habet acht! Bald entweicht die Nacht.*  
Take care! Take care! Soon the night will pass.  
6:38  Soars to a climax on the repeat of *"Habet acht!"* ("Take care!").

**9** [Orchestra]  
**7:19**  Peaceful Love leitmotif, soft and tender in the strings.

ISOLDE:
*Lausch', Geliebter!* Hark, beloved!  
7:45  Continuity is in the orchestra.

TRISTAN:
*Lass mich sterben!* Let me die!

ISOLDE:
*Neid'sche Wache!* Envious lookout!  
8:16  The leitmotif is developed and expanded in the orchestra, while the lovers declaim their lines freely.

TRISTAN:
*Nie erwachen!* Never awakening!

ISOLDE:
*Doch der Tag muss Tristan wecken?*  
But must not the day arouse Tristan?  
8:30

TRISTAN:
*Lass den Tag dem Tode weichen!*  
Let day give way to death!  
8:39

ISOLDE:
*Tag und Tod mit gleichen Streichen*  
Day and death, with equal force

*sollten unsre Lieb' erreichen?*  
would they not attack our love?

**10** TRISTAN:
*Unsre Liebe? Tristans Liebe?*  
Our love? Tristan's love?  
**9:08**  Tristan's longest solo speech of the scene. *continued*

| TEXT | TIME | LEITMOTIF / COMMENTS |
|------|------|----------------------|
| *Dein' und mein', Isoldes Liebe?* <br> Yours and mine, Isolde's love? | | |
| *Welches Todes Streichen könnte je sie weichen?* <br> What death blow could ever make it give way? | | |
| *Stünd' er vor mir, der mächt'ge Tod* <br> Were mighty death to stand before me | | |
| *wie er mir Leib und Leben bedroht',* <br> however he threatened my life, | | |
| *die ich so willig der Liebe lasse,* <br> which I would willingly yield to love, | | |
| *wie wäre seinen Streichen die Liebe selbst zu erreichen?* <br> how could his blows affect love itself? | **10:06** | The head of the Peaceful Love leitmotif repeats. |
| *Stürb' ich nun ihr, der so gern ich sterbe,* <br> Were I now to die, so gladly for love, | | |
| *wie könnte die Liebe mit mir sterben,* <br> how could love die with me, | | |
| *die ewig lebende mit mir enden?* <br> the ever-living perish with me? | | |
| *Doch stürbe nie seine Liebe,* <br> So, if his love could never die, | 10:44 | To simple accompaniment, with appoggiatura on first *"Liebe"* ("love"). |
| *wie stürbe dann Tristan seiner Liebe?* <br> how could Tristan die in his love? | | |
| 11 [Orchestra] | **11:29** | Peaceful Love leitmotif. Brief interlude. |
| ISOLDE: <br> *Doch unsre Liebe,* <br> Yet our love, | 11:34 | Isolde's response to Tristan's speech. Development of the Peaceful Love leitmotif in the orchestra. |
| *heisst sie nicht Tristan und Isolde?* <br> is it not called Tristan and Isolde? | | |
| *Dies süsse Wörtlein: und,* <br> This sweet little word "and," | | |
| *was es bindet, der Liebe Bund,* <br> binding as it does love's tie, | | |
| *wenn Tristan stürb', zerstört' es nicht der Tod?* <br> would not love destroy it if Tristan were to die? | | |

| TEXT | TIME | LEITMOTIF / COMMENTS |
|------|------|----------------------|
| TRISTAN:<br>*Was stürbe dem Tod, als was uns stört,*<br>What could death destroy but what hinders us,<br><br>*was Tristan wehrt, Isolde immer zu lieben,*<br>that hinders Tristan from loving Isolde<br><br>*ewig ihn nur zu leben?*<br>forever, and forever living but for her? | 12:31 | 4-note motive weaves its way through the strings. |
| ISOLDE:<br>*Doch dieses Wörtlein: "und," wär's zerstört,*<br>Yet this little word "and"—how might it be destroyed<br><br>*wie anders als mit Isoldes eignem Leben*<br>other than with Isolde's own life,<br><br>*wär' Tristan der Tod gegeben?*<br>if death were to be given Tristan? | | |
| [Orchestra] | 13:23 | Orchestral interlude. Soft string tremolos, melody in horn, then winds. |
| STANZA 1 | | |
| **12** TRISTAN:<br>*So starben wir, um ungetrennt,*<br>Thus we might die, undivided,<br><br>*ewig einig ohne End',*<br>one forever without end,<br><br>*ohn' Erwachen, ohn' Erbangen,*<br>never waking, never fearing,<br><br>*namenlos in Lieb' umfangen,*<br>embraced namelessly in love,<br><br>*ganz uns selbst gegeben, der Liebe nur zu leben!*<br>given entirely to each other, living only in our love! | **13:43** | **III. Parting song.** Leitmotif based on chromatic rising sequence. |
| STANZA 2 | | |
| ISOLDE:<br>*So stürben wir, um ungetrennt . . .*<br>Thus we might die, undivided . . .<br><br>TRISTAN:<br>*ewig einig ohne End'* . . . forever united without end . . . | **14:35** | Second stanza, in alternating voices between the lovers. Climbs steadily toward greater and greater climax.<br><br>*continued* |

| TEXT | TIME | LEITMOTIF / COMMENTS |
|---|---|---|

**ISOLDE:**
*ohn' Erwachen* . . . never waking . . .

**TRISTAN:**
*ohn' Erbangen* . . . never fearing . . .

**BOTH:**
*namenlos in Lieb' umfangen*
embraced namelessly in love,

*ganz uns selbst gegeben,*
given entirely to each other,

*der Liebe nur zu leben!* living only in our love!

**13** BRANGÄNE:
*Habet acht! Habet acht!* Take care! Take care!    15:25    Identical to the soaring last line of her earlier speech.

*Schon weicht dem Tag die Nacht.*
Night is already giving way to day.

**14** [Orchestra]    **16:05**    Peaceful Love leitmotif in the strings.

TRISTAN:
*Soll ich lauschen?* Must I listen?    16:12    The continuity remains in the orchestra.

ISOLDE:
*Lass mich sterben!* Let me die!

TRISTAN:
*Muss ich wachen?* Must I awake?    16:36

ISOLDE:
*Nie erwachen!* Never awaken!

TRISTAN:
*Soll der Tag noch Tristan wecken?*    16:51
Must day yet rouse Tristan?

ISOLDE:
*Lass den Tag dem Tode weichen!*    17:00
Let day give way to death!

TRISTAN:
*Des Tages Dräuen nun trotzen wir so?*    17:12
Shall we then defy day's threats?

ISOLDE:
*Seinem trug ewig zu fliehn.*    17:18    Foreshadowing of the impending climax.
To forever escape its treachery.

| TEXT | TIME | LEITMOTIF / COMMENTS |
|------|------|----------------------|
| TRISTAN:<br>*Sein dämmernder Schein verscheuchte uns nie?*<br>Its dawning light never to banish us? | | In swirling strings, the orchestra grows increasir.gly agitated. |
| ISOLDE:<br>*Ewig währ' uns die Nacht!*<br>For us may night last forever! | | |
| [Orchestra] | | Surging with full orchestra. |
| **15** BOTH:<br>*O ew'ge Nacht, süße Nacht!*<br>O endless night, sweet night! | **17:47** | "Lively, with rising energy." The orchestral texture continues to grow more complex. |
| *Hehr erhabne Liebesnacht!*<br>Glorious, exalted night of love! | | |
| *Wen du umfangen, wem du gelacht,*<br>Those whom you embrace, on whom you smile, | | |
| *wie wär' ohne Bangen aus dir er je erwacht?*<br>how could they ever awaken from you without dismay? | | |
| *Nun banne das Bangen, holder Tod,*<br>Now banish fear, sweet death, | | |
| *sehnend verlangter Liebestod!*<br>ardently desired death in love! | 18:25 | |
| *In deinen Armen, dir geweiht,*<br>In your arms, devoted to you, | | |
| *ur-heilig Erwarmen, von Erwachsens Not befreit!*<br>ever sacred glow, freed from the need to wake! | | |
| **16** TRISTAN:<br>*Wie sie fassen, wie sie lassen, diese Wonne . . .*<br>How to grasp, how to relinquish, this bliss . . . | **18:50** | Parting Song leitmotif, sung with more urgency. |
| BOTH:<br>*fern der Sonne, fern der Tage Trennungsklage!*<br>far from the sun, far from the day's lamentations at parting! | 18:59 | |
| ISOLDE:<br>*Ohne Wähnen . . . Without delusions . . .* | 19:08 | A new wave of sound. Parting Song and Love Declaration leitmotifs developed simultaneously.<br>*continued* |

| TEXT | TIME | LEITMOTIF / COMMENTS |
|------|------|----------------------|

**TRISTAN:**
*sanftes Sehnen;* tender yearning;

**ISOLDE:**
*ohne Bangen* . . . without fears . . .

**TRISTAN:**
*süss Verlangen. Ohne Wehen* . . .
sweet longing. Without grieving . . .

**BOTH:**
*hehr Vergehen.* Exalted oblivion.

**ISOLDE:**
*Ohne Schmachten* . . . Without languishing . . .

**BOTH:**
*hold Umnachten.* enfolded in sweet darkness.

**TRISTAN:**
*Ohne Meiden* . . . Without separating . . .

**17** **BOTH:**
*ohne Scheiden, traut allein, ewig heim,*      **19:41**     Parting Song leitmotif. Begins another
without parting, dearly alone, ever at one,               wave of sound. Voices overlap to create a
                                                      continuous melody.
*in ungemessnen Räumen übersel'ges Träumen!*
in unbounded space, most blessed of dreams!

**TRISTAN:**
*Tristan du, ich Isolde, nicht mehr Tristan!*
You Tristan, I Isolde, no more Tristan!

**ISOLDE:**
*Du Isolde, Tristan ich, nicht mehr Isolde!*
You Isolde, I Tristan, no more Isolde!

**BOTH:**
*Ohne Nennen, ohne Trennen,*                 20:16
No names, no parting;

*neu' Erkennen, neu' Entbrennen;*
newly perceived, newly kindled;

**18** *endlos, ewig, einbewusst;*            **20:32**     Series of frenzied climaxes built on
ever, unendingly, one consciousness;               repeating orchestral appoggiaturas.

*heiss erglühter Brust höchste Liebeslust!*     21:00      A final climb to a cathartic climax.
supreme joy of love glowing in our breast!

                                                   21:14      Overpowering climax, King Mark bursts
                                                      on the scene.

## THE MUSIC CRITIC

Today many small-town newspapers have writers who report on the arts in weekly or daily columns. Newspapers and magazines with large circulations usually have a staff writer whose only job is to report on musical events. (This is also true of some campus newspapers.) Major papers, such as the *New York Times* and the *Chicago Sun-Times,* have music critics who specialize in art music, popular music, or jazz, and magazines like *Rolling Stone* devote much of their space to music (see Figure 23.4). We expect all these critics to tell us what music was played, who played it, and how many people were in attendance. We also expect them to tell us whether the music was any good and how well it was played. (The same holds true for record reviews, which are often more important to performers than are reviews of live concerts.) In other words, critics *evaluate* as well as *describe.*

FIGURE 23.4  From stereos to CDs: Since it began as a newspaper in San Francisco during the late 1960s, *Rolling Stone* has evolved with the changing musical world it covers. It remains one of the most serious popular forums for rock criticism.

Earlier ages were not without writers who commented on the aesthetic issues of their day. For example, during the early seventeenth century, Giovanni Battista Doni (1595–1647), a Florentine intellectual, published several treatises in which he advocated a revival of what he believed to be the musical practices of the ancient Greeks. But most of the issues discussed were of interest to only a small group of sophisticates. So long as the audience for music was essentially restricted to the aristocracy, there was little need for published criticism. Court composers received rapid feedback from their patrons, and probably talked to them regularly.

By the end of the eighteenth century, however, music-making had become more widespread, and several popular periodicals appeared. Although there was no true middle class as yet, there was a growing class of bankers and merchants who employed large staffs to run their enterprises. Those city folk, along with the hordes who were flocking into the cities, made up a substantial audience of music lovers and amateur performers eager to read about the latest compositions and forthcoming concerts.

One of the first successful music journals was the *Allgemeine musikalische Zeitung* (*General Music Newspaper,* Figure 23.5), which was founded in 1798 and continued to be published for half a century. It was owned by the music publishing house of Breitkopf & Härtel in Leipzig, which used the journal to promote sheet-music sales in its retail outlets. The *AMZ* maintained music correspondents in Vienna, Paris, Berlin, Milan, and other important cities throughout Europe, and it often published accounts of events within a few months. Today we get reports within hours, but in the early nineteenth century

FIGURE 23.5 In this famous issue of the *AMZ*, the critic and composer E.T.A. Hoffmann described music as "the most romantic of all the arts—indeed, one might contend, the only purely romantic art." He went on to cite Beethoven as the composer who had most penetrated music's "innermost being." That same month, Beethoven wrote to Breitkopf and Härtel, his publisher: "You, being more humane and cultivated than any other music publishers, should also make it your aim not merely to pay the artist a pittance, but to put him in a position where he can develop, in tranquility, what he has in him and what other people expect of him."

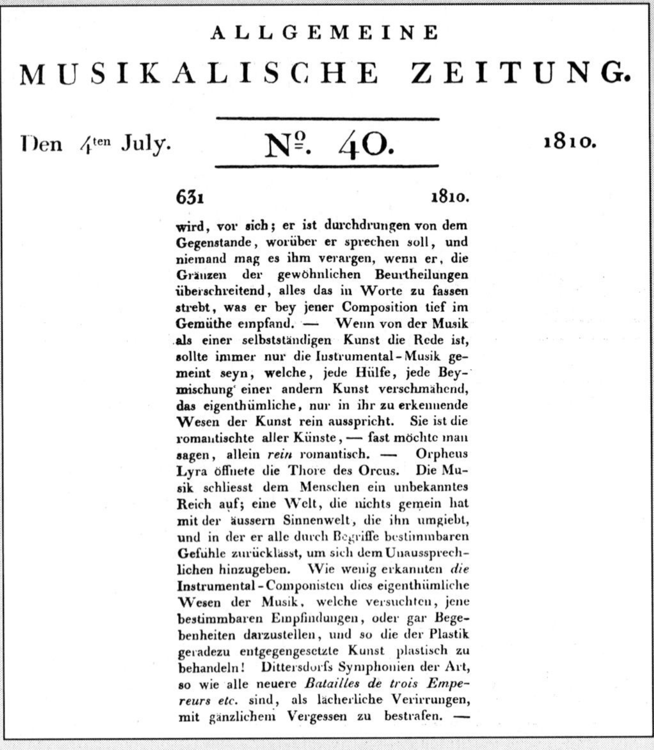

ALLGEMEINE

# MUSIKALISCHE ZEITUNG.

Den 4ten July.    N⁰. 40.    1810.

631    1810.

wird, vor sich; er ist durchdrungen von dem Gegenstande, worüber er sprechen soll, und niemand mag es ihm verargen, wenn er, die Gränzen der gewöhnlichen Beurtheilungen überschreitend, alles das in Worte zu fassen strebt, was er bey jener Composition tief im Gemüthe empfand. — Wenn von der Musik als einer selbstständigen Kunst die Rede ist, sollte immer nur die Instrumental-Musik gemeint seyn, welche, jede Hülfe, jede Beymischung einer andern Kunst verschmähend, das eigenthümliche, nur in ihr zu erkennende Wesen der Kunst rein ausspricht. Sie ist die romantischte aller Künste, — fast möchte man sagen, allein *rein* romantisch. — Orpheus Lyra öffnete die Thore des Orcus. Die Musik schliesst dem Menschen ein unbekanntes Reich auf; eine Welt, die nichts gemein hat mit der äussern Sinnenwelt, die ihn umgiebt, und in der er alle durch Begriffe bestimmbaren Gefühle zurücklasst, um sich dem Unaussprechlichen hinzugeben. Wie wenig erkannten *die* Instrumental-Componisten dies eigenthümliche Wesen der Musik, welche versuchten, jene bestimmbaren Empfindungen, oder gar Begebenheiten darzustellen, und so die der Plastik geradezu entgegengesetzte Kunst plastisch zu behandeln! Dittersdorfs Symphonien der Art, so wie alle neuere *Batailles de trois Empereurs etc.* sind, als lacherliche Verirrungen, mit gänzlichem Vergessen zu bestrafen. —

to have reports published within two or three months was considered extraordinary.

Among the early music critics writing for the *AMZ* was the German E. T. A. Hoffmann (1776–1822), who wrote a series of influential essays on Beethoven's music. Like most of the writers published by the *AMZ*, Hoffmann was a critic only by avocation; he earned his living variously as a lawyer, a judge, a composer, and a music director. The first fully "professional" music critic was probably Eduard Hanslick (1825–1904) (Figure 23.6). Born near Vienna, Hanslick had trained to become a lawyer, but he began to write pieces about music in his early twenties, and for much of his life writing about music in popular journals was a major source of income. He was also one of the first to give public lectures on music for members of the emerging middle class, whose appetite for music was lively but whose background was limited.

FIGURE 23.6 Eduard Hanslick, music critic. As long as there are critics, musicians will continue to complain about them. In 1969, Igor Stravinsky described a dream about music critics: "They were small and rodent-like with padlocked ears, as if they had stepped out of a painting by Goya."

Hanslick had an unprecedented influence on the musical taste of his time. Unlike most critics today, he reviewed the music itself rather than the performances. In 1846, early in his career, he wrote an article on *Tannhäuser* that Wagner saw fit to praise. Gradually, however, he came to feel that Wagner had overstepped the proper bounds of music; Hanslick was bothered by Wagner's obsession with mythological figures and by his "excessive" use of such dissonant harmonies as the diminished seventh. In several books on a wide variety of topics, Hanslick championed absolute music, arguing that it did not depend on external associations for coherence. He was largely responsible for setting the supporters of Brahms (his ideal composer) against the supporters of Wagner. In 1876 he wrote from Bayreuth:

This much we can say with considerable certainty: that the style of Wagner's *Ring* will not be the music of the future, but at the most one music among many—perhaps only as a catalyst for new developments that will draw upon the past. For Wagner's newest reforms consist not of an enriching, an extension, or a rejuvenation of music—in the sense that it was in the art of Haydn, Mozart, Beethoven, Weber, and Schumann—but on the contrary of a reversal and a distortion of the fundamental laws of music, a style at odds with human hearing and sensibilities.

Brahms and other friends of Hanslick knew that he had a blind spot when it came to Wagner (whose lifestyle did not correspond to Hanslick's own conservative bent). And Wagner had certainly done nothing to earn Hanslick's affections. After years of barely civil exchanges in Vienna prompted by Hanslick's negative reviews of *Lohengrin* in 1858, Hanslick declared that he was willing to learn from Wagner. In November 1862 he was invited to the Viennese home of a Dr. Standhartner to hear Wagner read the "poem" of his newest music drama, *Die Meistersinger von Nürnberg*. This opera describes a sixteenth-century singing competition in which a pedantic stickler for rules—and the butt of many jokes—is a narrow-minded town clerk and critic whose name in Wagner's manuscript was Veit Hanslich (Wagner later changed the name to Sixtus Beckmesser). Hanslick apparently showed up in good faith, only to find himself exposed to ridicule by Wagner and his friends. He fled from the house, and from then on the estrangement was permanent. To Hanslick's credit, he never mentioned this ugly incident in his writings, though his judgments of Wagner's music continued to be severe. Few critics writing today can claim the breadth and depth that Hanslick exhibited.

# *Chapter 24*

## NATIONALISM;
## THE TWILIGHT
## OF ROMANTICISM

As the nineteenth century neared its close, many of the countries of Europe sought to throw off foreign influences and assert their own cultural identity. At the same time, many centers of political and cultural power were growing weak and self-indulgent. A kind of twilight descended in music, and in other arts as well.

We look first at three composers whose music reflects the rising tide of nationalism. Then we turn to a composer whose music alludes subtly, but unmistakably, to the twilight of Romanticism.

## NATIONALISM OUTSIDE THE EUROPEAN MAINSTREAM

Nationalism, as we have seen, was a powerful force in the political and cultural life of Germany, Italy, and France. Its influence was even stronger outside the European mainstream—in Poland, Bohemia (part of present-day Czechoslovakia), Norway, Denmark, and Russia (see the map on page 373). The people in these lands hungered not only for political freedom but for cultural expressions that would reflect their unique heritage. They wanted their own music—music that did not sound like the music of Beethoven or Wagner.

During the latter half of the nineteenth century several gifted composers in eastern Europe and Scandinavia responded to that desire. Among them were the Bohemians Bedřich Smetana (1824–1884) and Antonín Dvořák (1841–1904), the Norwegian Edvard Grieg (1843–1907), and the Dane Carl Nielsen (1865–1931). Among the Russians were Mikhail Glinka (1804–1857), Alexander Borodin (1833–1887), Mily Balakirev (1837–1910), Modest Musorgsky (1839–1881), Peter Tchaikovsky (1840–1893), and Nikolai Rimsky-Korsakov (1844–1908).

Although some listeners claim they can sense what is peculiarly "Czech" or "Russian" about certain works, it is difficult to identify nationalist characteristics with certainty. The native folk music that inspired these composers was unharmonized music based on melodic patterns drawn from nontraditional scales. Those patterns suggested novel harmonic combinations, and the rhythms and instrumentation of folk music encouraged composers to experiment with novel sounds. It was the composers with limited training in composition who were most likely to build the harmonies and sounds of folk music into their works.

The blending of folk music and art music proceeded in subtle and complex ways. What emerged was music quite distinct from the music of the early Romantic composers, as we will see in the works of three of the best-known nationalist composers.

## BEDŘICH SMETANA (1824–1884)

Smetana, the first Bohemian composer to achieve an international reputation, was born in a small village in eastern Bohemia, which was then part of the Austro-Hungarian empire. His father, who spoke German at home, was a master brewer in the service of Count Waldstein, one of Beethoven's patrons. Smetana made his public debut as a pianist at the age of 6—playing, predictably, not a Czech work but an arrangement of an overture by a French composer.

When Smetana was 14, he was sent to school in the capital city of Prague, whose rich musical life proved more exciting than schoolwork. He sought out concerts and operas, wrote chamber music, and, in 1840, attended a dazzling solo concert by Liszt. After his father recalled him from Prague to finish his schooling, he eked out a living as a piano teacher. During the Prague Revolution of June 1848, he returned to the capital, helped man the barricades, and wrote patriotic marches.

The uprising was soon suppressed, however, and in 1856 Smetana accepted a teaching position in Sweden. Following the defeat of the Austrians by Napoleon III in 1859, he returned to Prague once again. With the Austrians gone, the climate was more favorable for Czech composers. Even so, Smetana was slow to gain recognition, partly because his countrymen suspected him of being a disciple of Liszt, whose modernist tendencies were well known.

Smetana achieved recognition at last as a composer of nationalist operas. He completed the first one in 1863 (when he was over 40) and over the next two decades wrote seven more. Encouraged by Count Jan Harrach, a nobleman who awarded prizes for the best operas on Czech themes, Smetana wrote an opera about courtship and marriage in a peasant village (*The Bartered Bride*, 1866) and another about the mythological founding of the Czech nation (*Libuše*, 1869–1872).

### ✳Smetana: *The Moldau* from *Má Vlast* (*My Fatherland*) (1874)

While he was writing *Libuše,* Smetana hit on the idea of composing a vast cycle of six symphonic poems (page 403) on the subject of *Má Vlast* (*My Fatherland*). During the seven years it took him to complete the cycle, he was afflicted with the secondary stages of syphilis and his health grew steadily worse. Gradually deafness set in.

Each of the six symphonic poems of *Má Vlast* deals with some aspect of Czech life:

   I.  *Vyšehrad,* a huge rock over the river Vltava (Moldau), by tradition the seat of the ancient Bohemian kings.

  II.  *Vltava* (transliterated as "The Moldau"), a river running north from the southernmost tip of Bohemia into the Elbe River.

 III.  *Šárka,* a wild valley near Prague where, in the fourteenth century, a group of Amazons (warrior women) were said to have slaughtered a band of men in vengeance for their unfaithfulness.

 IV.  *From Bohemia's Woods and Fields,* which Smetana described as "depicting Czech life in work and dance."

  V.  *Tábor,* a town in southern Bohemia where the Czech reformer Jan Hus had been burned at the stake.

 VI.  *Blaník,* a forested hill in southern Bohemia where, according to legend, a troop of knights lies sleeping, waiting to come to the aid of their country in time of need.

The second of these symphonic poems, *The Moldau* (Listening Guide 50), has captured the imagination of generations of listeners. It is a remarkably suggestive representation of a mighty river and the life along its banks. Although many nineteenth-century tone poems are only vaguely programmatic, Smetana is very specific about what each passage represents. For example, he begins with a murmuring theme, which he calls "First source of the Moldau," that flows along without interruption. In the opening passage he passes the theme back and forth between two flutes:

Later he expands the orchestration to include clarinets, in what he calls the "Second source of the Moldau." Here we can sense the river rising from its modest beginnings.

Over this running accompaniment Smetana imposes a slower but equally flowing melody in the violins:

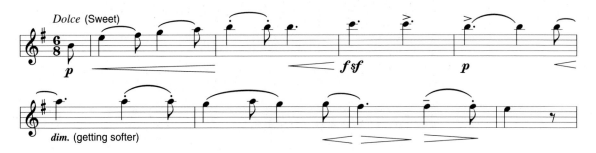

Most of the harmonies that underlie this melody are minor chords. But as the melody reaches its peak (bar 3 in the example), Smetana harmonizes it with a major chord and gives it a loud dynamic and a *sforzando* (a strong accent, from the Italian for "forcing") to suggest the rising power of the river. The first section ends with a "Forest hunting" scene in which hunting calls in the horns and trumpets mingle with the murmuring theme in the violins.

Formally, *The Moldau* consists of four sections. The first and last are dominated by water themes. The second and third depict episodes in Bohemian life. The second section, "Village wedding," is built around a dancelike tune in duple meter. Although the underlying harmonies are simple enough, Smetana enlivens the tune by displacing the tonic chord from the first measure (where it would be expected) to the second measure of each 4-bar half. This displacement, coupled with a well-placed syncopation, throws the tune delightfully off-balance.

Smetana calls the third section "Moonlight—Dance of the water nymphs." Bohemia is a land of lakes, and its folklore is rich in tales of water fairies and water sprites. Here Smetana carries a slow-moving melody in muted strings over a faster-moving variation of the original "source" music (played again by alternating flutes). The soft rippling of the harp and a dynamics range from *p* to *ppp* give this section a shimmering, magical quality.

In the fourth section the stream surges into a mighty river. Smetana suggests "The rapids of St. John" with a heavy infusion of brass, timpani, and rapidly repeated diminished-seventh chords. He moves on to a rousing restatement of the full melody, now entirely in the major mode, labeled "The Moldau, mighty stream." Such contrasts between major and minor permeate Smetana's music. Although there are precedents in the music of Mozart and Schubert, Smetana makes these modal contrasts a central part of his "nationalistic" language.

Finally, in the coda, Smetana recalls a theme, a broad chorale, that he had used in his first symphonic poem, *Vyšehrad*.

Smetana moves from section to section of *The Moldau* with smooth transitions, bringing half a dozen themes together into a coherent statement without resorting to sonata form. There is a sincerity about this music that has proved irresistible to Czechs and non-Czechs alike.

# Listening Guide 50

## SMETANA: *The Moldau* from *Má Vlast* (*My Fatherland*)

CD 6, TRACK 1
TAPE 6A, TRACK 1
DURATION: 12:24

*The four sections of this work suggest a travelogue rather than a traditional symphonic movement. Smetana's labels for the themes appear in bold italic type.*

*Form: Sectional (4 sections plus coda)*

| LOCATION | TIME | COMMENTS |
|---|---|---|
| **1** SECTION I | | |
| ***First source of the Moldau*** | **0:00** | Continuous, murmuring figure in the flutes. |
| ***Second source of the Moldau*** | 0:28 | Clarinets join with the flutes, still *piano*. |
| Moldau theme | 1:11 | Lyrical theme in strings and winds, primarily in the minor mode but with coloristic patches of major. The long second half of the theme repeats in its entirety. |
| ***Forest hunting*** | **3:03** | Brass fanfares accompanied by murmuring figures in the violins. |
| **2** SECTION II | | |
| ***Village wedding*** | **4:06** | Introduced by long-held tones in the French horns. Duple-meter tune presented in successive variations, first in the strings and winds, and then more prominently in the winds. |
| **3** SECTION III | | |
| ***Moonlight—dance of the water nymphs*** | **6:01** | A slow, lyrical melody in the strings over murmuring figures in the flutes. Ends with an urgent, crescendo passage in the winds that anticipates the return of the Moldau theme. |
| **4** SECTION IV | | |
| Moldau theme | **8:43** | Return, identical to the theme in Section I (though without the internal repeats). |
| ***The rapids of St. John*** | 9:34 | Loud brass, timpani, and rapidly repeated diminished-seventh chords, later piccolo and cymbals as well. |
| ***The Moldau, powerful stream*** | 10:50 | The Moldau theme triumphantly rendered in the major mode by the full orchestra. |
| [Coda] ***Vyšehrad theme*** | **11:21** | Broad chorale-like theme in the full orchestra representing the great rock along the Moldau. |

## RUSSIAN NATIONALISM

From its very beginnings, Russia has embraced countless cultures and ethnic loyalties. Armenians, Belorussians, Estonians, Georgians, Latvians, Lithuanians, Moldavians, Ukrainians, Poles, Slovaks, Serbs, Croatians, and Siberians—all have participated in this remarkable mix. With the adoption of the Greek Orthodox religion around Kiev during the tenth century, a strong Byzantine influence further enriched the cultural diversity of the country.

Following the consolidation of the Russian state in the fifteenth century, distrust of foreign ways retarded economic development, and autocratic rulers seized political power. Serfdom—a form of slavery in which everyone born in a certain area belonged to the landowner—became legal in the seventeenth century. At last Peter the Great (czar from 1689 to 1725) opened Russia up to the West, and for the next century and a half Western music, especially Italian opera, enjoyed a vogue in Moscow and St. Petersburg.

By the second half of the nineteenth century, Russian composers had tired of music that had little to do with the Russian soul or the Russian character. Perhaps the first composer to incorporate Russian themes into his music was Mikhail Glinka, who has been called the father of Russian music. To compensate for his lack of formal music education, Glinka went to Berlin for training. In his operas *A Life for the Tsar* (1834–1836) and *Ruslan and Lyudmila* (1837–1842), he struggled to wed Western styles to the rhythmic vigor and harmonic boldness of Russian folk music. In the Bridal Chorus from *A Life for the Tsar,* for example, he gave symphonic expression to melodies rooted in Russian folksong. Only with the next generation, however, did Russian composers create a truly Russian music.

## MODEST MUSORGSKY (1839–1881)

Born into a family that numbered both landowners and serfs, Modest Musorgsky grew up in comfortable circumstances. With the liberation of the serfs in 1861, however, his family wealth declined and he took various civil service jobs to support himself. A chronic alcoholic, he was unable to hold a job for more than a few years, and he died in a military hospital at the age of 42.

During his brief career, Musorgsky struggled to complete two mammoth operas on Russian subjects: *Boris Godunov* (1868–1874), the loosely historical story of a sixteenth-century czar who was said to have murdered the rightful heir to the Russian throne, and *Khovanshchina* (1872–1880), a story of treason within the imperial family at the end of the seventeenth century. He failed to complete either opera, however, and the Russian composers Nikolai Rimsky-Korsakov (1844–1908) and Dmitri Shostakovich (1906–1975) revised them heavily in an effort to "finish" them. Rimsky-Korsakov, though a great admirer of Musorgsky, found in his music "absurd, disconnected harmonies, ugly part-writing, [and] strikingly illogical modulations," which he felt obliged to "correct." Not until 1975 was Musorgsky's original score for *Boris Godunov* published, revealing a work of striking originality.

## ✳Musorgsky: *Pictures at an Exhibition* (1874)

Another work of Musorgsky's that has been better known in arrangements by others (especially the lush 1922 orchestration by the French composer Maurice Ravel) is a suite of piano pieces called *Pictures at an Exhibition*. Musorgsky's suite, though modeled on piano cycles like Schumann's *Carnaval*, has a novel structure. It depicts in musical terms a visit to an exhibition of paintings and drawings by Musorgsky's friend Victor Hartmann, who had died suddenly the year before at the age of 39. Hartmann belonged to a circle of Russian artists who took as their subjects Russian history, folklore, and everyday life. The 10 pictures Musorgsky selected for his suite range from a sketch for ballet costumes ("Ballet of the Chicks in Their Shells," No. 5, Figure 24.1) to a sketch for "The Great Gate of Kiev" (No. 10, Figure 24.2), which Hartmann had entered in a competition to commemorate an unsuccessful attempt to assassinate the czar (no gate was ever built).

Musorgsky prefaces the suite with a "Promenade" that suggests his arrival at the exhibition. As he strolls from picture to picture, he varies the Promenade theme several times. Its 2-bar thematic kernel, which shifts back and forth between 5/4 and 6/4 meter, suggests the ponderous gait of the composer, who weighed over 200 pounds. But its irregularity is characteristic of much of Musorgsky's music:

*Nel modo russico* (In the Russian mode)

What is "Russian" about this idea? For one thing, though it is nominally in the key of B-flat Major (B♭ is the third pitch in the preceding example), the theme does not cadence on a tonic B♭ chord until the very end of the 24-bar Promenade. More striking, the leading tone of A natural, which in Western harmony is crucial to defining a key, does not appear at all. Finally, the theme exhibits a rough, "off-balance" symmetry: pitches 1–3 correspond approximately to the last four pitches, and the theme begins and ends with the same two pitches. Moreover, the 3-note slurred figure occurs on each side of the bar line. This rough symmetry is characteristic of Russian folksong but is rare in Western art music.

Musorgsky's development of the Promenade theme also differs from Western

FIGURE 24.1 (left) Musorgsky's friend Victor Hartmann was a minor painter at best, but his paintings triggered the composer's imagination. The "Chicks in Their Shells" was an actual costume sketch for a ballet.

FIGURE 24.2 (right) The event which Hartmann's "The Great Gate of Kiev" was to commemorate was not permitted to be mentioned, presumably because it might give others ideas.

practice. He extends the initial 2-bar theme to 24 bars in a succession of small, irregular blocks, and in subsequent appearances he subjects it to a series of free variations. For example, after viewing Hartmann's picture of the Parisian catacombs (No. 8), Musorgsky strolls on to the next painting deep in thoughts of mortality. To reflect this mood, he harmonizes the theme with somber octave tremolos. He calls this version, in nonidiomatic Latin, *"Con Mortuis in Lingua Mortua"* ("With the Dead in a Dead Language").

Musorgsky's treatment of each of the pictures is highly evocative. In No. 1, *Gnomus,* he uses three themes in a series of disconnected outbursts to suggest the erratic movements of a carved wooden nutcracker. No. 2, *Il Vecchio Castello* (*The Old Castle*), which is played entirely over a tonic pedal tone (a drone), suggests a troubadour singing a mournful melody outside an old Italian ruin that Hartmann had visited in the 1860s. Once again, there is no trace of the leading tone. No. 3, *Tuileries,* subtitled *Dispute of Children after Play,* describes Hartmann's painting of the Tuileries Gardens in Paris, with a group of quarreling children in the foreground.

On his way back from western Europe in 1869, Hartmann had stopped off at the Polish town of Sandomir, where he observed scenes in the Jewish ghetto. No. 4, *Bydlo* (Polish for "cattle"), represents a lumbering oxcart with enormous wooden wheels traveling along a muddy road. At the close Musorgsky suggests the dying clatter of the cart as it recedes into the distance. No. 6, titled *Two Polish Jews, One Rich, the Other Poor,* describes the pompous posturings of a rich man and the obsequious responses of a beggar, who end up talking at the same time.

*Chapter 24   Nationalism; The Twilight of Romanticism*   487

No. 5, which is cast in the form of a miniature scherzo and trio, is a delicate yet spirited representation of dancing chicks not yet out of their shells. In No. 7 Musorgsky describes Hartmann's painting of peddlers and their pushcarts in the bustling marketplace of Limoges, a medieval cathedral city that Hartmann had visited. Musorgsky suggests the peddlers' lively chatter with a torrent of perpetual motion. In the margin of his score he imagines what they are saying:

> The Great news: Monsieur de Puissangeout has just found his lost cow, The Fugitive. But the good gossips of Limoges are not in complete agreement on the subject because Mme. de Remboursac has just acquired a fine new set of false teeth, while Monsieur de Panta-Pantaléon's nose, which is in his way, remains the color of a [red] peony.

No. 8 describes a watercolor by Hartmann showing himself and a friend in the Roman catacombs in Paris. To suggest the setting, Musorgsky uses a series of dissonant, long-held chords and their eerie echoes. No. 9, *The Hut on Fowl's Legs,* refers to Hartmann's painting of a witch in Slavic folklore who lives in a hut supported by four chicken feet and who eats human bones ground up with a mortar and pestle. Musorgsky's bravura music portrays the witch thundering through the air.

In No. 10, *The Great Gate of Kiev,* Musorgsky transforms the Promenade theme into a triumphal procession (complete with clanging bells) that brings the whole composition to a rousing conclusion.

## PETER TCHAIKOVSKY (1840–1893)

Unlike Musorgsky, Tchaikovsky had no desire to escape Western influences. After studying for a career in the civil service, Tchaikovsky attended the St. Petersburg Conservatory, where he received a Western-oriented training. With the encouragement of its director, Anton Rubinstein, he did well and graduated with a silver medal in 1866. Tchaikovsky's first works were criticized by his former teachers for being too unpolished and by a group of intensely nationalist Russian composers (to which Musorgsky belonged) for being too Western in form and expression. Before graduating, Tchaikovsky accepted a position as teacher of harmony at the newly formed Moscow Conservatory, where he remained for many years.

The members of "The Five," as the group of Russian nationalist composers was called, continued to question Tchaikovsky's talents, mainly because of his Western training. However, one member of that group, Mily Balakirev, eventually recognized Tchaikovsky's extraordinary gifts and encouraged him to complete his first masterpiece, the fantasy overture *Romeo and Juliet* (1869). Over the next 24 years, most of Tchaikovsky's works were based on Western models: six symphonies, three string quartets, three piano concertos, a violin concerto, and several grand operas. His last three symphonies, the first of his piano con-

certos (in B-flat Minor, Op. 23), and his violin concerto (in D Major, Op. 35) have long been staples of the concert repertoire. But the premiere of several of these works met with a stormy reception.

Perhaps Tchaikovsky's most original contributions were in music for ballet. **Ballet** is the theatrical presentation of group or solo dancing of great precision to a musical accompaniment, usually with costumes and scenery and conveying a story or theme. Introduced by the French in the early eighteenth century, ballet had flourished in France and Italy throughout the eighteenth and nineteenth centuries, both as an independent entertainment and as an interlude during an opera. Even Beethoven had once composed a ballet, but the form had never entered the mainstream of musical development. With the encouragement of the dancers at the Bolshoi Theater in Moscow, however, Tchaikovsky demonstrated that ballet music was worthy of the same serious attention accorded other genres.

He began his first important ballet, *Swan Lake,* in 1871 as a domestic entertainment for his sister's children and their friends. Several years later he received a commission to expand and complete the work for the Bolshoi Theater. He went on to compose two other ballet masterpieces, *Sleeping Beauty* (1889) and *The Nutcracker* (1892; Figure 24.3); the Christmas theme of *The Nutcracker* has made it a holiday staple for countless ballet companies around the world.

Tchaikovsky's personal life reads like a novel by Dostoevsky. For almost 15 years his chief patroness, Madame Nadezhda von Meck, provided him with generous financial support on condition that they never meet. On the two occasions when they happened to cross paths, they both averted their eyes. In his late thirties Tchaikovsky, a homosexual, succumbed to the pleadings of a young woman who threatened to commit suicide unless he married her. Though he had never met her, he agreed to the marriage and soon suffered a nervous breakdown. He died at the age of 43. Various explanations have been offered for his early death. According to one, he died of cholera. According to another, he committed suicide at the suggestion of a school disciplinary board investigating his liaison with the young nephew of an aristocrat.

## COMPOSERS IN THE MOVIES

Before the advent of "talkies" in the late 1920s, a solo pianist or organist (sometimes a full orchestra) played live music to accompany the silent movies. Then, during the 1930s, movie studios began to commission composers to write musical scores that were carried directly on the film track. These first film composers wrote music very much in the late Romantic style of Tchaikovsky and Mahler (more about film music in Chapter 29).

The lives of famous composers—especially Romantic composers—have long attracted filmmakers. One of the first of the musical "bio-pics" (biographical pictures) was Columbia Pictures' *A Song to Remember* (1945), a movie based *very* loosely on the life of Frédéric Chopin and his liaison with George Sand (pen name of Aurore Dudevant). Chopin, who in real life stood less than 5 feet 7 inches tall and weighed under 100 pounds, was played by a swashbuckling leading man, Cornel Wilde. George Sand, his trouser-wearing, cigar-smoking lover, was played by Merle Oberon, who usually played a *femme fatale* (a woman to whom men are "fatally" attracted). Any connection between the script of writer Sidney Buchman and actual events in Chopin's life was strictly coincidental. In commenting on the film, one critic wrote: "It is the business of Hollywood to shape the truth into box-office contours." Film critic James Agee remarked: "As infuriating and funny a misrepresentation of an artist's life and work as I have seen." In 1945, with the war over and with millions of Americans enjoying unaccustomed leisure time, movie producers wanted to ensure that the first exposure of American audiences to "classical" music was not overly intellectual. They succeeded.

The British director Ken Russell has frequently turned to the lives of composers for his films. After directing short biographies of Richard Strauss and the English composer Sir Edward Elgar for BBC Television, he directed three bio-pics based on popular Romantic composers: *The Music Lovers* (1970), about the life of Tchaikovsky; *Mahler* (1974); and *Lisztomania* (1975). *The Music Lovers* is a sensationalist account of Tchaikovsky's homosexuality. *Mahler,* the most successful of the three, is a horror film based on the composer's obsession with death. *Lisztomania,* though its premise is the intriguing notion of Liszt as a pop star, ended up, according to one critic, as "a welter of arbitrary gags." Even so, Russell at least tried to deal with these composers in contemporary terms.

Luciano Visconti's film *Death in Venice* (1971) is based on the novella by the German author Thomas Mann. A middle-aged German composer on holiday in Venice becomes infatuated with a silent young boy and stays on in Venice too long to escape the approaching plague. Visconti hints that the composer is Gustav Mahler and uses the haunting Adagietto from Mahler's Fifth Symphony as a backdrop to the visual glories of Venice. Though the treatment is sometimes tedious, the overall effect is moving.

Perhaps the most successful bio-pic of a composer is Milos Forman's 1986 film adaptation of Peter Shaffer's play *Amadeus* (1980), based on the life of Mozart. In writing the play, though Shaffer consulted sources associated with Mozart (especially letters), he ignored many facets of Mozart's character in order to picture him as a divinely gifted composer with an obnoxious and infantile personality. In fact, the theatrical premise of the play is that God is capricious in deciding who will be a genius and who will be a mediocrity. Salieri, the court composer, is elegant and urbane but possesses only modest musical talents. In both the play and film, Mozart is a bumbling fool on whom God has squandered genius. Ironically, the most eloquent lines are delivered by the embittered Salieri, who is the true focus of the action. Discussing his revision of the play between the London and Washington premieres, Shaffer remarked: "Dramatically speaking, Salieri seemed to me to be too much the observer of the calamities he should have been causing. Now, in this new version, he seems to me to stand where he properly belongs—at the wicked center of the action."

The film, shot in Prague (one of the few European cities that have preserved their eighteenth-century look), creates a rich period atmosphere while retaining much of Shaffer's witty dialogue. Was Mozart poisoned by Salieri? Almost certainly not. Does Shaffer present a balanced picture of Mozart? No. But dramatically the film is a brilliant success because Shaffer has focused on an issue of universal appeal. In so doing he has also shown the relevance of the past to the present. Moreover, *Amadeus* brought Mozart's music to millions of people who had never heard it before. In short order the sound-track album "went gold," and "Amadeus" and "Mozart" became household words.

## Tchaikovsky: Fantasy Overture, *Romeo and Juliet* (1881)

The plays of Shakespeare, especially *Romeo and Juliet,* held a special fascination for many Romantic composers, including Tchaikovsky. His *Romeo and Juliet* fantasy overture is a fusion of Western forms and his highly personal treatment of themes. He himself styled this work a "fantasy overture," suggesting that he regarded its form as unique. Although *Romeo and Juliet* follows the traditional thematic pattern of sonata form, the theme of what appears to be the secondary area of the exposition does not return in the tonic key in the recapitulation (though a fragment does return in that key in the coda).

The lengthy introduction opens with a somber, elegaic chorale in the winds—doubtless a reference to Friar Lawrence, who tries to counsel the young lovers. The winds are soon reinforced by the strings and harp. As the theme repeats, it grows more urgent and intense. Through an accelerando it leads without break into the Allegro exposition. This blurring of the divisions between sections conceals the seams within Tchaikovsky's rather transparent forms.

The theme of the principal area is open-ended: It begins "off the tonic" and unfolds irregularly. Its minor mode and its explosive rhythms, punctuated by short rests, suggest the conflict between the warring Montagues and Capulets. A brief fugal episode—a kind of contrapuntal sparring—intensifies the sense of conflict. Without transition, Tchaikovsky moves directly to a pedal point that seems to be leading up to the conventional key for the secondary area (the relative major). Instead, he sidesteps into an unexpected key and has the English horn introduce a gently descending, poignant melody:

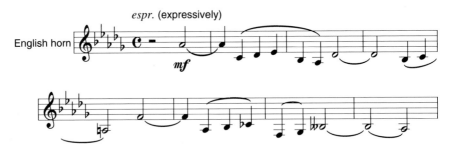

This *a*-phrase of what is obviously Romeo and Juliet's love theme begins on what proves to be its second pitch; a few bars later the theme trails off without cadencing (measure 8 above). After a brief *b*-phrase with a "waiting" quality, the flutes and oboes restate the opening more fully (*a'*-phrase), with a sighing countermelody in the horns. Finally, Tchaikovsky extends the theme in true Romantic style (*a''*-phrase), carrying it higher and higher (against its descending tendencies) until he reaches a soaring climax—although the strings remain muted and never play louder than *piano*. The climax is followed by a gentle closing passage in the harp.

Tchaikovsky launches the development abruptly by returning to the conflict theme, which soon displaces Friar Lawrence's conciliatory chorale. We sense that the lovers are headed for disaster. The theme climaxes at the moment of recapitulation in a tumultuous but abridged tonic restatement of the conflict theme. Perhaps to symbolize that the young couple's dilemma cannot be resolved, the restatement of the love theme does not occur in the tonic. Tchaikovsky omits its first *a*-phrase but replaces the soft dynamics of the subsequent phrases (*b-a'-a"*) with a new *fortissimo* climax and adds fresh closing material that returns to the minor mode.

The first of the two codas revives the conflict theme once again, this time in a more emphatic manner than before. The second coda, in a mixture of major and minor, returns to the tempo of the introduction. It recalls the love theme and finally brings it together with Friar Lawrence's chorale, which now sounds like a benediction for the entombed lovers. Without resorting to programmatic explanations, Tchaikovsky has managed to convey the dramatic essence of Shakespeare's play.

FIGURE 24.4 Franz Joseph, Austrian emperor for 68 years, remarked to Theodore Roosevelt, "You see in me the last monarch of the old school." The assassination in 1914 of Franz Ferdinand, his nephew and Hapsburg heir, sparked World War I.

## THE TWILIGHT OF ROMANTICISM

At twilight we reflect on the events of the dying day. As the nineteenth century drew to a close, the continent of Europe seemed to slip into a twilight of its own. The monarchical, authoritarian, agrarian order that had prevailed for centuries was on the wane, and the end of an era seemed imminent.

This sense of twilight was especially strong in Austria, where the Austro-Hungarian empire was in steady decline. What had once been a powerful empire was now, under the aged Emperor Franz Joseph (Figure 24.4), an enfeebled state living on memories of an irretrievable past. In France, the mood was only slightly less escapist. The French chose to ignore the military buildup in Prussia and refused to adopt the mass-production technologies emerging in England. Empires that a century before had embraced the Enlightenment now turned their backs on the future.

The urge to escape showed itself in the popularity of the waltzes, quadrilles, gallops, and polkas of the Strauss family (Chapter 21). Though captivated by the trivial plot of *The Merry Widow,* the public expressed little concern for the oppression of national minorities, institutionalized anti-Semitism, or the plight of the working class. While Europe was plunging toward war, the old aristocracy lived complacently in a world of fantasy.

A series of destabilizing developments paved the way for the First World War. Each time with thin pretext, the Prussian Chancellor Otto von Bismarck waged successful wars against Austria (1866) and France (1870–1871). Those conflicts led to the unification of the German nation but sowed seeds of resentment in both of the defeated countries. Meanwhile, ethnic minorities in Poland, central Europe, and the Balkans were campaigning for greater freedom but were met with sterner repression.

In music, too, the old order was under siege. Triadic tonality underwent gradual dissolution, a trend hastened by the interaction between mainstream music and nationalist music. The decline of tonality was accompanied by an even greater emphasis on originality. Late Romantic composers strove to create music that sounded like no one else's, and any literal repetition of a musical idea was something to be avoided. Toward the end of the century, composers carried this obsession with originality to extraordinary lengths. Richard Strauss and Gustav Mahler, for example, wrote long symphonic works in which not a single idea, however brief, is ever repeated in exactly the same form.

At the same time, late Romantic composers prized unity. Often they would use a single theme (perhaps little more than a few notes), or at most a few themes, as the basis for extensive thematic elaborations that would tie a lengthy movement or even an entire work together.

To perform music of such complexity, huge orchestras were needed. A typical symphonic work by Tchaikovsky or Strauss calls for, in addition to a substantial increase in the usual number of strings, such instruments as the piccolo, English horn, bass clarinet, contrabassoon, tuba, harp, and a variety of percussion. Mahler's Symphony No. 8 (ca. 1906) requires such a vast orchestra and chorus that the work has been dubbed the "Symphony of a Thousand" (see Figure 4.17 on page 57).

All this complexity of texture and structure taxed the capacity of listeners as well as the stamina of musicians. Under the influence of Wagner, melodies grew so long that they were hard to hear as a coherent unit, and chromaticism permeated harmony more and more. New forms were created to support single movements that went on for as long as 40 minutes.

Some find late Romantic music, with its willful excesses, exhilarating; others find it self-indulgent. Richard Strauss (1864–1949) and Gustav Mahler, who came from very different backgrounds, epitomize the sense of twilight during these years—a combination of nostalgia for the past and a foreboding about the future. Strauss, the son of a famous horn player, began his career as a radical, taking the thematic complexity of the symphonic poem to unheard-of lengths and shocking the public with two avant-garde operas, *Salome* (1903–1905) and *Elektra* (1906–1908). But beginning with *Der Rosenkavalier* (*The Rose Cavalier*; 1909–1910), Strauss backed away from the implications of his own radicalism and adopted a voice that was deeply nostalgic about the Romantic twilight. Mahler was equally nostalgic, but he also maintained an adventurous spirit that gives his music a three-dimensional quality.

## GUSTAV MAHLER (1860–1911)

Gustav Mahler once described himself as "thrice homeless: as a native of Bohemia in Austria, as an Austrian among Germans, and as a Jew throughout all the world." Born to a brutal peddler and his crippled wife in Kalischt, Bohemia, Mahler's childhood was marred by family strife and poverty. His favorite brother,

Gustav Mahler

Otto, committed suicide; a second brother, Alois, was subject to delusions of grandeur from an early age; his sister, Justine, was obsessed with ritualistic fantasies of death.

Mahler must have been relieved when, at the age of 16, he was permitted to enroll in the Vienna Conservatory, where his classmates included Hugo Wolf (1860–1903), a gifted composer of *Lieder*. When Mahler was only 20, he won his first appointment, as conductor in the provincial town of Bad Hall. From that time on, he rose steadily as an opera conductor (Prague, Leipzig, Budapest, Hamburg). Finally, in 1897, he was named Director of the Vienna State Opera, the most sought-after musical post in the German-speaking world. To win the appointment, however, he had to renounce his Jewish heritage and agree to be baptized a Catholic.

In 1901 Mahler fell in love with Alma Schindler, the daughter of a well-known landscape painter and almost 20 years Mahler's junior. Though she was a composer herself, Mahler insisted after they were married that she give up her musical activities. He also insisted that she adjust her life to his own frenetic schedule, which included heavy conducting commitments during the fall, winter, and spring and furious bouts of composition during their summers in western Austria (Color Plate 11).

Mahler, too, was plagued by the emotional instability that brought such tragedy to his family. When he was 19 he wrote to Josef Steiner, a childhood friend:

> The fires of a supreme zest for living and the most gnawing desire for death alternate in my heart, sometimes in the course of a single hour. I know only one thing: I cannot go on like this!

During the summer of 1907, the death of his five-year-old daughter Maria and the discovery that he had a fatal heart condition deepened his depression.

Yet his indomitable will carried Mahler to remarkable achievements in the two genres he loved best: song and symphony. His entire output consists of about 45 songs, 10 symphonies, and an orchestral song cycle, *Das Lied von der Erde* (*The Song of the Earth*). Each symphony is a mammoth structure embodying his conviction that a symphony should be "a world unto itself." His Second, Third, Fourth, and Eighth Symphonies include vocal texts ranging from an anthology of folk poetry, *The Youth's Magic Horn* (Figure 24.5), to a medieval hymn, *Veni creator spiritus* (*Come, Creator Spirit*). Although many of his works call for hundreds of performers, Mahler sometimes used the orchestra as if it were a chamber ensemble. Along with Berlioz and Richard Strauss, he ranks as one of the greatest orchestrators of any age.

During his lifetime Mahler was known primarily as a conductor. Not until the American conductor and composer Leonard Bernstein recorded his complete symphonies in the 1960s was the magnitude of Mahler's achievement recognized. Mahler's symphonic output has often been compared with the nine symphonies of another Austrian, Anton Bruckner (1824–1896), though Bruckner was more indebted to Wagner and his emotional range was more limited.

## Mahler: First Movement from the Symphony No. 6 in A Minor (1903–1904)

Mahler completed his Symphony No. 6 during the summer of 1904, probably the most productive period of his life. Although this symphony is structured according to the four conventional symphonic movements (an Allegro, a Scherzo, a slow movement, and a rondo finale), each movement is on a vast scale. The enormous orchestra includes four flutes, four oboes, five of three varieties of clarinet, three bassoons and contrabassoon, four horns, four trumpets, three trombones, bass tuba, timpani, two snare drums, bass drum, glockenspiel, cowbells, xylophone, triangle, tambourine, harp, celesta (Mahler asks for two or more), and a huge complement of strings.

Mahler organized the first movement around a vigorous, almost ferocious, march in thematic sonata form. (Like Tchaikovsky's *Romeo and Juliet,* the theme of the secondary area does not return in the tonic key in the recapitulation.) The novel structure of this movement shows Mahler's delight in welding disparate ideas together. The energetic march is the opening theme:

Mahler contrasts this theme with a soft, mysterious chorale theme that is still part of the primary area:

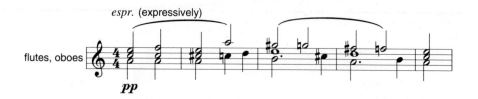

*espr.* (expressively)

flutes, oboes

*pp*

The secondary area introduces a lyrical, sweeping theme that Mahler said was meant to represent his wife, Alma:

*Schwungvoll* (Spirited)

violins

Mahler unifies these contrasting themes in subtle fashion. For example, in rhythm and general contour, bar 1 of Alma's theme (the full bar *after* the three upbeats) is identical to bar 3 of the march theme.

To make sure that the music would be played exactly as he intended, Mahler drew on his own extensive experience as a conductor and included a wealth of performance directions. There are, for example, five sforzandos in the first three bars (not counting the three pickups before bar 1!) of Alma's theme alone. Throughout this 20-minute movement, Mahler subjects the three themes to extensive development and transformation. For example, in the development section, the xylophone gives the march theme an eerie, ghostly quality. In the recapitulation, the chorale theme is played in "diminution," or twice as fast as in the exposition. The triumphant rush to the final cadence transforms Alma's lyrical theme into a march that is even more exuberant than it was at the opening of the movement. For sheer manic energy, Mahler's movement cannot be surpassed.

# Part Four

## THE TWENTIETH CENTURY

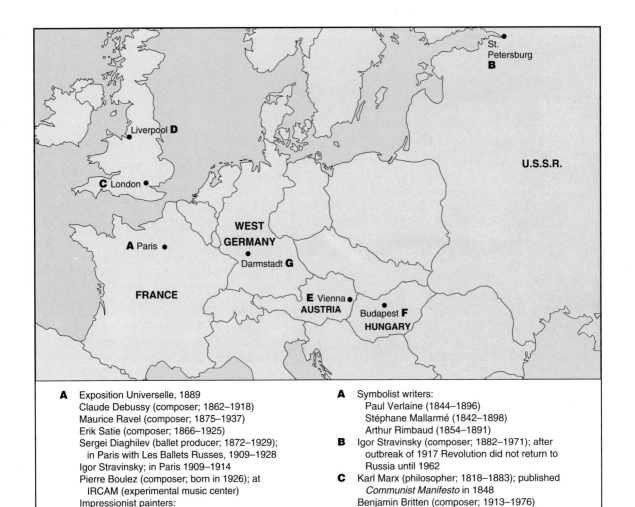

**A** Exposition Universelle, 1889
  Claude Debussy (composer; 1862–1918)
  Maurice Ravel (composer; 1875–1937)
  Erik Satie (composer; 1866–1925)
  Sergei Diaghilev (ballet producer; 1872–1929);
    in Paris with Les Ballets Russes, 1909–1928
  Igor Stravinsky; in Paris 1909–1914
  Pierre Boulez (composer; born in 1926); at
    IRCAM (experimental music center)
  Impressionist painters:
    Claude Monet (1840–1926)
    Pierre Auguste Renoir (1841–1919)
    Edgar Degas (1834–1917)
  Cubist painters:
    Pablo Picasso (1881–1973)
    Juan Gris (1887–1927)

**A** Symbolist writers:
    Paul Verlaine (1844–1896)
    Stéphane Mallarmé (1842–1898)
    Arthur Rimbaud (1854–1891)
**B** Igor Stravinsky (composer; 1882–1971); after
    outbreak of 1917 Revolution did not return to
    Russia until 1962
**C** Karl Marx (philosopher; 1818–1883); published
    *Communist Manifesto* in 1848
    Benjamin Britten (composer; 1913–1976)
**D** The Beatles (rock group formed in 1960)
**E** Arnold Schoenberg (composer; 1874–1951)
    Alban Berg (composer; 1885–1935)
    Anton Webern (composer; 1883–1945)
    György Ligeti (composer; born in 1923)
**F** Béla Bartók (composer; 1881–1945)
**G** Karlheinz Stockhausen (composer; born in 1928)

FIGURE 1  Europe in the twentieth century.

# THE AGE OF TECHNOLOGY

*A*s the new century dawned, industry and technology were transforming life in Europe (Figure 1) and America. Railroads crisscrossed Europe and swept passengers from city to city at speeds of up to 70 miles an hour. Mail could be sent farther and faster than ever before, at cheaper rates, and transatlantic steamers carried tens of thousands of immigrants to America.

The discoveries of researchers like the French scientist Louis Pasteur (1822–1895) were raising the level of public health. Knowledge about the role of germs in spreading disease, though still rudimentary, began to reduce the 50 percent infant-mortality rate that had plagued humanity for millennia. The English surgeon Joseph Lister (1827–1912) applied germ theory to surgical procedures, using carbolic acid and heat sterilization to diminish the incidence of postoperative deaths. Anesthesia, which had been introduced experimentally in England and America around the middle of the nineteenth century, now become widely available for surgical procedures. The smallpox vaccine had been discovered at the end of the eighteenth century, and vaccinations against other diseases now became widespread in industrialized countries; life expectancies rose steadily in western Europe and the United States.

In 1879 the American inventor Thomas Edison (1847–1931) produced his first incandescent light bulb. Soon electricity was introduced in Austria, and by the turn of the century electric power plants lighted most of the major cities of Europe. In 1876 Alexander Graham Bell (1847–1922), a Scot who emigrated to Canada and then to America, introduced a version of the telephone that was soon being used in business offices and homes. Guglielmo Marconi's (1874–1937) experiments with wireless telegraphy around the turn of the century, together with Sir John Fleming's (1849–1945) development of the electron vacuum tube and Lee de Forest's (1873–1961) invention of the amplification tube, led to the emergence of the radio. The first commercial radio station, KDKA in Pittsburgh, Pennsylvania, went on the air in 1920 (Figure 2).

In 1878 Edison introduced the first phonograph and made a brief recording with Johannes Brahms. In stiff German over a loud background of static, Brahms says, "Here is Dr. Brahms. Warm greetings to Dr. Edison." He then

FIGURE 2 (left)  With a dramatic immediacy, radio brought news, music, sports, and entertainment (including the original soap operas) into American homes. Here, Mrs. Jimmy Braddock listens to a prizefight; her husband won.

FIGURE 3 (right)  RCA Victor had the first million-seller recording: Enrico Caruso singing "*Vesti la giubba*" in 1903. Their logo became the most readily recognized trade-mark in music. (Why a dog instead of a cat?)

plays an abbreviated piano version of one of his Hungarian dances. In 1925, with the introduction of electrical recording techniques, RCA Victor introduced wind-up phonographs (the name for machines that played sound recordings) at an affordable price (Figure 3). During the twenties and thirties stores all over America were offering hundreds of both popular and classical "78s"* that established the reputations of composers and performers and offered listeners a convenient alternative to live music. The radio and the phonograph brought music of all kinds into the living rooms of America.

Not everyone shared in the economic and cultural gains of the great industrial powers, however. In many European cities, factory workers lived in squalid tenements (Figure 4). In his *Communist Manifesto* of 1848, the German philosopher Karl Marx (1818–1883) urged the working classes (the *proletariat*) to unite and throw off the bonds of corrupt capitalism. Marx showed how economic self-interest inevitably produced exploitation of the many by a wealthy few. His ideas found their most sympathetic reception among the lower social classes and in underdeveloped countries.

Frictions among the nations of Europe gave ominous warnings of approaching conflict. At the end of the nineteenth century, such matters as the French-

*Records that turned at 78 revolutions per minute (78 rpm). Each side carried up to about four minutes of music.

FIGURE 4  In urban slums, one room might be "home" to several families. Among the English working class, the death rate was double and life expectancy half of that in prosperous neighborhoods.

German dispute over the Rhineland had been settled by force rather than by treaty or negotiation. Now great standing armies faced each other across the Continent. By 1910 the Germans, French, English, Italians, Austrians, and Russians all had large professional armies supplemented by millions of trained civilian reserves. On the high seas, the Germans were challenging England's traditionally strong navy. With this vast buildup of troops and weapons, the outbreak of war was only a matter of time. One after another, nations entered into mutual defense alliances, advancing the prospect of conflict.

On June 28, 1914, a Bosnian revolutionary assassinated the heir to the Austro-Hungarian throne, setting in motion a calamitous chain of events, in which nation after nation declared war. In just over a month the Continent was engulfed in a war that over the next four years would kill more than 10 million and wound more than 20 million combatants—far more than in any previous conflict (Figure 5). Late in the war the United States intervened and tipped the balance in favor of the Allied powers of France, Great Britain, and Russia. (The Russian Revolution that broke out in 1917 had greatly reduced Russia's effectiveness as an ally.) American casualties were only a fraction of those suffered by the countries in which the war was fought.

For the first time in recorded history human beings had unleashed mass ter-

FIGURE 5 During the Battle of the Somme in 1916, pictured here, the British used tanks for the first time. The battle dragged on for months, with the Allied forces gaining a few thousand yards and losing several thousand soldiers.

ror—including poison gas, heavy artillery, and air raids—on a scale that threatened the future, if not the survival, of the species. That grim fact was not lost on world leaders. At the end of the war, President Woodrow Wilson of the United States crusaded tirelessly for the formation of an international body that would mediate global disputes and guarantee peace and security. His efforts led to the creation of the League of Nations in 1919. Sadly, in his valiant effort to satisfy the demands of the member states, Wilson's "Fourteen Points" were significantly weakened. Moreover, the U.S. Senate refused to ratify the Treaty of Versailles that followed Germany's surrender, and the United States never joined the League.

In 1933 Germany and Japan withdrew from the League of Nations. The rise of militaristic regimes in those two nations, and in Italy as well, made war once again only a matter of time. The Great Depression, precipitated by the collapse of the U.S. stock market in October 1929, created widespread unrest that military extremists in Japan and dictators Benito Mussolini (1883–1945) in Italy and Adolf Hitler (1889–1945) in Germany exploited to their own advantage. Whatever the underlying causes, the Second World War was set off by Hitler's unprovoked invasion of Poland in September 1939. The six-year struggle between the Axis powers of Germany, Italy, and Japan and the Allied forces of Great Britain, France, the USSR, and the United States finally ended when the Americans dropped atomic bombs on Hiroshima and Nagasaki in August

1945. That struggle brought death to 15 million combatants and to at least as many civilians. Among the civilians were two-thirds of Europe's Jews, brutally exterminated by Hitler's minions.

Today, some 50 years after that nightmare, remarkable technological strides continue to be made. We can now examine the recesses of the human brain without making an incision, or monitor a baby's neonatal development. We have found cures for many diseases that were fatal only a generation ago. A single farmer can cultivate acreage that would have required the labor of scores of workers in the nineteenth century.

Thanks to developments in electronics, consumers now have available everything from wristwatches to video cameras, from television sets to personal computers. Such products—especially the computer—are transforming everyday life in industrialized nations. Computers play a vital role in payrolls, inventory control, architectural design, real estate, banking, publishing, and scientific research. The day may soon come when school children will carry video encyclopedias the size of a lunch box that afford instant access to information on almost any subject.

Yet most people still live in heavily armed camps or in "Third World" countries impoverished by the burden of international debt. The superpowers have the capacity to destroy life on earth within minutes. The problems of feeding the hungry on an increasingly overpopulated planet seem more intractable than ever. Environmental pollution generated by the industrial nations is causing irreversible damage to the earth's fragile ecosystems. Governments continue to vacillate between taking unilateral action and using the United Nations to arbitrate global conflict.

All these events, and the paradoxes they raise, have profoundly affected the creation, reception, dissemination, and indeed the very *character* of our music. Whatever Romantic glow may have lingered into the first decade of this century was extinguished by the cataclysmic events that followed.

If the two world wars accomplished nothing else, they brought the people of all nations closer together. We no longer live as inhabitants of separate countries; instead, we are all members of what anthropologist Jan Myrdal has called the "global village." News from every corner of the earth is relayed almost instantaneously by satellite into our living rooms. Indeed, it is no longer very meaningful to speak of "Western culture" and "non-Western culture." Americans stir-fry their vegetables in Chinese woks, and inhabitants of mainland China wear American-style jeans. Worldwide exchanges are now common among all the arts, and the rhythms, instruments, and colors of music from Latin America, Africa, and Asia are now integral parts of our music (see map, Figure 6). The myriad musical styles that replaced Romanticism reflect the turbulence and the tragedy, the optimism and the despair, and most of all the remarkable variety of our age.

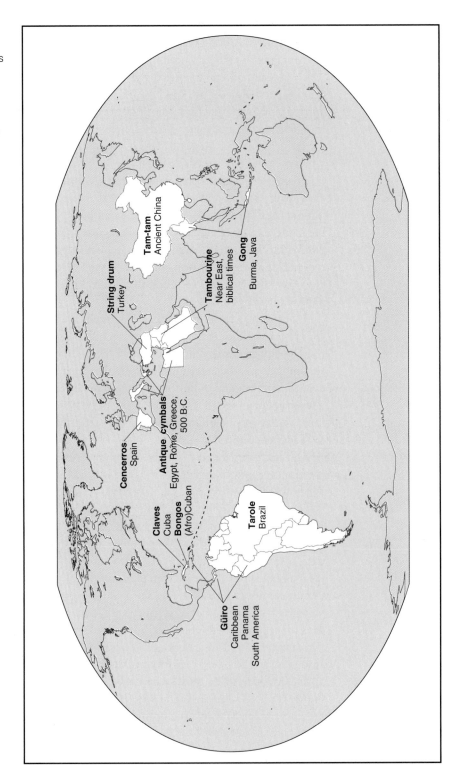

FIGURE 6 Our shrinking globe. The percussion instruments used in works such as Igor Stravinsky's *The Rite of Spring* (Chapter 25) and Edgard Varèse's *Ionisation* (Chapter 29) offer striking testimony to the internationalism of Western music.

Tam-tam
Ancient China

Gong
Burma, Java

String drum
Turkey

Tambourine
Near East,
biblical times

Cencerros
Spain

Antique cymbals
Egypt, Rome, Greece,
500 B.C.

Claves
Cuba
Bongos
(Afro)Cuban

Tarole
Brazil

Güiro
Caribbean
Panama
South America

# Chapter 25

## DEBUSSY AND STRAVINSKY IN PARIS

By the end of the nineteenth century the traditional musical genres had been stretched to their limits. Moreover, the forms that had nurtured the symphony and the string quartet—namely, the solo sonata and the piano concerto (especially the varieties of sonata form)—had reached a degree of formal complexity that demanded repeated hearings before a listener could perceive their structure. Wagner, drawing on the symphonic techniques of Beethoven and his successors, had created his own web of thematic and harmonic interrelationships. After Wagner, it seemed unlikely that any further integration of music, libretto, staging, and scenery could be achieved.

### AVANT-GARDE PARIS

For composers seeking new channels for their creative energies, Paris provided an ideal environment. Despite the Prussian humiliation of the French in 1871, Paris was still the cultural capital of the Western world. The city had a long tradition of welcoming artists from all over Europe, and, as Berlioz had learned, the French were often more hospitable to foreigners than they were to their own artists.

In 1873 a group of four Parisian painters that included Claude Monet (1840–1926) and Pierre Auguste Renoir (1841–1919) learned that their works had been rejected for an exhibition organized by the reigning academicians. Unwilling to accept this rebuff, the next year they sponsored their own exhibit, sparking the first of several dramatic ruptures in the visual arts. A critic pejoratively labeled them "impressionists" (see Color Plate 12). Over the next 13 years almost every French painter of note exhibited at least briefly with the Impressionists, including Edouard Manet (1832–1883), Camille Pissarro (1830–1903), and Edgar Degas (1834–1917). The Impressionists rejected realism and Romantic displays of emotion, seeking instead to depict fleeting, informal scenes from everyday life in broken, luminous textures of pure color. They viewed themselves more as scientific observers of reality than as vessels of artistic inspiration.

Met at first by hostile criticism, by the 1920s the Impressionists had achieved a widespread popularity that continues to this day. Despite their early reception, they altered the artistic landscape of Paris almost overnight and opened the way for other innovators. Paul Cézanne (1839–1906), for example, led Impressionism in a more analytical and abstract direction. An even bolder innovator was Paul Gaugin (1848–1903), who, after careers as sailor and stockbroker, turned to painting full-time and exhibited briefly with the Impressionists. To protest against the "disease" of civilization, he sailed from France and settled in 1891 on the island of Tahiti. Turning away from the representation of nature as the primary purpose of art, he embraced abstract symbols and figures that took nature only as their starting point. His bold paintings and their uncivilized settings brought together daring colors and shapes that were labeled "exotic" and "primitive" (Color Plate 13).

French literature kept abreast of painting. Taking their cue from the poetry of Charles Baudelaire (1821–1867), symbolist writers such as Paul Verlaine (1844–1896), Stéphane Mallarmé (1842–1898), and Arthur Rimbaud (1854–1891) reacted against the realism and naturalism of the period and focused on suggestion and allusion rather than on direct statement.

Bold new art movements continued to spring up in Paris during the early years of the twentieth century. Fauvists (after *fauve,* meaning "wild beast") such as Henri Matisse (1869–1954), Georges Rouault (1871–1958), Georges Braque (1882–1963), and Raoul Dufy (1878–1953) made up the French wing of Expressionism, a Franco-German movement in which the representation of objective reality was replaced by an inner, often tormented psychological vision. Asked Dufy: "Can I render not what I see, but what is, what exists for me, my reality?" An even more radical exponent, Maurice de Vlaminck (1876–1958), explained: "I wanted to burn down the École des Beaux-Arts ["School of Fine Arts," the center of French academic painting] with my cobalts and vermilions and I wanted to express my feelings with my brushes without troubling what painting was like before me."

Around 1907 a group of painters known as Cubists, including Braque, Juan Gris (1887–1927), and Pablo Picasso (1881–1973)—all living in Paris—rejected subjects charged with emotion in favor of abstract geometrical shapes that redefined traditional three-dimensional objects from several different points of view (Color Plate 16). Though founded in Italy, the movement called Futurism, with its worship of the kinetic machine, received a major exhibition in Paris in 1912. Meanwhile, the Trocadero Museum was sponsoring pathbreaking exhibits of "primitive" African art and artifacts (especially masks).

It was this remarkably avant-garde yet cosmopolitan Parisian mix that was to find its musical expression in the music of Claude Debussy and Igor Stravinsky. But first French music had to liberate itself from the suffocating grip of Wagnerism.

# WAGNERISM

By the end of the nineteenth century the dominant force in European music was what had become known as "Wagnerism." So pervasive was Wagner's influence on harmony, for example, that virtually all composers active at the end of the century sounded as if their music had passed through a Wagnerian filter. Under the spell of *Tristan und Isolde,* French composers like César Franck (1822–1890) and Emmanuel Chabrier (1841–1894) wrote music that resonated with Wagnerian chromaticism, instrumentation (especially the prominent use of brass), and leitmotifs. For a time Chabrier belonged to a small group of musicians known as *Le petit Bayreuth* ("The Little Bayreuth") who came together to study Wagner's scores.

Even composers who rejected Wagner's style fell under its influence. Georges Bizet (1838–1875), France's most original opera composer at the time, modeled his operas on those of Mozart, Verdi, and his teacher Charles Gounod (1818–1893). Yet French critics accused him of being either too Wagnerian or not Wagnerian enough. Bizet died a few months before his operatic masterpiece *Carmen* (1875) attained success, but the first reviews of this utterly un-Wagnerian work accused him of having sacrificed the vocal line to the harsh clamor of the orchestra. Bizet himself once accused Verdi, in *Don Carlos* (written for performance in Paris in 1867), of "trying to write Wagner."

Actually, the term *Wagnerism* was applied to a variety of social movements as well as to music. Wagner believed himself to be a cultural messiah, and his followers endorsed everything from vegetarianism and antivivisectionism, to Darwinism, to politics of both the extreme left and the extreme right. Between the opening of Bayreuth in 1876 and Wagner's death in 1883, scores of Richard Wagner Societies sprang up across Europe.

Wagner and the Wagnerians declared themselves the musical avant-garde—the defenders of the new and the adventurous—and they decried the preference of middle-class audiences for a small group of "classical" masterpieces by composers long dead (a dispute that still rages today). Probably no composer in history—not even Bach, Mozart, or Beethoven—exercised such a powerful influence on the music of his own time as Wagner did. Only against that background can we appreciate the achievement of Claude Debussy.

# CLAUDE DEBUSSY (1862–1918)

At the time of Claude Debussy's birth, his parents were running a china shop in a small village near Paris; later, his father worked as a traveling salesman and a clerk, his mother as a seamstress. When the young man's extraordinary musical talents became evident, his parents enrolled him in theory and piano classes at

Claude Debussy

the Paris Conservatory. For a brief time he considered pursuing a career as a pianist, but when he failed to receive the Conservatory's top awards he turned to composition. At the age of 22 he won the Prix de Rome, which enabled him to study for two years at the Villa Medici outside Rome. But the introspective, fastidious young composer was unhappy in the pretentious atmosphere there, and he returned to Paris as soon as he could.

Debussy remained in Paris for the rest of his life. Except for a series of stormy relationships (two of which led to marriage), Debussy's life was uneventful. From time to time his friends persuaded him to write music criticism for several of the music and literary journals that had sprung up in Paris, and his witty and often biting commentaries were eagerly anticipated and discussed.

Like other aspiring composers of the 1880s, Debussy fell at first under the spell of Wagner. At the Villa Medici he had played the score of *Tristan und Isolde* over and over. He made two pilgrimages to Bayreuth (in 1888 and 1889), where he heard Wagner's last opera, *Parsifal*. Fourteen years later he recalled "that period, when I was a Wagnerian to the point of forgetting the simplest principles of civility."

Over the years, Debussy's uncritical enthusiasm for Wagner waned. Although he never actually questioned Wagner's greatness as a composer, he was irritated by claims that Wagner was the greatest German musician who ever lived. "What about Bach?" he wrote. "Was he just a man who had lots of children?" He remarked sarcastically that Wagner "had created the system of leitmotifs for those who cannot find their way in a score." At last, Debussy came to see Wagner's music as a threat to the character of French music. Disputing the claim that Wagner's music dramas were "the artwork of the future," Debussy wrote that "Wagner was . . . a beautiful sunset that was mistaken for a sunrise."

Although his earliest compositions were clearly influenced by Wagner, Debussy soon developed a musical language that was very much his own. In fact, his goals were often the opposite of Wagner's. For example, Wagner's mature music always seems to be heading harmonically for a cadence that is then diverted, which in turn sets up another cadence that is also diverted. In *Tristan und Isolde*, as we have seen, this technique creates an intense sense of longing. Debussy, by contrast, used harmonies that seem to float weightlessly. He replaced the strong chordal movements outlined in Wagner's basses with soft stepwise motion and with chords that move in parallel. Rather than the strong dissonances that Wagner favored, Debussy used milder ones. (On the piano, contrast a typical Wagner chord with the notes C-E-G-B and a typical Debussy chord with the notes C-E♭-G-B♭). When Debussy did employ strong dissonances, he set them in lush orchestrations that softened their harsh outlines.

Debussy's themes, and the rhythms that propel them, are marked by equilibrium and balance rather than by Wagnerian surges. There is little counterpoint of the kind we associate with German or Austrian composers. Rather than building toward a single climax, Debussy's themes are made up of small repeating units whose effect is cumulative rather than climactic. Whereas Wagner would introduce an arresting idea and then subject it to symphonic development, Debussy's themes are more open-ended and undergo little development. The themes in a Debussy composition often sound as if they were derived from a common theme that is never fully articulated.

A gifted orchestrator, Wagner had introduced the Wagner tuba and other unfamiliar instruments into the orchestra. Still, like other German composers, he had favored the middle registers of the orchestra. Debussy spread his sounds out over a wider range than had any composer before him. He often omitted traditional instruments in favor of less common ones and combined instruments in unusual ways (doubling instruments, for example, at more than an octave apart).

Finally, whereas Wagner was a man of the theater who tried to portray actions and emotions specifically and literally, Debussy was a musician who scorned the notion that music could be concrete or specific. In reviewing a production of Wagner's *Ring,* he wrote: "How unbearable these people in skins and helmets become by the fourth night! . . . Remember they never appear without the accompaniment of their accursed leitmotif. Some of them even sing it! This suggests a harmless lunatic who, on presenting his visiting card, would declaim his name in song."

Debussy's reaction against Wagnerian emotionalism was altogether in keeping with the views of the Impressionist painters, and his rich orchestral colors and evocative titles soon led critics to label him a "musical Impressionist." One of the first works to suggest that label was Debussy's *Prelude to "The Afternoon of a Faun."*

### ✷Debussy: *Prelude to "The Afternoon of a Faun"* (1892–1894)

Debussy's *Prelude to "The Afternoon of a Faun"* (Listening Guide 51) is his best-known orchestral work. Following its Paris premiere in 1894, it was performed in Boston in 1902, in Berlin in 1903, in Vienna in 1907, and in London in 1908. By the outbreak of the First World War, it had become an international favorite with orchestras and audiences alike.

Though Debussy did not begin the *Prelude* until he was 30, it was his first major orchestral work. It was inspired by a poem written in 1876 by Stéphane Mallarmé, whose evocative use of the French language perfectly suited Debussy's style. Debussy had attended a number of Mallarmé's Tuesday evening gatherings, at which the poet had expounded a symbolist theory of poetry in which language served as a vehicle for suggestion rather than description, approaching the abstractness of music. Back in Berlioz's day, certain literary critics had described music as "a disagreeable noise made on purpose." Now the poet Paul Valéry, a contemporary of Debussy, observed that "poetry felt itself insufficient before the power and resources of the orchestra."

Mallarmé called his 111-line poem an *eclogue,* from the ancient Greek for a dialogue poem on a pastoral subject. A *faun* was a rural deity in Roman mythology who possessed the body of a man and the horns, ears, and tail (and sometimes the legs) of a goat. Mallarmé's faun is an erotic, seductive creature who dreams in free-association manner of encounters with nymphs. "Those nymphs, I want to make them perpetual," begins the faun. His anonymous respondent

# Listening Guide 51

## DEBUSSY: *Prelude to "The Afternoon of a Faun"*

CD 6, TRACK 2
TAPE 6A, TRACK 2
DURATION: 10:39

*For ease of identification, the theme played by the solo flute at the beginning of the* Pre-lude *is referred to throughout as the Languor Theme, with appearances numbered successively. Notice that the beginnings and ends of the themes are not emphasized; rather, they seem to melt into one another.*

*Form: Free ternary (A-B-A') with coda*

| | LOCATION | TIME | COMMENTS |
|---|---|---|---|
| 1 | *A*-Section | **0:00** | Languor Theme 1, solo flute. |
| | | 0:23 | As the theme pauses, horns, winds, and harp enter. |
| | | 0:36 | The end of the phrase repeats and slows. |
| | | 0:57 | Languor Theme 2, flute accompanied by soft tremolo strings. |
| | | 1:18 | The melody is extended further by the oboe. |
| | | 1:34 | A repeating figure dissolves through repetition. |
| | | 1:58 | Languor Theme 3, flute accompanied by harp and strings. |
| | | 2:36 | Languor Theme 4, flute accompanied by harp and strings. |
| | | 3:08 | Strongest internal cadence in the *Prelude*. |
| 2 | *B*-Section | **3:15** | Clarinet plays *B*-Theme 1, an animated takeoff on the Languor Theme. |
| | | 3:31 | The same theme is now repeated slightly higher. |
| | | 3:44 | *B*-Theme 2 in the oboe. |

asks, "Might not the girls you are describing be/Wishful figments of your mythopoetic senses?" But the faun dreams on of "The kiss, that softly reassures unfaithful lovers."

There is no narrative in either Mallarmé's poem or in Debussy's tone poem. Here Debussy was breaking with Wagner as well as with the programmatic tradition of Berlioz. It is not even clear what Debussy meant by calling the work a "prelude." Was it a prelude to the reading of Mallarmé's poem? Or a commentary on it? To make this nonnarrative, "formless" piece of music somehow hang together, he chose as his chief unifying device a theme that projects both sensuality and weightless equilibrium. The sensuality derives partly from Debussy's use, at the very opening, of a solo flute:

*Part Four The Twentieth Century*

| LOCATION | TIME | COMMENTS |
|---|---|---|
| | 4:06 | The theme builds toward a climax using repetition and sequence. |
| | 4:17 | Though seemingly on the way to a major climax, the phrase winds slowly down instead. |
| | 4:30 | A gradual ritard, accompanied by repeated figures in the horns. |
| | 4:45 | A bridge theme in the clarinet. |
| | 5:09 | *B*-Theme 3 in the winds, builds slowly. |
| | 5:46 | With an intensified accompaniment, the same theme begins to build toward a climax. |
| | 6:03 | The bridge theme continues toward a climax but sinks through repetition and a ritard back to earth. |
| | 6:35 | A solo horn plays the bridge theme while the violin recalls *B*-Theme 3. |
| **3** **A′-Section** | **7:02** | Languor Theme 5, flute solo with harp accompanying in major chords. |
| | 7:25 | The continuation resembles *B*-Theme 1. |
| | 7:38 | Languor Theme 6 in oboe, a slightly varied repeat of the previous appearance. Once again the theme winds down through repetition and a ritard. |
| | 8:19 | Languor Theme 7, flute with solo violin intermixing the bridge theme. |
| | 9:02 | Languor Theme 8, flute and solo viola. |
| **4** **Coda** | **9:29** | Second part of Languor Theme in the oboe, not heard since the second statement. |
| | 9:55 | A descending bass figure in the harps minimizes the sense of final resolution. |
| | 10:06 | Languor Theme 9, played in parallel by the muted horns; the final cadence fades to a distant echo. |

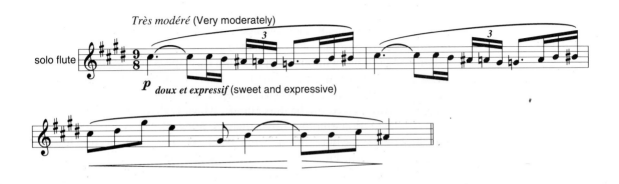

# Historical Window

## THE EXPOSITION UNIVERSELLE OF 1889

In Chapter 1 we remarked that it made little sense to try to cover Western music *and* non-Western music in a single volume. True, the origins of Western music were intertwined with developments in Byzantium, the Middle East, and elsewhere. But after about A.D. 1000, as Western music focused on polyphony, those influences pretty much vanished. Then, as modern technology began to shrink the globe, Western music once again grew more responsive to outside forces.

We find the best evidence of this trend in the trade fairs or expositions in Europe that had their origins in the medieval cloth fairs. Before the emergence of affordable transportation and mass marketing, these fairs gave people an opportunity to exchange merchandise and served as social centers for widely separated communities. During the eighteenth century, fairs in France and England began to feature goods produced in factories that used advanced manufacturing techniques. Manufacturers were eager to make their new products known to a public that had until now relied largely on door-to-door peddlers.

Much of what we know about the technological development of the piano, for example, derives from reports of expositions in Austria, France, and England. With its combination of wood, metal, cast-iron plate, moving parts, and high-tension wire, the late-nineteenth-century piano was considered one of the technological marvels of the age.

During the second half of the nineteenth century, the trade expositions became increasingly international in scope. A grand exposition held in 1851 in London at the "Crystal Palace" (Figure 25.1), a massive glass and steel structure erected especially for this month-long event, brought together products from more than a dozen industrial nations, including the United States. The French were especially keen on international expositions. In 1855, 1868, 1878, 1889, and 1900, a series of "Expositions universelles" in Paris displayed the cultural artifacts of non-Western nations as well as the products of industrialized nations. The famed Eiffel Tower (Figure 25.2) was commissioned and built for the exposition of 1889.

That 1889 exposition, which lasted several months, contained numerous pavilions through which the public could stroll and view the exhibits. One of the largest pavilions was devoted entirely to anthropology, the study of peoples and their cultures. Originating at the end of the eighteenth century, anthropology draws on biology, archaeology, psychology, linguistics, and geology to answer broad questions about the origins of humankind and the ways in which

Debussy worked slowly and car
tic standards. His one opera, *Pell*
became a regularly performed wo
Though he was not a virtuoso p
1894–1901), *Estampes* (*Engravi*
two books of preludes (1910–191
1915–1916) established him as o
the twentieth century. His three
Three Nocturnes for Orchestra (
and *Images* (1905–1912), all bea

It was with the *Prelude to "The*
broke the stranglehold of Wagne
He proudly signed his last works
Debussy, French musician). He h
soon to erupt in full force.

## LES BALLETS RUSSES

Even more radical experiments a
experiments was a restless Russia
1929; Figure 25.4). Born to a m
died a few days after his birth, you
section of St. Petersburg. There h
(who, for a pittance, accompanied
studying law, though with little er
ing, the theater, and music. He o
art that came to the attention of t
wealthy patrons. In 1898 he foun
with contemporary art inside and
ballets at the Imperial Theater in
quent trips to the West, usually t
publicized exhibition of Russian
received "historical concerts" of
performances of Musorgsky's *Bor*

Diaghilev—now one of Europ
something to Paris that the Fren
Ballet. The company had risen to
Tchaikovsky, but recently a young
had introduced more expressive a
headed by two superstars, Anna Pa
said, "She doesn't dance, she floa
25.5). Diaghilev renamed the con

Uncertain whether Parisian au

FIGURE 25.4 Impresario Sergei Diaghilev had a talent for attracting and promoting talent. He greeted the stormy response to *The Rite of Spring* by saying, "Exactly what I wanted."

FIGURE 25.1 (left) At the world's first international exhibition, Joseph Paxton's Crystal Palace in London covered 19 acres of Hyde Park.

FIGURE 25.2 (right) The engineer Alexandre Gustave Eiffel was commissioned to create a symbol of the Paris Exhibition of 1889. Some Parisians called his tower a "junkman's Notre Dame." Today, a TV antenna tops it.

societies are bound together. In the latter half of the nineteenth century, with the first important studies of preliterate, non-Western peoples, anthropology emerged as a serious discipline. Visitors to the anthropology pavilion at the 1889 exposition saw exhibits on the ancient Egyptians, the Aztecs, China, Japan, India, Nepal, Tibet, and prehistoric humans in Africa.

The exposition also attracted hordes of Western and non-Western musicians who performed in the open air or in tents and booths along the Champs de Mars and the Esplanade des Invalides. There were tribal dancers from Africa, choirs from Finland, gypsies from Hungary, a Vietnamese (Annamite) theater, and folk singers from Spain, the Middle East, and Rumania. The Russian composer Nikolai Rimsky-Korsakov presented two concerts of his own music and music by Balakirev and Musorgsky, inaugurating a relationship between French and Russian composers that had grown very close by the end of the century. Visitors to this remarkably diverse exposition were seeing and hearing expressions of exotic cultures for the first time.

Claude Debussy, with his composer friend Paul Dukas, spent many hours strolling through the exhibits and listening to the outdoor musicians. Debussy

*continued*

FIGURE 25.3 The instruments of a few gamelan orchestras have made their way to the United States. At universities such as UCLA, students can learn to perform as a member of these exotic ensembles.

was especially taken by the mus[...]
The Bĕdayas was a ceremonial [...]
performed by nine female danc[...]
stylized movements without d[...]
small orchestra called a *gamela[...]*
percussion instruments, includ[...]
assortment of gongs. The gong[...]
7-note *pelog* scale, both of whic[...]
A small two-string fiddle provid[...]
by the delicate, veiled sounds [...]
had ever heard before. His comp[...]
for the next 30 years, from the a[...]
*of a Faun*" to the scale pattern[...]
diverse instruments."

We can still marvel at the div[...]
can safely say that the "internati[...]
year. Consequently our account[...]
increasingly global frame of refe[...]

LO

5 Ri[...]

6 Pr[...]

7 Tl[...]

8 D[...]

# *Chapter 26*

## EXPRESSIONISM AND SERIALISM IN VIENNA

Defeated by the Prussians in 1871, the French had abandoned any illusion that they were a major military power. Moreover, having been governed by short-lived regimes since the rise of Napoleon in the 1790s, they had become accustomed to political instability. So, as the century neared its end, Parisians focused on what they had always done best: fashion, art, theater, and music. Embracing a future that might help them forget an often humiliating past, they extended a warm welcome to the "modernists" who were taking unprecedented approaches to musical composition.

As the nineteenth century drew to a close, the Hapsburg dynasty had been in power for more than six centuries. At its height under Charles V in the sixteenth century, the Hapsburgs had ruled much of Europe, but since that time their power and influence had steadily declined. Early in the century Napoleon had twice occupied Vienna, the Hapsburg capital, and yet, following the end of the Napoleonic Wars in 1813, the Hapsburgs managed to hang on for another century.

With his white handlebar mustache and medal-bedecked uniform, Emperor Franz Joseph (Figure 24.4, page 493), who ruled from 1848 until his death in 1916, symbolized the glory that had once been Austria's. Already an anachronism among world leaders by the end of the century, Franz Joseph was like a marble statue perfectly preserved in a museum. Unlike the French, who embraced the future, the Austrians viewed the future with *Angst* (anxiety). Hugo von Hofmannsthal (1874–1929), a leading Austrian author and playwright, wrote, "We must take leave of a world before it collapses."

To dispel their anxiety, many Austrians pretended that the empire was alive and well and simply ignored the mounting evidence of decline. Others, rejecting the route of escapism, turned to art in the hope of making some sense of the decline—or at least of responding to it in some fashion. In this effort they were joined by other German artists distressed by the militarism of a newly unified Germany. Together they engaged in several short-lived movements that reflected the *Angst* of the dying century.

# SECESSIONISM, FREUD, AND EXPRESSIONISM

It was not only in France that unorthodox artists found themselves excluded from the established academic associations. In Berlin, Munich, Vienna, London, and even in New York City, rebellious young artists "seceded" from the Establishment and set up loosely defined organizations of their own. Unlike the French Impressionists, however, who had substituted a more disciplined view of nature for the excesses of Romanticism, this new generation of Secessionists sought to intensify their visual images and strove to distort nature rather than represent it. One of the most influential of their early styles was *art nouveau* ("new art"), which was introduced in the decorative arts—especially furniture, jewelry, and book design and illustration—in England during the 1880s. In Germany the style became known as *Jugendstil* ("youth style") and in Austria simply as *Secessionstil* ("secession style"). This was a richly ornamental, highly symbolic style that often featured exotic characters drawn from the world of dreams.

The leading Austrian exponent of art nouveau was Gustav Klimt (1862–1918), one of the 19 founders in 1897 of the Austrian Secession, and its first president. In a panel he painted in 1898 for the home of a wealthy Viennese music lover, Klimt portrays Music as a Greek priestess holding an ancient *kithara*, the instrument of Apollo. Accompanying the priestess, who represents classical order and balance, are the Sphinx (a child-eating mother) and Silenus, a companion of Dionysius, the god of wine—both of them symbols of irrational passion. These figures stare out at the viewer impassively, as if in a dream. Music stands as a mysterious presence bridging the gap between these seemingly isolated forces. In 1903 Klimt and his colleagues staged an extravagant exhibition designed to resemble an ancient temple and housing a statue of Beethoven by the Leipzig sculptor Max Klinger (1857–1920). The statue incorporates several kinds of colored marble, precious stones, ivory, bronze, and polished gold (Color Plate 14). Beethoven emerges as a mythic hero, and art seems to provide a refuge from the harsh realities of life. This was a new way of viewing both artists and art.

Meanwhile, two brilliant young Viennese architects, Otto Wagner (1841–1918) and Adolf Loos (1870–1933), were redefining the urban landscape. Under the influence of the Secessionists, they rejected the heavy symbolism that had characterized Viennese architecture throughout the nineteenth century, and in its place they substituted *function.* Their designs, which featured aluminum, poured concrete, and other modern materials, became models for industrial and residential architecture all over Europe (Figure 26.1).

The frequency of the dream motif in Secessionist art tied in to the work of the Viennese physician Sigmund Freud (1856–1939; Figure 26.2). In 1900 Freud published a seminal paper, *The Interpretation of Dreams,* in which he proposed that dreams are subconscious commentaries on reality. Over the next 15 years Freud and his disciples—several of whom started their own schools of what Freud called *psychoanalysis*—explored the subconscious and its contents. They

FIGURE 26.1 In 1896, Louis Sullivan, a pioneering American architect, said, "Form ever follows function," and many twentieth-century designers (such as Adolf Loos, whose work is shown here) have sworn by Sullivan's dictum—with mixed results.

FIGURE 26.2 At the age of 70, Freud assessed his achievement: "The poets and philosophers before me discovered the unconscious; what I discovered was the scientific method by which the unconscious can be studied."

concluded that childhood traumas and infantile attachments are the source of certain destructive patterns of behavior known as "neuroses." Although Freud and his followers sought to help their patients exorcise, or at least adjust to, their neuroses, their work—especially in this age of anxiety—focused attention on the dark, mysterious side of the human mind, to which many artists were drawn.

These Expressionist artists took their cue from the *fauves* in Paris but added a generous dose of German melancholy and *Angst*. Oskar Kokoschka (1886–1980), the most talented painter and writer among the Viennese Expressionists, ridiculed the Secessionists' concern with the decorative arts, and in his poetry, drama, and drawings explored the basic, instinctual dimensions of human behavior. In his play *Murderer, Hope of Women,* he treats the relationship between the sexes as a struggle to the death, with neither male nor female able to break the murderous bond between them. The force and the violence of Kokoschka's drama derive at least in part from his reaction against a repressed society that was out of touch with its own feelings.

Between 1890 and the outbreak of the First World War in 1914, Secessionism, Expressionism, escapism, modernism, and the revolutionary views of Sigmund Freud kept the intellectual life of Vienna in a state of ferment. Into that ferment was born an artist and musician whose sense of mission was to alter the course of music forever.

**COLOR PLATE 13**

*Paul Gauguin abandoned his family and a prosperous career as a stockbroker to rediscover humankind's links to nature, first among peasants in western France and later in Tahiti. He portrayed the two figures in* Words of the Devil *in a self-consciously primitive manner that seems to resonate in Stravinsky's orchestration of* The Rite of Spring. *(The standing figure represents Eve.)*

**COLOR PLATE 14**

It is hard to imagine a
more idealized repre-
sentation of a creative
artist than Max
Klinger's statue of
Beethoven, created for
the fourteenth Vienna
Secession exhibition in
1902. Klinger con-
ceived the idea in 1885
and spent the next sev-
enteen years assembling
and integrating the
materials, which in-
clude alabaster, ivory,
mother of pearl, and
several types of marble.
The casting of the
bronze throne in 1901,
a continuous process,
took nineteen hours.
With the determined
expression of the defiant
hero, Klinger's
Beethoven is godlike, an
immortal genius whose
life transcends time
and place.

**COLOR PLATE 15**
*The clownish profile in Schoenberg's* The Critic *depicts not only Schoenberg's natural aversion to music critics but also his view of* *human behavior as governed by subconscious and often dark impulses, giving this painting its macabre quality.*

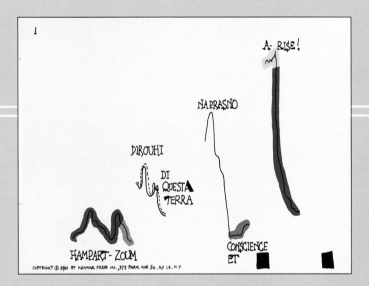

**COLOR PLATE 16**

*"Art is meant to disturb. Science reassures,"
said the Cubist painter
Georges Braque. In
Violin and Palette, he
presents the curves of
the violin from several
perspectives simultaneously. The instrument's strings are no
longer sound generators
but lines creating abstract geometric planes.*

**COLOR PLATE 17**

*Following the first page
of the score to John
Cage's* Aria *is easier
than you might think:
Dark blue = jazz; red =
lyric contralto; black
with parallel dotted
lines = Sprechstimme;
purple = Marlene
Dietrich; yellow =
coloratura. What are
the two "noises" that
vocalist Berberian
makes at the black
squares?*

# ARNOLD SCHOENBERG (1874–1951) AND ATONALITY

FIGURE 26.3 Schoenberg made innovation sound inevitable when he wrote, "Once, in the army, I was asked if I was really the composer Arnold Schoenberg. 'Somebody had to be,' I said."

Like Debussy and Stravinsky, Arnold Schoenberg (Figure 26.3) contributed to the transition from Romanticism to modernism in music. Debussy and Stravinsky deflected the course of music from the great Austro-German tradition—the tradition of Bach and Beethoven and Wagner. Schoenberg carried that tradition to its logical conclusion. Indeed, he saw himself as someone who preserved and extended the tradition, not—as many of his critics were to charge—as someone bent on destroying it.

Schoenberg was born in Vienna in 1874 to parents of Hungarian and Czech ancestry. His father ran a shoe shop and the family lived on the edge of poverty. Yet somehow his parents arranged for young Arnold to take violin lessons from the time he was 8, and by the time he was 10 he was arranging all the music he could get his hands on. Unable to afford concert tickets, he and a few friends formed a small chamber ensemble in which Schoenberg advanced his knowledge of music. He studied musical form in a music encyclopedia, but, except for some informal lessons from his future brother-in-law, Alexander von Zemlimsky, he was entirely self-taught as a composer. To support himself, he orchestrated more than 6,000 pages of operettas and took on composition pupils, two of whom—Alban Berg (1885–1935) and Anton Webern (1883–1945)—were to become major composers in their own right. In 1911 Schoenberg published his *Harmonielehre* (*Harmony Method*), which is as much a comprehensive history as a textbook and is still widely consulted. He was also a gifted painter whose haunting portraits of human faces—Schoenberg called them "visions"—hinted at the macabre inner world of the Expressionists (Color Plate 15). Both his music and his paintings were reproduced in the short-lived (1911–1914) but influential periodical of the German Expressionists, *Der blaue Reiter* (The Blue Rider, named after a painting by Wassily Kandinsky [1866–1944]).

By the time Schoenberg reached his mid-twenties, he had emerged as one of the most talented composers of a generation that included Mahler, Richard Strauss, Debussy, Stravinsky, and Bartók. Schoenberg's early works, among them the string sextet *Verklärte Nacht* (*Transfigured Night,* 1899) and the tone poem *Pelleas und Melisande* (1902/1903), show a mastery of late Romantic styles, especially that of Brahms, whom he admired. Until about 1907, Schoenberg's style did not differ radically from that of his two greatest Austrian contemporaries, Mahler and Richard Strauss. Strauss, in his early operas, and Mahler, in his last symphonies, had pushed Wagner's chromaticism to its limits, but neither composer had abandoned tonality.

Schoenberg—whose music had been well received by Viennese audiences—could easily have continued along this late-Romantic path, but he felt compelled to follow a new one. "I am being forced in this direction. . . . I am obeying an inner compulsion which is stronger than any upbringing," he wrote to a friend. Schoenberg was just enough younger than Strauss and Mahler to be more strongly attracted to the Expressionists than to the Secessionists. Unlike Mahler, who did not live long enough to reveal whether he would have evolved in more radical directions, or Strauss, who backed off from the implications of his own early style, Schoenberg decided to take the plunge.

For over 200 years, the system of tonality had served as a framework for virtually every form of Western music. Although the level of dissonance had declined during the Viennese period, it had risen steadily throughout the nineteenth century, reaching its culmination in the music of Wagner. Because dissonances require resolutions, each of which takes time, the rise in the level of dissonance had led to the writing of longer and more complex pieces. Eventually, however, dissonance rose to such a level that it threatened to overwhelm the very foundations of tonality, in which all harmonic movement ultimately must return to the tonic triad, a point of consonant repose.

At the end of 1907, Schoenberg began writing movements in which many of the dissonances are left unresolved. Perhaps coincidentally, it was at this time that he first became acquainted with the music of Debussy. Schoenberg's Quartet No. 2 begins in F-sharp Minor, but in its last movement he introduces a part for a soprano singing a text by the poet Stefan George. The soprano's first line is, "I feel breezes from other planets, the visions blow over me through the darkness. . . ." For these prophetic words, Schoenberg wrote music with no key signature and—more important—in *no key*. Although at its very end the movement returns dutifully to F♯, Schoenberg had made a break that soon became irreversible. About the same time, he wrote a cycle of songs on George's *Das Buch der hängenden Garten (The Book of the Hanging Garden)*, in which he wrote similarly "atonal" passages to describe the decay of a garden (a device Austrian artists used to symbolize the decay of their own society). Although Schoenberg failed to come up with a satisfactory alternative, he was never happy with the term *atonal*, which he compared to calling swimming "the art of not drowning."

Between 1908 and 1913 Schoenberg was astonishingly productive, even though he was writing in a style that was almost as foreign to him as it was to his audiences. Many years later he described this period with a grim metaphor: "Personally I had the feeling as if I had fallen into an ocean of boiling waters, and not knowing how to swim or get out in another manner, I tried with my legs and arms as best I could." He soon abandoned the idea of ending otherwise atonal pieces with tonal cadences, and he criticized composers who paid lip service to tonality in that way.

One of his largest works during this time was *Erwartung (Expectation*, 1909), which Schoenberg called a "monodrama." In this work a distraught woman wanders along a moonlit path in a half-waking, half-dreaming state, looking for her beloved, whom she fears she may have murdered. There are no triadic harmonies, much less tonal passages, in this entire 40-minute work. Nor are there any recognizable themes. Yet *Erwartung*, which Schoenberg wrote in 19 days, has a riveting power that transcends its utter lack of traditional materials.

During this turbulent period, Schoenberg believed that he was following the path charted by Wagner and his predecessors. And yet, in both his subject matter and musical expression we sense a spirit of rebelliousness, a conscious rejection of the comfortable escapism of Viennese society. The Viennese had emerged as the most conservative—even reactionary—audience in Europe, viewing themselves as the guardians of the great tradition from Bach to Brahms. Unlike the Parisians, who took music less seriously and who cultivated scandal with a theatrical flair, the Viennese were not the least bit amused by the music of Schoenberg and his pupils Berg and Webern (see the Historical Window on page 562). Their rejection only deepened Schoenberg's contempt for a society he viewed as corrupt. We turn now to two Expressionist works by Schoenberg that chronicle his departure from traditional tonality.

## Schoenberg: *Vergangenes (The Past)* from *Five Pieces for Orchestra*, Op. 16 (1909)

Almost all orchestral works had been either symphonies or tone poems until 1909, when Schoenberg presented a group of orchestral movements simply titled *Five Pieces*. This was not a slap at the symphonic tradition, which Schoenberg revered, but at middle-class expectations of what an orchestral work should be called. At the urging of his publisher, Schoenberg gave each of the movements an evocative title: I, *Premonitions;* II, *The Past;* III, *Colors* (originally subtitled "Summer Morning on a Lake," later dropped); IV, *Culmination;* and V, *The Obligatory Recitative.* Although Schoenberg used the large, post-Romantic orchestra favored by Mahler, none of the movements lasts more than five minutes—a remarkable departure from the mammoth structures Mahler was writing at the time.

The second of the pieces, *Vergangenes* (*The Past;* Listening Guide 53), is both a personal evocation of some dimly remembered event (perhaps only in a dream) and a wistful farewell to the age of tonality. Schoenberg uses the orchestra as a gigantic chamber ensemble, scoring almost all of the string parts for solo instruments. Except for a few measures of an aborted climax, the dynamic level rarely rises above *mp* (medium soft). Schoenberg assigns a prominent role to the only percussion instrument in the piece, the *celesta,* a small keyboard instrument shaped like an upright piano whose hammers strike a series of resonating steel plates to produce a bell-like but veiled sound. The instrument, invented in 1886, had been made famous six years later by Tchaikovsky in his *Dance of the Sugar Plum Fairy* from *The Nutcracker.* Whereas Tchaikovsky had used the celesta to evoke a fairy-tale atmosphere, Schoenberg uses it to suggest a dreamlike state somewhere between illusion and reality.

In its external structure, *Vergangenes* is in ternary form. Although there are no distinct cadences, the opening *A*-Section is separated from the *B*-Section by long-held notes and by the new material that follows. Moreover, the return of the abridged *A′*-Section is well articulated. But the material within each section is quite untraditional. The solo cello opens over a tonic pedal tone in the trombone with what might be called a motive, but scarcely a theme:

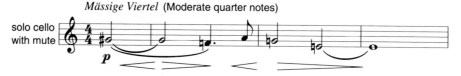

SCHOENBERG: *Vergangenes (The Past)*
from *Five Pieces for Orchestra*, Op. 16

CD 6, TRACK 4
TAPE 6B, TRACK 1
DURATION: 4:32

*Although the boundaries of the three sections are reasonably clear, Schoenberg's use of this traditional form has little to do with its Baroque or even Romantic origins. The ideas within the sections resemble motives more than self-contained themes, and they drift in and out of focus. All are open-ended, and none is resolved.*

*Form: Ternary*

| LOCATION | TIME | COMMENTS |
|---|---|---|
| **1** *A*-SECTION | | |
| Motive 1 | **0:00** | Solo cello with mute, answered by low woodwinds. Over a tonic pedal in the trombone. |
| | 0:16 | Vague elaboration of Motive 1 in high woodwinds, ending in a fermata and brief silence. |
| | 0:47 | Over a soft pedal point in the celesta (echoed by piccolo and flute), fragmentary motives in faster note values and a more contrapuntal texture. |
| | 1:22 | Long-held notes, which prepare the return of |
| Motive 1 | 1:28 | Motive 1 in the winds and trumpet (interrupted briefly by a pause at 1:36). Fades to another brief pause. |

This motive, Motive 1, is "open-ended"—that is, like the past itself, it has no clear beginning or end. Only its second and third notes are consonant with the pedal tone D, the key that is evoked but never established. The phrase that follows seems to be vaguely based on this opening motive, but it pauses before reaching any goal. A longer phrase unfolds around a shadowy pedal point in the celesta, piccolo, and flute. Only after it dissolves into long-held notes does Motive 1 return to "frame" the *A*-Section, where it is played—with an unexpected pause in the middle—by trumpet and English horn over a tonic pedal in the cellos. Nowhere is there any clear sense of meter or key. The fragmentary ideas and the hazy contrapuntal texture give the whole section an eerie quality.

The *B*-Section begins with what seems to be a more clear-cut idea (Motive 2):

| | LOCATION | TIME | COMMENTS |
|---|---|---|---|
| **2** | *B*-SECTION | | |
| | Motive 2 | **1:52** | Short, floating motive at varying speeds subjected to dense imitation. Marked *ppp* and "extremely delicate." Repetitive but unrelated lines with no sense of meter. |
| | Motive 3 | 2:48 | Overlapping ostinato in the celesta. Contrasting ostinato in the bassoon played at different speeds. |
| | Motive 2 | 3:33 | Motive 2 returns in slower form with hazy, dreamlike texture. Struggles toward a climax from 3:52–3:58, but fades away. |
| **3** | *A'*-SECTION | | |
| | Motive 1 | **4:21** | Motive 1 returns in the oboe, with horns playing a 2-note tonic/dominant pedal point. |
| | | 4:32 | Motive 1 "completes" itself, sliding upwards into a *major triad*—which then disappears. |
| | + Motive 3 | 4:46 | Dim echoes of Motive 1 in clarinet and trumpet, but over the ostinato of Motive 3. |
| | Motive 2 | 5:03 | Minus its first two, and its last, notes, Motive 2 appears in three closely spaced imitations. |
| | (Motive 1) | 5:23 | The beginning of Motive 1 is left suspended, suggesting an infinite past. |

But Schoenberg immediately subjects this idea to the first of a series of "free" imitations—that is, imitations that preserve only a shadowy similarity to the original idea:

The imitations that follow are now faster, now slower. The motive seems to emerge briefly from the shadows, only to disappear.

The middle of the *B*-Section (itself a miniature ternary form) is built around a delicate but ghostly ostinato (Motive 3) in the celesta:

Although each measure is repeated, as always happens in ostinato, the pattern itself is irregular and is punctuated by the imitation in the left hand. When Motive 2 returns in the strings, it struggles to achieve a climax, reaching the only *forte* in the movement. But after sticking on the same melodic peak three times in a row, it sinks back in exhaustion, cueing the return of the *A*-Section.

With the return of Motive 1 in the oboe, something entirely unexpected happens. Instead of closing on the dissonance that marked its first appearance in the opening *A*-Section, Motive 1 now slides up two more notes to F#, creating a major tonic triad with the pedal tones D and A in the horns. With this surprising touch, at the juncture in the movement that most resembles a recapitulation, Schoenberg evokes two centuries of tonal harmony. But no sooner does this pure tonic triad appear than it too vanishes, leaving us to wonder whether we really heard it.

The *A′*-Section, rather than resolving the uncertainties of the first two sections, blurs all three motives together. Motive 1 plays over the ostinato in the celesta (Motive 3), and Motive 2 returns minus its first two and its last notes. In the concluding bars we seem to hear the beginning of Motive 1, but it soon recedes into the echoing past.

Schoenberg's *Vergangenes* is more than a work without tonality or meter or clear-cut themes. Rather, it is a work full of references to the traditional techniques of tonality, imitation, ostinato, and ternary form. It is a poignant farewell to a musical—and a political—age.

### Schoenberg: *"Nacht"* ("Night"), from *Pierrot lunaire (Pierrot of the Moon)*, Op. 21 (1912)

Poetry played an important role in Secessionist and Expressionist art, and poetry and vocal music play an equally important role in Schoenberg's music. With the 1912 premiere of *Pierrot lunaire (Pierrot of the Moon)* in Berlin, where Schoenberg was living, even Schoenberg's critics had to concede that he had created a remarkable marriage of Expressionist poetry and music; many viewed *Pierrot lunaire* as his first undisputed masterpiece.

The figure of Pierrot emerged during the sixteenth century in Italian street theater (*commedia dell' arte,* or "comedy of art") and, along with his comrades, provided a frequent source of Romantic inspiration (Schumann's piano cycle *Carnaval* is one of the best-known examples). From Pierrot's habit of falling in love, or becoming "moonstruck," the Belgian Albert Giraud (1860–1929), a symbolist poet, derived the notion of *Pierrot lunaire.* With its graphic, grotesque images, Giraud's symbolism is a natural fit with Schoenberg's Expressionism. Giraud was more interested in the moon's power to drive us insane than in its "moonstruck" qualities.

Reflecting his interest in numerology, Schoenberg selected 21 of Giraud's poems (translated from French to German by Schoenberg's friend Otto Hartleben) and divided them into three groups of seven each. (Schoenberg believed that numbers had external significance—he managed to be born and to die on Friday the 13th!) As in many of his Expressionist works, the performing forces in *Pierrot lunaire* are untraditional. Five instrumentalists play eight instruments—piano, flute (also piccolo), clarinet (also bass clarinet), violin (also viola), and cello.

These instruments are joined by what Schoenberg called *Sprechstimme,* or "speech-voice," a vocal delivery intermediate between speech and song. It was probably stimulated by singing styles present in turn-of-the-century popular song, especially cabaret music. Schoenberg notated the rhythms of the pitches precisely and instructed the performer to follow them as if they were being sung. He further instructed the performer to land exactly on each pitch but then to depart from it immediately (either up or down). Schoenberg notated *Sprechstimme* by placing an **x** on the stem of a note. His pupil Berg used *Sprechstimme* occasionally (and to great effect in *Wozzeck*), but for Schoenberg it became a regular feature of his style. In *Pierrot lunaire, Sprechstimme* gives Pierrot's lines an eerie, often sinister quality.

The form of all 21 of Giraud's poems is the *rondel,* a flexible medieval poetic form akin to the rondo in music. In Giraud's case, the first two lines of the first stanza serve as the last two lines of the 4-line second stanza and the 5-line third stanza. In *"Nacht"* ("Night"; Listening Guide 54), the poem that begins Part II of *Pierrot lunaire,* the underlying image is of "dark, black, giant moths" which "kill the sunlight" and turn day into a nightmarish darkness. To suggest the darkness, Schoenberg uses only the bass clarinet, cello, and the piano in its lower registers.

In spite of the poem's structure, Schoenberg does not resort to large-scale musical repetition in his setting. Instead, he organizes it around a passacaglia (as in the Brahms *Variations on a Theme by Haydn,* Chapter 21)—the movement's subtitle. Schoenberg interprets passacaglia very freely. His pattern is only three notes long:

# Listening Guide 54

## SCHOENBERG: *"Nacht"* ("Night"), from *Pierrot lunaire (Pierrot of the Moon)*, Op. 21

CD 6, TRACK [5]
TAPE 6B, TRACK 2
DURATION: 2:23

*Stanzas 1 and 2 are separated by a pause, and stanzas 3 and 4 are separated by a brief instrumental interlude. There are no large-scale repetitions of material as one might expect in the setting of a strophic poem. The unity is provided by the continuous presence of the 3-note passacaglia figure and the chromatic line.*

*Form: Through-composed (free passacaglia)*

| STANZA / TEXT | TIME | COMMENTS |
|---|---|---|
| **1** STANZA 1 | | |
| | **0:00** | Instrumental introduction with four low statements of the 3-note passacaglia in closely spaced imitation. |
| *Finstre, schwarze Riesenfalter töteten der Sonne glanz.* Dark, black, giant moths kill the sunlight. | 0:21 | Descending chromatic line in voice. Slow-moving passacaglia moves through the instruments. |
| *Ein geschloßnes Zauberbuch ruht der Horizont,* A closed magic book rests on the horizon, | 0:35 | The passacaglia played twice as fast in the instruments. |
| *verschwiegen.* silenced. | 0:49 | While the cellist plays the descending chromatic line, the vocalist sings the passacaglia theme for the only time—at its original pitch and, coincidentally, her lowest pitches. Both are barely audible. |

He introduces the passacaglia in the bass of the piano at the beginning. And yet the register is so deep, and the imitation that follows so closely spaced, that we are only dimly aware of it. Nevertheless, the 3-note pattern is present either in the voice or in an instrument (and, occasionally, shared among instruments) in every measure of the movement. It occurs at four different speeds and in inversion (played upside down) and retrograde (played backwards). The passacaglia

| STANZA / TEXT | TIME | COMMENTS |
|---|---|---|
| **2** STANZA 2 | | |
| *Aus dem Qualm verlorner Tiefen steigt ein Duft,* <br> From the fumes of lost depths wafts an aroma, | **0:58** | Passacaglia in the bass clarinet and piano. Cello begins eerie tremolos "on the bridge" at 1:02. |
| *Erinnerung mordend!* <br> murdering memory! | 1:06 | Delivered by the vocalist in unnatural upward swoops. The instrumentalists swoop up and down on the chromatic lines. |
| *Finstre, schwarze Riesenfalter* <br> Dark, black, giant moths <br><br> *töteten der Sonne Glanz.* <br> kill the sunlight. | 1:09 | Sustained crescendo to *fff*. The bass clarinet imitates the cello tremolos by flutter-tonguing. |
| (Interlude) | 1:19 | The rhythmic activity decreases, the music grows dramatically softer, and all the instruments rise to their highest notes. The cellist bows "at the finger board." |
| **3** STANZA 3 | | |
| *Und von Himmel erdenwärts senken sich mit schweren Schwingen* <br> And from heaven earthwards sink with heavy oscillations | **1:26** | From its "heavenly" peak, the piano part sinks "earthwards," symbolized by the passacaglia in retrograde-inversion. |
| *unsichtbar die Ungetüme auf die Menschenherzen nieder . . .* <br> invisibly the monsters down onto the hearts of men . . . | 1:35 | The voice makes the chromatic descent, continued by the tremolo cello. The passacaglia also descends in a spiral of interlocking statements in the piano and bass clarinet. |
| *Finstre, schwarze Riesenfalter.* <br> Dark, black, giant moths. | 1:51 | The last few bars in the piano replicate the opening. A parting shot by the cello and bass clarinet announces that the movement is over. |

is often "answered" by a 4- or 5-note chromatic descent (or, later, ascent), heard in the voice at its first entrance and soon shared among the instruments as well. The focus is almost entirely on the linear quality of these two ideas; very little of *"Nacht"* can be analyzed in traditional harmonic terms.

To heighten the bizarre atmosphere of the poem, Schoenberg uses several unusual instrumental techniques. For the first stanza he has the cellist play rapid tremolos *am Steg* ("at the bridge"), which produces a more nasal, less resonant sound. In the short interlude between stanzas two and three, the cellist plays *am Griffbrett* ("at the finger board"), producing a distant, ethereal sound. In this same interlude, Schoenberg instructs the pianist to keep the dampers raised all the way through, creating a dreamlike blur. To imitate the cello's tremolos in the first stanza, he has the bass clarinettist use "flutter-tonguing." With this technique the clarinettist, by rolling an "r" at the tip of the tongue, can approximate the speed of note repetition that a string player achieves with the bow.

"*Nacht*" presents a paradox that flavors many of Schoenberg's Expressionist works. On the one hand, the absence of tonality rules out traditional formal schemes, producing a through-composed work. On this basis the work seems to teeter on the edge of chaos. On the other hand, with almost 100 repetitions of the same 3-note figure in a work that lasts less than 150 seconds, "*Nacht*" is more highly organized at the motivic level than the vast majority of tonal works that preceded it.

## ANTON WEBERN (1883–1945)

In the fall of 1904, Schoenberg took on as a composition pupil a 21-year-old musicology student at the University of Vienna. A slight, intensely serious young man, Anton Webern was also studying harmony, counterpoint, cello, and piano with a private instructor. He made rapid progress in composition under Schoenberg's direction, and in 1908 he wrote a Passacaglia for Orchestra as an informal graduation exercise. After earning his Ph.D. degree, he published his dissertation in the form of an edition of Renaissance music. For the next decade Webern earned a precarious living conducting orchestras in small German and Austrian towns, although conducting was one of the few areas in which he had no formal training. Most of the works he conducted were operettas, and yet the music he was composing during this period seemed to some even more "advanced" than Schoenberg's.

In 1918 Webern moved back to Vienna, where he conducted both the state-supported workers' orchestra and workers' chorus. He was deeply committed to music education and to the cause of the "new music." He remained in close touch with Schoenberg until the latter left for Berlin in 1925. In 1927 Webern received a regular conducting appointment with the orchestra of the Austrian state radio. When the Nazis came to power, they abolished the workers' organizations and Webern was obliged to support himself and his family with routine editorial work. He spent the Second World War in isolation on the outskirts of Vienna. While visiting his family in western Austria only a few weeks before the war ended, he was accidentally shot dead by an American soldier who was carrying out a raid on Webern's son-in-law, a suspected black marketeer.

Even as a student, Webern had matched Schoenberg's radical experiments step for step and was developing a distinctive style along the way. That style, which is marked by enormous concentration, was to have a profound influence on the course of twentieth-century music. Although Schoenberg, in *Vergangenes,* had cut Mahler's mammoth structures down to about five minutes, those movements could still be related quite comfortably to instrumental or song movements from the eighteenth or nineteenth centuries. Webern intensified Schoenberg's quest for concentration. Chopin and other Romantics had cultivated the miniature, but the scope of such works was conspicuously modest. The power of Webern's music is that it manages to say so much in so little time.

## Webern: Nos. 3 and 4 from *Five Pieces for Orchestra,* Op. 10 (1911–1913)

While Schoenberg was writing his *Five Pieces for Orchestra,* Webern decided to compose a set of his own. These pieces show both the profound influence of Schoenberg and the individuality of Webern. Although, like Schoenberg, he was urged to supply programmatic titles, Webern published his *Five Pieces* with nothing but tempo markings. His core orchestra is even more unusual than Schoenberg's: single winds and brass and one of each member of the string family. For No. 3 (headed "Very slow and extremely quiet"; Listening Guide 55), he called for clarinet, horn, trombone, and solo violin, viola, and cello. In addition, he called for the following instruments:

- *Harmonium:* a small reed organ patented in 1842 and designed for use by amateurs.
- *Mandolin:* a plucked string instrument with a rounded body, made popular in the seventeenth century.
- *Guitar:* a plucked string instrument with a flat back, popular since the Renaissance.
- *Celesta:* the small keyboard instrument used in Schoenberg's *Five Pieces.*
- *Harp:* a plucked string instrument with strings perpendicular to the soundboard, dating back to the Middle Ages.
- *Large and small snare drums:* high-pitched, ·penetrating drums generally found in military bands.
- *Bells:* There were no standard sizes, though Webern calls for "a few deep ones."
- *Cow bells:* the kind used in Austria to keep track of straying animals.

The harp and the bells were sometimes used in opera orchestras; Webern may have got the idea for the cow bells from Mahler's use of them a few years earlier in the third movement of his Sixth Symphony. The harmonium, mandolin, and guitar were "domestic" instruments·whose presence in an orchestra would have seemed ludicrous.to Viennese audiences. In fact, that is true of more than half the instruments here.

Nor does Webern treat the ensemble like a traditional orchestra. In No. 3, the ternary form of the piece is delineated entirely by instrumental textures. What

# *Listening Guide 55*

## WEBERN: Nos. 3 and 4 from *Five Pieces for Orchestra*, Op. 10

CD 6, TRACKS ⑥–⑦

TAPE 6B, TRACKS 3–4

DURATION: 1:59

### *No. 3*

*The three sections are defined entirely by the texture of the sounds rather than by harmony, melody, rhythm, or any other traditional element. Although there are no absolute silences in the piece, the background of snare drum, bells, and cow bells is almost inaudible; such passages are treated here as "silences." The snare-drum rolls at the end replace the conventional cadence.*

*Form: Ternary (textural)*

| | LOCATION | TIME | COMMENTS |
|---|---|---|---|
| 1 | *A*-Section | **0:00** | Tremolos in mandolin, guitar, celesta, and harp. |
| | | 0:06 | While tremolos continue, violin plays a slow 4-note motive, marked "sweetly." |
| | | 0:20 | Tremolo figures fade away to brief silence. |
| 2 | *B*-Section | **0:26** | Horn plays a 3-note motive, marked "expressively" and fading to another brief silence. |
| | | 0:39 | Flurry of motives in clarinet, mandolin, guitar, and cello, ending in a soft 4-note fragment for the viola, marked "very sweetly." Another brief silence. |
| 3 | *A'*-Section | **0:48** | Beginning with the almost inaudible mandolin, the hypnotic tremolo pattern returns, now played higher. |
| | | 1:00 | Muted trombone plays a 4-note motive. |
| | | 1:39 | Three snare-drum rolls replace the traditional cadence. |

DURATION: 0:29

### *No. 4*

*There are only four events in this highly concentrated movement.*

*Form: Through-composed*

| | | TIME | COMMENTS |
|---|---|---|---|
| | | 0:00 | Opens with a 6-note figure in the mandolin, marked "sweetly." |
| | | 0:05 | Viola (playing harmonics), clarinet, trumpet, and trombone respond softly. |
| | | 0:17 | Following the snare drum, the harp, celesta, clarinet, and mandolin play repeated notes. |
| | | 0:23 | Out of the repeated notes comes a brief 5-note motive in the violin, marked "like a breath" and giving the movement a sense of finality. |

might be regarded as the *A*-Section features tremolos (plucked rather than bowed) in the mandolin and guitar, and in the *B*-Section the winds and brass play short, overlapping motives. The return of the *A*-Section is marked by the return—imperceptible at first—of the tremolo figures. This purely textural return is as dramatic as any tonal/thematic return in a traditional form. To signal the end of the movement, Webern sounds three snare-drum rolls, which substitute nicely for a traditional cadence. Except for the mandolin and guitar, each instrument plays only once during the piece; when all the instruments have had their turn, the movement is over.

In No. 4, Webern's concentration assumes the brevity of an aphorism—a tersely phrased statement of a truth. Aphorisms are paradoxical; they state the truth more completely in a few words than it could be stated in many words. For example:

| DESCRIPTION | APHORISM |
|---|---|
| "Persons in a depressed state often make an effort to drag others down to their own level of unhappiness." | Misery loves company. |
| "Sometimes we have a better perspective on an event after it has taken place." | Hindsight is 20/20. |

No. 4, which contains only four closely spaced events, opens with a brief motive in the mandolin. The viola (playing harmonics) and the clarinet, trumpet, and trombone respond briefly, but without really "answering" the mandolin. The harp, celesta, clarinet, and mandolin then play a series of irregularly spaced, repeated notes. Finally, the viola offers a wistful motive that seems to complete the opening motive in the mandolin. Even one more note would be a note too many.

Webern's music expresses a powerful reaction against Romanticism. For two centuries instrumental works had grown longer and longer, orchestras larger and larger, and thematic relationships more and more complex. Webern dispatched these aspects of Romanticism like someone blowing down a house of cards.

## ALBAN BERG (1885–1935)

Alban Berg

In the autumn of 1904 Schoenberg placed an ad in a Viennese newspaper in the hope of attracting composition students for private instruction. One of the few responses was from a young man who showed Schoenberg some songs his brother had written. Impressed, Schoenberg agreed to take on the brother, 19-year-old Alban Berg, thereby inaugurating a relationship that was to endure for three decades. Because Berg was poor, Schoenberg charged him nothing the first year.

Berg's father, the son of a factory worker, had come to Vienna from Bavaria in 1867, when he was 21. He soon set up a successful business as a book importer and exporter and married the daughter of a court jeweler. The youngest of their four children was Alban, who inherited from his energetic Viennese mother his talent in both music and the graphic arts. Berg's passion for music emerged when he was 14, and he began to attend every concert and opera performance he could. His father died when Alban was 15, and the family's economic situation grew desperate. Only through the intervention of a well-to-do aunt was Berg able to remain in school. So preoccupied was he with music that he failed his first set of graduation exams; years later he wondered how he had ever passed.

Unlike his fellow student Webern, Berg had had almost no formal training in music before he met Schoenberg, to whom he looked for fatherly guidance as well as instruction in music. At his mother's urging, Berg began work as an accountant in the Viennese civil service. He discharged his duties conscientiously but spent his free time composing music. In 1906 his mother received an inheritance that enabled Berg to devote all his time to music.

From the very beginning of their association, the lives of Schoenberg, Berg, and Webern were inextricably interwoven. In 1930 Berg wrote to Schoenberg, "I never let an occasion pass without emphasizing with pride that you are *the* teacher of my life." The bond was strengthened by the hostility with which almost all the performances of their music were greeted. On March 31, 1913, for example, a concert was scheduled that included Berg's *Five Songs on Picture Postcard Texts of Peter Altenberg* (a minor Viennese poet and writer). The notion of a huge Romantic orchestra playing in a freely atonal style to accompany the vocalist's aphoristic, sometimes whimsical lines was too much for the Viennese audience. Shortly after Berg's songs began, a riot broke out. The police had to be summoned and the rest of the concert was canceled.

Schoenberg, Berg, and Webern were never appointed to a post at any of Vienna's musical institutions, such as the Vienna Conservatory or the Royal Academy of Music and Dramatic Art. Once, in 1910, the Academy invited Schoenberg to teach a theory course outside its regular curriculum. But when word got out, speeches were made in the Austrian Parliament criticizing even that temporary appointment. Despite the animosity directed toward them (which, in Schoenberg's case, included virulent anti-Semitism), only Schoenberg, who taught in Berlin three times between 1912 and 1933 before emigrating to the United States, ever left the environs of Vienna for any length of time. Berg's life was made easier by his marriage in 1911 to Helene Nahowski, who for 25 years proved a sympathetic, understanding companion and guaranteed the privacy he needed to compose.

## Berg: Act III from *Wozzeck* (1917–1922)

In May 1914 Berg attended several performances in Vienna of a play written in 1836 by Georg Büchner (1813–1837), a young German academic. Overwhelmed by its dramatic power, he resolved to turn it into an opera. The play is based on the true story of a German drifter turned soldier who, worn down by the hardships and abuses of military life, murders his girlfriend, whom he suspects of being unfaithful. Büchner viewed this act of murder as the inevitable outcome of a life spent in degradation and poverty. For the first time in German theater not only was the hero a member of the forgotten class but also the play itself was a scathing indictment of society.

The incident on which the play is based had occurred as early as 1821. Büchner's father was a physician who served on the editorial board of a scholarly journal that published the medical report that led to Johannes Woyzeck's* beheading in a public square in Leipzig in 1824. The incident aroused passionate debate among intellectuals, some of whom advanced the then-novel argument that Woyzeck—who had suffered for years from visions and hallucinations—was not responsible for his actions at the time he murdered his girlfriend.

While still a student, Büchner founded the Society for the Rights of Man in his native Darmstadt and distributed pamphlets giving facts and figures that underscored the disparity between rich and poor. In 1835 he was forced to flee to Strasbourg and, eventually, to Switzerland. He wrote to his fiancée:

> I studied the history of the [French] Revolution. I felt myself crushed by the terrible fatalism of history. I find in human nature a horrifying sameness in the human condition, an inescapable force, granted to all and to no one. The individual [is] merely foam on the waves, greatness sheer chance, the mastery of genius a puppet play, a ludicrous struggle against an iron law.

While serving as professor of anatomy at the University of Zurich, Büchner began sketching a play based loosely on the Woyzeck story. After drafting a series of terse, independent scenes, he contracted a typhus infection and died at the age of 24. His prophetic manuscript was discovered only in the first decade of the twentieth century and was reconstructed in the form that Berg had seen.

Berg's health was always frail—he inherited his father's heart condition and suffered from asthma—and when he was first called for military duty at the outbreak of the First World War he was declared physically unfit. After being called a second time he was accepted, only to suffer a physical breakdown during combat training. Eventually he was assigned to the War Ministry, where he served out the war. All these experiences made a powerful impression; he wrote of Wozzeck to Helene in 1918: "There is something of myself in his character, since I have been spending these war years just as dependent on people I hate, have been in chains, sick, captive, resigned, in fact humiliated."

It took Berg almost six years to complete *Wozzeck*. From Büchner's 26 loosely ordered scenes, Berg chose 15, which he divided into three acts of five scenes each. Although the scenes are loosely chronological, there is no direct continuity, and often there are only vague hints to how much time has elapsed between them. The events in the course of Wozzeck's self-destruction occur in random fashion.

*In the version of the play Berg saw in Vienna, Woyzeck's name was mistakenly transcribed as *Wozzeck*.

Act I paints a grim picture of Wozzeck's life. His captain, whom Wozzeck has to shave every morning, reproaches him for the "immorality" of his unwed relationship with his girlfriend, Marie. While collecting firewood with a fellow soldier, Wozzeck experiences hallucinations. To support Marie and their young son, he submits to dietary experiments conducted by a sadistic, pseudoscientific army doctor. (Presumably the experiments caused the hallucinations.) In the final scene Marie succumbs to a manly Drum Major (identified only by this name), whom she has admired as he strutted by.

In Act II, Wozzeck's fragile world begins to crumble. He sees Marie wearing a new pair of gold earrings, which she lamely claims to have found. The captain and the doctor ridicule Wozzeck about Marie's affair with the Drum Major. Marie refuses to let Wozzeck touch her any longer. When he follows her to a dance, he sees her carrying on openly with the Drum Major. Later, the Drum Major beats up Wozzeck back at the barracks.

In Act III, Marie, now guilt-ridden, reads the New Testament story in which Jesus forgives the adultress. In the second scene Wozzeck murders her while they are walking near a pond. Distraught, Wozzeck goes to the local tavern where he makes bold advances toward one of the tavern girls. When she notices blood on his hand and arm, Wozzeck flees back to the scene of the murder, where, in the course of trying to hide the knife, he becomes obsessed with the bloody images of moon and water. In an attempt to wash himself clean, he walks into the water and drowns. The captain and doctor overhear his struggle but merely exchange comments without trying to help. In the last scene, as Marie's child sits on his hobby horse, the neighborhood children enter and call out: "Hey you, your mother is dead! . . . Let's go look." Uncomprehending, the child follows them offstage.

Like Schoenberg, Berg was concerned about how to give coherence to a work lacking traditional tonality. Berg, whose style was more eclectic and overtly Romantic than that of Schoenberg or Webern, chose to draw, paradoxically, on several operatic and symphonic traditions. In the idiom of Schoenberg's *Erwartung,* he makes each scene naturalistic; there are no arias or ensembles to interrupt the action. He does, however, introduce snatches of folk song, sung in distorted fashion. And he uses recurring phrases modeled on Wagnerian leitmotifs, such as the cry *"Wir arme Leut'!"* ("We poor people!") sung sometimes by Wozzeck, sometimes by Marie. Moreover, to link the scenes in each act he uses a symphonic interlude, sometimes of Wagnerian proportions, that gives emotional expression to the action that has taken place and anticipates the action to come.

Berg suggests Wozzeck's abnormality with frequent stretches of *Sprechstimme* (which Berg calls "rhythmic declamation"), yet he also has Wozzeck sing and speak. The suggestion is that Wozzeck has no clear identity. Marie, though trapped, is more normal; her part is written for a lyric soprano of the sort we might find in a Verdi opera. Her passages are the most tonal and the most lyric. The boastful Drum Major is a Wagnerian *Heldentenor* ("heroic tenor"). Perhaps the most unusual treatment is reserved for the captain and the doctor, who do a great deal of speaking over the music, as in melodrama. The music evokes a

TEXT

You
    s

's ist
It's

3   Wei:
      n
Say,
      v

MA
Zu
At l

WO
Un

      1
And

4   MA
Ich

WO
Fü

Un
An

Un
An

[P
he

5   W
Wl

De
I v

we
if l

mood but is not synchronized with the speaking voices, a practice familiar to us from movies.

Taking his cue from Büchner, Berg models the Drum Major, the doctor, and the captain on one-dimensional characters from comic opera. Although by conventional standards their behavior is outrageous, their brutal treatment of Wozzeck seems somehow "normal" because Wozzeck never protests. (Berg could not have foreseen the similarities between the doctor's experiments and the medical experiments conducted in Nazi concentration camps.)

To satisfy the need for organization, Berg assigns a formal model to each act and scene. He calls Act I "Five Character Studies," which consist of a "suite," a "rhapsody," a "march and lullaby," a "passacaglia," and a "rondo." He calls Act II a "symphony in five movements," which consists of a "sonata movement," a "fantasy and fugue," a "largo," a "scherzo," and a "rondo martiale." Act III consists of five "inventions." J. S. Bach and his contemporaries used the term *invention* to describe a short piece (usually for keyboard) written in contrapuntal style. Berg, however, uses the term in the general sense of "freely inventive." His inventions include a "theme and variations," an "invention on a tone," an "invention on a rhythm," an "invention on a six-[note] chord," and an "invention on an eighth-note rhythm." Although these organizational devices seem to have satisfied Berg's need for order, the listener is scarcely aware of most of them. The most apparent ones are those based on ostinatos or repeating figures, such as the obsessive repetition of the note B in Scene 2, in which Wozzeck murders Marie.

Act III unfolds with terrifying swiftness. In Scene 1, Marie reads from the Bible, one of the few times she employs *Sprechstimme*, alternating with sung outbursts of remorse. To hold the frequent mood shifts together, Berg uses a brief, delicate theme, which functions more like a motive and serves as the basis for a set of free orchestral variations:

The first, fifth, and sixth variations begin with clear statements of the motive, but the beginnings of the others are scarcely detectable. For the bleak nursery rhyme that seems to foretell the deaths of Marie and Wozzeck, Berg reverts briefly to a poignant minor tonality. The scene ends with Marie reading the passage in which Mary Magdalen falls on her knees and begs forgiveness from Jesus. For this Berg supplies a free fugue based on a variation of the motive. Marie begins the fugue alone (but in *Sprechstimme!*), the only time she shares the orchestra's material.

The thick brass chords in the brief orchestral interlude following Scene 1 hint of the tragedy to come but soon dissolve to a low, menacing B in the double basses (where Listening Guide 56 begins). Throughout Scene 2 this note migrates nervously up (as high as the piccolo) and down, foreshadowing the murder Wozzeck is about to commit. Berg expresses the violence of the murder

*(Text continues on page 560.)*

| TEXT | TIME | COMMENTS |
|------|------|----------|
| *Aber ich darf nicht!* <br> But I may not! | 2:13 | Menacing, accompanied by a 4-note repeating figure in the horns. |
| *Was zitterst?* <br> You're trembling? | 2:20 | Xylophone plays steady beats. |

**6**   MARIE:

| TEXT | TIME | COMMENTS |
|------|------|----------|
| *Der Nachttau fällt.* <br> The night dew is falling. | **2:23** | Voice imitates the harp. |
| WOZZECK *[Whispering to himself]:* <br> *Wer kalt ist, den friert nicht mehr!* <br>     *Dich wird beim Morgentau nicht frieren.* <br> Whoever is cold will freeze no more in the <br>     cold morning dew. | 2:27 | Eerie string accompaniment. |
| MARIE: <br> *Was sagst Du da?* <br> What did you say? | 2:42 | Followed by brief silence. |
| WOZZECK: <br> *Nix.* <br> Nothing. | 2:46 | Unaccompanied. |
| *[A long silence. The moon rises.]* | 2:53 | The B throughout the entire orchestra, with slowly rising chords to accompany the rising moon. |

**7**   MARIE:

| TEXT | TIME | COMMENTS |
|------|------|----------|
| *Wie der Mond rot aufgeht!* <br> How red the rising moon is! | **3:06** | Slowly and rising. |
| WOZZECK: <br> *Wie ein blutig Eisen! [He draws a knife.]* <br> Like a bloody dagger! | 3:16 | Slowly, rising, and menacing. |
| MARIE: <br> *Was zitterst? [Leaps up] Was willst?* <br> What glistens? What do you want? | 3:24 | With terror. Soft, slow strokes begin in the timpani. Panic-stricken outbursts in the xylophone. |

**8**   WOZZECK:

| TEXT | TIME | COMMENTS |
|------|------|----------|
| *Ich nicht, Marie! Und kein andrer auch* <br>     *nicht!* <br> Not me, Marie! Then no one else either! | **3:30** | Shouting. Timpani strokes rise to a deafening level. |

| TEXT | TIME | COMMENTS |
|------|------|----------|
| *[He stabs her in the throat with the knife.]* | | |
| MARIE: | | |
| *Hilfe!* Help! | 3:34 | Screaming (on a high B). Chaotic scurrying in the orchestra, gradually giving way to mournful chords in the strings. |
| *[She sinks down. Wozzeck bends over her. Marie dies.]* | | |
| WOZZECK: | | |
| *Tot!* Dead! | 3:52 | Low monotone. Timpani strokes cease. Orchestra grows silent. |
| *[Startled, he rises and rushes away in silence.]* | | |

| | | | |
|---|---|---|---|
| **9** | CHANGE OF SCENE | **4:09** | Soft B in the orchestra makes long crescendo. |
| | (Interlude) | | |
| | | 4:24 | Loud dissonance in the orchestra overlaps with loud knocking at the door, introducing the syncopated rhythm on which the next scene is based. |
| | | 4:33 | A second, even longer crescendo on B. |

SCENE 3: INVENTION ON A RHYTHM

| | | | |
|---|---|---|---|
| **10** | *[A tavern. Night. Dim light. Whores, among them Margret, and young men dance a fast polka. Wozzeck sits at one of the tables.]* | **4:44** | Barroom piano plays raucous tune using the Rhythm. |
| | WOZZECK: | | |
| | *Tanzt Alle; tanzt nur zu, springt,* Dance, everyone; dance away, jump, | 4:48 | Shouting, like a man possessed. |
| | *schwitzt und stinkt, es holt Euch doch noch einmal der Teufel!* sweat, and stink, the devil will fetch you again! | | |
| | *[He hurls a glass of wine to the ground, shouting over the piano.]* | | |
| **11** | *Es ritten drei Reiter wohl an den Rhein,* Three riders rode along the Rhine, | **5:02** | Attempts to sing a folk song but is sabotaged by the Rhythm in strings, horns, and piano. |
| | *Bei einer Frau Wirtin da kehrten sie ein.* They turned off at the hostesses. | | |

*continued*

| TEXT | TIME | COMMENTS |
|------|------|----------|
| *Mein Wein ist gut, mein Bier ist klar,*<br>My wine is good, my beer is clear, | 5:10 | |
| *Mein Töchterlein liegt auf der . . .*<br>My little daughter lies on the . . . | | Voice trails away. |
| *Verdammt! [Jumps up] Komm, Margret!*<br>Damnation! Come, Margret! | 5:18 | Sudden change of mood. Pianist again plays tune to Rhythm. |
| *[Dances a few steps with Margret. Suddenly stands still.]* | 5:21 | |
| *Komm, setz Dich hier, Margret!*<br>Come, sit down here, Margret! | 5:24 | Drunken and belligerent. Ugly orchestral sounds. |
| *[Leads her to a table and pulls her onto his lap]* | | |
| *Margret, du bist so heiss—*<br>Margret, you are so hot— | 5:33 | Eerie trills "on the bridge" of all the strings. |
| *[Presses her to him, then lets go]* | | |
| *Wart nur, wirst auch kalt werden!*<br>Just wait, you'll also get cold! | 5:41 | Eerie trilled chords in winds and brass. |
| | 5:49 | Strings play "smeared" chords. |
| *Kannst nicht singen?* Can't you sing? | 5:53 | Imploring with trombone echo. |
| 12 MARGRET *[Accompanied by piano player on stage]:* | | |
| *In's Schwabenland, da mag ich nit,*<br>To Swabia I don't want to go, | **5:56** | In the Rhythm, while pianist plays an unrelated "accompaniment." |
| *Und lange Kleider trag ich nit,*<br>And I won't wear long dresses, | | |
| *Denn lange Kleider, Spitzeschuh,*<br>For long dresses, high heels, | 6:09 | |
| *Die kommen keiner Dienstmagd zu.*<br>Don't become a servant girl. | | |
| WOZZECK:<br>*Nein! keine schuh, man kann auch blossfüssig in die Höll' geh'n.*<br>  *Ich möcht heut raufen, raufen . . .*<br>No! no shoes, for one can also go to hell barefooted!<br>  Today I'd like to fight and tussle . . . | 6:21 | Angrily. Chilling chords in horns. |

**13** MARGRET:
*Aber was hast Du an der Hand?*      **6:35**      Very low, muffled accompaniment.
But what is that on your hand?

WOZZECK:
*Ich? Ich?* Me? Me?      6:42      Losing all confidence.

MARGRET:
*Rot! Blut!*      6:45      Low, starts rising. Ominous string and wood-
Red! Blood!                      wind accompaniment to the Rhythm.

WOZZECK:
*Blut? Blut?*      6:48      Throughout this accusatory passage, the
Blood? Blood?                     music rises in both pitch and volume.

*[People gather around her.]*

MARGRET:
*Freilich . . . Blut!* Indeed . . . blood!      6:50

**14** WOZZECK:
*Ich glaub', ich hab' mich geschnitten da an*      **6:53**      All vocal phrases built on the Rhythm.
    *der rechten Hand . . .*
I believe I cut myself there on the right
    hand . . .

MARGRET:
*Wie kommt's denn zum Ellenbogen?*      6:58      Interrupts Wozzeck before he finishes.
Then how come it's on your elbow?

WOZZECK:
*Ich hab's daran abgewischt.*      7:02      Increasingly hysterical.
I wiped myself there.

YOUNG MEN:
*Mit der rechten Hand an rechten Arm?*      7:05      Interrupt Wozzeck.
With your right hand on the right arm?

WOZZECK:
*Was wollt Ihr? Was geht's Euch an?*      7:06      Angrily.
What do you want? What business is it of
    yours?

MARGRET:
*Puh! Puh! Da stinkt's nach Menschenblut!*      7:07      Slowly but firmly.
Pooh pooh! It reeks of human blood!

WOZZECK:
*Bin ich ein Mörder?* Am I a murderer?      7:09      All at once.

*continued*

| TEXT | TIME | COMMENTS |
|------|------|----------|
| **YOUNG MEN:** | | |
| *Blut, Blut, Blut, Blut!* | | |
| Blood, blood, blood, blood! | | |
| **WHORES:** | | |
| *Freilich, da stinkt's nach Menschenblut!* | 7:09 | |
| Indeed, it reeks of human blood! | | |
| **WOZZECK:** | | |
| *Platz! oder es geht wer zum Teufel!* | 7:12 | |
| Cool it! Or else someone goes to the devil! | | |
| *[Wozzeck storms out.]* | | |
| CHANGE OF SCENE | 7:19 | Curtain falls. Music climbs to a peak. |
| (Interlude) | **7:25** | Sudden rest followed by ferocious drum roll and last statement of the Rhythm in the brass. |
| | 7:32 | Another sudden rest, followed by fast irregular repetitions of the 6-note chord, fading to a brief rest. |

with 34 slow timpani strokes that build to a tremendous crescendo and then fade as Marie's life drains away. Berg has Marie die on her highest and most dramatic note (a B, naturally). Although *Sprechstimme* is Wozzeck's normal mode of expression, Berg has both Wozzeck and Marie sing throughout this chilling scene, giving it a sense of unreality. The interlude consists of two electrifying orchestral crescendos on the B. The first ends with Wozzeck pounding on the tavern door in the rhythm that characterizes Scene 3. The second leads to a wildly distorted tune on the tavern piano, which reinforces that rhythm:

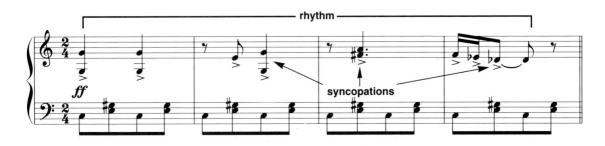

The three consecutive syncopations in this rhythm reflect Wozzeck's agitated state. Berg repeats the rhythm at different speeds throughout the scene, often overlapping in the voice and orchestra.

In a somewhat Romantic vein, Wozzeck's singing over the dance music at the beginning of the scene is reminiscent of the parlando at the beginning of Verdi's *Rigoletto* (Chapter 22). When Wozzeck turns to folk song ("Three riders rode along the Rhine"), the syncopated rhythm defeats his attempts to achieve the rollicking movement of the song. The nonsensical folk song that Margret, the tavern girl, sings at Wozzeck's insistence ("To Swabia I don't want to go, And I won't wear long dresses") suggests keys that bear no relation to the piano accompaniment.

The scene reaches a climax when, over four simultaneous versions of the syncopated rhythm, a chorus of men and women join in Margret's insistent questioning about the blood on Wozzeck's hand. Wozzeck flees, his agitation mounting. After a dramatic pause (where Listening Guide 56 ends), a terrifying drum roll announces the scene in which Wozzeck will meet his death.

Berg builds Scene 4 around an ingenious harmony that consists of six notes:

**six-note chord**

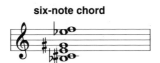

It would be hard to assemble any six notes that contain fewer triadic combinations than these. No single major or minor triad can be found among them, and only two pairs even belong to the same major or minor triad: the top and bottom notes (B♭ and F), and the two middle notes (E and G♯). The harmony throughout the scene has a static quality that suggests Wozzeck's inability to escape his predicament. Later, when Wozzeck tries to wash himself clean, the 6-note chord symbolizes the blood he cannot wash away. In murdering Marie (who, because of her infidelity, was already "dead" to Wozzeck), Wozzeck has ensured his own destruction.

As Wozzeck wades into the pond, the 6-note chord climbs higher and higher to suggest the deepening water. Because a continuous rise would soon elevate the pitches beyond the audible range, Berg overlaps the top of each ascent with a fresh start in the bass. With this ingenious stroke he creates, for 30 full seconds, the aural illusion that the music is climbing continuously. As Wozzeck drowns, the captain and the doctor enter and hold a matter-of-fact conversation that is all the more eerie for being entirely spoken. Here the music functions like the sound track in a movie.

Wozzeck's death is not even noticed by any of the drama's participants. Instead, Berg offers in the last orchestral interlude his personal commentary on the tragedy he has unfolded. He begins softly in the strings and moves on to a huge catharsis that includes the only tonal cadence in the entire opera. The thick brass chords that were hinted at between the first two scenes of Act III now

## THE SOCIETY FOR PRIVATE MUSICAL PERFORMANCES

Composers had been getting bad reviews ever since regular music criticism began to appear around 1800. (See the Historical Window in Chapter 23 on page 477.) Beethoven, Schumann, Brahms, and Mahler had all received their share. But the hostility with which performances of works by Schoenberg, Berg, and Webern were greeted in Austria and Germany was unprecedented. The concert-going public was convinced that these composers were intent on undermining, even destroying, centuries of musical tradition. The music critics agreed. Schoenberg wrote:

> Important musicians who care about their calling cannot write for our papers. In Paris it is possible, and since Berlioz many, such as Debussy and Dukas, have written daily criticism. But among us a musician goes to a newspaper only when he is unfit to be even a "professor" of singing or the piano. . . . If a court reporter has once been a choirboy, that is enough qualification to review music.

Matching the public disdain was the lack of interest in contemporary music displayed by the major musical institutions of the city, such as the Vienna State Opera and the Vienna Philharmonic. When Richard Strauss took over the State Opera from Gustav Mahler in 1907, he had already begun his stylistic retreat and did nothing to help Schoenberg. Mahler, on his departure from Vienna in 1910, wrote to his wife: "After I am gone who will be there to protect poor Schoenberg?"

Disgusted with audiences and critics, in 1918 Schoenberg made a bold move. With Berg and Webern and many other composers and musicians, he founded the *Verein für musikalische Privataufführungen* ("Society for Private Musical Performances"). Berg, who drafted the prospectus for the Society, set forth the following provisions (italics in the original):

> The Society, founded by Arnold Schoenberg in 1918, has this purpose: to give artists and friends of art a real and precise knowledge of modern music. . . . It is not a society for composers but only for the audience. If joy and pleasure in some of the performed works are aroused, thereby encouraging composer and composition, this must be viewed as a side effect. . . . In the planning of programs, no attention can be paid to this . . . because our purpose is restricted to giving as perfect a representation [of modern music] as possible.
>
> 1. In the selection of works for performance, *no specific style is preferred*. From

Mahler and Strauss to the very youngest, the total spectrum of modern music is to be represented. . . .

2. *The preparation of works* takes place with a care and thoroughness not found in today's concert life, where . . . one has to make the best of . . . an insufficient number of rehearsals. . . . The number of rehearsals in the Society is always determined by the goal of achieving utmost clarity and fulfillment. . . . Unless the ground rules of a good performance are fulfilled, namely *clarity and precision*, the works cannot and must not be performed in the Society. . . .

The Society commands . . . ways and means to achieve complete comprehension in a music performance, namely:

1. *By frequent repetition*. Every work is not performed just once, but is repeated in different concerts, in general two to four times, until it can be [fully] understood.

2. The same goal will be pursued in *introductory discussions* of the works performed.

3. The performances themselves are removed from the corrupting influence of publicity. Members of the Society are encouraged not to sit in judgment. . . . Public judgment takes away from this purpose, since:

(a) the *performances* are not *public*. . . . Guests are excluded (with the exception of those living abroad). Reviews of the performances in newspapers as well as all advertising of the works or artists are prohibited.

(b) At the performances, *expressions of approval, of displeasure and of gratitude are not permitted.* The only success that the author can have is the one that ought to be the most important for him—that he can make himself understood.

(c) The *performers* are primarily of the kind that have placed themselves at the disposal of the Society—out of interest to the cause. Through strict selection, mere virtuosity is excluded. . . .

No organization in the history of music had ever set itself more sternly against concert-going traditions. Although the rampant postwar inflation in Austria led to the dissolution of the Society in 1921, for three full seasons it exercised an influence that has persisted throughout the century. The Society sponsored a total of 122 concerts with music by 48 composers, most of them living, and made possible professional performances of works that might otherwise have been performed poorly or not at all. At these concerts many Viennese heard the music of Debussy and Stravinsky for the first time. The practice, widespread today, of offering lectures before the event got its start at the Society's concerts. The very existence of such an organization, however, evidenced the ominous alienation that had set in between composer and audience.

achieve full expression, with an overpowering effect. With this catharsis, Berg releases the flood of feelings the tragedy has aroused.

Instead of leaving us with this cathartic release, Berg directs us back to the painful reality of the drama. In Scene 6, the cruel words of the neighborhood children ("Hey you, your mother is dead!") are accompanied by a 2-note rhythm, to which Marie and Wozzeck's child, rocking on his hobby horse, sings "hop hop" as if in a trance. As the boy moves off to view his mother's body, we sense that his life will prove to be as wretched as his father's.

The premiere of *Wozzeck* took place in Berlin on December 14, 1925. Since that time the opera has commanded the attention of audiences all over the world (in spite of the Nazis' attempts to suppress it during the 1930s and 1940s). Following its premiere, critics were quick to credit Berg with all sorts of radical reforms, especially his blending of traditional and modern elements. In 1928, in a popular music periodical, he replied:

> I did not dream of reforming the art of opera with the composition of *Wozzeck*. This was not my intention when I began it, nor do I regard the finished work as a model for future operatic directions—neither my own nor that of other composers. . . .
>
> Aside from the desire to write good music, to realize musically the intellectual content of Büchner's immortal drama, to transform his poetic language into a musical one, I imagined at the moment when I decided to write an opera nothing more than to give the theater what belongs to it. That meant forming the music in such a way that it is always conscious of its duty to serve the drama.

In this goal Berg succeeded admirably.

## THE DEVELOPMENT OF SERIALISM

From 1914 to 1923 Schoenberg completed very little music. Beyond the disruption caused by the First World War, he realized that he could not sustain the style he had developed before the war without a more solid foundation. Gradually he arrived at a solution that he called the "method of composing with twelve tones which are related only with one another." That system eventually came to be known as *serialism,* which simply means the arrangement of notes in a series.

According to Schoenberg's method, each composition is based on the linear arrangement of the 12 tones of the chromatic scale in a particular order (of which there are almost infinite possibilities). In the United States such arrangements are called *tone rows.*

Schoenberg permitted three variants of the "basic set" of 12 notes, which he called "row forms":

- *Inversion:* Beginning on the first note of the original row, each interval is reversed. For example, if the basic set begins on A and the second note is B♭

(a half step higher), then the inversion will also begin on A, but the second note will be G♯, a half step lower.

- *Retrograde:* The row is played backward, from the twelfth note and proceeding to the first note.
- *Retrograde-Inversion:* The row is played backward and the intervals are inverted.

Schoenberg also permitted these four row forms (the basic set and the three variants) to be transposed to any of the 11 other notes of the chromatic scale. In all, there could be up to 12 transpositions of four different row forms, making possible 48 different row forms for each composition.

Schoenberg made it clear that his new system addressed melody more readily than harmony. "The basic set functions in the manner of a motive," he wrote. He was aware that there was nothing new about applying inversion or retrograde or even retrograde-inversion to a motive; J. S. Bach, in his *Art of Fugue,* had done that two centuries earlier. So in a sense Schoenberg was simply extending tradition. But he felt that the power of the row to create an unprecedented degree of "comprehensibility" raised his method "from a mere technical device to the rank and importance of a scientific theory." Schoenberg was as eager to demonstrate the natural rightness of his system as Rameau had been to demonstrate the natural rightness of tonality in the eighteenth century (see page 204).

Schoenberg warned composers that they could not simply invent a tone row and start composing:

> The introduction of my method of composing with twelve tones does not facilitate composing; on the contrary, it makes it more difficult. Modern-minded beginners often think they should try it before having acquired the necessary technical equipment. This is a great mistake. The restrictions imposed on a composer by the obligation to use only one set in a composition are so severe that they can only be overcome by an imagination which has survived a tremendous number of adventures.

Schoenberg was using his new method sporadically as early as 1921, and by 1923 it had become his exclusive means of composing. He continued to consolidate and refine the method over the rest of his life. In his later years, for example, he relaxed the absolute prohibition he had once imposed against the use of octaves, in the belief that an octave might make a particular tone sound like a tonic. And he developed row forms in which various portions of the row were themselves motivically related to other portions of the row. To do so he simply partitioned the 12 notes into two groups of six notes (called "hexachords"), three groups of four notes ("tetrachords"), or four groups of three notes ("trichords").

Schoenberg composed an impressive list of serial works: for piano (Suite for Piano, Op. 25; Piano Pieces, Op. 33), chamber ensemble (Serenade, Op. 24; String Quartets Nos. 3 and 4; the String Trio, Op. 45; the Fantasy for Violin and Piano, Op. 47), orchestra (Variations for Orchestra, Op. 31; Violin Concerto, Op. 36; Piano Concerto, Op. 42), and an opera, *Moses und Aaron* (of which only two acts were completed). As the titles of these works suggest, Schoenberg sought to integrate traditional forms with his advanced serial techniques. This desire to integrate the present and the past was part of a larger movement often referred to as *neoclassicism,* which we will explore in the next chapter.

Although the intensity of the early criticism of Schoenberg's works abated, Schoenberg continued to meet with hostility. Ultimately, however, he came to be recognized as a composer on a level with Stravinsky and Béla Bartók (whose music we explore in Chapter 29), and his reputation was greatest among composers and professional musicians.

In 1933 Schoenberg emigrated to the United States. After teaching for a year in Boston, he settled in Los Angeles, where from 1936 to 1943 he taught at the University of California, Los Angeles. His private pupils ranged from film composers such as David Raksin to avant-garde composers such as John Cage.

After its introduction in the 1920s, Schoenberg's serial method was to influence for the next 50 years most important composers of art music at some time in their careers. But the greatest influence on the development and spread of serial music was exercised by Schoenberg's pupil Webern.

## Webern: Symphony, Op. 21 (1928)

Both Berg and Webern put Schoenberg's serial method to use, each in his own way. Berg, eclectic and Romantic as usual, created a tone row in his Violin Concerto that contains no fewer than four alternating minor and major triads. And Webern used the method to achieve even greater concentration and integration than Schoenberg had.

In 1927 Webern wrote to Schoenberg that he was working on "something for orchestra, a little symphony." The notion of Webern writing a symphony might seem surprising, but he wanted to demonstrate that he could use the serial method to reinterpret large instrumental forms. He set out to compose a three-movement work. After he had completed two movements, however, he decided that the symphony itself was also complete. As in many of Schoenberg's serial works, the external form of both movements is traditional: The first is in a binary form and the second is a theme and variations.

Webern's thematic treatment, however, is highly unusual. His basic set is a row with special properties:

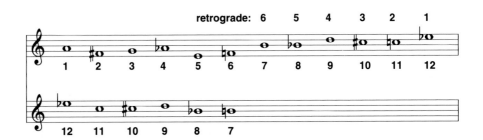

*Part Four   The Twentieth Century*

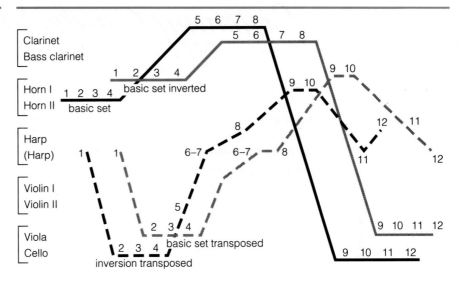

FIGURE 26.4 Evaluating the impact of serialism, Webern said in 1933 that the past 25 years had seen "an advance greater than has ever taken place before in the history of music."

The 12 notes of the basic set are numbered below the first stave. The second half of the row is a transposed version in retrograde of the first half. The numbers above the first stave show the retrograde as part of the basic set, while the second stave shows these same notes in true retrograde below the parallel notes in the basic set. The interval of transposition (the interval between the first and last notes of the row) is a tritone, which divides the octave exactly in half. For Webern, such rows—called "combinatorial"—had an almost mystical unifying power. A keen student of plant life, Webern related this kind of composition to an essay by Goethe on the *Urpflanze* (primeval plant), in which "the root is really nothing other than the stalk, the stalk nothing other than the leaf, the leaf again nothing other than the blossom: variations of the same idea."

Webern's unprecedented desire for organization begins in the first movement (Listening Guide 57) with the orchestral pairings: clarinet and bass clarinet, two horns, harp (which serves as its own "pair"), first and second violins, viola and cello. (Webern authorized anywhere from one to four players per string part.) He organizes his first movement as a pair of canons in which each of the paired instruments plays one of the canonic voices. The first canon consists of the basic set followed at a distance of two measures by the basic set in inversion. The second canon, which begins just one measure after the first, uses a transposition of the basic set in inversion and the same transposition from the basic set. No single instrument plays more than four consecutive notes of any row. Only the harp plays two notes simultaneously, each time dividing the row exactly in half. This complex counterpoint can best be shown with a diagram of the first 14 measures, which constitute one statement of the various row forms, or about half of this first half of the binary form (see Figure 26.4).

Not even a highly trained listener can follow all four separate lines simultane-

# Chapter 27

AMERICAN MUSIC COMES OF AGE

When the first Europeans landed on the shores of North America, between one and two million native Americans had been living there for at least 25,000 years. The Europeans, believing they had reached the East Indies, called them "Indians." It now appears that the Indians had migrated to North America from Asia across what is now the Bering Strait. There were at least six major groups, each with its own complex culture and with music at the heart of its rites and ceremonies.

In 1606, in the English village of Scrooby (in Nottinghamshire), a congregation of Puritans, most of them farmers with little or no education, broke away from the Church of England and set up a separatist church. By 1608, they had made their way to Leiden, Holland, where they hoped to earn a livelihood and find religious tolerance. Life there was harder than they had expected, however, and they began to fear that their children would take to Dutch ways. So some of them made the bold decision to sail across the Atlantic to "America," named after the Italian explorer Amerigo Vespucci.

On the eve of their departure in 1620, they shared a communal meal followed by the singing of Psalms, a collection of free-verse poems in the Old Testament. Later, one of the participants recalled: "We refreshed ourselves, after tears, with singing of Psalms, making joyful melody in our hearts as well as with the voice, there being many of our congregation very expert in music; and indeed it was the sweetest melody that ever mine ears heard." When the 102 settlers sailed into Plymouth Bay aboard the *Mayflower* (see the map in Figure 27.1), they carried their psalm books with them.

## EARLY AMERICAN MUSIC

For many years the music the New England settlers played and sang was mainly religious music. During the 1770s, Yankee tunesmiths like William Billings (1746–1800) wrote four-part settings of popular hymns, often in the form of "fuguing tunes"—so called after the musical imitation with which the last line of text was treated. Singing schools, where people could learn to read music,

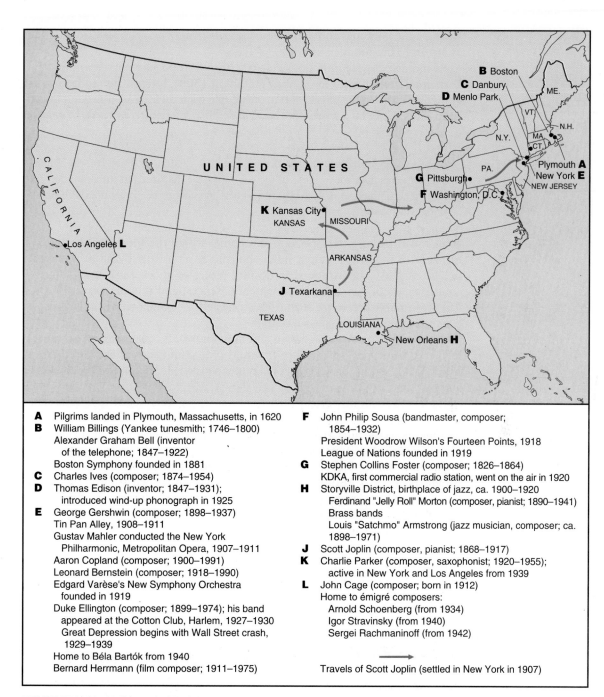

**A** Pilgrims landed in Plymouth, Massachusetts, in 1620
**B** William Billings (Yankee tunesmith; 1746–1800)
 Alexander Graham Bell (inventor
 of the telephone; 1847–1922)
 Boston Symphony founded in 1881
**C** Charles Ives (composer; 1874–1954)
**D** Thomas Edison (inventor; 1847–1931);
 introduced wind-up phonograph in 1925
**E** George Gershwin (composer; 1898–1937)
 Tin Pan Alley, 1908–1911
 Gustav Mahler conducted the New York
 Philharmonic, Metropolitan Opera, 1907–1911
 Aaron Copland (composer; 1900–1991)
 Leonard Bernstein (composer; 1918–1990)
 Edgard Varèse's New Symphony Orchestra
 founded in 1919
 Duke Ellington (composer; 1899–1974); his band
 appeared at the Cotton Club, Harlem, 1927–1930
 Great Depression begins with Wall Street crash,
 1929–1939
 Home to Béla Bartók from 1940
 Bernard Herrmann (film composer; 1911–1975)

**F** John Philip Sousa (bandmaster, composer;
 1854–1932)
 President Woodrow Wilson's Fourteen Points, 1918
 League of Nations founded in 1919
**G** Stephen Collins Foster (composer; 1826–1864)
 KDKA, first commercial radio station, went on the air in 1920
**H** Storyville District, birthplace of jazz, ca. 1900–1920
 Ferdinand "Jelly Roll" Morton (composer, pianist; 1890–1941)
 Brass bands
 Louis "Satchmo" Armstrong (jazz musician, composer; ca.
 1898–1971)
**J** Scott Joplin (composer, pianist; 1868–1917)
**K** Charlie Parker (composer, saxophonist; 1920–1955);
 active in New York and Los Angeles from 1939
**L** John Cage (composer; born in 1912)
 Home to émigré composers:
 Arnold Schoenberg (from 1934)
 Igor Stravinsky (from 1940)
 Sergei Rachmaninoff (from 1942)

→ Travels of Scott Joplin (settled in New York in 1907)

FIGURE 27.1 Musical history in America.

sprang up in churches and at denominational colleges like Harvard (founded in 1636) and Yale (founded in 1701).

As more and more immigrants arrived from Europe (the population of New York grew from 30,000 in 1775 to 60,000 in 1800), interest shifted from religious music to secular music, and many people tried their hand at making music themselves. In 1810 a writer for the Philadelphia *Mirror of Taste and Dramatic Censor* reported:

> Almost every young lady and gentleman, from the children of the judge, the banker, and the general, down to those of the constable, the huckster and the drummer, can make a noise upon some instrument or other, and charm their neighbors with something which courtesy calls music.

Most music-making took place in the home, where the most popular instruments were the piano, guitar, flute, and "fiddle" (violin). By 1820 American publishers had issued more than 15,000 pieces of sheet music consisting of arrangements of patriotic songs, marches, dances, and sets of easy variations. They also published more than 500 "songsters"—pocket-sized collections of texts to be sung to well-known tunes.

Art music was rarely performed and little known. Occasionally virtuoso performers (known as "professors") would play compositions imported from Europe, but in the busy new country people had little time for music from abroad.

As time passed, however, gifted American composers began to appear. The country's first great songwriter was Stephen Collins Foster (1826–1864). Born to a middle-class Pittsburgh family, Foster received no encouragement in what his father regarded as his "strange talent." Foster wrote about 200 songs, most of them sentimental love songs. From "I Dream of Jeannie with the Light Brown Hair" to "Beautiful Dreamer"—his last published song (1864)—his songs combined simple harmonies with memorable melodies. In "Beautiful Dreamer," notice how the continuous rhythms of bar 3 are set up by the broken pattern of bars 1 and 2:

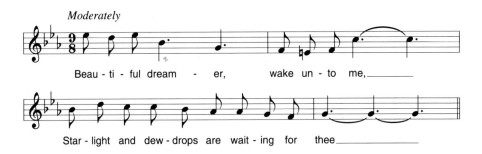

Foster wrote some of his songs for the minstrel troupe of E. P. Christy. Minstrel shows, performed by whites in blackface, were a popular form of entertainment from the 1820s until a decade or so after the Civil War. The stereotype of the black as a plantation "Jim Crow" or a ludicrous Broadway "Dandy Jim" reflected the unabashed racism of the times, and yet minstrel shows gave the public some idea, distorted though it was, of the music that would eventually find its way into the uniquely American music called jazz. A Unionist during the Civil War, Foster wrote two antislavery songs: "We Are Coming, Father Abraham," and "We're a Million in the Field."

A few composers of art music also appeared on the scene. Anthony Philip Heinrich (1781–1861) emigrated to America from Bohemia around the age of 30. After working as a merchant in Philadelphia, he moved in 1817 to what he described as "the solitary wilds and primeval forests of Kentucky." There he embarked on a surge of creative activity that lasted for almost 40 years. During that time he produced an astonishing variety of songs, programmatic piano pieces (*The Dawning of Kentucky,* with voice and violin), and symphonies (*The Cliffs of Plymouth* and *To the Spirit of Beethoven*). Heinrich described his music as "full of strange ideal somersets [somersaults] and capriccios [whims]." His exuberant style was probably little appreciated during his lifetime, and his music is rarely performed today.

The first American composer to command international attention was John Philip Sousa, the son of a Portuguese father and a German mother.

## JOHN PHILIP SOUSA (1854–1932)

The origins of the modern military march date back to the bands of the French Revolution, but John Philip Sousa, known as "The March King," raised the march to a level of popularity matched in Europe only by the waltz.

Sousa grew up in Washington, D.C., and while still a teenager he enlisted in the U.S. Marine Band. A skillful violinist, he turned down opportunities to study in Europe and chose instead to direct theater orchestras in Philadelphia. In 1880 he was named director of the U.S. Marine Band, and over the next 12 years he did much to raise its performance standards. In 1892 he relinquished that post and formed his own Sousa's Band (Figure 27.2), which he continued to conduct almost to his death 40 years later.

Sousa and his band made four European tours, and Sousa became one of the world's best-known musicians. A fine conductor and a busy one, he still found time to write operettas, novels, and an autobiography. He also helped to develop the sousaphone, a bass tuba that is still used by marching bands at halftime shows across America.

### Sousa: March, "The Stars and Stripes Forever" (1897)

Probably no march is more familiar to Americans than Sousa's "Stars and Stripes Forever" (Listening Guide 58). Recalling his return from a European vacation in 1896, Sousa wrote in his autobiography:

FIGURE 27.2 From 1879
to 1892, Sousa led the
U.S. Marine Band and
played for five presidents
at the White House. He
then launched a lucrative
career touring with his
own band, shown here.

I began to sense the rhythmic beat of a band playing within my brain. . . . Throughout the . . . voyage, that imaginary band continued to unfold the same themes, echoing and re-echoing the most distinct melody. I did not transfer a note of that music to paper while I was on the steamer, but when we reached shore I set down the measures that my brain-band had been playing for me.

For "The Stars and Stripes Forever" Sousa used a structure that was to serve him well throughout his career. All his marches open with a brief "curtain," probably intended to command the listeners' attention. The first two "strains" (as each brief section was called; referred to here as *A* and *B*) are in the tonic key and repeat immediately after their first appearance. The tuneful *C*-Strain moves suddenly to the subdominant key. This strain functions in much the same way as a trio in a minuet or a scherzo. Moreover, the band is sharply reduced, as it often is in an orchestral trio.

Instead of returning to the opening strains in the da capo manner, Sousa follows the *C*-Strain with a dramatic "break" dominated by the brass, creating a sense of anticipation. The break leads to a soft restatement of the *C*-Strain, embellished by a spirited countervoice in the piccolos. After a second break, the *C*-Strain repeats once again. This time Sousa pulls out all the stops. The trumpets blare forth the principal melody while the trombones address the piccolos with a countermelody of their own. The march ends with a brief but powerful cadence. Unlike almost every other closed form, Sousa's marches typically end in the subdominant rather than in the tonic key.

# *Listening Guide 58*

## SOUSA: March, "The Stars and Stripes Forever"

CD 3, TRACK ⬚12⬚
TAPE 3B, TRACK 7
DURATION: 3:20

*This typical Sousa march form begins with two repeating strains (A and B) in the tonic key. A contrasting strain (C) in the subdominant key is followed by a "break" in the lower brass, which sets up an embellished return of C. Another restatement of the break leads to a climactic restatement of C in the full ensemble.*

*Form: Sectional (A-A-B-B-C-break-C-break-C)*

| | LOCATION | TIME | COMMENTS |
|---|---|---|---|
| 1 | Curtain | **0:00** | Syncopated brass followed by dramatic snare-drum roll. |
| | A-Strain | **0:04** | Snappy, upbeat melody played by trumpets and piccolo. Second half of phrase softer with *forte* echoes. |
| | A-Strain repeated | 0:18 | Same as above. |
| 2 | B-Strain | **0:32** | Two parallel phrases more boisterous than A, reinforced by snare-drum rolls. |
| | B-Strain repeated | 0:47 | Same as above. |
| 3 | C-Strain | **1:02** | Sudden switch to soft, lyrical theme in reduced ensemble, underpinned by a catchy rhythm in the snare drum. |
| | Break | 1:32 | Blaring trombones create a keen sense of anticipation. |
| 4 | C-Strain | **1:55** | Full ensemble, soft. To the main theme in the brass, Sousa adds a saucy countermelody in the piccolo. |
| | Repeat of break | 2:24 | As before. |
| 5 | C-Strain | **2:47** | Full ensemble, loud. A final triumphant statement includes trumpets and snare-drum rolls. |

The *A*- and *B*-Strains, which are only half as long as the *C*-Strain, occur twice in quick succession rather than in the three separate, and hence more dramatic, statements of *C*. As in many of Sousa's marches, the piece stands or falls on this strain:

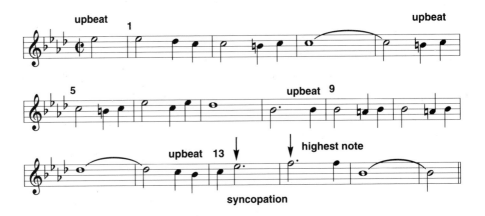

Although this theme seems simple enough, its structure is quite sophisticated. It consists of two varied 16-bar phrases—the first of which is shown above. Each of the four subphrases (bars 1–4, 5–8, 9–12, 13–16) begins with an upbeat that is varied slightly each time. The rhythms of the first subphrase are square; the second and third subphrases are linked by the first dotted rhythm (m. 8); the final subphrase introduces a syncopation (m. 13, arrow), and in the next bar the highest note of the theme appears. (Notice that the rhythms of bars 13 and 14 are a mirror image.) Sousa concludes the 16-bar phrase with a descent through its widest leap. In the repeat of the phrase, he introduces chromatic harmonies that render the final cadence all the more satisfying.

Much of the appeal of Sousa's marches arises from his colorful orchestration. Although bands numbering hundreds (and sometimes thousands) of musicians were common at the time, Sousa insisted on a tight ensemble of only 48 players, including 25 reeds (clarinets, saxophones), 16 brasses (cornets, trumpets, trombones, sousaphones), 6 percussion (snare drum, bass drum, cymbals), and—surprisingly—one string bass. The bass was possible because the band usually performed on a concert stage rather than in march formation. The march soon spawned a ballroom dance known as the "two-step," which rivaled the march in popularity.

## CHARLES IVES (1874–1954)

Charles Ives (Figure 27.3) was a staunch New England Yankee whose stubborn adherence to an eclectic but highly original style met with strong resistance during his lifetime. Ives stands as the first important American composer of art music and one of the most original composers of the twentieth century.

Ives's father, George, had served during the Civil War as the youngest bandmaster in the Union Army. After settling down in Danbury, Connecticut, he gave instruction on various instruments, trained and conducted church choirs, and directed bands at town concerts and other events. Charles's first composi-

FIGURE 27.3 "Beauty in music," noted Charles Ives, "is too often confused with something that lets the ears lie back in an easy chair."

tions may date from his twelfth year (the dating is uncertain), and at the age of 14 he was the youngest salaried church organist in the state. But he still found time to pitch for his high school baseball team.

In 1894 Ives entered Yale University, where he studied theory and composition with Horatio Parker, an American composer and church musician trained in Europe. Parker's view of "modern" music extended little beyond Brahms, a view that sometimes caused friction between teacher and pupil. Parker gave Ives a solid grounding in composition, however, as is evidenced by Ives's First Symphony, written while he was still an undergraduate.

Ives's father died only a few months after Charles entered Yale. In later life Ives often spoke of his father's role in his musical development. For example, he credited his father with introducing him to such techniques as mixing meters, devising exotic harmonies, using quarter tones and microtones (intervals smaller than Western half steps), accompanying a tune in one key with a tune in a different key, and building collage-like textures. It now seems doubtful, however, that George Ives was as innovative a musician as his son claimed.

After graduating from Yale (with a D+ average), Ives entered the new field of life insurance and, with a sympathetic partner, built up a prosperous business with which he supported his wife, Harmony, and, later, their adopted daughter, Edith. But music remained Ives's obsession. He was especially preoccupied with "originality" and spoke harshly about almost all the music of the past. Even Debussy, wrote Ives, would have been better off if he had "hoed corn or sold newspapers for a living."

Deploring the preference of American audiences for European music, Ives once wrote:

> Many American composers, I believe, have been interested in working things out for themselves to a great extent, but it seems to be the general opinion that, unless a man has studied most of his life in a European conservatory, he has no right (and does not know how) to throw anything at an audience, good or bad.

Ives set down his opinions in a series of essays he called *Memos.* The cryptic, aphoristic tone of these pieces reveals a mind that was fiercely critical and independent. Here are some excerpts:

ON MUSIC

> A Symphony written only to amuse and entertain is likely to amuse only the writer—and him not long after the check is cashed.
>
> Beauty in music is too often confused with something that lets the ears lie back in an easy chair.
>
> Initial coherence today may be dullness tomorrow.
>
> The trouble with modern music is that [it is] . . . too intellectual.
>
> Is it the composer's fault that man has only ten fingers?
>
> I have with much practice been able to keep five, and even six, rhythms going on in my mind at once, so that I can hear each one exactly by leaning toward it, changing the ear in each measure. . . .

Why tonality as such should be thrown out for good, I can't see. Why it should be always present, I can't see.

The way I'm constituted, writing soft stuff makes me sore—I sort of hate all music.

Why do I like these things? . . . Are my ears on wrong?

ON MUSIC'S FUTURE

The time is coming, but not in our lifetime, when [music] will develop possibilities inconceivable now—a language as transcendent that its heights and depths will be common to all mankind.

In some century to come . . . school children will whistle popular tunes in quarter-tones.

Throughout his *Memos*, Ives wove a rough chronology of his music. Because so little of that music was published, or even performed, during his lifetime, scholars have tended to rely pretty much on his own datings. According to his account, he wrote almost all of his music between 1896 and 1916. "As I look back," he wrote, "I find that I did almost no composing after 1918"—the year in which he had suffered a serious heart attack. It seems, however, that in order to appear even more innovative he dated numerous works earlier than they had in fact been composed. And he continued to tinker with many of them—especially the songs—for many years after their initial composition.

Even after 1930, Ives was still claiming that he was unfamiliar with Stravinsky's *The Rite of Spring* or with any of Schoenberg's music. On his handwritten score of "Putnam's Camp" from *Three Places in New England,* he made a comment on the election of 1908 and mentioned the date 1912. But other evidence suggests that he completed this piece shortly before its premiere in 1931. In fact, it seems likely that he was still writing music at least into the 1930s. We may never know to what extent (if any) he was influenced by the music of Debussy, Stravinsky, Schoenberg, and Bartók. But the originality of his music is evident no matter when he wrote it.

If we had only the titles of Ives's compositions to go on, we might assume that he was unabashedly Romantic. Many of his pieces carry such extramusical, programmatic titles as *Washington's Birthday, The Gong on the Hook and Ladder, The Fourth of July, Decoration Day,* and *Southpaw Pitching.* Yet the compositions themselves are not so much *about* those topics as they are dreamlike reminiscences of Ives's boyhood. Just as memories are made up of bits and pieces of past events, Ives's music is a blend of disparate and seemingly contradictory styles— a blend that perhaps only a non-European composer could have achieved. The nostalgic, retrospective nature of much of Ives's music may remind us of Brahms or Mahler,* but its working out takes innovative forms.

One of Ives's most original techniques was the piling up of several unrelated textures in the manner of a collage, with several ideas proceeding at different speeds and sometimes in different directions. Into these musical collages he

*Once, while in his publisher's office, Mahler expressed admiration for an unidentified score of Ives's that he happened to pick up.

introduces snatches of folk songs, popular tunes, marches, and hymns. Although in a sense Ives was a populist composer who spoke the language of the common people, his distortions of such popular music shocked many of his early listeners.

Ives also composed in many traditional genres. His first major publication, in 1922, was a group of 114 songs. Some of them evoke the tunes of Stephen Foster or the nineteenth-century European *Lied*. Still others are radical experiments of Ives's own devising. He also wrote two sonatas for piano, four for violin and piano, two string quartets, and four symphonies. He wrote no operas, a form he regarded as effeminate. Some of his orchestral pieces are for a small orchestra of the pickup variety that might be found in a small-town theater. Others are for large symphonic orchestras, often supplemented by a battery of unusual percussion.

Although his music received sporadic performances, Ives was not really discovered until the 1930s, by the American composer Henry Cowell. Along with another pioneer of American music, Nicholas Slonimsky, Cowell championed the performance of Ives's music through the American Composers Alliance and other organizations. At the time of Ives's death, however, few of his works had been performed. His larger orchestral works called for unusual groupings of performers, and their fiendish difficulty demanded costly rehearsal time that few orchestras were willing to underwrite. Since Ives's death in 1954, however, more and more of his music has found a place in the regular repertoire.

## Ives: "Putnam's Camp, Redding, Connecticut" and "The Housatonic at Stockbridge" from *Three Places in New England* (1912?–1930?)

One of the few of Ives's orchestral works that received a public performance during his lifetime was his *First Orchestral Set*, which he subtitled *Three Places in New England*. Although he may have sketched the three movements of this work many years earlier, he did not complete them until 1931. Of the second movement, "Putnam's Camp" (Listening Guide 59), Ives wrote in his *Memos*:

> Once upon a "4th of July," some time ago, so the story goes, a child went there on a picnic, held under the auspices of the First Church and the Village Cornet Band. Wandering away from the rest of the children past the camp ground into the woods, he hopes to catch a glimpse of some of the old soldiers. As he rests on the hillside of laurel and hickories, the tunes of the band and the songs of the children grow fainter;— when . . . over the trees on the crest of the hill he sees a tall woman standing. She reminds him of a picture he has of the Goddess of Liberty,—but the face is sorrowful— she is pleading with the soldiers not to forget their "cause" and the great sacrifices they have made for it. But they march out of the camp with fife and drum to a popular tune of the day. Suddenly a new national note is heard. Putnam is coming over the center,— the soldiers turn back and cheer. The little boy awakes, he hears the children's songs and runs down past the monument to "listen to the band" and join in the games and dances.

# Listening Guide 59

## IVES: "Putnam's Camp, Redding, Connecticut"
### from *Three Places in New England*

CD 6, TRACK 10
TAPE 6B, TRACK 7
DURATION: 5:55

*The form is a shadowy outline rather than a clear-cut shape. The chief means of organization is a collage texture in which snippets of familiar material appear and disappear.*

*Form: Free ternary*

| LOCATION | TIME | COMMENTS |
|---|---|---|
| **1** *A*-SECTION | | |
| Curtain | **0:00** | *Fortissimo,* full orchestra, music remains off-balance. |
| Main March Theme | 0:11 | Begins in the strings, with off-balance syncopations. |
| | 0:21 | A second "band," playing snatches of "The British Grenadiers," seems to march by in the opposite direction. |
| Repeat of March Theme | 0:52 | Trumpets and winds added to strings. |
| Snippets of popular tunes | 1:01 | First in the violins, then in the trumpets. |
| "Yankee Doodle" | 1:06 | Fragments in the trumpet, flute, and violin. |
| Parlor music | 1:11 | Sudden change to a soft, sweet violin melody accompanied by clarinet and bassoon. |
| Snippets, including "Bringing in the Sheaves" | 1:20 | Strings plus staggered winds and brass. |
| Dissonant dissolve | 1:43 | Predominantly strings and piano, fading gradually to a pause. |
| **2** *B*-SECTION | | |
| The Dreaming Child | **2:17** | Soft, slow-moving chords in strings with thematic snippets in the winds. |
| | 2:38 | Snippets of "The British Grenadiers" in the trumpet. |
| Snippets of popular tunes | 2:51 | Collage texture in which lyrical winds are answered by staccato strings, dissolving to oom-pah-pah accompaniment. |
| Various marches | 3:27 | Collage texture includes "The British Grenadiers" in the flute. |
| | 3:53 | Brass issue a stirring fanfare which degenerates into chaos. |
| Parlor music | 4:15 | As in the *A*-Section, and equally unprepared. |
| Another curtain | 4:26 | Clarinets, then blaring brass. |
| **3** *A'*-SECTION | | |
| Main March Theme | **4:37** | Most prominent voice initially is a trombone countermelody, soon joined by what seems a convention of marching bands, all moving in different directions. |
| Repeat of March Theme | 5:13 | Main March Theme is more audible, but the triumphant parade continues. |
| Cadential flourish | 5:48 | Starts with the 4-note opening of "The Star-Spangled Banner," then cuts off abruptly. |

Ives organizes the piece in free ternary form (the return of *A* is quite abbreviated), with the dream sequence providing the middle section.

The first march tune (called the Main March Theme in Listening Guide 59) was apparently Ives's own invention. The irregularly placed accents carry a hint of parody:

The second tune is of British origin. Known as "The British Grenadiers," it was first set to words in 1779 by a captain in one of General Putnam's regiments. Here is one of the verses:

That seat of science, Athens,      [*A*]
    And earth's great mistress, Rome,
Where now are all their glories?      [*A*]
    We scarce can find the tomb.
Then guard your rights, Americans,      [*B*]
    Nor stoop to lawless sway,
Oppose, oppose, oppose, oppose      [*A*]
    My brave America.

Ives's treatment of these two simple tunes is anything but simple. Using the collage technique, he brings in snippets of other marches and popular songs. We hear bits of "Yankee Doodle," the hymn "Bringing in the Sheaves," and domestic "parlor music." The two *A*-Sections are charged with excitement, and the pandemonium of the climax is extraordinarily effective. To achieve this effect Ives called for a large orchestra that includes organ, piano, celesta, two harps, gong, and cymbals. In less than six minutes, Ives transports us from the holiday atmosphere of a Fourth of July celebration to a dreamlike reverie and back again.

Commenting on "The Housatonic at Stockbridge," the last movement of *Three Places in New England,* Ives wrote:

> *The Housatonic at Stockbridge* was suggested by a Sunday morning walk that Mrs. Ives and I took near Stockbridge, the summer after we were married. We walked in the meadows along the river, and heard the distant singing from the church across the river. The mist had not entirely left the river bed, and the colors, the running water, the banks and elm trees were something that one would always remember.

This movement is organized around a haunting refrain theme introduced by the French horn and the English horn. Its opening faintly suggests the opening of Beethoven's Fifth Symphony:

The movement then proceeds through a tortured, late-Romantic melody, to a dreamy episode colored by the undamped harp and celesta, and finally to a cathartic crescendo and accelerando. Unlike Baroque ritornello forms, in which the refrain theme remains intact, Ives's refrain theme is overwhelmed in the course of the movement and reappears only as a haunting echo in the codetta.

Although both of these works demand the capabilities of the most highly trained orchestra and conductor, they have begun to find a place in concert halls all over the world. Ives's influence on twentieth-century music is acknowledged even by those who are still uncomfortable with his unique mix of the homespun and the avant-garde.

## AARON COPLAND (1900–1990)

Aaron Copland (Figure 27.4) was the first American composer of art music to achieve international fame. Although his music passed through several stylistic phases, all of it has a directness, a strength, and a clarity that sound distinctly American.

FIGURE 27.4  In *What to Listen for in Music,* Aaron Copland wrote, "A great symphony is a man-made Mississippi down which we irresistibly flow from the instant of our leave-taking to a long foreseen destination. Music must always flow."

Copland's parents emigrated from Russia to Brooklyn, where his father set up a retail store and became president of the oldest synagogue. Aaron, the youngest of five children, showed an early aptitude for music and—without encouragement from his family—attended concerts by the newly formed New York Symphony at the Brooklyn Academy of Music. He studied music with Rubin Goldmark (1872–1936), a teacher with conservative tastes, but he soon turned his attention to the exotic scores of Debussy, Musorgsky, and Ravel.

Unlike Ives, Copland was receptive to European music. In 1920 he set off for Europe with barely enough money to pay for his passage and a few months of food and lodging. He went to Paris and sought out Nadia Boulanger (1887–1979), a distinguished teacher who was to tutor several generations of America's most talented composers and conductors. Boulanger insisted that her students master the standard repertoire but at the same time encouraged them to follow their own bent. Curiously, it was while Copland was abroad that he established contact with his American roots. By the time he returned to America in 1924, he was familiar not only with the music of Debussy and Stravinsky but with American jazz as well. One of his first works, *Music for the Theatre* (1925), and a piano concerto from 1926 are shot through with the sounds and rhythms of jazz.

Copland also composed works in a complex, dissonant style, including the Piano Variations (1930). But with the onset in that same year of the Great Depression, Copland felt he should write music that spoke to the widest possible audience. About the masses who wanted music that they could comprehend immediately, Copland said: "It made no sense to ignore them and to continue writing as if they did not exist. I felt that it was worth the effort to see if I couldn't say what I had to say in the simplest possible terms." Over the next two decades, Copland's music incorporated cowboy songs, revival hymns, folk tunes, and his own jazz-influenced brand of tonality. He looked to American subjects for inspiration, as in his ballets *Billy the Kid* (1938), *Rodeo* (1942), and *Appalachian Spring* (1944). He wrote overtures, symphonies, and film scores (*Of Mice* and Men, *Our Town*, *The Red Pony*). He also wrote two popular books on music, *What to Listen for in Music* and *Our New Music*.

Around 1950 Copland began writing serial music. Nevertheless, during the 1960s younger members of the American avant-garde came to regard him as overly traditional despite his experiments with serialism, which many of them had begun to abandon. But Copland's stature as the quintessentially American composer remains undiminished.

## Copland: Suite from *Appalachian Spring* (1944)

In 1943 the Elizabeth Sprague Coolidge Foundation commissioned Copland to compose a ballet for Martha Graham's modern dance company (Figure 27.5). He decided to build the work around "a pioneer celebration in spring around a newly built farmhouse in the Pennsylvania hills in the early part of the last century":

> The bride-to-be and the young farmer-husband enact the emotions, joyful and apprehensive, their new domestic partnership invites. An older neighbor suggests now and then the rocky confidence of experience. A revivalist and his followers remind the new householders of the strange and terrible aspects of human fate. At the end the couple are left quiet and strong in their new home.

In typical anti-Romantic fashion, Copland scored the original ballet music for only 13 players. The work proved to be enormously popular, however, and in 1945 he converted it into an independent suite for full orchestra, omitting only "those sections in which the interest is primarily choreographic."

The narrative line in Copland's score is scarcely stronger than that in Stravinsky's *Rite of Spring*. Instead of telling a story, Copland conjures up a series of moods and emotions that might have been felt by a pioneer couple at the start of their life together. He divides the suite into eight sections (several of which are themselves subdivided), each headed by a brief description and with changes in tempo and mood marking the transition from one section to the next.

**Section 1:** "Introduction of the characters (bride, groom, a neighbor, revivalist preacher and his flock) one by one, in a suffused light." Beginning on a single tone in the second violins and viola, Copland expands the strings both up and down in long-held, static tones that suggest a vast, still landscape just before dawn. He bases much of the thematic material of the suite on a simple triadic "motto" theme (labeled "very slowly"), which is first enunciated in the clarinet a few seconds into the hushed introduction:

*p Semplice* (Simply) "white" tone

"White tone" means an open, neutral color, free of vibrato, corresponding to Copland's "suffused light." The lyrical solos in the violin, oboe, and bassoon that introduce each character also give this opening section an air of intimacy. The melodies shift freely in and out of focus, and the line between melody and accompaniment is blurred. The clarinet theme returns to frame this section (and returns at the end of the suite to frame the entire work).

**Section 2:**  Allegro. The sudden introduction of an angular, leaping theme expands on the triadic motto. The "vigoroso" strings and piano (punctuated by three single tones in the xylophone) crackle with a percussive energy:

Copland's use of square (nondotted) rhythms such as these gives the score much of its vitality and freshness. The emergence of a tender, hymnlike theme out of this pulsating texture is as delightful as it is unexpected. Copland needs three stages. In stage 1, the rising arpeggios of the introduction are expanded, as in this passage from the Allegro:

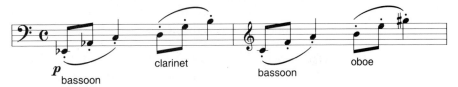

In stage 2, the horns and trombones expand the germinal arpeggio from three to five notes:

Stage 3 grows directly out of a restatement of stage 2. The trumpet begins aggressively, but by measure 6 the theme has emerged as a warm, lyrical melody whose syncopations nevertheless give it a slightly jazzy feel:

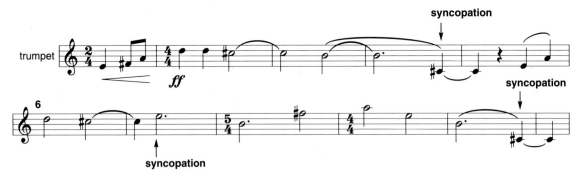

Copland subjects this theme to the thematic transformation favored by the Romantics. Its numerous repetitions (in Sections 3, 4, 6, and 8) give the music a reflective, often poignant air. Following the practice of late-Romantic composers, Copland avoids repeating any of his themes literally, relying instead on variation, fragmentation, and extension.

**Section 3:** "Duo for the Bride and her Intended—scene of tenderness and passion." Copland juxtaposes these emotions, alternating between tender passages in the winds and passionate, chromatic outbursts in muted strings. The hymnlike theme returns twice and even occurs in inversion (in the flute).

**Section 4:** "Quite fast. The Revivalist and his flock. Folksy feeling—suggestions of square dances and country fiddlers." After a tentative beginning in the oboe, the square rhythms of Section 2 turn into a literal square dance, though one with many more rhythmic surprises than in traditional fiddle tunes. Copland builds to a large climax that dissolves briefly to a plaintive recall in the oboe and flute of the hymnlike theme.

**Section 5:** "Still faster. Solo dance of the Bride—presentiment of motherhood. Extremes of joy and fear and wonder." Along with an exuberant new theme built on a cadence pattern (in short-short-short / LONG - [LONG] rhythms), Copland transforms the angular, leaping theme of the first Allegro into a jazzy theme built on scales. Bright instrumental voices scurry past each other in marked syncopation. After another climax, the cadential theme repeats slowly and emphatically.

**Section 6:** "As at first. Transition scene to music reminiscent of the Introduction." Copland recalls both the hymnlike theme (in a high solo violin) and the triadic theme that opened the suite (now played by the flute).

**Section 7:** "Calm and flowing. Scenes of daily activity for the Bride and her Farmer-husband." Now follows the emotional climax of the suite, a set of free variations on the Shaker hymn "Simple Gifts." This appealing tune follows the familiar *a-a-b-a* pattern. Copland's treatment is cumulative, moving from a solo clarinet (Theme) down a whole step to oboe and bassoon (Variation 1), back up a whole step to strings in imitation (Variation 2), and to the brass in a brisk tempo (Variation 3). A compressed Variation 4 plays each of the phrase-pairs simultaneously. The section ends with a grand statement of the first two phrases (*a* and *a'*) in the full orchestra (Variation 5), with powerful descending octaves in the bass.

**Section 8:** "The Bride takes her place among her neighbors." A chordal theme in the muted strings, marked "like a prayer," repeats four times to varying cadences, only the last of which comes to rest. After a final recall of the hymnlike theme in the flute and violin, the suite ends by recalling the hushed mood of the introduction, with the triadic theme finally back in the clarinet. By coming full circle, Copland has suggested the daily rhythms that will govern the newlyweds' lives.

## JAZZ: A UNIQUELY AMERICAN MUSIC

Not even the most farseeing prophet could have predicted the course of American music after 1900. Who, for example, could have predicted a Charles Ives? And who could have foreseen the remarkable confluence of musical elements that led to jazz?*

As the twentieth century opened, the United States was already an industrialized society with all its attendant social benefits and ills. The country had scarcely begun to integrate the millions of descendants of slavery into the mainstream of national life. African-Americans were still denied the right to vote in

---

*The origins of the term *jazz* are obscure. Some claim that it derives from the French word *jaser,* meaning "to have an animated conversation"; others, that the root word *jass* comes from the African Gold Coast or even from the Arab world; still others, that it originated in vaudeville or that it refers to the sex act. Though the word first appeared in print in 1917, it seems to have been in use at least a decade earlier.

most areas of the South, where unconstitutional voting tests would not be outlawed until the second half of the twentieth century. Few had access to the education and employment that most whites took for granted, and most continued to live in abject poverty.

The music that came to be known as jazz was in part a response to the institutionalized oppression that persisted long after the abolition of slavery. Conscious of their rich cultural traditions, African-Americans expressed themselves in music of their own devising. And yet the musicians who played jazz were racially integrated from the very beginning. Black or white, they seemed relatively free of prejudice. Black musicians were willing to share their music with anyone who was interested and able. In "Congo Square" in New Orleans, black and white musicians came together every Sunday for a round of music-making. Yet many of the early consumers of jazz—especially the white owners of nightclubs and their patrons—clung to the old segregationist ways.

Countless styles came together in the mix that became jazz. From the descendants of slaves came West African drumming, the spiritual, the blues, the field holler, and work songs. From the European-American tradition came popular songs and ballads, Western harmony, closed structures like the march, and instruments like the clarinet, trumpet, cornet, trombone, and bass.

What emerged was something new. Jazz sounded like no other music. Its strongly accented duple meter, coupled with unprecedented rhythmic freedom in the melody lines, invited listeners to dance, and countless thousands did. During the years before the First World War, Debussy, Schoenberg, and Stravinsky were all composing music that broke with tradition, but nothing they wrote was as startlingly new as jazz. Despite its varied roots, jazz is the only major musical style that is uniquely American.

Unlike art music, which was set down in precisely notated scores, jazz relied on oral tradition. Today, jazz historians study old recordings rather than old scores. Because jazz is at base an improvisatory style, there have been thousands and thousands of jazz "composers." The greatest improvisers—musicians like Louis Armstrong (1898–1971)—have inspired countless imitators, but from the very beginning it was individual style that counted.

Jazz has evolved continuously from the moment it emerged, and the constant pressure to remain contemporary may help explain its rapid evolution. We turn now to several of the stages in that development.

## RAGTIME

In 1899 the American novelist Rupert Hughes noted that something called *ragtime* was "sweeping the country like a plague of clog-hopping locusts." Hordes of itinerant black pianists were playing their music in saloons and dance halls across America and making simplified arrangements for sale as sheet music. The ragtime mania lasted almost until the First World War. Ragtime was not quite jazz, but it incorporated certain features that would find their way into jazz.

## Scott Joplin (1868–1917): "Gladiolus Rag" (1907)

FIGURE 27.6  Interest in Scott Joplin revived in 1974 when a popular movie, *The Sting,* featured five of his ragtime songs. The movie's score and title song won Academy Awards, and the soundtrack sold more than 2 million copies.

Ironically, the man who did most to popularize ragtime spent much of his life trying to win recognition as a composer of operas. Scott Joplin (Figure 27.6) grew up in Texarkana, Texas, the son of hardworking, musical parents. At the age of 7 he became obsessed with a piano he had discovered in the neighborhood. His parents managed to scrape together enough money to buy him a square piano* of his own. His mother, who took in laundry, spread word of his prowess throughout the white community. There is some evidence that a German "professor" (as instrumental teachers in small towns were commonly called) befriended Joplin in his early teens and introduced him to the "classics," including opera.

At age 14, Joplin rejected his father's insistence that he learn a trade and struck off on his own. He traveled about through Texas, Louisiana, Missouri, Arkansas, and Kansas, playing the piano in nightclubs, saloons, poolhalls, and brothels. He also led a vocal group for a short time. Along the way he got to know many white musicians from whom he picked up certain techniques that entered into the stylistic amalgam known as ragtime.

The harmonies of ragtime are essentially those used by Schubert and the first generation of German Romantics, and the structure of most rags adheres closely to that of Sousa's marches. (Joplin would have had ample opportunity to hear Sousa's music performed.) The regular, powerful beats by the left hand also are reminiscent of Sousa's marches. To these influences Joplin added a fresh melodic style based on systematic syncopation—the "ragged time." He may have been influenced by a practice in slave music known as "patting Juba," in which a regular percussive beat gave support to a syncopated melody.

In ragtime, there are three types of syncopation. In one type, the first or second beat of a bar is either silent (as shown by the rest in this excerpt from the *A*-Section of Joplin's "Gladiolus Rag," Listening Guide 60) or is tied over from the preceding beat (as in the second beat of the second bar):

*A piano of rectangular shape, larger than a spinet but smaller than a grand. The square piano was popular during the second half of the nineteenth century but ceased production entirely after the First World War.

Contrasting with this rather mild type of syncopation is a second, more dramatic type. Here the accent occurs on the second of the four fast notes (known as sixteenths) that make up each bar, as in the first beat of the *D*-Section from the "Gladiolus Rag":

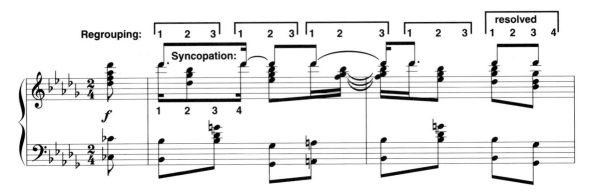

This example also contains the third, and most complex, type of syncopation, in which a pattern of regrouping takes place. In this instance, three beats of four fast notes per beat are rearranged via the high note (the one whose stem is up) into four beats of three fast notes per beat. This creates an exhilarating tension with the regular pulse in the left hand, which is resolved on the last beat of the second bar.

The connection between ragtime and marches is evident. Many rags carried the heading *Tempo di marcia* ("In march tempo"), and several ragtime composers wrote marches as well. Sousa, in turn, incorporated certain ragtime features into his march arrangements. Another form that depended on syncopation was the *cakewalk*, a dance of black origin that was popular in minstrel shows. For a brief time the cakewalk was the rage of Europe, inspiring Debussy to write a piano piece called "Golliwog's Cakewalk" for his suite *Children's Corner*.

Though ragtime was not the invention of any one composer, Scott Joplin was its first great exponent. Between 1899, when he published his best-seller "Maple Leaf Rag," and his death in 1917, he published more than three dozen rags. Joplin represents the "classic" strain of ragtime. Unlike other ragtime composers, he insisted that his rags be played in a dignified manner, preferably on a well-tuned grand piano. (Many of his published pieces carry this heading: "Note: Do not play this piece fast / It is never right to play ragtime fast.") The "Gladiolus Rag" shows Joplin's mastery of the cumulative form, in which each of the four successive themes generates a more powerful forward motion.

Around 1907 Joplin settled in New York City, where he published a tutor, the *Rag Time Instructor*. He also worked on a three-act opera, *Treemonisha*, about a woman abandoned as an infant who overcomes severe obstacles and leads her people to freedom through education. Joplin never managed to get *Treemonisha* produced, though it has been produced in recent years. (An earlier opera, *A Guest of Honor*, apparently disappeared without a trace en route to the U.S. Patent Office.)

# Listening Guide 60

## JOPLIN: "Gladiolus Rag"

CD 6, TRACK 11
TAPE 6B, TRACK 8
DURATION: 4:25

*The form of Joplin's "Gladiolus Rag" parallels that of many Sousa marches. The gentle A-Strain repeats immediately, followed by the B-Strain and its repeat. Then the first strain—poised at the center of the form—repeats once, followed by two further strains and their repeats. Like most Sousa marches, the "Gladiolus Rag" ends in the key of the subdominant rather than the tonic and builds cumulatively to a climax in the last strain.*

*Form: Sectional (A-A-B-B-A-C-C-D-D)*

| | LOCATION | TIME | COMMENTS |
|---|---|---|---|
| 1 | A-Strain | **0:00** | A tender, syncopated melody divided between an antecedent phrase and a strong repeated cadence. |
| | A-Strain repeated | 0:31 | Embellished slightly. |
| 2 | B-Strain | **1:01** | Louder, with a more directed bass line that includes linking chains of four or eight rapid notes. Divided again between an antecedent and a cadential phrase. |
| | B-Strain repeated | 1:30 | |
| 3 | A-Strain | **1:59** | A return to the calm, sweet atmosphere of the opening. |
| 4 | C-Strain | **2:29** | Modulates to the subdominant, softer than either of the preceding strains. Nevertheless, the melody is doubled at the octave, giving it a certain brilliance. |
| | C-Strain repeated | 2:58 | |
| 5 | D-Strain | **3:26** | The climax of the piece, with powerful bass lines and melodic syncopations on three of every four beats. |
| | D-Strain repeated | 3:54 | |

# Historical Window

## THE NEW ORLEANS BRASS BAND

The French who settled in New Orleans brought with them a keen interest in music-making. And following the abolition of slavery, African-Americans poured into the town, bringing their own rich musical heritage. Not surprisingly, the Creoles—offspring of Europeans and blacks—turned out to be great music-makers themselves.

The popularity of brass bands in New Orleans dates back to the end of the eighteenth century. As time passed, it became customary for a marching band to accompany funeral processions on their way to and from the cemetery. In 1819 a visitor to New Orleans described these parades as "peculiar alone among American cities." In 1838 the New Orleans *Daily Picayune* spoke of the "real mania in this city for horn and trumpet playing." People in other cities went to church on Sunday, but in New Orleans they spent the day listening to the marching bands, which grew more numerous as the day wore on. "The sabbath in New Orleans exists only in its Almanacs," observed an alarmed visitor. One Episcopalian minister was obliged to dismiss his congregation because he could no longer be heard. Each year during Mardi Gras the clamor became downright deafening, and when President Garfield died in 1881 more than 16,000 people turned out to march to the bands.

Notices of parades appeared regularly in the local newspapers. Almost any occasion would bring the marchers out: a wedding, a funeral, an election, a national holiday, a holy day, a visiting dignitary, the laying of a cornerstone, the dedication of a statue. Parades took place at almost any hour of the day or night, and almost any organization could sponsor a band: militia companies, war veterans (of the Revolutionary War and the War of 1812), freemasons, benevolent societies, fire companies, workers' societies. Records show that almost two dozen professional bands were active during the first decade of the twentieth century, with names like The Excelsior Brass Band, The Tuxedo Brass Band, The Onward Brass Band, and the all-white Reliance Brass Band.

A photograph of the The Onward Brass Band taken in 1905 (Figure 27.11) shows its 12 members and their instruments: three cornets, clarinet, two horns, baritone horn, two trombones, one double bass (we assume the bass player did not march with the others), snare drum, and bass drum. All the musicians are wearing white starched uniforms, and some of them appear to be in their teens or early twenties.

The player who is credited with first playing jazz in New Orleans was the cornetist Buddy Bolden (1877–1931), whose band was one of the most celebrated in New Orleans. The regular Buddy Bolden Band was a dance band (it

FIGURE 27.11 In the 1880s, brass bands in New Orleans played marches from scores, but by 1900, jazz was common on the streets and the musicians improvised. "Every Sunday there was a parade in New Orleans," Jelly Roll Morton recalled. "They would have from two to eight and ten parades on Sunday. I've never seen it so small they only had one."

included three double bassists), but, augmented by additional musicians, it performed as a marching band as well. For funerals the band would improvise on hymns like "What a Friend We Have in Jesus" on the way to the cemetery and then would turn to more upbeat tunes like "Oh Didn't He Ramble" as it marched away. The structure of Morton's "Dead Man Blues" reflects this practice: The mournful introduction represents the march to the cemetery, while the rest of the piece represents the march back.

According to legend, Buddy Bolden's band was so familiar in the Storyville district that the "working girls" could recognize it by its signature theme, the second strain of a piece called "Sensation Rag." Bolden was also reputed to be the loudest cornet player who ever lived. It was said that he could poke his horn through a hole in the fence of the Johnson Amusement Park and play a call that would signal to people in the Lincoln Amusement Park several miles away that his band was about to perform.

In 1922 Armstrong was invited to join Oliver's Creole Jazz Band in Chicago, and it was here that he won his fame. Soon horn players from all over the Midwest were flocking to learn the secrets of "hot" jazz. After marrying Lillian Hardin, the pianist in Oliver's band, Armstrong embarked in 1925 on a series of recordings with his "Hot Five" (or "Hot Seven") that are milestones in the history of jazz. The verse/chorus structure of the 12-bar blues was well suited to the three-minute limit of the 78-rpm record that had just been introduced, and Armstrong was the first jazz musician whose reputation rested as much on recordings as on live performances.

One has the impression that there was nothing Armstrong could not do on the trumpet, whether playing rapid riffs (in the stop-and-start melodic style of jazz) or sustaining a high note for what seems an endless time. His vocal style was smooth, mellow, and relaxed. Although he was one of the first black artists to perform regularly in places like New York's Carnegie Hall and Boston's Symphony Hall, Armstrong endured with graciousness and dignity the prejudice that was the lot of most black people. In Europe he was lionized, and by the time of his death in 1971 America had finally come to recognize him as a national treasure.

"West End Blues" (Listening Guide 62), a breakthrough piece from the twenties, shows Armstrong at his most inventive. From the daring opening solo he moves instinctively to the right note to prepare the first full chord and then turns directly to the slow, languorous beat of the first chorus. The harmonic pattern is more chromatic and complex than that of Morton's "Dead Man Blues," and Armstrong and pianist Earl "Fatha" Hines (1903–1983) move in and out of it at will. In Armstrong's two solo choruses (the first and last), he uses an unprecedented variety of rhythms and a wide melodic span. Note how the first chorus builds steadily toward the final triplet ascent, making the trombone solo that follows seem almost superfluous. His emphasis is less on syncopation than on a spontaneous flow of melody that transcends the schematic blues pattern.

The third chorus exploits the call-and-response pattern that was characteristic of West African music and that by now had become a regular feature of New Orleans jazz. The call is sounded by the clarinet and the response is carried by the vocals. In more subtle fashion, Armstrong incorporates a portion of the second half of his opening solo note for note into the solo that follows the long-held note in the final chorus (often called the "out chorus"). The resulting sense of cohesion was much admired by Armstrong's followers.

## SWING BANDS

In the early days of jazz, ensembles rarely consisted of more than seven musicians. During the 1920s, however, as jazz won wider acceptance, a demand arose for larger ensembles suited to the spacious dance halls that were opening in cities across the country. At the same time, some of the better-known groups began to

# Listening Guide 62

## ARMSTRONG: "West End Blues"

CD 7, TRACK 3
TAPE 7A, TRACK 3
DURATION: 3:17

*This piece marked a new phase in the evolution of New Orleans jazz, in which the melody lines begin to move independently of the harmonic blues pattern. (The Bars column shows the location within the 12-bar-blues scheme.)*

*Form: 12-bar blues*

| | LOCATION | TIME | BARS | COMMENTS |
|---|---|---|---|---|
| 1 | Curtain | **0:00** | | Improvised solo by Armstrong, leading to prearranged jazz chord (at 0:13) with the entire ensemble. |
| | Chorus 1 | **0:15** | 1–4 | Simple statement with steady piano harmonies as the founda- |
| | | 0:28 | 5–8 | tion. Builds to melodic triplets in last phrase. |
| | | 0:39 | 9–12 | |
| 2 | Chorus 2 | **0:50** | 1–4 | Trombone, with tremolo piano and metallic percussion |
| | | 1:02 | 5–8 | accompaniment. |
| | | 1:13 | 9–12 | |
| | Chorus 3 | **1:24** | 1–4 | Clarinet echoed by Armstrong vocals on "wah-doo-wah" |
| | | 1:36 | 5–8 | syllables. |
| | | 1:48 | 9–12 | |
| 3 | Chorus 4 | **1:59** | 1–4 | Solo piano, steady left hand with free melody in the right hand. |
| | | 2:10 | 5–8 | Embellishes and varies harmonies in last two phrases. |
| | | 2:22 | 9–12 | |
| | Chorus 5 | **2:32** | 1–4 | Trumpet holds high B-flat for four bars. |
| | ("Out Chorus") | 2:45 | 5–8 | Trumpet makes a virtuoso descent. |
| | | 2:56 | 9–12 | Begins in solo piano and is interrupted after three bars by the trumpet . . . |
| | (Codetta) | **3:08** | | leading to three smooth, chromatic final chords. |

offer full programs on concert stages. These ensembles were known as "swing bands" or "big bands" (though such a band might have as few as 12 players).

## Duke Ellington (1899–1974): "Harlem Air Shaft" (1940)

Many people regard Edward Kennedy "Duke" Ellington as the greatest jazz composer of all time, and one of the most gifted American composers of the twentieth century. Ellington's father, a White House butler, supported his son's

FIGURE 27.12 Duke Ellington's elegant big band sound enjoyed decades of success. Commenting on a form of jazz that rebelled against his style, Ellington said, "Playing 'bop' is like playing Scrabble with all the vowels missing."

interest in music. After studying ragtime in Washington, the young Ellington moved to New York in 1923 with his 12-member Washington band (in which he was the pianist). By 1927 the band was playing regularly in the famous Harlem Cotton Club (Figure 27.12).

With this large ensemble, Ellington relied less on improvisation and began to write out many of his arrangements. Some of his roughly 6,000 compositions are 12-bar blues; others follow the popular song form *a-a-b-a* (known as the 32-bar form); and still others depart altogether from standard forms. He also wrote scores for over 50 films, numerous musical comedies, and an opera.

Ellington's harmonic language sometimes suggests that of Debussy or Ravel, and his orchestrations are far smoother and more sophisticated than those of the rougher ensembles that preceded him. He created exquisite, unusual textures and gave his soloists sensitive support during improvisations. Although the saxophone had been used only sparingly in New Orleans jazz (and slightly less so in its tamer offshoot, Dixieland), Ellington gave that instrument, especially the baritone and alto sizes, a prominent place in his music.

By the 1940s Ellington's band had grown to 19 players. Between 1943 and 1952 he presented a series of annual concerts in Carnegie Hall, and in 1971 he made a triumphant tour of the Soviet Union. After his death in 1974 the band was taken over by his son, Mercer Ellington (b. 1919).

Ellington wrote "Harlem Air Shaft" (Listening Guide 63) at the height of his career. Commenting on the title, he wrote:

> So much goes on in a Harlem air shaft [an open ventilating area in tenements]. You hear fights, you smell dinner, you hear people making love. You hear intimate gossip floating down. You hear the radio. An air shaft is one great big loudspeaker. . . .

# *Listening Guide 63*

## ELLINGTON: "Harlem Air Shaft"

CD 7, TRACK 4
TAPE 7A, TRACK 4
DURATION: 2:56

*For this piece Ellington used a 14-member orchestra, including Ellington on piano, Cootie Williams on trumpet, Johnny Hodges on alto saxophone, Jimmy Blanton on bass, and Sonny Greer on drums. Several of these talented musicians went on to become important soloists in their own right. The lower-case letters in the Location column refer to the phrases within each theme.*

*Form: Three a-a-b-a themes connected by a bridge*

| | LOCATION | TIME | COMMENTS |
|---|---|---|---|
| **1** | Curtain | **0:00** | Brush establishes upbeat tempo. |
| | | 0:05 | Saxophones in smooth parallel harmonies. |
| | | 0:10 | Unexpected cadential progression that sets up Theme *A*. |
| | THEME *A* | | |
| | *a* | **0:15** | Tune in saxophones with muted trumpet counterpoint. |
| | *a'* | 0:25 | |
| | *b* | 0:35 | Strong parallel chords in the saxophones answered by the plunger trombone. |
| | *a'* | 0:45 | |
| | Bridge | 0:55 | Begins with dramatic rest and long-held saxophone chords. The smooth saxophones are challenged by the trumpet. |
| | | 1:05 | Another unexpected rest, followed by an extension and heightening of the preceding dialogue. |
| | | 1:24 | Another rest, followed by a spirited dialogue that sets up Theme *B*. |
| **2** | THEME *B* | | |
| | *a* | **1:35** | The brass play the most regular of all the themes, answered by a swinging, wailing clarinet in improvisation. |
| | *a* | 1:44 | The clarinet response is even more complex. |
| | *b* | 1:54 | Long syncopated chords held by the brass. The clarinet dissolves into rapid trills. |
| | *a* | 2:04 | Clarinet peaks with three ascending arpeggiated triplets. |
| **3** | THEME C | | |
| | *a* | **2:14** | Trumpets play a softer variant of their counterpoint to Theme *A*, while the muted cornet responds. |
| | *a* | 2:24 | Different counterpoint from the cornet. |
| | *b* | 2:33 | The trumpets emerge, prompting an energized response from the clarinet. |
| | *a'* | 2:43 | The full orchestra joins in on a series of sassy, repeated chord pairs, leading directly to the final cadence. |

This spirited piece is organized around three variations on a driving 32-bar song pattern. Ellington places a dramatic bridge between Themes *A* and *B*, punctuated by three unexpected rests. Note the careful balance he strikes between the prearranged parts (Theme *A*) and the solos (trumpet in the bridge, clarinet in Theme *B*, muted cornet and clarinet in Theme *C*). Along the way, he resorts to both contrapuntal and call-and-response textures.

Ellington had an enormous influence on the other big bands of the day. Band leaders like Fletcher Henderson, Paul Whiteman, and Count Basie borrowed heavily from his bag of orchestration tricks, though they were rarely as bold or adventurous. By mid-century, however, many younger musicians had grown impatient with what they saw as the blandness and the predictable harmonies and rhythms of the big band sound. The stage was set for the rise of bebop.

## BEBOP

*Bebop* or *bop* is a style of jazz singing in which the performer sings rapid lines to nonsense syllables, commonly known as *scat*. The phrases often end in a LONG-short pattern sung to the syllables "BEE-bop" (or sometimes "RE-bop"). The term was quickly applied to purely instrumental jazz as well. The practitioners of bebop were making a social as well as a musical statement. They wanted to distance themselves from the more staid elements of jazz as practiced by the swing bands, and they showed hostility toward anyone who refused to accept their new style of jazz. Jazz was now old enough to become politicized; it had come of age.

One bebop player remarked that his group played certain songs "just to keep the other guys off the stand, because we knew they couldn't make these chord changes." The foremost trumpeter of bebop, Dizzy Gillespie (b. 1917), once told an interviewer that "the modulations we manufactured were the weirdest, especially if some new cat walked in with his horn and tried to sit in with us." This was a jazz of cool alienation. Its most brilliant practitioner was the saxophonist Charlie "Bird" Parker.

### Charlie "Bird" Parker (1920–1955): "Bloomdido" (1950)

Parker's life was short but intense. Born in Kansas City, Kansas, he received an alto saxophone as a present from his mother when he was 11. By 17 he was playing professionally. In 1941 he met Dizzy Gillespie, and together they pioneered the new bebop style. Parker was plagued by alcohol and drug addiction throughout his adult life, but he remained determined to realize his potential as a jazz artist.

Though obsessed with technical virtuosity, Parker used a hard-edged, aggressive style that forbade listeners to be indifferent to his art. He wanted no one to

# Listening Guide 64

## PARKER: "Bloomdido"

CD 7, TRACK 5
TAPE 7A, TRACK 5
DURATION: 3:26

*Five musicians take part in this remarkable performance recorded in June 1950: Charlie Parker on alto saxophone, Dizzy Gillespie on trumpet, Thelonious Monk on piano, Curley Russell on bass, and Buddy Rich on drums. The prearranged frame—a tight ensemble between saxophone and trumpet—contrasts dramatically with the open-ended structure of the improvised choruses. The phrase structure of the choruses, though obscured by complex harmonies and overlapping phrases, is built around a 12-bar pattern.*

*Form: Improvised choruses with introduction and frame*

| | LOCATION | TIME | COMMENTS |
|---|---|---|---|
| 1 | Introduction | **0:00** | Driving hi-hat (suspended cymbals) sets up syncopated piano. |
| 2 | FRAME | | |
| | *a*-phrase | **0:09** | Saxophone and trumpet play jaunty 12-bar tune in rapid unisons, |
| | *a'*-phrase | 0:22 | accompanied by bass and hi-hat. |
| 3 | CHORUS 1 | **0:34** | Saxophone improvisation. Chord changes hard to discern. Bass and percussion maintain the beat while the piano fills in harmonies. Four statements of the 12-bar pattern. |
| 4 | CHORUS 2 | **1:25** | Trumpet improvisation. Harmonies even more elaborate. Three statements of the 12-bar pattern. |
| 5 | CHORUS 3 | **2:06** | Piano improvisation, with driving bass and steady hi-hat rhythms. Lean, spare piano texture. Two statements of the 12-bar pattern. |
| | DRUM SOLO | 2:30 | Extensive cross rhythms between snare drum and hi-hat, designed to dazzle the audience. Amounts to two statements of the 12-bar pattern. |
| 6 | FRAME | | |
| | *a*-phrase | **2:55** | Identical to opening. |
| | *a'*-phrase | 3:08 | Dies out abruptly on the fourth beat of the twelfth bar, with the drummer providing a last, delayed "downbeat." |

dance to his music, and he saw to it that only a few insiders were aware of the source of his improvisations. In short, he insisted that his art be appreciated for its own sake.

In 1945 Parker and the trumpeter Dizzy Gillespie made a series of historic recordings in New York that are regarded as the birth of bebop. In 1950, three-fifths of this group (with newcomers Thelonious Monk on piano and Buddy Rich on drums) had a New York reunion for another series of bebop recordings. "Bloomdido" (Listening Guide 64) was apparently named after August Bloom, a Buffalo-based disc jockey. This practice was quite popular in an era when such persons wielded great influence on what was heard and what was not. The 25-second frame that brackets the three choruses of "Bloomdido" is a prearranged duet of great rhythmic subtlety between Parker and Gillespie. For the two-plus minutes in between, Parker and Gillespie improvise with disciplined abandon over the regular, driving beat of the bass and drums (especially the hi-hat—suspended cymbals). Although the choruses are built around repetitions of a flexible 12-bar pattern, they are progressively shortened and their junctures intentionally blurred. Rich, in his free improvisation, takes us to the edge of loss of control but never steps over the line. This is white-knuckle music that combines shock with exhilaration.

## MODERN JAZZ

Like other forms of contemporary music, jazz has evolved steadily over the years. The fifties brought the "cool" jazz of trumpeter Miles Davis (b. 1926); the sixties brought the "free jazz" of saxophonist Ornette Coleman (b. 1930; heavily influenced by avant-garde composers of art music); and the seventies brought the jazz of "fusion." The jazz of the eighties and nineties is impossible to label. Indeed, as with art music, jazz has settled into a more tolerant pattern, with New Orleans jazz and free jazz, bebop and cool jazz existing side by side. Miles Davis, for example, has absorbed every style from bebop on, producing successful albums over almost a 40-year period. Today we must speak of a variety of jazz styles rather than of one dominant style. Younger artists like trumpeter Wynton Marsalis (b. 1961; Figure 27.13) seem more interested in cultivating an intelligent audience for jazz than in restricting it to an elite group. He has given jazz instruction to students at Harvard, and his sessions have been broadcast on public television.

During the seventies and eighties, jazz often drew on art music, though without sacrificing its own identity. A talented practitioner of this "new eclecticism" is the composer and pianist Keith Jarrett, born in 1945 in Allentown, Pennsylvania. Jarrett's first professional experience was with Fred Waring's Pennsylvanians, a musically conservative big band. After attending the Berklee College of Music (which has a strong program in jazz) in Boston, Jarrett moved to New York in 1965. Shunning commercial appearances, he was relatively unknown

until he was "discovered" in a small club, the Village Vanguard. In the late sixties he formed a quartet with saxophonist Charles Lloyd (b. 1938), and between 1969 and 1971 he worked with Miles Davis.

In the early 1970s Jarrett began to give solo piano recitals. The styles he brought to these improvisations encompassed almost every variety of twentieth-century music, rooted in—but by no means restricted to—jazz. Jarrett has appeared in the Soviet Union, and one of his best-known albums was recorded at the huge opera house in Cologne. In more recent years he has performed piano concertos by Béla Bartók and Samuel Barber. Like other jazz performers today, Jarrett continues to follow an independent course. For example, after some experiments with Davis in the early seventies, he has declined to play electronic instruments. The independent spirit of such musicians opens up intriguing possibilities for jazz in the 1990s.

# Chapter 28

## RESPONSES TO JAZZ;
## NEOCLASSICISM

*J*azz has become so deeply rooted in our consciousness that it is hard to imagine our musical world without it. Although other forms of popular music have gained wider acceptance, jazz has influenced almost every dimension of contemporary music. Here we explore its influence on European and American art music. In Chapter 30 we consider its influence on popular music.

FIGURE 28.1 James Reese Europe introduced jazz to the Continent when he and his band performed in France in 1918.

## JAZZ AND ART MUSIC

In 1918 a black lieutenant serving in the machine-gun battalion of the 15th Regiment, James Reese Europe (1881–1919; Figure 28.1), was asked to recruit a "369th Infantry Band." Back in 1905 in New York, he had taken part in the first public concert of "syncopated music" (later to be known as jazz). And in 1912 his black musicians' union, the Clef Club, had given a concert in Carnegie Hall with 125 musicians playing mandolins, bandoras, harp-guitars, banjos, violins, saxophones, tubas, cellos, clarinets, baritones, trombones, cornets, timpanis, drums, basses, and 10 pianos. J. R. Europe had also served as accompanist for the ballroom dancers Irene and Vernon Castle, and the Castles credited him with inventing the foxtrot, a moderately adventurous ballroom dance in duple meter, in 1913.

J. R. Europe later said that he recruited the reed players for the infantry band from Puerto Rico and the other musicians from the United States. His repertoire included blues, ragtime arrangements by the bandsman W. C. Handy (1873–1958), and the cakewalk. In 1918 the band traveled to Paris, where its performances created a stir, especially among musicians. European bands tried to imitate J. R. Europe's syncopated style, but without success.

The French composer Darius Milhaud (1892–1974) heard jazz for the first time in London in 1920 when he attended a performance by the Billy Arnold Band. In 1922, on his way home from South America, he visited Harlem. That visit was the inspiration for his masterful blend of jazz and symphonic music in the ballet *The Creation of the World* (1923), scored for a small ensemble of saxophones, trumpet, and trombone.

Jazz suited the mood of the Continent, where memories of the World War were still painfully fresh. Audiences had little interest in the lush symphonies of the Romantic composers, and in any case the great symphony orchestras had lost many of their musicians on the battlefield. The bright new sounds of jazz brought a promise of happier times ahead.

### Stravinsky: "Three Dances" from *A Soldier's Tale* (1918)

In 1918, when J. R. Europe's band arrived in Paris, Igor Stravinsky was living in exile in Switzerland. There he met the Swiss conductor Ernest Ansermet (1883–1969), who shared with him a collection of sheet music he had assembled during a recent tour of the United States. Ansermet had already heard Sidney Bechet's "Southern Syncopated Orchestra." But in his *Expositions,* Stravinsky wrote:

> My knowledge of jazz was derived exclusively from copies of sheet music, and as I had never actually heard any of the music performed, I borrowed its rhythmic style not as played, but as written. I *could* imagine jazz sound, however, or so I liked to think. Jazz meant, in any case, a wholly new sound in my music, and *A Soldier's Tale* marks my final break with the Russian orchestral school in which I had been fostered.

Stravinsky had organized much of *The Rite of Spring* around the unit pulse, where most rhythmic groupings are irregular. But in the "Three Dances" from *A Soldier's Tale* (Listening Guide 65) he sets syncopated melodies against accompaniments that are regular—at least in the short run. While preserving the characteristic rhythms of each dance, he handles the larger rhythmic organization freely. For example, a tango is ordinarily organized around a 5-note rhythm in the percussion:

This pattern recurs regularly throughout the dance. But in Stravinsky's version of the tango, the pattern never establishes a regular succession. Sometimes it begins on the first beat and at other times on the second beat, always separated by rests of irregular length. Occasionally Stravinsky breaks the pattern up, perhaps sounding only the third and fifth notes. Although he makes constant reference to a syncopated melody and a rhythmic accompaniment, he never fixes the regular repetitions that mark the traditional tango.

# Listening Guide 65

## STRAVINSKY: "Three Dances" from *A Soldier's Tale*

CD 7, TRACK 6
TAPE 7A, TRACK 6
DURATION: 6:23

*The dances grow increasingly complex. The simple alternating structure of the tango (A-B-A'-B') gives way in the waltz to more varied phrase repeats and a grafting of Theme C onto D (shown by an arrow in the Location column). The ragtime is unified by the framing Theme E and by the cadential combination of Themes G and F. The italicized text in the Comments column is a translation of the French original spoken by the narrator.*

*Form: Sectional*

| LOCATION | TIME | COMMENTS |
|---|---|---|
| **1** TANGO | | |
| Theme *A* | **0:00** | The violin's slinky thirds are accompanied by characteristic but unpredictable tango rhythms in the drums. |
| | 0:26 | *"The princess opens her eyes."* <br> *"The princess rises from her bed."* |
| Theme *B* | 0:57 | Dark, legato melody in the violin accompanied by a murmuring ostinato in the clarinet. |
| Theme *A'* | 1:12 | Violin and drums once again, joined at the end by the clarinet. |
| Theme *B'* | 1:51 | Violin, clarinet, and percussion. <br> *"The princess dances [with the soldier]."* |
| **2** WALTZ | | |
| Theme *C* | **2:13** | Ornately embellished violin melody, oom-pah-pah accompaniment with bassoon on weak beats. |

Stravinsky scored the "Three Dances" for clarinet, bassoon, cornet, trombone, violin, double bass, and percussion—closer to a contemporary jazz ensemble than to a conventional chamber group or symphony orchestra. *A Soldier's Tale* marks a decisive step in Stravinsky's departure from the oversized orchestras and theatrical effects of his earlier works.

Back in 1915 Stravinsky had met the Swiss novelist Ferdinand Ramuz, with whom he collaborated on several song translations from Russian into French. Neither of them had much money, so they decided to create a work that would

| LOCATION | TIME | COMMENTS |
|---|---|---|
| Theme C′ | 2:23 | More active violin; bass and bassoon make an abrupt cadence at the end of the phrase. |
| Theme D | 2:39 | The trumpet and clarinet add sporadic countermelodies; a second abrupt cadence. |
| Theme D′ | 3:11 | The tune and the accompaniment seem to be in different keys. |
| → C | 3:16 | D′ is drafted directly onto C. |
| Theme C″ | 3:27 | The clarinet and trumpet introduce elaborate countermelodies. |
| Coda | 3:54 | The clarinet's dotted rhythms do not mesh with the violin's overwrought melody. The waltz leads into the ragtime without a cadence. |
| **3**  RAGTIME | | *"The princess alone."* |
| Theme E | **4:15** | Violin tune in parallel thirds with frequent syncopations. Abrupt cadence at the end of the phrase. |
| Theme F | 4:35 | Scurrying voices punctuated by a major arpeggio in the trombone. |
| Themes G and F | 4:43 | A cadential combination of a 4-note ascending scale in the bassoon and the trombone arpeggio. |
| Theme G | 4:58 | Repeat of the ascending pattern in the bassoon. |
| Theme H | 5:07 | A lyrical violin melody suggests the middle "trio" section found in many ragtimes. |
| Theme I | 5:18 | A disjunct violin melody punctuated by jazzy trombone smears. |
| Theme H′ | 5:30 | The lyrical melody is out of phase with the percussion. |
| Theme F′ | 5:41 | The violin part only, reinforced by drums in matching rhythms—not characteristic of ragtime. |
| Themes F and G | 5:50 | The trombone/bassoon cadence pattern returns. |
| Upbeat | 5:56 | Repeated dotted rhythms create a sense of anticipation. |
| Coda | 6:00 | The trumpet, supported by the trombone, provides a lyrical countermelody (based on the A-Section) that leads to a final, off-balance, cadence. |

be simple to produce in a small theater or even outdoors. In looking through a collection of Russian folk tales that Stravinsky had brought with him, Ramuz was intrigued by a story about "the soldier who deserts and the wily Devil who comes to claim his soul."* Ramuz wrote his own version of this story, with the

---

*There are many versions of this theme, ranging from Goethe's *Faust* to Weber's *Der Freischütz* to Stephen Vincent Benét's *The Devil and Daniel Webster.*

action related by a narrator, with dialogue between the soldier and the devil, and with pantomime by the soldier, the devil, and the princess.

Stravinsky provided nearly continuous music to accompany the telling of *A Soldier's Tale*. The work is divided into two parts of three scenes each. In the fifth scene the soldier appears with his fiddle and tries to heal the princess of the land with his music. As he plays a tango, a waltz, and a ragtime, the princess rises from her sickbed and dances.

The tango, a duple-meter dance, had been imported around 1907 from Argentina to Paris, where it was popularized by a ballroom dance instructor named Camille de Rhynal. In the tango, the dancers glide across the floor with their upper bodies rigid and their thighs touching suggestively (Figure 28.2). In lighthearted fashion, Stravinsky caricatures the *machismo* of the dance and its erotic, often tragic overtones. In Theme *B*, he reduces the accompaniment to a murmuring clarinet. His two-theme (*A* and *B*) organization is typical of the tangos that were being played in Paris at the time.

The waltz, whose popularity had begun to wane, provides a break from the duple-meter tango (and gives the percussion a breathing spell). Although Stravinsky alludes to the ONE-two-three rhythm of the waltz throughout most of the dance, his melodies do not depend on a regular beat. Indeed, the melody often seems to be in a different key. Moreover, its phrase structure bears little resemblance to the symmetrical 4-, 8-, and 16-bar phrases typical of the waltz. Instead of smooth cadences, the bass and bassoon cadence abruptly at the end of Themes *C'* and *D*, sure to throw even the most skillful dancers off-balance.

In the ragtime, Stravinsky takes even greater liberties by constantly undercutting the regularity of its bass pattern. Few listeners would feel the urge to dance or march to this music. Still, the melody, centered in the violin, reflects ragtime's characteristic syncopations, though here they are more unpredictable than in typical ragtime. An abbreviated cadence pattern shared by trombone (Theme *F*, a 4-note descending arpeggio) and bassoon (Theme *G*, a 4-note rising scale pattern) does further violence to the regularity of ragtime but fits right into Stravinsky's adaptation, which lies somewhere between paraphrase and caricature.

The "Three Dances" represent a dramatic departure from Stravinsky's earlier style. He uses the materials of jazz to achieve a fresh alternative to both post-Romanticism and the stridency of *The Rite of Spring*.

## GEORGE GERSHWIN (1898–1937)

Nowhere was the response to jazz more enthusiastic than in the United States. Jazz was a way of playing rather than a defined repertoire of music, and from the very beginning musicians drew much of their material from the popular songs turned out by New York City's Tin Pan Alley.*

In the early years of the twentieth century, people relied on sheet music to keep them abreast of the latest songs (Figure 28.3). By 1910, sheet-music sales were already in the millions, and they continued to be brisk until the appearance of 78-rpm records and regular radio broadcasts around 1930. Tin Pan Alley publishers interviewed hordes of composers and lyricists every day, searching for that elusive hit that would bring fame and fortune to all. To encourage prospective customers to buy their music, publishers employed "pluggers," pianists who sat in adjoining rooms and pounded out the newest tunes (usually singing the lyrics as well).

It was into this bustling world that Jacob Gershvin (Gershwin's birth name) was born a few months before the turn of the century. His parents, who had fled Russia in 1891 to escape persecution, were living in a poor Jewish neighborhood on Manhattan's Lower East Side. As a boy, George (as he came to be called early on) spent his time playing on the streets. Then in 1910 his family bought an upright piano and his interest turned to music. After outgrowing his neighborhood piano teacher, he studied theory, harmony, counterpoint, and orchestration with a succession of teachers that included pianist Edward Kilenyi (1884–1968) and theorist Joseph Schillinger (1895–1943). Though he had little money, he managed to attend concerts in Carnegie Hall, Cooper Union, City College, the Waldorf Astoria, and the Brooklyn Academy of Music, as well as the Ziegfeld Follies, band concerts at Coney Island, jazz sessions at Harlem clubs—anywhere music was being performed. When he was 15, he got a job as a song plugger at Remick's, a Tin Pan Alley publisher.

Before he was 17, Gershwin (Figure 28.4) had published his first song, and by the time he was 20 he had written his first big hit, "Swanee," and his first musical, *La La Lucille*. He was interested in both art music and jazz, and he experimented with a movement for string quartet and a one-act "jazz opera"

*Located originally at 28th Street and Sixth Avenue, "Tin Pan Alley" later moved to the Brill Building near 49th Street. The phrase may be related to the "tinny" sound of the pianos used by arrangers and songwriters.

FIGURE 28.3 (left) Before records and radio, people depended on sheet music to learn the hits. Tin Pan Alley publishers supplied tunes by the thousands and hired pianists to plug their music, hoping to catch the public's attention.

FIGURE 28.4 (right) The sophisticated songs of George Gershwin, shown here at his Beverly Hills home, were as popular as the earlier sentimental ballads of Tin Pan Alley. According to Gershwin, "True music . . . must repeat the thought and inspirations of the people and the time. My people are Americans. My time is today."

(*Blue Monday Blues,* 1922). Soon he was collaborating on Broadway musicals with distinguished (mostly European-trained) composers: Victor Herbert, Sigmund Romberg, Jerome Kern, and Irving Berlin.

Gershwin's big break came when bandleader Paul Whiteman commissioned him to write *Rhapsody in Blue* for piano and jazz band in 1924. Gershwin had had little experience with orchestration, so Whiteman asked his arranger, Ferde Grofé, to orchestrate the piece. Gershwin performed the *Rhapsody* in 1924 with Whiteman at Aeolian Hall and became famous overnight. Starting in 1927 he gave concerts at the Lewisohn Stadium on the campus of City College that attracted as many as 17,000 listeners, with thousands more turned away. Soon he was the most sought-after performer/composer in the country.

Denying that there was any real difference between popular music and "concert" (art) music, Gershwin accepted a commission from the Metropolitan Opera for an opera, *The Dybbuk,* based on a Jewish folk tale. (He never composed the opera.) He turned out a series of popular song hits, including "Oh, Lady Be Good!," "The Man I Love," "Fascinating Rhythm," "Someone to Watch Over Me," "'S Wonderful," "Embraceable You," "I Got Rhythm," and "Strike Up the Band." During this time he was also composing concert works: the Concerto in F, the Second Rhapsody, the *Cuban Overture,* and Preludes for Piano. His tragically early death at age 38 from a brain tumor deprived the world of a quintessentially American voice.

Gershwin's most ambitious work was the opera *Porgy and Bess,* which he composed in 1934–1935 to a libretto by his older brother Ira, with whom he often collaborated. The opera is based on the story of a crippled black beggar on Catfish Row in Charleston, South Carolina.

### Gershwin: From Act I, Scene 1 of *Porgy and Bess* (1935)

People still debate whether *Porgy and Bess* is a musical, an operetta, or an opera. By any reasonable definition it is an opera that incorporates elements of art music, jazz, and popular song in a natural, unaffected manner. Although Gershwin never claimed that it was a jazz opera, the influence of jazz is apparent on almost every page.

The Introduction opens with an energetic passage soon followed by a syncopated theme that leads into the "Jasbo Brown blues." (Jasbo Brown is the pianist at the local dance hall.) After an alternating succession of four further themes, a chorus enters on "wah-doo-wah"—first tentatively and then in a long, hypnotic crescendo with the orchestra. As it rounds out the Introduction, the chorus already seems part of the action to come.

A colorful bridge in winds, strings, and xylophone sets up Clara's opening song, "Summertime" (where Listening Guide 65 begins), which Gershwin called a lullaby. Its two strophes (the second reinforced by a wordless women's chorus) are based on the sighing alternation of two adjacent chords:

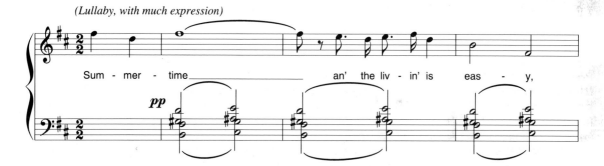

Clara's cheerful account of life on Catfish Row contrasts sharply with the crap game that follows, in which men with nothing to lose gamble away money they haven't got.

During the crap game, Gershwin moves deftly from the declamation characteristic of spirituals (Mingo: "Oh, nobody knows . . . ; Chorus: "Roll dem bones"), to symphonic development (orchestral bridges between speeches), to natural speech-song (Jake and Serena), to spoken speech (Robbins: "There you go again. Lissen what I say"; Sporting Life: "Damn you, give me dem bones!"), and finally to lyrical snatches that sound as though they should develop into a full-fledged song but never do (Robbins: "I works all de week; Sunday got to pray . . ."). Before Porgy or Bess ever appears, Gershwin has created a vivid picture of the hard life in which men must choose between baling cotton and trying to eke out a living as fishermen.

In a daring move, Gershwin imposes a reprise of "Summertime" over the continuing crap game. Audiences expected composers to repeat a good tune, but Gershwin succeeds both in pleasing his audience and in moving the drama

*(Text continues on page 618.)*

# *Listening Guide 66*

## GERSHWIN: From Act I, Scene 1 of *Porgy and Bess*

CD 7, TRACK [7]
TAPE 7A, TRACK 7
DURATION: 10:44

*Gershwin's opera blends three centuries of European operatic history with jazz and popular American song. Our excerpt revolves around two set pieces (Clara's "Summertime" and Jake's "A Woman Is a Sometime Thing") that are integrated into a natural dramatic flow. Ira Gershwin's dialect spellings represent his attempt to capture the flavor of the language on Catfish Row. Some critics have found the results excessive, even a caricature. You will hear that some performers in this recording ignore the directions.*

*Form: Continuous action organized around set pieces*

| | TEXT | TIME | LOCATION / COMMENTS |
|---|---|---|---|
| **1** | [Orchestral bridge] | **0:00** | Winds, xylophone. |
| | SONG, "SUMMERTIME" | | |
| | CLARA: | | |
| | Summertime an' the livin' is easy, Fish are jumpin', an' the cotton is high. | **0:17** | Stanza I/*A*: languorous melody over gently oscillating chords. |
| | Oh yo' daddy's rich, an' yo' ma is good lookin', So hush, little baby, don' yo' cry. | 0:42 | Stanza I/*A'*: returns to the tonic key. Orchestral coloring in English horn, flute, and xylophone. |
| | One of these mornin's you goin' to rise up singin', Then you'll spread yo' wings an' you'll take the sky. | 1:08 | Stanza II/*A*: sung with more intensity and wordless chorus in background. |
| | But till that mornin' there's a nothin' can harm you With Daddy an' Mammy standin' by. | 1:32 | Stanza II/*A'*: vocal melody doubled by the winds; "by" extended with a peak high note. |
| **2** | *[The lights fade, then come up on the crap players.]* | **2:20** | Agitated, untuned piano with bongo drum, accelerating tempo. |
| | MINGO: | | |
| | Oh, nobody knows when de Lord is goin' to call, | 2:32 | Over held string chord. Delivered like the improvised part of a spiritual. |
| | CHORUS: Roll dem bones, roll! | 2:44 | Four-part jazz harmonies. |
| | SPORTING LIFE: It may be in the summertime an' it may be in the fall, | 2:50 | Over another held chord; the melody descends on "fall." |
| | CHORUS: Roll dem bones, | 3:06 | Four-part jazz harmonies. |
| | SPORTING LIFE: But you got to leave yo' baby an' yo' home an' all, so roll dem bones! | 3:11 | Lyrical line leads to the chorus on "roll . . ." |

| TEXT | TIME | LOCATION / COMMENTS |
|------|------|---------------------|
| ALL:<br>Oh my brudder, Roll dem bones! | 3:20 | Extended treatment of jazzy harmonizations. |
| *[The crap shooters throw the dice.]* | 3:52 | Agitated, then marchlike. |
| **3** JAKE:<br>Seems like these bones don't give me nothin' but boxcars tonight.<br>It was the same two weeks ago an' the game broke me; I don't like that kind o' luck! | **4:26** | The dialogue is based on free melody delivered in a conversational tone. |
| SPORTING LIFE:<br>Damn you, give me dem bones! | 4:50 | Shouted *(Sprechstimme)*. |
| MINGO:<br>What do you say to these, Jake? | 4:54 | String pedal creates suspense. |
| JAKE:<br>Them's the same cockeyed bones what clean the game out last Saturday night; if they rolls in this game, I rolls out. | 4:58 | Free melody. |
| SERENA:<br>Honey boy! | 5:15 | Serena's lyrical plea countered by Jake. |
| JAKE:<br>Come on down, Robbins, we're waiting for you. | | |
| SERENA:<br>Honey, don't play tonight. Do like I say. | | |
| ROBBINS:<br>I been sweatin' all day. Night time is man's time. He's got a right to forget his troubles. He's got a right to play. | **5:27** | Free melody. Orchestra illustrates "troubles" and "play." |
| SERENA:<br>If you hadn't been drinkin' you wouldn't talk to me that way. You ain't nebber hear Lord Jesus say nuttin' about got to play. | 5:44 | Lyrical free melody over slow-moving chords. |
| ROBBINS:<br>There you go again. Lissen what I say. | 6:03 | Spoken. |
| **4** I works all de week; Sunday got to pray.<br>But Saturday night a man's got a right to play. | **6:08** | Begins like a song, but soon reverts to free melody. |
| MEN:<br>A man's got a right to play. | | Chorus serves as an echo.   *continued* |

| TEXT | TIME | LOCATION / COMMENTS |
|---|---|---|
| **ROBBINS:** Yes sir, that's right. | | |
| That ole lady of mine is hell on savin' money to join the buryin' lodge. | | Free melody. |
| I say spend it while you is still alive and kickin'. | | Orchestra scurries on "kickin'." |
| *[Jim enters, saunters up to the group, with several children following.]* | | More dice-throwing. |
| **JIM:** Lord, I is tired this night, I'm done with cotton. | 6:46 | Suggests a song but never becomes one. |
| **5**   **JAKE:** Better come along with me on the Sea Gull. | **6:57** | Free melody. |
| I got room for another fisherman. | | |
| **JIM:** That suit me. | | |
| This cotton hook done swung its last bale of cotton. Here, who wants a cotton hook? | | Spoken; notated like Schoenberg's *Sprechstimme.* |
| *[Throws the hook to the floor; the children dive for it.]* | | The orchestra dives with the children. |
| Reprise of "Summertime" over the crap-game music | 7:27 | The piano recalls the oscillating harmonies of "Summertime." |
| **6**   **CLARA:** Summertime an' the livin' is easy, | **7:34** | Clara's song is now superimposed over the gritty crap game. |
| Fish are jumpin', an' the cotton is high. | | |
| **CRAP SHOOTERS:** Seven come, | | |
| seven come to pappy! | | The two activities take place simultaneously, but on two separate dramatic and musical planes. |
| Throw dat beautiful number! | | |
| Come seven to me! Yeah, man! | | |
| I'll bet yo' wrong. Gettin' hot! | | |
| **CLARA:** Oh yo' daddy's rich, | 7:58 | |
| an' yo' ma is good lookin', | | |
| So hush, little baby, don' yo' cry. | | High, held peak note on "cry." |
| **CRAP SHOOTERS:** Come seven! Shoot! | | |
| Made it! He made it! | | |
| Ol' man seven come down from heaven! | | |

| TEXT | TIME | LOCATION / COMMENTS |
|---|---|---|
| **7** JAKE:<br>What, that chile ain't asleep yet?<br>Give him to me. I'll fix him for you. | **8:29** | Driving rhythms to sudden stop.<br>Delivered unaccompanied. |
| SONG, "A WOMAN IS A SOMETIME THING" | | Jake sings a set piece of three stanzas,<br>each divided into a "verse" and a<br>"chorus." Suspended cymbal, snare<br>drum, and muted trumpet suggest a<br>dance band. |

| TEXT | TIME |
|---|---|
| **8** STANZA 1 | |
| JAKE (Verse):<br>Listen to yo' daddy warn you, 'fore you start a travelling, | **8:48** |
| Woman may born you, love you, an' mourn you, | |
| (CHORUS) But a woman is a sometime thing, Yes, a woman is a sometime thing. | 9:02 |
| MINGO:<br>Oh, a woman is a sometime thing. | |
| **9** STANZA 2 | |
| JAKE:<br>Yo' mammy is the first to name you, an' she'll tie you to her apron string. | **9:17** |
| Then she'll shame you and she'll blame you til yo' woman comes to claim you, | |
| (CHORUS) 'Cause a woman is a sometime thing, Yes, a woman is a sometime thing, | 9:23 |
| SPORTING LIFE:<br>Oh, a woman is a sometime thing. | |
| **10** STANZA 3 | |
| JAKE:<br>Don't you never let a woman grieve you Jus' 'cause she got yo' weddin' ring. | **9:46** |
| She'll love you and deceive you then she'll take yo' clo'es an' leave you, | |
| (CHORUS) 'Cause a woman is a sometime thing, Yes, a woman is a sometime thing, | 9:59 |
| ALL:<br>Yes, a woman is a sometime thing. | |
| JAKE:<br>There now, what I tells you; He's asleep already. *[Baby wails.]* | |

forward. His dramatic juxtaposition highlights the depressing future that awaits Clara and her baby.

To deepen the contrast, Gershwin follows "Summertime" with Jake's animated but cynical song, "A Woman Is a Sometime Thing." In a society where men have low self-esteem and despair of supporting their families, women can be viewed as oppressors. Each of the three verses speaks of male resentment: the woman who "may born you," the "mammy" who'll "tie you to her apron string," and the wife who'll "love you and deceive you then . . . take yo' clo'es an' leave you."

This song is the counterpart of an aria in a more formal opera. Its verse-chorus structure (repeated three times) was common in the popular songs of the time, with the chorus providing the melodic "hook" that follows each verse. Bright syncopations and regular duple meter lend a jazzy feel. To add suspense, Gershwin introduces each chorus with a long-held upbeat (supported by a chain of orchestral syncopations):

The strong-beat accents in the chorus contrast with the weak-beat syncopations in the orchestra. Nowhere in this opening scene is there a full cadence or

*Part Four   The Twentieth Century*

an awkward transition. Gershwin has achieved a dramatic continuity that Verdi or Wagner might have admired, and he has done so with a unique blend of jazz and popular song.

## MUSICAL THEATER IN AMERICA

Americans have always looked to the musical theater for entertainment. At the end of the eighteenth century, the "Old American Company" toured from town to town with more than a hundred musical shows in its repertory. The most popular form of musical entertainment was the ballad opera imported from England. John Gay's *The Beggar's Opera*, produced in London in 1728 and soon thereafter in America, delighted audiences with its satirical attacks on public officials and its bawdy humor. Also popular were the *pasticcio*, in which music by famous composers was arranged around a new story, and the *burletta*, in which a classical legend or a historical event was treated in outlandish fashion.

The first truly American form of musical theater was the minstrel show. After the Civil War, black entertainers began to perform their own minstrel shows (Figure 28.5). One of the most famous was James Bland (1854–1911), a singer who accompanied himself on the banjo and improvised freely as he sang. Although fewer than 40 of his songs are known, he is said to have written more than 600, including "Carry Me Back to Old Virginny," "In the Evening by the Moonlight," and the popular "walkaround," "O, Dem Golden Slippers."

By the end of the nineteenth century, vaudeville had become America's favorite form of entertainment. Vaudeville consisted of a string of unrelated acts, one after another. Showmen like Tony Pastor in Paterson, New Jersey, and George Gottlieb in New York City built lavish theaters in which off-color language was banned and entertainment was suited to women and children. A typical "act" consisted of a 10-minute sketch with singers, dancers, actors, comedians, magicians, or animals (monkeys, dogs, and elephants were especially popular). A standard offering was the "nine-act bill," in which the first half built from a "dumb act" (an act that could not be spoiled by latecomers) to a "headliner." The eighth act was a comedy act that marked the high point of the show, and the last act was usually a "sight act" that patrons could catch on their way out.

Tin Pan Alley provided the vaudeville entertainers with an endless supply of popular songs, many of which are still familiar today: Charles Harris's sentimental "After the Ball" (1892), Harry Dacre's waltzlike "A Bicycle Built for Two" (1892), Charles Lawlor's "Sidewalks of New York" (1894), Charles Ward's "The Band Played On" (1895), James Thornton's "When You Were Sweet Sixteen" (1898), Lamb and Tilzer's "A Bird in a Gilded Cage" (1900), and George M. Cohan's "You're a Grand Old Flag" (1906).

Most of these songs had the same structure: a verse (which described a sentimental or tragic situation) followed by a chorus (which expressed reactions to the situation and provided the song's melodic hook). This structure is evident even without the music:

FIGURE 28.5 When James Bland toured Europe, he performed without the blackface makeup common in American minstrel shows.

The ballroom was filled with fashions throng,
It shone with a thousand lights,
And there was a woman passed along,
The fairest of all the sights,
A girl to her lover then softly sighed,
There's riches at her command;
But she married for wealth, not for love he cried,
Though she lives in a mansion grand.

CHORUS

She's only a bird in a gilded cage,
A beautiful sight to see,
You may think she's happy and free from care,
She's not, though she seems to be,
'Tis sad when you think of her wasted life,
For youth cannot mate with age,
And her beauty was sold,
For an old man's gold,
She's a bird in a gilded cage.

The showmen who produced vaudeville (and its racier spinoffs, burlesque and the revue) built hundreds of theaters throughout the country for the hundreds of touring shows. But by the late 1920s, movies (especially the new talkies) had stolen their audiences away, and by the 1930s most of the great vaudeville houses had closed their doors.

Even during the heyday of vaudeville, however, Americans continued to patronize shows imported from Europe and England. The comic operas of Gilbert and Sullivan, beginning with the Boston premiere of *H.M.S. Pinafore* in 1878, attracted enthusiastic audiences. People with a taste for opera were delighted to find that they could now understand what the singers were saying. Immigrant composers were quick to respond: the Irish Victor Herbert (1859–1924), the Hungarian Sigmund Romberg (1887–1951), and the Czech Rudolf Friml (1879–1972) cleverly adapted the Viennese operetta to the American stage. Among Victor Herbert's English-language operettas were *The Red Mill, Naughty Marietta,* and *Babes in Toyland.* Many of his songs, such as "Ah, Sweet Mystery of Life," became household standards. Romberg wrote almost 80 shows (including *The Student Prince, The Desert Song,* and *The New Moon*) and over 2,000 songs. Friml, though less prolific, was no less successful with *Rose-Marie* (1924) and *The Vagabond King* (1925). None of these composers wrote anything that remotely resembled jazz, but they all contributed to what was to emerge as the "American musical."

The American musical drew on all the forms of musical theater. But what set it apart as an authentically new form was its blending of European operetta with the language of jazz and the popular song. In 1927, Jerome Kern (1885–1945), a native New Yorker, electrified the musical world with *Show Boat,* with lyrics by

Oscar Hammerstein II (1895–1960). Based on the novel by Edna Ferber, it deals with life along the Mississippi in the 1880s. Many of the principal characters are poor southern blacks who are presented not as stereotypes or Jim Crows but as believable human beings.

Sixteen years later, Hammerstein began to work with the composer Richard Rodgers (1902–1979), with whom he created a series of musical-theater masterpieces. Rodgers had studied with the European composers Henry Krehbiel and Percy Goetschius, but he particularly admired the music of Victor Herbert and Jerome Kern. His first important collaborator was Lorenz Hart (1895–1943), with whom he wrote *Pal Joey* (1940), an appealing musical despite its unsavory characters and cynical story. After Hart's death, Rodgers linked up with Hammerstein. Together, Rodgers and Hammerstein turned out *Oklahoma* (1943), *Carousel* (1945), *South Pacific* (1949), *The King and I* (1951), *Flower Drum Song* (1958), and *The Sound of Music* (1959), making the 1940s and 1950s the golden age of the American musical. Hammerstein's insistence on the integrity and realism of the drama, coupled with Rodgers's gift for capturing a dramatic situation in a few notes and then extending them into an entire song, led to the creation of works that have survived thousands of professional and amateur productions and have been made into memorable films.

The American musical theater continues to thrive. Its vigor is most evident in the works of Leonard Bernstein and Stephen Sondheim.

## LEONARD BERNSTEIN (1918–1990)

Leonard Bernstein

Born in Lawrence, Massachusetts, Bernstein attended Harvard University, where he received a broad education in the liberal arts, including music. After graduation in 1939, he studied at the Curtis Institute in Philadelphia and went on to study conducting with Serge Koussevitsky at Tanglewood, the summer home of the Boston Symphony. On November 13, 1943, on short notice, he replaced Bruno Walter as conductor of the New York Philharmonic in a concert that included works by Schumann, Strauss, and Wagner. His performance was acclaimed by the critics and launched Bernstein's career as a major conductor.

Bernstein was a respected pianist, composer, and teacher. His talents as a composer ranged from jazz to musical theater to art music. He became conductor of the New York Philharmonic in 1958 and was named laureate conductor for life in 1969. He was largely responsible for the revival of interest in the symphonies of Gustav Mahler and was a tireless advocate of American music. His own works included the ballet *Fancy Free* (1944), the musicals *On the Town* (1944) and *West Side Story* (1957), the opera *Trouble in Tahiti* (1952), the film score for *On the Waterfront* (1954), the comic operetta *Candide* (1956), the "theater piece" *Mass* (1971), and three symphonies.

Bernstein was extraordinarily successful in bridging the gap between popular American music and art music. In the introduction to his book *The Infinite Variety of Music* (1966), he comments on the dilemma faced by American music:

Everyone says that this is a critical moment in the history of music. I agree, but double in spades: it is a *scary* moment. The famous gulf between composer and audience is not only wider than ever: it has become an ocean. What is more, it has frozen over, and it shows no immediate signs of either narrowing or thawing.

He suggested a possible reason for that gulf:

And so to the inescapable conclusion. All forms that we have ever known—plainchant, motet, fugue, or sonata—have always been conceived in *tonality,* that is, in the sense of a tonal magnetic center, with subsidiary tonal relationships. This sense, I believe, is built into the human organism; we cannot hear two isolated tones, even devoid of any context, without immediately imputing a tonal meaning to them. . . . It has occasionally occurred to me that music could conceivably exist, some distant day, ultimately detached from tonality. I can't hear such music in my head, but I am willing to grant the possibility. Only that distant day would have to have seen a fundamental change in our physical laws, possibly through man's detaching himself from this planet.

Bernstein's commitment to tonality is evident in his brilliant musical *West Side Story.*

## Bernstein: Two Excerpts from *West Side Story* (1957)

For a long time Bernstein had wanted to create a musical based on *Romeo and Juliet.* The opportunity came when the playwright Arthur Laurents came up with a story built, not around two rival families, but around two rival New York City street gangs. Jerome Robbins, who had many successes in theater and film to his credit, served as choreographer (Figure 28.6).

The story is simple enough. A local gang called the Jets, led by Riff, is locked in a turf war with a gang of recent arrivals from Puerto Rico, the Sharks, led by Bernardo. Tony, an erstwhile Jet, falls in love with Maria, Bernardo's sister, whom he meets at a dance in the local gym. Maria returns his love. Though they realize that their own people will never accept their union, they dream of a future together. Riff and Bernardo meet in a one-to-one battle that turns into a full-scale rumble between the two gangs. Tony is drawn in and is stabbed to death. No resolution is suggested, and as the curtain falls the audience understands that the senseless violence will continue.

The lyrics, by Stephen Sondheim,* are witty, fast-paced, and unsentimental. Two of the most compelling numbers in the two-act musical are "America" and "Tonight" (Listening Guide 67), both from the first act. In "America," Rosalia (a Shark girlfriend) sings of the delights of her native Puerto Rico, while Anita (Bernardo's girlfriend) counters with the pleasures of life in Manhattan. The

---

*Sondheim himself is now the leading composer of Broadway musicals, with such works as *A Little Night Music* and *Sweeney Todd* to his credit.

FIGURE 28.6 *West Side Story* was Stephen Sondheim's first job as a lyricist. He doubted he could handle the assignment: "I can't do this show," he said. "I've never been that poor and I've never even *known* a Puerto Rican."

number begins with a dreamy, floating introduction that builds gradually to a chorus based on the rhythm of the huapongo, a popular Caribbean dance that alternates between compound duple and simple triple meter:

Instead of following the standard verse-chorus structure, in which the chorus would follow the first verse, Bernstein leads off with the chorus. As the number continues, the choruses seem to enfold each verse. In Sondheim's lyrics, Rosalia's "tropical breezes" becomes Anita's "tropic diseases." Rosalia's "hundreds of flowers in full bloom" becomes Anita's "hundreds of people in each room!" The spontaneity of the verses (matched by Bernstein's treatment of the words "diseases" and "hurricanes") contrasts delightfully with the rhythmically tight choruses. The final chorus begins *pianissimo* and then builds to an electrifying climax.

The structure of "Tonight" is more complex. The song is first heard as the climax to the love duet sung by Tony and Maria after their meeting. Its warm, arching melody (organized in the familiar *a-a-b-a* pattern) is set off by the catchy, syncopated rhythms of another Caribbean dance, the duple-meter beguine:

(*Text continues on page 630.*)

# *Listening Guide 67*

## BERNSTEIN: Two Excerpts from *West Side Story*

CD 7, TRACKS 8 – 9
TAPE 7A, TRACKS 8-9

DURATION: 4:46

### Act I, "America"

*The form of "America" is closely related to that of American popular song—a "verse" (the initial exchange between Rosalia and Anita), followed by a "chorus"—an alternation repeated three times.*

*Form: Three verse / choruses with introduction*

| TEXT | TIME | LOCATION / COMMENTS |
|---|---|---|
| **1** ROSALIA:<br>Puerto Rico,<br>You lovely island,<br>Island of tropical breezes.<br>Always the pineapples growing,<br>Always the coffee blossoms blowing. | **0:00** | Complex but steady "rhythm-of-six" background consisting of claves playing a 2-bar syncopated pattern, güiro playing 2-beat groups, and guitar playing 3-beat groups. |
| ANITA *[mockingly]:*<br>Puerto Rico,<br>You ugly island,<br>Island of tropic diseases.<br>Always the hurricanes blowing,<br>Always the population | 0:31 | Rosalia and Anita sing to the 2-beat rhythm of the güiro, which meanwhile drops out. The music illustrates both "diseases" and "hurricanes." |
| *[rhythmically]* growing,<br>And the money owing,<br>And the babies crying,<br>And the bullets flying. | 0:52 | As Anita repeats the music of Rosalia's last line, the disembodied beat takes on a metrical character, with the maracas providing regular syncopations. |
| I like the island of Manhattan.<br>Smoke on your pipe and put . . . | 1:04 | Declaimed broadly over slow-moving harmonies. |
| that in! *[Tempo di Huapongo]* | 1:15 | Rapid dance, accompanied by guitars, that alternates between measures of 2- and 3-beat groupings (matched by the girls' clapping). |
| **2** GIRLS *[except Rosalia]:*<br>I like to be in America!<br>O.K. by me in America!<br>Ev'rything free in America<br>For a small fee in America! | **1:19** | CHORUS. Catchy, rhythmically clear; the heart of the number.<br>Each metric level in "America" has become clearer and more regular. |

| TEXT | TIME | LOCATION / COMMENTS |
|---|---|---|
| **3** ROSALIA:<br>I like the city of San Juan. | **1:33** | VERSE 1. Continues the repartée between Rosalia and Anita. Exclamations from the other girls at the end of the first exchange add to the naturalness of the dialogue. |
| ANITA:<br>I know a boat you can get on. | | |
| ROSALIA:<br>Hundreds of flowers in full bloom. | | |
| ANITA:<br>Hundreds of people in each room! | | Spoken in a low, guttural voice. |
| GIRLS *[except Rosalia]*:<br>Automobile in America,<br>Chromium steel in America,<br>Wire-spoke wheel in America,<br>Very big deal in America! | **1:45** | CHORUS. Maracas added to the orchestra. The descending arpeggios to which the first three "Americas" are sung set up the upward leap in the fourth repeat. |
| **4** ROSALIA:<br>I'll drive a Buick through San Juan. | **2:00** | VERSE 2. Continues the subject matter of the preceding chorus. |
| ANITA:<br>If there's a road you can drive on. | | |
| ROSALIA:<br>I'll give my cousins a free ride. | | |
| ANITA:<br>How you get all of them inside? | | |
| GIRLS *[except Rosalia]*:<br>Immigrant goes to America,<br>Many hellos in America,<br>Nobody knows in America,<br>Puerto Rico's in America! | **2:12** | The tambourine now provides the rhythm. |
| [Instrumental interlude] | 2:23 | Melody in muted trumpet. The girls dance and shout. |
| [Instrumental chorus] | 2:49 | In the brass, with girls chattering in the background. |
| **5** ROSALIA:<br>I'll bring a TV to San Juan. | **3:03** | VERSE 3. |
| ANITA:<br>If there's a current to turn on! | | |

*continued*

| TEXT | TIME | LOCATION / COMMENTS |
|---|---|---|
| ROSALIA:<br>I'll give them new washing machine.<br><br>ANITA:<br>What have they got there to keep clean? | | |
| GIRLS *[except Rosalia]*:<br>I like the shores of America,<br>Comfort is yours in America,<br>Knobs on the doors in America,<br>Wall-to-wall floors in America! | **3:15** | CHORUS. |
| [Instrumental interlude] | 3:29 | Varied from the earlier interlude, especially by the addition of percussion. |
| [Instrumental chorus] | 3:55 | Same as the earlier brass chorus. |
| **6**   ROSALIA:<br>When I will go back to San Juan<br><br>ANITA:<br>When you will shut up and get gone!<br><br>ROSALIA:<br>Ev'ryone there will give big cheer!<br><br>ANITA:<br>Ev'ryone there will have moved here! | **4:09** | VERSE 4. |
| [Chorus, *pianissimo*] | **4:21** | CHORUS: Piccolo, xylophone, girls. |
| [Chorus with full orchestra] | **4:31** | A final climactic statement, led by the screaming trumpets. |

DURATION: 3:38

## Act I, "Tonight" (Reprise)

*Bernstein first contrasts the harsh gang music of the Jets and Sharks with a reprise of Tony's love song. He then weaves the two into a single musical texture that nevertheless maintains two dramatic planes.*

Form: A → B / A + B

| | | |
|---|---|---|
| [GANG MUSIC]<br>**1**   Curtain | **0:00** | Introduces a 3-note ostinato. |
| RIFF:<br>The Jets are gonna<br>have their day—Tonight. | 0:07 | Sung in a menacing tone with a 3-note duh-duh-DUM burst on "-night." |

| TEXT | TIME | COMMENTS |
|---|---|---|
| BERNARDO:<br>The Sharks are gonna have their way—Tonight. | | |
| RIFF:<br>The Puerto Ricans grumble: "Fair fight."<br>But if they start a rumble,<br>We'll rumble 'em right. | | |
| SHARKS:<br>We're gonna hand 'em a surprise<br>Tonight. | 0:24 | Exact duplicates, suggesting that the rival gangs are on a collision course. |
| JETS:<br>We're gonna cut 'em down to size<br>Tonight. | | |
| SHARKS:<br>We said, "O.K., no rumpus,<br>No tricks."<br>But just in case they jump us,<br>We're ready to mix . . .<br>Tonight! | 0:42 | Still over the ostinato, sung in an even more menacing fashion. |
| BOTH:<br>We're gonna rock it tonight,<br>We're gonna jazz it up and have us a ball!<br>They're gonna get it tonight;<br>The more they turn it on,<br>the harder they'll fall! | | The orchestra maintains a driving, steady, often syncopated beat, supplying the 3-note bursts. |
| JETS:<br>Well, they began it! | 0:57 | The antiphonal exchange is a further reminder that each group holds the other responsible for their mutual enmity. |
| SHARKS:<br>Well, they began it! | | |
| BOTH:<br>And we're the ones to stop 'em<br>once and for all<br>Tonight! | | |
| ANITA:<br>Anita's gonna get her kicks<br>Tonight.<br>We'll have our private little mix<br>Tonight.<br>He'll walk in hot and tired, So what? | 1:08 | Sung in a sultry, erotic voice to the same music as the Jets and Sharks. The parallel between the gangs and Anita's desire is a perfect foil to the love song Tony is about to recall. |

*continued*

| TEXT | TIME | COMMENTS |
|------|------|----------|
| Don't matter if he's tired,<br>As long as he's hot . . . | | |
| [TONY'S LOVE SONG] | | |
| **2**   Tonight! | **1:25** | (*A*) Dovetailing with Anita's final "tonight,"<br>Tony begins a reprise of "Tonight." |
| TONY [*warmly*]:<br>Tonight, tonight<br>Won't be just any night,<br>Tonight there will be no morning star. | | |
| Tonight, tonight, I'll see my love tonight,<br>And for us, stars will stop where they are. | 1:38 | (*A'*) Higher and more fervent than the first *A*. |
| Today the minutes seem like hours,<br>The hours go so slowly,<br>And still the sky is light. | 1:51 | (*B*) The strings play in canon with the voice. |
| Oh moon, grow bright,<br>And make this endless day endless night! | 2:04 | (*A''*) Ends on a climax that is immediately<br>undercut by the orchestra. |
| [GANG MUSIC] | | |
| RIFF [*to Tony*]:<br>I'm counting on you to<br>be there<br>Tonight.<br>When Diesel wins it fair and square<br>Tonight.<br>That Puerto Rican punk'll Go down,<br>And when he's hollered "Uncle"<br>We'll tear up the town! | 2:23 | The 3-note ostinato and the raw declamation<br>quickly displace the elation of Tony's love<br>song. |

[GANG MUSIC AND TONY/MARIA'S LOVE SONG SIMULTANEOUSLY]

| TEXT | TIME | COMMENTS |
|------|------|----------|
| **3**   MARIA:<br>Tonight, tonight   [*A*] | **2:40** | RIFF:<br>So I can count on you, boy? |
| | | TONY [*abstractedly*]:<br>All right. |
| Won't be just any night, | | RIFF:<br>We're gonna have us a ball. |
| | | TONY:<br>All right. |

| TEXT | TIME | COMMENTS |
|------|------|----------|
| | | RIFF:<br>Womb to tomb! |
| Tonight there will be no morning star. | | TONY:<br>Sperm to worm! |
| | | RIFF:<br>I'll see you there about eight. |
| | | TONY:<br>Tonight. |
| | | JETS:<br>We're gonna rock it tonight! |
| Tonight, tonight, I'll see my   [A']<br>love tonight, | 2:52 | SHARKS:<br>We're gonna jazz it tonight! |
| | | ANITA:<br>Tonight, tonight,<br>Late tonight, We're gonna mix it tonight. |
| And for us, stars will stop where they are. | | SHARKS:<br>They're gonna get it tonight! |
| [TONY joins MARIA] | | |
| Today the minutes seem like hours,   [B] | 3:06 | ANITA:<br>Anita's gonna have her day,<br>Bernardo's gonna have his way tonight. |
| The hours go so slowly, | | SHARKS:<br>They began it, And we're the<br>ones to stop 'em once and for all! |
| And still the sky is light. | | JETS:<br>They began it, we'll stop 'em [etc.] |
| (MARIA/TONY):<br>Oh moon, grow bright,   [A"] | 3:19 | JETS/SHARKS:<br>The Jets/Sharks are gonna have their day,<br>we're gonna rock it tonight, Tonight! |
| And make this endless day endless night<br>Tonight. | | ANITA:<br>Tonight, this very night,<br>we're gonna rock it tonight, Tonight! |

Strictly speaking, the reappearance of "Tonight" later in the first act is a reprise. But Bernstein, recalling Gershwin's reprise of "Summertime" in *Porgy and Bess,* ingeniously set it over the gang music that dominates the scene. The scene opens with a series of threats (carrying Sondheim's clever word plays) in which the Sharks and the Jets vow revenge in phrases that all end with the word "tonight"—on the same ascending interval with which the love song begins. While the gangs taunt each other, first Tony and then Maria repeat their love duet. The musical overlay of the two worlds foreshadows the tragedy to come. (Bernstein's handling of this scene also recalls Verdi's quartet from *Rigoletto.*)

*West Side Story* is a masterful blending of jazz, symphonic music, popular song, and operatic ensembles. It holds a special place in American musical theater.

## NEOCLASSICISM

Jazz was not the only new style to emerge after the First World War. Even before the outbreak of war in 1914, Romantic composers had begun to sound a lingering farewell to a vanishing era. Mahler's last major works—the Symphony No. 9

(1908–1909), the song cycle *The Song of the Earth* (1908–1909), and the incomplete Symphony No. 10 (1910)—are all in a sense prolonged valedictories. Indeed, the final song of *The Song of the Earth* is titled "The Farewell."

The Romantics had extolled emotion over rational thought, but now that view seemed suspect. To many people, emotion as expressed in nationalistic upheavals and political assassinations was itself a cause of war. The dark side of the Romantic vision, in works like Wagner's *Tristan und Isolde,* had become all too real in the years just past, and in the aftermath of war Europeans and Americans alike longed for a brighter future.

Composers were now prepared to break with trends that had governed music for over two centuries. For example, from about 1700 to 1914 the trend had been to larger and larger ensembles:*

- Baroque concerto grosso, ca. 1700            10–15 players
- Early Classical orchestra, ca. 1760          15–20 players
- Late Classical orchestra, ca. 1820           30–40 players
- Romantic orchestra, ca. 1850                 40–60 players
- Romantic orchestra, ca. 1900                 60–80 players
- "Post-Romantic" orchestras of Mahler,        80–100 players
  Schoenberg, and Stravinsky, 1900–1914        (not counting vocal soloists and chorus)

At the war's end, none of Europe's major orchestras—the Vienna Philharmonic, the Berlin Philharmonic, the Concertgebouw Orchestra of Amsterdam, the London Philharmonic—was fully staffed, and it would be several years before any of them returned to full strength. In any event, few composers were interested in creating huge works on the scale of post-Romantic symphonies; most were ready to embrace smaller ensembles.

The shift in musical taste extended to the very nature of the music itself. Nineteenth-century instrumental music had often dealt with extramusical ideas, as in program music, character pieces, and tone poems. Composers and critics alike had accepted the notion that music should express emotions and ideas, and Mahler had even supplied extramusical programs for his early symphonies to satisfy the demands of his audience.

Stravinsky, in his *Autobiography* (1936), summarized his view of such music. Of Beethoven's *Eroica* (Third) Symphony, he wrote:

> What does it matter whether the *Third Symphony* was inspired by the figure of Bonaparte the Republican or Napoleon the Emperor? It is only the music that matters.

Stravinsky also broke with the nineteenth-century view of how music should be interpreted. To the Romantics, interpretation was a personal affair, with performers and conductors more or less free to put their own imprint on a musical work. Mahler, one of the great late-Romantic conductors, once said:

*These figures are only averages.

All the most important things—the tempo, the total conception and structuring of a work—are almost impossible to pin down. For here we are concerned with something living and flowing that can never be the same even twice in succession. That is why metronome markings are inadequate and almost worthless; for unless the work is vulgarly ground out in barrel-organ style, the tempo will already have changed by the end of the second bar. . . . Whether the overall tempo is a degree faster or slower often depends on the mood of the conductor. . . .

Stravinsky disagreed:

Music should be transmitted and not interpreted, because interpretation reveals the personality of the interpreter rather than that of the author, and who can guarantee that such an executant will reflect the author's vision without distortion?

Stravinsky was urging a return to absolute music (see page 414), which seemed to demand less interpretation. He was not alone in this view. In 1920 the Italian composer and virtuoso pianist Ferruccio Busoni (1866–1924) wrote an open letter to a German music critic in which he outlined a "Youthful Classicism": "I mean the idea that music is music, in and for itself, and nothing else. . . ." Busoni advocated "the casting off of what is 'sensuous' and the renunciation of subjectivity (the road to objectivity, which means the author standing back from his work . . .)." In the twenties, German art critics coined the phrase *Neue Sachlichkeit* (new objectivity) to describe the work of visual artists who had rejected Expressionism.

In 1917 a young Russian composer, Sergei Prokofiev (1891–1953), had published a work titled "Classical Symphony," an overtly tonal work that makes constant reference to the style of the Viennese classicists, particularly Haydn's. Although Prokofiev had been influenced by Stravinsky's *Rite of Spring* (which he had heard in London in 1914) and was criticized by the Soviets for being too "modernist," in this work he set out to evoke the past in a spirited twentieth-century manner. The Classical Symphony itself soon became a classic.

In 1917 the French composer Erik Satie (1866–1925) wrote a parodistic *Sonatine bureaucratique* for piano based on a keyboard sonatina by the Italian composer Muzio Clementi (1752–1832), a contemporary of Mozart's. Not surprisingly, Stravinsky also was drawn to the music of pre-Romantic composers. In 1919/20 he wrote the music for a ballet, *Pulcinella,* based on works by the Italian Baroque composer Giovanni Battista Pergolesi (1710–1736).

Throughout the 1920s Stravinsky continued to write works that evoked memories of pre-Romantic music, though his references to that music were subtle and highly personal. For example, his Serenade in A for piano (1925) includes movements titled Hymne, Romanza, Rondoletto, and Cadenza Finale.* (That same year, Schoenberg also wrote a Serenade, replete with such movements as

*This work was commissioned by Columbia Records. Each movement was limited to three or four minutes so that it would fit on one side of the 10-inch 78-rpm records that had just come onto the market.

FIGURE 28.7 To get the sounds of modern life into *Parade,* for which Pablo Picasso designed the sets, Eric Satie included a typewriter and a revolver in the orchestra.

March and Menuett.) In works like these, Stravinsky viewed the past through a kaleidoscopic prism, incorporating and transforming elements that struck his fancy without regard to their traditional, "proper" function.

Much of the music composed after the outbreak of the First World War is parodistic or satirical in tone. Satie's ballet *Parade* (1917), created in collaboration with the French artist Jean Cocteau (1889–1963), includes sirens and grotesquely costumed animals (Figure 28.7). Stravinsky subtitled *The Card Game* (1937) "a ballet in three deals." Instead of writing a piano concerto, the Swiss composer Arthur Honegger (1892–1955) wrote a "concertino" (1925) that poked fun at virtuosity.

Whether or not they drew on the music of the past, works composed in the twenties and thirties sound leaner, more economical, and more astringent than late-Romantic works. No longer did orchestral textures depend on a lush group of strings—violins, violas, cellos, double basses. Instead, composers favored the reedier, brassier sound of the jazz ensemble, even in works that otherwise show little jazz influence.

Given the rich variety of the music written in the postwar period, critics had a hard time finding a term to describe it. They rejected *anti-Romantic* as too limited and negative. At last, perhaps with Busoni and Prokofiev in mind, they settled on the term *neoclassicism*. That term is regrettably imprecise. *Classical* suggests something whose beauty is timeless and unchanging; so *neoclassical* suggests something that is "newly timeless"—a logical contradiction.

Presumably *neoclassicism* was meant to suggest a revival of the formal proportions and economical means that had governed the music of the Viennese Classicists, especially Haydn, Mozart, and Beethoven. But, as we have seen, the term

# *Historical Window*

## THE BOSTON SYMPHONY

The earliest established orchestras in Europe date from the 1840s. There were occasional concerts in the United States well before that time, but they were too irregular to support a large ensemble of musicians year-round. Until late in the century, visiting virtuosos were obliged to round up their own orchestras as they traveled from city to city.

Bostonians had been enthusiastic supporters of art music for many years. The great Beethoven biographer Alexander Wheelock Thayer (1817–1897; Figure 28.8) was a Bostonian, and in 1815 a group of Bostonians founded the Handel and Haydn Society to perform the oratorios of those composers—often with an orchestra of 100 and a chorus of 750. The Harvard Musical Association, established in 1837, supported a semiprofessional orchestra that gave frequent concerts. In 1869 and 1872 the bandleader Patrick Gilmore staged two "Peace Jubilees" in Boston. The first program was performed by 1,000 instrumentalists and a chorus of 10,000. For the second there were twice as many performers, along with artillery. One of the participants was Johann Strauss, Jr., who always seemed to know where the action was.

In 1881, a 47-year-old banker from New York, Henry Lee Higginson, founded the Boston Symphony, whose mission was to "play the best music in the best way and give concerts to all who could pay a small price." Because there were few schools of music or conservatories in the country at the time, most of the 68 charter members of the BSO (as the Boston Symphony Orchestra is affectionately called) were Germans trained in Europe. Another German, Georg Henschel, who was only 31, was hired as the orchestra's first conductor. In its first season the BSO offered 20 public rehearsals on Friday afternoons and 20 concerts on Saturday evenings—a practice that was soon abandoned as impractical.

For a sometimes baffled audience, Henschel conducted the U.S. premieres of several Brahms symphonies, which one critic described as "an incomprehensible terror." Henschel soon decided to play serious music during the first half of a concert and lighter music during the second half. Attendance in the BSO's second season numbered more than 100,000 people. In 1900, Boston's Symphony Hall was opened, an auditorium that is still regarded as one of the most acoustically perfect in the world.

In October 1917 the BSO became the first American orchestra to record for the recently invented phonograph. (The recording was made for Victor—later RCA Victor.) After the recording session, one ecstatic critic declared about the

FIGURE 28.8 Alexander Wheelock Thayer interviewed many people who knew Beethoven; more than a century after its publication, Thayer's biography of Beethoven is still widely consulted.

FIGURE 28.9 From 1911 to 1914, Pierre Monteaux was the conductor for the Ballets Russes. In 1963 he conducted *The Rite of Spring* on the fiftieth anniversary of its Paris premiere.

players: "There was never anything like them before, there can never be anything quite like them again."

In 1919, when the French conductor Pierre Monteux (1875–1964) took over the orchestra, one of his first acts was to replace the European-trained musicians with American musicians. (By this time Boston had a first-class music school, the New England Conservatory.) With his white handlebar mustache and dignified bearing (Figure 28.9), Monteux was for many Bostonians the very model of the "classical musician." As time passed, Monteux introduced Boston audiences to music by Stravinsky and other contemporary composers and raised the quality of the orchestra to a level matched by only a few European orchestras.

Over its long history the Boston Symphony has had only 13 conductors. All of them have kept up the orchestra's reputation for supporting contemporary music (though the orchestra never performed any of Charles Ives's music during his lifetime). (The Ives recording in your record set is by the Boston Symphony Orchestra under American-born conductor Michael Tilson Thomas.)

In 1924 Arthur Fiedler (1894–1979), a young violinist with the BSO, formed an ensemble with 25 colleagues called the "Boston Sinfonietta." Their self-proclaimed mandate was to carry symphonic music to remote parts of New England. After staging a series of large outdoor concerts, in 1930 Fiedler was named conductor of the "Boston Pops," the summertime wing of the BSO. Over his 40-year tenure, Fiedler (who bore an uncanny resemblance to Monteux) stood as a cultural institution in his own right, and the Boston Pops became a familiar presence in radio, television, and recording studios. After Fiedler's death, leadership of the Boston Pops passed to the well-known film composer John Williams (b. 1932), who wrote the music for the films *The Towering Inferno, E.T.,* and *Indiana Jones and the Temple of Doom.*

*Classicism* was applied to that music only long after the style itself had vanished. Moreover, composers like Stravinsky never really revived sonata form or the other stylistic conventions of the Viennese Classicists. Rather, their references to those conventions are oblique, nontraditional, and eclectic. And they drew not just from the Classicists but from the Baroque *(Pulcinella)* and from the nineteenth century (Stravinsky's ballet score, *The Fairy's Kiss* [1928], based on melodies by Tchaikovsky). Still, the term *neoclassicism* has endured, and it at least suggests the dramatic shifts in musical styles that set in during the postwar period.

### Stravinsky: Third Movement from the *Symphony of Psalms* (1930)

Stravinsky's *Symphony of Psalms* (Listening Guide 68) was "composed to the glory of God and dedicated to the Boston Symphony (see the Historical Window on page 634) on the occasion of the fiftieth anniversary of its existence." The work may have been partially a response to his return in 1926 to the Russian Orthodox faith into which he had been born. Stravinsky explained his choice of title:

> I was looking for a brief title that would seize the special character of my *Symphony*. In short, this is not a symphony into which I have put some psalms which are sung, but on the contrary, it is the singing of psalms which I symphonize, and that is difficult to say in two words.

For his texts, Stravinsky chose parts of Psalms 28 and 39 for the first and second movements, and the entire Psalm 150 for the third movement. The second movement is a fugue, and the third movement serves as the climax of the work.

Though Psalm 150 is a psalm of celebration, Stravinsky's setting is remarkably restrained. Instead of including the full string section of a Romantic orchestra, Stravinsky omits the violins and violas altogether. His heavy use of winds and brass (the only percussion is the timpani) gives the movement a solemn, austere sound, starting with the opening curtain and the hushed "Alleluia." The vocal melodies reflect the narrow range, medieval modality, and rhythmic smoothness of plainchant, but they are even more static and repetitive, as in "Praise, Praise, Praise the Lord" near the very beginning (Theme *B*):

The pitches of the first three repetitions seem to belong to E-flat Major, while the theme cadences ambiguously in C Major. Throughout the movement Stravinsky alludes, as here, to traditional tonality. However, instead of opposing two contrasting keys in the manner of earlier tonal composers, Stravinsky balances keys in a kind of static equilibrium that he referred to as "poles of attraction." Although these keys—C Major/Minor and E-flat Major (less often, B-flat Major)—are related, they would not have appeared simultaneously in a traditional tonal work.

Underlying the movement's solemnity is a certain joyousness created by Stravinsky's use of ostinatos. Some of them, called free ostinatos, are free in both rhythm and in the succession of pitches, as in the outlining of a C-major triad in the bass at the opening:

The vocal line, shown in the first example, favors the notes of the minor scale. Clashes such as this between the major and minor modes were characteristic of Stravinsky's style during the 1920s and 1930s.

In the majestic coda (the longest section of the movement), a long, symmetrical ostinato repeats almost 11 times. Here is a single statement:

This ostinato divides neatly into two halves. The third measure is a retrograde of the first measure; the fourth measure is an inversion of the second measure.

Another composer might have responded literally to the sound suggested by the text of the coda ("Praise him on the joyful cymbals"), but Stravinsky's hushed setting is more dramatic. Over the ostinato Stravinsky lays a static, hypnotic melody (Theme *E*) organized like a more elaborate version of Theme *B* from the opening *A*-Section (shown above). Like Theme *B*, a cluster of notes belonging to the orbit of E-flat Major gravitate at the end of Theme *E* to the pitch C, expressing equilibrium rather than resolution:

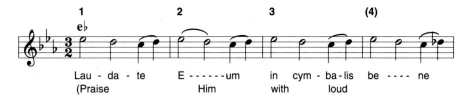

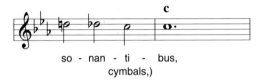

so - nan - ti - bus,
cymbals,)

Stravinsky builds the movement around a sturdy ternary form, rounding out the coda with the opening of the *A*-Section (Themes *A* and *B*) and ending on the same ambiguous cadence. The returning *A*-Section, abridged and reorchestrated, contains some brilliant flourishes in the piano and brass. At key points throughout the movement (just before the return of the *A*-Section, for example) the music surges toward a climax, only to pull back suddenly—another anti-Romantic element.

Borrowing from a theme introduced by the horns in the opening *A*-Section (Theme *C*), the pulsating *B*-Section presents the most striking declamation in the movement:

Lau - da - te Do - mi - num     in     vir - tu - ti - bus     Ej - us
(Praise     the     Lord     for     His     mighty     acts.)

Although the rapid bursts and long pauses between syllables that characterize such lines violate almost every rule of Latin declamation, Stravinsky achieves a powerful effect by celebrating the sheer sound of the words, divorced from their traditional meanings. In so doing he created one of the most popular choral works of the twentieth century.

# Listening Guide 68

## STRAVINSKY: *Symphony of Psalms,* Third Movement

CD 7, TRACK [10]
TAPE 7B, TRACK 1
DURATION: 11:00

*Stravinsky uses traditional elements—ternary form, ostinatos, a chantlike vocal style, and triadic harmonies—in a highly individual fashion, producing a style that is at once archaic and contemporary. Only those themes which recur at different points in the movement have been assigned letter names: Theme A, Theme B, and so forth. Themes appearing in brackets are sung; the others are played by the orchestra. Theme C—the source of the most distinctive vocal declamation—is the only theme that appears in both the orchestra and the chorus.*

*Form: Ternary plus coda*

| | TEXT / LOCATION | TIME | COMMENTS |
|---|---|---|---|
| 1 | Opening curtain | **0:00** | A suspended cadence in the winds. |
| | *A*-SECTION | | |
| | *Alleluia* [Theme *A*] Alleluia. | **0:10** | A restrained 3-note ascent that pauses but does not cadence. |
| | *Laudate, laudate, laudate Dominum* [Theme *B*] Praise, praise, praise the Lord | 0:16 | Over a free ostinato, the chorus declaims a repetitive theme that leads to an ambiguous cadence containing two of the three notes of a C-Major triad. |
| | *in sanctis Ejus.* in His sanctuary. | 0:43 | Mixture of the major and the minor modes. |
| | *Laudate Eum in firmamento virtutis Ejus,* Praise Him in the firmament of His power, | **1:00** | A more extended version of Theme *B*. The notes of the ostinato belong to a C-Major triad; the choral parts gravitate toward E-flat Major; |
| | *Laudate Dominum.* Praise the Lord. | 1:42 | these are another manifestation of Stravinsky's "poles of attraction." |
| 2 | Theme *C* | **2:03** | Alternates between sharp repeated chords in the horns and an ostinato in the bass. |
| | | 2:11 | The ostinato moves briefly to the trumpet before embarking on a crescendo. |
| | Theme *D* | 2:28 | The orchestra surges on the wings of the rapid triplets. |
| | | 2:33 | The strident trumpet pushes the triplets even harder. |
| | | 2:39 | The triplets climax in five powerful brass chords. |

*continued*

| TEXT / LOCATION | TIME | COMMENTS |
|---|---|---|
| **3** B-SECTION | | |
| *Laudate Eum in virtutibus Ejus.*<br>Praise Him for His mighty acts. | **2:47** | Intoned in chantlike fashion by the sopranos and altos over a narrow range. |
| *Laudate Dominum in virtutibus Ejus.* [Theme C]<br>Praise the Lord for His mighty acts.<br><br>*Laudate Dominum in sanctis Ejus.*<br>Praise the Lord in His sanctuary. | 3:06 | Over a 2-note free ostinato, the chorus sings a variant of Theme *C* (introduced by the horns in the *A*-Section). |
| *Laudate Eum secundum multitudinem magnitudinis Ejus.*<br>Praise Him according to His most excellent greatness. | 3:17 | Borrowing from the ostinato, the basses (joined by the tenors and altos) sing another static phrase while the winds supply a chattering commentary. |
| *Laudate Eum in sono tubae.*<br>Praise Him with the sound of the trumpet. | **3:41** | The sopranos finally enter, and the section soars to a repetitive but exhilarating climax that breaks off abruptly without a cadence. |
| [Retransition] | 4:01 | Suddenly soft, followed by a passage similar to that which opened the movement. |
| **4** A'-SECTION | | |
| *Alleluia* [Theme *A*] | **4:15** | Identical to the opening "Alleluia." |
| *Laudate Dominum, laudate Eum.*<br>Praise the Lord, praise Him. | **4:22** | A new, aggressive choral texture over traces of Theme *C* in the brass. |
| [Orchestral bridge] | 4:30 | Static arpeggios in the winds, piano, and brass. |
| *Laudate dominum.*<br>Praise the Lord. | 4:39 | The chorus sings Theme *C* (played by the horns in the opening *A*-Section). |
| *Laudate Dominum, laudate Eum.* [Theme C]<br>Praise the Lord, praise Him. | 5:02 | Theme *C* in the chorus, to which Stravinsky adds the triplets from Theme *D*. |
| Theme *D'* | 5:09 | A solo horn blasts out a jerky version of the earlier triplets. |
| | 5:14 | The brass triplets are even more dramatic than in the original *A*-Section. |
| | 5:22 | The five chords of the *A*-Section are expanded to seven. |
| Theme *C* | 5:29 | The repeated chords are played in slow motion. |

**5**  CODA

| | | |
|---|---|---|
| *Laudate Eum in timpano et choro,*<br>Praise Him with drums and choirs, | **5:42** | Beginning in the sopranos, a series of gently dotted, ascending arpeggios over an ostinato. |
| *Laudate Eum in chordis et organo,*<br>Praise Him with strings and instruments, | 6:15 | Stravinsky adds a rising scale in the sopranos and moves toward a climax. |
| *Laudate Eum in cymbalis*<br>    *bene sonantibus.*   [Theme *E*]<br>Praise Him with loud cymbals. | 6:45 | Suddenly soft. Solemn, repetitive vocal theme, identical in structure to Theme *B*, over a new, symmetrical 4-bar ostinato. |
| *Laudate Eum in cymbalis*<br>    *jubilationibus.*   [Theme *E*]<br>Praise Him with joyful cymbals. | 7:15 | Repeats in slightly varied form. |
| *Laudate Dominum.*<br>Praise the Lord. | 7:45 | Tenors and basses intone their monotone syllables as pure sounds, independent of meaning. |
| *Laudate Dominum*<br>Praise the Lord. | 8:24 | Stravinsky adds rising sopranos and altos, building toward another climax. |
| *Omnis spiritus*<br>    *laudat Dominum.*   [Theme *E*]<br>Let everything that breathes praise the<br>    Lord. | **8:44** | Suddenly soft. Theme *E*, still over the ostinato. |
| *Omnis spiritus*<br>    *laudat Dominum.*   [Theme *E*]<br>Let everything that breathes praise the<br>    Lord. | **9:13** | Theme *E* one last time. |
| [Orchestral bridge] | 9:42 | Slow rising scale over the 4-bar ostinato. As in the retransition, the music dies away. |

| | | |
|---|---|---|
| **6**  *Alleluia*   [Theme *A*] | **10:16** | Identical to the opening of the *A*-Section. |
| *Laudate, Dominum.*   [Theme *B*]<br>Praise the Lord. | 10:24 | Stravinsky ends on the tentative, C-Majorish cadence of Theme *B*. |

# Chapter 29

## ÉMIGRÉS AND
## TRADITIONALISTS

Nothing in Europe's long history compares with the extraordinary growth in population and emigration that took place during the nineteenth and twentieth centuries. From 1800 to 1950, the population of Europe soared from about 200 million to almost 700 million. With the accompanying rise in industrial productivity, the standard of living and life expectancy of Europeans also rose to new levels.

Yet between 1840 and the outbreak of the Second World War, more than 60 million Europeans—about one in five—left their native country in search of a better life. Some fled to escape religious persecution and some to escape the ravages of the Franco-Prussian War (1870–1871), the First World War (1914–1918), or the Russian Revolution (1917). Others, like the Irish, left to escape famine and poverty. Many were seduced by rumors of the riches that could be had for the taking in distant lands. One rumor was more reliable than the others: The demand for labor overseas far outstripped the supply. Musicians, no less than farmers and factory workers, responded to the lure of emigration.

More than half of the 60 million European émigrés between 1840 and 1940 came to the United States. Until the end of the First World War, America's doors were wide open, and almost anyone who could scrape together the money for passage and who had no serious communicable disease on arrival at Ellis Island was assured of an opportunity to make it in America. Then in 1921, and again in 1924, the United States passed laws that imposed immigration quotas on selected countries. Hardest hit were the countries of eastern and southern Europe, from which the flow of immigrants had been heaviest.

The Second World War threw Europe into even greater chaos than had the First. Although the first war had caused millions of casualties, there had been no systematic program of extermination like that carried out by the Nazis against the Jews. Nor had there been anything like the fierce aerial bombing attacks launched in 1940 by the Germans against the British and later carried on by the Allies against Germany and its partners. Again faced with war and persecution, many Europeans turned to the United States for refuge.

## THE ÉMIGRÉS

Within three years after the outbreak of the Second World War in 1939, the three most influential composers of the first half of the twentieth century—Arnold Schoenberg, Igor Stravinsky, and Béla Bartók—had all emigrated to America. Their careers were well advanced at the time of their emigration, and the dislocation they suffered reflects the fragility of life in the twentieth century. Before discussing Bartók and his American years, we turn to an earlier émigré composer who wrote almost all of his important music in America.

## EDGARD VARÈSE (1883–1965)

FIGURE 29.1 Edgard Varèse gave many of his works titles drawn from physics and mathematics. For example, *Density 21.5*—the specific weight of platinum—refers to the platinum flute of Georges Barrère, for whom Varèse composed the piece.

Edgard Varèse (Figure 29.1) was born in Paris but spent his childhood in the small Burgundian town of Le Villars. At the age of 19 he left home and returned to Paris. Though penniless, he reveled in his new freedom and made the acquaintance of the artist Pablo Picasso, the sculptor Auguste Rodin, the writer Guillaume Apollinaire, and the composers Debussy and Ravel. He studied theory and composition at the Paris Conservatory.

In 1908 Varèse accepted a position in Berlin directing a mixed chorus, but he failed in his attempts to find full-time employment. In December 1915, frustrated by his inability to make ends meet, he set sail for New York with 80 dollars in his pocket, hoping like countless others to find a better life. Up to this point, Varèse had composed only a few works, which he later destroyed. On his arrival in the United States, he won considerable success as a conductor, directing works of Berlioz in New York and Cincinnati.

Two years after his arrival, in an article published in a literary magazine, Varèse expressed his view of what music should be:

> Our alphabet is poor and illogical. Music, which should be alive and vibrating, needs new means of expression and science alone can infuse it with youthful sap. . . . I dream of instruments obedient to thought—and which, supported by a flowering of undreamed-of timbres, will lend themselves to any combination I choose to impose and will submit to the exigencies of my inner rhythm.

To advance that vision, in 1919 Varèse founded the New Symphony Orchestra, an ensemble whose purpose was to present "futurist" music. The orchestra's debut in New York City drew a hostile response from traditionalist critics, whose dean, Henry Krehbiel, described the concert as "unrelieved and dissonant clashing of keys, reiteration of unmeaning rhythmical figures, paucity of melody and monotonous striving for unwonted combination of instrumental timbres." Unnerved by such criticism, Varèse's supporters on the orchestra's board urged more orthodox programming. Varèse, enraged by their timidity, resigned, and a year later the orchestra was dissolved.

Undaunted, Varèse joined with the harpist/composer Carlos Salzedo to found the International Composers' Guild. As with Schoenberg's Society for Private Musical Performances (page 562), admission was limited to subscribers. The Greenwich *Villager* declared the Guild's first concert in 1921 "a historical event of the first magnitude in the world of music this side of the Atlantic." In the third concert, two songs by Varèse were favorably reviewed. But the honeymoon was brief. Reviewing a performance the next season of Varèse's newest work, *Hyperprism*, a critic accused him of causing "peaceful lovers of music to scream in agony, to arouse angry emotions, and tempt men to retire to the back of the theater and perform tympani concertos on each other's faces. . . ."

Throughout the seven years of the Guild's existence, Varèse campaigned tirelessly on behalf of the new music and introduced New York audiences to works by Schoenberg, Stravinsky, and dozens of other living composers. To the charge that with his own music he was forcing listeners to endure his experiments, Varèse replied: "I have always been an experimenter. But my experiments go into the wastepaper basket. I give only finished works to the public." Commenting on the emerging gulf between composers and audiences, he declared:

> There has always been a misunderstanding between the composer and his generation. The commonplace explanation of this phenomenon is that the artist is ahead of his time; but this is absurd. The fact is the creative artist is representative in a special way of his own period; and the friction between himself and his contemporaries results from the fact that the masses are by disposition and experience fifty years out of date.

By the time Varèse completed *Ionisation* in 1931, supporters of the new music were rallying around him, and his works were being performed in Paris and other European cities. In 1940 he wrote:

> I prefer to use the expression "organized sound" and avoid the monotonous question: "But is it music?" "Organized sound" seems better to take in the dual aspect of music as an art-science, with all the unconditional recent laboratory discoveries which permit us to hope for the unconditional liberation of music. . . .

Varèse's words were prophetic. With the *Poème électronique*, composed when he was 73 for the 1958 World's Fair in Brussels, Varèse emerged as a pioneer in the use of electronic technology in music. Toward the end of his life, his works were being regularly performed and recorded, and in 1955 he was elected to the prestigious National Institute of Arts and Letters. At last he had been vindicated for his passionate commitment to the music of his time and to his own role in shaping it.

### Varèse: *Ionisation* (1929–1931)

*Ionisation* (Listening Guide 69) is one of Varèse's most original works. The title refers to the process by which atoms and molecules gain or lose electrical charges through the addition or loss of electrons. In an ingenious musical parallel, Varèse

# Listening Guide 69

## VARÈSE: *Ionisation*

CD 7, TRACK 11
TAPE 7B, TRACK 2
DURATION: 4:55

*Varèse's "organized sounds" are based on a rhythmic/textural "theme" that develops through the mutation of various cells. The sectional boundaries between the "free variations" in which these mutations occur are frequently blurred.*

*Form: Free variations*

| | SECTION | TIME | COMMENTS |
|---|---|---|---|
| 1 | Introduction | **0:00** | A heterogeneous mix dominated by bass drum, snareless drum, gong, tam-tam, soft sirens, cymbals, maracas, and triangle. |
| 2 | Theme | **0:26** | Crisp rhythmic figure in the snare drum that features rapid 4-note upbeats followed by extended syncopations. |
| | (Introduction) | 0:38 | Interrupted by a varied repeat of the opening bars. |
| 3 | Free Variation 1 | **0:51** | Mutated Cells 1 and 4 in the tarole, which then spread to the castanets and sleigh bells. |
| | | 1:04 | Played more aggressively by the snare drum, and then extended to güiro, Chinese blocks, castanets, and maracas. |
| 4 | Free Variation 2 | **1:55** | Powerful unison drum outburst in rapid rhythms. Includes mutations of Cells 1 and 4. |
| | | 2:11 | Slower rhythms punctuated by slow triplets (derived from Cell 4) in the bass drum. |
| 5 | Free Variation 3 | **2:31** | Cells 1 and 3 in the triangle and other metallic instruments, surrounded by maracas and sirens. |
| | | 2:46 | Joined by the snare drum. |
| | | 2:55 | A series of overlapping sirens leads to a high-pitched climax. |
| 6 | Free Variation 4 | **3:21** | Drums and castanets play powerful bursts derived from Cell 2, alternating with delicate statements in the Chinese blocks. |
| | | 3:35 | Amidst organized chaos, the snare drum repeats the opening theme. |
| | | 3:44 | Bass drum stroke followed by sudden *pianissimo* in the tarole. |
| | | 3:47 | Short, powerful bursts of Cell 2. |
| 7 | Coda | **3:51** | Blurred by the siren, the three pitched instruments enter. The bells play a quasi-melody while disconnected fragments of all four cells seemingly disperse, in a dramatic diminuendo, to the far corners of the universe. |

*Chapter 29 Émigrés and Traditionalists*       645

treats the thematic material of *Ionisation* as rhythmic cells that gain and lose notes.

Varèse dedicated *Ionisation* to Nicolas Slonimsky (b. 1894), another émigré and a champion of new music. Slonimsky conducted the premiere of the work in 1933.* Except for the brief appearance of three pitched instruments (piano, tubular bells, and glockenspiel) in the last few bars, the piece is scored entirely for nonpitched instruments. The 13 percussionists play 26 different instruments whose European, African, Asian, Latin American, and Near Eastern origins reflect the global nature of twentieth-century music. In addition to familiar instruments like bass drum, cymbals, and snare drum, these include anvils (metal bars), bongos (Afro-Cuban drums), castanets (cup-shaped pieces of wood connected by a cord and struck together), cencerro (a clapperless Spanish bell struck with a drum stick), Chinese cymbal (a metal disc struck with a wooden stick), Chinese blocks (hollow rectangular blocks), claves (cylindrical hardwood sticks from Cuba), fouet (two slabs of wood with hand grips designed to imitate the sound of a whip cracking), glockenspiel, gong (heavy metal disc from Java and Burma, struck with a soft mallet), güiro (a hollow gourd with raised frets over which a switch is rubbed), maracas (a pair of gourd rattles), siren (hand-operated rotating discs that produce a high, wailing sound), sleigh bells, string drum (an African instrument that imitates a lion's roar when a rosined cord is pulled through a membrane), tambourine, tam-tam (similar to the gong), tarole (a high-pitched Brazilian snare drum), and tubular chimes.

*Ionisation* is organized around rhythm and texture rather than melody or harmony. Following a brief introduction, a rhythmic theme is first stated in the snare drum:

After this first statement, the theme reappears only twice in its original form. Varèse subdivides the theme into rhythmic cells (the four most frequent divisions are shown above) which he subjects to continuous "mutation" in a series of "free variations."[†] *Mutation* refers to the gradual alteration of the rhythmic cells by the addition or removal of single pitches or by a shift in rhythm (for example, a shift from four fast notes to five fast notes in the same period of time).

Each cell can be combined in any sequence with any other, and each free variation incorporates rhythmic and textural mutations of the original theme.

---

*Slonimsky has edited several important reference books, including *Baker's Biographical Dictionary of Musicians* (1958–1978); the humorous *Lexicon of Musical Invective* (1952, 1965)—which contains negative reviews of great composers from Beethoven's time to the present—and the *Lectionary of Music* (1989), a "reading reference work" that contains a goldmine of information about common and arcane terms.

[†]Varèse himself did not use this term.

For example, Variation 1 opens with the tarole playing Cells 1 and 4, followed by the snare drum playing the original theme, portions of which are then passed to the bongos, Chinese blocks, maracas, and castanets. Other instruments embellish the theme with textural commentary. Variation 2 opens with a dramatic *fortissimo* outburst derived from Cells 1 and 4. Variations 3 and 4 make use of Cells 2 and 3. The three pitched instruments—piano, tubular chimes, and glockenspiel—usher in the coda, which fades into silence.

## BÉLA BARTÓK (1881–1945)

FIGURE 29.2 An artist of unflinching views, Bartók wrote to a friend when he was 25 that "human frailty has been the primary cause of our belief in gods."

Béla Bartók (Figure 29.2) was the first composer from eastern Europe (excluding Russia) to achieve international stature. He was born in a small Hungarian village that today lies in Romania. Both of Bartók's parents were accomplished musicians. As a child, he was fascinated by the gypsy music played in his home, and when he was five he persuaded his parents to let him take piano lessons. He made his first public appearance as a pianist at age 11, performing a movement of a Beethoven sonata and a piece of his own, *The River Danube*.

Though the family had little money, Bartók managed to win a series of scholarships, and by his mid-teens he had composed several large-scale works (all of which have disappeared). At 18 he entered the Academy of Music in Budapest, where his compositions often bewildered the faculty. A teacher commented on one of his slow movements: "In an Adagio there must be love; but in this movement there is no sign of love."

Bartók published his first work, *Four Songs*, in 1902. His enthusiasm for the tone poems of Richard Strauss now led him to take up composition more seriously. He felt an increasing urge to "create something specifically Hungarian in music"—an urge that his German-trained teachers tried to discourage. He saw himself as a citizen of an oppressed nation, and he swore to "devote every part of my life, always and in every way, to one good: the good of the Hungarian nation and of the Hungarian fatherland." Following a performance of his programmatic, nationalistic *Kossuth* Symphony in 1904, Bartók became known almost overnight as a champion of Hungarian music.

In 1905 Bartók received a grant that enabled him to travel around Hungary studying its folk music, which he described as "a revelation." In the company of a fellow Hungarian composer, Zoltán Kodály (1882–1967), he recorded hundreds of Slovak, Romanian, and Hungarian folk songs (Figure 29.3) on unwieldy wax cylinders which he later transcribed. Bartók wrote:

> I wanted to do two things: to bring back the spirit of folk song, and to harmonize the melodies in modern style. I tried to make them easy to play on the piano, and, although I made use of modern means of expression, not to take away their national flavor. It was presenting the past in the mode of expression of the present, like a Hamlet in contemporary costume.

FIGURE 29.3 Starting in 1906, Bartók made recordings of folk music by using an Edison phonograph. Here he records Slovak peasants in Darazs in 1907. Bartók also recorded Arabian music in North Africa.

Bartók was struck by the sharp differences between folk music and Western art music. The basic building block of much folk music, for example, is the 5-note pentatonic scale rather than the Western diatonic scale:

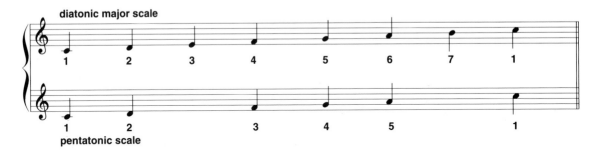

Bartók also discovered whole-tone and other exotic scales. Folk music became an integral part of his musical language, along with a radical treatment of dissonance, orchestration, and form. He was as skillful as Beethoven in building complex structures from simple materials, and he favored the thematic clarity and lean, muscular textures he had discovered in folk music. Even in his most dissonant and complex works, he maintained a sense of tonality, though not traditional triadic tonality. His harmonic language derives from relationships among intervals rather than among triads. This peculiar mix set Bartók's music apart from that of his contemporaries.

Both Bartók and Kodály soon became professors at the Academy of Music, where Bartók continued to teach for over 30 years. During a concert tour in 1922, Bartók met Stravinsky in Paris. By that time Stravinsky had come to believe that music expressed nothing beyond itself, and he had little sympathy for Bartók's programmatic leanings. Bartók toured the United States in 1927–1928 (beginning with a concert in Carnegie Hall). After several weeks of touring, he concluded that "this country is so vast but so uniform!" He wrote to his mother: "It is very interesting to come here once, but now I have had enough."

By 1937 Bartók had established himself as one of the world's preeminent composers. Over the years he composed a series of orchestral masterpieces, including *The Miraculous Mandarin* (1919), *Dance Suite* (1923), Music for Strings, Percussion, and Celesta (1936), two violin concertos, and two piano concertos. His six string quartets (the last completed in 1939) reestablished the vitality of this genre and extended the frontiers of string writing and formal organization. His Sonata for Two Pianos and Percussion (1937) and *Contrasts* for violin, clarinet, and piano (1938; premiered by the American jazz clarinetist Benny Goodman [1909–1986]) are monuments of twentieth-century chamber music. For his youngest son, Peter, Bartók composed a six-volume set of 153 graded piano pieces, which he called *Mikrokosmos* (1926–1939). These pieces—divided between folk-song arrangements and original compositions—were the first guide for the beginning pianist to be written in a twentieth-century language. Several of them are regularly performed in the concert hall.

Despite the disruption of his field studies during the First World War and hostile treatment by Hungary's postwar government, Bartók managed to retain his professorship at the Academy of Music and continued to flourish until about 1935. But the rise of fascism in Europe proved unbearable for Bartók and his second wife, the pianist Ditta Pásztory, and they watched with horror as the Republican forces in the Spanish Civil War (1938) were crushed. The death of Bartók's mother in January 1940 broke his last bond with his homeland, and in October he and his wife played a farewell concert to a packed hall in the Academy before leaving Budapest for the United States.

Like many other émigrés, Bartók never adapted to life in America. As he had in Europe, he refused to teach composition for fear that it would sap his creative energies. Following his arrival, he gave a well-publicized concert in New York that was favorably reviewed by the *New York Times*. In the months that followed, however, he felt increasingly ignored. The few concert requests that came his way were not enough to support his family. Though he was invited to study a collection of Yugoslav folk songs at Columbia University, he grew depressed over the commercialism of American culture. In 1942 he showed the first signs of leukemia. About this time, two Hungarian compatriots, the violinist Joseph Szigeti (1892–1973) and the conductor Fritz Reiner (1888–1963), secretly arranged a commission for him to compose a new orchestral work, the five-movement Concerto for Orchestra. Bartók completed the work during a period of remission at his retreat at Lake Saranac in upper New York State, which the American Society for Composers, Authors, and Publishers (ASCAP) had made available to him. ASCAP also provided him with the best medical care, but Bartók died of his illness in September 1945.

### Bartók: Concerto for Orchestra, First and Fourth Movements (1944)

The five movements of the Concerto for Orchestra (Listening Guide 70) explore every facet of Bartók's art. *Concerto* refers to Bartók's treatment of instruments "in a soloistic manner" (as he remarked), rather than to any organized exchange between soloist and orchestra. He organizes the movements in symmetrical fashion. The first and last are large Allegros, and each contains striking fugato passages that make use of such contrapuntal devices as stretto and inversion. Bartók titled the second movement, which functions as a scherzo, the "Presentation of the Pairs." In succession, pairs of bassoons, oboes, clarinets, flutes, and muted trumpets present themselves just as couples might in a folk dance. The fourth movement, described by Bartók as an "Interrupted Intermezzo," also draws on the style of folk music and, in tempo and mood, balances the second movement. He places the atmospheric "Elegia," an example of the "night music" for which Bartók is well known, at the center of the Concerto and strengthens the symmetry among movements by thematic relationships between them—strongest between the first and third movements.

**First Movement.** In this movement, as in others, Bartók gave sonata form a new lease on life. Rather than organizing the movement around tonality, however, he organizes it around themes, often in unusual relationships. For example, he uses the transition theme as both the retransition and as the final cadence—functions that would have been highly unlikely in a traditional tonal structure.

Bartók's fondness for structural symmetries led to an emphasis on the interval of the fourth, whose augmented form (the tritone) divides the octave exactly in half:

He delighted in playing off the tritone against the perfect fourth, a half step smaller, and structures the opening movement around these two adjacent intervals, beginning with the interlocking perfect fourths of the slow introduction:

These bare unison statements alternate with delicate violin tremolos that expand and contract symmetrically in both directions. With each repetition, the tempo of the unison passages and the intensity of the tremolo responses increase. A tentative flute melody based on a neighboring half step gains momentum with each repetition of the tremolo, climaxing in a passionate outburst in the strings. This leads to the accelerating repetition of an ostinato in the low strings that anticipates the symmetrical primary theme of the exposition:

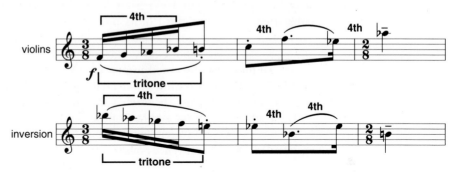

The second half of the theme inverts the first half almost exactly. The first four notes of bars 1 and 4 each outline a perfect fourth and all five notes outline a tritone. Even the succession of pitches here is symmetrical, alternating between whole and half steps (this alternation, known as the *octatonic scale*, was favored by Stravinsky as well).

The transition reassembles many of the pitches of the primary theme:

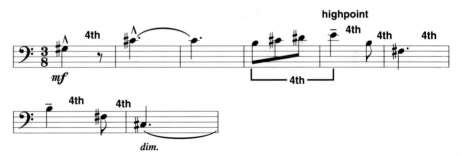

The first part of the phrase ascends via perfect fourths to the high point (placed exactly in the middle) and then descends symmetrically via further perfect fourths. Only the secondary theme deviates from that structure. But its static alternation between two adjacent pitches (over an equally static drone) derives from the flute theme of the introduction. The closing theme extends the secondary theme.

The development returns to the primary theme, placing a tranquil variant of bars 2 and 3 exactly in the middle. The retransition, modeled on the modest transition theme of the exposition, grows through fugal imitation in the brass to a brilliant climax (characteristically, its second half is a loose inversion of its first half). To compensate for the focus on the primary theme in the development, that theme is truncated in the recapitulation, leading almost directly to the secondary and closing themes, both of which Bartók varies over the exposition. The opening of the coda is similar to the development and concludes just as it does, with the transition theme unexpectedly serving as the final cadence. Despite this high degree of thematic unity, Bartók achieves a wide range of expression.

**Fourth Movement.** The fourth movement, ironically labeled "Interrupted Intermezzo" (an intermezzo is itself an interruption), emphasizes contrast rather than unity. The third of its three themes parodies the march from the *Leningrad* Symphony of the Russian composer Dmitri Shostakovich (1906–1975), whose wartime popularity had irked Bartók. Both this and the first theme are interrupted and dismissed in mid-course. Once again, Bartók provides an unexpected ending by stating the first bars of the bridge theme that links Themes *A* and *C* and then leaving the listener suspended in mid-air.

The shifting, hypnotic *a*-phrase of the *A*-Theme revolves around the tritone in its first half before descending unexpectedly via a perfect fourth at the end, again balancing these two intervals:

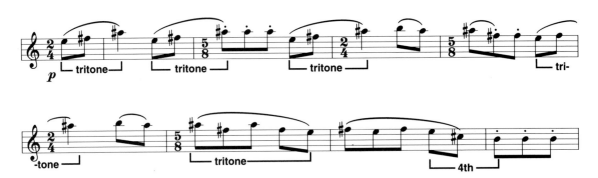

In the *a-a'-b-a″* shape of Theme *A*, the *b*-phrase is simply an inversion of the *a*-phrase. The irregular alternation between bars of four beats (those marked 2/4) and bars of five beats (those marked 5/8) gives the tune an unsteady, tottering quality.

As a result, the intensely lyrical *B*-Theme that follows is all the more unexpected. Bartók's orchestration of the theme's three appearances is highly individual. The violas play the theme the first time, accompanied by two harps and timpani—an unorthodox combination. To the immediate *forte* repetition Bartók adds full strings and English horn in a low, throaty register. In the final appearance, rather than providing the lush, sweeping climax that the theme invites, he has the first violins and violas play the theme *piano* with mutes and has the other strings strum guitarlike pizzicatos, creating a poignant effect. The saucy march parody (Theme *C*) reaches three separate climaxes, only to evoke each time guffaws from the orchestra. Each of the three themes is enhanced by its juxtaposition to the other two.

The power of Bartók's music stems not only from his ability to infuse highly organized themes and structures with energy and passion but also, as with Haydn and Mozart a century and a half earlier, from his ability to integrate popular and serious styles.

### BARTÓK:  Concerto for Orchestra, First and Fourth Movements

CD 8, TRACKS ①–②

TAPE 8A, TRACKS 1–2

DURATION: 9:01

#### First Movement

*In his use of sonata form, Bartók pays little heed to the harmonic framework of eighteenth- and nineteenth-century composers. Instead, he relies on rich interrelationships among themes generated by intervals. In this guide we refer to the generating theme of the movement, stated at the outset by the low strings, as the Fourth Theme. The transition theme—traditionally a kinetic passage of limited thematic interest—holds the structure together by providing both the retransition and the final cadence.*

*Form: Thematic sonata form*

| | LOCATION | | TIME | COMMENTS |
|---|---|---|---|---|
| 1 | INTRODUCTION | | | Andante ma non troppo (Moderately slow). |
| | Fourth Theme 1 | | **0:00** | Cellos and basses play a soft, legato series of interlocking fourths. |
| | Tremolo 1 | | 0:20 | Upper strings play tremolos in a series of expanding and contracting intervals, ending with a flourish in the flutes. |
| | Fourth Theme 2 | | 0:34 | Cellos and basses; the range expands. |
| | Tremolo 2 | | 0:48 | A fourth higher than before. |
| | Fourth Theme 3 | | 1:04 | Cellos and basses; the range expands further. |
| | Tremolo 3 | | 1:20 | A flute theme based on half steps is added to the texture. |
| | Fourth Theme 4 | | 1:37 | Though still *pianissimo*, the rhythms are twice as fast as before. |
| | Trumpets | | 1:48 | Muted inversion of the flute theme over the Fourth Theme. |
| | Strings | | 2:19 | Passionate outburst based on the flute theme, played again over the Fourth Theme. |
| | Ostinato | | 2:36 | A repeating, accelerating pattern built around fourths; the rhythm is reinforced by the timpani. |
| 2 | EXPOSITION | | | Allegro vivace (Fast and lively). |
| | Primary Theme | *A* | **3:04** | Strings. First bar derived from the ostinato figure. The second half of the first phrase inverts the first half. |
| | | *B* | 3:19 | Lyrical expansion of Theme *A*. |
| | Transition | | 3:47 | *Forte* in the trombone and derived from the Fourth Theme. Dissolves in the flute to *pianissimo*. |
| 3 | Secondary Theme | *A* | 3:59 | In the oboe, based on neighboring whole steps derived from the introduction. |
| | | *A'* | 4:24 | Clarinets with harp accompaniment. |
| | Closing Theme | *A* | 4:40 | Flutes, oboes; based on the secondary theme. |
| | | *A'* | 4:57 | Lower strings answered by upper winds; disquieting mood. |

*continued*

| LOCATION | TIME | COMMENTS |
|---|---|---|
| **4** DEVELOPMENT | | |
| Primary Theme *A* | **5:17** | Based on mm. 1 and 4, passing through the entire orchestra. |
| Primary Theme *A* | 5:29 | Based on mm. 2 and 5; uses stretto. |
| Tranquilo [Tranquilly] | 5:47 | Clarinet plays lyrical variant of bars 2 and 3 of Theme *A*. |
| Primary Theme *A* | 6:24 | Strings, *fortissimo*. |
| **5** Retransition | **6:26** | The brass expand considerably on the transition. |
| **6** RECAPITULATION | | |
| Primary Theme *A* | **7:12** | Telescoped from almost a minute in the exposition to a few seconds here. |
| Secondary Theme *A* | 7:19 | Varied from the exposition, and now in the clarinet. |
| *A'* | 7:44 | Varied from the exposition, and now in the flutes and oboe. |
| Closing Theme *A* | 8:11 | Flutes and oboes play a slower, dreamier version than in the exposition. |
| *A'* | 8:19 | Ominous and unsettling. |
| **7** CODA | | |
| Primary Theme *A* | **8:38** | *Fortissimo* and highly charged, intensified by the string tremolos. |
| **8** Transition | 8:53 | All of the brass playing *fortissimo*. |

DURATION: 4:01

## Fourth Movement: (Intermezzo Interrotto) [Interrupted Intermezzo]

*The simple outer form of this movement conceals a rich and varied thematic structure. In keeping with the movement's title, the themes are riddled with breaks that range from dreamy "dissolves" to dramatic interruptions. All three themes, including the parody of Shostakovich in Theme C, are rooted in eastern European folk music.*

*Form: Sectional (A-B-A-C-B-A)*

| | | | |
|---|---|---|---|
| **1** | Curtain | **0:00** | Strings in fierce octaves. |
| | Theme *A* | | |
| | *a* | **0:06** | The oboe plays a soft, lyrical theme in shifting meters. |
| | *a'* | 0:16 | Flute, clarinet, and bassoon. |

| LOCATION | TIME | COMMENTS |
|---|---|---|
| *b* | 0:26 | Flute accompanied by harp. An inversion of the *a*-phrase. |
| *a"* | 0:42 | Oboe with flute countermelody. |
| **2**  Theme *B* | | |
| *a* | **0:55** | Lush, singing theme in viola and harp, *forte*. |
| *a'* | 1:10 | Full orchestra, *forte*. |
| **3**  Theme *A* | | |
| *a* | **1:30** | Oboe and strings, *piano*. |
| Bridge | 1:41 | Strings, *piano*. A simple bass pattern repeated three times. |
| **4**  Theme *C* (parody) | | |
| *a* | **1:49** | Folklike march tune in clarinet, with an accelerando. |
| | 2:02 | Guffaws in brass, strings, and winds. *Fortissimo* to *piano*. |
| | 2:09 | Jazzy, irreverent trombone smear. |
| *a'* | 2:13 | Strings with shimmering accompaniment. |
| | 2:25 | Guffaws from brass, strings, and winds. *Fortissimo* to *piano*. |
| *a* | 2:30 | Tuba and strings in inversion, dissolving into chaos. |
| **5**  Theme *B* | | |
| *a* | **2:45** | Muted bowed strings playing in octaves, plus strummed pizzicato strings and harp. |
| **6**  Theme *A* | | |
| *b* | **3:01** | Fragments tossed from oboe to flute to clarinet. |
| *a* | 3:14 | English horn. Dissolves into a fermata. |
| *b* | 3:22 | Flute and strings. Dissolves into a quasi-cadenza. |
| "quasi-cadenza" [like a cadenza] | 3:35 | Flute over a held string chord. |
| *b* | 3:49 | Fragment tossed from oboe to bassoon to flute. |
| **7**  Bridge | **3:56** | Strings, *piano*. The first of the three preceding repetitions functions unexpectedly as the final cadence. |

## MUSICIANS AND WAR

During the Middle Ages and the Renaissance, army commanders often took a small group of musicians (Guillaume de Machaut, for one) along with them to brighten the hours between battles, and in the seventeenth century military bands supplied marching soldiers with a steady beat and spirited melodies. A ragtag fife-and-drum corps kept pace with soldiers during the American Revolution (Figure 29.4).

Many composers have eulogized the victims of war. Benjamin Britten based his *War Requiem* (1961) on poems by Wilfred Owen, a British soldier who was killed in combat a week before the armistice that ended the First World War. Others have written music to celebrate happier occasions, such as the *Nelson Mass* that Joseph Haydn composed in 1798 to celebrate Lord Nelson's victory over the French fleet at Abu Qir, Egypt.

The career of Heinrich Schütz was dominated by the Thirty Years' War (1618–1648). Schütz's employer, the Duke of Saxony, was a Protestant prince struggling to throw off the domination of the Holy Roman Empire. Even before Saxony entered the war, its resources were being siphoned off, and in the late 1620s Schütz complained to the Duke that his musicians "have been given barely one month's pay in the space of a year." By the time Saxony joined the war in 1631, the nearly three dozen singers and instrumentalists whom Schütz relied on at the court had dwindled to almost none. In 1641 he pleaded with the Duke to let him train eight boys as singers and instrumentalists, but no action seems to have been taken. When the war ended in 1648, Schütz, now in his mid-sixties, wrote to the Duke that his ensemble of court musicians "has gone completely to ruin in these perilous times, and I in the meanwhile have grown old."

In the twentieth century, scarcely a composer or a musical institution of note has been untouched by war. After a long illness, Claude Debussy died in March 1918 during a fierce German bombardment of Paris. Igor Stravinsky's life was transformed by the revolution in his native Russia and by two world wars. Alban Berg and Arnold Schoenberg served briefly in the Austrian Army during the First World War, and Edgard Varèse served in the French army. All three were discharged because of ill health. At the end of 1916, just before the Russian Revolution broke out, Sergei Rachmaninoff was forced to flee Russia. Anton Webern was accidentally killed near the end of the Second World War by an American soldier in an occupied zone of Austria.

The First World War weakened most of Europe's great orchestras and led to the closing of many conservatories of music. During the Second World War,

FIGURE 29.4 *The Spirit of '76.* War and music have a long association; as the novelist Arthur Koestler observed, "The most persistent sound which reverberates through men's history is the beating of war drums."

when Richard Strauss was recording several of his works with the Vienna Philharmonic, the absence of many of the orchestra's regular musicians resulted in understandably poor performances. In fact, the Philharmonic was referred to in those years as the *Witwenorchester* ("Widows' Orchestra").

Life has not been much easier for those composers who managed to escape the arena of war. In 1933 Schoenberg and his family fled the Nazis and stopped briefly in France before traveling to the United States. Like many other refugees, he tried to adjust to the American way of life but found it bewildering. Writing to a European friend about job prospects, he advised:

> Be very careful. Here they go in for much more politeness than we do. Above all, one never makes a scene; one never contradicts; one never says: "to be quite honest," but if one does, one takes good care not really to be so. Differences of opinion are something one keeps entirely to oneself. . . . Everything must be said amiably, smiling, always with a smile.

Eventually, Schoenberg managed to adjust to life in America. Bartók never did. While still in Budapest, he had written prophetically to a friend:

*continued*

It is surely unpleasant enough for me to live so near the clutches of the Nazis—which means, entirely in their clutches; but if I could live elsewhere, it wouldn't be any easier. . . .

After emigrating to America over a tortuous route that took them through France and Spain (much of their luggage was confiscated, though some of it caught up with them almost a year later), the Bartóks tried gamely to adjust to life in America. But two years after their arrival, Bartók wrote in his faltering English to a friend in Seattle:

Our situation is getting daily worse and worse. All I can say is that never in my life since I earn my livelihood (that is from my 20th year) have I been in such a dreadful situation as I will be probably very soon. . . . I am rather pessimistic, I lost all confidence in people, in countries, in everything.

Many other talented musicians uprooted by the war have found refuge in the United States: the violinist Jascha Heifetz (1901–1986), the pianist Artur Schnabel (1882–1951; the foremost Beethoven interpreter of his day), the composer/pianist Sergei Rachmaninoff (1873–1943), and many of the principal players in American symphony orchestras.

Regardless of their political affiliations, artists in many countries have spoken out on issues of war and peace. Ives spoke with characteristic bluntness:

Who makes war? The People? NO, THE POLITICIANS. . . .
Who gets it in the neck? The Politicians? NO, THE PEOPLE.

Three decades of cultural exchanges between the United States, eastern Europe, the Soviet Union, and China have done much to dispel distrust based on ignorance and superstition. The string of mostly peaceful democratic revolutions that took place during the latter half of 1989 offers some hope. If a playwright (Bronislav Havel) can be elected prime minister of a country (Czechoslovakia) that a few months earlier was controlled by a rigid totalitarian regime, then a world free of war may one day become a reality.

# TRADITIONALISTS

Although many composers embraced the new styles of the 1920s, several of the most popular did not. The differences among these traditionalists loom larger than the similarities, but they had at least one trait in common: All were committed to one form of tonality or another. Moreover, most of them cultivated such traditional genres as concerto, symphony, and opera. Whereas bold innovators regularly attract attention in studies of musical style, more traditional composers tend to be overlooked and undervalued. Their contributions to musical life are well worth our attention, however.

FIGURE 29.5  Of Sergei Rachmaninoff, Stravinsky recalled, "He was the only pianist I have ever seen who did not grimace. That is a great deal."

### Sergei Rachmaninoff (1873–1943): *Rhapsody on a Theme of Paganini* (1934)

A brooding and intense man, Sergei Rachmaninoff (Figure 29.5) somehow managed to shun the lure of modernism. His wealthy father had squandered much of his fortune before Sergei was born, and when Rachmaninoff was nine the family estate was sold and the family moved to the imperial capital of St. Petersburg. Rachmaninoff revealed his musical talent in informal lessons with his mother, and he was enrolled in the St. Petersburg Conservatory at an early age. There he met Tchaikovsky, who had a powerful influence on him. On his graduation in 1891 he was awarded the Conservatory's Gold Medal, only the third time it had been conferred. At the age of 18 he was already regarded as a world-class pianist and a composer of great promise.

Rachmaninoff's best-known piano piece was (and still is) the Prelude in C-sharp Minor, which he composed in 1892. Over the years, audiences demanded this piece so frequently as an encore that he came to detest it. His First Symphony (1895) met with sharp criticism, and he sank into a long depression, the first of recurring mood swings that persisted throughout his life. In 1900, after recovering, he returned to composing and completed his second, and most popular, piano concerto in 1901. He made his London debut in 1899 and toured America for the first time in 1909.

A brilliant concert pianist, Rachmaninoff specialized in the Romantic repertoire, especially the works of Schumann, Chopin, Liszt, Scriabin, and, of course, his own. In 1921 the Rachmaninoffs bought a large house in Manhattan, where they employed Russian servants and a Russian chef and entertained their Russian friends. Over the next two decades Rachmaninoff toured the world as a concert pianist and continued to write works for piano, orchestra, or both. (He also wrote operas, none of which has entered the standard repertory.)

Although Rachmaninoff must have been familiar with the music of his countrymen Stravinsky, Prokofiev, and Shostakovich, and with the works of Schoenberg and Bartók, in his own compositions he adopted a post-Romantic style that remained essentially unchanged throughout his career. His achievement is a reminder that great music is not the exclusive domain of innovators.

Rachmaninoff performed his *Rhapsody on a Theme of Paganini* for piano and orchestra, composed in 1934, in Baltimore for the first time. For his theme, he chose the last of the 24 caprices that Paganini had published as Op. 1. In that caprice, Paganini had used the theme as the basis for a set of 11 virtuosic variations. Earlier, Brahms and Liszt had used the same theme. The shape of the theme recalls bar form: an opening 4-bar *a*-phrase that repeats, and an 8-bar *b*-phrase that descends through an octave:

Rachmaninoff opens his *Rhapsody* with a dramatic curtain based on the 4-note "turn" figure at the end of bar 1. He then uses the bass line for the first variation (a trick used by Beethoven in the last movement of his *Eroica* Symphony). The five variations that follow (nos. 2–6) remain mostly within the tempo and style of Paganini, though Variation 6 introduces coquettish starts and stops.

The second group of variations (nos. 7–10) incorporate the *Dies irae* from the Mass for the Dead. For Variation 9, Rachmaninoff directs the strings to play *col legno* (with the wood of the bow), recalling Berlioz's Witches' Sabbath (page 391). Here he takes greater liberties with Paganini's harmonies and phrase structure, though he never abandons the theme entirely.

The third group of variations (nos. 11–15) modulates away from the home key, as in a sonata movement, moving first to the minor and then to the major mode. Variations 11 and 12 (the last labeled "Tempo di Minuetto") serve as a slow interlude, and Variation 15 is a breakneck scherzando played by the soloist. The fourth group (nos. 16–18) modulates, as in a development, to the keys most remote from the tonic. Variations 16 and 17, in the minor mode, create a sense of anticipation and longing that are fulfilled in Variation 18, which builds to a lyrical climax.

The fifth (nos. 19–22) and sixth (nos. 23–24) groups of variations reestablish, by way of a short bridge, the original theme, tempo, and key. Here Rachmaninoff introduces two fiery cadenzas of the sort common in concertos. A final statement of the *Dies Irae* combines the chorale texture of Variation 7 with the march tempo of Variation 10. The work ends with a brief coda in which fireworks give way to a return of the opening mode.

There is nothing especially innovative about this set of variations—in fact, it could have been composed anytime after 1890. Yet it is elegantly constructed and overflows with sparkling melodies. Though it has been performed countless times, it has kept its freshness over the years.

## Benjamin Britten (1913–1976): *Peter Grimes* (1945), Act III, End of Scene 1 through Scene 2

England had produced many talented composers over the years, the most talented of whom was Henry Purcell in the seventeenth century. But with the rise of instrumental music and opera in Italy at the end of that century, followed by the domination of Austro-German composers in the eighteenth and nineteenth centuries, English composers had long been overshadowed by their contemporaries on the Continent.

Then, in the twentieth century, several acclaimed English composers emerged: Edward Elgar (1857–1934), Frederick Delius (1862–1934), Ralph Vaughan Williams (1872–1958), William Walton (1902–1983), Michael Tippett (b. 1905), Benjamin Britten (1913–1976), and Peter Maxwell Davies (b. 1934). With the exception of Davies, these composers have favored rather conservative styles, as had most English composers of the past. Of the group, Benjamin Britten has gained the most lasting popularity.

Throughout his career, Britten gave careful consideration to *context:*

> When I am asked to compose a work for an occasion, great or small, I want to know in some detail the conditions of the place where it will be performed, the size and acoustics, what instruments or singers will be available and suitable, the kind of people who will hear it, and the language they will understand—and even sometimes the age of the listeners and performers. . . . It is the easiest thing in the world to write a piece virtually or totally impossible to perform—but . . . that is not what I prefer to do; I prefer to study the conditions of performance and shape my music to them.

Britten created an impressive body of music for children and young people, notably his *Young Person's Guide to the Orchestra*. His eclectic style draws freely on a variety of nineteenth-century and early twentieth-century styles. During his early career Britten composed a wide range of instrumental and vocal music, but as he matured he concentrated almost exclusively on music for the theater, producing 11 operas that reinterpret Romantic opera in twentieth-century terms.

After graduating from the Royal College of Music in 1934, Britten sensed that the music he had been studying was insular and provincial. After hearing a performance of *Wozzeck*, he announced that he was planning to study with Berg. His family and teachers dissuaded him from doing so, however. In 1939 he emigrated to America with the tenor Peter Pears, his lifelong companion. While browsing in a Los Angeles bookstore, Britten came across a copy of *Peter Grimes*, a poem by the British pastor and poet George Crabbe. The story sparked his interest and reminded him of his English roots. Britten returned to Britain in 1942, and during the crossing he began a choral work called *A Ceremony of Carols*. That work was the first in a series that brought new life to English music.

Back in England, Britten set to work on an opera based on Crabbe's poem, and the premiere of *Peter Grimes* took place in June 1945. Peter Grimes, the antihero of Britten's opera, is an alienated fisherman in a small fishing town on the eastern coast of England. We learn that, before the action begins, Grimes's young apprentice has been lost at sea. As the opera opens, a court finds that the boy died of "accidental circumstances." But the townspeople are suspicious and advise Grimes to choose an older man as the boy's replacement. Unable to find a fisherman willing to work with him, Grimes takes on an orphan boy as apprentice. A sympathetic widow, Ellen Orford, and a retired merchant skipper, Balstrode, try to befriend Grimes but are rebuffed. When Grimes hears a group of townspeople approaching his remote hut, he accuses the boy of carrying tales and orders him to gather up the nets and prepare to launch their boat. In his haste, the boy falls from a steep cliff near the hut and Grimes flees. When the townspeople enter the hut, although Balstrode notices the boy's Sunday clothes lying in a heap, there seems to be nothing amiss.

In Scene 1 of Act III (where Listening Guide 71 begins), no one has seen Grimes or his apprentice or his boat for two days. During a dance at Moot Hall, Mrs. Sedley—a busybody widow—bursts into The Boar (a local pub) looking for Swallow, a lawyer and the mayor of the borough. Auntie, The Boar's proprietress, fears that Mrs. Sedley's shouting will hurt business and orders her to leave. The women trade insults. During this encounter Britten adopts Verdi's practice of *parlante* ("speaking"), with the dialogue delivered over a background of dance music. Britten has the clarinet play a galop, an extremely fast ballroom dance popular in the nineteenth century. The melody constantly threatens to fly out of control, suggesting the emotional tension of the scene. Mrs. Sedley at last manages to tell Swallow that she has spotted Grimes's boat and demands an investigation.

Mrs. Sedley points out the boat to the nearsighted Swallow, who orders Carter Hobson, the borough constable, to send a posse to Grimes's hut. When Hobson protests that Grimes is still at sea, the clarinet theme turns briefly into a watery ripple before returning to the galop. While Hobson is trying to round up his posse, Mrs. Sedley savors these developments in a private reverie—the same kind of multilevel ensemble we heard in the Quartet from *Rigoletto*. A lengthy chorus follows, in which the townspeople serve as protagonist, as in Berlioz's *The Trojans*. The syncopated accompaniment of the galop continues, and the townspeople join in an elaborate fugato (recalling a similar passage at the end of Verdi's opera *Falstaff*). One last furious phrase of the galop climaxes in an unexpectedly lush "Ha, ha, ha!" chorus over a descending bass pattern. The section ends with menacing shouts of "Peter Grimes!" interrupted by snatches of the frantic galop.

In the orchestral interlude that follows (the sixth interlude in the opera, sometimes played as a separate suite), Britten provides a transition from the angry

*(Text continues on page 670.)*

# *Listening Guide 71*

### BRITTEN: *Peter Grimes*, Act III,
### End of Scene 1 through Scene 2

CD 7, TRACK 12
TAPE 7B, TRACK 3
DURATION: 20:26

*Despite Britten's open borrowing of various techniques of Romantic opera (parlante, multilevel ensembles, protagonist choruses, fugato, a mad scene) in earlier scenes, these final scenes unfold seamlessly in an individual and compelling style.*

*Form: Through-composed*

| TEXT | TIME | COMMENTS |
|---|---|---|
| **1** MRS. SEDLEY:<br>Mr. Swallow! Mr. Swallow! I want the lawyer Swallow! | **0:00** | In parlante style, dialogue occurs over the galop in the background. |
| AUNTIE:<br>What do you want? | 0:22 | The galop melody is carried by the syncopated clarinet, while Mrs. Sedley and Auntie carry on their parlante argument. |
| MRS. SEDLEY:<br>I want the lawyer Swallow! | | |
| AUNTIE:<br>He's busy! | | |
| MRS. SEDLEY:<br>Fetch him please, this is official. Bus'ness about the Borough criminal. Please do as I tell you! | | |
| AUNTIE:<br>My customers come here for peace, for quiet, away from you and all such nuisances! | 0:35 | Auntie's highly chromatic melody reflects her annoyance. |
| MRS. SEDLEY:<br>This is an insult! | 0:44 | Singing simultaneously, the women show their contempt for each other.<br>The syncopated rhythms of the galop continue in the background. |
| AUNTIE:<br>You'll find as long as I am here, you'll find that I always speak my mind! My customers come here, they take their drink, they take their ease. | | |
| SWALLOW:<br>Hi! What's the matter? Tell me what's the matter. What is it? What's all this noise about? Hi! | **0:57** | Swallow enters and his cries add to the tumult. The passage ends with Auntie going back inside The Boar and slamming the door. |

| TEXT | TIME | COMMENTS |
|------|------|----------|

**MRS. SEDLEY:**
I'll have you know your place, you baggage!

**AUNTIE:**
As long as I am here, you'll find that I will speak my mind! Good night!

**MRS. SEDLEY:**
Look!

**SWALLOW:**
I'm short-sighted, you know.

**MRS. SEDLEY:**
Look! It's Grimes's boat, back at last!

**SWALLOW:**
That's different! Hey! Is Hobson there? Is Hobson there?

1:06 — While they discuss in parlante the reappearance of Grimes's boat, the clarinet plays a fast and furious version of the galop melody. The drumbeat adds to the urgency.

**HOBSON:**
Ay, ay, sir!

**MRS. SEDLEY:**
Good, now things are moving, and about time too!

**SWALLOW:**
You're constable of the Borough, Carter Hobson.

**HOBSON:**
Ay, ay, sir!

**SWALLOW:**
As the mayor, I ask you to find Peter Grimes! Take whatever help you need.

1:16 — Hobson answers Swallow in crisp military fashion. While the two men talk, Mrs. Sedley savors her pleasure in the renewed search for Grimes.

**HOBSON:**
Now what I claims is he's out at sea.

The clarinet melody briefly takes on a rippling character to suggest the ocean.

**SWALLOW:**
But there's his boat.

The drumbeat is replaced by an ominous pedal point that suggests the bottomless depths of the sea.

**HOBSON:**
Oh! We'll send a posse to his hut.

| TEXT | TIME | COMMENTS |
|---|---|---|
| SWALLOW:<br>If he's not there, you'll search the shore, the marsh, the field, the streets, the Borough. | | |
| HOBSON:<br>Ay, ay, sir!<br>Hey there! Come out and help!<br>Grimes is around! Hey there! Come on! Come on! | 1:43 | While Hobson engages in "action," Mrs. Sedley withdraws to a "psychological" plane. |
| MRS. SEDLEY:<br>Crime, that's my hobby, is by cities hoarded. Rarely are country minds lifted to murder, the noblest of my crimes which are my study. And now the crime is here and I am ready! | | |
| **2**    CHORUS:<br>Who holds himself apart, lets his pride rise.<br>Him who despises us we'll destroy!<br>And cruelty becomes his enterprise.<br>Him who despises us we'll destroy!<br>*[Mrs. Sedley and others join in]* | **2:00** | The chorus expresses the citizens' intolerance of nonconformists. The syncopated galop rhythm continues to provide continuity. |
| Our curse shall fall on his evil day!<br>We shall tame his arrogance! Who holds, etc. Our curse shall fall on him! Him who despises us we'll destroy! | 2:43 | |
| | **3:17** | The chorus drives the point home with an elaborate fugato. |
| [Furious galop] | 3:57 | The brass and percussion play *fortissimo*. |
| **3**    Ha, ha, ha!<br>We'll make the murd'rer pay, we'll make him pay for his crime! | **4:03** | In an unexpectedly lush, triadic passage, the chorus seems to revel in its hatred. |
| Peter Grimes! [repeated] | 4:45 | Interrupted by snatches of the galop. |
| Peter Grimes! | 5:20 | Follows a dramatic rest. |
| Grimes! | 5:28 | Foghorns represented by muted French horns. |
| **4**    INTERLUDE VI:<br>     Drumroll, flute | **5:45** | Furious orchestral outburst dies to solo flute. |

*continued*

| TEXT | TIME | COMMENTS |
|---|---|---|
| Pizzicato strings | 6:17 | Foghorns continue. |
| 3 violins, oboe | 6:31 | Poignant melody in high register. |
| Clarinets (crescendo and decrescendo) | 6:59 | Pale echoes of the galop rhythms. |
| Oboe, crescendo | 7:24 | Built on string tremolos. |
| Rich chord | 7:57 | Widely spaced, *fortissimo*. |
| CHORUS *[distant]*: Peter Grimes! | 8:22 | Tuba as foghorn; the chorus continues. |

**5** GRIMES:

| | | |
|---|---|---|
| Steady! There you are! Nearly home! | **8:30** | Grimes sings in a halting recitative, recalling mad scenes in Romantic opera. |
| GRIMES *[continuing]*: What is home? Calm as deep water. Where's my home? Deep in calm water. Water will drink my sorrows dry, and the tide will turn. | 8:35 | Sung unaccompanied. Throughout this scene we become aware that Grimes has lost his grip on reality. |
| CHORUS *[distant]*: Grimes! | 9:12 | The crowd is never far away. |
| GRIMES: Steady! There you are! Nearly home! The first one died, just died. The other slipped, and died . . . and the third will . . . | | Grimes recalls the fate of his two apprentices and hints at the fate of a third. He feels more and more like a caged animal. |
| "Accidental circumstances." | **9:35** | A direct reference to the court's finding in Act I. |
| Water will drink his sorrows, my sorrows dry, and the tide will turn. | 9:38 | Unaccompanied. |
| CHORUS *[distant]*: Peter Grimes! | 9:55 | |
| GRIMES: Peter Grimes! Here you are! Here I am! Hurry, hurry! Hurry! Hurry, hurry! Now is gossip put on trial. | 10:04 | Grimes lashes out angrily at the distant crowd. |
| Bring the branding iron and knife, for what's done now is done for life! | 10:11 | Sung unaccompanied in a singsong, nonsense fashion. As the scene progresses, Grimes darts from one subject to another. |

| TEXT | TIME | COMMENTS |
|---|---|---|
| Come on! Land me! "Turn the skies back and begin again." | 10:23 | A poignant reminder of Ellen Orford's words of hope in Act I. |
| **6** CHORUS: *[distant]:*<br>Peter Grimes! | **10:46** | |
| GRIMES:<br>"Old Joe has gone fishing and young Joe has gone fishing and you'll know who's gone fishing when you land the next shoal!" | | A reference to a folk song in Act I, Scene 2. Such capricious changes of mood are typical of mad scenes. |
| CHORUS *[distant]:*<br>Peter Grimes! Grimes! | | |
| GRIMES:<br>Ellen! Give me your hand. There now, my hope is held by you. If you take it away, if you . . . | 11:10 | A last reference to Ellen Orford's compassionate support. |
| Take away your hand! The argument's finished, friendship lost, gossip is shouting, ev'rything's said. | 11:41 | Grimes suddenly turns angry. |
| CHORUS *[distant]:*<br>Peter Grimes! | 11:47 | The chorus functions as a kind of ritornello. |
| GRIMES:<br>To hell with all your mercy! To hell with your revenge. And God have mercy upon you! | | A lyrical but bitter attack on both those who defended him and those who attacked him. |
| CHORUS *[distant]:*<br>Peter Grimes! Peter Grimes! | 12:07 | Faster and more urgent than before. |
| GRIMES:<br>Do you hear them all shouting my name? D'you hear them? D'you hear them? | | Almost spoken. |
| Old Davy Jones shall answer: Come home, come home! | 12:15 | A lyrical, passionate outburst. |
| CHORUS *[closer]:*<br>Peter Grimes! | 12:28 | The mob comes closer. |

*continued*

| TEXT | TIME | COMMENTS |
|------|------|----------|
| GRIMES:<br>Peter Grimes! Grimes! Peter Grimes! | | Grimes joins in the mob's calls; he has become his own persecutor. |
| 7 ELLEN:<br>Peter, we've come to take you home. O come home out of this dreadful night! See, here's Balstrode. Peter, don't you hear me? | **13:17** | Ellen sings unaccompanied in order to get through to Grimes. But he can no longer be reached. |
| CHORUS [distant]:<br>Peter Grimes! Grimes! Peter! Peter! | 13:41 | For an agonizing moment, Balstrode and Ellen listen with Grimes to the mob. |
| GRIMES:<br>What harbour shelters peace, away from tidal waves, away from storms! What harbour can embrace terrors and tragedies! Her breast is harbour, too, where night is turned to day. | 13:58 | Grimes musters his energies to sing three parallel phrases expressing his deep desire for peace and his awareness of impending death. |
| 8 BALSTRODE:<br>Come on, I'll help you with the boat.<br>ELLEN:<br>No.<br>BALSTRODE:<br>Sail out til you lose sight of land. Then sink the boat. D'you hear? Sink her. Good-bye, Peter. | **15:14** | In one of the few spoken stretches in the opera, Balstrode's words convey a finality that even the music cannot. Balstrode knows—and Ellen must acknowledge—that there will be no reasoning with the crowd. Neither asks how the second apprentice died. |
| [Dawn comes to the Borough.] | 15:44 | The return of Interlude I brings the opera full circle; nothing has changed. |
| 9 CHORUS:<br>To those who pass the Borough sounds betray the cold beginning of another day. And houses sleeping by the waterside wake to the measured ripple of the tide. | **16:59** | Progresses from a solo soprano, to all the sopranos, to all the sopranos and the altos. The deep major harmony that underlies this passage is mixed with the high notes in the violins from the minor mode. |

| TEXT | TIME | COMMENTS |
|------|------|----------|
| SWALLOW:<br>There's a boat sinking out at sea, coast guard reports. | 18:00 | Delivered matter-of-factly. The deep harmony symbolizes the unchanging nature of the sea. |
| FISHERMAN:<br>Within reach? | | Swallow and the fisherman do not protest; both sing on the same major chord. |
| SWALLOW:<br>No. | | |
| FISHERMAN:<br>Let's have a look thro' the glasses. | | |
| CHORUS:<br>Or measured cadence of the lads who tow some entered hoy to fix her in her row. Or hollow sound that from the passing bell to some departed spirit bids farewell. | **18:18** | Sung by the tenors and basses, representing the fisherman. A "hoy" is a small craft used to ferry passengers between a large ship and shore. |
| AUNTIE *[comes to pub door]*:<br>What is it? | 18:56 | Auntie and the fisherman Boles dismiss the sinking as a rumor. Grimes's death will leave no mark on this tightly knit community. |
| BOLES:<br>Nothing I can see. | | |
| AUNTIE:<br>One of these rumors! | | |
| *[The nieces emerge and begin to polish the brasses outside The Boar.]* | | |
| **10** ALL:<br>In ceaseless motion comes and goes the tide, flowing it fills the channel broad and wide. Then back to sea with strong majestic sweep, it rolls in ebb yet terrible and deep. | **19:06** | As the new day begins, the community acknowledges the supremacy of the ocean, the "anchor" of their precarious existence. Life, like the tide, is a "ceaseless motion." The music flows and ebbs. |
| *[The curtain falls slowly.]* | 20:15 | Britten withdraws the comforting major harmony and leaves us with a bittersweet minor. |

mob to the disoriented Grimes. Britten's mood painting here is cinematic (earlier, Britten had written scores for documentary films). As Grimes staggers onto the stage, we hear the angry chorus in the distance.

In the second part of this scene, Britten presents a version of the Romantic "mad scenes" that were popular in the operas of the 1830s and 1840s. For example, in Donizetti's *Lucia di Lammermoor*, the distraught heroine goes mad when she is forced to marry a man she does not love. Such scenes were usually delivered in a halting recitative with only meager accompaniment, with sharp changes of mood and with distorted echoes of earlier speeches. Britten uses similar devices in this powerful scene.

When Ellen Orford and Captain Balstrode find Grimes, Balstrode—in the only unaccompanied speech in the opera—orders him to "sail out til you lose sight of land. Then sink the boat." In his understated farewell, Balstrode saves Grimes from being torn apart by the approaching mob.

In the final scene, the same interlude music that preceded Act I ushers in the dawn. A rich mixture of minor-chord tones in the upper register, a major chord in the middle register, and deep pedal tones suggest the deep, unchanging sea. Someone has sighted a boat sinking offshore, but no one asks whose it is. Grimes's death has changed nothing, and life goes on.

The parallels between *Peter Grimes* and Berg's *Wozzeck* are obvious. Both deal with antiheroes crushed by impersonal, external forces. For Berg, however, Wozzeck is a symbol of oppressed humanity, whereas Britten is more concerned with the personal tragedy of Peter Grimes. Although we condemn the intolerance of the townspeople toward Grimes, we never quite give him our sympathy or trust—he may be guilty of unstated evils after all. Britten refrains from passing judgment and simply lets the story play itself out to its tragic conclusion.

## MUSIC FOR FILMS

Traditional musical styles have found perhaps their most enduring home in the twentieth century in music for films, one of the few areas where art music and pop music interact freely. A sound track by Prince seems no more novel to movie audiences than a sound track by Aaron Copland or Leonard Bernstein.

The silent films of the early 1900s were generally accompanied by a theater organ (Figure 29.6). The organist worked in a pit in front of the screen where he or she could observe the action and improvise music to suit the situation—soft, tender harmonies for a love scene and rapid, vigorous music for a chase. Many of these early films were less than 30 minutes long and were shot from a single camera angle. Since the plots were predictable, the organists simply drew on a collection of special effects as needed.

The American director D. W. Griffith (1875–1948), a pioneer in film technique, introduced the fade-in and fade-out, the long shot and the close-up, and the moving-camera shot. His elaborate 1915 film *The Birth of a Nation* was the

FIGURE 29.6 By 1910, grand movie palaces (like the Alabama Theatre in Birmingham pictured here) featured the "Mighty Wurlitzer" organ, designed to reproduce the sounds of an orchestra.

first full-length film masterpiece. Such films were shown in ornate movie houses across the country accompanied by a live orchestra that played a mix of familiar and original pieces. By the 1920s, when going to the movies had become a national pastime, hundreds of musicians earned their living playing in movie theaters. In 1927 *The Jazz Singer*, starring Al Jolson, was the first film to include spoken dialogue, and in 1928 *Lights of New York* was the first all-talking picture. By 1938 more than 80 million Americans were going to the movies every week—some 65 percent of the population.

The studios that had sprung up to meet the demand for new movies now began to hire staff composers who could turn out music on a tight schedule. Typically, a composer would watch the rough take of each scene and then would go off to compose suitable music for it—all in the same day. The music was copied overnight, rehearsed briefly the next day, and recorded in a single take by a studio orchestra. The music for many early films was written by teams of anonymous composers.

FIGURE 29.7 Among the many movies Max Steiner scored are *King Kong, A Star Is Born, Sergeant York, Casablanca,* and *The Treasure of the Sierra Madre.*

The first generation of successful film composers consisted almost entirely of European émigrés, whose music is rooted in the post-Romantic idiom of Mahler and Strauss. The greatest of these composers was Max Steiner (1888–1971; Figure 29.7), who was born and raised in Vienna. At the age of 13, he completed an eight-year course of study in one year and went on to study with Mahler. By the age of 16 he was a professional conductor. He emigrated to the United States in 1914 and earned his living conducting and orchestrating Broadway musicals.

In 1929, when studios began to commission music for the new talkies, Steiner moved to Hollywood. Between 1929 and 1965, he scored almost 200 films for RKO and Warners. He pioneered the use of theme music, derived from the Wagnerian leitmotif—notably "Tara's Theme" from *Gone with the Wind.*

Among the other European composers who found their way to Hollywood was Erich Korngold (1897–1957), another Austrian prodigy who knew Mahler. Even native-born American composers, like Alfred Newman (1900–1970), studied with Europeans. For two decades (1940–1960), as head of the music department at 20th Century Fox, Newman composed the music for 250 films, including *The Hunchback of Notre Dame* and *Wuthering Heights* (both 1939), *Cry of the City* (1948), and *The Robe* (1953). That music won him nine Academy Awards. Like Steiner and Korngold, Newman's greatest debt is to Mahler, who was composing "cinematic" music before movies even existed.

Several major composers of art music have also written for film, including Aaron Copland, William Walton, and Sergei Prokofiev—even Schoenberg explored the possibility. Yet the most successful film composers have been those who were willing to accept a supporting role by enhancing the action taking place on the screen. Among the most original of those composers was Bernard Herrmann.

## Bernard Herrmann (1911–1975): Music from the Film *Journey to the Centre of the Earth* (1959)

FIGURE 29.8 Starting at the top: Bernard Herrmann wrote his first movie score for *Citizen Kane*. Of all the directors and producers he worked for, Herrmann said Orson Welles was the only one who knew anything about music.

Bernard Herrmann (Figure 29.8) was born in New York City, where he studied with European-trained composers. By the time he was 20, he was leading his own chamber orchestra in performances of works by American composers. From 1942 to 1959 he was chief conductor of the CBS Symphony Orchestra, and between 1941 and 1971 he composed the scores for 50 films.

Herrmann set high standards for himself and refused to work under pressure. He sometimes specified unusual ensembles. For the score of *Psycho* (1960), for example, he used only strings. He regarded music as an essential element of film, not just an embellishment. He once remarked:

> I would say that every director has a dream—that is, to make a film without music. But it is not possible. . . . You see, cinema is an illusion, and it is the combination of the camera, photography, music, and, of course, the word that creates the illusion of what is known as cinema.

Herrmann was a post-Romantic in both training and disposition, but his film scores are unmistakably individual. Commenting on his score for *Journey to the Centre of the Earth* (1959; Listening Guide 72), based on the novel by Jules Verne, he wrote:

> I decided to evoke the mood and feelings of inner Earth by using only instruments placed in low registers. Eliminating all strings, I utilized an orchestra of woodwinds and brass, with a large percussion section and many harps. . . . I wanted to create an atmosphere with absolutely no human contact and I eliminated all strings as a way of doing it.

# Listening Guide 72

## HERRMANN: From the Film
### *Journey to the Centre of the Earth*

CD 8, TRACK 3
TAPE 8B, TRACK 1
DURATION: 15:01

*The success of this evocative score results in large part from Herrmann's skillful exploitation of brass, wind, and electronic colors. Themes as such play a secondary role.*

*Form: Episodic, with unifying chorale*

| LOCATION | TIME | COMMENTS |
|---|---|---|
| **1** **Mountain Top and Sunrise (Prelude)** | | |
| Fanfare | **0:00** | A 5-note call in the brass with two distant echoes. |
| Arpeggios | 0:33 | In the harps, cascading in overlapping patterns. |
| Ascent | 0:52 | From the depths, contrabassoon up to trumpets. |
| Chords | 1:31 | Sunburst in the organ, brass, timpani, harps. |
| Arpeggios | 1:49 | In the harps, cascading in overlapping patterns. |
| **2** **The Grotto: Descent** | **2:13** | Massive chords in the organ, descending relentlessly. |
| Cymbal crashes | 3:41 | Four, evenly spaced, announcing the arrival at the earth's core. |
| **3** **The Giant Chameleon and The Fight** | | |
| Trills | **5:22** | Descending trills over the cascading harp arpeggios. |
| More trills | 5:43 | In winds and trumpet over harp and bassoon. |
| Pedal point | 5:54 | Low, giving way to slow brass chords. |
| Chorale | 6:19 | In the muted trumpet, echoed by the clarinets. |
| Chorale | 6:43 | Alternation between the brass and wind echoes. |
| Waiting | 7:08 | Bass clarinet, other winds. |
| Chorale | 7:37 | Muted trumpets. |
| Cadence | 7:50 | Three sudden, harsh chords in the brass and clarinets. |
| **4** **The Shaft** | | |
| Chorale | **8:08** | Eerie, ghostly textures, from organ to *ondes martenot*. |
| **5** **Finale** | | |
| Bleating ↔ Chorale | **11:00** | Alternation between the *ondes martenot* and the chorale. |
| Chorale ↔ Bleating | 12:00 | Low (timpani and *ondes martenot*), rising and falling. |
| Final ascent | 13:04 | Relentlessly rising, dissonant. |
| Chorale | 14:13 | Full brass triads (announced by percussion) with organ echoes. |

### Pierre Boulez (b. 1925): *Le marteau sans maître*
### (The hammer without a master) (1954)

Pierre Boulez was born in a small town in the Loire Valley in south-central France. His father, a wealthy industrialist, decided that his son, who had a special aptitude for mathematics, should become an engineer. At the age of 17 Boulez flouted his father's wishes and tried to enroll in the Paris Conservatory rather than in the Polytechnical School. Although he failed the Conservatory's keyboard entrance exam, he was soon admitted and joined the famous harmony and analysis classes of Olivier Messiaen (b. 1908). Messiaen, an organist and composer, had devised a system of rhythm based on the music of India and used the songs of birds as a source of thematic ideas. His wide-ranging classes touched on music from Beethoven to the present day and attracted talented young composers from all over Europe. Although Boulez's developing style diverged from that of his teacher, Messiaen quickly recognized Boulez's ability to analyze complex musical scores and encouraged him to follow his own bent.

Boulez rejected the work of the French neoclassicists Francis Poulenc (1899–1963) and Darius Milhaud (1892–1974) and argued, first, that atonality, and later, serialism, were the only proper paths for a contemporary composer to follow. Anything else, he said bluntly, was "of no use." In 1949 he published a brief article titled "Schoenberg Is Dead," the first of many articles he was to publish on contemporary music. In this article Boulez pointed out what he regarded as a logical contradiction in Schoenberg's experiment. He admitted that the serialization of pitch was an innovation of great historical importance, but he complained that Schoenberg had cloaked this radical notion in "a reactionary attitude: . . . the persistence of accompanied melody, for example; of counterpoint based on a principal part and secondary parts." In short, Boulez declared that Schoenberg's music was "stereotyped writing representing . . . the most ostentatious and obsolete romanticism." Boulez replaced romanticism with "asceticism." Citing Webern's more radical experiments, he mused that "perhaps one could generalize the serial principle to the four sound-constituents: pitch, duration, intensity and attack, timbre"—known as "total serialism."

This is exactly what Boulez did in a 35-minute, nine-movement work that he introduced at a contemporary music festival in Baden, Germany, in 1955. In *Le marteau sans maître* (The hammer without a master) he took as his text three brief Surrealist poems by a contemporary French poet, René Char (see Listening Guide 73). Surrealism, founded by a French poet in 1924 under the influence of Freud, explored the language of dreams, in which words have associations and implications but no set meanings. There are many associations here—"red" and "knife" with "corpse," "workhorses" with "caravan" or even "prison"—but few literal meanings. Moreover, there is no punctuation to help us group the words into ideas. The music works in much the same way—by the association of sounds rather than by the grouping of discrete phrases.

Boulez integrates and interweaves the three poems into three quasi-independent song cycles. He scored the work for alto flute (a larger, deeper version of the standard flute), xylophone, vibraphone, percussion, guitar, and viola. The

# *Listening Guide 73*

BOULEZ: Movement III, "the furious artisan,"
from *Le marteau sans maître* (The hammer without a master)

CD 8, TRACK 4
TAPE 8A, TRACK 3
DURATION: 2:26

*In this setting, Boulez stresses words that earlier composers would have underplayed
("the," "at," "of," "and"; shown below in capital letters). The breaks in the vocal line
(shown by ruled lines in the Time column) do not reflect any regular musical structure.
Although the movement is notated with great precision, it has an improvisatory air.*

*Form: Through-composed*

| | TEXT | TIME | COMMENTS |
|---|---|---|---|
| 1 | CURTAIN | 0:00 | Flute solo, rhythmic bursts in wide leaps. |
| | *LA roulotte rouge*<br>THE red caravan | 0:12 | Solo voice, similar though independent line. |
| | *AU bord*<br>AT the edge | 0:22 | Flutter-tonguing in flute. |
| | *DU clou*<br>OF the prison | 0:28 | Characterized by wide leaps. |
| 2 | *ET cadavre dans le*<br>AND a corpse in the | 0:42 | Largely duet texture begun by the flute, with lines that are similar yet independent. |
| | *PANIER*<br>BASKET | 0:58 | A long melisma, overlapping with . . . |
| 3 | | 1:16 | . . . the flute, which moves to flutter-tonguing. |
| | *et chevaux DE labours*<br>and horses OF work<br>(i.e., workhorses) | 1:19 | |
| | *dans le fer À CHEVAL*<br>in the shoes OF HORSES<br>(i.e., horseshoes) | 1:28 | The vocal line slows. |
| | | 1:42 | A long "melisma" in the flute. |
| 4 | *je rêve LA tête*<br>I dream, THE head | 1:46 | Angular line. |
| | *sur LA pointe de mon*<br>on THE point of my | 1:58 | Vocal line rises to "THE" instead of "point." Final "cadential" flutter-tongue in flute, played "without nuance." |
| | *couteau LE Pérou*<br>knife, THE Peru | | |

percussionist employs a battery of instruments (clearly derived from Varèse): snare drum, two pairs of bongos, maracas, claves, tubular chimes, triangle, tam-tams, and suspended cymbal. Such unconventional groupings of instruments had become the norm for avant-garde composers. Unlike the string quartet or the piano trio of earlier days, contemporary music ensembles invariably include several performers who play "as needed." In four of the nine movements an alto voice sings Char's poems (the third poem is sung twice). Hence the sonority of the work is primarily in the alto range—a range that Romantic composers had seldom explored. Each movement of *Le marteau* calls for a different group of instruments. For example, movement III calls for only alto flute and voice, whereas movement VII calls for the entire ensemble.

The five purely instrumental movements (I, II, IV, VII, and VIII) serve as preludes, postludes, or commentaries on the four texted movements (III, V, VI, and IX). Movement III·(the vocal setting of "the furious artisan" outlined in Listening Guide 73) is a good illustration of Boulez's style. The musical language of this brief movement is overtly anti-Romantic. Almost all of the expressive melismas in the vocal line (shown in capital letters in the translation) occur on insignificant words like "the" or "and." Moreover, Boulez breaks the lines into parts, further undermining the "meaning" of the text. And nowhere does he repeat even a small musical phrase.

Bursts of rhythmic activity employing wide intervals (most often sevenths and ninths, which are slightly smaller or larger than an octave) demand extreme agility on the part of the singer. The flute employs the technique of flutter-tonguing, in which the performer rolls an *r* on the tip of the tongue to produce a rapid, staccato barrage of sound. The singer and the flute are not in conflict, but their commentaries seem largely independent of one another. As a result, there is almost no sense of harmony and consequently no sense of dissonance. The dynamics gradations are as wide as those in a Romantic work (from *pp* to *ff*), but they occur so rapidly that long lines never develop.

Except in a general sense, it is impossible to grasp the serialization that Boulez assures us underlies his work. Yet the perfection of the musical language somehow captures the elusive imagery of the poetry. The precision, almost abstraction, of the singing reflects the nervous images in the text, and the rhythmic bursts and the absence of any conventional pulse give the music a rhapsodic, improvisatory quality well suited to the dreamlike state.

Some people complain that Boulez is antimusical. Actually, he is one of the most distinguished conductors of our time, excelling in his interpretations of works by Debussy, Berg, and Mahler as well as contemporary works. So his musicality can hardly be questioned. After leading the New York Philharmonic for several turbulent seasons, Boulez was named by the French government in 1978 as head of its experimental music center known as IRCAM (Figure 30.1). In the United States avant-garde composers like Milton Babbitt (b. 1916) have carried Boulez's serial experiments in other directions. Boulez's published opinions have kept him at the center of debates on contemporary music, and his outspoken views (for example, that "the solution of the problem of opera" is "to blow up

FIGURE 30.1 The Institute for Research and the Coordination of Acoustics and Music (IRCAM), headed by Pierre Boulez, promotes collaboration between musicians and scientists in generating new music.

the opera houses") have sometimes obscured his unsentimental analysis of contemporary music and culture.

## THE ELECTRONIC AGE

The electrification of the world has revolutionized the way music is created, performed, and consumed. In fact, we seem to be nearing the time when electronic instruments will be more common than acoustic* instruments. We already live in an electronic age of radios, tape recorders, cassette decks, Walkmen, electronic keyboards, and synthesizers (see the Historical Window on page 686). If someone were suddenly to pull the plug, much of our music-making would cease.

Electronic instruments have been around almost as long as the first commercial use of electricity itself. In 1876, the year in which Alexander Graham Bell introduced the telephone, Elisha Gray (1835–1901) introduced a 2-octave "musical telegraph." In 1915 Lee de Forest (1873–1961) patented a simple electronic piano (though apparently he never built it). The first electronic instrument to be put to use was the "Theremin," invented by a Russian radio engineer and cellist of French descent, Léon Thérémin (b. 1896), who introduced it in 1920. In this remarkable monophonic instrument, the frequency of the pitch is controlled by the distance of the performer's hand from a vertical antenna. As early as 1924, composers were using the Theremin in orchestral works, and in 1929 RCA began to manufacture the instrument in the United States. Subsequently, a French inventor, Maurice Martenot (1898–1980), invented an even

*Acoustic instruments are instruments that produce sound without benefit of electricity.

FIGURE 30.2 With a key-
board and separate
speaker cabinet, the
*ondes martenot* produces
only one note at a time.

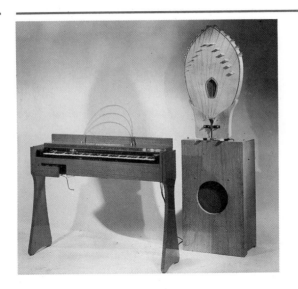

more versatile instrument called the *ondes martenot* ("Martenot wave"; Figure
30.2) With a range from below that of the contrabassoon to above that of the
piccolo, and with a wailing tone resembling the human voice, the *ondes martenot*
has been used by several generations of composers, including Varèse and Boulez.
The instrument is still being manufactured today.*

Starting in the 1930s, electronic instruments were used for a wide variety of
orchestral, stage, and film music. The sound of these instruments usually differed
dramatically from the sound of acoustic instruments, but in other respects the
works composed for them were in rather conventional forms. Karlheinz Stockhausen, a young German composer, was the first to use the new sounds to create
a new musical language.

### Karlheinz Stockhausen (b. 1928): *Song of the Youths* (1954–1956)

Orphaned during the Second World War, Karlheinz Stockhausen spent the last
years of the war working as a stretcher-bearer, farmhand, and rehearsal pianist.
While in high school he studied the violin, oboe, and piano and seemed headed
for a career in music education. Then, in 1951, he spent the summer at the
contemporary music institute in Darmstadt and heard the music of Webern for
the first time. Like Boulez, Stockhausen was attracted to Webern's serial aesthetic, and in 1952 he moved to Paris to study with Messiaen. There he became
interested in the physical nature of sound and after returning to Cologne started
to work at a studio for electronic music that his mentor, the critic and composer
Herbert Eimert (1897–1972), had recently set up.

---

*As we have seen, Bernard Herrmann used the *ondes martenot* in his score for the movie *Journey to
the Centre of the Earth*.

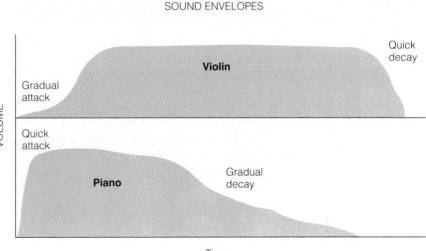

FIGURE 30.3  Stockhausen created *Song of the Youths* for five groups of loudspeakers, surrounding the audience, with the music moving freely among these sound sources. This was the first serial music to use physical space as a compositional element.

Determined to apply the principles of "total serialism" to electronically generated sounds, Stockhausen began to manipulate the simple sounds produced by a sine-wave generator. A sine-wave generator produces only the *fundamental* of a pitch, whereas an ordinary tone consists not only of the fundamental (which determines the perceived pitch) but of a series of higher frequencies known variously as *overtones, harmonics,* or *partials.* It is these higher frequencies that determine the color or timbre of the tone. Sounds produced by a sine-wave generator are described as "neutral" or "cool."

Stockhausen manipulated his sounds by passing them through simple filters or capacitors. He then transferred them to a tape recorder, a device that had become available just after the war. Every sound has a certain pattern of attack, volume, duration, and decay, known collectively as its *envelope* (Figure 30.3). With the tape recorder, Stockhausen found that he could alter the natural envelope of a sound by, for example, playing the tape backward or at different speeds. And he could superimpose one tone over another by *overdubbing** or could add an echo to a tone. He could quite literally remove the attack, duration, or decay of a tone simply by *splicing* it out.

After numerous experiments, Stockhausen created a work he called *Song of the Youths* (Listening Guide 74), which many regard as the first masterpiece of electronic music. Since the work was intended to be performed in Cologne Cathedral, Stockhausen chose as his subject the *"Benedicte"* ("Blessing"), a medieval *canticle* (literally, "song") sung at important church festivals. In a visionary story recounted by the Old Testament prophet Daniel, three young Israelites refuse to bow down before King Nebuchadnezzar's golden image and

---

*A tape consists of numerous tracks, each of which can carry its own sounds. By assembling up to 15 tracks of a single voice, Stockhausen was able to create a crowd effect.

# *Listening Guide 74*

## STOCKHAUSEN: *Song of the Youths*

CD 8, TRACK 5
TAPE 8A, TRACK 4
DURATION: 13:00

*This work is a product of texture and timbre. Its 13-minute length is part of Stockhausen's elaborate symbolism. Although we hear fragments of the sung canticle, there is little melody in the traditional sense and only fleeting moments of chordal harmony. The words vary from easily understood to incomprehensible sources of pure sound. "Group" in the Comments column refers to Stockhausen's clustering of overdubbed voices.*

*Form: Through-composed (3 sections)*

| | SECTION / TEXT | TIME | COMMENTS |
|---|---|---|---|
| **1** | Curtain | **0:00** | Burst of electronic sounds, like an opening flourish. |
| | SECTION 1 | **0:11** | First entrance of voices. Disembodied fragments of high-pitched solo and group sounds coming from many directions. |
| | | 0:40 | A rare "chord" in the voices, leading to a long decrescendo. |
| | | 1:01 | Begins from near silence, followed by group voices. |
| **2** | *Preiset den Herrn*  Praise the Lord | **1:07** | The first snatch of understandable text. The electronic sounds come in staccato bursts. |
| | *Schaden ihr alle herum*  They have all sinned | 1:33 | Sung in close, jumbled imitation by many solo voices. |
| | *Preiset den Herrn*  Praise the Lord | 1:56 | Solo voice surrounded by group sounds. |
| | *Schaden ihr alle herum*  They have all sinned | 2:05 | Begins an irregular but steady increase in excitement. |
| | | 2:35 | An unexpected pause and a final group outburst. |
| **3** | SECTION 2 | **2:41** | Another dramatic pause, then a "choral" burst and a long-held tone in the solo voice. Text fragments sung in drawn-out syllables. |
| | *Prei — set*  Praise | 2:51 | The electronic background is quieter and cooler. |
| | *den — Herrn*  the — Lord | 3:02 | Sounds travel across stereo channels. |
| | *Son — ne*  Sun  *und — Mond*  and — moon | 3:10 | Fragmented voices, a sense of stillness. Long stretch of purely electronic sounds. |
| | *Preiset den Herrn*  Praise the Lord | 3:37 | Text follows sudden burst of sound. |
| | *des Himmels*  of heaven | 3:45 | Solo voice. |
| | *Ster — ne*  Stars | 3:50 | Solo voice. |

| SECTION / TEXT | TIME | COMMENTS |
|---|---|---|
| *al — le Re — gen*   all rain | 4:00 | Different solo voices on separated single syllables. |
| *und — Tau*   and — dew | 4:09 | Intermixed with low, slow tones and bursts. |
| *den Herrn — Preiset*<br>the Lord — Praise | 4:22 | Solo voice. |
| | 4:30 | Sudden bursts. |
| *ihr Win — de*   all winds | 4:46 | Only electronic sounds from 4:54 to 5:16. |
| *und Som — mersglut*<br>and sum — mer's heat | 5:36 | Group voices, followed by longer text segments played backward. |
| *Käl — te*   Cold | 5:57 | Solo voice singing widely separated syllables. |
| *und star — rer Win — ter*<br>and numb Win — ter | | |

**4**  SECTION 3

| | TIME | COMMENTS |
|---|---|---|
| | **6:22** | Opens with long passsage of electronic sounds. |
| | 6:40 | Decelerating and accelerating rattlelike effects. |
| | 6:53 | Group voices re-enter, high and distant. |
| *Frost und Eis*   Frost and ice | 7:18 | Group voice in imitation (over *"Preiset den Herrn"*). |
| | 7:29 | Rattlelike effects. |
| | 7:52 | Disembodied, distorted chorus with rattlelike effects. |
| | 8:23 | A series of rattlelike effects. |
| *Preiset — den — Herrn*<br>Praise — the — Lord | 8:49 | Disconnected, unearthly. |
| *Preiset — und Eis — und Frost*<br>Praise — and ice — and frost | 9:31 | Group and solo voices. Highly distorted fragments of text. |
| | 10:25 | Sudden pauses punctuated by single chords. |
| *Frost — und — Eis*<br>Frost — and — ice | 10:40 | Disconnected solo syllables. |
| *Schaden ihr —*<br>All have sinned —<br>*des Herrn*   The Lord<br>*und*   and | | |

**5**  CODA

| | TIME | COMMENTS |
|---|---|---|
| | 11:40 | Long pause, leading to long-held group chord. In this final section, the text is largely incomprehensible. |
| | 12:56 | A final cadential flourish that seems to mirror the opening. |

are thrown into a "burning fiery furnace." When the youths survive the flames, they sing a song of thanksgiving, and Nebuchadnezzar grants them "great power in the land of Babel."

In its Latin original, and in the free German translation Stockhausen used, the song consists of two-line verses, each beginning with "Praise the Lord."* Of the more than 20 verses, Stockhausen drew largely from four:

Praise the Lord, sun and moon;
Praise the Lord, stars of heaven.

Praise the Lord, all rain and dew;
Praise the Lord, all winds.

Praise the Lord, fire and summer's heat;
Praise the Lord, cold and numb winter.

Praise the Lord, frost and ice;
Praise the Lord, night and day.

Stockhausen wanted to bring together "into a single sound both sung notes and electronically produced ones," and he wanted to see how "sung sounds can appear like electronic sounds, and . . . electronic sounds can appear like sung sounds." So he began by recording a young boy speaking parts of the canticle and singing other parts as they would be performed in a service. He then subjected the tape to countless manipulations. Finally he mixed the voice with electronic sounds produced by his sine-wave generator and by various tone-modifying devices. The result is a work that is deeply moving and yet detached and otherworldly—a fitting metaphor of the technological age.

Because *Song of the Youths* exists only on tape, we have to accept on faith Stockhausen's statement that it is a work of total serialism. In a modern electronic studio (see the Historical Window on page 686) such a work could be assembled in a few days, but in Stockhausen's time the editing had to be done by mechanical splicing and re-recording; it took him almost two years to produce the work. He designed it originally to be played over five clusters of loudspeakers set far apart in the giant Cologne Cathedral. Today we can hear it in the recorded stereo version that Stockhausen prepared in 1968.

Although the work has no clear structure, a progression of textures and a textual division divide it into three main sections preceded by a brief curtain and followed by a coda. The first section consists of largely unintelligible groups of sounds interrupted by bursts of electronic sound. From time to time we can hear the phrase "Praise the Lord" sung by the unaltered solo voice.

The second section, which is noticeably slower, introduces fragments, of the first three verses in long, drawn-out syllables. Here the stretches of purely electronic sounds are cooler and more distant than those in the first section. The third section opens with another long stretch of electronic sounds marked by rattlelike effects that slow down and speed up. The text of this section is drawn

---

*The German version changes the Latin for "Bless the Lord" to "Praise the Lord." In the Middle Ages, *praise* was the equivalent of *bless*.

from the fourth of the verses. In the course of the piece we can make out fragments of text that move from "sun" and "summer's heat" to "winter" and "frost and ice." Yet the words also function as sources of pure sound that at times are barely distinguishable from the purely electronic sounds.

This revolutionary work brought Stockhausen international fame while he was still in his mid-twenties and had a strong influence on subsequent composers of electronic music. For example, the American composer Morton Subotnick (b. 1933), in his 1967 album *Silver Apples of the Moon*, used electronic music to attract a surprisingly large audience of popular-music fans to an ostensibly art-music album.

Stockhausen has continued to pioneer. His *Zyklus* ("Cycle"; 1959) is a composition for 12 percussionists sitting in a circle; the players start on any page they choose and continue to play until they come back to their starting point. In *Sternklang* ("Star Sound"; 1971) he uses a large outdoor park as an integral part of the compositional structure. In what he calls "process planning," he has written pieces that specify the basic musical colors but leave many of the choices about pitch and rhythm up to the performer. Such works have been dubbed "open forms" (anticipated in literature by James Joyce's open-ended novel *Finnegans Wake*) and were especially popular in the 1960s among American composers such as Earle Brown (b. 1926). Throughout his works, Stockhausen mixes electronic sounds and acoustic sounds in bold and novel ways. Unlike Boulez, whose musical language is precise and tightly organized, Stockhausen encourages composers to surrender some of their control to the performers.

## THE BIRTH OF ROCK 'N' ROLL

Jazz, despite its profound influence on twentieth-century music, has never achieved the worldwide impact of rock 'n' roll. Still less than half a century old, rock 'n' roll and its various offshoots have created the largest music business the world has ever known.

Rock 'n' roll is rooted in many American styles—primarily rhythm & blues, but also jazz, stride, boogie-woogie, gospel music, swing, folk music, ethnic ballads, and Tin Pan Alley. Its nearest source was the postwar rhythm and blues created by artists like Muddy Waters (1915–1983) and Bo Diddley (b. 1928). During the 1920s most blues had been released on so-called race records purchased mostly by blacks. But by 1950 the popularity of urban midwestern blues—now called rhythm & blues—had become so great that it was being played by radio stations around the country and was available on several record labels.

At the end of 1954, disc jockey Alan Freed (1922–1965), whose favorite composer was Wagner, took his popular rhythm & blues radio show, which he called "The Moondog Show," from Cleveland to station WINS in New York City. When a local street musician who called himself "Moondog" sued Freed over the use of his name, Freed switched to "The Rock and Roll Show." The

# *Historical Window*

## THE HOME ELECTRONIC MUSIC STUDIO

The instrument that revolutionized the writing of electronic music is the synthesizer, which can create (synthesize) a wide variety of sounds in response to the user's instructions. During the 1950s, when the first primitive synthesizers were built, the equipment needed to produce rather simple sounds had to be housed in buildings several stories high. Then, in 1964, the American inventor Robert Moog (b. 1934) introduced a console-sized synthesizer (Figure 30.4). Moog took advantage of the new transistor, the first of a series of tiny devices called *semiconductors* that perform the functions of large, heat-generating vacuum tubes. Today a chip the size of a thumbnail can do what it took more than a million vacuum tubes to do only 30 years ago. The synthesizer has bridged the gap between composers of art music and composers of popular music.

At first Moog and others sold their synthesizers only to universities and other centers of experimental music. But in 1971 the pop group Emerson, Lake, and Palmer included in their concerts a rock version of Musorgsky's *Pictures at an Exhibition* played on the Moog (as the synthesizer itself came to be called). Overnight, the Moog became famous. The Moog and similar machines were prohibitively expensive, however; moreover, they were strictly monophonic. Programming them required plugging and unplugging dozens of *patch cords*, and only eight successive pitches could be programmed at a time.

As time passed, inventors came up with more versatile units that were marketed at affordable prices by several American companies in the early 1970s. For example, Arp (with its model 2600), EMu (pronounced E-mew), and Oberheim (with its Prophet 5) marketed systems that were cheaper and more powerful (two or four voices). (Moog responded with his still monophonic "mini-Moog" but eventually sold his company.) Now that the programming could be done more quickly, musicians like Herbie Hancock (b. 1940) began to use the new systems in live concerts and for recordings.

Earlier, in the late 1950s, the Hammond Organ Company had equipped some of its electronic organs with "draw bars" that permitted the performer to adjust, rather crudely, the intensity of overtones and the consequent timbre of sounds. These were really primitive synthesizers. The Japanese preempted the Hammond draw bars and combined them with the more sophisticated electronics of the Arp and EMu models to create portable, inexpensive machines. In 1982 the Yamaha DX-7, selling for under $2,000, provided FM synthesis ("frequency-modulation" synthesis), interchangeable sound cards (each containing 32 different sounds), and the capacity to program up to 16 voices. Moreover, by connecting the keyboard synthesizer to a personal computer, one could edit music on-screen.

FIGURE 30.4   Robert Moog (left) and Keith Emerson with Emerson's custom Moog synthesizer in 1974. Five years earlier, Walter Carlos's "Switched-on Bach" was the first record featuring a Moog synthesizer to achieve popular success.

For years, American companies had been exploring ways to make it possible for personal computers and synthesizers to talk to one another. In 1982 they settled on an industrywide standard for the "Music Instrument Digital Interface"—known as MIDI—that made it possible to store music as binary digital bits. Now a single keyboard could talk to a whole chain of synthesizers (each with its characteristic sound qualities), and keyboardless synthesizers selling for under $1,000 appeared on the market. These machines provided greater capabilities for *sequencing* (programming a series of sounds) than any of the early units had provided.

The rapid pace of innovation persisted. In 1984 the Australian company Fairlight introduced *sampling,* the capacity of a synthesizer to hear a single sound (recorded through a microphone) and then store and reproduce the timbre of that sound over the entire audible range. This advance made it possible to approximate more closely the sounds of acoustic instruments like the piano. High-end sampling systems like the "Synclavier" marketed by New England Digital cost between $45,000 and $100,000. Less expensive sampling synthesizers that offer many of the same features, like the EMu Emulator, are now available.

Another breakthrough came in 1988. Until that time, synthesizers could record only a single timbre at a time, even though they might have as many as 16 voices. Today, "multitimbral" synthesizer keyboards like the Korg M-1, the Akai S-900, and the Roland can record up to eight timbres simultaneously. These synthesizers sell for under $3,000. And the keyboardless Proteus model from Emulator offers 32 voices and 16 simultaneous timbres for under $1,000.

*continued*

More sophisticated methods of sampling ("pulse-code modulation," or PCM) make possible even closer approximations to complex acoustic sounds.

How much would it cost an aspiring musician to set up a modest but complete electronic music studio? Assuming that an amplifier and speakers are already on hand, a personal computer, MIDI interface and keyboard, synthesizer, and mixing console could be had for under $5,000 in 1991. An excellent composing and recording studio can be set up for under $25,000. In such a studio an aspiring composer could create, record, and edit works whose technical quality would be almost indistinguishable from works produced in a million-dollar studio. Even composers who write for acoustic instruments can now hear what their music sounds like before anyone else hears it. So popular are these new low-cost, high-tech studios that two magazines, *Electronic Musician* and *Music Technology*, have sprung up to keep readers abreast of the latest developments.

Personal-computer technology is helpful in teaching and learning about music as well. With a CD-ROM drive (a CD-player that talks to a computer), we can link text, graphics, or video to a specific musical passage. And since every form of information—text, still images, moving pictures, sound—can be stored in a single digital format, we can now access the world in a "multimedia" way. In short, we are experiencing a revolution as far-reaching as that brought about by the introduction of printing almost 500 years ago.

name stuck. The music Freed played, targeted mainly at teenagers, had a strong duple meter with the accents falling on beats 2 and 4 of a 4-beat bar (called the *backbeat*); it was earthy and humorous rather than formal and pretentious; and it was meant for dancing. Teenagers tuned into Freed's show by the millions.

In 1955, Bill Haley's (1925–1981) "Rock Around the Clock" was used as the title song of the movie *The Blackboard Jungle*, in which unruly teens destroy their teacher's priceless jazz collection record by record. From that time on, many Americans associated rock 'n' roll with the new social disease of juvenile delinquency.

It was about this time that black artists like Fats Domino (who weighed 224 pounds and stood 5′5″ tall) and Chuck Berry (who was more Native American than black) emerged as rock 'n' roll stars. As with jazz, it was not so much the songs they sang as the way they delivered them that won them popularity. For example, one of Fats Domino's biggest hits, "Blueberry Hill," had already been a pop song back in the 1930s. But his driving, rhythmic bass, pulsating chordal piano, and raspy delivery gave the song new life. And Chuck Berry's first big hit,

"Maybelline," was an arrangement of a noncopyrighted tune, "Ida Red." Berry's rapid-fire oom-PAH percussion rhythms, in which the weak part of the beat was more heavily accented than the strong part, soon became a staple of the emerging rock 'n' roll style. Another common feature was the verse-verse-bridge-verse structure, a variation of the *a-a-b-a* theme structure that had endured from the Classical period to Tin Pan Alley (where it was called 32-bar song form). As dance music, rock 'n' roll took two forms, known simply as "fast" and "slow." The slow numbers were generally ballads—that is, songs with a narrative. Chuck Berry characterized early rock 'n' roll in a celebrated song:

> That's why I go for that rock 'n' roll music,
> Any ol' way you choose it,
> It's got a backbeat you can't lose it,
> Any ol' time you use it,
> It's gotta be rock 'n' roll music,
> If ya' wanna dance with me.

All rock 'n' roll bands included at least one vocalist, one guitarist (who was soon playing the new "electric" guitars designed to fill large amphitheaters), and one percussionist (invariably the loudest and therefore positioned at the back of the stage).

In 1954 Elvis Presley (1935–1977), a 20-year-old truck driver, made his first recordings with Sun Records. His early style sounded like a cross between Dean Martin, gospel, and country. Soon, however, he developed a simple, highly rhythmic delivery (dubbed *rockabilly*) that would win him dozens of gold records over the next two decades. Presley was not a songwriter himself, and he built his repertory on many varieties of popular music. When he appeared on the Ed Sullivan TV show in 1956, he captured 80 percent of the viewing audience. *Love Me Tender*, the first of his 30 films, was released that same year.

Presley's success prompted other young performers to try their hand. A young bespectacled Texan, Charles "Buddy" Holly (1938–1959), unlike most of his contemporaries, wrote his own material. Beginning with "That'll Be the Day," he composed a series of fresh songs, including "Oh Boy," "Peggy Sue," and "It's So Easy to Fall in Love," that became rock classics. Holly's death in 1959 in a plane crash was a severe blow to American music.

Rock 'n' roll sales fell off in the late 1950s, in part because of Presley's departure to the army. But by this time it had become an international movement.

## ROCK IN THE 1960s: THE AGE OF THE BEATLES

The bleak English seaport of Liverpool might seem an unlikely starting place for a rock group that would dominate popular music for years to come. But rhythm & blues had long been popular in that city. And many young Liverpudlians who worked on the Cunard Line ships invariably returned from the States with the latest rhythm & blues and early rock 'n' roll recordings, which the Liverpool bands immediately set out to imitate.

In 1956, John Lennon (1940–1980), a restless 16-year-old, formed a Liverpool band called the Quarry Men. The next year, while his band was playing at a church festival, Lennon happened to meet Paul McCartney (b. 1942), a reserved, well-mannered teenager. McCartney's father was a part-time musician who had bought Paul his first guitar. Lennon was impressed with Paul's musical talents (for one thing, he could tune a guitar) and invited him to join the Quarry Men. The next year they were joined by George Harrison (b. 1943), a guitarist who had been picking out Buddy Holly tunes on his own.

With drummer Pete Best and guitarist Stuart Sutcliffe, the group played small Liverpool clubs as "Johnny and the Moondogs," then as "The Silver Beatles," and, in 1960, as the "Beatles" (doubtless an intentional misspelling). Soon they embarked on a grueling two-month, seven-hour-a-night stint in rough-and-tumble Hamburg. (Sutcliffe died of a brain hemorrhage caused by a mugging in Hamburg.) Although Lennon and McCartney had begun to write songs together from the time they met, their repertoire consisted mainly of songs by Fats Domino, Ray Charles, Elvis Presley, Chuck Berry, and Jerry Lee Lewis.

On their return to Liverpool, the Beatles caught the attention of Brian Epstein, who was managing the record department in his father's furniture store. Epstein immediately set about polishing their rough image. He also introduced them to George Martin, an EMI record producer, who later became known as "the fifth Beatle" for his role in producing their albums.

For their first recording session, in 1962, the Beatles brought in drummer Richard Starkey (known around Liverpool as Ringo Starr; b. 1940), a member of a rival Liverpool band. Instead of having one member of the band serve as lead and the rest as backup, Martin had them perform as equals. Harrison usually played lead guitar, Lennon rhythm guitar, and McCartney bass guitar. Their very first album rose to the top of the British pop charts, and the Beatles were invited to play first at London's Palladium Theatre and then before the Queen. Their second album had sold 2.5 million copies in England and Europe before Capitol Records released the first Beatles song in the United States. By the time the Beatles arrived in New York, in February 1964, that song, the single "I Want To Hold Your Hand," had sold 1.5 million copies. Their first New York concert drew 55,000 fans (an unprecedented number at the time). They played to capacity crowds throughout the country (Figure 30.5) and before the end of the year had made their first world tour, appearing in 50 cities on four continents.

Over the next two years Beatlemania swept the world, and the group toured endlessly in a valiant effort to keep up with demand. When they appeared on BBC's first worldwide television special, "Our World," they were seen by more than 200 million viewers. But the pace could not be maintained, and on August 29, 1966, the Beatles played their last live concert, in San Francisco's Candlestick Park, and then retired to the recording studio.

Between 1962 and 1970 the Beatles composed more than 200 songs of high quality. More than 80 percent of those songs were written by Lennon and

FIGURE 30.5 The Beatles' live performances evoked hysterical responses—a reaction dubbed "Beatlemania"—from teenage girls (many now mothers of college students). Some fans refused to accept the group's breakup as final; despite various rumors of reunion, Paul McCartney said, "You cannot reheat a soufflé."

McCartney, the rest by Harrison. With this impressive output, the Beatles demonstrated that rock performers could be creative artists as well. Between 1963 and 1970 the Beatles released a series of albums that revealed their astonishing musical and emotional growth. The first were "mop-top" albums (a reference to their early hairdos), including *With the Beatles, The Beatles Second Album* (containing the irreverent "Roll Over, Beethoven"), and *Beatles for Sale.* Their style grew increasingly complex in the albums released between 1964 and 1970 (when they disbanded):

1. *Help!* (1964, from their second movie)
2. *Rubber Soul* (1965)
3. *Revolver* (1966)
4. *Sgt. Pepper's Lonely Hearts Club Band* (1967)
5. *Magical Mystery Tour* (1968)
6. *The Beatles* (1968; known as "The White Album")
7. *Abbey Road* (1969)
8. *Let It Be* (1970)

Each album has its own special character. The songs through *Help!*, mostly straight rock 'n' roll on themes of adolescent love, adhere mainly to the standard 32-bar song form. In the mid-1960s the Beatles began to experiment with Eastern religion. They also began to experiment with drugs, which they used for the purpose of achieving expanded awareness.

### The Beatles: *Sgt. Pepper's Lonely Hearts Club Band* (1967)

When the Beatles gave up public performances in 1966, many people assumed that they were through. But the release of the album *Sgt. Pepper's Lonely Hearts Club Band* on June 2, 1967, proved the rumors false. Listeners to rock stations that summer heard almost nothing but the 35 remarkable minutes of this album, which the Beatles had produced over five months at the then unheard-of cost of $100,000.

*Sgt. Pepper* was the first "concept album" in rock 'n' roll history. The theme was drawn from English vaudeville, and the song "Being for the Benefit of Mr. Kite" was taken almost verbatim from a circus poster. The songs focus on loneliness ("A Little Help from My Friends," "When I'm Sixty-Four," "Within You, Without You") and on alienation ("Getting Better," "Fixing a Hole," "She's Leaving Home," "Good Morning," "A Day in the Life").

The Beatles use a wide range of musical techniques in this album. As in a Romantic song cycle, the songs are grouped around a key, E Major. The album opens with the rising noise of the audience. We hear the tuning of the strings (suggesting a symphony orchestra), which then launch into a rhythm & blues treatment of the theme song. Nowhere among the 13 songs is there a single unadorned 32-bar song form. Instead, each song consists of three (occasionally four) endlessly varied strophes. These include opening phrases of *a-a-b* ("Being for the Benefit of Mr. Kite"; "When I'm Sixty-Four"), *a-b-b* ("Lovely Rita, Meter Maid"; "She's Leaving Home"), and *a-b-c-a'* ("Getting Better").

The phrase structure is highly elastic. "Fixing a Hole" opens with four regular bars followed by an unexpected 2-bar extension, appropriately on the last syllable of "wander-ing." Although the entire phrase turns out to be eight bars long, it sounds anything but regular.

Even bolder is the treatment of meter. At a time when duple meter was standard in rock 'n' roll, Lennon and McCartney wrote "She's Leaving Home" as a poignant triple-meter waltz. The verses of "Lucy in the Sky with Diamonds" are in triple meter, while the choruses are in duple. When, in "Mr. Kite," "Henry the Horse" is described as "dancing the waltz," the music shifts dramatically from duple to triple meter. "Within You, Without You," a song for sitar and tabla (an obvious reference to the Beatles' experiences in India), has no meter at all in the Western sense. "Good Morning" careens back and forth between measures of four, five, and three beats. Clearly, *Sgt. Pepper* is not music for dancing.

The songs are in a variety of styles. "Lovely Rita, Meter Maid" is in honky-tonk style, and "With a Little Help from My Friends," "Fixing a Hole" (with harpsichord!), and "When I'm Sixty-Four" are in English dancehall style. "She's Leaving Home," with its harp-and-string quartet accompaniment, suggests art music. The harmonies range from simple and diatonic ("When I'm Sixty-Four") to the jazzily dissonant chorus of "Sgt. Pepper's Lonely Hearts Club Band."

The frequent blending of two or more sounds, along with the special effects, serve to tie the album together. The title song is mixed directly into "With a Little Help," and the carillon effects at the end of "Mr. Kite" create a dizzying blend of triple over duple meter. The animal sounds at the end of "Good Morning" lead directly into the reprise of the title song.

*Sgt. Pepper* changed the landscape of rock music. After its appearance, bands could no longer go into a studio and simply record the songs they had played on the road and call it an album. Album production became as important as opera staging.

## ROCK IN THE 1970s AND 1980s

Rock 'n' roll reflected not only the musical tastes but also the political turbulence of the 1960s. The assassination of President John F. Kennedy in November 1963 (and of his brother Robert in 1968); the deepening American involvement in Vietnam between 1964 and 1969; the civil rights movement; the assassination of Dr. Martin Luther King, Jr., in 1968; and the police slaying of war protesters at Kent State University in 1970 led many young people to rebel against what they viewed as a bankrupt society. In songs like Bob Dylan's "Blowin' in the Wind" (1962) and "The Times They Are a-Changin' " (1964) and Joan Baez's rendering of "We Shall Overcome," American youth found powerful expressions of their alienation. But the gathering of some 300,000 young people in 1969 at a rock concert near Woodstock, New York, turned out to be the last major statement of social protest by the rock movement. With that unifying force gone, boundaries between the various forms of rock grew more rigid.

The Woodstock performers themselves had given hints of the deepening split between "hard" rock (Janis Joplin [1943–1970], Jimi Hendrix [1942–1970]) and "soft" or "folk" rock (Simon and Garfunkel; Crosby, Stills, and Nash). In the 1970s *heavy metal* bands began to thunder rebellion and defiance from vast outdoor stages. The style persisted into the 1980s as *punk*. The Motown sound, based on gospel and rhythm & blues by Berry Gordy, Jr., found its most eloquent spokesperson in Stevie Wonder. Singer/songwriters like James Taylor carried on the folk tradition of Joan Baez. The vacuum left by the Beatles' retirement was partially filled by sophisticated mainstream rockers like Elton John, and Michael Jackson carried on with the lavishly produced stage shows introduced by Motown. Bruce Springsteen keeps hard rock alive, and in this wide spectrum there is still room for sentimental balladeers like Barry Manilow. But these artists have little in common, and their audiences, too, have become more and more segmented.

Even so, there has been a certain coalescence of generic styles, if not of personal styles. Synthesizers have blended the regular beat of disco with rhythm & blues, and funk has merged the Motown sound with the rougher rhythms of Jimi Hendrix. Reggae is a blend of Jamaican rhythms and instruments with rock, and Christian rock blends old-fashioned rock 'n' roll with a message. In short, rock survives in a variety of rich, vigorous forms, though it is no longer a unifying force. Today, in fact, many people no longer distinguish between rock and pop. This fragmentation in rock music is not unlike the fragmentation we have noted in art music.

The long-range effects of video are still difficult to predict, although the video craze sparked by MTV in the early eighties continues unabated. The best videos have introduced elements of opera into their mix of music, scenario, and dance; the worst try to hide the blandness of the music behind slick visual effects. Nor can we as yet predict the impact of electronic technology on rock, though the electronic workplace seems to have become a cradle of creativity. It remains to be seen whether technology will open up new musical vistas or encourage the recycling of old ones.

## THE PIONEER SPIRIT

Even before Heinrich and Ives, many composers in the United States were given to experimentation. One indirect reason might be that they lacked training in traditional European art music. But a more direct reason is that they were responding to the pioneer spirit that has typified life in America from the beginning. The desire to experiment with new sounds has been especially keen in the twentieth century.

After Ives, one of the most daring American experimentalists was Henry Cowell (1897–1965). Cowell grew up in a small town in the San Francisco foothills where he had little opportunity for formal music instruction. Though self-taught, he made the bold decision to become a composer, and by the time he was 17 he had written more than a hundred pieces. One of them, *The Tides of Manaunaun* (after an Irish god), is a piano piece in which the right hand plays a modal melody while the left forearm sounds huge clusters of tones in the bass. At a Carnegie Hall recital in 1924, Cowell astonished the audience with his unorthodox keyboard techniques, which included banging on the keys with his fists and scraping the strings inside the piano with his fingers. Bartók wrote to him asking for permission to use his clusters of closely spaced notes, and Cowell later met both Bartók and Schoenberg during a European concert tour. In 1929 he was the first American composer to be invited to visit the USSR, where his performances electrified his audiences but stunned the authorities.

Cowell set up a publishing house called New Music Edition to publish the works of American composers, and he campaigned tirelessly to get Ives's music performed. He traveled about the world in search of ethnic music and advocated the internationalization of music.

A more eclectic experimentalist was Harry Partch (1901–1974), another Californian who was largely self-taught in music. Dissatisfied with Western scales and Western instruments, Partch devised new scales (one of which has 43 tones) and created instruments on which to play them (Figure 30.6). Although he received little recognition during most of his life, his achievement was recognized in his later years.

FIGURE 30.6 Harry
Partch with his gourd tree
and cone gongs. His in-
struments include the blue
rainbow, Castor and Pol-
lux, crychord, zymo-xyl,
boo, cloud chamber
bowls, and spoils of war.

## John Cage (b. 1912): *Aria with Fontana Mix* (1958)

The most influential American experimentalist of the twentieth century is John
Cage. Born and raised in Los Angeles, Cage graduated as valedictorian from Los
Angeles High School and then traveled to Europe to study music, visual art, and
architecture. He studied with both Cowell and Schoenberg and served for a time
as accompanist with a dance group. In 1938 he joined a dance school in Seattle,
where he met the dancer and choreographer Merce Cunningham (b. 1919),
with whom he has collaborated for over 50 years (Figure 30.7).

Bored by the sounds of the traditional orchestra, Cage began to write compositions for percussion and for the "prepared" piano. He prepared the piano
by placing various objects between the piano strings, thereby altering their natural timbre. In 1942, after coming across a collection of electronic sound effects
at a Chicago radio station, he began to use electronic sounds, such as *white noise,*
in which every audible frequency is present at approximately the same intensity.
A study of Eastern rhythms led him to incorporate additive rather than dynamic
patterns into his music, and after reading the *I Ching* (the Chinese "Book of
Changes"), he adopted "chance" as a compositional element.

Cage has published several collections of essays that reflect his thinking about
music. Among them are *Silence* (1961), *A Year from Monday* (1967), *Empty
Words* (1979), *Themes and Variations* (1982), and *I–VI* (1990), a series of lectures delivered at Harvard. Central to his thinking is the Zen notion that our

# Listening Guide 75

LIGETI: *Lux aeterna* for 16-Voice
A Capella Mixed Chorus

CD 8, TRACKS 7
TAPE 8B, TRACK 3
DURATION: 7:50

*Because the coordination between Text and Times is only approximate, we have linked the times to the changes in register noted in the Comments column. There are no male voices in the first half, whereas the second half is dominated by male voices. The return of the sopranos near the end echoes the return of the opening lines.*

*Form: Through-composed*

| | TEXT | TIME | COMMENTS |
|---|---|---|---|
| 1 | *Lux aeterna*<br>Let eternal light | **0:00** | Opens on unisons in alto register, gradually widening in both directions. |
| 2 | *luceat eis Domine*<br>shine on them, O Lord, | **1:42** | The sopranos enter on a sustained high note. |
| | *cum sanctis tuis in aeternum*<br>with thy saints in eternity, | 2:32 | The altos re-enter. |
| 3 | *quia pius es.*<br>for Thou art merciful. | **3:12**<br>4:05 | The tenors enter.<br>Full vocal sonority at the midpoint. |
| | *Requiem aeternam dona eis*<br>Grant them eternal rest, | 5:21 | The female voices gradually give way to male voices. |
| 4 | *Domine*<br>O Lord, | **5:46** | The basses re-enter. |
| 5 | *et lux perpetua luceat eis.*<br>and let perpetual light<br>    shine on them. | **6:17** | The sopranos re-enter (as at 1:42), but gradually give way to the deeper registers. The sounds die away slowly. |

*aeterna* is the penultimate section. This setting is for 16 separate vocal parts. Because most of the degrees of the chromatic scale are present in each sonority, Ligeti's harmonic structures more closely resemble bandwidths of sound than conventional harmonies defined by consonance or dissonance. Ligeti transforms harmony into shifting bands of light and color that are perfectly suited to this text.

*Lux aeterna* is organized as a strict canon (both Penderecki and Ligeti have been influenced by J. S. Bach). The first six female voices enter at close time intervals and with the same pitch on the word "Lux." There is no melody or even rhythm in the traditional sense. Instead, the music unfolds in slow, overlapping phrases. The slowly enunciated words serve only as sources of color.

The form is continuous, with a series of dramatic entries that change the register of the prevailing sonority. The first half is dominated by the higher vocal ranges. At almost exactly the midpoint Ligeti achieves a full, balanced sonority and then shifts toward the lower registers. The last soprano entries echo the earlier entries and then give way to male voices. The overall effect is one of a deep serenity, and the long diminuendo on the final chord (which lasts almost 20 seconds) fades into silence.

## Ellen Taaffe Zwilich (b. 1939): "Eyesight" from *Passages* for Soprano and Instrumental Ensemble (1981)

A number of contemporary American composers have carved out a style for themselves by drawing on a wide range of styles that might ordinarily be thought of as incompatible. One of the most successful at integrating diverse styles is Ellen Taaffe Zwilich. Born in Miami, Florida, she learned violin at an early age and studied at the Juilliard School, where she also studied composition with Roger Sessions (1846–1985) and Elliott Carter (b. 1908), two distinguished American composers. Zwilich has written a large number of symphonic and chamber works, most of them in response to commissions from orchestras (including the Indianapolis Symphony and the San Francisco Symphony) and chamber groups (especially Musica Viva in Boston). Her Symphony No. 1 earned the 1983 Pulitzer Prize in music.

Zwilich's early works, such as the song cycle *Einsame Nacht* (Lonesome Night), were in an austere, often harsh style. In *Passages* (Listening Guide 76), based on the poetry of the American poet A. R. Ammons, Zwilich brought six poems together to create a stylistically varied cycle in which voice and instruments share equally. The poems pose major questions about life and death, though in an aphoristic and almost offhand way.

The ensemble includes a traditional piano quartet (piano, violin, viola, cello), three kinds of flute (played alternately by one performer), clarinet and bass clarinet, and a mixed battery of percussion (including marimba, vibraphone, bells, gong, tam-tam, cymbals, and timpani). The blending of traditional and nontraditional instrumental groups is typical of Zwilich's style.

"Eyesight" (the first song in the cycle) is a metaphoric poem about the coming of spring, particularly how easily it—and, by extension, life—can be missed. At one level it contains the kind of word painting we associate with the sixteenth-century madrigal: lush vocal climaxes on both occurrences of "spring" and the use of high harmonics in the viola to accompany "mountain." Third-based harmonies with clear tonal allusions, the recurrence and reshaping of thematic material (especially in the instrumental interludes and coda), and the drawn-out buildup to "are gone" suggest Romanticism. The coloristic use of percussion, the viola harmonics, and the abstract accompanimental figures of Interlude 2

# *Listening Guide 76*

## ZWILICH: "Eyesight" from *Passages* for Soprano and Instrumental Ensemble

CD 8, TRACK 8
TAPE 8B, TRACK 4
DURATION: 3:24

*Zwilich organizes this song around three instrumental interludes that provide the thematic and harmonic material that holds the song together. The allusions to traditional harmony are both referential (alluding to a Romantic past) and functional.*

*Form: Through-composed*

| | LOCATION/TEXT | TIME | COMMENTS |
|---|---|---|---|
| 1 | It was May before my attention came to spring and | **0:00** | Voice in duet with the flute. Delicate opening surges to a climax on the word "spring," supported in a rich chord by the piano, strings, and clarinet. |
| | my word I said to the southern slopes | 0:15 | Text sung over the preceding held chord. Static. |
| | I've missed it, | 0:22 | Sung in emphatic rhythms, doubled by the piano. |
| | [Interlude 1] | 0:24 | Short bursts (including an echo of "I've missed it" in the piano). |
| | | 0:34 | Sudden pedal point in piano and vibraphone. Oscillating figures in flute, clarinet, and violin. |
| 2 | it came and went before I got right to see: | **0:43** | Lyrical vocal line over continuing pedal point. Same oscillating figures in flute, clarinet, and violin. |
| | [Interlude 2] | 0:52 | Lyrical continuation breaks into staccato arpeggios at 0:59. |

and the coda evoke the abstract language of Webern and Boulez. Yet the music has a coherence that reveals a composer with a clear and particular vision. Zwilich's many admirers credit her with reinvigorating tonality and Romantic thematic treatment. Some enthusiasts have gone so far as to speak of the "New Romanticism" represented by composers like Zwilich. Critics predictably speak of "recycling."

| LOCATION/TEXT | TIME | COMMENTS |
|---|---|---|
| | | Settles into ostinato-like accompaniment between clarinet and violin at 1:12. |
| 3  don't worry, said the mountain, try the later northern slopes | **1:16** | Voice accompanied by orchestral bells and a viola melody made up of high harmonics. |
| or if you can climb, climb into spring: spring ah la | 1:27 | Romantic climb to full-blooded climax on "spring." |
| [Interlude 3] | 1:44 | Arpeggiated figures in solo piano, soon joined by bursts from flute and clarinet. Reverts at 1:55 to earlier ostinato-like accompaniment. |
| 4  but said the mountain it's not that way with all things, | **2:00** | Accompanied again by the orchestral bells and the high harmonics in the viola. Cello pizzicatos follow "things." |
| some that go . . . | 2:15 | Sung on two alternating pitches, answered by pizzicato cello. |
| | 2:24 | Text repeats, answered by pizzicato cello. |
| | 2:30 | Text repeats yet a third time. |
| are gone. | 2:35 | Long melisma on "are." "Gone" sung simultaneously with striking of the hand bell. |
| 5  [Coda] | **2:44** | The same pedal point and oscillating harmonies of Interlude 1. The flute plays the melody sung at "it came and went." |
| | 2:59 | Similar to the staccato arpeggios at 0:59. The high viola harmonic treated as a pedal point, under which Zwilich adds a final, "major-mode" cadence. |

# MINIMALISM

One of the most popular but controversial languages devised by American composers is *minimalism*, also known as *pattern music, pulse music,* or *trance music.* Detractors call it "stuck-record music." Minimalism grew out of the impatience of many composers with the complexities of post-Webernian serialism. There are several varieties of minimalism, but all are based on *static* states.

For almost a thousand years Western music has relied on dynamic states that progress toward a single goal. The minimalists, influenced by non-Western philosophy and music, have rejected this search for what they regard as artificial goals and have turned to the repetitiveness of Indian ragas, African drumming, and the Balinese gamelan.

The landmark minimalist work is the 1964 *In C* by Terry Riley (b. 1935). The work consists of 53 motives, none more than a few measures in length and all more or less consonant with C. Except for a piano, the ensemble consists only of melody instruments. Each instrumentalist plays each of the 53 motives as often as he or she wants and continues until all of them have been played. The rhythmic "glue" is provided by steady eighth-note pulses in the top C-octave of the piano.

Steve Reich (b. 1936), a member of the ensemble that made the historical CBS recording of this work, later moved to San Francisco to experiment on his own. He discovered that when he played the same tape loop on two different machines, the slight differences in speed between them would gradually shift the passage in and out of phase. Using this phasing technique, he produced two unusual works. *It's Gonna Rain* (1965) takes its text from a live street sermon about the Flood delivered by an itinerant preacher in San Francisco's Union Square. In *Come Out* (1966), he extracted a single phrase from the taped testimony of 19-year-old Daniel Hamm, a youth arrested on murder charges in the 1964 Harlem riots. Describing his beating at the hands of the police, Hamm related how, in order to be attended to, "I had to, like, open the bruise up and let some of the bruise blood come out to show them." (The police were treating only those with visible bleeding.) When applied to the last five words—"come out to show them"—Reich's phasing technique created a haunting account of this incident. Drawing on his study of African drumming, Reich went on to develop a style of considerable rhythmic subtlety and complexity.

In a 1968 essay, "Music as a Natural Process," Reich wrote: "I do not mean the process of composition, but rather pieces of music that are, literally, processes." He added, "To facilitate closely detailed listening a musical process should happen extremely gradually."

In 1966 Reich assembled an ensemble of acoustic instruments called "Steve Reich and Musicians" to perfect the precise rhythmic style his music required. Although the music is repetitive, Reich writes out all his compositions in scores. Among his works are the 85-minute *Drumming* (1971) and the jazz-influenced *Music for Eighteen Musicians* (1976), of which more than 20,000 records were sold in the first year.

One of Reich's classmates at the Juilliard School in the 1950s was Philip Glass (b. 1937). After meeting again in 1967, they worked closely together for several years. Glass uses a mostly electronic ensemble and employs "additive" rhythmic techniques rather than phasing. He is particularly interested in the theater, and his best-known works are three theater pieces about "historical figures who changed the course of world events through the wisdom and strength of their inner vision." Those works are *Einstein on the Beach* (1976), *Satyagraha* (1980; about Gandhi's nonviolent struggle in India), and *Akhnaten* (1983; about an Egyptian pharaoh martyred for his monotheistic beliefs).

Glass and Reich have attracted a large crossover audience of listeners whose main interest is in rock. In fact, the rock star David Bowie made a minimalist pop album, *Low,* in 1977. This is one of several encouraging signs that the gap in our time between art music and popular music can be bridged.

## John Adams (b. 1947): "News Has a Kind of Mystery" from *Nixon in China* (1987)

John Adams, a younger contemporary of Reich and Glass, grew up in Massachusetts. He studied clarinet with his father and later with a member of the Boston Symphony and majored in composition at Harvard. In 1978 he became new-music adviser to the San Francisco Symphony (a model since copied by other major orchestras). With works like *Phrygian Gates* (1977, piano), *Harmonium* (1980, chorus and orchestra), and *Harmonielehre* (1984–1985, orchestra), Adams has attracted national attention.

Adams's minimalist opera *Nixon in China* (1987; Figure 30.9; Listening Guide 77) is based on President Nixon's historic visit to China in February 1972. The premiere of the opera (followed by a production on public television) aroused extraordinary public interest. The idea for the opera was suggested by Peter Sellars (b. 1958), a brilliant young director. The text, created by librettist Alice Goodman in rhymed couplets, is a sober account that portrays Nixon as variously heroic, statesmanlike, boorish, gallant, visionary, and paranoid.

Nixon's "arrival aria" at the end of Act I, Scene 1 is set as a kind of "simultaneous reminiscence." Though still on Air Force One as it approaches Peking, Nixon is already anticipating how his visit will be viewed by historians and constituents back home. Throughout the scene Adams displays his fondness for traditional word painting by matching both voice and accompaniment to such key words as "quietly," "transforming," and "tranquility."

Adams's rate of harmonic change is brisk and variable, allowing for a broad range of expression. Bright orchestral colors accompany Nixon's expansive lines ("It's prime time in the U.S.A."), but the accompaniment turns erratic and

## ADAMS: "News Has a Kind of Mystery" from Act I of *Nixon in China*

CD 8, TRACK 9
TAPE 8A, TRACK 5
DURATION: 6:39

*The scene divides into two main parts, each headed by up-tempo "news" music. Adams varies the accompaniment to reflect the moods expressed in the text.*

*Form: Sectional, with repetitions*

| LOCATION/TEXT | TIME | COMMENTS |
|---|---|---|
| **[FIRST PART]** | | |
| 1 NIXON: | **0:00** | Steady, driving rhythms; oscillating triadic harmonies. Considerable repetition of words. |
| News has a kind of mystery; | | |
| When I shook hands with Chou En-lai | 0:24 | |
| On this bare field outside Peking | | |
| Just now the whole world was listening. | | |
| | | |
| CHOU: | | |
| May I— | | Nixon sings over Chou's voice. |
| | | |
| 2 NIXON: | **0:46** | "Quietly" sung as a soft melisma. |
| And though we spoke quietly | | |
| The eyes and ears of history | | |
| Caught every gesture— | | |
| | | |
| CHOU: | | |
| —introduce— | | |
| | | |
| NIXON: | | |
| And every word, | | |
| transforming us as we, transfixed,— | 1:16 | Elaborate melisma on "transforming." |
| | | |
| CHOU: | | |
| —the Deputy | | |
| Minister of Security. | | |
| | | |
| NIXON: | | |
| made history. | | |
| The eyes and ears of history | 1:39 | Melisma on "eyes and ears." Syncopated brass to convey the heroism of both leaders. |
| As we made history. | | |
| | | |
| CHOU: | | |
| May I— | | |
| | | |
| 3 NIXON: | | |
| On our flight over from Shanghai | **1:53** | Accompaniment more muted. |

| LOCATION/TEXT | TIME | COMMENTS |
|---|---|---|
| CHOU:<br>The Minister— | | |
| NIXON:<br>the countryside<br>Looked drab and gray. "Brueghel," Pat said.<br>"We came in peace for all mankind," I said,<br>and I was put in mind<br>Of our Apollo astronauts simply— | 2:09<br>2:24 | Woodwind flourishes hint at the painter Brueghel's embellished style.<br>Warm, lyric phrase for the repetitions of "I said."<br>Dramatic harmonic shift on "astronauts." |
| CHOU:<br>—of the United States | | |
| NIXON:<br>achieving a great human dream. | | |

4  We live in an unsettled time.        **2:39**     Hushed and anxious, with muted trumpet.

| LOCATION/TEXT | TIME | COMMENTS |
|---|---|---|
| Who are our enemies? | 2:52 | Parallels musically the preceding line. |
| Who are our friends? | | |
| The Eastern Hemisphere | 3:07 | Dramatic slowdown, with more exotic orchestration. |
| Beckoned to us, and we have flown | | |
| East of the sun, west of the moon | | |
| Across an ocean of distrust | | |
| Filled with the bodies of our lost; | 3:27 | Rhythmic pulses almost disappear on repetitions of "tranquility." |
| The earth's Sea of Tranquility. | | |

[SECOND PART]

| LOCATION/TEXT | TIME | COMMENTS |
|---|---|---|
| 5   News! It's prime time in the U.S.A. | **3:53** | Recapitulates the beginning music. |
| It's yesterday night. | | |
| They watch us now; | 4:13 | Syncopated rhythms replace driving rhythms. |
| The three main networks' colors glow | | |
| Livid through drapes onto the lawn. | | |
| Dishes are washed and homework done, | 4:25 | New pattern of syncopated accompaniment. |
| The dog and grandma fall asleep, | | |
| A car roars past playing loud pop, is gone. | 4:33 | Sudden loudness on "pop." |
| As I look down the road | 4:42 | Steady rhythms return. |
| I know America is good at heart. | | |
| An old cold warrior | | |
| Piloting towards an unknown shore | | |
| through shoals. | | |
| 6   The rats begin to chew the sheets. | **5:04** | Highly irregular accompaniment, sudden groans in the brass; chorus echoes the words. Textual repetition to suggest an obsession. |

*continued*

| LOCATION/TEXT | TIME | COMMENTS |
|---|---|---|
| There's murmuring down below. | 5:22 | The chorus anticipates Nixon's observation. Much textual repetition. |
| Now there's ingratitude! | 5:33 | Syncopated accompaniment. No textual repetition. |
| My hand is steady as a rock. | 5:37 | No textual repetition. |
| A sound like mourning doves reaches my ears, Nobody is a friend of ours. | 5:43 | Lyrical, over a syncopated background. No textual repetition. |
| The nation's heartland skips a beat As our hands shield the spinning globe From the flame-throwers of the mob. | 5:54 | Sudden loud syncopation on "skips." |
| **7** We must press on. | **6:09** | Unusual dotted-rhythm accompaniment. |
| We know we want— | 6:13 | Slow, legato accompaniment, reflecting Nixon's indecision. |
| KISSINGER: Mr. President— NIXON: | 6:21 | Spoken in a group monotone. |
| What?—Oh yes— | 6:31 | Spoken. |

muted for the darker lines ("The rats begin to chew the sheets"). Since the melody is always carried by the voices against the orchestral accompaniment, there is some danger of tedium. Adams avoids monotony, however, by making frequent changes in texture and by paying careful attention to the dramatic details. *Nixon in China* has already been performed by four major opera companies, and may turn out to be one of the few post-war operas to gain a permanent place in the repertoire.

The modified minimalism practiced by Adams and other composers has had a powerful effect on American music. For example, the "New Age" music that sprang up in the 1980s owes much of its near-hypnotic style to minimalism. Some critics have suggested that Adams has tempered minimalism with the New Romanticism.

## OTHER CONTEMPORARY STYLES AND TRENDS

In our survey of postwar styles, we have omitted mention of many important composers whose works fall outside the categories we have explored. Elliott

Carter (b. 1908), for example, is regarded by many as the most accomplished American composer of the postwar period. Carter writes in a dissonant, chromatic style yet shuns serial procedures. His most important innovation is the use of refined rhythms to create large forms. In a process that has been dubbed "metrical modulation," Carter moves from one section to another by subtle shifts in the pulse rate. His Double Concerto for Harpsichord and Piano (1961) has proved popular with both performers and audiences. For the American bicentennial, the Boston Symphony Orchestra commissioned Carter to write the colorful *Symphony of Three Orchestras,* and string players regard his three string quartets as the most important since Bartók's. Carter's views on contemporary music and culture have been published as *Flawed Words and Stubborn Sounds.*

Another American, George Crumb (b. 1929), has developed a passionate, theatrical style whose extramusical dimensions are allied to Romanticism. He has attracted a wide audience with his Pulitzer-Prize-winning *Echoes of Time and the River* for orchestra (1967), *Black Angels* for electric string quartet (1970; "a kind of parable on our troubled contemporary world"), and the song cycle *Ancient Voices of Children* (1970), a setting of poetry by the martyred Spaniard Federico Garciá Lorca (1899–1936). Along with composers like George Rochberg (1918), Crumb draws on both traditional and contemporary techniques. For example, *Black Angels* contains an electrified version of Schubert's song *Death and the Maiden,* and another passage emulates a sixteenth-century English dance, the pavane. Such use of discrete styles that shift frequently during a composition can be regarded as "stylistic modulation."

The Italian-born composer Luciano Berio (b. 1925), identified with the European avant-garde, writes music that incorporates elements from the Italian Baroque to Puccini, from folk song to avant-garde instrumental techniques. Berio has also practiced stylistic modulation. The third movement of his *Sinfonia* (1968) is a kind of gloss on the Scherzo movement from Mahler's Second Symphony, interspersed with quotations from works by Beethoven, Debussy, Stravinsky, and Berg.

Ruth Crawford Seeger (1901–1953) studied at the American Conservatory of Music in Chicago, where she became friends with the poet Carl Sandburg (1878–1967). She went on to study with Cowell, who recommended her to Charles Seeger, a well-known teacher in New York. Seeger was at first reluctant to take on a woman student, a bias, he admitted, based on the "absence of mention of them in the histories of music." (But the absence is hardly surprising, since most of the histories were written by men.) But she soon became his best student, pursuing an avant-garde style worthy of Webern. In 1930 she received a Guggenheim Fellowship and traveled to Europe, where she was warmly received by Berg, Bartók, and Ravel. While in Berlin she wrote her best-known work, a String Quartet. Later, she married Seeger, her former teacher. In time, she gave up her career as a composer and turned to research on American folk music.

The role and importance of women in American music continues to grow. In the 1940s only a few women were enrolled in conservatories and other professional music schools. By 1990 more than a third of those enrolled were women, and the number of women in major orchestras has increased correspondingly. In the pop-music world, female singer/songwriters regularly top the charts.

Although change has been slower to come in the area of art music, several of America's leading composers are women. Joan Tower (b. 1938) rose to national prominence in 1981 with a dazzling 16-minute orchestral work, *Sequoia*. Although she began as a serialist, she has evolved toward a freer, more individual style. In 1969 Tower founded a contemporary ensemble, the Da Capo Chamber Ensemble. As both pianist and composer, Tower has taken the group all over America and abroad. She has lobbied tirelessly to have contemporary music included in mainline, prestige series instead of consigned to underbudgeted, poorly publicized contemporary series—what Tower calls "ghetto series." For most composers of art music, however, the barriers to widespread success remain considerable.

## WHERE ARE WE HEADED?

Although no one can predict what the musical future holds, we can point to four current social and musical trends that seem likely to continue.

### Segmented Audiences

In the eighteenth century, composers could use the current musical language of the day in full confidence that their audiences would understand it. That was still largely true even a hundred years ago. Today, however, the proliferation of musical languages and the segmentation of audiences have destroyed that confidence. Go into almost any record store and you will find the bins labeled for the guidance of many discrete audiences (see page 3). That segmentation is carefully observed by the organizations that make music available to the public. For example, MTV and the Chicago Symphony direct their appeals to very different audiences. MTV concentrates on viewers between the ages of 13 and 25. These music-lovers wear the latest fashions featured by specialty chains, have food tastes faster than gourmet, drive Camaros or Corollas rather than Buicks or BMWs, and spend much of their limited income on entertainment. By contrast, subscribers to the Chicago Symphony are typically between 30 and 60, buy their clothes at boutiques or department stores, eat in upscale restaurants, drive the "B" cars rather than the "C" cars, and allocate their larger incomes to a variety of obligations and indulgences.

True, the segmentation of audience and marketing opens up opportunities for composers and performers who would never be heard were the world of music more homogeneous. But it also fosters narrowness of taste and conformity in listening habits. Ironically, the more varied our musical fare becomes, the narrower many individual tastes seem to grow.

## Centrifugal Styles

Early rock 'n' roll was based almost exclusively on a single style derived from rhythm & blues. In the last 35 years, however, that style has spawned a whole range of rock styles. Each new style has spun off from another, and advocates often view their new style as incompatible with other styles.

A similar trend is apparent in art music as well. It is unlikely, for example, that there will ever be an aesthetic reconciliation between the avant-garde and the minimalists, though both ultimately derive their languages from the tonal music of the eighteenth and nineteenth centuries. Even Beethoven's most controversial works failed to polarize his audiences the way contemporary music has polarized ours. Few contemporary critics feel qualified to comment on the whole range of contemporary music.

## Vanishing Boundaries

Paradoxically, in this time of stylistic fragmentation and polarized opinions, it is often more difficult to distinguish between art music and popular music, between avant-garde music and traditional music. Whereas composers of art music took the stylistic and technological lead for many centuries, in our century much of the innovation—especially in the use of electronic technologies—is taking place in pop music and home electronic studios. Composers of art music have begun to borrow from the vast range of sounds and techniques routinely heard in pop music, movie soundtracks, and even jingles. This cross-fertilization is perhaps the most encouraging current evidence in contemporary music of a stylistic rapprochement.

## More Technology

Music composed on computers and synthesizers has entered the mainstream of musical life. The electrification and computerization of music is far more advanced than most people realize. The majority of film scores today are composed, and sometimes even recorded, at electronic work stations, and most music for television and advertising is now prepared on synthesizers. Synthesizer ensembles have replaced acoustic musicians from Las Vegas to Broadway. Few rock groups today venture on stage without an electronic orchestra. And, as we have seen, composers of art music regularly rely on synthesizers as well.

Although the traditional symphony orchestra is not about to disappear, the music it performs in the future is likely to reflect the influence of technological advances, just as the music written for piano during the nineteenth century reflected technological advances in the making of pianos.

## Dynamic Stasis

In 1967 the writer Leonard Meyer spoke of what he called the "probability of stasis" in the arts. Meyer meant a condition in which many different styles compete for an audience but in which no single style predominates. In a condition of stasis, there is vigorous internal activity, but the system as a whole does not advance. Although certain assumptions in Meyer's construct—for example, that "the rate of [scientific] change is probably slowing down"—can, more than two decades later, be challenged, his basic model seems to have held up. We might say that Western music today is in a state of "dynamic stasis." Activity is restless and constant, and the influence of non-Western musics is fostering stylistic pluralism, as we have seen in the music of Debussy, Varèse, the Beatles, and Adams.

At the same time, composers have become more modest in their expectations. Instead of seeking universal acceptance, they seem willing to settle for a secure reputation with a limited audience. It is probably no longer possible for a single composer to dominate the musical world as Beethoven did. To entertain that possibility would surely require the sacrifice of much of the musical diversity that we now enjoy, and very few people would be willing to make that sacrifice if it entailed the demise of their favorite type of music. In the end, the desire for a single dominating figure or style may represent a nostalgic longing for a simpler and less stressful past.

Yet the freedom to explore musical diversity, both past and present, is there as it has never been before. With this freedom goes the responsibility of making choices. It is not just a matter of which albums will be in your record collection or which stations you will tune in, but of what kind of relationship you will forge between yourself and one of humankind's most direct and powerful means of expression.

# GLOSSARY

*The glossary focuses on technical terms that recur throughout the text. Terms that appear only once can be accessed through the index. Most persons, musical style periods, and historical terms are also listed in the index.*

**absolute music**  Instrumental music without any explicit literary or pictorial associations, as opposed to *program music.*

**a cappella**  (ah ka-*pel*-uh) Music for voices alone, without instrumental accompaniment.

**accelerando**  (ak-sell-e-*ran*-doh) Getting faster.

**accent**  A conspicuous, sudden emphasis given to a particular sound, usually by an increase in volume.

**accidental**  A notational sign in a score indicating that a specific note is to be played as a flat (♭), a sharp (♯), or a natural (♮). The most common accidentals (flats and sharps) correspond to the five black notes in each octave of the keyboard.

**accompaniment**  The subordinate material or voices that support a melody.

**acoustics**  (1) The science of sound; (2) the art of optimizing sound in an enclosed space.

**adagio**  Quite slow tempo.

**allegro; allegretto**  Fast tempo; slightly fast tempo.

**alto**  (1) The lowest adult female voice; (2) the second-highest voice in a four-part texture.

**andante; andantino**  Moderately slow (walking) tempo; a little faster than andante.

**antiphon**  Originally, a plainchant that framed the singing of a psalm. The term derives from the early practice of singing psalms "antiphonally"—that is, with two or more alternating choirs.

**appoggiatura**  A strong-beat dissonance that resolves to a consonance; used as an expressive device in much tonal music.

**aria**  In opera or oratorio, a set piece, usually for a single performer, that expresses a character's emotion about a particular situation.

**arioso**  A singing style between aria and recitative.

**arpeggio**  (ar-*pej*-yio) A chord whose individual notes are played successively rather than simultaneously.

**arrangement**  An orchestration of a skeletal score or a reorchestration of a finished composition.

*ars nova*  The "new art" of fourteenth-century France; refers to the stylistic innovations, especially rhythmic, of composers around 1320.

**articulation**  The manner in which adjacent notes of a melody are connected or separated.

**art song**  A song focusing on artistic rather than popular expression.

**a** (ah) **tempo**  At the original tempo.

**atonality; atonal**  The absence of any sense of tonality.

**augmentation**  The restatement of a theme in longer note values, often twice as long (and therefore twice as slow) as the original.

**avant garde**  In the arts, on the leading edge of a change in style.

**ballade**  (1) One of several types of medieval secular songs, usually in A-A-B form; (2) a type of nineteenth-century character piece for piano.

**ballad opera**  A popular eighteenth-century English dramatic form characterized by spoken dialogue on topical themes interspersed with popular or folk songs.

**ballata**  A type of fourteenth-century Italian secular song, similar to the French virelai.

**ballet**  The theatrical presentation of group or solo dancing of great precision to a musical accompaniment, usually with costumes and scenery and conveying a story or theme.

**bar**  Same as *measure.*

**baritone**  Adult male voice of moderately low range.

**basic set**  The underlying tone row in a serial composition.

**bass**  (1) The lowest adult male voice; (2) the lowest voice in a polyphonic texture.

**bass clef**  The clef (𝄢) in the upper staff that shows pitches mostly *below* middle C.

**basse danse**  A popular Renaissance court dance for couples.

**bassoon**  A double-reed woodwind with low range.

**beam**  In musical notation, the heavy line (or lines) connecting notes of short duration.

**beat**  The regular pulse that provides the basic unit of musical time; often compared to the human heartbeat or pulse.

**bebop**  A cool, complex style of jazz that developed in the mid-1940s, closely associated with Charlie ("Bird") Parker.

**bel canto**  A style of singing that emphasizes the sensuous beauty of the voice, cultivated especially in Italian opera between 1800 and 1850.

**binary form**  A musical form consisting of two "unequal" halves (A-B), each of which is generally repeated. In rounded binary form, the theme that opened the first half returns in the second half.

**blue note** In blues singing or jazz, the deliberate off-pitch lowering of certain pitches.

**blues** (1) A form of African-American folk music, characterized by simple, repetitive structures and a highly flexible vocal delivery; (2) the style of singing heard in the blues.

**bow** In string playing, a bundle of bleached horsehairs stretched tautly between the ends of a wooden stick. To produce a sound, the bow is drawn over one or more of the strings.

**branle** A high-stepping Renaissance group dance.

**brass** A family of instruments with cup-shaped mouthpieces through which the player blows into a series of metal tubes. Usually constructed of brass or silver.

**bridge** (1) A passage connecting two sections of a composition; (2) on string instruments, a small piece of wood that holds the strings above the body.

**cadence** (*kay*-dunce); **cadential** The musical punctuation that separates phrases or periods, creating a sense of rest or conclusion that ranges from momentary to final.

**cadenza** An improvised passage for a soloist, usually placed within the closing ritornello in a concerto movement.

**canon** (1) Strict imitation, in which one voice imitates another at a staggered time interval; (2) a piece that uses canon throughout, such as "Row, Row, Row Your Boat."

**cantata** A Baroque genre for voice(s) and instruments on a sacred or secular poem, including recitatives, arias, and sometimes choruses.

**cantus firmus** ("fixed melody") A pre-existing plainchant or secular melody incorporated into a polyphonic composition, common from the twelfth through the sixteenth centuries.

**castrato** A male singer castrated during boyhood to preserve his soprano or alto vocal register. Castratos played a prominent role in seventeenth- and eighteenth-century opera.

**CD-ROM** Compact disc-read only memory. A compact-disc technology that enables a personal computer to access digitally text, still images, moving pictures, and sound.

**celesta** A small keyboard instrument invented in 1886 whose hammers strike a series of resonating steel plates to produce a bell-like but veiled sound. Used by composers from Tchaikovsky to Boulez.

**cell** In certain twentieth-century compositions, a brief, recurring musical figure that does not undergo traditional motivic development.

**chamber music** Music played by small ensembles, such as a string quartet, with one performer to a part.

**chance music** A type of contemporary music in which some or all of the elements, such as rhythm or the interaction among voices, are left to chance.

**chanson** (French, "song") The most popular form of secular vocal music in northern Europe during the late fifteenth and early sixteenth centuries.

**character piece** A short Romantic piano piece that expresses a single overall mood.

**choir** (1) A vocal ensemble with more than one singer to a part; (2) a section of an instrumental ensemble, such as a brass choir.

**chorale** (1) A German hymn, especially popular in the Baroque; (2) a polyphonic setting of such a hymn, such as those by J. S. Bach.

**chord** A group of three or more pitches sounded simultaneously.

**chordal style** An alternate term for *homophony.*

**chorus** (1) Same as *choir*; (2) each varied repetition of a 12-bar blues pattern; (3) the principal section of an American popular song, following the *verse(s).*

**chromatic** A descriptive term for melodies or harmonies that use all or most of the twelve degrees of the octave.

**chromatic scale** The pattern that results when all twelve adjacent semitones in an octave are played successively.

**clef** In musical notation, a symbol at the beginning of a staff that determines the pitches of the lines and spaces. The most common clefs are *treble* (𝄞) for indicating pitches mostly above middle C and *bass* (𝄢) for indicating pitches mostly below middle C.

**closing area** In a movement in sonata form, the final stage in an exposition or recapitulation that confirms the temporary or home key with a series of cadences.

**coda** The optional final section of a movement or an entire composition.

**combinatorial** A descriptive term for tone rows in which the second half is a transposed version of the first half.

**compound meters** Duple or triple meters in which the individual beats are subdivided into triple units.

**computer (personal)** Electronic device with screen display that performs a variety of tasks in response to instructions transmitted through a typewriter keyboard. When connected to a synthesizer and printer, computers can aid in the creation, playback, and printing of music.

**concertino** The solo group in a Baroque concerto grosso.

**concerto** An instrumental composition for orchestra and soloist (or a small group of soloists).

**concerto grosso** The principal variety of Baroque concerto, for a small group of soloists (the concertino) and a larger ensemble (the ripieno).

**conjunct motion**  Melodic motion by half steps or whole steps.

**consonance**  Intervals or chords that sound relatively stable.

**countermelody**  A melody that contrasts with or complements another melody.

**counterpoint; contrapuntal**  A texture that combines two or more rhythmically independent voices.

**countersubject**  In a fugue, a subsidiary theme that appears regularly in counterpoint with the subject.

**continuo**  (1) In Baroque music, the harmonization of the figured bass; (2) the instrument(s) that play the continuo, most often cello plus harpsichord or organ.

**crescendo**  Getting louder.

**Cubism**  An avant-garde French art movement of the early twentieth century, marked by a fascination with abstract geometrical shapes.

**cyclicism**  The incorporation of a single theme into two or more movements of a multi-movement composition.

**da capo**  ("from the head [beginning]") A performance direction to repeat music from the beginning of a piece up to a designated point.

**da capo aria**  An aria in A-B-A form, in which the final A is indicated only by the performance direction *da capo*.

**declamation**  The manner in which words are set to music, especially with respect to rhythm and accent.

**degree**  A more precise term for *note* when referring to the steps of a scale.

**developing variation**  A Romantic technique in which melodies are developed through extension and elaboration rather than Classical fragmentation.

**development**  (1) The process of manipulating musical themes through techniques such as fragmentation, sequence, and reharmonization; (2) the section in a sonata-form movement devoted to that process.

**diatonic**  Describes music made up of the seven pitches of the diatonic scale, which contains five whole steps and two half steps.

**Dies Irae**  ("Day of wrath") A section of the Requiem Mass. Used by Berlioz in the last movement of his *Symphonie fantastique*.

**digital**  A descriptive term for laser technology in which information of all kinds is stored as a series of binary bits, each of which is either "on" or "off."

**diminuendo**  Getting softer.

**diminution**  The technique of embellishing a simple melody with systematically smaller note values (most commonly by half), thus seeming to speed up the melody.

**disco**  A style of popular dance music characterized by slick, ostinato-like rhythms and propulsive, repetitive lyrics.

**disjunct motion**  Melodic motion by a leap rather than by a step.

**dissonance**  Intervals or chords that sound impure, harsh, or unstable.

**dominant**  (1) The fifth degree of the diatonic scale; (2) the triad built on this degree; (3) the key oriented around this degree.

**dominant seventh chord**  A dominant triad with an added seventh degree—for example, G-B-D-F.

**dotted rhythm**  The alternation of LONG and short notes, named after the notation ( ♩. ♪) used to record them.

**downbeat**  A strong or accented beat, most frequently the first beat of a measure.

**draw bars**  Primitive synthesizer-like controls used on Hammond organs in the 1950s.

**drone**  A sustained tone (a kind of permanent pedal point) over which a melody unfolds.

**duet**  A composition for two performers.

**duple meter**  The regular grouping of beats into twos (STRONG-weak). The most common duple meters have two or four beats per measure.

**dynamics**  The relative softness or loudness of a note or passage.

**electronic music**  Music in which some or all of the sounds are produced by electronic generators.

**embellishment**  An ornamental addition to a simpler melody.

**ensemble**  (1) A group of performers; (2) a musical number in an opera, oratorio, or cantata sung by two or more performers; (3) the extent to which a group of performers coordinate their performance.

**entry**  In an imitative texture, the beginning of each statement of the theme.

**envelope**  The graphic representation of a sound's attack, duration, and pattern of decay.

**episode**  (1) In a fugue, a freer passage between full statements of the subject; (2) in ritornello form, a freer concertino passage between ripieno statements of the ritornello.

**espressivo**  Expressively.

**estampie**  A type of early instrumental (perhaps dance) music consisting of independent sections strung together.

**étude**  A musical piece designed to address a particular technical problem on an instrument.

**exposition**  The first section of a movement in sonata form.

**expression** (1) The general character of a passage or work; (2) the blend of feeling and intellect brought to a performance by the performer.

**Expressionism** A short-lived Austro-German art movement at the beginning of the twentieth century, marked by a focus on the dark, mysterious side of the human mind.

**Fauvism** The French version of Austro-German Expressionism.

**fermata** In musical notation, a sign (⌢) indicating the prolongation of a note or rest beyond its notated value.

**figure** (1) In Baroque and Classical music, the numbers below a staff designating the harmonies to be filled in above; (2) a general term for a brief melodic pattern.

**figured bass** The Baroque system of adding figures to a bass line, indicating what harmonies are to be improvised on each beat.

**final** In plainchant, the concluding note in a mode; corresponds roughly to the tonic note in a tonal scale.

**finale** (1) The last movement of an instrumental work; (2) the large ensemble that concludes an act in an opera.

**fine arts** The realm of human experience characterized as aesthetic rather than practical or utilitarian, including music, painting, dance, theater, and film.

**fingerboard** A piece of wood extending from the body of a string instrument; the strings are attached to the end of the fingerboard.

**flat** (1) In musical notation, a sign (♭) indicating that the note it precedes is to be played a half step lower; (2) the term used to specify a particular note, for example, B♭.

**FM synthesis** Frequency-modulation synthesis; a superior version of electronic synthesis introduced in the consumer market by Yamaha in 1982.

**folk music** Music indigenous to a particular ethnic group, usually preserved and transmitted orally.

**form** A term used to designate standardized musical shapes, such as binary form or sonata form.

**forte; fortissimo** Loud; very loud.

**fortepiano** The wooden-framed eighteenth-century piano used by Mozart, Haydn, and their contemporaries.

**fragmentation** The technique of developing a theme by dividing it into smaller units, most common in the music of the Viennese Classicists.

**frequency** In acoustics, the number of times per second that the air carrying a sound vibrates as a wave.

**fret** A raised strip across the fingerboard of a stringed instrument, designed to produce a specific pitch when stopped at that point.

**frottola** A light, popular Italian song, a precursor of the Italian madrigal.

**fugato** A fugal passage within a composition.

**fugue** A polyphonic composition that makes systematic use of imitation, usually based on a single subject, and that opens with a series of exposed entries on that subject.

**full cadence** An emphatic cadence at the end of a musical period.

**fundamental** The basic pitch of a tone.

**gamelan** A small Javanese orchestra consisting mainly of metal percussion instruments.

**genre** The term used to identify a general category of music that shares similar performance forces, formal structures, and/or style—for example, "string quartet" or "12-bar blues."

**glissando** Rapid sliding from one note to another, usually on continuous-pitch instruments such as the trombone or violin, but also on discrete-pitch instruments such as the piano or harp.

**ground (bass)** A repeating pattern, usually in the bass, over which a melody unfolds, as in Dido's lament from Purcell's *Dido and Aeneas*.

**half cadence** An intermediate cadence, usually on the dominant chord, within a musical period.

**half step (semitone)** The interval between any two adjacent notes on a keyboard; the smallest interval in common use in Western music.

**harmonic** (1) In acoustics, a synonym for *overtone* or *partial;* (2) in string playing, a high-pitched, whistling tone made by bowing a lightly stopped string.

**harmonic minor scale** The scale that results from flatting the third and sixth degrees of the major scale.

**harmonic rhythm** The rate at which harmony changes and the degree of regularity with which it changes.

**harmonize** To provide a melody with a chordal accompaniment.

**harmony** (1) In general, the simultaneous aspects of music; (2) specifically, the simultaneous playing of two or more different sounds.

**harpsichord** A Baroque keyboard instrument in which the strings are plucked by quills.

**head** The beginning of a theme.

**heavy metal** A descriptive term for rock bands since the 1970s whose heavily amplified electric and percussion sounds have been associated with youthful rebellion and defiance.

**heterophony** (heter-*off*-ony) A texture in which two or more variations of the same melody are performed simultaneously, common in folk music.

**hexachord**  the six usable degrees of the modal scale, often used to organize Renaissance music.

**hocket**  In late medieval polyphony, the alternation of short melodic phrases (or even single notes) between two voices.

**homophony; homophonic**  (ho-*mof*-ony; homo-*fon*-ick) Texture in which all the voices move more or less together (often referred to as the *chordal style*).

**hymn**  A simple religious song in several stanzas, sung in a church service by the congregation.

**idée fixe**  (French, "fixed idea") Term used by Berlioz for the theme representing his beloved in every movement of his *Symphonie fantastique.*

**imitation**  The successive repetition in different voices of a single musical idea.

**Impressionism**  A French art movement of the late nineteenth century that rejected Romanticism in favor of fleeting, informal scenes from everyday life.

**improvisation**  The spontaneous, on-the-spot creation of music, preserved today largely in jazz but common in Western music well into the nineteenth century.

**incidental music**  Music performed before and during a play to intensify the mood.

**intermedio**  In the Renaissance, a musical entertainment between the acts of a play.

**interpretation**  The manner in which a performer carries out a composer's performance directions.

**interval**  The acoustical distance between two pitches, usually reckoned by the number of intervening scale degrees.

**introduction**  A passage or section, often in a slow tempo, that prepares the way for a more extended section.

**inversion**  The playing of a melody upside down, with upward intervals played downwards and vice versa, most common in contrapuntal and serial music.

**irregular meter**  The mixture at a single rhythmic level of more than one metric grouping.

**jazz**  A style of performance developed largely by African-Americans after 1900; the most original form of American music in the twentieth century.

**jongleur; jongleuress**  (zhong-*ler*; zhong-ler-*ess*) Male and female musical minstrels of the Middle Ages.

**key**  (1) In tonal music, one of twelve possible tonalities organized around a triad built on the main note; (2) on a keyboard, a lever pressed down to produce sound.

**key signature**  Sharps or flats placed at the beginning of a staff to indicate the key of a passage or work.

**K. numbers**  The common method of referring to works by Mozart, after the chronological catalogue first published by Ludwig Köchel in 1865.

**largo; larghetto**  Very slow tempo; less slow than largo.

**legato**  The smooth, seamless connection of adjacent notes in a melody.

**Leitmotiv**  A term adopted by Wagner's disciples to designate the "leading motives" in his operas; translated as *leitmotif.*

**libretto**  A "little book" that contains the complete text of an opera, oratorio, and so forth.

**Lied**  (German, "song") A vocal piece dating back to the polyphonic Lied of the fourteenth century. The solo German Lied, accompanied by piano, reached its zenith during the nineteenth century.

**line**  A general term for a discrete voice or part in a vocal or instrumental composition.

**liturgical drama**  A sung religious dialogue that flourished during the eleventh and twelfth centuries. Liturgical in spirit even when performed outside the formal liturgy, liturgical dramas were the most elaborate form of medieval music.

**lyre**  An ancient plucked string instrument in the shape of a box (Figure 5.1), whose association with music (especially with the mythological character Orpheus) is so strong that the word *lyric* is derived from it.

**madrigal**  A vocal form that arose in Italy during the sixteenth century and developed into the most ambitious secular form of the Renaissance.

**madrigalism**  An alternate term for *word painting*, reflecting the frequent use of word painting in the Renaissance madrigal.

**major mode**  One of two colorings applied to a key, characterized by the major scale and the resulting predominance of major triads. Generally sounds bright and stable.

**major scale**  A pattern of seven (ascending) notes, five separated by whole steps, with half steps between the third and fourth and the seventh and eighth degrees.

**major seventh**  A highly dissonant interval a half step smaller than an octave.

**major third**  An interval consisting of four half steps; a major third forms the bottom interval of a major triad.

**major triad**  A triad consisting of a major third plus a minor third bounded by a perfect fifth.

**march**  A military style (or piece) characterized by strongly accented duple meter and clear sectional structures.

**Mass**  (1) The central worship service of the Roman Catholic Church; (2) the music written for that service.

**mazurka**  Polish folk dance in rapid triple meter with strong offbeat accents.

**measure (bar)** The single recurrence of each regular pattern in a meter, consisting of a strong first beat and weaker subsidiary beats and set off in musical notation by vertical lines known as bar lines.

**melisma; melismatic** (muh-*liz*-muh; mel-iz-*mat*-ic) Technique of singing in which a single syllable receives many notes.

**melody** (1) The aspect of music having to do with the succession of single notes in a coherent arrangement; (2) a particular succession of such notes (also referred to as *tune, theme,* or *voice*).

**meter** The organization of strong and weak beats into a regular, recurring pattern.

**metronome** Mechanical (or, today, electrical) device that ticks (or blinks) out regular tempos from about 40 to 208 beats per minute.

**metronome marking** A number, usually placed at the top of a piece, that indicates tempo by telling how many beats of a certain note value will be heard per minute, for example, ♩ = 60.

**mezzo** (*met*-zoh) Medium, as in *mezzopiano* (medium soft).

**microtones** Intervals smaller than a half step.

**MIDI** Acronym for "musical instrument digital interface," the industrywide standard adopted in 1982 that permits personal computers and synthesizers to talk to one another.

**miniature** A descriptive term for a short Romantic piece, usually for piano.

**minimalism** A contemporary style marked by steady pulse, simple triadic harmonies, and insistent repetition of short melodic patterns.

**minor mode** One of two colorings, generally dark and unstable, applied to a key, characterized by the minor scale and the resulting predominance of minor triads.

**minor scale** The scale in which the third and sixth degrees are the lower of two options. The melodic minor scale raises the sixth and seventh degrees in ascending passages and lowers them in descending passages.

**minor third** An interval consisting of three half steps; a minor third forms the bottom interval of a minor triad.

**minor triad** A triad consisting of a minor third plus a major third bounded by a perfect fifth.

**minuet** A seventeenth-century court dance in moderate triple meter that later served as the model for the third movement of Classical instrumental works.

**mode** (1) In the Middle Ages, a means of organizing plainchant according to orientations around the seven-note diatonic scale (corresponding to the white notes on a keyboard); (2) in the tonal system, one of the two colorings, called major and minor, that may be applied to any of twelve keys.

**modulation** The process of changing keys in a tonal work, as in "the modulation from C major to F minor."

**molto allegro** Very fast tempo.

**monody** A style of accompanied solo singing that evolved in the early Baroque in which the meaning of the text was expressed in a flexible vocal line.

**monophony; monophonic** (mo-*nof*-ony; mo-no-*fon*-ick) A musical texture consisting of a single voice, as in plainchant.

**Moog** Robert Moog, American inventor of early synthesizers. During the 1970s his most popular synthesizer was itself known as "the Moog."

**morality play** In the Middle Ages, a monophonic drama set to music to illustrate a moral point, such as the struggle between good and evil. An example is Hildegard of Bingen's *Play of the Virtues* (pages 79–82).

**motet** A descriptive term for the several varieties of polyphonic vocal music, mostly sacred, from the Middle Ages to the present.

**motive** The smallest coherent unit of a larger musical idea.

**movement** A self-contained, largely independent portion of a larger piece, such as a symphony or concerto.

**MTV** A cable TV service introduced in the 1980s devoted to heavily produced videos of current popular hits.

**multimedia** Rapidly developing technology that enables information of all kinds—text, still images, moving pictures, sound—to be stored and retrieved on a single digital medium, such as CD-ROM or videodisc.

**multi-timbral** A descriptive term for the ability of a synthesizer to record different timbres simultaneously.

**music** Broadly speaking, sounds organized to express a wide variety of human emotions.

**musical theater (musical)** A hybrid form of twentieth-century American musical entertainment that incorporates elements of vaudeville, operetta, jazz, and popular song.

**music drama** Wagner's designation for his operas.

**musicology** The scholarly study of music and its historical contexts.

**musique concrète** Natural sounds that have been recorded electronically.

**mute** A mechanical device used with string and brass instruments to muffle the tone.

**nationalism** A nineteenth-century political movement that led in music to the frequent use of national folk songs, styles, and historical subjects.

**natural** (1) In musical notation, a sign (♮) indicating that the preceding accidental applied to this note is to be cancelled; (2) the name given to such a note, for example, C♮.

**neoclassicism** A twentieth-century movement characterized by a selective and eclectic revival of the formal proportions and economical means of eighteenth-century music.

**neumatic** In plainchant, a style in which each syllable of text receives several notes.

**neume** The stemless symbols used in medieval sources to notate plainchant (see Figure 4.12).

**nocturne** ("night piece") A nineteenth-century character piece for piano.

**non-imitative counterpoint** Same as *unequal-voiced counterpoint.*

**non-legato** The slight separation of adjacent notes.

**note** (1) A sound with a specific pitch and duration; (2) in musical notation, the symbol (e.g., ♩) for such a sound; (3) a single key on a keyboard.

**octave** The interval in which one pitch is doubled (or halved) in frequency by another pitch. The octave is found in virtually all music systems.

**Office (Divine)** The eight daily worship services, apart from the Mass, in the Roman Catholic Church.

**ondes martenot** An early electronic instrument invented in the late 1920s by Maurice Martenot.

**opera** A drama set to music; the dominant form of Western music from the seventeenth through the nineteenth centuries.

**opera buffa** A comic form of eighteenth-century Italian opera featuring everyday characters involved in outlandish plot intrigues.

**opera seria** A serious, heroic form of eighteenth-century opera featuring historical or mythological figures in stereotypical plots stressing the tension between love and duty.

**operetta** A light, entertaining version of Romantic opera with spoken dialogue between numbers.

**opus** A "work"; opus numbers were introduced by publishers in the seventeenth century to identify each of a composer's works.

**oratorio (English)** A musical entertainment usually on a sacred subject and including recitatives, arias, choruses, and an overture.

**orchestration** The designation of what instruments are to play what voices or notes in a composition. The process of orchestrating is often referred to as *scoring.*

**Ordinary of the Mass** In the Roman Catholic liturgy, the five items (Kyrie, Gloria, Credo, Sanctus, Agnus Dei) that are part of every celebration of the Mass.

**organ** An instrument in which air forced through pipes by mechanical means is controlled by one or more keyboards, including a foot-operated pedal keyboard.

**organum** The earliest type of medieval polyphonic music, in which voices were added above a plainchant.

**ornament** An embellishment, such as a trill, used to decorate a melodic line.

**ostinato** A brief pattern repeated over and over again at the same pitch, often in the bass.

**overtones** The spectrum of the higher-pitched frequencies that accompany the fundamental of any pitch and determine its tone color (also called *harmonics* or *partials*).

**overture** An instrumental piece that precedes a dramatic work such as an opera (some overtures are nevertheless independent compositions).

**paraphrase** The practice by Renaissance composers of embellishing or elaborating a cantus firmus in polyphonic vocal works.

**parlante** Nineteenth-century operatic style in which the voices declaim in a rapid, speechlike manner against a backdrop of melody and accompaniment.

**part** (1) One of the voices in a polyphonic work; (2) the written music for a single player in an ensemble.

**partial** Same as *overtone.*

**passacaglia** Baroque technique in which a brief melodic idea repeats over and over while the other voices are varied freely.

**passage work** Descriptive term for figuration consisting of rapid runs and scales, common in keyboard music.

**patch chords** On early synthesizers, the cables required to connect various components.

**PCM** Pulse-code modulation. A more sophisticated method of sampling introduced into the consumer synthesizer market in the late 1980s.

**pedal board** An organ's foot-operated keyboard.

**pedal point** Long-held tones, usually in the bass of a polyphonic passage.

**pentatonic scale** A five-note scale found in numerous non-Western musics and adopted as an exotic element by many twentieth-century Western composers.

**percussion** Instruments, either tuned or untuned, that produce sounds by being struck, rattled, or scraped. Common percussion include drums, cymbals, and bells.

**performance directions** Words or symbols provided by composers to instruct performers in *how* their music is to be played, including articulation, dynamics, expression, and phrasing.

**period** The musical equivalent of a paragraph.

**period instrument** An instrument of a type that was in use at the time a work was originally performed.

**phrase** The coherent segments that make up a melody; roughly equivalent to a sentence in prose.

**phrasing** The manner in which a performer organizes and presents the parts of a composition.

**piano** A keyboard instrument whose tone is produced by hammers striking strings tightly stretched over a large soundboard. A foot pedal controls the damping of the strings.

**piano; pianissimo** Soft; very soft.

**piano trio** A chamber work for piano and two other instruments, usually violin and cello.

**pitch** (1) The high and low of sounds, measured in acoustical frequencies; (2) a particular note, such as middle C.

**pizzicato** Playing a string instrument that is normally bowed by plucking the strings with the finger.

**plainchant (plainsong, Gregorian chant)** Monophonic unison music sung during Catholic church services since the Middle Ages.

**poles of attraction** A term introduced by Stravinsky to describe the harmonic equilibrium of his neoclassical works.

**polyphony; polyphonic** (po-*lif*-ony; poly-*fon*-ick) A musical texture in which the individual voices move independently of one another.

**polyrhythm** A texture in which the rhythms of various voices seem to exist independently of one another.

**pop** A generic term for popular music in contemporary America, overlapping but not identical with rock.

**postmodern** A term adopted around the mid-1970s to describe our current eclectic, experimental age.

**prelude** An introductory piece (though Chopin and other nineteenth-century composers wrote independent preludes).

**premiere** The first public performance of a musical or dramatic work.

**prepared piano** In contemporary music, the modifying of a traditional grand piano by such techniques as placing various objects between the strings.

**presto; prestissimo** Very fast; extremely fast.

**primary area** In a movement in sonata form, the first stage in an exposition; establishes the tonic key with one or more themes.

**program music** An instrumental work associated explicitly by the composer with a story or other extramusical idea.

**Proper of the Mass** The parts of the Mass that vary from day to day according to the church calendar.

**punk** A descriptive term adopted by the most rebellious heavy metal bands and their followers.

**quarter tone** Half a semitone.

**quartet** (1) A piece for four singers or instrumentalists; (2) a group of four singers or instrumentalists.

**quintet** (1) A piece for five singers or instrumentalists; (2) a group of five singers or instrumentalists.

**ragtime** A type of popular American music, usually for piano, that arose around 1900 and contributed to the emergence of jazz.

**range** The pitch distance between the lowest note and the highest note of an instrument, a composition, or an individual part.

**recapitulation** The third principal section of a movement in sonata form whose function is to resolve the harmonic conflicts set up in the exposition and development.

**recitative** A flexible style of vocal delivery employed in opera, oratorio, and cantata and tailored to the accents and rhythms of the text.

**reduction** The compression of a complex, multi-stave score onto one or two staves.

**reed** In wind instruments such as the clarinet and oboe, a small vibrating element made of cane that serves as all (double reed) or part (single reed) of the mouthpiece.

**register** The relative location within the range of a voice or an instrument, such as "the piercing upper register of the oboe."

**resolution** A move from a dissonance to a consonance.

**rest** (1) in music, a brief silence; (2) in musical notation, a sign indicating such a silence (e.g., ♪).

**retransition** In sonata form, the passage that leads from the harmonic instability of the development to the stability of the recapitulation.

**retrograde** Playing a theme backward.

**rhythm** (1) The pattern in time created by the incidence and duration of individual sounds; (2) used more loosely to refer to a particular rhythm, for example, "a dotted rhythm."

**rhythm & blues (R&B)** A term coined in 1949 to describe the heavily rhythmic urban blues cultivated mainly by midwestern African-American musicians.

**rhythmic background** The subdivisions of beats within a regular meter.

**rhythmic foreground** The regular beats provided by meter.

**ripieno** The largest of the two instrumental groups in a Baroque concerto grosso.

**ritard; ritardando** Slowing down the tempo.

**ritornello** (Italian, "the little thing that returns") A recurring theme in eighteenth-century arias and concertos.

**ritornello form** Baroque instrumental form based on recurrences of a ritornello.

**rock 'n' roll (rock)** Style of popular vocal music, often for dancing, that developed in the United States and England during the 1950s, characterized by a hard, driving duple meter and amplified instrumental accompaniment. Currently the most widespread musical style in the world.

**rondo** A musical form in which a main theme alternates with other themes or sections, for example, A-B-A-C-A.

**round** A simple sung canon in which all voices enter on the same note after the same time interval.

**rubato** "Robbed" time; the subtle pressing forward and holding back the tempo in performance.

**sampling** The capacity of a synthesizer to extrapolate from a single example a homogeneous timbre over a wide pitch range.

**scale** An array of fixed, ordered pitches bounded by two notes an octave apart. The common Western scales contain seven notes; in non-Western cultures, scales may contain fewer or more than seven notes.

**scherzo** (Italian, "joke") A faster, often humorous transformation of a minuet, introduced into symphonies by Beethoven.

**score** The complete musical notation of a composition, especially for an ensemble; the individual parts are lined up vertically.

**scoring** The process of orchestration.

**secondary area** In a movement in sonata form, the theme or group of themes that follows the transition and establishes the new key in the exposition.

**semitone** Same as *half step*.

**sequence** (1) The repetition of a musical idea at progressively higher or lower pitches; (2) a form of medieval chant.

**sequencing** On a synthesizer, programming a series of sounds.

**serialism** The technique, introduced by Schoenberg, of basing a composition on a series, or tone row. Boulez and others have extended serialism to rhythm and timbre.

**shape** The interrelationship through time of the parts or sections of a piece. Standardized shapes are commonly referred to as *forms*.

**sharp** (1) In musical notation, a sign (♯) indicating that the note it precedes is to be played a half step higher; (2) the means of designating particular notes, for example, F♯.

**simple meter** A meter in which the main beats are subdivided into twos, such as 2/4 or 3/4.

**Singspiel** ("sung play") German folk or comic opera in which arias, ensembles, and choruses are interspersed with spoken dialogue.

**slur** (1) In musical notation, a curved line connecting notes that are to be played legato; (2) in performance, the playing of legato.

**sonata** A chamber work in several movements; in the Baroque, typically for three parts (the continuo part normally requiring two instruments); in later periods, for one or two instruments.

**sonata-concerto form** A hybrid of Baroque ritornello form and sonata form often used in the Classical concerto.

**sonata form** A musical form or style, originating in the eighteenth century, based on successive stages of stability, tension, and resolution; the most influential form developed during the age of tonality.

**sonata-rondo form** A synthesis of sonata and rondo forms, especially popular in finales of Classical instrumental works.

**song cycle** A collection of poems set to music and tied together by mood or story line.

**sonority** A general term for sound quality, either of a brief moment or of an entire composition.

**soprano** (1) The high woman's (or boy's) voice; (2) the highest voice in a polyphonic texture.

**spinning-out** A translation of the German *Fortspinnung*, in reference to the single-minded use in Baroque music of a brief motive to generate a long, continuous phrase.

**Sprechstimme** A vocal delivery, developed by Schoenberg, intermediate between speech and song.

**staccato** (1) In musical notation, a dot placed above a notehead to indicate that it is to receive only about half its regular value; (2) in performance, the pronounced separation of adjacent notes.

**staff** (plural, *staves*) In musical notation, the five horizontal lines on which one or more voices are notated.

**stanza** In vocal works, poetic units two lines or longer of equal length and accent pattern, often sung to the same music.

**stem** In musical notation, the vertical line attached to a notehead.

**stop** On the organ, hand-operated levers that activate different means of sound production, thereby varying the tone color.

**stop (double, triple, quadruple)** In string playing, the sounding of two, three, or four strings at once.

**stretto** In a fugue, beginning an entry of a subject before a previous entry has finished.

**string quartet** (1) Ensemble consisting of two violins, viola, and cello; (2) a work composed for this ensemble.

**strings** Family of bowed or plucked instruments in which thin strings are stretched over a wooden frame.

**strophic form** Vocal form in which each stanza of a poem is set to the same music.

**structure** A term often used in music to mean shape or form.

**style** The result of the interaction among rhythm, melody, harmony, texture, color, and shape that gives the music of a particular period or composer its distinctiveness.

**stylistic modulation** In contemporary music, the shifting among discrete styles (for example, Renaissance and Viennese Classicism) within the same composition.

**subdominant** (1) The fourth degree of the diatonic scale; (2) the triad built on this degree; (3) the key oriented around this degree.

**subject** The main theme of a fugue.

**suite** (1) A work consisting of a collection of dances, popular in the Baroque; (2) an abbreviated version of a longer work, for example, the suite from the film *Star Wars*.

**swing** (1) A style of jazz playing whose flexible, improvised rhythms resist notation; (2) name used to describe big band jazz from the 1930s and 1940s.

**syllabic** In plainchant, a style in which each syllable of text receives a single note.

**symbolism** French literary movement of the late nineteenth century favoring suggestion and allusion rather than realism or naturalism.

**symphonic poem** Same as *tone poem*.

**symphony** A large orchestral composition in several movements; a dominant form of public music in the eighteenth and nineteenth centuries.

**syncopation** The accenting, within a well-defined meter, of weaker beats or portions of beats.

**synthesizer** An electronic device that can create a wide variety of sounds in response to the user's instructions.

**system** A group of staves connected by a brace, indicating that they are to be played simultaneously.

**tail** The end of a theme.

**tailpiece** The holder to which the strings are attached at the lower end of the body of a string instrument.

**tango** A duple-meter dance from Argentina that was popular in Paris in the early twentieth century.

**tempo** (Italian, "time") The speed of a piece of music, usually reckoned by the rate of its beats.

**tenor** (1) The high male voice; (2) the second-lowest voice in a four-part texture; (3) the long-held voice in a medieval organum.

**ternary form** A three-part musical structure (A-B-A) based on statement (A), contrast (B), and repetition (A).

**texture** The musical weave of a composition, such as *homophonic* or *contrapuntal*.

**thematic anticipation** The Romantic practice of introducing fragments of a theme before presenting it in its entirety.

**thematic transformation** A Romantic technique that preserves the essential pitch identity of a theme while altering its rhythm or character.

**theme** A self-contained melodic idea on which musical works are frequently based.

**theme and variations** Popular form in which a theme is followed by variations that preserve the phrase lengths and harmonization of the theme while varying its rhythms, melodies, and textures.

**through-composed** A descriptive term for a song or an instrumental movement in which there is no large-scale repetition.

**timbre** (*tam*-burr) Same as *tone color*.

**time signature** The two numbers that appear in a score immediately after the clefs. The upper number indicates how many beats each measure is to receive; the lower number indicates the value of the note that receives each beat.

**toccata** An improvisatory style of keyboard music especially popular during the Baroque.

**tonality; tonal** A harmonic system in which triads are arranged hierarchically around a central triad called the tonic.

**tone** A more general term for pitch or note.

**tone cluster** The simultaneous sounding of adjacent pitches.

**tone color (timbre)** The acoustical properties of a sound, including its envelope and the distribution of overtones above the fundamental.

**tone poem (symphonic poem)** A piece of orchestral program music in one long movement.

**tone row** In serial music, the ordering of all twelve notes of the chromatic scale to serve as the basis of a composition.

**tonic** (1) The first degree, or central note, of the diatonic scale; (2) the triad built on this degree; (3) the key oriented around this degree.

**total serialism** The application of serial techniques to all aspects of musical style.

**transcription** An arrangement, usually for a solo instrument such as a piano, of an orchestral or vocal work.

**transition** In a movement in sonata form, the unstable stage in an exposition that undertakes the modulation from the tonic to the new key.

**transpose; transposition** To move a passage (or section or entire work) from one pitch level to another.

**treble clef** The clef (𝄞) in the upper staff that shows pitches mostly *above* middle C.

**tremolo** In string playing, repetitions of a tone produced by rapid alternation between up-and-down strokes of the bow.

**triad** A chord consisting of three pitches constructed around intervals of interlocking thirds (on the white notes, this amounts to every other note).

**trill** Musical ornament that consists of two notes a half step or a whole step apart played in rapid alternation.

**trio** (1) A work for three performers; (2) the second section of a Baroque dance such as a minuet.

**trio sonata** A Baroque sonata for two treble instruments and continuo, generally requiring four performers.

**triple meter** The regular grouping of beats into threes, as in a waltz.

**triplet** The grouping of three notes per beat, usually in contrast to the standard grouping of two notes per beat.

**tritone** A dissonant interval consisting of three whole steps, known in medieval music as "the devil in music."

**trope** An addition to the plainchant, usually in the form of new text set to either existing or new music.

**troubadors; trouvères** Poet/musicians, usually aristocratic, active in southern and northern France during the Middle Ages.

**tune** A less formal term for a melody, especially a catchy melody.

**tutti** (Italian, "all") The full ensemble.

**under-third cadence** A fourteenth-century cadence, closely associated with Francesco Landini, in which the melody proceeds from the seventh to the sixth degree of the modal scale before rising a third to the tonic note.

**unequal-voiced counterpoint (non-imitative counterpoint)** A musical texture in which independent voices of different character compete for attention.

**unison** A descriptive term for music sung or played at the same pitch by two different voices or instruments.

**unit pulse** A rhythmic technique in which meter is replaced by a focus on the shortest rhythmic value.

**upbeat** A weak or unaccented beat that anticipates a strong downbeat.

**variation** (1) Generally, an altered version of a rhythm, motive, or theme; (2) in theme and variations, each regular section following the theme, in which the phrase lengths and harmonization remain true (or close) to the theme while the rhythms, melodies, and textures change.

**verismo** A descriptive term for a realistic, often sensational, type of late-Romantic Italian opera, whose disreputable characters are caught up in lust, greed, betrayal, or revenge.

**vernacular dramas** A sung monophonic play presented in the Middle Ages by roving minstrels, who freely mixed secular texts, instrumental music, and plainchant.

**verse** One of two sections (verse and bridge) of many American popular songs, especially common in the sequence verse-verse-bridge-verse.

**vibrato** On string instruments, small but rapid fluctuations in pitch used to intensify a sound.

**virtuosity** In a composition, a focus on exceptional technical demands; in a performance, a focus on exceptional technical display.

**virtuoso** A performer with exceptional technical skills.

**voice** (1) The human voice; (2) an independent line in any polyphonic piece.

**walking bass** A Baroque pattern in which a bass part moves steadily in constant rhythms.

**waltz** A popular nineteenth-century dance in moderate to fast triple meter.

**white noise** Sounds containing every audible frequency at approximately the same intensity.

**whole step (whole tone)** An interval equal to two half steps.

**whole-tone scale** An exotic non-Western scale employed by Debussy and other Western composers.

**woodwinds** A family of instruments, constructed largely of wood, that produce sound by means of blowing air across an aperture or through a vibrating reed.

**word painting** A technique that became prominent in the Renaissance, in which musical figures are used to represent specific images—falling, sighing, weeping, rejoicing, and so forth.

# CREDITS

# INDEX

*This index is restricted to important movements, persons, works, and terms to facilitate study and review. Concise definitions of all musical terms are in the glossary. Although typically only the first appearance of technical terms is cited, hard-to-trace terms (for example, fugato) are indexed throughout the book. Works discussed extensively are listed by title, by composer, and—where appropriate—by genre. **Boldface** page numbers designate the main biographical entry for each composer; italic page numbers indicate illustrations (illustrations of composers are not listed separately). The abbreviation T.E. stands for Tape Example and refers to the elements tape packaged with the book. C.P. stands for Color Plate.*

absolute music, 267, 414
academy (concert), 291, 335–37, *337*
*a cappella*, 150
accelerando, 409
accent, 24, T.E. 13a–b
accidental, 29
accompaniment, 30
Adams, John, 703–6
    "News Has a Kind of Mystery," *Nixon in China*, 703–6, *703*
allemande, 217
*"Alma redemptoris mater,"* 75–77
*Amadeus* (Shaffer), 491
American Revolution, 201, 656
Angeles Quartet, *300*
Ansermet, Ernest, 607
*"An Silvia"* (Schubert), 361–63
answers in fugue, 226
antiphon, 75
*Appalachian Spring* (Copland), 584–87, *585*
appoggiatura, 310, 462, 464, 468–70, 476
*Aria with Fontana Mix* (Cage), 696–97, C.P. 17
arioso, 239
Armstrong, Louis, 594, 598
    "West End Blues," 598–99
arpeggio, 33, T.E. 30
*ars nova*, 100, 102, 109, 127
*ars subtilior*, 115
art music, definition of, 10
art song, 357
articulation, 51
Artusi, Giovanni Maria, 163, 177
Athens, 63
atonality, 538
Attaignant, Pierre, 152–53
augmentation, 355
Augustine, St., 67
aulos, 11, *11*
*"A una amante infidele"* (Countess of Dia), 83–85
"Autumn," *Four Seasons, The,* Op. 8 (Vivaldi), 214–15
avant-garde, 509, 675
Babbitt, Milton, 678
Bach, Carl Philipp Emanuel, 266, 270
Bach, Johann Christian, 266
Bach, Johann Sebastian, 8, *14,* 14–15, 204, **207–8,** 234, 250, 296, 349, 408, 698, *Art of Fugue, The,* 226, 565
    Brandenburg Concerto No. 2 in F Major, 208–13
    Cantata No. 78, *Jesu der du meine Seele,* 251, 254–59
    *Concerto in the Italian Style,* 30
    Prelude in C Minor, 17
    Prelude in C-sharp Major, 36
    Toccata and Fugue in D Minor, 227–30
*"Baisez moy"* (Josquin), 136–38
ballade, 108
    *"Dame, comment qu'amez"* (Machaut), 109–10

ballata, 111, 116–17
    *"Cara mie donna"* (Landini), 111, 114–15
    *"O rosa bella"* (Dunstable), 116–18
ballet, 489, *489,* 519–21
Ballets Russes, Les, 519–21
bar form, 83, 89
Bardi, Count Giovanni de', 163–64
bar lines, 56
Baroque, 162, C.P. 8
    early style, 163–64
    late style, 203–6
basic set, 564
bass clef, 56
basse danse, 139, 141
Bartók, Béla, **647–49,** 658
    Concerto for Orchestra, 650–55
    Dance in Bulgarian Rhythm, 22–23
    "Minor Seconds, Major Sevenths," 36
Bayreuth, 462, *463*
beams (notation), 58
beat, 18, T.E. 4
Beatles, The, 689–91, *691*
    *Sgt. Pepper's Lonely Hearts Club Band,* 692–93
bebop, 602
Beethoven, Ludwig van, 265, 296, **333–35, 338, 346–48,** *378,* 535
    Andante of G-Major Piano Sonata, Op. 14, No. 2, 18, 20–21
    *Eroica* Symphony, 335, 338, 631
    Piano Concerto No. 4 in G Major, Op. 58, 343–45
    Piano Sonata in C Minor, Op. 111, 348–49, 354
    Scherzo from E-flat Major Piano Sonata, 25
    String Quartet in C-sharp Minor, Op. 131, 355–56
    Symphony No. 5 in C Minor, Op. 67, 338–43, 383, 582
    *Waldstein* Sonata, 21
bel canto, 433
Bell, Alexander Graham, 501
Bellini, Vincenzo, 382, 433
    *Norma,* 433–34
Benedict, 66
Berg, Alban, 537, **549–50,** 656
    *Wozzeck,* 550–61, 564
Berio, Luciano, 707
Berlin, Irving, 612
Berlioz, Hector, 379, 414, **382–84**
    style of, 384–85, 395
    *Symphonie fantastique,* 378, 385–87, 390–92, 398–99, 416
    *Trojans, The,* 372
Bernstein, Leonard, 621–22
    *West Side Story,* 622–30
Berry, Chuck, 688–89
Billings, William, 570
binary form, 217
Binchois, Gilles, 127
    Rondeau, *Je ne vis onques le pareille,* 127–29
"Bird in a Gilded Cage, A," 619–20

Bismarck, Otto von, 375, 493
Bizet, Georges, 453, 509
    *Carmen,* 453, 509
Black Plague, 150, 201
Blake, William, 371, *372*
Bland, James, 619
"Bloomdido" (Parker), 603–4
Blow, John, 192
    *Venus and Adonis,* 192
blue notes, 593
blues, 592–93
Bolden, Buddy, 596–97
Boston Symphony, 634–35
Boulanger, Nadia, 583
Boulez, Pierre, 676, 678–79
    *Le marteau sans maître,* 676–79
Bourbon family, 159, 201
*bourée,* 222
Bowie, David, 702
Brahms, Johannes, 333, 378, 396, 414, 416, **424,** 501–2
    Variations on a Theme by Haydn, Op. 56a, 425–26
Brandenburg Concerto No. 2 in F Major (Bach), 208–13
*branle,* 140–42, *140*
Braque, Georges, C.P. 16
brass, 46, T.E. 45a–d
brass bands, New Orleans, 428, 596–97, *597*
Britten, Benjamin, 661
    *Peter Grimes,* 661–72
Brunelleschi, Filippo, 120
Büchner, Georg, 550–51
Busoni, Ferruccio, 632
Byzantine Church, 73
*caccia,* 111
    *"Con bracchi assai,"* 111–13
Caccini, Giulio, 164, 185
    *Le nuove musiche,* 164
cadence, 30–31, T.E. 23–24
cadenza, 294–95, 342, 344, 417, 655, 660
Cage, John, 695
    *Aria with Fontana Mix,* 696–97, C.P. 17
cakewalk, 590
*calata,* 139–41
canon, 111, 136
canonic chanson
    *"Baisez moy"* (Josquin), 136–38
*canso,* 89
cantata, 250–51
    chorale 251
    Cantata No. 78, *Jesu der du meine Seele* (Bach), 251, 254–59
cantus firmus, 146
*Canzoni e Sonate* (Gabrieli), 167–69
*Capriccio del Soggetto scritto sopra l'Aria di Ruggiero* (Frescobaldi), 170–71, 176
*"Cara mie donna"* (Landini), 111, 114–15

723

*Carmen* (Bizet), 453, 509
Carter, Elliott, 706–7
Castiglione, Baldassare, 123
*Castor et Pollux* (Rameau), 238–45
castrato, 235
CD-ROM, 688
cell
    in *Ionisation* (Varèse), 646
    in *Rite of Spring, The* (Stravinsky), 530
chamber music, 205–6
chance music, 695
character piece, 413
Charlemagne, 66, *66*
Charles the Bold, 126, 128
child labor, 374, *375*
choirboys (Notre Dame), 106–7
Chopin, Frédéric, 380, **406–7**, 416
    Étude in G-sharp Minor, Op. 25, No. 6, 408–9
    Mazurka in D Major, Op. 33, No. 2, 409
    Nocturne in E Major, Op. 62, No. 2, 410–11
    Prelude in A Major, 34
    style of, 407–8
chorale, 38–39, 251, T.E. 39
chord, 33
chordal style, 105
Christianity, spread of, 64–65
chromatic harmony, 35, T.E. 33
chromatic scale, 28, T.E. 17
Civil War, American, 375
Classical, derivation of, 264–65
classical music, 9–10
"classicizing" style, 357, *358*
clausula, 99
Clementi, Muzio, 632
closing area, definition of, 268
coda, definition of, 269
codex, 67
Coleridge, Samuel, 371
colonialism, 375
*color*, 105
Columbus, Christopher, 119
combinatorial, 567
compound meter, 21–22, T.E. 11a–b
computers, 505, 687–88
"*Con bracchi assai*" (Firenze), 111–13
Concert Étude after Paganini, *La Campanella*, (Liszt), 404–6
concertino, 206
concerto
    Baroque, 206
    Classical, 287
Concerto for Orchestra (Bartók), 650–55
concerto grosso, 206–7
concerto ripieno, 206
consonance, 35–36, 125, T.E. 34
continuo, 164–65, *165*, 204, 267
contrast (musical), 53
Copland, Aaron, 582–84
    *Appalachian Spring*, 584–87, *585*
copyright, 359
Corelli, Arcangelo, 193, 206, 234, 252
*cori spezzati*, 167, 180
Cosimo de' Medici, 122–23, *123*
countersubject, in a fugue, 226
Countess of Dia, 83
    Troubador song, "*A una amante infidele*," 83–85
country music, 5
courante, 217
Cowell, Henry, 694
Crawford (Seeger), Ruth, 707
criticism, music, 477–79, *477*
Crumb, George, 707
Crystal Palace, 516–17, *517*

Cubism, 508, 533
da capo, 221–22
"*Dame, comment qu'amez*" (Machaut), 109–10
dance music, Renaissance, 139
Danhauser, Joseph, *378*
Darwin, Charles, 374
Davis, Miles, 604
"Dead Man Blues" (Morton), 593–95
Debussy, Claude, **509–11, 519**, 517–18, 656
    Prelude to "The Afternoon of a Faun," 511–15, 518
    *Voiles*, 17,
decay, acoustical, 30
deceptive cadence, 464
Delacroix, Eugéne, 372, C.P. 9
Depression, Great, 504
*deus ex machina*, 239
developing variation, 379
development, in sonata form, definition of, 268–69
Diaghilev, Sergei, 519–21
diatonic harmony, 35
Diderot, Denis, 201, 374
*Dies irae*, 391–92, 660
digital, 687
diminished seventh chord, 348, 459
diminution, 169, 355
dissonance, 35–36, 125, T.E. 35
Divine Office, 66, 75
Dolmetsch, Arnold, 172–73
dominant, 34
Domino, Fats, 688
Donatello, 120, *120*
Donizetti, Gaetano, 382, 433, 670
double-reed instruments, 44
doubling, 33
downbeat, 20
drone, 50, 69
Dryden, John, 231–32
Dufay, Guillaume, 127
    Motet, "*Supremum est mortalibus bonum*," 143–46
    Rondeau, "*Je ne vis onques le pareille*," 127–29
Dunstable, John, 116
    Ballata, "*O rosa bella*," 116–18
duple meter, 19
duplum, 96
duration, in rhythm, 16
Dylan, Bob, 693
dynamics, 17
"early music" movement, 172–75
Edison, Thomas, 501
Eiffel Tower, 516, *517*
Eleanor of Aquitaine, 83
electronic music, 679–80
electronic music studios, 686–87
"*El grillo*" (Josquin), 134–36
Ellington, Duke, 599–600, *600*
    "Harlem Air Shaft," 600–602
*Empfindsamkeit*, 266
English madrigal
    "Those sweet delightful Lilies" (Weelkes), 138–39
Enlightenment, 201–2, 231, 262
envelope, 681
episodes
    in a fugue, 226
    in a ritornello form, 209
equal-voiced counterpoint (imitative counterpoint), 39, 285, T.E. 40
*Essercizii musici* (Telemann), 224–25
estampie, 92–94
Esterháza, 271, *272*
Esterházy family, 271–72
étude, 394, 398, 407–8
    Concert Étude after Paganini, *La Campanella* (Liszt), 404–6

Étude in G-sharp Minor, Op. 25, No. 6 (Chopin), 408–9
Eugenius IV, Pope, 143
Europe, James Reese, 606–7, *606*
exposition
    in a fugue, 226
    in sonata form, 268
Exposition universelle (1889), 516–17
expression, musical, 52
Expressionism, 536–37
"Eyesight," *Passages* (Zwilich), 699–701
"*Fammi combattere*," *Orlando* (Handel), 234–37
fantasia, 225
Fantasy Overture, *Romeo and Juliet* (Tchaikovsky), 492–93, 496
fascism, 649
Fauvism, 508, 536
"Feast of the Pheasant, The," 132
fermata, 22
Fiedler, Arthur, 635
figured bass, 164–65
film
    composers in, 490–91
    music, 490, 670–72
    music from *Journey to the Centre of the Earth* (Herrmann), 672–74
finale
    in instrumental music, 269
    in opera, *The Marriage of Figaro*, 310, 316–27, 329–32
final, in medieval modes, 75
fine arts, 11–12
Firenze, Giovanni da, 111
    Caccia, "*Con bracchi assai*," 111–13
First World War, 502–3, *504*
*Five Pieces for Orchestra*, Op. 10 (Webern), 547–49
*Five Pieces for Orchestra*, Op. 16 (Schoenberg), 539–42
folk song, music, 529, 531, 647–48, *648*
*formes fixes*, 105, 108, 111, 127
form, musical, 53
Foster, Stephen Collins, 572–73
*Four Seasons, The*, Op. 8 (Vivaldi), 214–17
fragmentation, 269, 299, 339–41, 379
Franz Joseph, Emperor, 493, *493*, 534
frequency, acoustical, 27
Frescobaldi, Girolamo, 171
    *Capriccio del Soggetto scritto sopra l'Aria di Ruggiero*, 170–71, 176
Freud, Sigmund, 535–36, *536*
"*Freue dich*" (Schütz), 180–82
Friedrich, Caspar David, 374
Friml, Rudolf, 620
frottola, 134
    "*El grillo*" (Josquin), 134–36
fugato, 227, 349, 650, 662, 665
fugue, 226–27, 343, 355, 392, 553, 636
    Toccata and Fugue in D Minor (Bach), 227–30
full cadence, 31
fundamental, 40, 681
Gabrieli, Giovanni, **166–67**, 180
    Sonata XIX, from *Canzonie Sonate*, 167–69
*galant*, 266
Galilei, Galileo, 161
galliard, 140, 142
Gama, Vasco da, 119
gamelan, 518, *518*
Gardiner, John Eliot, 175
Gauguin, Paul, 508, 533, C.P. 13
Gay, John
    *Beggar's Opera, The*, 245, 619
George I, King of England, 218, 234
Gershwin, George, 611–12
    *I Got Rhythm*, 16–17
    *Porgy and Bess*, 612–19
    *Rhapsody in Blue*, 612

"Someone to Watch Over Me," 32
*Gesamtkunstwerk,* 462
gigue, 217
Gilbert and Sullivan, 620
Gilmore, Patrick, 634
Giotto, C.P. 3
"Gladiolus Rag" (Joplin), 589–91
Glass, Philip, 702
Goethe, Johann Wolfgang von, 264
Gothic architecture, 68, *68,* 162
Goya, Francesco, 262, *262*
grace note, 58
grand opera, 382, 434
Greek music, 69–71
Greenberg, Noah, 173
Gregorian chant, 73
Gregory the Great, Pope, 73, *74*
*"Gretchen am Spinnrade"* (Schubert), 363–64,
    368–70
Griffith, D. W., 670–71
Grofé, Ferde, 612
ground (bass), 193, 255
Guido of Arezzo, 74
Gustavus Adolphus, King of Sweden, 159
Gutenberg, Johann, 152
half cadence, 31
half step, 28
Halle, Adam de la, 79
Hammerstein, Oscar, II, 621
Handel, George Frideric, **233–34, 252–53,** 349
    *"Fammi combattere," Orlando,* 234–37
    *Messiah,* 246–50
    Suite in D Major, *Water Music,* 218–23, 270
Hanover, House of, 234
Hanslick, Eduard, 478–79, *479*
Hapsburg family, 159, 201, 261, 534
"Harlem Air Shaft" (Ellington), 600–602
harmonic, 395, 549, 699
harmonic minor scale, 29
harmonic rhythm, 36, T.E. 36, 37
harmony, 26, 33–36
harpsichord, 166, *166*
Hart, Lorenz, 621
Haydn, Joseph, 265, **270–72,** 335, 656
    compared with Mozart, 283–85
    in London, 280–82
    Piano Sonata in E-flat Major, 32
    Piano Sonata in E Minor, 22, 37
    String Quartet in D Major, 300–303
    Symphony No. 100 in G Major, "Military,"
        273–79, 282–83
heavy metal, 693
Heinrich, Anthony Philip, 573
hemiola, 303
Hendrix, Jimi, 693
Henry IV, King of France, 183
Herbert, Victor, 612, 620–21
Herrmann, Bernard, 672
    Music from *Journey to the Centre of the Earth,*
        672–74
Hermann of Reichenau, 77
heterophony, 69–70, 92, 531
hexachord, 174
Hildegard of Bingen, 79, 82
    *Ordo virtutum,* 79–82
Hines, Earl "Fatha," 598
Hitler, Adolf, 504
hocket, 105
Hoffmann, E. T. A., 376, 478–79
Hofmannsthal, Hugo von, 534
Hogarth, William, 262, C.P. 7
Hogwood, Christopher, 174–75, *175*
Holly, Charles "Buddy," 689
homophony, 39, T.E. 25a
Honegger, Arthur, 633
"Housatonic at Stockbridge, The" (Ives), 582
Hugo, Victor, 371, 374

humanism, 119
hurdy-gurdy, 303, *303*
idée fixe, 387, 390–91
imitation (imitative counterpoint), 39, 126,
    T.E. 40
imperialism, 375
Impressionism, 507–8, C.P. 12
improvisation, 225, 291, 294–95, 344, 417, 588
incidence, in rhythm, 16
Industrial Revolution, 48, 263
instrumental melody, 30, T.E. 21–22
instrumental music
    early Baroque, 166
    medieval, 92
    Renaissance, 139
intermedio, 183
intermezzo, 304
interpretation, 52, T.E. 49
interval, 27
inversion, 36
*Ionisation* (Varèse), 644–47
IRCAM, 678, *679*
irregular meter, 22, T.E. 12a–b
Isaac, Heinrich, 127–28
    Lied, *"Isbruck, ich muss dich lassen,"* 127,
        129–31, 133
*"Isbruck, ich muss dich lassen"* (Isaac), 127,
    129–31, 133
Islam, 64
isorhythm, 104
Ives, Charles, 576–79, 635
    "Housatonic at Stockbridge, The," 582
    "Putnam's Camp, Redding, Connecticut,"
        579–82
Janissary music, 273, *273,* 279, 283
Jarrett, Keith, 604–5
jazz, 5, 587–607, 611
*"Je ne vis onques le pareille"* (Binchois or Dufay),
    127–29
Jennens, Charles, 246
*Jesu der du meine Seele,* Cantata No. 78 (Bach),
    251, 254–59
Johnson, Samuel, 202
Joplin, Scott, 589
    "Euphonic Sounds," 25
    "Gladiolus Rag," 589–91
Josquin Desprez, 131–34, 426
    Canonic chanson, *"Baisez moy,"* 136–38
    Frottola, *"El grillo,"* 134–36
    *Missa L'homme armé super voces musicales,*
        146–50
Joyce, James, 685
*Journey to the Centre of the Earth,* music from the
    film (Herrmann), 672–74
Kern, Jerome, 612
    *Show Boat,* 620–21
key, 34
keyboard instruments, 47–48, T.E. 47a–b
kithara, 71
Klinger, Max, C.P. 14
Kodály, Zoltan, 647–48
*La bohème* (Puccini), 453–57
*La Campanella* (Liszt), 404–6
Landini, Francesco, 111
    Ballata, *"Cara mie donna,"* 111, 114–15
Landini (under-third) cadence, 114
Landowska, Wanda, 174, *174*
*La serva padrona* (Pergolesi), 304–5
legato, 51
Lehár, Franz, 428
leitmotif, 461
*Le marteau sans maître* (Boulez), 676–79
Leonardo da Vinci, 120–21, *122*
Leoncavallo
    *I Pagliacci,* 453
Léonin (Master), 96–97
libretto, 183–84

Lied
    *"An Silvia"* (Schubert), 361–63
    *"Gretchen am Spinnrade"* (Schubert), 363–64,
        368–70
    *"Isbruck, ich muss dich lassen"* (Lassus), 127,
        129–31, 133
    polyphonic, 129
    *"Rastlose Liebe"* (Schubert), 365, 370
    Romantic, 357, 360
Ligeti, György, 697
    *Lux aeterna,* 697–99
Lister, Joseph, 501
Liszt, Franz, 376, *378,* **398–404,** *403*
    Concert Étude after Paganini, *La Campanella,*
        404–6
    *Rigoletto* transcription, 446–47
    transcription of *Symphonie fantastique,*
        398–99, 446–47
liturgical dramas, 78–79
Locke, John, 201
Loos, Adolf, 535
Louis XIV, King of France, 160, *160,* 202
Louis XV, King of France, 202, C.P. 5
Louis XVI, King of France, 202
Ludwig II, King of Bavaria, 372
Lully, Jean-Baptiste, 237
Luther, Martin, *122,* 123, 130
*Lux aeterna* (Ligeti), 697–99
Machaut, Guillaume de, 102, 108, 656
    Ballade, *"Dame, comment qu'amez,"* 109–10
    *Mass of Notre Dame,* 102–5
Machiavelli, Niccolò, 122
madrigal
    English, 138
    Italian, 176
    *"Zefiro torna"* (Monteverdi), 177–79
madrigalism, 138, 176
"mad scene," 433, 670
Magellan, Ferdinand, 119
*Magnus Liber,* 96
Mahler, Gustav, 55, 494–96, 537, 578
    composing hut, C.P. 11
    Symphony No. 6 in A Minor, 496–97
major mode, 34, T.E. 30–31a, 32
major scale, 28, T.E. 18
major third, 33
major triad, 33
Mallarmé, Stéphane, 508, 511
maps
    Age of Enlightenment, 200
    Age of Revolution, 260
    Age of Romanticism, 373
    ancient world, 62
    Europe in 1648, 158
    medieval world, 65
    our shrinking globe, 506
    Renaissance, 124
    twentieth century, 500
    United States, 571
*maqâm,* 29, T.E. 20
Marcellus II, Pope, 151
march, 19, *19,* 573, *574,* 579, 581, 590, 596–97
mariachi music, 5, *6*
Marian antiphon, 75–77
Maria Theresa, Empress, 261, 290
Marie de' Medici, 183
*Marriage of Figaro, The* (Mozart), 306–32, *307*
Marsalis, Wynton, 604
Marx, Karl, 502
Mary, mother of Jesus, 75, C.P. 2
Mary of Burgundy, 128
Mass, 72
    settings, 102, 146
*Mass of Notre Dame* (Machaut), 102–5

Maximilian, Holy Roman Emperor, 128, 261
mazurka, 407, *408*
　Mazurka in D Major, Op. 33, No. 2
　　(Chopin), 409
measure, 18
Medici
　family, 122, 159
　Cosimo de', 122, *123*
medieval drama, 78–79
Mei, Girolamo, 164
melisma, 77, 154
melismatic organum, 96
melodic minor scale, 29
melodrama, 458
melody, 26–32
Mendelssohn (Henselt), Fanny, 420–21
Mendelssohn, Felix, 378, 414, **418–19**, 420–21
　Piano Trio in D Minor, Op. 49, 419, 423
mensural rhythm, 74
*Messiah* (Handel), 246–50
meter, 18, T.E. 5–7c
metronome, 23, *23*
metronome markings, 23–24
Meyerbeer, Giacomo, 382, 434
　*African Girl, The, 435*
Michelangelo, 120, *121*
microtone, 577
MIDI, 687–88
*mijwiz,* 50, *50,* T.E. 48b
Milhaud, Darius, and jazz, 606–7
"Military," Symphony No. 100 in G Major
　　(Haydn), 273–79, 282–83
minimalism, 701–2
Minnesänger 82, 89
　Song, *"Unter der linden an der heide"*
　　(Vogelweide), 89–92
minor mode, 34, T.E. 31b, 32
minor scale, 28–29, T.E. 19a–b
minor third, 33
minor triad, 33
minstrel show, 619
minuet, 222, 267, 342
*Missa L'homme armé super voces musicales*
　　(Josquin), 146–50
mode
　in plainchant, 74–75
　rhythmic, 99
　in tonality, 34
modulation, 36–37, 268, T.E. 38
*Moldau, The* (Smetana), 482–84
monastery, medieval, 66–67, 86–88, *87*
Monet, Claude, C.P. 12
monody, 163
monophony
　definition of, 38
　monophonic music, 69–94
monothematicism, 278
Monteux, Pierre, 635, *635*
Monteverdi, Claudio, 163, **176–77**
　Madrigal, *"Zefiro torna,"* 177–79
　*Orfeo,* 184–91
mood swings, 384, 388–90, 415
Moog, Robert, 686, *687*
morality play, 79
Morton, Ferdinand "Jelly Roll," 593
　"Dead Man Blues," 593–95
　Red Hot Peppers, The, *594*
motet
　medieval, 99–100
　　*"O mittisima/Quant voi—Virgo
　　　Virginum—Haec dies,"* 100–102
　Renaissance, 143
　　*"Supremum est mortalibus bonum,"* 143–46
motive, 32, T.E. 29

Mozart, Leopold, 289
Mozart, Wolfgang Amadeus, 7–8, 265, **289–91,**
　408, 432
　in letters, 296–97
　operas, 305–6
　*Marriage of Figaro, The,* 306–32, *307*
　Piano Concerto in C Major, K. 467, 291–95,
　　298–99
　Piano Sonata in C Major, 36
　Symphony No. 41 in C Major, K. 551, 283–85
　Variations on *Ah, vous dirai-je, Maman,* 36
MTV, 694
Munrow, David, 174
music, definition of, 9
musica ficta, 105
musical theater, 619–21
musica recitativa, 164
music drama, 461
musique concrète, 696
Musorgsky, Modest, 485–86
　*Pictures at an Exhibition,* 486–88, *487*
Mussolini, Benito, 504
mutation, 646
*"Nacht,"* Pierrot lunaire, Op. 21 (Schoenberg),
　542–46
Napoleon Bonaparte, 262–63, *263,* 335, 338
nationalism, 375, 480–81
　Russian, 485
neoclassicism, 264, 566, 630–33, 636
Nero, 71
*Neue Zeitschrift für Musik,* 416, 424
neumatic, melody, 77
neumes, 55, *76*
New Age music, 5
*New Magazine for Music,* 416, 424
Newman, Alfred, 672
New Orleans, 592
New Romanticism, 700, 706
"News Has a Kind of Mystery," *Nixon in China*
　(Adams), 703–6
Nijinsky, Vaslav, 519, *520*
*Nixon in China* (Adams), 703–6, *703*
Nocturne in E Major, Op. 62, No. 2 (Chopin),
　410–11
Nocturne in F Major, Op. 15, No. 1 (Chopin), 54
non-imitative (unequal-voiced) counterpoint, 39
non-legato, 41
non-Western music, 9, 29, 49–51, *506,* 516–18,
　646
*Norma* (Bellini), 433–34
Norrington, Roger, 175
notation, 54, *55–58*
Notker Balbulus, 88
Notre Dame (Paris), 96, *97*
　choirboys, 106–7
octatonic scale, 528–29
octave, 27–28, T.E. 16
Offenbach, Jacques, 428
*"O mitissima/Quant voi—Virgo virginum—Haec
　　dies,"* 100–102
ondes martenot, 674, 680, *681*
opera
　Classical, 304–5
　Romantic, 380
　late Baroque, 232–33
　origins of, 183
　public opera houses, 194–96, *196*
opera buffa, 305
operetta, 428
opposition theme, 531–32
oratorio (English), 245–46
orchestra, instruments of, *42–43*
orchestration, 51, 384
Ordinary (of Mass), 72
*Ordo virtutum* (Hildegard of Bingen), 79–82
*Orfeo* (Monteverdi), 184–91
organ, 48, *48, 227*

theater, 670, *671*
organum, 95–96
organum quadruplum, 97
*Orlando* (Handel), 234–37
*"O rosa bella"* (Dunstable), 116–18
Orpheus, 69–70, *70,* 184–85
Orthodox (Byzantine) Christianity, 64, 73
ostinato, 255, 529–30, 532–33, 542
overtones, harmonics and partials, 40, 95, 681
Paganini, Nicolò, *378,* **394–95,** *395,* 398, 406,
　415
　Solo Violin Caprice, Op. 1, No. 9, 396–97
Palestrina, Giovanni Pierluigi da, 150
　*Pope Marcellus Mass,* 151, 154–57
parallel organum, 96
paraphrase mass, 146
Paris
　avant-garde, 507–8
　medieval, 96–97
　nineteenth century, 380–82, *381*
Parker, Charlie "Bird," 45, 602, 604
　"Bloomdido," 603–4
parlante, 436, 444
Partch, Harry, 694, *695*
Parthenon, 63, *64*
passacaglia, 425–26, 543
*Passages* (Zwilich), 699–701
passage work, 166
passamezzo, 140, 142
Pasta, Giuditta, 431, *432*
pedal chords, 529
pedal point, 228, 348
pentatonic (scale), 528, 532, 648
percussion, 46, T.E. 46a–m
performance directions, 51
performance practice, 172
Pergolesi, Giovanni Battista, 632
Peri, Jacobo, 185
period, musical, 30
period instruments, 48–49
Pérotin, Master, 97
　Four-voiced organum, *Viderunt omnes,* 97–99
*Peter Grimes* (Britten), 661–70
Petrarch, Francesco, 120, 138
Petrucci, Ottaviano, 152–53, *153*
Philip II, King of Spain, 159
Philip the Good, 126–27, 132–33
phrase, 30
phrasing, 52
piano
　fortepiano, Classical, 287, 350–53, *351, 353*
　manufacturers, Pleyel and Erard, 400–401, *401*
　Romantic, 397–98
Piano Concerto in A Minor, Op. 54 (Schumann),
　416–18
Piano Concerto in C Major, K. 467 (Mozart),
　291–95, 298–99
Piano Concerto No. 4 in G Major, Op. 58
　　(Beethoven), 343–45
Piano Sonata in C Minor, Op. 111 (Beethoven),
　348–49, 354
Piano Trio in D Minor, Op. 49 (Mendelssohn),
　419, 423
*Pictures at an Exhibition* (Musorgsky), 486–88,
　*487*
*Pierrot lunaire,* Op. 21 (Schoenberg), 542–46
pitch, 27
pizzicato, 40
plainchant, 73–78
Plato, 70–71
Pleyel, Ignace, 377
"poles of attraction," 637
polonaise, 407
polyphony, 39
polyrhythm, 526, 528, 530, 533
Pompei, 264, *264*
Ponte, Lorenzo da, 306–10

*Pope Marcellus Mass* (Palestrina), 151, 154–57
popular music, 10, 426–27
*Porgy and Bess* (Gershwin), 612–19
postmodernism, 697
Pouplinière, Jean-Joseph Le Riche de la, 238
Prelude to *"The Afternoon of a Faun"* (Debussy), 511–15, 518
prepared piano, 695
Presley, Elvis, 689
primary area, definition of, 268
"primitive" art, 508
program music, 214, 414
   *Symphonie fantastique* (Berlioz), 385–87, 390–92
Prokofiev, Sergei, 521
Proper (of Mass), 72
Puccini, Giacomo, 449, 452–53
   *La bohème,* 453–57
pulse-code modulation (PCM), 688
punk rock, 693
Purcell, Henry, 191–92
   *Dido and Aeneas,* 192–93, 196
"Putnam's Camp, Redding, Connecticut" (Ives), 579–82
Pythagoras, 70
*qin,* 49, *50*
quadrivium, 70
quarter tone, 577
Rachmaninoff, Sergei, 396, 659
   *Rhapsody on a Theme of Paganini,* 660–61
radio, 501, *502*
ragtime, 588–91, 610–11
   "Gladiolus Rag" (Joplin), 589–91
Rainey, Ma, 592–93
Rameau, Jean-Philippe, 204, **236–38**
   *Castor et Pollux,* 238–45
range, 30, 75
rap music, 3
*"Rastlose Liebe"* (Schubert), 365, 370
Ravel, Maurice
   *Daphnis and Chloe,* 521
   *Pavane for a Dead Princess,* 31
RCA Victor, 502, *502*
recapitulation, definition of, 269
recitative, 184, 190–91, 312–13, 327–28
   simple, 235
Red Hot Peppers, The, *594*
Reformation (Protestant), 123
reggae, 3
Reich, Steve, 702
Renaissance, 119–123
   musical style traits of, 125–26
repetition, musical, 53
rest, 31
retransition, definition of, 269
*Rhapsody on a Theme of Paganini* (Rachmaninoff), 660–61
rhythm, 16–25, T.E. 1–14b
rhythm & blues, 685, 709
*Rigoletto* (Verdi), *432,* 436–46, *445*
   Liszt transcription, 446–47
Riley, Terry, 702
Rimsky-Korsakov, Nikolai, 517, 522, 529
ripieno, 206
ritard, 31
*Rite of Spring, The* (Stravinsky), 524–533, *525, 578*
ritornello
   Baroque, 185
   medieval, 111
ritornello form, 209, 287
Robbins, Jerome, 622
rock 'n' roll, 1, 685, 688–94
Rodgers, Richard, 621
Roerich, Nicholas, 524
Romance in G Minor (Wieck), 30, 411–13
*Roman de Fauvel,* 100

Romanesque architecture, 67, *67*
Romans, 63
romantic, derivation of, 371
Romanticism, 371–74
   style traits of, 377–80
   twilight of, 493–94
Romberg, Sigmund, 612, 620
Rome, ancient, 63–64
*Romeo and Juliet* (Tchaikovsky), 492–93, 496
rondeau, 108
   *"Je ne vis onques le pareille"* (Binchois or Dufay), 127–29
rondo form, 270
Rossini, Giaocchino, 346, *378,* 380, 431
   *The Barber of Seville,* 307
Rousseau, Jean-Jacques, 374
Russell, Ken, 490
St. Cecilia, 231
St. Gall, 86–88, *87,* C.P. 1
St. Mark's, Venice, 166–67, 169
St. Peter's, Rome, 150, *151*
Salieri, Antonio, 358–59, 491
Salomon, Johann Peter, 272, 281
sampling, 687
Sand, George, *378,* 380, 406–7, *407*
*sarabande,* 217
Satie, Erik, 521, 632
   *Parade,* 633, *633*
scale, 28–29
   Greek, 70
scherzo, 342
Schiller, Friedrich von, 264
Schoenberg, Arnold, 537–39, 656–57, C.P. 15
   *Erwartung,* 538
   *"Nacht," Pierrot lunaire,* Op. 21, 542–46
   *Vergangenes, Five Pieces for Orchestra,* Op. 16, 539–42
Schubert, Franz, 265, 346, 357–59
   *"An Silvia,"* 361–63
   *"Gretchen am Spinnrade,"* 363–64, 368–70
   Impromptu in G-flat Major, 31
   *"Rastlose Liebe,"* 365, 370
   Waltz in A Major, 19
Schubertiad, 366–67, *366*
Schumann, Robert, **415–16,** 420–22
   *Carnaval,* 31, 415, 543
   Piano Concerto in A Minor, Op. 54, 416–18
Schütz, Heinrich, **178–80,** 656
   *"Freue dich,"* 180–82
score, 51
scoring, 51
Scott, Sir Walter, 372
Secessionism, 535
secondary area, definition of, 268
Second World War, 334
sequence, T.E. 26b
   medieval, 88
   melodic/harmonic, 31
sequencing, electronic, 687
*Sgt. Pepper's Lonely Hearts Club Band* (The Beatles), 692–93
serialism, 564–66
Shakespeare, William, 123, 383, 419, 435
shape, musical, 53, T.E. 50a–b
single-reed instruments, 44
Singspiel, 305
Slonimsky, Nicholas, 646
Smetana, Bedrich, 481
   *Moldau, The, Má Vlast,* 482–84
Smith, Bessie, 592–93, *593*
Smithson, Harriet, 383
smorzando, 409
Society for Private Musical Performances, 562–63
*A Soldier's Tale,* "Three Dances" (Stravinsky), 607–11
solo concerto
   Baroque, 207, 213

Classical piano concerto, 287–88
Romantic piano concerto, 416–18
Solo Violin Caprice, Op. 1, No. 9 (Paganini), 396–97
sonata
   early Baroque, 167
   late Baroque, 206
   piano sonata, 348
   Piano Sonata in C Minor, Op. 111 (Beethoven), 348–49, 354
   Sonata XIX, from *Canzoni e Sonate* (Gabrielli), 167–69
sonata-concerto form, 288
sonata form, 267–69
sonata-rondo form, 288
Sondheim, Stephen, 622
song cycle, 360
*Song of the Youths* (Stockhausen), 681–85
soul music, 3
Sousa, John Philip, 573, *574,* 589, 590
   "Rifle-Regiment March, The," 19
   Stars and Stripes Forever, The, 573–76
spinning-out, 204
Sprechstimme, 543, 552–53, 560, 696–97
staccato, 51
staff (staves), 56
stanza, poetic, 83
"Stars and Strips Forever, The" (Sousa), 573–76
Steiner, Max, 671
stem, notation, 58
Stockhausen, Karlheinz, 680
   *Song of the Youths,* 681–85
Storyville, New Orleans, 592–93, *592*
Stradivari, Antonio, 218–19, C.P. 6
Strauss, Johann, Jr., 427–28, 634
   Waltz, *Voices of Spring,* Op. 410, 428–30
Strauss, Richard, 494, 537, 652, 647
   *Don Quixote,* 378
Stravinsky, Igor, 522–24, *523*
   *Firebird, The,* 520–21, 523
   *Petrushka,* 521
   *Rake's Progress, The,* 262
   *Rite of Spring, The,* 524–33, *525,* 578
   "Three Dances," *A Soldier's Tale,* 607–11
   *Serenade in A,* 32
   *Symphony of Psalms,* 636–41
Striggio, Alessandro, 184
string quartet, 299
   String Quartet in C-sharp Minor (Beethoven), 355–56
   String Quartet in D Major (Haydn), 300–303
strings, 40, *41, 44,* T.E. 42a–d
strophic form, 83
strophic variations, 164
style, musical, 59
subdivision of beats, 20–21, T.E. 8–10
subdominant, 34
subject, in a fugue, 226
Subotnick, Morton
   *Silver Apples of the Moon,* 685
suite
   Baroque, 206, 217
   Suite in D Major, *Water Music* (Handel), 218–23
Suppé, Franz von, 428
*"Supremum est mortalibus bonum"* (Dufay), 143–46
swing bands, *594,* 598–99
syllabic writing, 77
symbolism, 508
symphonic poem, 403, 482
*Symphonie fantastique* (Berlioz), *378,* 385–87, 390–92, 416

727

symphony
  anatomy of, 269–70
  Symphony, Op. 21 (Webern), 566–68
  Symphony No. 5 in C Minor, Op. 67
    (Beethoven), 338–43, 383, 582
  Symphony No. 6 in A Minor (Mahler), 496–97
  Symphony No. 41 in C Major, K. 551
    (Mozart), 283–85
  Symphony No. 100 in G Major, "Military"
    (Haydn), 273–79, 282–83
*Symphony of Psalms* (Stravinsky), 636–41
syncopation, 25, T.E. 14a–b
synthesizer, 686–88
*tactus,* 23
"Take Me Out to the Ball Game," 34
talea, 104
tango, 607–8, 610, *610*
Tchaikovsky, Peter, 488–89
  Fantasy Overture, *Romeo and Juliet,* 492–93,
    496
technology and music, 501–2, 505, 679–80
Telemann, Georg Philipp, 208, **223–24,** 250
  Trio Sonata in A Minor, *Essercizii musici,*
    224–25
tempo, 23–24
tenor in medieval music, derivation of, 97
ternary form, 54
texture, 38–39
Thalberg, Sigismond, 400–402
Thayer, Alexander Wheelock, 634, *634*
Theater-an-der-Wien, *287*
thematic anticipation, 379, 467
thematic transformation, 379
theme, 32, T.E. 28
theme and variations, 176, 425
  *Capriccio del Soggetto scritto sopra l'Aria di*
    *Ruggiero* (Frescobaldi), 170–71, 176
  Piano Sonata in C Minor, Op. 111, second
    movement (Beethoven), 354
  String Quartet in C-sharp Minor, Op. 131,
    fourth movement (Beethoven), 355–56
  Variations on a Theme by Haydn, Op. 56a
    (Brahms), 425–26
Theremin, 679
Thirty Years' War, 159
"Those sweet delightful Lilies" (Weelkes),
  138–39
"Three Dances," *A Soldier's Tale* (Stravinsky),
  607–11
*Three Places in New England* (Ives), 579–80
through-composed, 116
timbre (tone color), 39–40
time signature, 56
Tin Pan Alley, 426, 611, 619
toccata, 225
  Toccata and Fugue in D Minor (Bach), 227–30
tonality, 34, 193, 204
tone color (timbre), 40

tone row, 564–65
*tornada,* 89
total serialism, 676
Tower, Joan, 708
transcription, 446
  Act III Quartet from *Rigoletto* (Liszt), 446–49
transition, definition of, 268
treble clef, 56
*trecento,* 109, 111
triad, 33, 125
trio sonata, 223
  Trio Sonata in A Minor, *Essercizii musici,*
    (Telemann), 224–25
triple meter, 19–20
triplum, 96
*Tristan und Isolde* (Wagner), 463–76, *465,* 510
tritone, 177
trope, 78, 99
troubadors, 82
Troubador song, *"A una amante infidele"*
  (Countess of Dia), 83–85
trouvères, 82
tune, 32, T.E. 27
tuning, 204
Turkish bands, 273, *273,* 279, 283
Turner, William, 374, C.P. 10
U2, *4*
Uffizi Gallery, Florence, 122, *123*
under-third (Landini) cadence, 114, 118, 144–46
unequal-voiced (non-imitative) counterpoint, 39,
  285, T.E. 41
unit pulse, 531
upbeat, 20
*"Unter der linden an der heide"* (Vogelweide),
  89–92
Varèse, Edgard, 643–44, 656
  *Ionisation,* 644–47
variation, definition of, 53
Variations o.1 a Theme by Haydn, Op. 56a
  (Brahms), 425–26
vaudeville, 619
Venice, 166–67, 194–96, C.P. 3
Verdi, Giuseppi, 434–36
  Italian unification, 450–52, *452*
  *Rigoletto,* 436–46, *445*
*Vergangenes,* Five Pieces for Orchestra, Op. 16
  (Schoenberg), 539–42
verismo, 452–53
vernacular drama, 79
Versailles, 160–61, *161*
Viardot, Pauline, 431, *432*
vibrato, 49
*Viderunt omnes* (Pérotin), 97–99
Vienna
  around 1800, 263–64
  around 1900, 534–36, *536*
Viennese Classical style, 266–67
  public vs. private music, 286–87

Vincenzo I, Duke, 177
violin, 166
*virelai,* 108
virtuosity, 393–94
Vitry, Philippe de, 100
Vivaldi, Antonio, 213
  "Autumn," *Four Seasons, The,* Op. 8, 214–17
Vogl, Johann Michael, 367, *367*
voice-leading, 105
*Voices of Spring,* Op. 410 (Johann Strauss, Jr.),
  428–30
Voltaire, François, 202, *202*
*vox organalis,* 96
*vox principalis,* 96
Wagner, Otto, 535
Wagner, Richard, 376, 379, 460–63, 510–11
  *Ring of the Nibelung, The,* 372
  *Tristan und Isolde,* 463–76, *465*
Wagnerism, 509
walking bass, 235, 255
Walther von der Vogelweide, 89
  Minnesänger Song, *"Unter den linden an der*
    *heide,"* 89–92
waltz, 428–29, *429,* 610
  *Voices of Spring,* Op. 410 (Strauss), 428–30
war, 656–58, *657*
Washington, D.C., neoclassical design, 264, *265*
*Water Music,* Suite in D Major (Handel), 218–23
Weber, Carl Maria von, 346
  *Der Freischütz,* 374, 458–59, *459*
Webern, Anton, 537, 546–47, 675
  *Five Pieces for Orchestra,* Op. 10, 547–49
  *Symphony,* Op. 21, 566–68
Weelkes, Thomas, 138
  English madrigal, "Those sweet delightful Lil-
    ies," 138–39
"West End Blues" (Armstrong), 598–99
*West Side Story* (Bernstein), 622–30, *623*
Whiteman, Paul, 612
white noise, 695
whole step, 28
whole-tone scale, 528, 648
Wieck (Schumann), Clara, 411–12, 415–16,
  **420–22**
  Romance in G Minor, 30, 411–13
Williams, John, 635
women in music, 79, 83, 420–22
  Alma Schindler (Mahler), 495, 707–8
woodwinds, 44–45, *45,* T.E. 44a–e
word painting, 126, 136, 138, 176, 181, 185, 699
Wordsworth, William, 371
*Wozzeck* (Berg), 550–61, 564
*Youth's Magic Horn, The,* 495, *496*
"Zefiro torna" (Monteverdi), 177–79
Zwilich, Ellen Taaffe, 699
  "Eyesight, *Passages,* 699–701
zydeco, 5

728